READINGS

Professional Essays

Student Essays

Student Sketches

The Curious Writer

Concise Edition

Second Edition

Bruce Ballenger

Boise State University

New York San Francisco Boston
London Toronto Sydney Tokyo Singapore Madrid
Mexico City Munich Paris Cape Town Hong Kong Montreal

Senior Vice President and Publisher: Joseph Opiela
Director of Development: Mary Ellen Curley
Associate Development Editor: Erin Reilly
Senior Supplements Editor: Donna Campion
Senior Marketing Manager: Sandra McGuire
Production Manager: Savoula Amanatidis
Project Coordination and Text Design: Elm Street Publishing Services
Electronic Page Makeup: Integra Software Services, Pvt. Ltd.
Cover Design Manager: John Callahan
Cover Image: © 2006 by Pearl Publishing Co. All rights reserved.
Photo Researcher: Vivette Porges
Senior Manufacturing Buyer: Roy L. Pickering, Jr.
Printer and Binder: Worldcolor Book Services—Taunton, MA
Cover Printer: Phoenix Color Corporation

For permission to use copyrighted material, grateful acknowledgment is made to the copyright holders on pp. 452–454, which are hereby made part of this copyright page.

Library of Congress Cataloging-in-Publication Data
Ballenger, Bruce P.
The curious writer / Bruce Ballenger.—Concise ed., [2nd ed.].
p. cm.
Includes index.
ISBN-13: 978-0-205-62024-1
1. English language—Rhetoric—Handbooks, manuals, etc.
2. Interdisciplinary approach in education—Handbooks, manuals, etc.
3. Academic writing—Handbooks, manuals, etc. I. Title.
PE1408.B37 2007c
808'.042—dc22

2007046159

Please visit us at www.ablongman.com

ISBN-13: 978-0-205-62024-1
ISBN-10: 0-205-62024-8

4 5 6 7 8 9 10—WCT—11 10 09

Contents

Chapter 4
Writing a Personal Essay 87

Chapter 7
Writing an Argument 201

Chapter 8
Writing a Critical Essay 249

Chapter 9
Research Techniques 301

Chapter 11
Revision Strategies 415

PREFACE

A few years ago, the Carnegie Foundation asked a group of leading scholars, teachers, and intellectuals to investigate the current state of undergraduate education at America's research universities. The Boyer Commission report was unequivocal about the problems: "The experience of most undergraduates at most research universities is that of receiving what is served out to them. In one course after another they listen, transcribe, absorb, and repeat, essentially as undergraduates have done for centuries." The investigators called for a "new model" of undergraduate education that would "turn the prevailing undergraduate culture of receivers into a culture of inquirers, a culture in which faculty, graduate students, and undergraduates share an adventure of discovery. . . ." In particular, they added, "The first year of university experience needs to provide new stimulation for intellectual growth and a firm grounding in inquiry-based learning."

The "adventure of discovery" is what many of us love about writing. Our students often enter our composition classrooms with little experience using language as a tool of learning. Then we help them understand that writing can be a means for finding out what they didn't know they knew, and that the process of revision can lead to a fresh way of seeing things; pretty soon even some resistant writers welcome the invitation to sit down and write. They've discovered that they can write to learn.

Most of us *already* teach inquiry, although not all may realize it. For instance, our writing classes invite students to be active participants in making knowledge in the classroom through peer review workshops. When we ask students to fastwrite or brainstorm, we encourage them to suspend judgment and openly explore their feelings or ideas. And when we ask students to see a draft as a first look at a topic, and revision as a means of discovering what they may not have noticed, we teach a process that makes discovery its purpose. Indeed, most composition classrooms create a "culture of inquirers" rather than passive recipients of what their teachers know.

That's why the Boyer Commission's call for an inquiry-based freshman year resonated with me and so many others. Initially, I saw its relevance to one of the most common writing assignments in the composition course—the research paper—and this led me to write my book *The Curious Researcher.* But an inquiry-based approach can and should permeate every assignment in the entire sequence of freshman writing courses. I also thought that although much of what we already do involves inquiry-based learning, we should explicitly make the spirit of inquiry—its practices, methods, and purposes—the focus of the writing course, generating ideas that students can apply not only in our classrooms but in their work in other disciplines.

INQUIRY IN THE WRITING CLASSROOM

Historically, composition teachers have struggled to decide what besides reading and writing skills students could export to their other classes and, later, into their lives. Often we vaguely refer to "critical-thinking" skills. *The Curious Writer* offers a comprehensive approach for teaching *inquiry*. This idea also may seem vague until you consider the following.

First, think about what is required to create a culture of inquirers in the composition course. How do we create the learning environment that will foster such a culture? I believe there are at least five key features of an inquiry-based classroom on nearly any subject.

1. *Create an atmosphere of mutual inquiry.* Students are used to seeing their teachers as experts who know everything that students need to learn. But in an inquiry-based classroom instructors are learners, too. They ask questions not because they already know the answers but because there might be answers they haven't considered.
2. *Emphasize questions before answers.* The idea that student writers begin with an inflexible thesis or a firm position on a topic *before* they engage in the process of writing and thinking is anathema to inquiry-based learning. Questions, not preconceived answers, lead to new discoveries.
3. *Encourage a willingness to suspend judgment.* Student culture at most schools works against this. Papers get written at the last minute, multiple deadlines in multiple classes compete for students' time, and multiple-choice tests or lecture courses imply that there is one true answer and the teacher knows it. To suspend judgment demands that we trust the process that will lead us to new insights. This requires both faith in the process and the time to engage in it. The composition course, with its emphasis on process, is uniquely suited to nurture such faith.
4. *Introduce a strategy of inquiry.* It's not enough to simply announce that we're teaching an inquiry-based class. We have to introduce students to the *strategy of inquiry* we'll be using. In the sciences, the experimental method provides a foundation for investigations. What guidance will we give our students in the composition course? *The Curious Writer* features a strategy that is genuinely multidisciplinary, borrowing from science, social science, and the humanities.
5. *Present inquiry in a rhetorical context.* An essay, a research project, an experiment, any kind of investigation is always pursued with particular purposes and audiences in mind. In an inquiry-based class, the *situation* in which the inquiry project is taking place is always considered.

You'll find all of these elements of inquiry-based learning integrated in *The Curious Writer.* For example, each "Inquiry Project" leads students toward writing subjects that offer the most potential for learning. Rather than write about what they already know, students are always encouraged to choose a topic because they want to find out more about it. In addition, the discussion questions that follow the student and professional essays are crafted to do more than simply test their comprehension of the piece or reduce it to a single theme. In many cases, questions are open ended and can lead students in many directions as they analyze a reading. *The Curious Writer* maintains a voice and persona throughout the book that suggests that I am working along with the students as a writer and a thinker, which is exactly the experience of mutual inquiry I try to create in my classes. Finally, *The Curious Writer* is organized around a strategy of inquiry that is present in every assignment and nearly every exercise. Introduced in the first three chapters, I call on the model often in every subsequent chapter. The inquiry strategy is the thematic core of the book.

THE INQUIRY STRATEGY OF *THE CURIOUS WRITER*

A strategy of inquiry is simply a process of discovery. In the sciences, this process is systematic and often quite formal. The model I use in this book borrows from science in some ways through its insistence on continually looking closely at the "data" (sensory details, facts, evidence, textual passages, and so on) and using it to shape or test the writer's ideas about a subject. But the heart of the model is the alternating movement between two modes of thinking—creative and critical—in a dialectical process. One way of describing this is shifting back and forth between suspending judgment and making judgments (see Figure A).

To help students see how questions can help them see their writing subjects in new ways, I offer four categories of questions—those that explore, explain, evaluate, and reflect—and return to these frequently, particularly in the early stages of the inquiry process. These will be most evident in the follow-up questions to the many readings throughout *The Curious Writer.* A strategy of inquiry is useful only if it makes sense to students; I've tried very hard, particularly in the first section of the book, to make the model comprehensible.

OTHER FEATURES

Because the inquiry-based approach is central to *The Curious Writer*, it's crucial for students to work through the first three chapters before moving on to the "inquiry projects." The range of assignments in this part should satisfy the needs of most composition instructors. If your university is lucky enough to have a two-semester sequence, *The Curious Writer* includes assignments suitable for both courses, including personal, argument, and research essays.

The book's focus on genres of writing also makes it appealing for advanced composition courses. For example, assignments such as the review and proposal help students see how to apply what they've learned to distinct rhetorical situations and help them to understand how those situations shape the genres.

In recent years, I've become interested in reading strategies, a topic that I never mentioned as a novice teacher. There was simply so much to say about the

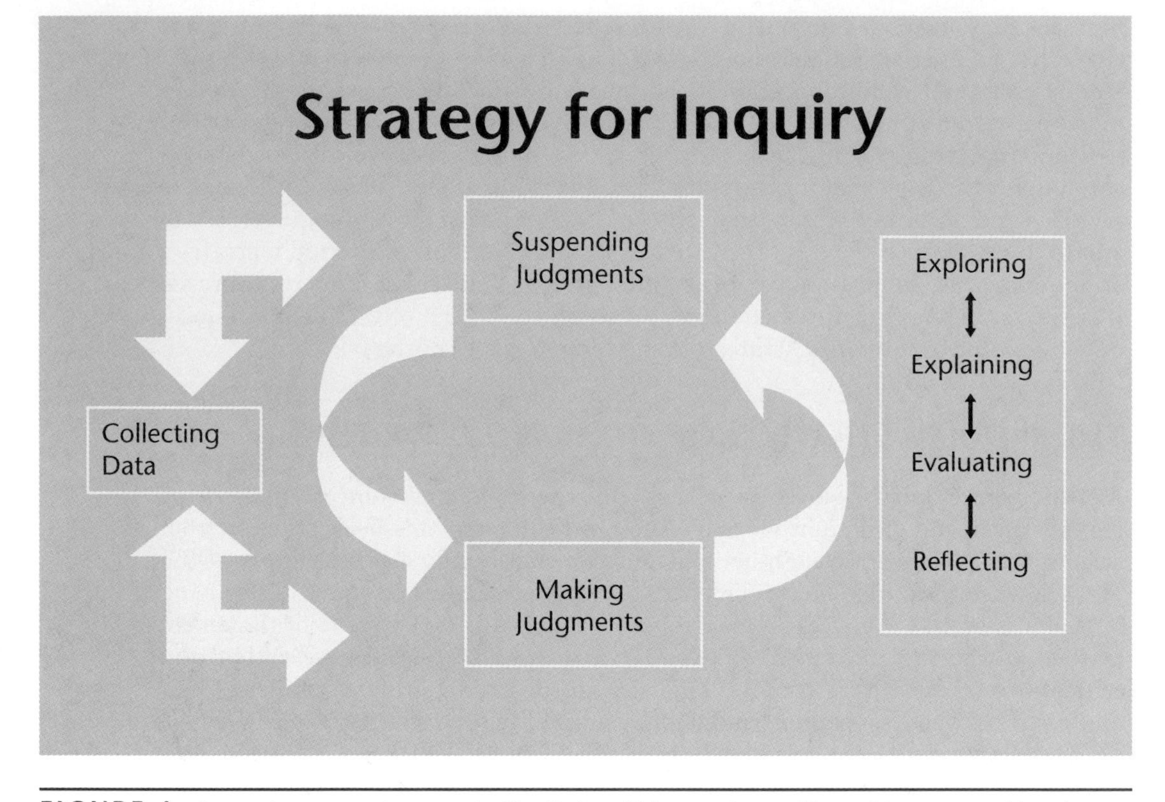

FIGURE A In nearly every assignment in *The Curious Writer,* students will use this strategy of inquiry.

writing process that I didn't think reading was a topic that should get much airtime. Yet as in writing, students bring many prior beliefs and assumptions about reading into our classrooms, and because reading is always an important part of teaching writing, I've come around to talking more about it. *The Curious Writer* reflects this. Chapter 2, "Reading as Inquiry," is devoted to the topic. The best thing about this is that the inquiry model I promote for writing applies just as easily to reading. I've also expanded the discussion to reading images. This emphasis on visual rhetoric echoes the latest developments in composition in response to the growth of the Web and the growing visual literacy of our students.

Finally, the approach of *The Curious Writer* grows in part from my own scholarship on research writing, particularly the criticism that research is too often isolated in the writing course. Students understandably get the idea that research is reserved only for the research paper if they're asked to do it only when they're assigned a research project. This book makes research a part of every assignment, from the personal essay to the proposal, emphasizing that it is a useful source of information, not a separate genre.

This is the third textbook I've written with the "curious" moniker. Because all are inquiry-based, the word is a natural choice. And although I'm very interested in encouraging my students to be curious researchers, readers, and writers, I also hope to remind my colleagues who use the books that we should be curious, too. We should model for our students our own passion for inquiring into the world. We should also celebrate what we can learn from our students, and not just about writing, or the many topics they might choose to write about. I'm curious every time I walk into the writing classroom what my students will teach me about myself. That's a lifetime inquiry project for all of us, as teachers and as people.

NEW TO THE SECOND EDITION

I have made a number of changes to the second edition in an effort to refine the book further. These changes, many made at the request of the book's users and reviewers, include the addition of sixteen new readings (eleven professional and five student); new material on visual analysis in Chapter 2; a clarified and streamlined discussion of the four ways of inquiring in Chapter 3; expanded treatment of revision in each of the inquiry project chapters, new material on the literacy narrative in Chapter 4; expanded treatment of formal argument techniques in Chapter 7; and new and improved versions of the *Seeing the Form, Writing with Computers,* and *Inquiring into the Details* features throughout the book.

APPROACHES TO TEACHING WITH THE BOOK

I organized the book to span, if necessary, a two-semester composition course, though it can easily be adapted to one semester. Typically, in a two-semester sequence the first course focuses on writing process, exposition, critical analysis, writing to learn, and so on. The second semester often focuses on argument and research. A single-semester composition course tries to combine them all. Fortunately, *The Curious Writer* is extremely flexible, with ample material to keep students busy for one or two semesters.

Sequence

Whether you use this book for one course or two, it's wise to introduce *The Curious Writer* to students by first working through the first three chapters because this section lays the foundation for all that follows. The many exercises in these chapters will help students experience firsthand what we mean by inquiry. I've organized chapters in an order that roughly follows typical composition courses, beginning with genres that draw heavily on students' personal experiences and observations and then moving them outward toward other sources of information and encounters with other people's experiences and ideas. In a one-semester course, for example, you might begin with the personal essay, followed by the review, and then the argument or research essay. This builds nicely by challenging students to work with more sources of information and leads to a more sophisticated understanding of persuasion and rhetoric. A two-semester course has the luxury of more assignments, of course, allowing you to potentially use most of the Inquiry Projects.

Certain assignments clump together. For example, while arguably all writing is persuasive, the following genres are most explicitly so: proposal, review, argument, critical essay, and often the research essay. A course that focuses on argument might emphasize these assignments. A research-oriented course might exploit the wealth of material with a strong emphasis on outside sources, including the proposal, review, argument, and research essay. A single-semester composition course that attempts coverage of critical thinking and writing as well as research and argument might begin with personal essay and then cover persuasion through the review or critical essay, move on to the argument, and finish with the research essays.

Integrating the Research and Revision Sections

An unusual feature of the book is its treatment of research skills and revision. Research is an element of every assignment but it receives special attention in Chapters 9 and 10, in which students are introduced to research strategies and skills. Hopefully, you will find that this section, particularly Chapter 9, "Research Techniques," is immediately relevant because students will be encouraged to consider research angles in every assignment they tackle. Consider assigning this chapter early in your course, particularly the sections on developing a working and focused knowledge of a subject.

Similarly, revision is an element of every assignment. That's hardly a novel idea, but what is unusual is that *The Curious Writer* devotes an entire chapter of the book to revision. Like the section on research, the chapter on revision is relevant to students from their very first assignment. The first half of Chapter 11, "Revision Strategies," is a useful introduction to what it means to revise, and you might assign this material early on in your course. The chapter also features specific revision strategies that your students will use in every assignment.

Using the Exercises

Learning follows experience, and the exercises in *The Curious Writer* are intended to help students make sense of the ideas in the text. I often plan the exercises as an in-class activity, and then assign the relevant reading to follow up that experience. Sometimes the discussion following these in-class exercises is so rich that some of the assigned reading becomes unnecessary. The students get it without having to hear it again from the author. More often, though, the reading helps students deepen their understanding of what they've done and how they can apply it to their own work.

However, assigning all of the exercises isn't necessary. Don't mistake their abundance in the book as an indication that you must march your students in lockstep through every activity or they won't learn what they need to.

The Curious Writer is more flexible than that. Use the exercises and activities that seem to emphasize key points that *you* think are important. Skip those you don't have time for or that don't seem necessary. If you're like me, you also have a few rabbits of your own in your hat, exercises and activities that may work better with the text than the ones I suggest.

ACKNOWLEDGMENTS

I owe the success of the first edition of *The Curious Writer* to many people, particularly my Development Editor, Adam Beroud, whose savvy judgment, sharp eye, and imaginative thinking influenced me every step of the way. He's been similarly helpful with this second edition. None of the *Curious* books would be possible if the Senior Vice President and Publisher of Pearson Longman, Joe Opiela, weren't a force behind them.

I've also been fortunate to have the help of other bright and generous people, particularly my colleague and friend Michelle Payne, with whom I coauthored an inquiry book. I'm a lucky author to have a partner in these projects with such a rich understanding of what I'm trying to do, and what I might do better.

In addition to Michelle, I've benefited from the insights of other colleagues as well, including Devan Cook, Brock Dethier, Bonnie Sunstein, Elizabeth Chiseri-Strater, Mike Mattison, Karen Uehling, Gail Shuck, Lad Tobin, and many others in the field whose work informed my understanding of how writers get better.

My students always contribute to my work. Several whose own exemplary writing is featured here include Julia Arrendondo, Lana Kuchta, Amy Garrett-Brown, Julie Bird, Kelly Sundberg, Gina Sinisi, Ben Bloom, and Christy Claymore.

Reviewers of books like these can be crucial to their development. I was lucky enough to have some excellent reviewers for the second edition, including the following: Melissa Batai, Triton College; Jennifer Black, McLennan Community College; Mark Browning, Johnson County Community College; Jo Ann Buck, Guilford Technical Community College; Jason DePolo, North Carolina A&T State University; John Christopher Ervin, University of South Dakota; Greg Giberson, Salisbury University; Nels P. Highberg, University of Hartford; William Klein, University of Missouri–St. Louis; Mary C. Leahy, College of DuPage; Lynn Lewis, University of Oklahoma; Steve Luebke, University of Wisconsin–River Falls; Michael Lueker, Our Lady of the Lake University; Jacqueline L. McGrath, College of DuPage; Betty Porter, Indiana Wesleyan University; Kristie Rowe, Wright State University; Kathleen J. Ryan, University of Montana; and Heath Scott, Thomas Nelson Community College.

Finally, I want to thank my daughters, Rebecca and Julia, who allow themselves to be characters in all of my books. They are both actors, and like good theater people, they are more than willing to play their parts in these texts, no matter what role I assign. I'm especially grateful to Karen, my wife, who has endured multiple editions of these books and their hold on my attention, which has often come at her expense. She's the beacon I follow through this blizzard of words, always guiding me home.

BRUCE BALLENGER

Writing as inquiry is an invitation to wonder again.

Writing as Inquiry

1

What You'll Learn in This Chapter

- Why it pays to spend time thinking about your writing process.
- Why learning to write well often involves *unlearning* things you already believe.
- How understanding rhetoric will help you analyze writing situations.
- What it means to be a writer who is motivated by a spirit of inquiry.
- How to harness both creative and critical ways of thinking to come up with new ideas.

Just the other night I was writing a card to my old friend Linda, someone I went to college with and haven't seen in twenty-five years. As I wrote, my words scribbled in a heavy black pen, she began to appear before me again. I saw her in geology class, a few rows up, wearing a black raincoat and rubber boots, carefully putting her straight black hair behind an ear so she could see her notes. I hadn't seen her so clearly in years, and the writing brought her back. Most of us have had this experience—the power of words to summon images, memories, and feelings—which is why we sometimes indulge, often with pleasure, in writing letters, cards, and e-mails to friends and family.

Yet many of us admit that we really don't like to write, particularly when forced to do it, or we clearly prefer certain kinds of writing and dislike others: "I just like to write funny stories" or "I like writing for myself, and not for other people" or "I hate writing research papers." I can understand this, because for years I felt much the same way. I saw virtually no similarities between my note to Linda and the paper I wrote for my philosophy class in college. Words that had power in one context seemed flimsy and vacant in another. One kind of writing was fairly easy; the other was sweating blood. How could my experience as a writer be so fundamentally different? In other words, what's the secret of writing well in a range of contexts *and* enjoying it more? Here's what I had to learn:

1. All writing can offer the joy of discovery, the opportunity to speak and be heard, and the satisfaction of earned insight.
2. A key to writing well is understanding the *process* of doing it.

I'm not really sure they are particularly novel, but both ideas were a revelation to me when I finally figured them out late in my academic career, and they changed the way I wrote for good. These two insights—that the pleasures of writing can span genres and situations, and that thinking about *how* we write matters—are guiding principles of this book. After they read *The Curious Writer,* I won't guarantee that haters of writing will come to love it, or that lovers of writing won't find writing to be hard work. But I hope that by the end of the book you'll experience some of the same pleasures I found writing to my friend Linda in most writing situations, and that you'll be able to adapt your own writing process to meet the demands of whatever situation you encounter.

The process of becoming a more flexible and insightful writer must begin by exploring what you already believe it means to write well and learning a bit about how we can talk about writing as a process. In this chapter, I'll also introduce you to an idea that will be at the heart of every activity and assignment in *The Curious Writer:* the habits of mind and practices that will encourage you to adopt the "spirit of inquiry" as a motive for writing. This may sound a bit lofty and abstract. But by chapter's end I hope you'll recognize some practical implications of this approach that will help you with any writing assignment.

MOTIVES FOR WRITING

Why write? You could probably build a long list of reasons in a minute or two, perhaps beginning facetiously: "Because I *have* to!" But as you consider the many situations that call for writing and the purposes for doing it, I suspect that most will fall under a broad and obvious category: to say something to someone else. I'm less confident that you will see another broad motive for writing, partly because it gets less attention: we write to *discover* what we want to say.

These two motives for writing—to *share* ideas with others and to *discover* what the writer thinks and feels—are equally important.

But both these motives may arise from a still deeper spring: a sense of wonder and curiosity or even confusion and doubt, a desire to touch other people, or an urge to solve a problem. These feelings can inspire what I call the *spirit of inquiry,* a kind of perspective toward the world that invites questions, accepts uncertainty, and makes each of us feel some responsibility for what we say. This inquiring spirit should be familiar to you. It's the feeling you had when you discovered that the sun and a simple magnifying glass could be used to burn a hole in an oak leaf. It's wondering what a teacher meant when he said that World War II was a "good" war and Vietnam was a "bad" war. It's the questions that haunted you yesterday as you listened to a good friend describe her struggles with anorexia. The inquiring spirit even drives your quest to find the best DVD player, an effort that inspires you to read about the technology and visit *Consumer Reports Online.*

BELIEFS ABOUT WRITING

Most of us have been taught about writing since the first grade. We usually enter college with beliefs about how best to write a paper, which rules govern school writing, and even how to improve at composing. As I mentioned earlier,

I've learned a lot about writing since my first years in college, and a big part of that learning involved unraveling some of my prior beliefs about writing. In fact, initially, I'd say that my development as a writer had more to do with *unlearning* some of what I already knew than it did with discovering new ways to write. Actually, that's one of the central findings of learning theorists: When learners have considerable prior knowledge of a subject, they often need to reexamine their beliefs to determine whether those beliefs are accurate or helpful. Until they do this, any new learning in the subject can be limited. In keeping with this philosophy, we need to evaluate what you already believe about writing. Only after you articulate your beliefs can you begin to examine whether those beliefs are obstacles or aids to new learning about writing.

EXERCISE 1.1

What Do You Believe?

STEP ONE: From the following list, identify *the one belief* about writing that you agree with most strongly, and *one* that you're convinced isn't true.

1. Writing proficiency begins with learning the basics and then building on them, working from words to sentences to paragraphs to compositions.
2. The best way to develop as a writer is to imitate the writing of the people you want to write like.
3. People are born writers. Either you can do it or you can't.
4. The best way to develop as a writer is to develop good reading skills.
5. Practice is the key to a writer's development. The more a writer writes, the more he or she will improve.
6. Developing writers need to learn the modes of writing (argument, exposition, description, narration) and the genres (essays, research papers, position papers, and so on).
7. Developing writers should start with simple writing tasks, such as telling stories, and move to harder writing tasks, such as writing a research paper.
8. The most important thing that influences a writer's growth is believing that he or she can learn to write well.
9. The key to becoming a better writer is finding your voice.

STEP TWO: Spend five minutes writing in your notebook or journal about *why* you agree with the one belief and disagree with the other. This is an open-ended "fastwrite." You should write fast and without stopping, letting your thoughts flow in whatever direction they go. Try not to think about what you want to say before you write it, and don't worry about whether you're writing well or making sense (see the following "One Student's Response" for an example).

Journal Prompts

- *When* did you first start agreeing or disagreeing with the belief? Can you remember a particular moment or experience as a student learning to write that drove this home?
- *What* do you mean, exactly, when you say you agree or disagree with the belief? Can you explain more fully why you think the belief is true or false?
- *Who* was most influential in convincing you of the truth or falsity of the belief?

Rules for Fastwriting

1. There are no rules.
2. Don't try to write badly, but give yourself permission to do so.
3. To the extent you can, think through writing rather than before it.
4. Keep your pen moving.
5. If you run out of things to say, write about how weird it is to run out of things to say until new thoughts arrive.
6. Silence your internal critic to suspend judgment.
7. Don't censor yourself.

ONE STUDENT'S RESPONSE

JON'S JOURNAL

EXERCISE 1.1

STEP TWO

I agree that writing is a natural human activity that we are all capable of. Anyone capable of thinking understands language. That's truly all that one needs to begin. The only problem that arises is that writing for one's self contains limitations. He is the rare person that can be satisfied with his own praise. There is something within the human spirit that understands that other people may know more than we do. This drives us on for a response from others. This requires a set standard for communication. This, in turn, requires rules. These are things that a successful writer must learn.

I don't agree with the next statement about imitation. Mr. Studabacher is a good man and a good writer and he pushes this theory a little bit. He says that we should learn to borrow without plagiarism. Imitation can only be a beginning—a starting block for the creation of our own voice and ideas . . .

INQUIRING INTO THE DETAILS

JOURNALS

Throughout *The Curious Writer,* I invite you to write in a journal. Some people hate journals. These are usually students who were forced to keep a journal in some class and found it a chore, or who tried to keep a journal at home and had little to show from the experience but blank pages. If you suffer from this condition, use a notebook instead of a journal. The two terms are synonymous. It's not what you call it that counts—it's what you do inside it!

Why do I want you to use a journal? One reason is that it is easier to write freely in this medium than it is when confronting the first page of a rough draft. Also, it's okay to write badly in journals and, as you will see later in this chapter, that's a good thing.

What kind of journal should you use? That's up to you. The writer Natalie Goldberg advises that a journal with a cartoon character on the cover will help you take yourself and your writing less seriously, which will help loosen up your writing. Some students just use the ubiquitous spiral notebook, which works just fine. For a variety of reasons, others find the digital journal best. They may be able to write faster and with more ease using a keyboard instead of pen; keeping a journal on the computer might even be required if you're taking your class in a computer lab.

Unlearning Unhelpful Beliefs

You shouldn't be surprised when I say that I have a lot of theories about writing development; after all, I'm supposedly the expert. But we are *all* writing theorists, with beliefs that grow out of our successes and failures as students who write. Because you don't think much about them, these beliefs often shape your response to writing instruction without your even knowing it. For example, I've had a number of students who believe that people are born writers. As far as I can tell, they mean that there is some kind of writing gene that some folks have and some don't. This belief, of course, would make any kind of writing course a waste of time because writing ability would be a genetic problem.

A much more common belief is that learning to write is a process of building on basics, beginning with words, and then working up to sentences, paragraphs, and perhaps whole compositions. This belief was very common when I was taught writing. I remember slogging my way through Warriner's *English Grammar and Composition* in the seventh and eighth grade, dutifully working through chapter after chapter, beginning with parts of speech, parts of sentences, sentences, and then paragraphs. It wasn't until page 377 that I was urged to write a whole composition, a topic whose section was the smallest in the book.

Along with a lot of experts on writing instruction, I don't think that this foundational approach to writing development is very effective. I know it didn't help me become a better writer, and while I can still diagram a sentence, that's never a skill I call on when I'm composing. As a matter of fact, fifty years of research confirms that teaching formal grammar separately from writing essays is largely a waste of time. Despite this, formal grammar instruction persists, testimony to the subversive power of common sense. (Isn't it common sense that we should always learn the basics first?)

Unlearning involves rejecting common sense if it conflicts with what actually works.

Unlearning involves rejecting common sense *if* it conflicts with what actually works. Throughout this book, I hope you'll constantly test your beliefs about writing against the experiences you're having with it. Pay attention to what seems to work for you and what doesn't; mostly, I'd like you at least initially to play what one writing instructor calls the believing game. Ask yourself, *What do I have to gain as a writer if I try believing this is true?*

The Beliefs of This Book

One of the metaphors I very much like about writing development is offered by writing theorist Ann E. Berthoff. She said learning to write is like learning to ride a bike. You don't start by practicing handlebar skills, move on to pedaling practice, and then finally learn balancing techniques. You get on the bike and fall off, get up and try again, doing all of those separate things all at once. At some point, you don't fall and you pedal off down the street. Berthoff said writing is a process that involves *allatonceness* (all-at-once-ness), and it's simply not helpful to try to practice the subskills separately. This is one belief about writing development shared by this book. Obviously, then, *The Curious Writer* is nothing like Warriner's *English Grammar and Composition,* but what other beliefs *does* it embrace?

Any number of beliefs—the importance of critical thinking, the connection between reading and writing, the power of voice and fluency, and the need to listen to voices other than your own—all guide the structure of this book. One belief, though, undergirds them all: *the most important thing that influences a writer's growth is believing that he or she can learn to write well.* Faith in your ability to become a better writer is key. From it grows the motivation to learn how to write well.

Faith isn't easy to come by. I didn't have it as a writer through most of my school career because I assumed that being placed in the English class for underachievers meant that writing was simply another thing, like track, that I was mediocre at. For a long time, I was a captive to this attitude. But then, as a college freshman, I wrote a paper I cared about and the writing started to matter, not because I wanted to impress my instructor but because I discovered something I really wanted to say, and say well. I didn't settle for mediocrity after that.

As someone who wasn't too keen on writing for a very long time, I know how difficult it is to develop compelling reasons to write, particularly when the writing is required. I had to learn, among other things, that my teacher wasn't responsible for supplying the motivation (though I acknowledge that deadlines can help). I had to find a way to approach a writing assignment that made it seem like an opportunity to learn something.

It turns out that the way you *initially* see a writing assignment—any assignment, really—influences your attitude toward it. To illustrate this point, consider the following questions. Which one of the two responses *best* describes your own feelings when confronted with a writing assignment?

Which opening question are you most likely to ask yourself?

❑ How can I be successful at this?	❑ What can I learn?

How do you feel when problems arise as you're writing?

❑ I don't have the necessary skills.	❑ I expect challenges.

How do you view your instructor?

❑ Someone who should tell me exactly what he or she wants.	❑ Someone who can help solve my writing problems.

What do you consider your main goal?

❑ I want to show I'm a decent writer.	❑ I want to develop my writing skills.

It may have been hard to limit yourself to just these responses because our attitudes are much more complex than this. You may also have found yourself checking the responses in both columns. But if your choices tended toward the left column, it's likely that your attitude toward writing is driven by *performance* goals. In other words, you want to perform well on a writing assignment for your instructor, for your peers, for your friends, for yourself. If you found yourself agreeing with the items in the right column, *learning goals* seem to dominate how you feel about writing assignments; that is, you are less interested in how well you perform than you are in developing your writing abilities. You see the challenge of a writing assignment as a learning opportunity.

There is nothing wrong with your attitude if it leans more toward performance than learning. Each type of goal has its place. Just remember this about performance-oriented writing: along with the desire for success inevitably comes anxiety about failure. Fearfulness is not a very comfortable place from which to write or to learn. If you're willing to consider making learning rather than performance goals a priority as you work through *The Curious Writer*, you're much more likely to develop your writing abilities. And you might even find that you can use writing in ways you never thought possible. Consider, then, beginning your study of college writing with the opening question, *What can I learn?*

INQUIRING INTO THE DETAILS

PORTFOLIOS

One method for evaluating your development as a writer is to use a *portfolio,* which is a collection of work you assemble throughout a semester and submit to your instructor at the end of the course. If your instructor uses portfolios, he or she may grade some of your work as you go along, but will mainly assess your writing abilities by reviewing the total body of work in your portfolio. This means that until you hand in your final drafts, everything is pretty much a work in progress, and for much of the course you can focus on learning goals—say, finding new methods to begin and end your essays, or improving your editing skills. Performance goals, such as getting a decent grade, become a priority only at the end of the course.

WRITING SITUATIONS AND RHETORICAL CHOICES

Good writing is good writing, right? Well, it depends on the situation. For instance, here's what a friend of my daughter wrote as a comment on her blog the other day:

> im happy to be back w/ u guys it was a too long of a weekend- dancing friday then? u hailey and i runnin tomorrow- sounds fun 2 me

This isn't necessarily bad writing for MySpace.com and sites like it. The message uses online conventions that most of us are familiar with—text messaging abbreviations like "u" for *you* and "2" for *two*—and it possesses a level of informality and intimacy that seems appropriate for its context. Would it be good writing for a college essay? Obviously not.

Part of learning to write well, then, isn't simply learning how to craft transitions, organize information, and follow grammatical rules; it's learning to recognize that each writing situation asks you for something different. Actually, you know this already. You know, for example, that composing a letter to a landlord who refuses to return your security deposit will be fundamentally different from a letter to your sister describing your problem with the landlord. What you may not know is what to call this kind of knowledge: rhetoric.

One way of analyzing any writing situation is by using *the rhetorical triangle,* which reveals the dynamic relationships among the writer, the subject, and the reader (see Figure 1.1).

What the triangle implies is pretty straightforward—to write effectively, you must simultaneously address three main factors: your own perspective as the writer, the topic you are writing about, and the people you are writing for. The word *rhetorical,* of course, comes from *rhetoric,* the classical term for the study and practice of written and verbal communication. In fact, the rhetorical triangle

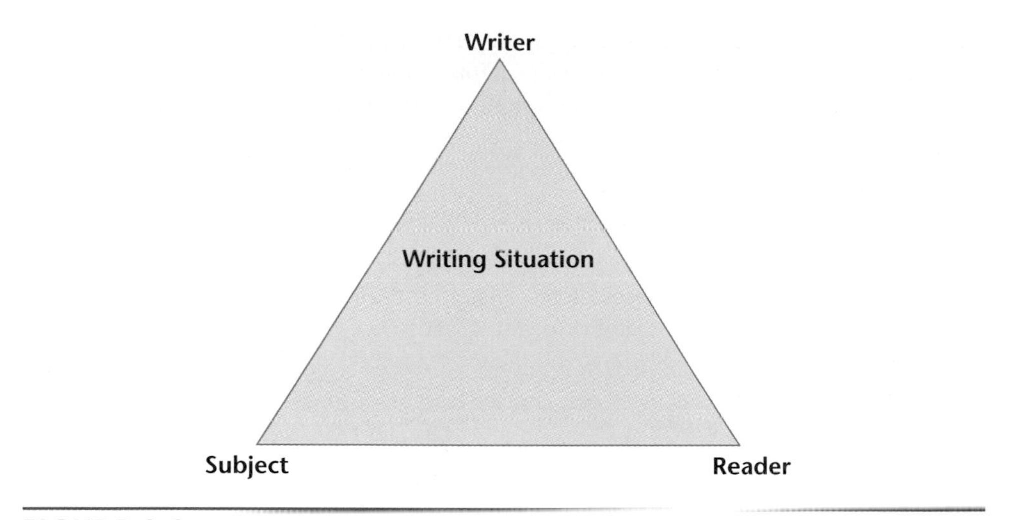

FIGURE 1.1 The rhetorical triangle.

has its origins in ancient Greece and the thinking of Aristotle, who first set down the principles of effective communication more than 2,000 years ago.

The three legs of the rhetorical triangle come together to shape the writing situation. The particularities of each leg—the writer, the subject, and the reader—determine the context of the writing situation. Consider again the security deposit problem. In that scenario, one thing is clear: both of the proposed letters has a distinct—and different—*audience*. While the writer and the subject would seem to be the same for both letters, given the different audiences, the approach will be fundamentally different. In the letter to the landlord, the writer might adopt a formal, even legalistic tone. The letter would be specific about what the writer is asking and when. The letter to the writer's sister would likely be informal, possibly more emotional. Its purpose would be to enlist a sibling's emotional support, not to persuade a landlord to return $500.

I'm pretty sure this is intuitively obvious to you. What may not be apparent is that you can use the same rhetorical knowledge to understand all kinds of writing situations, including academic ones. For example, consider next the opening two paragraphs from a writing assignment in Political Science 141: Contemporary Political Ideologies.

> This assignment aims to encourage students to connect the arguments being made by the thinkers in class to the issues and themes of our politics today. It aims to help students understand the relevance of political thinking for our political practice. Students are encouraged to share their judgments about the authors, only after they have shown that they understand the authors as the authors would understand themselves.
>
> Use one of the following questions as the basis for a short essay. Your essay should be lucid and concise, and your argument should be thoroughly supported by

> relevant citations and allusions from the texts at hand. Grammar, spelling, punctuation, and syntax should be perfect . . . Your paper is to be three to five pages in length, double-spaced, typed, and stapled in the upper left-hand corner. Please number your pages. A title page with an appropriate title must also be included, and all title pages should show what question the student is answering.

Using your own instincts about the rhetorical situation in this example, answer the following questions:

1. How would you characterize the instructor, and, based on that characterization, what kind of reader do you think he might be?
2. If you were in this class, how might your analysis of the rhetorical situation influence your approach the writing assignment?

Writing well involves evaluating situations like these using your rhetorical knowledge. *The Curious Writer* offers you tools to help analyze various writing and reading situations and explores a range of choices that might be appropriate in each, choices that will make you a more persuasive writer and a more sophisticated reader.

HABITS OF MIND

When I first started teaching writing, I noticed a strange thing in my classes. What students learned about writing through the early assignments in the class didn't seem to transfer to later assignments, particularly research papers. What was I doing wrong, I wondered? Among other things, what I failed to make clear to my students was how certain "essential acts of mind" were present in every assignment, from the very first to the very last. What bound the writing course together was the idea of academic inquiry and the habits of mind—or *dispositions*, as one writer describes them—that lead students to see how writing can be a process of discovery.

Start with Questions, Not Answers

A lot of people think that writing is about recording what you already know, which accounts for those who choose familiar topics to write on when given the choice. "I think I'll write about ______________," the thinking goes, "because I know that topic really well and already have an idea what I can say." Unfortunately, the result of writing about what you already know is too often an uninspired draft full of generalizations and clichés.

What do you do about this problem? *Make the familiar strange.* This means finding new ways to see what you've seen before. For years, I've asked some of my writing students to take photographs of any subject they want. Predictably, most students choose to take pictures of familiar things—their rooms or apartments, the trees outside the window, campus buildings, local landscapes—and they almost always take one picture of each subject. The result is that these photographs are rarely surprising. They see these familiar subjects in very familiar ways. But when I ask them to return to a single subject and take multiple pictures of it there are almost always surprises, and fresh ways of seeing the subject.

It's apparent that there are multiple ways of seeing the same thing, and of course this is one thing that we often admire about good writing—it offers a perspective on something familiar that we hadn't considered before. One of the ways writers accomplish this is by using questions. Questions shift a writer's perspective on a subject much as distance, angle, and light alter a photographer's ways of seeing a tree or a building.

Therefore, in an inquiry-based approach to writing, you'll choose a writing topic that raises questions about how you think or feel over one that you have all figured out. Almost any topic can raise interesting questions. *There are no boring topics, only boring questions.* The key is to approach any topic with a sense of wonder and curiosity: *Why are houseflies so hard to kill? What distinguishes the cultures of skaters and snowboarders? When do most marriages fail and what can be done about it? Why do young people join gangs?*

Suspend Judgment

What's one of the most common problems I see in student writers? Poor grammar? Lack of organization? A missing thesis? Nope. *It's the tendency to judge too soon and too harshly.* A great majority of my students, including really smart, capable writers, have powerful internal critics, or as the novelist Gail Godwin once called them, "Watchers at the Gates." This is the voice you may hear when you're starting to write a paper, the one that has you crossing out that first sentence or that first paragraph over and over until you "get it perfect." As you'll see later, this voice isn't demonic; you need it. "Watchers at the Gates" are, as Godwin said, "excellent critics after inspiration has been captured" and "dependable, sharp-eyed readers of things already set down." The problem, of course, is that many of us allow our Watchers to keep us from setting down much of anything. The blank page or screen offers nothing for our internal critics to scrutinize except the glaring failure to get words on the page or screen in the first place.

I've seen bad writing transform students who once hated writing into people who see writing as a useful tool for thinking, and even a source of pleasure.

The only way to overcome this problem is to suspend judgment. In doing so, you essentially tell your Watchers this: *It's okay to write badly.*

I never try to write badly, of course, but whenever I'm stuck in the middle of something, or can't figure out what to say or where to begin, or even when I don't have a clue about my subject, I simply start writing. Sometimes it's absolutely horrible. But just as often, there's a glint of an idea, or direction, or topic, and away I go, trying to keep up with the vein of thought branching in all directions. The British novelist E. M. Forster once said, "How do I know what I think until I see what I say?" I've come to have a lot of faith in this idea. Rather than trying to use my journal the way I used to—to try to write beautiful, eloquent prose—I use the journal simply to think things through; that the prose sometimes stinks doesn't bother me anymore.

We know how powerful our internal critics can be, insisting that every word be spelled right, and every thought sharp. Our Watchers can't abide bad writing. One of the conditions that makes bad writing possible for me is that my Watchers are not voices I honor in my journal, at least not when I want to use my journal to think something through.

Now I know it must seem odd that a book on writing would talk about the virtues of writing badly, but it can be a useful tool for solving all kinds of writing problems. I encourage you to use this approach throughout *The Curious Writer.* I've seen bad writing turn slow writers into faster ones, procrastinators into initiators. I've seen bad writing help students who always wrote short papers begin to generate longer, more thoughtful essays. Best of all, I've seen bad writing transform students who once hated writing into people who see writing as a useful tool for thinking, and even a source of pleasure.

Conditions That Make "Bad" Writing Possible

1. Willingness to suspend judgment.
2. Ability to write fast enough to outrun your internal critic.
3. Belief that confusion, uncertainty, and ambiguity help thought rather than hinder it.
4. Interest in writing about "risky" subjects, or those that you don't know what you want to say about until you say it.

Search for Surprise

One of the key benefits of writing badly is *surprise.* This was a revelation for me when I first discovered the virtues of bad writing in graduate school. I was convinced that you never pick up the pen unless you know what you want to say, which may account for my struggles with journal writing. Suddenly I stumbled on a new way to use writing—not to *record* what I already knew about a subject, but to *discover* what I actually thought. This way of writing promised a feast of surprises that made me hunger to put words on the page.

EXERCISE 1.2

A Roomful of Details

STEP ONE: Spend ten minutes brainstorming a list of details based on the following prompt. Write down whatever comes into your mind, no matter how silly. Be specific and don't censor yourself.

> Try to remember a room you spent a lot of time in as a child. It may be your bedroom in the back of the house at the edge of the field, or the kitchen where

your grandmother kneaded bread or made thick red pasta sauce. Put yourself back in that room. Now look around you. What do you see? What do you hear? What do you smell?

STEP TWO: Examine your list. If things went well, you will have a fairly long list of details. As you review the list, identify one detail that surprises you the most, a detail that seems somehow to carry an unexpected charge. This might be a detail that seems connected to a feeling or story. You might be drawn to a detail that confuses you a little. Whatever its particular appeal, circle the detail.

Brainstorming

- Anything goes.
- Don't censor yourself.
- Write everything down.
- Be playful but stay focused.

STEP THREE: Use the circled detail as a prompt for a seven-minute fastwrite. Begin by focusing on the detail: What does it make you think of? And then what? And then? Alternatively, begin by simply describing the detail more fully: What does it look like? Where did it come from? What stories are attached to it? How does it make you feel? Avoid writing in generalities. Write about specifics—that is, particular times, places, moments, and people. Write fast, and chase after the words to see where they want to go. Give yourself permission to write badly.

One Student's Response

MARGARET'S JOURNAL

EXERCISE 1.2

STEP THREE

Detail: Pillows that spelled our names

The pillows that spelled our names sat on our beds against the wall. I slept on the top bunk, I think. Mostly I think I wanted the bunk that she got—if she was on the bottom then I wanted it. If she wanted the top then that was inevitably the coolest bunk. My pillows spelled out "Margy" in red, green fabric, with white lace tracing the edges. They were ugly, Christmassy shades, antiquish. Freckly. Our mom made them just for us girls, not the three boys. I didn't get my whole name spelled out because it is eight letters long, but Chelsea got all seven of hers. Her colors were blue-yellow, a color scheme that to this day I find elegant and beautiful. Her colors were fresh and alive and mine seemed dusty, old, plain, like my old-lady name . . . But they were fun, they made bed-making an exercise in identity, these are my colors—red, green, brown like my hair and eyes and freckles and hers were gold like her almost white blond hair and bright blue eyes. This is us . . .

"Did anything surprise you?" That's one of the first questions I ask my students after an open-ended fastwriting exercise. With any exercise, some students answer, "No, nothing surprised me." But almost always an equal number of students nod, or simply ignore the question because they haven't stopped writing even after the time is up. This is the experience I most want my students to have, particularly early in a writing course, because they discover, often for the first time, that they can write to learn more about something.

You may experience at least three kinds of surprise after completing a fastwriting exercise like the preceding one:

1. Surprise about *how much* writing you did: "I never thought I had that much to say about that." Even if the writing doesn't lead to an essay or provide material for an assignment, this discovery is crucial. Remember, the fastwriting was prompted by just one detail. "Who would have guessed that I could write three pages about a broken old chair!"

2. Surprise about discovering an *unexpected topic:* The poet Richard Hugo wrote that there were two kinds of these—triggering topics and generated topics. Writers often begin with one idea about their subject, but the writing leads them to another, better idea, one they wouldn't have discovered without following the trail of words.

3. Surprise about discovering a *new way of understanding a topic:* Consider Margaret's response to Exercise 1.2 in the preceding "One Student's Response." Margaret writes about embroidered pillows she and her sister received from their mother, a seemingly innocuous detail until her writing suddenly takes a reflective turn: *they made bed-making an exercise in identity* . . . Quite unexpectedly, Margaret has discovered a new way of understanding her childhood bed pillows.

The kind of surprises you encounter doing this sort of writing may not always be profound. They may not even provide you with obvious essay topics. With any luck, though, by hunting for surprises in your own work you will begin to experience the pleasure of writing *to learn.* That's no small thing, particularly if you've always believed that writers should have it all figured out before they pick up the pen.

Finally, remember that *the more you look, the more you see.* Memories, texts, objects, data, experiences, art, whatever, are all much more likely to yield surprise if we prolong our gaze, resisting the temptation to rush to easy conclusions.

INQUIRING INTO THE DETAILS

INVENTION STRATEGIES

Perhaps without knowing it, you have already practiced some writing techniques designed to help you generate material. These *invention strategies* include fastwriting, listing, brainstorming, questioning, and even conversation. You can use these techniques in any writing situation when you need to gather more information, find a topic, or explore what you think. We call on these strategies often in the exercises and assignments that follow.

At first, spending time doing all this writing and thinking before you actually begin a draft may seem like a waste of time. After all, your goal is to finish the assignment. But if you want to find a focused topic that means something to you and write it with enough information, then invention strategies such as fastwriting will prove invaluable. They produce the raw material that can be shaped, like clay on a potter's wheel, into something with form and meaning. But really the best thing about invention strategies is that they often generate material that is ripe with surprise.

Invention Strategies

- ***Fastwriting:*** The emphasis is on speed, not correctness. Don't compose, don't think about what you want to say before you say it. Instead, let the writing lead, helping you discover what you think.
- ***Listing:*** Fast lists can help you generate lots of information quickly. They are often in code, with words and phrases that have meaning only for you. Let your lists grow in waves—think of two or three items and then pause until the next few items rush in.
- ***Clustering:*** This nonlinear method of generating information, also called *mapping,* relies on *webs* and often free association of ideas or information. Begin with a core word, phrase, or concept at the center of a page, and build branches off it. Follow each branch until it dies out, return to the core, and build another. (See page 105.)
- ***Questioning:*** Questions are to ideas what knives are to onions. They help you cut through to the less obvious insights and perspectives, revealing layers of possible meanings, interpretations, and ways of understanding. Asking questions complicates things but rewards you with new discoveries.

- ***Conversing:*** Conversing is fastwriting with the mouth. When we talk, especially to someone we trust, we work out what we think and feel about things. We listen to what we say, but we also invite a response, which leads us to new insights.
- ***Researching:*** This is a kind of conversation, too. We listen and respond to other voices that have said something or will say something if asked about topics that interest us. Reading and interviewing are not simply things you do when you write a research paper but activities to use whenever you have questions you can't answer on your own.
- ***Observing:*** When we look closely at anything, we see what we didn't notice at first. Careful observation of people, objects, experiments, images, and so on generates specific information that leads to informed judgment.

WRITING AS A PROCESS

Hunting is not those heads on the wall. This is the title of an essay by Amiri Baraka, a writer and intellectual, who argues that the *process* of bringing art into being is the essential element of a creative act, not the end product. In other words, the *act* of painting, not the painting itself, matters most. I wouldn't go quite that far when describing writing—the process and the final product are inseparable—but generally students pay far too little attention to the writing process in their rush to get the writing done. The result is that rich possibilities, including new ideas and perspectives, are short-circuited before they have a chance to be explored. The key to writing well is to understand the writing process. That way we get more control over it.

Recognizing the Challenges

All writers, including those who publish, face challenges in their writing. The difference between an experienced writer and a less experienced one is that the experienced writer recognizes the challenges and has figured out ways to solve them.

Consider, for example, the process of John McPhee, a writer of creative nonfiction articles and books on topics ranging from birch bark canoes to oranges. Pulitzer Prize winner McPhee is of the "stone-kicking school" of journalism; its philosophy is that if you want to discover the story you want to tell, you must spend a lot of time just hanging around with the people who know something about your subject. McPhee does this, spending as much as a year interviewing and observing people and things, as well as reading up on his subject. The result of this kind of investigation is pages and pages of notes, a mother lode of information, and this is McPhee's writing challenge: how to organize all that information and find the story he wants to tell. Over the years, McPhee has worked this out. When his notes get lengthy, he organizes them by topic in three-ring binders, and then he transfers the topics to index cards, which he

The writer John McPhee, winner of the Pulitzer Prize.

posts on a bulletin board above his desk. McPhee constantly plays with the order of the cards, experimenting with different beginnings, middles, and ends, constantly on the hunt for a structure that will bring all the information to life. When he finds it, he begins writing the piece, following the trail he worked out on the bulletin board in front of him.

John McPhee established this process through trial and error. He stuck with the strategies that seemed to improve the results and abandoned the strategies that didn't. I offer you this story not because McPhee's process is one I recommend. It's an approach that's peculiar to this one writer in a particular situation, a writer who must figure out how to organize a tremendous amount of information in a meaningful way. I want to suggest that if you recognize your writing challenges as solvable issues that are often related to *how* you approach a particular writing task, then you will become a more versatile and more skilled writer. Seeing the link between writing challenges and the writing process means that most writers can improve if they become more aware of *how* they approach a particular writing situation that creates the challenges for them.

EXERCISE 1.3

What Is Your Process?

Take a moment and analyze your own writing challenges. The following questions might help you develop a profile of your writing process in certain situations, and help you identify problems you might want to address by altering your process.

STEP ONE: Complete the Self-Evaluation Survey.

Self-Evaluation Survey

1. When you're given a school writing assignment, do you wait until the last minute to get it done?

   Always——Often——Sometimes——Rarely——Never

2. How often have you had the experience of learning something you didn't expect through writing about it?

   Very often——Fairly often——Sometimes——Rarely——Never

3. Do you generally plan out what you're going to write before you write it?

   Always——Often——Sometimes——Rarely——Never

4. *Prewriting* describes activities that some writers engage in before they begin a first draft. Prewriting might include freewriting or fastwriting, making lists, brainstorming or mapping, collecting information, talking to someone about the essay topic, reading up on it, or jotting down ideas in a notebook or journal. How much prewriting do you tend to do for the following types of assignments? Circle the appropriate answer.

   - A personal essay:

     A great deal——Some——Very little——None——Haven't written one
   - A critical essay about a short story, novel, or poem:

     A great deal——Some——Very little——None——Haven't written one
   - A research paper:

     A great deal——Some——Very little——None——Haven't written one
   - An essay exam:

     A great deal——Some——Very little——None——Haven't written one

5. At what point in writing an academic paper do you usually get stuck? Check all that apply.

   ❑ Getting started

   ❑ In the middle

   ❑ Finishing

   ❑ I never get stuck (go on to Question 9)

   ❑ Other ______________________________

6. If you usually have problems getting started on an academic paper or essay, which of the following do you often find hardest to do? Check all that apply. (If you don't have trouble getting started, go on to Question 7.)

   ❑ Deciding on a topic

   ❑ Writing an introduction

❑ Finding a good place to write
❑ Figuring out exactly what you're supposed to do for the assignment
❑ Finding a purpose or focus for the paper
❑ Finding the right tone
❑ Other ______________________

7. If you usually get stuck in the middle of a paper, which of the following causes the most problems? (If writing in the middle of a paper isn't a problem for you, go on to Question 8.)

❑ Keeping focused on the topic
❑ Finding enough information to meet page length requirements
❑ Following my plan for how I wanted to write the paper
❑ Bringing in other research or points of view
❑ Organizing all my information
❑ Trying to avoid plagiarism
❑ Worrying about whether the paper meets the requirements of the assignment
❑ Worrying that the paper just isn't any good
❑ Messing with citations
❑ Other ______________________

8. If you have difficulty finishing an essay or paper, which of the following difficulties are typical for you? Check all that apply.

❑ Composing a last paragraph or conclusion
❑ Worrying that the paper doesn't meet the requirements of the assignment
❑ Worrying that the paper just isn't any good
❑ Trying to keep focused on the main idea or thesis
❑ Trying to avoid repeating yourself
❑ Realizing you don't have enough information
❑ Dealing with the bibliography or citations
❑ Other ______________________

9. Rank the following list of approaches to revision so that it reflects the strategies you use *most often to least often* when rewriting academic papers. Rank the items 1–6, with the strategy you use most often as a 1 and least often as a 6.

____ I usually just tidy things up—editing sentences, checking spelling, looking for grammatical errors, and other proofreading activities.

____ I mostly look for ways to reorganize existing information in the draft to make it more effective.

____ I generally try to fill holes by adding more information.

____ I do more research.

____ I often completely change the focus or even the main idea in the revision, rewriting sections, adding or removing information, and rearranging the order of things.

____ I rarely do any rewriting at all.

10. Finally, do you tend to impose a lot of conditions on when, where, or how you think you write most effectively? For example, do you need a certain pen, do you always have to write on a computer, must it be quiet or noisy, or do you often write best under pressure? Do you need to be in certain kinds of places to write effectively? Or can you write under a range of circumstances, with few or no conditions? Circle one.

    Lots of conditions——Some——A few——No conditions

    If you do impose conditions on when, where, or how you write, list some of those conditions here:

    1.
    2.
    3.
    4.

STEP TWO: In small groups, discuss the results of the survey. Begin by picking someone to tally the answers to each question. Post these on the board or a sheet of newsprint so they can be added to the class totals. Analyze the results for your group. In particular, discuss the following questions:

- Are there patterns in the responses? Do most group members seem to answer certain questions in similar or different ways? Are there interesting contradictions?
- Based on these results, what "typical" habits or challenges do writers in your class seem to share?
- What struck you most?

Thinking About Your Process

We are creatures of habit. This applies to writing, too. Even experienced writers have deeply ingrained habits, some of them quite sensible, some quirky. Donald Murray always works in the morning and always in his basement office with a view of the river. Novelist Mitch Wieland always writes with a No. 2 pencil and a yellow legal pad; only later does he compose on the computer. Some writers must smoke, chew gum, or drink. Some must write in bed. Rachel, a former student, always came to class on the day a draft was due with dark circles under her eyes; she insisted that the only way she could write good papers was to pull an all-nighter before the assignment was due.

When we do something more than a few times we often develop habits like these. Sometimes we don't even think about them. But we develop other habits with some awareness—waiting until the last minute to write a draft seemed to work for Rachel the first time she tried it, an accidental strategy she first used when she forgot a paper was due and was forced to crank it out at the last minute. Likewise, Mitch Wieland developed his fondness for pencils and legal pads to draft a short story or novel early on without much deliberation. He likes the way he thinks with a pencil in his hand, and perhaps the feel and sound of the lead scratching on paper.

The habits we consciously develop become less conscious as time goes on, and pretty soon it isn't even a question whether television and schoolwork mix well together, or if last-minute drafts are the only way to compose. When we *do* scrutinize these habits, we often immediately assume that they are part of the best—if not the *only*—way to proceed with a task. "It's always worked for me," Rachel said every time.

However, reflecting on *how* we do something is as central to intellectual activities as it is to athletic ones. Coaches often help a tennis player deconstruct and then revise a backhand, or a swimmer refine a flip turn, but consider how infrequently we do this kind of reflection when it comes to our academic writing. *Metacognitive thinking,* or thinking about thinking, is a fairly sophisticated intellectual activity but it's an essential one for this simple reason: *the more we think about a process, the more control we get over it.*

Reading and writing are two processes that are central to life—including academic life—and the time you spend reflecting on how you engage in both activities is time well spent. That's why the composition course emphasizes discussion and analysis of the writing process, and will include many moments like the one I had with Rachel after she told me that she wrote her best stuff at the last minute.

"Are you sure?" I asked.

"I think so," she said. "But I never really thought about it much."

The survey you completed is the beginning of reflection on your own writing process. You will do this kind of reflection again and again throughout this book so that by the end you will have written a narrative of thought that tells the story of your reading and writing processes, and how you change those processes to produce better writing more efficiently.

Linear Versus Recursive Models

No single writing process—a kind of recipe every writer can follow—will reliably produce "good" writing. But certain elements of the writing process are fairly common to all writers. What distinguishes one writer's process from another's is *when* they invoke an element and in what situations. Timing is crucial in the writing process, as in any process from making fudge to building space shuttles. But what are these elements of the writing process? Many experts have proposed models to describe it. You may be familiar with some of them. For example, one of the simplest models for the writing process is depicted in Figure 1.2, which shows a linear process that moves, step by step, from prewriting to writing to rewriting. Typically, prewriting represents things a writer does to generate information and clarify intention. The term from classical rhetoric that roughly equates with prewriting is *invention*. As we discussed earlier, prewriting can include a range of activities from brainstorming and fastwriting to note taking, conversation, and formal research. Writing is the process of producing the draft. Rewriting, of course, is revision and all that it entails, from tidying up sentences to entirely changing a paper's focus or even its topic.

FIGURE 1.2 A linear model of the writing process.

The only problem with the linear model is that it moves in one direction, and most writing theorists agree that the writing process just doesn't work that way. Instead, movement within the process proceeds in a *recursive* fashion—that is, it moves back and forth from one stage to the next. Writers do not simply march forward, step by step, completing one stage of the writing process and then moving on to a subsequent stage. Writing, like life, is more complicated than that. For example, I initially drafted this chapter fairly quickly, relying on what I already knew about writing process models. Only later did I consult the books on my shelf and collect more information about the writing process—double-checking what I had said and adding information I may not have thought of at the time of my initial draft. When I have some background knowledge about my subject my approach often is to draft *and then* prewrite *and then* rewrite.

In other words, writers don't always begin at the "beginning" of the writing process, and they may return to a step they've already attempted. Sometimes they leap over a step or return to it later. A better description of the writing process, then, looks like Figure 1.3.

Dialectical Thinking

The recursive model of the writing process focuses on the back-and-forth movement between the different stages of process. The sort of thinking writers do as

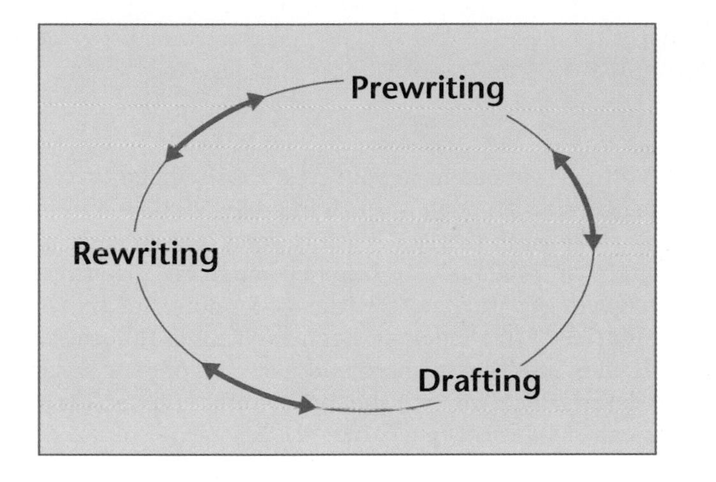

FIGURE 1.3 A recursive model of the writing process.

they move through the process also is done in a back-and-forth manner, but instead of moving between the different stages of the process, *dialectical thinking* shifts between two contrasting modes of thought, one creative and the other critical.

The word *dialectical* has several meanings, many of which focus on the relationship between opposing ideas or forces. In dialectical thinking, the relationship between creative and critical modes of thought is important. Why? Because the interplay between the creative and the critical can foster new and deeper ways of understanding.

Dialectical thinking does not come naturally to most people and, while you might think otherwise, the critical mode of thought isn't the problem. I mentioned earlier that most writers have strong internal critics—the "Watchers at the Gates" who are quick to criticize and judge. "That's a stupid sentence," they hiss. "You really don't know what you're trying to say, do you?" The critical self is all too present for most of us. What we tend to be less aware of is our creative self. This side may surface in a fastwrite that uncovers an unexpected subject, or in the pleasure of making lists of places you remember from childhood. Much like children, our creative selves are playful, open to surprise and discovery.

One of the key benefits of writing badly is surprise.

Unfortunately, for many writing students these two selves are often at war with each other. This is a pity. Imagine the results if you could get the creative and the critical to collaborate. As a writer, you could be both playful *and* judgmental, open things up *and* narrow them down. That's the key to dialectical thinking when it's applied to the writing process.

EXERCISE 1.4

Practicing Dialectical Thinking

STEP ONE: Think of a moment in your past that seemed typical for you. Perhaps you spent time sitting on a bench in a bay window reading or playing football at the park down the street. Possibly you grew up with an alcoholic parent, and would wait anxiously for him to come home. Use this moment as the topic of a fastwrite. Write quickly without stopping, but try to remain within the boundaries of this moment. Begin writing in the present tense, putting yourself back into this moment and using all of your senses. Describe the moment in detail. Don't worry if the tense shifts and don't try to explain the moment's meaning. Just keep writing.

STEP TWO: Reread your initial fastwrite, underlining words, lines, or passages that seem significant in some way. Now compose a short paragraph that begins with the following words:

As I look back on this moment now, I realize that . . .

STEP THREE: After completing your short paragraph, skip a few lines in your journal and compose a response to one or more of the following questions about your writing experience.

- How differently, if at all, would you have approached the fastwrite if you knew that you would read the results aloud to others?
- Did you imagine an audience other than yourself?
- What, if anything, surprised you?
- What problems arose during the fastwrite, if any, and how did you resolve them?
- Was there anything different about the ways you approached the writing from the ways you usually do?

ONE STUDENT'S RESPONSE

JON'S JOURNAL

EXERCISE 1.4

STEP ONE

Birds chirp overhead as the squirrels quickly dash through the branches like schoolchildren would burst through the door at recess. Directly behind me, Aunty Val is hanging her laundry out to dry. Directly in front of me lies the sort of structure that all children would dream of having. It's as tall as my house! A rope dangles from the top down to the ground. I have never climbed this to the top and I don't think that I ever will. If I ever got to the top of this structure, I would climb the wooden ladder built on the side. Or maybe take the few steps up to the monkey bars, swing to the end, and try to climb up from there. But I rarely paid any attention to this structure at all. Today is no exception. I am sitting in the sandbox with my springer spaniel and the dismembered corpses of hundreds of GI Joes that felt the heat of battle and now lay in shallow, unmarked sand graves . . . I can hear my brothers and the neighbor kid fight over who shot first, why he didn't die, and whether or not he was wearing Kevlar. That was the beauty of the GI Joes, they didn't whine, or cheat. When it was their time they simply snapped and died. Then, they were satisfied with mass burials . . .

STEP TWO

As I look back on this moment now, I realize that as a child, I was extremely self-contained. I could keep myself entertained as easily, if not better than I could be entertained by others. I wonder what changed between now and then? Now, I hate being alone . . .

Writing with Computers

KNOWING WHEN TO STEP AWAY FROM THE COMPUTER

Computers make many time-consuming tasks more efficient, but there are times when it's important to step away from the computer.

- Some writers prefer the experience of writing with paper and pen. If a computer makes you feel disconnected from your writing or makes you feel anxious, then by all means step away from it.
- Some invention strategies are best done with paper and pen. For instance, one of your invention strategies might be carrying a small notepad and pen with you and jotting notes about your ideas and observations as you go about your day. Doing this with a computer, even a very small one, would be unnatural.
- Computers are tools of both productivity and recreation. Many writers sit down with great intentions of working diligently and find themselves checking their e-mail, visiting social networking sites, shopping, or playing games. Thus, the computer can become a source of procrastination or a scapegoat for avoiding the apprehension of starting a new project. Either way, if you are distracted when sitting down at a computer, it may be best to step away.
- Sitting down at a computer without initial thinking, note taking, and invention causes writers to bypass one of the most critical stages of writing. While it is perfectly fine to use the computer to invent, we must distinguish invention and drafting. Skipping the invention stage and jumping into drafting may seem productive at first, but it usually results in a shallow draft that will require substantial revision. When you start a new writing project, choose an invention strategy that works for you before sitting down at the computer to write a first draft.

Calling the two opposed modes of thought creative and critical is a helpful shorthand for the different *types* of thought. But let's look at this idea more closely. When students reflect on their experience with Exercise 1.4, they often say that Step One and Step Two were quite different. In Step One, when they plunged into a fastwrite remembering a moment from their past, the writing often led them to unexpected places. They remembered surprising details, or discovered a new subject, or found a new way of seeing something they'd seen before. This is a kind of *creative thinking;* it is open ended, digressive, and often surprising. It might even engage feelings as well as thoughts. Step Two of Exercise 1.4 begins with the phrase, *As I look back on this moment now . . .*, and this frame often thrusts writers into a much more reflective, thoughtful, and detached stance. When writers are instructed to *compose* rather than fastwrite—that is, think about what they're going to say before they say it—their writing process frequently slows down, their language becomes more precise, and the writing becomes more focused. This is *critical thinking.*

Combining these two modes of thinking gives both thinking and writing more range and depth. Creative thinking creates the conditions for discovery—new insights or ways of seeing—while critical thinking helps writers refine their discoveries and focus on the most significant of them.

Figure 1.4 lists other ways you can visualize creative and critical thinking. In narrative writing, for instance (the kind of writing you likely did in the previous exercise), creative thinking helps you generate information about *what*

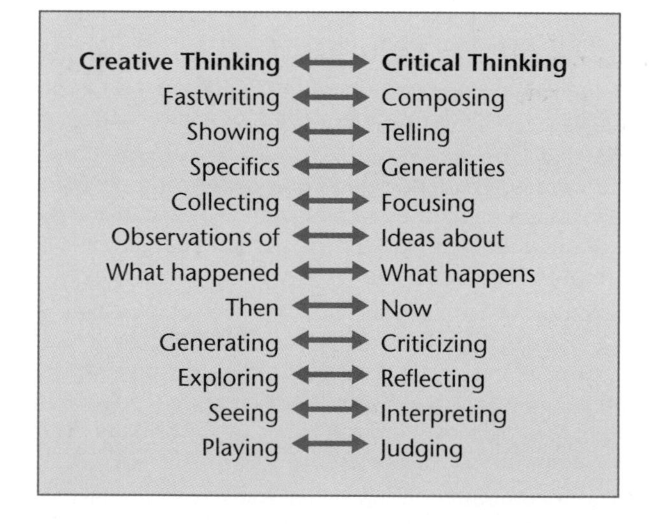

FIGURE 1.4 When writers use dialectical thinking, they move back and forth between two opposing modes of thought—the creative and the critical. One seems playful and the other judgmental; one feels open ended and the other more closed. Certain activities such as fastwriting or brainstorming promote one mode of thought, and careful composing or reflection promotes another.

happened, while critical thinking may lead you to insights about *what happens.* Note in the excerpt from Jon's journal how a seemingly meaningless scene describing play with toy soldiers acquires substance when Jon is forced to place the experience in perspective. Jon finds a larger significance in his simple recollection by shifting to critical thinking. Likewise, in research writing, investigators often move back and forth between their *observations of* things and their *ideas about* them. More broadly speaking, when we think creatively we collect, and when we think critically we evaluate what we have collected.

Note that in Figure 1.4 double-ended arrows link each of the two pairs. The process is *dialectical*; it consists of a back-and-forth movement between the two opposing modes of thought. Many writers do this instinctively. As they compose, they constantly shift between contrasting modes of thought, from collecting to focusing, from generating to criticizing, from showing to telling, from exploring to reflecting, from believing to doubting, from playing to judging.

Certain activities—such as fastwriting and composing—encourage one way of thinking or the other. Learning to balance these opposing forces is what dialectical thinking is all about. In practice, however, many beginning writers give too much emphasis to either one mode of thinking or the other, a tendency that accounts for many of the challenges these writers face within their own writing processes.

Spend too much time locked in the critical mode of thinking and your internal critic takes over. This voice pinches off the flow of material generated by creative thinking. The writing then comes slowly and painfully, and it rarely yields surprise. Topics are abandoned before the writer has fully explored their potential. Working from scarcity, the writer is compelled to use all the material he or she has at hand, often resulting in writing that feels forced, incomplete, or obvious.

On the other hand, give too much free rein to creative thinking and the artist runs wild. The problem here isn't scarcity but rather overabundance. It's a poverty of riches, for without a critical eye to provide shape and direction, the writer cannot present all of his or her material in a coherent and meaningful fashion.

Other challenges result when writers fail to move back and forth between creative and critical modes. One excursion into creative thinking followed by a second into critical thinking is rarely enough to produce good writing. Writers need to move back and forth between the two modes until they come to see their topics in interesting ways that differ from what they might have creatively or critically thought about the topic when they started the writing process.

Put simply, the goal of this dialectical thinking is to address a question that ultimately all writing must answer:

So what?

So what? can be a pretty harsh question, and I find that some students tend to ask it too soon in the writing process, before they've fully explored their topic or collected enough information. That may have been your experience when you suddenly found yourself high and dry, forced to reflect on possible meanings of a moment you've written about for only eight minutes. When you can't come up with an answer to *So what?,* the solution is usually to generate more information.

There's another danger, too. In their enthusiasm to answer *So what?,* some writers seize on the first convenient idea or thesis that comes along. This abruptly ends the process of inquiry before they've had a chance to explore their subjects. These writers squander the opportunity to be surprised by what they discover.

EXERCISE 1.5

Overcome Your Own Challenges

STEP ONE: Consult again the Self-Evaluation Survey you completed in Exercise 1.3. Based on what you've learned so far, answer the following questions:

- What are the biggest challenges to your writing process?
- How can you overcome these challenges?

USING WHAT YOU HAVE LEARNED

When I was in college I used to say this to anyone who asked how I felt about writing: *I don't like writing but I love having written.* What I meant, of course, is that I often felt satisfaction with the product of writing—the paper or essay—but didn't like the work that it took to produce it. This belief didn't help me improve as a writer because it prevented me from finding things about the process that could actually be okay, and even pleasurable, things like discovery. I never imagined surprise was possible. I hope this chapter initiated a reexamination of your own beliefs about writing. I hardly expect a revolution in your thinking, but maybe one or two things you once thought were true of writing may at least be in doubt, particularly if you think those beliefs get in the way of your progress. Carry that openness to revise your thinking into every assignment in this book and you may be surprised at what you can do.

You now know more about your writing process. You've identified what seems to go well and when you get into trouble. The habit of reflecting on your process will be invaluable as you face each new writing situation because each one presents different problems and choices. Understanding the basic rhetorical principles—considering how to present yourself to particular audiences on particular subjects—will help. You already know more than you think about rhetoric.

You'll also have the chance to try out dialectical thinking, a process that may seem a little dizzying. In a way, it should, because both the writing process and dialectical thinking involve a great deal of back-and-forth movement, the sort of mental gymnastics you perform with the pen in your hand or your fingers on the keyboard.

Does it feel natural? Probably not. At least not yet. But I hope you'll find that your understanding of the writing process becomes more intuitive as you read further in the book. You may modify your writing process, add a step here or skip one there, prolong the process or cut it short, depending on the writing situation and your rhetorical concerns. Whatever you do, though, you need to make choices based on an understanding of how they will influence your process. This is the key to making you a productive, confident writer.

On Saturday mornings across America, students read a passage on an aptitude test and answer a question about it by darkening a circle on a bubble sheet. In contrast, reading to inquire opens a conversation with a text in which the words on the page are only a part of the dialogue between the author and the reader.

Reading as Inquiry

Here's what you might be thinking as you read this sentence: *this is a chapter about reading (in a textbook about writing) and I'm really hungry and could eat some potato chips and I already know about reading; I've been reading for years; this guy has a strange way of opening a textbook chapter how does he know what I'm thinking, he probably doesn't want to know* . . . Okay, so I don't know exactly what you're thinking. But I do know that you're not simply sitting there decoding the meaning of each word I've written. For one thing, you're reading faster than that, looking at chunks of language. However, a lot of what is going on in your head isn't directly related to the words here. You are thinking about what kind of book you are reading—the textbook genre—and making mental predictions about what is going to come next. You are thinking about the subject—"reading as inquiry"—and considering what you may already know about it. And you are thinking about your purpose in reading these sentences or this book, trying to use that purpose as a guide to help you navigate my meaning and its relevance to you. However, I'm probably wrong about the potato chips.

I hope the image you get of reading from this account is that what *you* bring to the reading situation is much more powerful than the words on the page. Experienced readers are aware of this, and like experienced writers, they can bring this knowledge to a range of reading situations and make choices about *how* to read. This rhetorical knowledge of reading is especially important in college. First, you'll be reading a lot, and you'll be introduced, in classes across campus, to new genres and specialized writing that are entirely new to you. Sometimes you might feel as if you're in a wrestling match with texts whose moves are so novel that they threaten to pin you every time you confront them. But you can learn the moves, and in many cases you already know them. My students fret about writing. But they don't seem to get very worked up

What You'll Learn in This Chapter

- How your existing beliefs about reading might be obstacles to reading rhetorically.
- What connections exist between the writing and reading process.
- How to use the double-entry journal to encourage dialectical thinking.
- How to apply some of the same strategies to reading pictures that you do to reading texts.
- How to understand the unique grammar of images.
- How to design the "look" of your writing.

about the challenges of reading. As you've seen, however, reading is complex, and in this chapter I'll show you how the writing process involves some of the same mental activities and even similar rhetorical choices used in reading. I'll also show you how writing can help you read better.

When we think of reading we usually associate the act exclusively with written texts, but so many of the images we encounter are, like written texts, crafted to communicate and persuade and so, whether we recognize it or not, we read images, too. In this chapter we'll use images as a metaphor to talk about all kinds of reading strategies, but we'll also focus on the unique grammar of visual literacy and how images work to influence a "reader."

MOTIVES FOR READING

Why read? In the case of best-selling popular fiction such as *The Da Vinci Code* or the Harry Potter books, the answer seems pretty clear: these are entertaining books. But pleasure is not a motive that seems to apply to most academic reading—we usually regard such reading as something we have to do to study for the test or write the paper. However, reading to inquire, while not always a source of pleasure, can offer the satisfaction of surprise and discovery, just as writing to inquire can. This is because what's behind an encounter with a text can be a desire to answer a question that interests you. Reading to inquire is, like writing to inquire, an open-ended process in which you set out to discover what you think, and along the way welcome confusion and ambiguity as a natural condition of the search. In other words, you never read just to collect information; you read to have a conversation with the information. You go back and forth between what an author says and what you think about what he or she says. *Does this help answer a question I've posed? Does it inspire me to see things differently? Does it complicate what I already believe?*

Reading with the spirit of inquiry turns books, essays, and articles into one side of a dialogue that you're having with yourself and an author.

Reading with the spirit of inquiry turns books, essays, and articles into one side of a dialogue that you're having with yourself and an author. The meaning of a text (or an image) isn't fixed forever—engraved in stone tablets like a message from above—but worked out between the two of you, the author and the reader. This turns reading into a much more complicated intellectual activity, but it also makes reading more interesting because you create the conditions for surprise, for learning, and for discovery.

BELIEFS ABOUT READING

Most of us aren't very aware of our reading strategies and habits. Why should we be? After all, isn't reading just reading? How many ways can you do it? The way we go about learning how to read, however, is similar to the way we learn how to write. We start at an early age, perhaps even before we get to school. Along with the learning, we acquire beliefs that inform our response to *how* we read. These beliefs, though, can help or hinder our progress as readers. Once again, then, we need to assess our beliefs. Only by understanding *how* we read in certain situations can we acquire more control over what we get out of the reading experience.

EXERCISE 2.1

What Do You Believe?

STEP ONE: From the following list, choose two qualities that you believe best characterize a "good" reader.

1. Needs to read things only once to understand what an author is saying.
2. Can find the hidden meanings in the text.
3. Takes notes while reading.
4. Reads slowly and carefully, and doesn't proceed unless she understands the meaning of every word.
5. Pays attention to his feelings about what he is reading.
6. Tries to find support for what she already believes.
7. Understands that all sources and all authors are biased.
8. Tries to find the author's theme or thesis.
9. Focuses mostly on the important parts of the text, such as the beginning, ending, and titles.
10. Pays most attention to details, facts, statistics.
11. Avoids reading things that don't interest him.
12. Reads with certain questions or goals in mind.

STEP TWO: Answer the following questions in your journal.

- Do you think you're a good reader? Why or why not?
- How would you describe your own reading habits and methods?

STEP THREE: Share the results of the previous two steps in a class discussion and then consider the following questions:

- Did you find that your beliefs were widely shared by others in the class?
- Did you find that others generally considered themselves competent readers?
- Did all competent readers have similar beliefs and reading habits?
- How important were your early reading experiences in shaping your beliefs about reading?

Most reading instruction seems to focus on comprehension—you know, the SAT- or ACT-inspired kind of situation in which you are asked to read something and then explain what it means. This often becomes an exercise in recall and vocabulary, an analytical challenge in only the most general way. Essentially, you train yourself to distinguish between specifics and generalities and to loosely follow the author's reasoning. In English classes, sometimes we are asked to perform a similar exercise with stories or poems—what is the theme or what does it mean?

Questions such as these send students off on what is essentially an archaeological expedition where they must dig for hidden meaning. The "right" answers to the questions are in the text, like a buried bone; you just have to find them. Sometimes the expedition is successful, sometimes not. The trouble with this type of exercise has less to do with its success rate than with the belief that it tends to foster, which is that *all meaning resides in the text and the reader's job is merely to find it.* This belief limits the reader's interaction with the text. If meaning is fixed within the text, embedded like a bone in antediluvian mud, then all the reader has to do is dig to find that meaning. Digging isn't a bad thing, but reading can be so much more than laboring at the shovel and sifting through dirt.

Only by understanding how we read in certain situations can we acquire more control over what we get out of the reading experience.

Our many experiences with reading in and out of school inevitably lead us to develop assumptions about what reading demands. That's why it's so crucial to draw those beliefs into the open where you can examine them in the light.

READING SITUATIONS AND RHETORICAL CHOICES

It's impossible to decide how you should read without knowing the reading situation. *What are you reading? Why are you reading it?* For example, consider the box score from the 2006 Major League Baseball All-Star Game, pictured here. Those who love baseball are familiar with this particular reading "genre" and how to decipher its meaning quickly and easily. A reader of this sort who is interested in how many runs batted in (RBIs) Alex Rodriguez had during the game knows exactly where to find this information. In the process, that reader might also cull additional relevant information about Rodriguez's performance, like at bats (ABs), statistics that illuminate the significance of his RBIs (or in this case, his lack of RBIs).

However, for a reader who is not a baseball fan and is unfamiliar with the conventions by which the sport communicates its statistics in print, interpreting the information in this box score would be a chore. Obviously then, reading in unfamiliar genres is not easy. Let's consider another, very different genre. For example, those not used to "reading" abstract art are often unmoved by a work like *One (Number 31, 1950).* Not surprisingly, students often have a similar reaction to academic writing, a reaction that can usually be summed up in two words: "It's boring!" But when you read rhetorically you learn not to stay with such initial reactions. You recognize that one reason you can't relate to the text is that you don't know the genre or its conventions. The language may be unfamiliar because you aren't the audience for whom the writing was originally intended.

AL All-Stars	AB	R	H	RBI	BB	SO	LOB	AVG
Suzuki, RF	3	0	0	0	0	1	0	.000
Dye, RF	1	0	0	0	0	0	0	.000
Jeter, SS	3	0	0	0	0	2	0	.000
Tejada, SS	1	0	0	0	0	0	0	.000
Ortiz, 1B	2	0	0	0	0	1	0	.000
Konerko, 1B	2	0	2	0	0	0	0	1.000
1-Lopez, PR-3B	0	1	0	0	0	0	0	.000
Rodriguez, 3B	2	0	0	0	0	0	0	.000
Glaus, 3B-1B	2	1	1	0	0	0	1	.500
Guerrero, LF	2	1	1	1	0	0	0	.500
Young, 2B	2	0	1	2	0	0	0	.500
Rodriguez, C	2	0	0	0	0	0	0	.000
Mauer, C	2	0	0	0	0	1	1	.000
Wells, CF	2	0	1	0	0	0	0	.500
Matthews, LF	1	0	1	0	0	0	0	1.000
Loretta, 2B	2	0	0	0	0	0	1	.000
Zito, P	0	0	0	0	0	0	0	.000
Kazmir, P	0	0	0	0	0	0	0	.000
Santana, P	0	0	0	0	0	0	0	.000
b-Thome, PH	1	0	0	0	0	0	1	.000
Ryan, P	0	0	0	0	0	0	0	.000
Rivera, P	0	0	0	0	0	0	0	.000
Rogers, P	0	0	0	0	0	0	0	.000
a-Ordonez, PH	1	0	0	0	0	1	0	.000
Halladay, P	0	0	0	0	0	0	0	.000
Sizemore, CF	2	0	0	0	0	1	1	.000
Totals	**33**	**3**	**7**	**3**	**0**	**7**	**5**	

a-Struck out for Rogers in the 3rd. b-Grounded out for Santana in the 8th.
1-Ran for Konerko in the 9th.

BATTING
2B: Glaus (1, Hoffman).
3B: Young (1, Hoffman).
HR: Guerrero (1, 2nd inning off Penny, 0 on, 1 out).
TB: Konerko 2; Glaus 2; Guerrero 4; Young 3; Wells; Matthews.
RBI: Guerrero (1), Young 2 (2).
2-out RBI: Young 2.
Runners left in scoring position, 2 out: Sizemore; Mauer.
GIDP: Glaus.
Team LOB: 3.

FIELDING
E: Lopez (1, fielding).
Outfield assists: Wells (Soriano at home).
DP: 3 (Rogers-Jeter-Ortiz, Loretta-Jeter-Ortiz, Young-Tejada-Konerko).

NL All-Stars	AB	R	H	RBI	BB	SO	LOB	AVG
Soriano, LF	2	0	1	0	0	0	0	.500
Webb, P	0	0	0	0	0	0	0	.000
Sanchez, SS-2B	2	0	0	0	0	0	0	.000
Beltran, CF	4	1	2	0	0	0	0	.500
Pujols, 1B	3	0	0	0	0	1	1	.000
Howard, 1B	1	0	0	0	0	0	1	.000
Bay, RF-LF	3	0	1	0	0	2	1	.333
Lee, LF	1	0	0	0	0	0	1	.000
Renteria, SS	2	0	0	0	0	0	1	.000
Arroyo, P	0	0	0	0	0	0	0	.000
Fuentes, P	0	0	0	0	0	0	0	.000
Turnbow, P	0	0	0	0	0	0	0	.000
b-Berkman, PH	0	0	0	0	1	0	0	.000
Cabrera, 3B	0	0	0	0	0	0	0	.000
Wright, 3B	3	1	1	1	0	0	1	.333
Gordon, P	0	0	0	0	0	0	0	.000
Hoffman, P	0	0	0	0	0	0	0	.000
Utley, 2B	2	0	1	0	0	0	0	.500
McCann, C	1	0	0	0	0	0	0	.000
Lo Duca, C	2	0	0	0	0	0	1	.000
Eckstein, SS	1	0	0	0	0	1	0	.000
Penny, P	0	0	0	0	0	0	0	.000
Oswalt, P	0	0	0	0	0	0	0	.000
a-Holliday, PH-RF	3	0	0	0	0	0	0	.000
Totals	**30**	**2**	**6**	**1**	**1**	**4**	**7**	

a-Grounded out for Oswalt in the 3rd. b-Walked for Turnbow in the 7th.

BATTING
2B: Beltran (1, Rogers).
HR: Wright (1, 2nd inning off Rogers, 0 on, 1 out).
TB: Soriano; Beltran 3; Bay; Wright 4; Utley.
RBI: Wright (1).
Runners left in scoring position, 2 out: Bay; Lee.
GIDP: Lo Duca; Renteria; Wright.
Team LOB: 2.

BASERUNNING
SB: Soriano (1, 2nd base off Halladay/Rodriguez), Beltran (1, 3rd base off Halladay/Rodriguez).

FIELDING
DP: (Wright-Sanchez-Howard).

AL All-Stars	IP	H	R	ER	BB	SO	HR	ERA
Rogers	2.0	3	1	1	0	1	1	4.50
Halladay	2.0	3	1	1	0	1	0	4.50
Zito	1.0	0	0	0	0	0	0	0.00
Kazmir	1.0	0	0	0	0	0	0	0.00
Santana	1.0	0	0	0	1	1	0	0.00
Ryan (W, 1-0)	1.0	0	0	0	0	1	0	0.00
Rivera (S, 1)	1.0	0	0	0	0	0	0	0.00

NL All-Stars	IP	H	R	ER	BB	SO	HR	ERA
Penny	2.0	1	1	1	0	3	1	4.50
Oswalt	1.0	0	0	0	0	1	0	0.00
Webb (H, 1)	1.0	0	0	0	0	1	0	0.00
Arroyo (H, 1)	1.0	1	0	0	0	0	0	0.00
Fuentes (H, 1)	1.0	0	0	0	0	1	0	0.00
Turnbow (H, 1)	1.0	1	0	0	0	0	0	0.00
Gordon (H, 1)	1.0	1	0	0	0	1	0	0.00
Hoffman (BS, 1)(L, 0-1)	1.0	3	2	2	0	0	0	18.00

WP: Halladay.
Pitches-strikes: Rogers 30-20, Halladay 22-13, Zito 8-7, Kazmir 9-6, Santana 11-5, Ryan 10-10, Rivera 17-12, Penny 36-24, Oswalt 13-7, Webb 16-10, Arroyo 10-7, Fuentes 9-8, Turnbow 14-8, Gordon 14-8, Hoffman 13-13.
Ground outs-fly outs: Rogers 3-2, Halladay 4-0, Zito 1-2, Kazmir 1-2, Santana 2-0, Ryan 1-1, Rivera 2-1, Penny 1-2, Oswalt 1-1, Webb 1-1, Arroyo 0-3, Fuentes 2-0, Turnbow 2-1, Gordon 2-0, Hoffman 3-0.
Batters faced: Rogers 8, Halladay 7, Zito 3, Kazmir 3, Santana 3, Ryan 3, Rivera 4, Penny 7, Oswalt 3, Webb 3, Arroyo 4, Fuentes 3, Turnbow 3, Gordon 4, Hoffman 6.
Umpires: HP: Jerry Crawford. 1B: Randy Marsh. 2B: Fieldin Culbreth. 3B: Jeff Nelson. LF: Mike Everitt. RF: Alfonso Marquez.
Weather: 79 degrees, cloudy.
Wind: 8 mph, R to L.
T: 2:33.
Att: 38,904.

Box score official statistics approved by Major League Baseball Office of the Commissioner

Box score from 2006 Major League Baseball All-Star Game.

One (Number 31, 1950). 1950. Oil and enamel on unprinted canvas, 8′10″ × 17′5 5/8″. Sidney and Harriet Janis Collection Fund (by exchange). (7.1968) Location: The Museum of Modern Art, New York, NY, U.S.A.

What do you do? Look for clues in the text about how to read it, prepare for the encounter by learning as much as you can about the text's subject, and always keep in mind your purposes for reading the piece in the first place. Only by keeping these things in mind can you make informed choices about *how* you should read. In this sense, reading situations demand the same sort of rhetorical choices that writing situations do. What's surprising, though, is that we rarely talk about choices when we discuss reading.

As a matter of fact, we rarely talk much about reading at all except to practice the reading skills that might help students do well on the reading comprehension section of the SAT or ACT. This is probably a good thing because those are high-stakes tests for college-bound students. But the Saturday morning computerized placement test is only one very specific rhetorical situation. Recall the rhetorical triangle—it also applies to reading situations.

In the reader's rhetorical triangle, the reader moves to the apex of the triangle and the writer (or text's author, in this case) moves down to one of the lower legs (see Figure 2.1). The reader's portion of the triangle includes the reader's purpose for reading the text and the particular habits and strategies he brings to his reading. The subject includes not only the main topic of the reading but the form or genre in which it is presented. The author's purpose shapes the third portion of the triangle. Combined, the three work to determine the context of each reading situation. The verbal SAT exam, for instance, in part involves reading short passages and answering multiple-choice comprehension questions. Speed is important. The significance of the test and the speed required to complete it influence the reader's portion of the triangle. So too does the subject, which is presented in the form of multiple-choice questions. The author's intent in composing the questions—to test comprehension—also shapes the reading situation.

A test situation differs greatly from one in which the same person is asked to read a Ralph Ellison short story and write a critical essay about it for her English

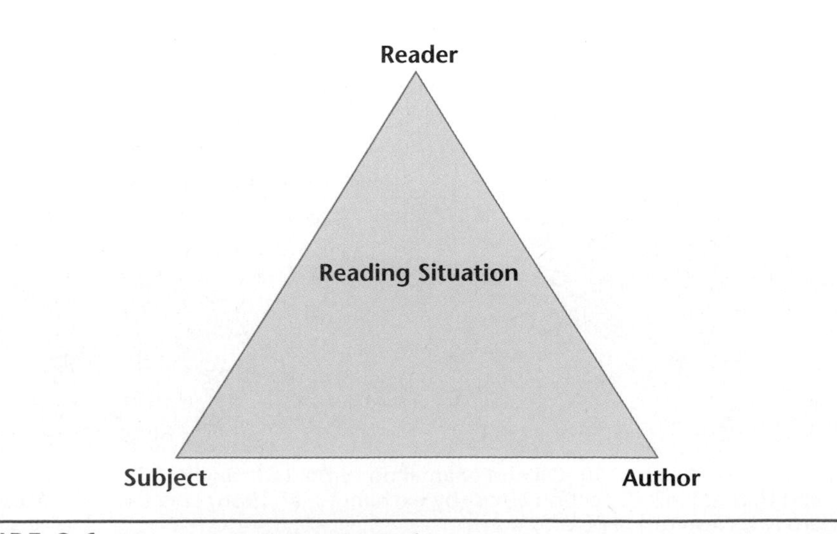

FIGURE 2.1 The reader's rhetorical triangle.

class. Here the author's perspective may be harder to interpret. The subject, presented in short-story form, is also likely to be more ambiguous in its message than multiple-choice questions. The reader also brings different reading habits to the text, reading slowly and perhaps repeatedly, to tease out the meaning.

Each reading situation, then, requires its own rhetorical choices. But how do you know which rhetorical choices to make? A recent study of reading strategies used by college undergraduates found that what distinguished academically successful readers from those who were less successful was agreement with the following statement: *I evaluate whether what I am reading is relevant to my reading goals.*[1] Students with lower GPAs generally didn't consider goals when they were reading and rarely varied their reading strategies. The less successful readers made the same rhetorical choices regardless of the reading situation. The more successful readers, on the other hand, tailored their rhetorical choices to address the needs of the reading situation.

READING AS A PROCESS

Rhetorical reading begins with understanding reading as a process. As with the writing process, the more we know about our own reading process, the more control we have over it and the more we are likely to get out of our reading. There's nothing difficult about understanding reading as a process, but doing so may challenge some of your existing beliefs about how reading works.

Linear Versus Recursive Models

In the last chapter, I discussed two models for understanding the writing process. The first model moved in one direction from prewriting to writing to rewriting. The second model moved back and forth among these three stages. The two models of the reading process that I want you to consider here operate in a similar fashion. The conventional model is linear—information flows in one direction from the text to the readers (see Figure 2.2). Here, while readers

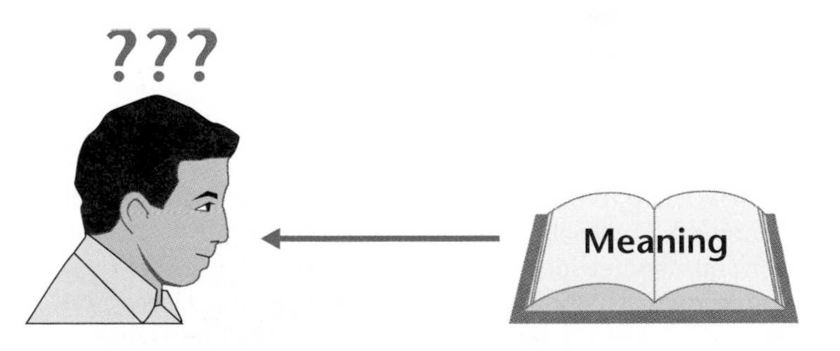

FIGURE 2.2 A linear model of the reading process.

1. Roman, Taraban, Kimberly Rynearson, and Marcel Kerr, "College Students' Academic Performance and Self-Reports of Comprehension Strategy Use," *Reading Psychology* 21, no. 4 (2000): 283–308.

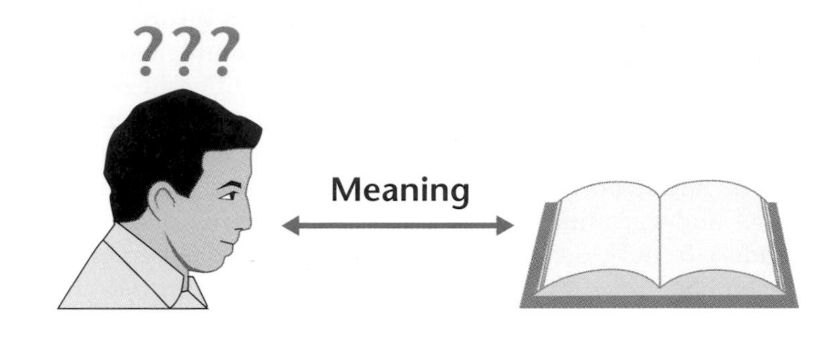

FIGURE 2.3 A recursive model of the reading process.

may have to actively dig within the text for information, the manner in which they receive the information is relatively passive. Meaning resides squarely within the text. Most reading comprehension tests exclusively evaluate this type of reading.

The second model is recursive. It suggests that our understanding of what a text means exists as a two-way *transaction* between the reader and author, the product of a back-and-forth dialogue between what the author is saying and what the reader thinks the author is saying (see Figure 2.3). In this model, the reader interprets, analyzes, reflects on, and thoroughly questions the information in the text; the meaning that emerges doesn't reside on the pages, but somewhere between the reader and the text. As you will see, the recursive model of the reading process often involves writing *while* you read. You will also learn that the back-and-forth movement represented by this model is guided by the reading situation and the rhetorical choices that the reader makes in response to the situation.

EXERCISE 2.2

Reading Strategies

Henry David Thoreau's *Walden*, a classic of American literature, is an account of his relatively brief time living in a one-room cabin on the shore of Walden Pond, just outside Concord, Massachusetts. The book continues to influence new generations of Americans, sometimes with tragic consequences. Writer Jon Krakauer's best seller *Into the Wild* is an account of a young man, Chris McCandless, who used *Walden* as his inspiration to live alone in Alaska, where he starved to death. The excerpt that follows is a famous passage from Thoreau's book in which he establishes his purposes for living alone. You can find a copy of this passage on the companion Web site (http://ablongman.com/ballenger) if you don't want to mark up your book.

STEP ONE: Read the excerpt as you normally would if your purpose was to understand what the author is saying.

WALDEN

"Where I Lived and What I Live For"

Henry David Thoreau

I went to the woods because I wished to live deliberately, to front only the essential facts of life, and see if I could not learn what it had to teach, and not, when I came to die, discover I had not lived. I do not wish to live what was not life, living is so dear; nor did I wish to practice resignation, unless it was quite necessary. I wanted to live deep and suck out all the marrow of life, to live so sturdily and Spartan-like as to put to rout all that was not life, to cut a broad swath and shave close, to drive life into a corner, and reduce it to its lowest terms, and, if it proved to be mean, why then to get the whole and genuine meanness of it, and publish its meanness to the world; or if it were sublime, to know it by experience, and be able to give a true account of it in my next excursion. For most men, it appears to me, are in a strange uncertainty about it, whether it is of the devil or of God, and have *somewhat hastily* concluded that it is the chief end of man here to "glorify God and enjoy him forever." 1

Still we live meanly, like ants; though the fable tells us that we were long ago changed into men; like pygmies we fight with cranes; it is error upon error, and clout upon clout, and our best virtue has for its occasion a superfluous and evitable wretchedness. Our life is frittered away by detail. An honest man has hardly need to count more than his ten fingers, or in extreme cases he may add his ten toes, and lump the rest. Simplicity, simplicity, simplicity! I say, let your affairs be as two or three, and not a hundred or a thousand; instead of a million count half a dozen, and keep your accounts on your thumb nail. 2

STEP TWO: It might seem criminal to distill such a rich passage into two or three sentences, but compose a summary in your journal. *In your own words,* explain what you understand Thoreau to be saying here. Identify, if you can, the main ideas you cull from the passage.

STEP THREE: Review the list of reading perspectives in the "Inquiring into the Details" box on page 41. Which perspectives did you use to complete the exercise? Also, list the reading behaviors you used, if any, to complete the previous two steps. Reading behaviors include underlining, highlighting, note taking, writing in the margin, listing, rereading, skimming, exploratory writing, conversing with others about the text, taking a break, or copying passages (see the accompanying list). When you are done, answer the following questions:

- Did you note any pattern to the way you used the behaviors (when, how much, which ones)? Were the perspectives you adopted pretty typical for you?
- Would you have used different behaviors or perspectives if your purpose had not been to summarize the passage but instead had been to write a one-page argument against the author's claims in the passage?

Types of Reading Behaviors

What do you actually *do*, if anything, when you read for school?

- Underline
- Highlight
- Make marginal notes
- Write in your journal
- Converse with someone about the text
- Reread
- Skim
- Take lots of breaks
- Copy down important passages or facts

A good first step to using the recursive model of the reading process is to find ways to *actively* interact with the text so that you're having a conversation with the material. Simple strategies such as underlining, highlighting, note taking, writing in the margins, listing, and rereading help begin this conversation. Doing nothing—the default mode for many readers—is the intellectual equivalent of being a couch potato. Conversations also work best when *both* participants listen and respond to each other—and as in any conversation, how you listen and respond depends on the stance or perspective you take toward what you're hearing.

The behaviors and perspectives that you use when reading depend on the rhetorical situation. For example, you'll likely mark up a poem in *The Longman Anthology of World Literature* differently from an article in *Sociology Quarterly.* If your motive is simply to summarize an article on Canada's drug laws, you'll ask yourself different questions than if you're analyzing the claims of an editorial on the ethics of downloading free music. But certain "essential acts of mind" occur in almost all reading situations, and you'll find them mighty familiar.

Inquiring into the Details

READING PERSPECTIVES

When we read, we always adopt certain perspectives toward a text, usually unconsciously. But one of the best ways to read strategically is to consciously *shift* our perspective while we read. Like changing lenses on a camera or changing the angle, distance, or time of day to photograph something, this shift in reading perspective illuminates different aspects of a text. Here are some of the perspectives you might take:

- ***Believing:*** What the author says is probably true. Which ideas can I relate to? What information should I use? What seems especially sound about the argument?
- ***Doubting:*** What are the text's weaknesses? What ideas don't jibe with my own experience? What are the gaps in the information or the argument? What isn't believable about this?
- ***Updating:*** What does this add to what I already know about the subject?
- ***Hunting and gathering:*** What can I collect from the text that I might be able to use?
- ***Interpreting:*** What might be the meaning of this?
- ***Pleasure seeking:*** I just want to enjoy the text and be entertained by it.
- ***Connecting:*** How does this information relate to my own experiences? What is its relationship to other things I've read? Does it verify, extend, or contradict what other authors have said?
- ***Reflecting:*** How was this written? What makes it particularly effective or ineffective?
- ***Resisting:*** This doesn't interest me. Why do I have to read it? Isn't *Survivor* on television right now?

Dialectical Thinking

The sort of thinking we do while engaged in the reading process is comparable to the thinking we do when involved in the writing process. We move back and forth between creative and critical modes of thought, shifting between specifics and generalities, collecting and focusing, narrating and criticizing, generating and reflecting. Many of the questions we asked for writing are the same for reading: *What does this mean? Why might this fact or detail be significant? How does this connect with what I already know? What do I understand from reading this that I didn't understand when I began? Is this believable and convincing?*

Like writers, readers often consider their motives before they plunge into the text. For example, one reader might begin with a particular purpose: He just bought a handheld computer and must read the instructions to find out how it works. In this particular reading situation, it wouldn't make much sense to use creative thinking to interpret the instructions. Instead, the reader, with clear purpose in mind, uses critical thinking to decipher the instructions and apply them to the task at hand. But many texts we read in college are either much less explicit or much more challenging to understand than the instructions to a handheld computer. Nor is the sense of purpose so obviously clear. How do we make sense of texts like these? Move back and forth between the two contrary modes of thought, trying to answer the same essential question that nags us as writers: *So what*? There are some very practical ways to encourage this kind of thinking when you read, including the *double-entry* or *dialogue journal*, which is introduced later in the chapter.

WRITING WITH COMPUTERS

REFLECTION AND DIALECTICAL THINKING ON A COMPUTER

The comments function of your word processor is a great tool for practicing reflection and dialectical thinking in electronic documents. If you're reading a Web site or other electronic source, you can copy the text into your word processor and use the comments function to make notes as you critically analyze the text while you are reading it. As a writer you can use the feature to reflect on your own writing without altering your draft. Some writers use the comments feature as they write their initial draft to make notes that they want to have available later. For instance, instead of spending ten minutes trying to revise a passage that seems a bit unclear, make a note to yourself saying you think it is unclear and then get back to writing your draft. This will prevent getting caught up with surface-level revision when your objective is to generate new ideas and text.

When you use the comments feature, you don't need to create a second file of your draft for making comments. Comments can be hidden by changing your display settings. In addition, the print menu has options to show or hide comments in printouts. These options allow you to have a presentable copy for your peer-editing groups and keep all of your comments in a single file with your draft.

Believing and Doubting

Another way to engage dialectical thinking is to move back and forth between believing and doubting the author's claims as we read. Writing teacher Peter Elbow introduced the terms *believing game* and *doubting game* to describe how we might look at texts or experiences.[2] Elbow argues that our tendency to doubt or be critical of what we hear or read is only half of what we need to be able to reason and inquire well. He suggests we also need to play the believing game, to "try on" accepting the truth of another's arguments, claims, or experiences, and to search for "virtues or strengths we otherwise might miss," even if we disagree.

2. Peter Elbow, "Methodological Believing and Doubting: Contraries in Inquiry," in *Embracing Contraries: Explorations in Learning and Teaching* (New York: Oxford University Press, 1986).

Believing and doubting are opposed stances, obviously, and adopting both of them when reading a book or an article isn't always easy, particularly when you have strong feelings about a topic or an author. But I think you'll be amazed at how the shift between the two sparks new ways of thinking.

Other stances were described in the "Inquiring into the Details: Reading Perspectives" box. These may come into play depending on what you're reading and why. But believing and doubting can be particularly useful, especially in academic situations.

EXERCISE 2.3

Practicing Dialectical Thinking

STEP ONE: Read the essay that follows.

THE IMPORTANCE OF WRITING BADLY

Bruce Ballenger

1 I was grading papers in the waiting room of my doctor's office the other day, and he said, "It must be pretty eye-opening reading that stuff. Can you believe those students had four years of high school and still can't write?"

2 I've heard that before. I hear it almost every time I tell a stranger that I teach writing at a university.

3 I also hear it from colleagues brandishing red pens who hover over their students' papers like Huey helicopters waiting to flush the enemy from the tall grass, waiting for a comma splice or a vague pronoun reference or a misspelled word to break cover.

4 And I heard it this morning from the commentator on my public radio station who publishes snickering books about how students abuse the sacred language.

5 I have another problem: getting my students to write badly.

6 Most of us have lurking in our past some high priest of good grammar whose angry scribbling occupied the margins of our papers. Mine was Mrs. O'Neill, an eighth-grade teacher with a good heart but no patience for the bad sentence. Her favorite comment on my writing was "awk," which now sounds to me like the grunt of a large bird, but back then meant "awkward." She didn't think much of my sentences.

7 I find some people who reminisce fondly about their own Mrs. O'Neill, usually an English teacher who terrorized them into worshipping the error-free sentence. In some cases that terror paid off when it was finally transformed into an appreciation for the music a well-made sentence can make.

8 But it didn't work that way with me. I was driven into silence, losing faith that I could ever pick up the pen without breaking the rules or drawing another "awk" from a doubting reader. For years I wrote only when forced to, and when I did it was never good enough.

9 Many of my students come to me similarly voiceless, dreading the first writing assignment because they mistakenly believe that how they say it matters more than discovering what they have to say.

10 The night before the essay is due they pace their rooms like expectant fathers, waiting to deliver the perfect beginning. They wait and they wait and they wait. It's no wonder the waiting often turns to hating what they have written when they finally get it down. Many pledge to steer clear of English classes, or any class that demands much writing.

11 My doctor would say my students' failure to make words march down the page with military precision is another example of a failed education system. The criticism sometimes takes on political overtones. On my campus, for example, the right-wing student newspaper demanded that an entire semester of Freshman English be devoted to teaching students the rules of punctuation.

12 There is, I think, a hint of elitism among those who are so quick to decry the sorry state of the sentence in the hands of student writers. A colleague of mine, an Ivy League graduate, is among the self-appointed grammar police, complaining often about the dumb mistakes his students make in their papers. I don't remember him ever talking about what his students are trying to say in those papers. I have a feeling he's really not that interested.

13 Concise, clear writing matters, of course, and I have a responsibility to demand it from students. But first I am far more interested in encouraging thinking than error-free sentences. That's where bad writing comes in.

14 When I give my students permission to write badly, to suspend their compulsive need to find the "perfect way of saying it," often something miraculous happens: Words that used to trickle forth come gushing to the page. The students quickly find their voices again, and even more important, they are surprised by what they have to say. They can worry later about fixing awkward sentences. First, they need to make a mess.

15 It's harder to write badly than you might think. Haunted by their Mrs. O'Neill, some students can't overlook the sloppiness of their sentences or their lack of eloquence, and quickly stall out and stop writing. When the writing stops, so does the thinking.

16 The greatest reward in allowing students to write badly is that they learn that language can lead them to meaning, that words can be a means for finding out what they didn't know they knew. It usually happens when the words rush to the page, however awkwardly.

17 I don't mean to excuse bad grammar. But I cringe at conservative educational reformers who believe writing instruction should return to primarily teaching how to punctuate a sentence and use *Roget's Thesaurus.* If policing student papers for mistakes means alienating young writers from the language we expect them to master, then the exercise is self-defeating.

18 It is more important to allow students to first experience how language can be a vehicle for discovering how they see the world. And what matters in this journey—at least initially—is not what kind of car you're driving, but where you end up.

STEP TWO: Carefully copy lines or passages from the essay that you found interesting, puzzling, provocative, or central to its argument, as you understand it. Copy these passages onto a blank page on the left side of your notebook or journal.

STEP THREE: PLAY THE BELIEVING GAME. To start with, assume the truth of the author's claims. *What evidence from your own experience or knowledge, or from the text itself, might lead you to believe some of the things said in the essay?* Explore this in a fastwrite on the right page of your journal, opposite the page on which you copied the passage. If the writing stalls, look left and find something to respond to in one of the quoted passages you collected.

STEP FOUR: PLAY THE DOUBTING GAME. Skip a few lines, and shift your stance to one that is critical of the essay's claims. What do you suspect might be the weakness of the argument? What do you know from your own experience and knowledge that contradicts the claims? What does the essay fail to consider? Do this in a fastwrite just below the one you completed from Step One. Again, if your pen slows, look on the left for quotations from the excerpt that will get you going again.

STEP FIVE: MAKE A CLAIM OF YOUR OWN. Based on what you've learned from these two contrary perspectives—believing and doubting—compose a paragraph that states what you believe about the idea that "bad" writing is important.

STEP SIX: REFLECT ON THE PROCESS. Reflect on your experience with this exercise. Make an entry in your journal that explores some of the following questions:

- What, if anything, do you understand about your reading habits or perspectives now that you didn't fully understand before this exercise?
- Which came more easily—doubting or believing? What perspectives on the topic might not have emerged if you hadn't been forced to shift stances?
- Can you see any similarities between your writing and reading processes? Differences?

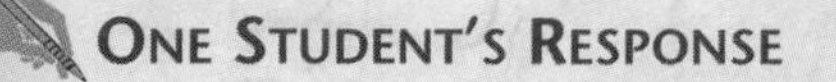

ONE STUDENT'S RESPONSE

TODD'S JOURNAL

EXERCISE 2.3

COLLECTING	FOCUSING
STEP TWO: Writing Down Quotations "I find some people who reminisce fondly about their own Mrs. O'Neill, usually an English teacher who terrorized them into worshipping the error-free sentence. In some cases that error paid off when it was finally transformed into an appreciation for the music a well-made sentence can make." "There is, I think, a hint of elitism among those who are so quick to decry the sorry state of the sentence in the hands of student writers." "If policing student papers for mistakes means alienating young writers from the language we expect them to master, then the exercise is self-defeating." "It is more important to allow students to first experience how language can be a vehicle for discovering how they see the world. And what matters in this journey—at least initially—is not what kind of car you're driving, but where you end up."	**STEP THREE: The Doubting Game** I know enough people who have had a strong grammar background to believe that this happens more often than the author implies. Some people really like to study grammar and mechanics, and isn't it common sense that you should learn the basics before you learn how to put them all together? I also wonder what the writer means about "elitism." What is elitist about helping students to write correctly, something that will help a lot of students get better jobs. After all, even if teaching grammar doesn't help some people write better, the world expects correctness. And writers quickly get into trouble if they can't punctuate, spell, or dangle their modifiers . . . **STEP FOUR: The Believing Game** On the other hand, making people afraid to write doesn't seem like a good idea either. In a way it can be elitist if grammar is taught as rules, handed down by the grammar god (someone invented by these "defenders" of the language). You get the impression that if you dangle a modifier you're a bad person. There's something moral about the whole thing that bothers me. I really like the idea that "policing" essays can be "alienating for your writers" because I've felt that way at times. I hand in a paper to a professor and I don't feel he or she has paid any attention to my ideas . . .

COLLECTING	FOCUSING
	STEP FIVE: Making a Claim So-called "bad" writing can be useful for some writers who struggle with perfection. But students who lack basic grammar skills will be punished for it in school and in the workplace. Therefore, teachers have an obligation to teach it. **STEP SIX: Reflecting on the Exercise** It was weird to shift stances. I really wanted to spend more time playing the "believing game" because I basically agreed with the article. This suggests that when I read something I agree with, I automatically read it looking for confirmation of what I already believe. The "doubting game" shook me out of that, and . . .

INQUIRING INTO THE DETAILS

THE DOUBLE-ENTRY JOURNAL

A double-entry journal is essentially a written dialogue between a reader and a text. As a reader you ask questions, make connections, and note memories and associations.

Here's how it works: You can either draw a line down the middle of a page to make two columns, or you can use the spine of your notebook for the line and use two opposing pages.

What the Text Says	What I Think
In the left column, write out the passages from the reading that confuse you, surprise you, make you think of other ideas, seem key to your understanding of what it says, and so on.	Then in the right column, write out your response to those passages. Sometimes you'll do a fastwrite, other times you may simply jot down quick thoughts.

(continued)

THE DOUBLE-ENTRY JOURNAL *(Continued)*

What the Text Says	What I Think
■ Jot down direct quotes, paraphrases, summaries, facts, claims. ■ Note page numbers next to each passage or summary/paraphrase. Put them in the far right margin next to the borrowed material or ideas.	Play the doubting game, questioning the source; play the believing game, trying to find its virtues, even if you disagree. ■ Shift to other reading perspectives. ■ Tell the story of your thinking about what you're reading: *My initial reaction to this is . . . but now I think . . . and now I think . . .* ■ List questions you have about the source's ideas; your emotional responses; other ideas or readings it connects to.

Continue this process for the entire reading, moving back and forth across the columns. Remember that you want to explore your response to a text, make connections to other works and your own writing, and analyze the writer's choices in terms of language, style, detail, and so forth. *Be sure to note all the bibliographic information from the source at the top of the page.*

Adapting to Unfamiliar Reading Situations

Studies on reading are unambiguous about one thing: What most affects readers' comprehension of a text is their prior knowledge of its topic. Texts on familiar subjects are clearly easier to read and respond to, but generally the reading you're required to do in college demands that you confront books and articles about things you may know little about. Frequently, these texts adopt the *discourse,* or language and conventions, of the field for which they were written, a field with which you may have little experience. Other times you'll be asked to read primary sources—the original writings of important thinkers—which may be written in the style and structure of another time or place. Reading situations such as these require us to modify our reading process.

Of course, it's quite common when reading in such situations to feel little connection to the author or her ideas, at least initially. *What is this person talking about? What does this mean to me? How boring!* In adapting our reading process to these rhetorical situations, then, the challenge is to use dialectical thinking to actively seek out the connections between your own experiences and knowledge and the author's text. The key is to use *writing* to help you to work out what you think about what you've read, focusing especially on what you find confusing, puzzling, or significant.

I realize that getting you to write as you read can be a tough sell. You're pressed for time, and you just want to get the reading done. But I'm confident that if you take a little time to use writing to hold up your end of the conversation with a text, you'll discover the pleasures of seeing the story of your own thinking unfold before you, and if you have to write about what you read, you're essentially beginning a draft. In other words, not only will you come up with better ideas, you may also work more efficiently.

EXERCISE 2.4

Further Practice: Untangling Academic Prose

Frequently you'll be asked to read some pretty difficult texts in your college classes, books or articles that are a thicket of ideas that may be hard to see through. Try using the dialectical thinking method to analyze the following passage, one that is typical of the kind of texts you'll encounter.

STEP ONE: COLLECT. As you read the following excerpt from David F. Noble's book, use the double-entry journal technique to collect lines or passages that you find significant, interesting, or puzzling. Carefully copy these on the left page of your journal. Consider reading the excerpt through at least once *without* taking notes and then begin collecting in your journal during the second or third reading.

THE FORCES OF PRODUCTION

A Social History of Industrial Automation

David F. Noble

1 It is a staple of current thinking about technological change that such a "successful" technology, having become dominant, must have evolved in some "necessary" way. Implicit in the modern ideology of technological progress is the belief that the process of technological development is analogous to that of natural selection. It is thus assumed that all technological alternatives are always considered, that they are disinterestedly evaluated on their technical merits, and that they are then judged according to the cold calculus of accumulation. Any successful technology, therefore—one which becomes the dominant and ultimately the only solutions to a given problem—must, by definition, be the best, for it alone has survived the rigors of engineering experimentation and the trials of the competitive marketplace. And, as the best, it has become the latest, and necessary, step along the unilinear path of progress.

2 This dominant "Darwinian" view of technological development rests upon a simple faith in objective science, economic rationality, and the market. It assumes that the flow of creative inventions passes progressively through three successive filters, each of which further guarantees that only the "best" alternatives survive. The first, the objective technical filter, selects the most scientifically sound solutions to a given problem. The second, the pecuniary rationality of the hard-nosed businessman, screens out more fanciful technical solutions and accepts only those which are practical and economically viable. The third, the self-correcting mechanism of the market, dooms the less savvy businessman and thus insures that only the best innovations survive.

3 But this facile faith assumes too much, and explains too little. It portrays technological development as an autonomous and neutral technical process, on the one hand, and a coldly rational and self-regulating economic process, on the other, neither of which accounts for people, power, institutions, competing values, or different dreams. Thus it begs and explains away all important historical questions: The best technology? Best for whom? Best for what? Best according to what criteria, what visions, according to whose criteria, whose visions?

STEP TWO: EXPLORE. When you feel satisfied that you've collected enough, use the lines or passages you've gathered on the left page as prompts for fastwriting on the right. When the writing stalls, skip a line, look to the left, and find something else to jump-start your writing. *When you can, write about your own observations and experiences with technology that might help you think about what Noble is trying to say. Tell stories.* Remember, questions, not answers, should direct your fastwriting. Keep writing until you feel you have a grip on some of what Noble seems to be saying about technology and your own response to his ideas.

STEP THREE: FOCUS. Adopt a critical mode of thinking for a moment. Use the writing and information you've collected so far to compose a paragraph response that summarizes, in your own words, Noble's argument and offers your own response to it. This response should complete the following sentence: *Based on my understanding, the most significant thing Noble has to say is . . .*

STEP FOUR: REFLECT. Finally, make an entry in your journal that reflects your experience with this exercise. The following questions may prompt your thinking:

- Did your reading process in this exercise differ significantly from the process you used when you read "The Importance of Writing Badly" in Exercise 2.3?
- What did you find most helpful about the double-entry journal method? What was least helpful?

- Can you connect any moments of insight or discovery in your journal with particular moves you made, perhaps asking a certain question or shifting the focus of your writing?
- How did you struggle with this reading? How did it come easily? What might you do differently when you encounter texts like these?

Inquiring into the Details

ENCOUNTERING UNFAMILIAR GENRES

An ad for the film *Memento.*

The only time most of us ever really pay attention to genre is when we encounter one that defies our expectations. When the low-budget film *Memento* was released several years ago, its puzzling narrative structure (beginning at the end of the story and proceeding to the beginning), its use of an unreliable narrator, and its alternation between black-and-white and color took audiences by surprise and generated lots of print by movie critics. Ultimately, the film became a phenomenal success, partly because its approach was so unexpected. *Memento* got people talking about a completely different way to think about filmmaking.

The response to the movie was so significant because we are a nation of moviegoers who are quite familiar with the genre, and *Memento* made us wonder how much we really know about film. These kinds of *Memento* moments happen to readers all the time, especially when we're in an academic setting and aren't familiar with the genres we're asked to read—a poem, a lab report, an academic argument, a minimalist painting. Our first response might be to question how well we can read, even though we've all been reading for a very long time.

One way of dealing with this is to simply apply reading strategies that we've used successfully in other genres. For example, because your verbal score on the reading comprehension portion of the SAT was so high, then why not approach reading the essay on the need for a new immigration policy the same way, and try to decode exactly what the writer must have meant and leave it at that? Well, your instructor will likely say, "Fine, but I want to know what you think about his argument."

A better approach when you encounter kinds of readings that are new to you is to let the reading situation be your guide.

- Ask yourself, *Why am I reading this? How is it relevant to my inquiry question?* or *What exactly is my instructor asking me to do with this text?*
- Are there clues in the text about how it might be efficiently read? For instance, do subheadings provide guidance? Is there a preface that reviews the argument? Does the concluding section have the most weight?
- Who is the intended audience for this text and what clues does that provide about the writer's purpose? Might that explain not only how she composed the text—its language, organization, and so on—and what she hoped to accomplish with it?
- Whenever possible, "frontload" before you read something challenging; that is, learn as much as you can about the subject and even the writer's relation to the subject. This knowledge will make a big difference in how much you understand.

"READING" THE VISUAL

That famous cliché—"a picture is worth a thousand words"—has apparently evolved slightly from the original Chinese proverb, "one picture is worth ten thousand words," but the theme is the same: images are more powerful than words. However, our experience tells us that this dichotomy is often false—verbal text *and* images, when used together, can be most powerful of all. Advertisers, perhaps the most skilled practitioners of modern rhetoric, know this well as they work to associate certain values or desires with a product by combining words and pictures. In the iPod advertisement on page 53, Apple has successfully married its famous silhouette images of young men and women to the pure white pleasure of the iPod. There is little text. But in this case it isn't needed because the association, by now, is firmly cemented in the public imagination. The success of our reading of this ad—and of any ad—has to do not only with its repetition but how it appeals to certain of our cultural

Chinese proverb.

Apple iPod advertisement.

values and beliefs. In this case, what are they? Answering that question must begin, as always, with another question: *Who is the intended audience here?*

Of course, you asked these same questions when analyzing verbal texts. These questions guide our reading of the visual, too, because reading images is also a rhetorical act. Why should we pay attention to this? For much the same reason we apply rhetorical knowledge to reading an article or essay: we can approach the reading with more understanding and on a more equal footing. Visual rhetoric gives us a language to talk about what we see, not simply to guard us from manipulation but to help us expose the assumptions we bring to our consumption of images. There's another reason, too. While you probably won't be designing advertisements this semester or next, you may have opportunities to craft how your writing looks, not just how it reads. We'll briefly explore both aspects of reading the visual—how images work and the "look" of writing—in the following section.

Learning the Grammar of Images

It's pretty obvious that images and texts have a lot in common. For example, a good picture is *composed*—the visual elements are arranged a certain way with a certain idea in mind. Images also have their own *grammar,* but rather than using words and syntax, images use color, lines, shape, and texture, all of which combine for a certain effect. The rhetorical reading triangle (Figure 2.1) applies to images as it applies to any other text because these elements—composition and grammar—are combined for a certain purpose and for a certain audience. And, just like writing, visual images take a range of forms, from advertisements to oil paintings, and each of these genres asks to be "read" differently (see Exercise 2.5).

Visual rhetoric gives us a language to talk about what we see, not simply to guard us from manipulation but to help us expose the assumptions we bring to our consumption of images.

Finally, the meaning of an image isn't fixed. Earlier in the chapter, I mentioned that we work out the meaning of what we read by having a conversation with it, one that is always conducted in a particular context. Each reader brings certain experiences and knowledge to a reading that influence what that reader thinks the text means. The same is true of reading images. For example, your reading of the 1950s advertisement for Wildroot Cream-Oil that follows will be quite different from the reading its designers intended.

For all of these reasons, the recursive process and dialectical thinking both apply to analyzing pictures just as they do to reading and writing texts.

Some Strategies for Reading Images

You can analyze images and written texts in many of the same ways, but because each has a different "language"—one works with words and the other with visual elements—the actual practices of analysis differ a bit. Here are some things to keep in mind:

- *Look closely.* Pictures, naturally, appeal to sight. Your skills of close observation, consequently, are probably as important when reading images as rereading is when analyzing a written text.
- *Find the subject.* Like a piece of writing, an image usually focuses on a particular visual subject that can be seen in the context of other elements of the picture. We intuitively look first at the very center of an image for the

An ad for Wildroot Cream-Oil Hair Tonic from the 1950s.

main subject, but some images may be designed to draw our eyes in other directions. Why would they do this? What might be the motive?

- *Understand the context.* It helps to know when and where an image was created. This knowledge helps shape our response and helps us understand the designer's motives. For example, knowing which magazine a particular advertisement appeared in also can provide valuable clues about purpose and audience. But the context of an image also includes the experiences and knowledge *the viewer* brings to the image, too. How might your interpretation of an image be influenced by your own history and historical vantage point and your own cultural beliefs and assumptions?
- *Understand the genre.* You are already an expert on the many forms that images take. You intuitively know that you should "read" an advertisement differently from an oil painting, a movie differently from a documentary photograph. Like written forms, visual genres give readers clues about how they should be read, and we typically know the purposes behind different forms. It's not hard, for example, to recognize the persuasive purpose of a car ad, but the purposes of other genres may be more ambiguous. For instance, what is the purpose of a painting by Van Gogh?
- *What's the story?* Images can tell stories, too. For example, the 1950s ad for Wildroot Cream-Oil on page 55 has a strong narrative element that isn't too hard to figure out: If you've got a really swell gal, she'll send you Wildroot instead of a letter because it's your hair she really cares about. Happy users of the product will also enjoy that "successful look," which has everything to do with sex appeal. Sometimes discovering the story in an image is a good starting point for analyzing its message: is this story designed to appeal to a certain audience? Does it reflect certain cultural values? Is the story current?
- *Analyze the interaction of words and pictures.* Web pages typically combine words and pictures. Some pictures have captions or are positioned carefully near certain text. Words and images are intended to work together—to *reinforce* each other. Notice how text and image elaborate on and extend a particular message. Also notice which element exploits emotions and which emphasizes reason.

EXERCISE 2.5

Reading Images

If an image is a kind of text that can be read like writing can, then the recursive reading model and dialectical thinking should help you analyze pictures, paintings, and ads, too. Try to apply those methods to the images that follow.

STEP ONE: Closely examine each of the five images that follow. Choose one you want to work with.

STEP TWO: Begin "reading" the image as you would a printed text, using the dialectical approach. Open your journal to two blank opposing pages. Begin on the left page and jump into the sea. Fastwrite about the image, letting the writing wander wherever it leads you. But begin with the following prompt: *When I first look at this picture, I think or feel_______. And then I think_______. And then . . . And then. . . .* Whenever the writing stalls, repeat the phrase *and then.* Write for five minutes without stopping.

STEP THREE: Now work on the right page with your more critical mind. Reread your fastwrite, and then try to focus your thinking about the picture by answering the question, *What story or stories does the image seem to be telling*? Remember that what makes a picture powerful is that it tells stories that transcend the moment the image captures, trying to say something larger about its subject, about our lives, or about a product. The most persuasive of these stories probably echo some cultural narrative we want to believe about ourselves, ideas about family, or patriotism, or racial harmony, or health, and so on.

STEP FOUR: Now return to the image, looking at it again closely. On the left page of your journal, collect information—specific details—from the picture or ad that seems to support the story or stories you believe the image inspires. Here's where it helps to know a little about the grammar of images.

- As you look at the pictures, pay attention to color. How does color contribute to feeling?
- What is the main visual subject? Where are your eyes drawn, and how is that accomplished?
- Are there clues about context, things like *when* or *where* the image was created?
- Are there rhetorical clues? What do you see in the image (or text) that suggests it targeted a particular audience? Does it include text or visual details that suggest a certain story, theme, or message?
- How does the image appeal to certain cultural values or beliefs? What are they? To what extent do you share these values and beliefs?

STEP FIVE: On the right page of your notebook, compose a 250-word response that explains, using supporting evidence from the picture you chose, your interpretation of its meaning and your analysis of how the image tries to communicate that meaning. Make sure you talk about rhetorical aspects of your image—what is it trying to do for what audiences?

Edward Hopper, *Nighthawks*, 1942. (Oil on canvas, 84.1 × 152.4 cm. Friends of American Art Collection, 1942.51. Reproduction, The Art Institute of Chicago.)

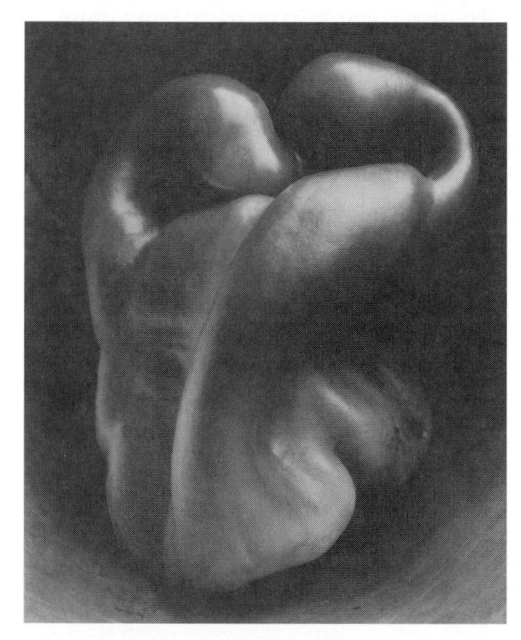

Edward Weston, *Pepper No. 30.*

A movie poster promoting the original 1933 film version of *King Kong*, starring Fay Wray.

Johnnie & Zeek from the Lower West Side series by Milton Rogovin. Photo courtesy of the Rogovin Collection (MiltonRogovin.com). Copyright 1952–2002 Milton Rogovin. All Rights Reserved.

C. R. Miller, *America's Strength, All of Us Pulling Together*, c. 1950.

The "Look" of Writing

Back in my typewriter days, I didn't think about how my writing looked except to worry over whether my whited-out corrections were ugly and my margins were straight. As you know, word-processing software opened a new world of graphic possibilities. It's a world you may not have much opportunity to explore in college because the format of your papers is often limited by the assignment. However, this is changing. Many instructors welcome some use of graphic elements *if they serve a useful purpose.* Does the graphic design of your work clarify your information and ideas, and, especially, does it make your argument more persuasive?

Five graphic elements are under your control:

1. Layout
2. Images
3. Graphic representations (charts, tables, graphics)
4. Color
5. Typefaces and fonts

This is too brief a treatment of visual rhetoric to explore these elements thoroughly, but we'll focus on a few key principles to give you an idea of how the visual and the verbal can work together to make writing persuasive.

Typefaces and Fonts. In the early days of computers, I could immediately tell which of my students owned a Mac. They were the students who handed in their papers with unusual fonts. PC users like me didn't mess with fonts much back then. Of course, all that has changed. The document I'm working on at this very moment includes at least four different fonts and sizes, and I'm constantly trying to manage them all. The reason, of course, is that how writing looks can influence how it is read. Imagine, for instance, I want to incorporate a concern for visual rhetoric in my course syllabus. The course is English 102, English Composition, and I'd like the syllabus to reinforce the idea that the class will be informal, intimate, and friendly. Which of the following fonts would be likely to suggest these?

1. Dr. Bruce Ballenger

   English 102: English Composition

   Course Syllabus

2. Dr. Bruce Ballenger

   English 102: English Composition

   Course Syllabus

3. Dr. Bruce Ballenger

English 102: English Composition

Course Syllabus

4. Dr. Bruce Ballenger

English 102: English Composition

Course Syllabus

The two broadest categories of fonts are *serif* and *sans serif.* Serif typefaces include flourishes that sans serif typefaces lack (see Figure 2.4). In general, graphic artists believe that serif fonts are more formal than sans serif. We also respond to certain typefaces because of our previous experience with them. For example, we naturally associate example 4 above, Old English, with old books, while those of us who have had experience working with typewriters usually recognize example 3, Courier. Figure 2.5, which associates various fonts with personality traits, takes this inquiry into the effect of fonts much further. It is based on a recent study of adjectives readers consistently associated with a certain typeface.

Layout. Of course, the typeface is only one aspect of the "look" of writing, and probably not the most important. Layout is perhaps the broadest category of graphic design, and in many cases may be the element least under your control with academic writing. Your papers in English, for example, will often be guided by the design prescriptions of the Modern Language Association (MLA), while in fields like education and psychology you'll toil under the guidelines of the American Psychological Association (APA). But even then, you can enhance the layout of your papers by adding bulleted lists and headings. If you've got more liberty to play with the graphic design of your work then there's a lot to consider. Begin by understanding the following four design principles suggested by Robin Williams[3] in *The Non-Designer's Design Book:*

FIGURE 2.4 Serif versus san serif fonts.

3. Robin Williams, *The Non-Designer's Design Book: Design and Typographic Principles for the Visual Novice* (Berkeley, CA: Peachpit Press, 1994).

	Top Three		
Stable	Times New Roman	Arial	Palatino
Flexible	Lisa	Giddyup	Palace Script
Conformist	Courier New	Times New Roman	Arial
Polite	Monotype Corsiva	Times New Roman	Palatino
Mature	Times New Roman	Courier New	Palatino
Formal	Times New Roman	Monotype Corsiva	Georgia
Assertive	Impact	Rockwell Xbold	Georgia
Practical	Georgia	Times New Roman	Palatino
Creative	Giddyup	Lisa	Palace Script
Happy	Lisa	Giddyup	Tekton
Exciting	Giddyup	Lisa	Palace Script
Attractive	Monotype Corsiva	Palace Script	Giddyup
Elegant	Monotype Corsiva	Palace Script	Giddyup
Cuddly	Lisa	Giddyup	Tekton
Feminine	Giddyup	Monotype Corsiva	Lisa
Unstable	Giddyup	Lisa	Palace Script
Rigid	Impact	Courier New	Futura Cond
Rebel	Giddyup	Lisa	Palace Script
Rude	Impact	Rockwell Xbold	Futura Cond
Youthful	Lisa	Giddyup	Tekton
Casual	Lisa	Tekton	Giddyup
Passive	Lisa	Giddyup	Tekton
Impractical	Giddyup	Palace Script	Lisa
Unimaginative	Courier New	Arial	Melior
Sad	Impact	Courier New	Futura Cond
Dull	Courier New	Melior	Helvetica
Unattractive	Impact	Courier New	Rockwell Xbold
Plain	Courier New	Impact	Rockwell Xbold
Coarse	Impact	Rockwell Xbold	Courier New
Masculine	Impact	Rockwell Xbold	Courier New

FIGURE 2.5 The results of a study that identified reader perception of the "personality" of various fonts.

Proximity. This principle concerns how much you "chunk" material and how well you use white or "negative" space. The idea here is that when you put similar or related things together they become an understandable "visual unit." For example, in the "Ten Things to Do" fact sheet about global warming below, notice how information about what actions to take is visually discrete from the information about the film, *An Inconvenient Truth*. There are at least two major visual units on the page, each containing related information.

Contrast. A page that lacks contrast is dull. Using different font types and sizes, colors, spaces, lines, and so on, establishes very noticeable (not subtle) contrasts. That isn't hard to see in the "Ten Things to Do" fact sheet. Notice the large, colored font with the black background that proclaims that there are

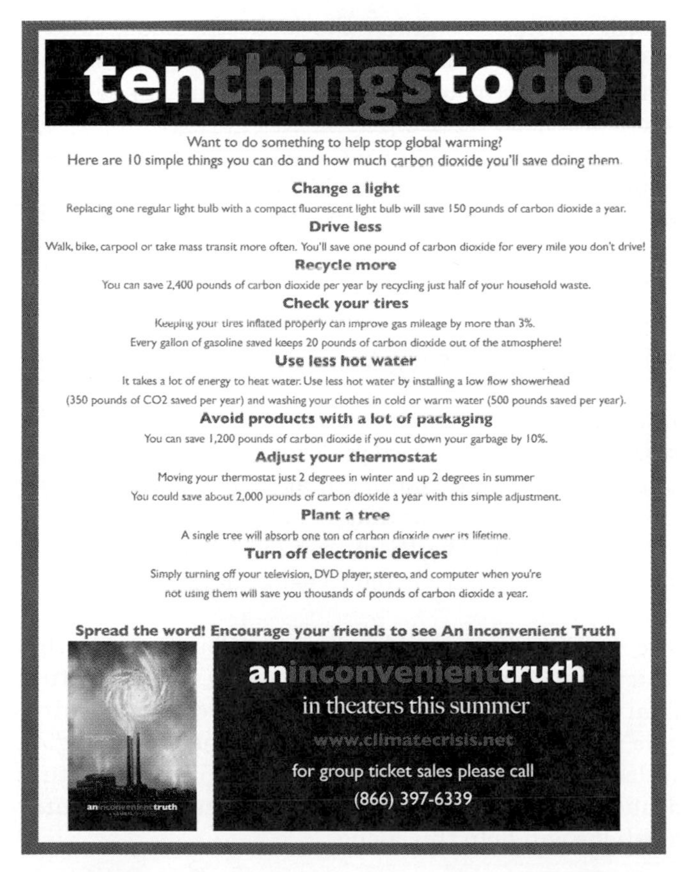

"Ten Things to Do" fact sheet accompanying Al Gore's global warming film, *An Inconvenient Truth.*

things you can do about the problem. This is a noticeable contrast from the list of activities, which use a smaller font size and lack the shading. At the bottom of the page, a black background and graphic again provides a striking contrast with the list of actions.

Repetition. Repeated design elements makes the page look unified; this is particularly important in multipage documents. Typically, we consistently use the same headings or subheadings, varying the size to signal a hierarchy of importance. But there are plenty of other things you can do, including repetition of colors, lines, boxes, white spaces, margins, bolding, and so on. It's not hard to see where the designers of the "Ten Things to Do" fact sheet use repetition. It's particularly striking, for example, in the repeated color pattern and font of the top head—"Ten Things to Do" and the head at the bottom, "An Inconvenient Truth."

Alignment. The eye loves order. When designing the look of a page, always consider arrangement of visual elements. You do this already when you use margins, or center titles, or align a table to the left or to the right. The key to alignment is the sense that there is a reason for the placement of everything on the page. Even visual elements that represent different material should all feel a sense of belonging to the single page, and alignment is the way we do this. For example, the "Ten Things to Do" fact sheet is aligned by centering most of the text. This is one of the most common methods of aligning material. You can also align edges of text chunks, or pictures and graphics.

USING WHAT YOU HAVE LEARNED

Inquiry-based writing and reading begins with an open-eyed sense of wonder. Instead of initially asking, *What should I say?* you ask, *What do I think?* You begin by trying to find questions that interest you, knowing that there isn't necessarily a single right answer. At the same time, you know that just as you open up possible meanings, at some point you need to narrow them. You are both creative *and* critical, moving back and forth between collecting and focusing, exploring and evaluating, narrating and reflecting.

As you continue in *The Curious Writer*, I'll encourage you to apply this process to nearly every assignment. Before long, it will become second nature to you; you'll find yourself naturally shifting back and forth between the creative and the critical, whether you're exploring a topic for an assignment, reading an essay that you'll discuss in class, or analyzing an advertisement. Techniques that you've already practiced such as fastwriting and listing, the double-entry journal, and generating questions will help this along.

Dorothea Lange's famous Great Depression–era photograph *Migrant Mother.*

Ways of Inquiring

In March 1936, while the Great Depression still gripped the nation, documentary photographer Dorothea Lange was driving along a quiet California road when she passed a sign that said, "Pea Picker's Camp." Lange already had finished a project for the federal Resettlement Administration that focused on migrant families devastated by the depression, but twenty miles after passing the sign she turned her car around to get just a few more photos. At the camp, Lange was "drawn like a magnet" to a mother and her children. Lange later recalled that she did "not remember how I explained my presence or my camera to her,"

> . . . but I do remember she asked me no questions. I made five exposures, working closer and closer from the same direction. I did not ask her name or her history. She told me her age, that she was thirty-two. She said that they had been living on frozen vegetables from the surrounding fields, and birds that the children killed. She had just sold the tires from her car to buy food. There she sat in that lean-to tent with her children huddled around her, and seemed to know that my pictures might help her, and so she helped me. There was a sort of equality about it.

Lange's last-minute decision to return to take a few more pictures proved opportune. Her image *Migrant Mother* is perhaps the most famous twentieth-century American documentary photograph, and it remains among the most requested pictures in the Library of Congress archive.

In the last chapter, we discussed the correlation between textual and visual literacy. A photograph, like an essay, involves composition and visual grammar. In Lange's photograph of the migrant mother, for example, she consciously arranged certain visual elements to create an emotional effect. Like writing, a good photograph is full of information, too. There are

What You'll Learn in This Chapter

- How questions create fresh perspective on any subject.
- How you can use certain categories of questions—those that explore, explain, evaluate, and reflect—to think more deeply about any subject.
- How you can combine question asking with dialectical thinking to discover what you want to say.

exactly three children in this picture surrounding Florence Thompson, and they are wearing similar rough-fabric clothing. None faces the camera. Florence's gaze seems fixed on some distant place, her mouth is set, and her brow seems furrowed. All of these details work together to say more than they say individually, to tell a story not just about the impact of the Great Depression but about motherhood and family.

You can develop your own interpretation of *Migrant Mother* using dialectical thinking, perhaps beginning by openly exploring how the picture connects with your own experiences and observations. This might lead you to focus on a "reading" of the photograph that emphasizes the anxieties of mothering or the shame of poverty in America. But there are ways to make the inquiry process a bit more methodological, ways that you can deliberately shift your perspective to see a subject freshly. How? Ask the right questions.

Years ago, I spent an afternoon taking photographs of an old wagon on a rolling New Hampshire hill. I got up early on a September morning hoping to take advantage of the slanting light and the shreds of mist that hung on the hayfield. I resolved to take an entire roll of the wagon, and I literally circled it, taking shot after shot. By the fourth or fifth shot, I started to see the wagon in ways I'd never seen it. I saw how the beads of dew covered the bleached wood of the wagon's wheel. I saw how the ironwork of the driver's bench created a shadow on the grass that was a tangle of geometric shapes.

What I'm describing is the process of revision. But the anecdote also comes to mind now because it illustrates how different questions shift your gaze on a topic. They help you circle the wagon, changing your angle and revealing certain aspects of the subject and not others. Behind each question is a different perspective.

All inquiry begins with questions. Indeed, the opening questions *we ask largely determine our response to a subject.*

In this chapter, I'll suggest four ways of seeing, each prompted by a different opening question. Combined with dialectical thinking, these stances—*exploring, explaining, evaluating,* and *reflecting*—are a foundation of inquiry-based learning that will help you with every assignment in this book, and in any situation in which you want to figure out what you think. We'll apply these ways of seeing to a range of texts, both written and visual, and I hope you'll find yourself circling the wagon in much the same way I did years ago.

OPENING QUESTIONS FOR INQUIRY

All inquiry begins with questions. Indeed, the *opening questions* we ask largely determine our response to a subject. These questions shape the stance we take toward both the writing process and the reading process. These opening questions are situational. For example, in writing they depend on our particular subject, on who we're writing for, and our purposes at any given moment in the process. Recall the rhetorical triangle from Chapter 1: the rhetorical choices we make are informed by the questions we ask in response to the writing situation. While opening questions vary from one writing situation to the next, we can group them into categories that conform to four different ways of inquiring into a subject: exploration, explanation, evaluation, and reflection. Each of these four ways of inquiring compels writers to take a different stance toward a subject, be it a text, a memory, an observation, a conversation, a photograph, or another process. Each shapes how writers see a subject (or themselves), much like taking a series of different photographs of the wagon on the hill that was mentioned earlier.

EXPLORATION

To explore is to see a topic with wide-eyed wonder. *What might this mean to me? What do I feel or think about this?* Through these questions, the writer can openly investigate his or her feelings and thoughts and find a personal point of attachment to the subject. This way of inquiring is easiest when you're writing on something about which you're uncertain. After all, it's not hard to suspend judgment when you don't have one. But exploration can also be useful when you want to reexamine what you already believe, when you're open to the possibility of changing your mind. Why would you want to do that? Because you can learn and discover things, even if you end up feeling more strongly about your initial belief.

This way of inquiring isn't just for fastwriting or journal work. Exploration can also inform much more publicly oriented inquiry into a subject. Historically, the personal essay is a genre that relies heavily on exploration (see Chapter 4, "Writing a Personal Essay"). Writers of personal essays constantly take measure of their emotional relationship with their subjects, much the way we do when we're writing for ourselves in our journals. This public performance of the inquiring *I* has an interesting effect on readers—we feel a sense of intimacy with the writer that is often absent in other writing genres. Ironically, questions that would seem to free us from concern for our audience can also wind up making our writing more accessible to that audience.

When should you try exploration as a way of inquiring?

1. When you want to discover what you think.
2. When you have time to take a more circuitous path to these discoveries.
3. When the topic is new to you or when you'd like to look critically at your existing ideas or beliefs about a subject.

Exploring Questions

- What does this mean to me, or how do I think or feel about it?
- What do I notice first? And then what? And then?
- What interests me most about this? What additional questions does it raise?
- How do my own personal knowledge and experiences affect the way I feel and what I see?
- What surprises me about the way I see or think about this?

EXPLANATION

We explain things all the time. This is something parents are acutely aware of, especially if they have a kid like my daughter Julia.

"Who are the Israelis?" she asks as we listen to National Public Radio on the way to school, "and why are they always talking about them?"

"Who is talking about them?"

"The people on the radio," she says. "They are always talking about the Israelis and the Palestinians."

How do I begin to explain a conflict that has its roots in several thousand years of history, one complicated by religious differences and political alliances that seem to defy resolution? What Julia knows seems much simpler: a Palestinian family in Gaza was killed by Israeli soldiers who were retaliating for a suicide attack in Jerusalem that killed thirteen. Do I begin by explaining Moses' exodus from Egypt and the Jews' historic claims to the Holy Land or the Muslims' conquest of the region in the seventh century? Or do I explain the creation of the Israeli state following World War II and the demise of Palestine? What I realize, as Julia impatiently waits for me to say something, is that I know much less than I thought I knew about the history of this conflict.

As this example suggests, we tend to use explanation with an audience in mind. But by explaining things to ourselves we can learn a lot, too, because this way of inquiring exposes gaps in our knowledge. Clearly, in attempting to explain the conflict between the Israelis and the Palestinians to my daughter I was forced to confront the limits of my own knowledge on the subject.

A common technique in psychotherapy is something called "say back." In couples counseling, for example, one partner may be required to listen carefully to his or her spouse talk, and then say back what he or she heard. The method is great for helping couples really listen to and understand each other, something that is ordinarily difficult to do amid life's daily distractions. The explanatory power of say back is much like the power of summarizing or paraphrasing something you've read or experienced. By challenging writers to use their own words, summarizing and paraphrasing allow writers to take possession of the information, to make it their own by articulating their understanding of the information in their own words. Summarizing and paraphrasing can also expose the gaps in our knowledge. You thought you understood a subject, but upon reading over your summary or paraphrase of the subject, you now aren't so sure that's the case. Is there another way to understand the subject so you can explain it better? Have you missed something you need to know in order to understand the subject?

This way of inquiring involves much more than simply reporting information. It's a way of clarifying thought, enhancing understanding, making useful comparisons, and exposing gaps. For me, trying to explain the Middle East conflict to Julia and writing this book were two experiences that involved discoveries that made them much more than mere recitations of fact and detail.

When should you try explaining as a way of inquiring?

1. When you want to understand what you think you know.
2. When you want to clarify that understanding for yourself and others.
3. When you want to define, describe, categorize, or compare things.

Explaining Questions

- What is this?
- What is its purpose?
- How does this work? Why does it work? How does this clarify things?
- What does it look like?
- How does it compare to something else?
- What do I understand this to be saying?

EVALUATION

To evaluate something is to judge it or to form an opinion about it. Evaluating things—restaurants, the quality of play in the NBA, the religious motives of terrorists such as Osama bin Laden—is something we all do naturally. These evaluations tend to lead us to do and say certain things to support our opinions or to make our claims convincing, first to ourselves and then to others. Indeed, evaluation is really the driving force behind argument.

As a way of inquiring, evaluation shares much with exploration. Both hinge on the writer's emotional response to a subject. Exploration, however, is much more open ended in its approach, more receptive to doubt and uncertainty about the subject. Evaluation, on the other hand, is focused exclusively on making and supporting a judgment about the subject. In sum, you use exploration when your purpose is *to discover* and you use evaluation when your purpose is *to prove,* although both ways of inquiring can be used together to great effect.

While we constantly evaluate things for ourselves, we usually reserve written evaluation for an audience. Our concern, then, is to persuade others to feel the same way we do about the subject. To do so, we usually have to clarify and elaborate on our thinking.

Indeed, because all evaluation stems from what are essentially subjective value judgments, a tension always exists between our *desire* to prove our point and our *need or willingness* to learn more about the subject. Most if not all issues worth arguing about are complex. In learning more about them, we can actually make it harder to prove our point. We might even be compelled to change our minds about the subject. This may be a good thing in terms of fostering a deeper understanding of the world, but it's bound to slow down the writing process. You may not have the time required to fully explore the complexities of a subject. Charged with evaluating the impact of the war in Afghanistan on the U.S. relationship with Uzbekistan or the meaning of the water imagery in Kate Chopin's story "The Awakening," you might feel compelled to come up with an assertion you can prove right away. Will you ignore evidence that doesn't support your claim? Will you allow the evidence to shape your understanding? Will you use it only to confirm your claim?

When used as a way of inquiring, evaluation should never be used merely to support a claim. Evaluation involves making judgments *and* testing them against the evidence. The discoveries that result should shape the claims you make. Evaluation, then, is essentially a form of dialectical thinking.

When should you turn to evaluation as a way of inquiring?

1. When you are more interested in proving something than finding more out about it.
2. When you're ready to judge the quality, relevance, or significance of something.
3. When you're looking for the reasons why you believe something is true.

Evaluating Questions

- What's my judgment about the value of this?
- What are my reasons?
- Do I see it the way most other people do?
- What's most convincing here? What's least convincing?
- What do I see that supports what I believe? What do I see that complicates or contradicts what I believe?

REFLECTION

Some of you may remember the television program *The Wonder Years.* Set in the turbulent 1960s, the show offered a glimpse of a boy and his middle-class family navigating the cultural upheavals of the time as well as the ordinary challenges of growing up. What was interesting about the show, though, was its narration. While viewers watched the boy Kevin deal with his family and friends in a changing society, the voice of a much older Kevin reflected on the meaning of those relationships and events, providing perspective that was unavailable to the boy while he was actually experiencing them.

As a way of inquiring, reflection is a lot like playing the part of the adult Kevin. Through reflection it is possible to increase the learning and self-knowledge we get from writing by looking back on the experience of writing and thinking about something. This means finding the right distance from which to see what's not necessarily apparent in the moments of engagement. It also means learning to ask the questions that help us see not just what we've written or what it means, but *how* we've done the writing and how we might be able to do it better. You've already had a fair amount of practice with this in *The Curious Writer* as you've reflected on the processes you used to complete the exercises and assignments. Indeed, one of the book's central claims is that only by reflecting on your process can you control it.

This way of inquiring may not yet come naturally to you. Reflection, in some ways, seems quite different from exploration, explanation, and evaluation. The object of reflection is not *what* you're writing or reading about, but *how* you are writing and reading about the subject. This way of inquiring requires us *to witness and report on ourselves.* Reflection is a form of self-assessment. By employing it, we can learn to identify and overcome our writing challenges. *What problems do you have in this writing situation? What might be some of the ways you could solve them? What's working? What's not? What's typical about your process? What's unique about your process in this situation?*

All of these questions force you backward, away from the immediate demands of the writing task, and encourage you to see *how* you write and think. Remember, writing *is* thinking. The payoff for reflecting is much more than figuring out when to resort to fastwriting or how to revise. It's discovering your patterns of thought and how they can be extended or changed to let you write with more insight.

When should you use reflection as a way of inquiring?

1. When you're interested in *how* you've done something and learning ways you can make the process better.
2. When you consistently have problems with the process.
3. When you're disappointed with the product.

Reflecting Questions

- What do I notice about how I think about or do this?
- How do I compare how I approach this task with how I approach another one?
- When did I have the most—and the fewest—problems?
- If I were going to do this again, what might I do differently?
- What do I understand now about how to do this that I didn't understand when I started?

PRACTICING INQUIRY

In Twin Falls, Idaho, a city of 38,000, people have taken to jumping off a bridge that spans the Snake River canyon. The Perrine Bridge, once the highest in the world, is 486 feet above the Snake, and it's a popular destination for BASE jumpers, thrill seekers who look for very tall stationary objects from which to jump with a parachute strapped to their backs. What fascinates me about this and other extreme sports is how successfully people apparently overcome the normal instincts that suggest, quite simply, that what you are about to do is a really, really bad idea because it could kill you.

Psychologists who study extreme athletes hear some of the same things over and over again. Some thrill seekers pursue extreme sports because life-threatening risk "makes them feel alive." Others talk about getting in a "zone" while climbing mountains or jumping off bridges, a feeling of being completely engaged in the moment. One study pointed to a particularly interesting finding: people with experience taking risks not only keep taking them but ultimately stop seeing what they do as all that risky.

While engaging in academic inquiry is hardly as risky as jumping off the Perrine Bridge, inquiry is also an activity that goes against instinct. It's a kind of thinking that will probably run counter to what you've learned in school so far. Rather than forming conclusions quickly, inquiry urges you to suspend judgment. Rather than avoiding uncertainty, inquiry works best when you accept ambiguity as a natural part of the discovery process. Rather than a quick look at a topic, inquiry involves a more prolonged engagement. What's the risk? That you'll become so wrapped up in your subject that you'll fail to open your parachute before you reach bottom. Fortunately, unlike BASE jumping, your life usually isn't at stake when you practice inquiry but your early drafts could be a real mess. But like an extreme athlete, the more you experience the open-ended approach to inquiry, the less risky it seems.

Rather than avoiding uncertainty, inquiry works best when you accept ambiguity as a natural part of the discovery process.

Before you move on to the writing assignments chapters of this book, you need to practice the four ways of inquiring. In preparation for that practice, first consider the following short reading.

How Much Should We Care What Happens to Animals?

1 Whenever my family packs bags for a trip we're all convinced that Bear, our yellow lab, is depressed. He curls up on his dog bed, tail tucked under his back legs, nose parked on the cushion, and looks up at us through his eyebrows. Only his eyes move, following our every movement. It's pathetic, and we all feel sorry for Bear, and guilty that we're daring to go somewhere without him. We imagine all of this, of course. We can't ask Bear how he's feeling. But like most pet owners and animal lovers across the world we naturally presume to believe that our animals feel some of the things we do—sadness, loneliness, joy, or in the case of cats, contempt. *Anthropomorphism* is the

To what extent do animals feel emotions as we do?

habit of attributing human qualities to non-human animals, and scientists rightly point out that this is often presumptuous and even arrogant. How can we know what an orangutan feels if we can't ask her?

2 But confronted with Bear's long face in the presence of luggage it's enormously hard not to sense feeling. I don't think I've ever met a pet owner who doesn't believe his pet can feel, or even think. The conversations between dog owners in the park down my street run the gamut: This pug is a loner, that collie loves only the owner's wife, this poodle is incredibly intelligent, and that lab is dopey. We often simply assume that the emotional landscapes of our pets are just like ours. Just look at that face!

3 However, this is more complicated than it seems. What do we mean by feeling or emotion? How do we define consciousness? In the absence of a means to communicate with a non-human animal, how can we determine the presence of feeling or thought? If we grant some animals like dolphins, dogs, cats, and the great apes special status because of their intelligence and emotionality, where do we draw the line? What other animals might deserve special consideration? And, of course, there's this question: who cares? If we can't definitively prove that an elephant can cry or a lab can be depressed, why worry about it? Well, think about it for a moment. If some animals can experience human-like emotion and others, including, say, a pig, are self-aware—I am this pig and not that one—then doesn't that raise some interesting ethical and moral questions? If we're able to determine, or even if we simply suspect, that an animal feels and thinks should we treat it differently? On the other hand, where do we draw the line? I suspect rats are plenty intelligent and are probably even good parents, but I much prefer them dead than alive.

The best inquiry projects deal with complicated issues like those that involve our treatment of animals. Such projects raise challenging questions and offer few simple answers. That's exactly what draws an inquiring writer to a subject—he might discover something new about what he thinks and add something to an important conversation. In the next few pages, you'll get a chance to try using the ways of inquiring discussed earlier by examining the controversy over whether non-human animals can feel and think, and in particular, whether their presumed feelings should influence how we treat them. I'm hoping that you'll find the topic interesting. Because many of us have pets, appreciate wildlife, and have definite attitudes about eating meat, this controversy touches us all in some way.

All inquiry projects are fueled by questions. An important part of the process, once you discover your topic, is to craft the questions that will initially power your investigation. In this case, I'll make it easy for you by providing the inquiry question that will get you started.

Those who argue about the "rights" of animals often claim that the issue comes down to this question:

> *Do people possess some inherent qualities that might make their lives have greater moral significance than the lives of other animals?*

In the exercises that follow, you'll pursue your own investigation into this question, exploring your own feelings, experiences, and ideas; explaining the significance of the issue; evaluating the evidence; and finally reflecting on the whole process.

EXERCISE 3.1

Exploring Within and Without

To explore is open things up rather than nail them down. More than any other method of inquiry, exploration asks that you suspend judgment, at least for a while, and ask, *What might this mean to me? What do I feel or think about this?* Changing your mind is fine. Don't hesitate to ask yourself questions you can't readily answer. Expect surprise and discovery.

STEP ONE: EXPLORING WITHIN. Return to the inquiry question. Do people possess some inherent qualities that might make their lives have greater moral significance than the lives of other animals? What are your first thoughts about it? Do you agree that human life has greater moral value than the lives of other animals? What questions does this raise for you personally? Fastwrite about this for five minutes, keeping your pen moving.

STEP TWO: EXPLORING WITHOUT. Explore your response to the following claim: *One of the things that distinguish people from other animals is that we think and they don't.* Fastwrite for three minutes. Begin by playing the "believing game"; that is, think about what makes sense to you about this claim. Then shift to the "doubting game," thinking more critically about this claim and what about it doesn't seem quite right to you.

STEP THREE: EXPLORING WITHIN AND WITHOUT. Consider the following passage from a recent article, which explores the new movement in the United States to extend animal rights to certain food items such as lobster and chickens. After reading the excerpt, fastwrite for five minutes about it. What are your first thoughts? And then what? And then?

IT DIED FOR US

Frank Bruni

Do oysters have little bivalve souls? Do they dream briny dreams, scream briny screams? On a level that I suppose is selfish and somewhat silly, I hope not, because they are alive when they are shucked right in front of us, their deaths more proximal than those of so many creatures we eat. 1

They don't thrash like the lobster in its scalding pot, but should we nonetheless worry about how they meet their end? And whether that end is a sufficiently compassionate one? 2

These questions seem less ridiculous than they once did. This month Whole Foods announced that it would no longer sell live lobsters, saying that keeping them in crammed tanks for long periods doesn't demonstrate a proper concern for animal welfare. The Chicago City Council recently outlawed the sale of foie gras to protest the force-feeding of the ducks and geese that yield it. California passed a similar law, which doesn't take effect until 2012, and other states and cities are considering such measures. 3

All of these developments dovetail with a heightened awareness in these food-obsessed times of what we eat: where it came from, what it was fed, how it was penned, how it perished. If the success of best sellers like *Fast Food Nation* and *The Omnivore's Dilemma* and stores like Whole Foods is any indication, more Americans are spending more time mulling the nutritional, environmental and, yes, ethical implications of their diets. 4

If you eat an animal, should you be morally concerned about the animal's welfare prior to its winding up on your dinner table?

5 They prefer that their beef carry the tag "grass fed," which evokes a verdant pasture rather than a squalid feed lot, and that their poultry knew the glories of a "free range," a less sturdy assurance than many people believe.

6 But these concerns are riddled with intellectual inconsistencies and prompt infinite questions. Are the calls for fundamental changes in the mass production of food simply elitist, the privilege of people wealthy enough to pay more at the checkout counter? Does fretting about ducks give people a pass on chickens? Does considering the lobster allow seafood lovers to disregard the tuna?

One Student's Response

DANIEL'S JOURNAL

EXERCISE 3.1

STEP THREE

The first thing I think about after reading this is that it really does raise "infinite questions" to consider where to draw the line. What animals are worthy of our concern and which aren't? Lobsters? And then I think that the whole movement to be concerned about what we eat is probably good. After all, until recently I never thought at all about eating organic food, and certainly had no idea about how chickens were raised. And then I think that the danger here is that we make everyone feel guilty about what they eat, and I'm not at all convinced that making people guilty makes them ultimately change what they do. And then I think that the agricultural industry does seem to respond to strong consumer movements; after all didn't the whole organic movement, which is now a multibillion dollar industry (I think), arise because more and more people demanded chemical free foods? If we make food ethics a part of our consumer demands, wouldn't the industry respond? And then I wonder again about the elitist thing mentioned in the article. Organic food is more expensive, and wouldn't ethically grown or raised chickens cost more? Doesn't that mean that some people can afford to care more and others simply don't have that choice?

EXERCISE 3.2

Explaining to Yourself, Explaining to Others

To explain is to ask, *What is this? How does it fit into what I know? How do I understand its significance?* Initially, we often ask ourselves these questions when we encounter something new. Later, we may need to explain what we know to others. When we explain things to ourselves, we do it privately, working things out in the absence of an audience. But an audience helps sharpen our thinking because to explain to others we must be clear and sensible.

STEP ONE: EXPLAINING TO YOURSELF. Review the information and ideas that you generated in the previous exploring exercise, particularly your entry from Step One, which asked for your "first thoughts" in response to the inquiry question: *Do people possess some inherent qualities that might make their lives have greater moral significance than the lives of other animals?* In your notebook, spend five minutes explaining to yourself how your thinking has evolved since then. Begin your fastwrite with the following phrase: *What I understand now about this question that I didn't understand then is . . .* See where this line takes you.

STEP TWO: EXPLAINING TO OTHERS. Craft a temporary thesis that reflects what you currently think about the inquiry question, explaining what you currently believe about the moral significance of what happens to people versus what happens to other animals.

One Student's Response

DANIEL'S JOURNAL

EXERCISE 3.2

STEP TWO

Overall, the lives of human beings have greater moral significance than the lives of other animals except those that show a recognizable human-like consciousness. Whales and other marine mammals and certain other primates should enjoy greater "rights" than other non-human animals.

EXERCISE 3.3

Evaluating the Arguments

Here are a few of the expert voices that are attempting to influence the debate about the inquiry question we're considering. Typically, when you do academic research you stride into an ongoing discussion about your topic, first trying to understand the conversation and then trying to find your own place in it. It's a two-step process: Listen carefully to what knowledgeable people are saying to make sure you understand it, and then make some judgments about what you find valid or questionable about their claims.

STEP ONE: Begin with an empty left page of your notebook. Then read each of the following four passages in turn, and *in your own words*, explain (paraphrase) what you understand the author's argument or point to be. Jot this down on the left page only, moving on to subsequent left pages as necessary.

1 "Although most humans may be superior in reasoning or in other intellectual capacities to nonhuman animals that is not enough to justify the line we draw between humans and animals. Some humans—infants and those with severe intellectual disabilities—have intellectual capacities inferior to some animals, but we would, rightly, be shocked by anyone who proposed that we inflict slow, painful deaths on these intellectually inferior humans in order to test the safety of household products. Nor, of course, would we tolerate confining them in small cages and then slaughtering them in order to eat them. The fact that we are prepared to do these things to nonhuman animals is therefore a sign of 'speciesism'—a prejudice that survives because it is convenient for the dominant group—in this case not whites or males, but all humans."[1]

* * *

1. Peter Singer, "Animal Liberation at 30," *New York Review of Books* (May 15, 2003), http://www.nybooks.com/articles/16276.

"I am a speciesist. Speciesism is not merely plausible; it is essential for right conduct, because those who will not make the morally relevant distinctions among species are almost certain, in consequence, to misapprehend their true obligations. The analogy between speciesism and racism is insidious. Every sensitive moral judgment requires that the differing natures of the beings to whom obligations are owed be considered. If all forms of animate life—or vertebrate animal life?—must be treated equally, and if therefore in evaluating a research program the pains of a rodent count equally with the pains of a human, we are forced to conclude (1) that neither humans nor rodents possess rights, or (2) that rodents possess all the rights that humans possess. Both alternatives are absurd. Yet one or the other must be swallowed if the moral equality of all species is to be defended. Humans owe to other humans a degree of moral regard that cannot be owed to animals. Some humans take on the obligation to support and heal others, both humans and animals, as a principal duty in their lives; the fulfillment of that duty may require the sacrifice of many animals. If biomedical investigators abandon the effective pursuit of their professional objectives because they are convinced that they may not do to animals what the service of humans requires, they will fail, objectively, to do their duty. Refusing to recognize the moral differences among species is a sure path to calamity."[2] 2

* * *

"People have always exalted certain 'higher' feelings that are claimed to single us out among animals. Only humans, it is said, feel noble emotions such as compassion, true love, altruism, pity, mercy, reverence, honor, and modesty. On the other hand, people have often attributed so called 'negative' emotions to animals: cruelty, pride, greed, rage, vanity, and hatred. At play here appears to be a seemingly unbearable injury to our sense of uniqueness, to our entitlement to the special nobility of our emotional life. Thus not only whether animals can feel, but what they feel, is used to strengthen the species barrier. What lies behind this 'us/them' mentality—the urge to define ourselves by proving we are not only different, but utterly different, including emotionally? Why should this distinction between man and beast be so important?"[3] 3

* * *

"The concept of the person belongs to the ongoing dialogue which binds the moral community. Creatures who are by nature incapable of entering into this dialogue have neither rights nor duties nor personality. If animals had rights, then we should require their consent before taking them into captivity, training them, domesticating them or in any way putting them to our uses. But there is no conceivable process whereby this consent could be delivered or withheld. 4

2. Carl Cohen, "The Case for the Use of Animals in Biomedical Research," *New England Journal of Medicine* 315, no. 4 (1986): 865–870.
3. Jeffrey Moussaieff Masson and Susan McCarthy, *When Elephants Weep: The Emotional Lives of Animals* (New York: Dell, 1995), pp. 26–27.

Furthermore, a creature with rights is duty-bound to respect the rights of others. The fox would be duty-bound to respect the life of the chicken and the whole species would be condemned out of hand as criminal by nature. Any law which compelled persons to respect the rights of non-human species would weigh so heavily on the predators as to drive them to extinction in a short while."[4]

STEP TWO: Now that you understand the arguments and ideas advanced by each of these four experts, determine which of them you find most compelling and how that might support or change your tentative thesis from Exercise 3.2. Begin by writing your tentative thesis on the top of the right page that faces your initial entry from Step One. Now fastwrite for seven full minutes on the right facing pages, using the following questions to focus for your thinking:

- Which of these claims or ideas do I find most persuasive? Which seem least persuasive? Why?
- What new questions do these authors raise for me?
- Which arguments seem to support what I initially believed in my thesis, and which challenged me to rethink my position?
- What do I believe now might be the best answer to the inquiry question?

STEP THREE: Finish by composing one or two paragraphs that best articulate your *current* thoughts on the inquiry question. What is your position on the question? What other questions do you have that you might investigate if you had more time? What do you understand now about the issue of speciesism that you didn't understand when you began?

ONE STUDENT'S RESPONSE

DANIEL'S JOURNAL

EXERCISE 3.3

STEP ONE

To be a "speciesist" is to insist that there are "essential" distinctions to be made between humans and other animals. The author argues that if we collapse these distinctions and distribute similar rights to all living things then we're stuck with a situation where the basic idea of "rights" is made meaningless, or we have to accept that a lab animal has the same rights as we do. The author believes that humans' "principal duty" is to each other. As a result, if other animals must suffer or even be sacrificed in the service of that duty, then this is the way things should be.

4. Roger Scruton, *Animal Rights and Wrongs* (London: Demos, 1996), p. 80.

EXERCISE 3.4

Reflecting on the Process

When athletes want to improve their performance—perfect their swing, improve their strategy at the track, improve the accuracy of their throw—they reflect on *how* they do something. The same idea applies to writing and thinking. If you want to get better at both, you set aside some time to consider what you did, how it worked, and what you might do differently.

STEP ONE: WHAT'S THE STORY? On a left page of your notebook, fastwrite the story of your experience writing and thinking about the inquiry question: *Do people possess some inherent qualities that might make their lives have greater moral significance than the lives of other animals?* Begin your fastwrite with the phrase, *When I first started investigating this issue, I began by . . .* When the writing stalls, use the phrase, *And then I . . .* Tell yourself the story of your experience until you feel there is nothing more to tell.

STEP TWO: On the right page of your notebook, begin with the following phrase and follow it for three minutes. Try to be specific as possible.

1. *As I reflect on my experience doing this, what I understand now about my methods of writing and thinking that I didn't understand when I began was . . .*

Finish by following this phrase for another three minutes:

2. *If I was going to do this again, I would . . .*

ONE STUDENT'S RESPONSE

DANIEL'S JOURNAL

EXERCISE 3.4

STEP ONE

When I first started investigating this issue I realized that it wasn't something I'd thought about at all, and I was a little surprised by the whole thing. I wasn't aware that there was all this controversy over whether a lobster has feelings or has rights. And then I spent some time working through the exercises, writing about what I thought, and I started to believe that maybe it was possible to think about this whole animal rights thing in a new way. I began to think that certain animals that have a consciousness might deserve some special consideration. And then I began to think about the whole idea of consciousness. What do I mean by that exactly? And how do you measure it? And then I thought this was something that would be interesting to research if I had more time . . .

SYMPHONIC INQUIRY

When we write, we rarely use just one of the four ways of inquiring. Instead, we explore, explain, evaluate, and reflect in concert, unconsciously shifting from one to the other. Even in a fastwrite, the seeming refuge of exploration, writers often use explanation, evaluation, and reflection as they circle a subject and discover their feelings and motives.

When you bring all four ways of inquiring together you achieve symphonic inquiry. But how do you do that? Learning the opening questions to ask yourself helps a lot. Soon, asking these questions becomes second nature. Taking time to reflect on how you're approaching a task also helps, particularly for an apprentice to inquiry-based learning. For instance, perhaps your essays come up a bit short on information and your instructor complains that your ideas are fairly obvious. Reflecting on this, you realize that you tend to short-circuit exploration in a rush to judgment. Next time, you try doing more open-ended writing in your journal before you try to come up with a thesis.

You're both a composer and the conductor of this orchestra, and your task is to create the music of surprise and discovery.

You also can incorporate some practical techniques into your reading and writing processes that promote symphonic inquiry. The double-entry journal, or some variation of it, can really help you shift back and forth between creative and critical thinking. You also might establish the habit of writing summaries or other explanations of the things you're reading in your notebook or in the margins of the article you're reading. Shifting from one way of inquiring to another is like shifting from one instrument to another. You're both a composer and the conductor of this orchestra, and your task is to create the music of surprise and discovery.

USING WHAT YOU HAVE LEARNED

The next few chapters introduce a range of genres and writing assignments. Although each has different features and purposes, I believe you'll find that the *process* of composing these essays draws heavily on what you've learned about writing in these first three chapters. Whether you're writing a personal essay or a research paper, some of the same things will guide you:

- The spirit of inquiry will guide your writing.
- You will use the power of questions to help you to see what isn't immediately obvious.
- You will employ constructive habits of mind, such as making the familiar strange, suspending judgment, and searching for surprise.
- You will make rhetorical choices based on the needs of the writing or reading situation.

- You will use dialectical thinking to guide your writing and reading processes, moving back and forth between the creative and the critical.
- You will use exploration, explanation, evaluation, and reflection to get the most out of your inquiry projects.
- You will experience the pleasure of using writing not only to say what you already know but to discover what you didn't know you knew.

Writing a personal essay is often like seeing an old picture of yourself. It thrusts you back into a particular time and place, but at the same time you see yourself from a certain distance, bringing knowledge and understanding to past events that you didn't have when they occurred. This publicity photograph of my mother, brother, and me in the 1950s returns me to that world and at the same time I see what I couldn't have seen then: a time when fathers were often missing from the picture while working mothers, like mine, had to move gracefully from family to job, proving themselves at both.

Writing a Personal Essay

What You'll Learn in This Chapter

- How personal essays can help you with academic writing.
- What distinguishes a personal essay from other forms.
- How to write a sketch.
- Why a confusing topic may be better than one you have all figured out.
- Questions for revising personal essays.

WRITING ABOUT EXPERIENCE

Most us were taught and still believe that we need to know what we are going to write before we actually pick up the pen or sit in front of the computer. My student Lynn was typical.

"I think I'll write about my experience organizing the street fair," she told me the other day. "That would be a good topic for a personal essay, right?"

"Do you think so?" I said.

"Well, yes, because I already know a lot about it. I'll have a lot to write about."

"Okay, but is there anything about this experience that you want to understand better?" I said. "Anything about it that makes you curious?"

"Curious? It was just a street fair," she said.

"Sure, but is there something about what happened that makes you want to look at the experience again? Is there a chance that you might learn something about yourself, or about street fairs, or about the community, or about people, or . . ."

Lynn was clearly sorry she asked. What I should have said was much more to the point: the best essay topics are those that are an itch you need to scratch. These tend not to be topics you have already figured out. While the topics can be familiar to you, the results of your inquiry are usually much better if you don't yet know what you think about your topics and you're interested to learn more about them. The best topics ask to be written about because they make you wonder *Why did I do that? What does that mean? Why did that happen? How did I really feel? What do I really think?*

Unlike most other forms of inquiry, the personal essay invites an initial display of confusion or uncertainty from writers regarding their subjects. In other words, writers do not have to have their subjects figured out when starting a personal essay. This form of inquiry is a vehicle for writers to work through their thinking and feeling on a subject directly in front of their readers.

As a form, the *personal* essay places the writer at center stage. This doesn't mean that once she's there, her responsibility is to pour out her secrets, share her pain, or confess her sins. Some essays do have these confessional qualities, but more often they do not. Yet a personal essayist, no matter the subject of the essay, is still *exposed.* There is no hiding behind the pronoun "one," as in "one might think" or "one often feels," no lurking in the shadows of the passive voice: "This paper will argue. . . ." The personal essay is first-person territory.

The personal essay is a vehicle for writers to work through their thinking and feeling on a subject directly in front of their readers.

In this sense, the personal essay is much like a photographic self-portrait. Like a picture, a good personal essay tells the truth, or it tells *a* truth about the writer/subject, and it often captures the writer at a particular moment of time. Therefore, the experience of taking a self-portrait, or confronting an old picture of oneself taken by someone else, can create the feeling of exposure that writing a personal essay often does.

But it does more. When we gaze at ourselves in a photograph we often see it as yanked from a larger story about ourselves, stories that thread their way through our lives and give us ideas about who we were and who we are. This is what the personal essay demands of us: we must somehow present ourselves truthfully and measure our past against the present. In other words, when we hold a photograph of ourselves we know more than the person we see there knew, and as writers of the personal essay, we must share that knowledge and understanding with readers.

MOTIVES FOR WRITING A PERSONAL ESSAY

Essai was a term first coined by the sixteenth-century French nobleman Michel de Montaigne, a man who had lived through occurrences of the plague, the bloody civil war between French Catholics and Protestants, and his own ill health. These were tumultuous and uncertain times when old social orders and intellectual traditions were under assault, and it proved to be ideal ferment for the essay. The French verb *essaier* means "to attempt" or "to try," and the essay became an opportunity for Montaigne to work out his thoughts about war, the education of children, the evils of doctors, and the importance of pleasure. The personal essay tradition inspired by Montaigne is probably unlike the essays you are familiar with in school. The school essay is often formulaic—a five-paragraph theme, or thesis-example paper—while the personal essay is an open-ended form that allows for uncertainty and inconclusiveness. It is more about the process of coming to know than presenting *what* you know. The personal essay attempts *to find out* rather than *to prove.*

It is an ideal form of inquiry if your purpose is exploratory rather than argumentative, and if you're particularly interested in working out the possible relationships between your subject and yourself. Because the personal essay is openly subjective, the writer can't hide. The intruding *I* confronts the writer with the same questions, over and over again: *Why does this matter to me? What do I make of it? How does this change the way I think of myself and the way I see the world?* Because of this, one of the principal dangers of the personal essay is that it becomes narcissistic; it goes on and on about what the writer thinks and feels, and the reader is left with that nagging question—*So what?* The personal essayist must always find some way to hitch the particulars of his or her experience to something larger—an idea, a theme, or even a feeling that readers might share.

On the other hand, one of the prime rhetorical advantages of the personal essay is its subjectivity. Because it is written with openness and honesty, the essay is often a very intimate form, inviting the reader to share in the writer's often concealed world. In the personal essay, we often get to see the face sweating under the mask. Honesty is one of the essay's primary virtues, and because the form allows for uncertainty and confusion, the writer doesn't need to pretend that he has *the* answer, or that he knows more than he lets on about his subject.

THE PERSONAL ESSAY AND ACADEMIC WRITING

In some ways, the personal essay might seem like a dramatic departure from the kind of academic writing you've done in other classes. Openly subjective and sometimes tentative in its conclusions, the personal essay is a relatively open form that is not predictably structured, like much academic writing. Additionally, the tone of the personal essay is conversational, even intimate, rather than impersonal and removed. If your sociology or economics professor will never ask for a personal essay, why bother to write one in your composition class?

It's a fair question. While the pleasures of personal essay writing can be significant, and reason alone to write essays, there are other important reasons to practice the form. The most obvious is that the essay, more than any other form, gives you an opportunity to use exploration as a method of inquiry, and to practice those habits of mind that are so important to academic inquiry: suspending judgment, tolerating ambiguity, and using questions to challenge easy assumptions.

But the purpose of writing personal essays in your composition class goes beyond this. For one thing, the essay emphasizes the *process* of coming to know about yourself and your subject, exposing your reasoning and the ways you use knowledge to get at the truth of things. Reflecting on these things in a personal essay can tell you a lot about how you think. The *dialectical thinking* required by the personal essay—the movement back and forth between critical and creative thinking—is a useful mental exercise for a range of academic situations. Finally, much of what you are asked to write in college depends on your

The dialectical thinking required by the personal essay—the movement back and forth between critical and creative thinking—is a useful mental exercise for a range of academic situations.

willingness to step forward and express a belief, make an assertion, or pose a relevant question. The personal essay is a form that puts the writer in the spotlight. You can't hide in the wings, concealed in the shadow of other people's opinions or someone else's findings. What *you* think is what the essay is all about.

FEATURES OF THE FORM

There are many different kinds of personal essays, of course, but certain conventions are present in most of them. Keep these in mind as you read the professional essays that follow. Which of the conventions listed here seem to be present? Can you detect any others?

- *Personal essays are usually written in the first person.* There is no pretense of scientific objectivity in personal essays. What makes them work is the tension between the subject and the writer as the writer reaches for new understandings.
- *The subject of the essay is often commonplace.* Although essayists sometimes write about dramatic things, they most often are interested in the drama of everyday life. Fine essays have been published, for example, about hats, houseflies, and summer lakes. The essayist's thoughts about such things may catapult her beyond the ordinary, but the topic is often humble.
- *Narrative is often the primary method of development.* Personal essays often tell two kinds of stories—they relate narratives of the writer's experiences and observations, and they tell the story of the writer's thinking about what those experiences and observations might mean.
- *The thesis can be implicit, and it frequently emerges late, rather than at the beginning, of the essay.* In some ways, the personal essay is the most literary of the academic forms—it tells stories, it relies heavily on details, it shows *and* tells. As a result, the meaning of an essay can be implied rather than stated directly, and because essays are often used to describe *the process* of coming to know something, insight is usually earned later rather than at the beginning of the telling.
- *Of the four sources of information, the personal essay relies on memory and observation most of all.* Because of the subjectivity of the essay, the writer often reports *what has happened* to her as a means to account for *what happens*. However, interview and research can enrich a personal essay by challenging the writer to consider other voices and other information.
- *The essay often mimics the dialectical process that helped the writer compose it, shifting back and forth from the then and now, what happened to*

what happens, and showing and telling. Because the personal essay, more than any other form of inquiry, often focuses on the process of coming to know, essays themselves often capture this process in action. See if you can see evidence of this movement in the essays that follow.

PERSONAL ESSAY

Naomi Shihab Nye is a poet, and the essay that follows, "Long Overdue," has some of the qualities of a poem—spare language, breaks or white spaces between sections of the narrative, and an emphasis on the line. That makes her essay unusual, yet compelling. Nye, the daughter of a Palestinian father and an American mother, writes here about confronting the prejudice of others and being unable to find the words to speak up.

While most of us have probably not been on the receiving end of bigotry, we commonly find ourselves offended by the words of others and unable to find the words to respond. In a larger sense, this essay explores those moments, as Nye attempts to write to the heart of the nagging question, *Why do we say nothing?*

LONG OVERDUE

Naomi Shihab Nye

A gardener stares at our raggedy front yard. More weeds than grass. The star jasmine vine has died in the drought, leaving its bony spine woven through the frets of the wire fence. A young hackberry presses too close to the house. A bedraggled pomegranate tree crowds the banana palms. 1

The gardener shakes his head. Hands on hips. He is large and blond as a Viking. He wears no shirt. When I ask what he thinks about laying flat stones on the beaten path from driveway to porch so we don't track in mud when it rains, he nods silently, then puts his arms out to embrace this troubled yard. "Long overdue." 2

Excuse me? And the trimming? What would he charge to take out that tree? Could he edge this flowerbed with smooth rounded river rocks while he's at it? He stares into my face. 3

Long, long, long overdue. 4

I laugh out loud. 5

His few well-chosen words come back to me for days. 6

That's how I feel about lives bereft of poetry. 7

That's how I feel about the whole Middle East. 8

The words we didn't say. How many times? Stones stuck in the throat. Endlessly revised silence. *What was wrong with me? How could I, a person whose entire vocation has* 9 *been dedicated one way or another to "the use of words," lose words completely when I needed them? Where does vocal paralysis come from? Why does regret have such a long life span?* My favorite poet William Stafford used to say. "Think of something you said. Now write what you *wish you* had said."

10 But I am always thinking of the times I said nothing.

11 In England, attending a play by myself, I was happy when the elderly woman next to me began speaking at intermission. Our arms had been touching lightly on the arm rest between our seats.

12 "Smashingly talented," she said of Ben Kingsley, whose brilliant monologue we'd been watching. "I don't know how he does it—transporting us so effortlessly, he's a genius. Not many in the world like him. " I agreed. But then she sighed and made an odd turn. "You know what's wrong with the world today? It's Arabs. I blame it all on the Arabs. Most world problems can really be traced to them."

13 My blood froze. Why was she saying this? The play wasn't about Arabs. Ben Kingsley was hardly your blue-blooded Englishman, either, so what brought it up? Nothing terrible relating to Arabs had happened lately in the news. I wasn't wearing a kef' fiyeh around my neck.

14 But my mouth would not open.

15 "Why *did so* many of them come to England?" she continued, muttering as if we were sharing a confidence. "A ruination, that's what it is."

16 It struck me then she might be a landlady having trouble with tenants. I tried and tried to part my lips. *Where is the end of the tangled thread? How will we roll it into a ball if we can't find an end?*

17 She chitted on about something less consequential, never seeming to mind our utterly one-sided conversation, till the lights went down. Of course I couldn't concentrate on the rest of the play. My precious ticket felt wasted. I twisted my icy hands together while my cheeks burned.

18 Even worse, she and I rode the same train afterwards. I had plenty of time to respond, to find a vocabulary for prejudice and fear. The dark night buildings flew by. I could have said, "Madam. I am half Arab. I pray your heart grows larger someday." I could have sent her off, stunned and embrassed, into the dark.

19 My father would say, *People like that can't be embarrassed.*

20 But what would he say *back to her?*

21 *Oh I was ashamed for my silence and I have carried that shame across oceans, through a summer when it never rained, in my secret pocket, till now. I will never feel better about it. Like my reckless angry last words to the one who took his own life.*

22 Years later my son and I were sitting on an American island with a dear friend, the only African American living among eighty or so residents. A brilliant artist and poet in his seventies, he has made a beautiful lifetime of painting picture books, celebrating expression, encouraging the human spirit, reciting poems of other African American heroes, delighting children and adults alike.

We had spent a peaceful day riding bicycles, visiting the few students at the schoolhouse, picking up rounded stones on the beach, digging peat moss in the woods. We had sung hymns together in the resonant little church. Our friend had purchased a live lobster down at the dock for supper. My son and I became sad when it seemed to be knocking on the lid of the pot of boiling water. "Let me out!" We vowed quietly to one another never to eat a lobster again. 23

After dinner a friend of our friend dropped in, returned to the island from her traveling life as an anthropologist. We asked if she had heard anything about the elections in Israel—that was the day Shimon Peres and Benjamin Netanyahu vied for prime minister and we had been unable to pick up a final tally on the radio. 24

She thought Netanyahu had won. The election was very close. But then she said, "Good thing! He'll put those Arabs in their places. Arabs always want more than they deserve." 25

My face froze. Was it possible I had heard incorrectly? *An anthropologist speaking. Not a teenager, not a blithering idiot.* I didn't speak another word during her visit. I wanted to, I should have, but I couldn't. My plate littered with red shells. 26

After she left, my friend put his gentle hand on my shoulder. He said simply, "Now you know a little more what it feels like to be black." 27

So what happens to my words when the going gets rough? In a world where certain equities for human beings seem long, long, long, overdue, where is the magic sentence to act as a tool? Where is the hoe, the tiller, the rake? 28

Pontificating, proving, proselytizing leave me cold. So do endless political debates over coffee after dinner. I can't listen to talk radio, drowning in jabber. 29

The poetic impulse—to suggest, hint, shape a little picture, to find a story, metaphor, scene—abides as a kind of music inside. Nor can I forget the journalist in Dubai who called me a donkey for talking about vegetables when there was injustice in the world. 30

I can talk about sumac too. When a friend asks what's that purple spice in the little shake-up jar at the Persian restaurant, tears cloud my eyes. 31

Is it good for you? 32

Are vegetables, in some indelible way, smarter than we are? Are animals? 33

But then the headlines take the power. The fanatical behavior. 34

Problem is, we can't hear the voices of the moderates, said the Israeli man, who assured me his home was built on a spot where Arabs had never lived. Where are *they*? Why *don't* they *speak louder?* 35

(They don't like to raise their voices.) 36

(Maybe they can't hear you either.) 37

The men haven't fixed it. Lose their turn. Their turn was long enough. Hanan stepped back. Anyone can understand why. Too many men. Pass the power to the women. And the children. And the eggplants. But it *was women who said stupid things both times to me.* No one exempt from stupidity. Is there a cure? 38

39 I love when the poet Wislawa said we have to honor anew those humble words *I don't know.*

40 Then we start out fresh. Like the soft dampness of a new morning.

41 I don't know. How. To tell the whole story. No one tells the whole story. No one knows it! *Still, don't those guys seem to talk forever?*

42 EVERY VIOLENT ACT SETS US BACK. SETS US BACK. Say it louder.

43 What to contain. To honor, leave unspoken. People will talk and talk while the almond tree is blooming. But something crucial is always too big, or too obvious, to say. Obviously, it is the thing which could save people, if we could only learn its name.

44 The gardener laid the stones. He cut the trees back. He turned over the soil around the plants so their roots could breathe. He used no language doing it. His skin glistened in the sun.

45 What he has suffered in his life remains a mystery to me. Rumors in the neighborhood say it has been much, and extreme. What did Aldous Huxley say toward the end of his life when someone asked him for advice? *After so much study, after so much research and discussion, it comes to this: be a little kinder to one another.*

46 Before leaving, the gardener mentioned the grass would grow up soon between the stepping stones to help them look much nicer, as if they had been there for years.

INQUIRING INTO THE ESSAY

Think about "Long Overdue" by shifting your perspective on it using the four methods of inquiry: exploring, explaining, evaluating, and reflecting.

1. After you've read through Nye's essay once, read through it again, but this time stop at every line break, or white space that divides each segment, and fastwrite in your journal for sixty seconds. Each time, begin with this phrase: *The most important thing I understand from this is . . .*" Use these multiple responses to compose the story of your understanding of the meaning of Nye's essay from beginning to end.
2. Explain what you take to be the significance of the repeated phrase *Long, long, overdue.*
3. Evaluate the effectiveness of the "line breaks" in this essay. We are used to unbroken narratives—this happened and then this happened and so on. "Long Overdue," like many contemporary personal essays, defies this expectation. What do you think about the effect of this on you as a reader?
4. An important part of academic inquiry—whether it's doing scientific research or writing a critical essay on literature—is trying to identify the prejudices you bring as an investigator to your project. Reflect on what prejudices you brought to your reading of this essay.

PERSONAL ESSAY

America is a nation of immigrants, and their stories often haunt their children. Judith Ortiz Cofer moved from Puerto Rico as a child with her family in the mid-1950s to a barrio in Paterson, New Jersey. There she became both part of and witness to a familiar narrative, that of the outsider who finds herself wedged between two worlds, two cultures, and two longings: the desire to return "home" and the desire to feel at home in the new place. While this is a story most immigrants know well, it is also a deeply personal one, shaded by particular places, prejudices, and patterns.

In "One More Lesson," Cofer describes both the places that competed for her sense of self—the Puerto Rico of her childhood, where she spent time as a child while her Navy father was away at sea, and an apartment in New Jersey where she would go when he returned.

ONE MORE LESSON

Judith Ortiz Cofer

I remember Christmas on the Island by the way it felt on my skin. The temperature dropped into the ideal seventies and even lower after midnight when some of the more devout Catholics—mostly older women—got up to go to church, *misa del gallo* they called it; mass at the hour when the rooster crowed for Christ. They would drape shawls over their heads and shoulders and move slowly toward town. The birth of Our Savior was a serious affair in our *pueblo*. 1

At Mamá's house, food was the focal point of *Navidad*. There were banana leaves brought in bunches by the boys, spread on the table, where the women would pour coconut candy steaming hot, and the leaves would wilt around the sticky lumps, adding an extra tang of flavor to the already irresistible treat. Someone had to watch the candy while it cooled, or it would begin to disappear as the children risked life and limb for a stolen piece of heaven. The banana leaves were also used to wrap the traditional food of holidays in Puerto Rico: *pasteles*, the meat pies made from grated yucca and plantain and stuffed with spiced meats. 2

Every afternoon during the week before Christmas Day, we would come home from school to find the women sitting around in the parlor with bowls on their laps, grating pieces of coconut, yuccas, plantains, cheeses—all the ingredients that would make up our Christmas Eve feast. The smells that filled Mamá's house at that time have come to mean anticipation and a sensual joy during a time in my life, the last days of my early childhood, when I could still absorb joy through my pores—*when I had not yet learned that light is followed by darkness, that all of creation is based on that simple concept, and maturity is a discovery of that natural law.* 3

It was in those days that the Americans sent baskets of fruit to our barrio—apples, oranges, grapes flown in from the States. And at night, if you dared to walk up to the hill where the mango tree stood in the dark, you could see a wonderful sight: a 4

Christmas tree, a real pine, decorated with lights of many colors. It was the blurry outline of this tree you saw, for it was inside a screened-in-porch, but we had heard a thorough description of it from the boy who delivered the fruit, a nephew of Mamá's, as it had turned out. Only, I was not impressed, since just the previous year we had put up a tree ourselves in our apartment in Paterson.

5 Packages arrived for us in the mail from our father. I got dolls dressed in the national costumes of Spain, Italy, and Greece (at first we could not decide which of the Greek dolls was the male, since they both wore skirts); my brother got picture books; and my mother, jewelry that she would not wear, because it was too much like showing off and might attract the Evil Eye.

6 Evil Eye or not, the three of us were the envy of the pueblo. Everything about us set us apart, and I put away my dolls quickly when I discovered that my playmates would not be getting any gifts until *Los Reyes*—the Day of the Three Kings, when Christ received His gifts—and that even then it was more likely that the gifts they found under their beds would be practical things like clothes. Still, it was fun to find fresh grass for the camels the night the Kings were expected, tie it in bundles with string, and put it under our beds along with a bowl of fresh water.

7 The year went by fast after Christmas, and in the spring we received a telegram from Father. His ship had arrived in Brooklyn Yard. He gave us a date for our trip back to the States. I remember Mother's frantic packing, and the trips to Mayagüez for new clothes; the inspections of my brother's and my bodies for cuts, scrapes, mosquito bites, and other "damage" she would have to explain to Father. And I remember begging Mamá to tell me stories in the afternoons, although it was not summer yet and the trips to the mango tree had not begun. In looking back I realize that Mamá's stories were what I packed—my winter store.

8 Father had succeeded in finding an apartment outside Paterson's "vertical barrio," the tenement Puerto Ricans called *El Building*. He had talked a Jewish candy store owner into renting us the apartment above his establishment, which he and his wife had just vacated after buying a house in West Paterson, an affluent suburb. Mr. Schultz was a nice man whose melancholy face I was familiar with from trips I had made often with my father to his store for cigarettes. Apparently, my father had convinced him and his brother, a look-alike of Mr. Schultz who helped in the store, that we were not the usual Puerto Rican family. My father's fair skin, his ultra-correct English, and his Navy uniform were a good argument. Later it occurred to me that my father had been displaying me as a model child when he took me to that store with him. I was always dressed as if for church and held firmly by the hand. I imagine he did the same with my brother. As for my mother, her Latin beauty, her thick black hair that hung to her waist, her voluptuous body which even the winter clothes could not disguise, would have been nothing but a hindrance to my father's plans. But everyone knew that a Puerto Rican woman is her husband's satellite; she reflects both his light and his dark sides. If my father was respectable, then his family would be respectable. We got the apartment on Park Avenue.

9 Unlike El Building, where we had lived on our first trip to Paterson, our new home was truly in exile. There were Puerto Ricans by the hundreds only one block

away, but we heard no Spanish, no loud music, no mothers yelling at children, nor the familiar *¡Ay Bendito!*, that catch-all phrase of our people. Mother lapsed into silence herself, suffering from *La Tristeza*, the sadness that only place induces and only place cures. But Father relished silence, and we were taught that silence was something to be cultivated and practiced.

10 Since our apartment was situated directly above where the Schultzes worked all day, our father instructed us to remove our shoes at the door and walk in our socks. We were going to prove how respectable we were by being the opposite of what our ethnic group was known to be—we would be quiet and inconspicuous.

11 I was escorted each day to school by my nervous mother. It was a long walk in the cooling air of fall in Paterson and we had to pass by El Building where the children poured out of the front door of the dilapidated tenement still answering their mothers in a mixture of Spanish and English: "Sí, Mami, I'll come straight home from school." At the corner we were halted by the crossing guard, a strict woman who only gestured her instructions, never spoke directly to the children, and only ordered us to "halt" or "cross" while holding her white-gloved hand up at face level or swinging her arm sharply across her chest if the light was green.

12 The school building was not a welcoming sight for someone used to the bright colors and airiness of tropical architecture. The building looked functional. It could have been a prison, an asylum, or just what it was: an urban school for the children of immigrants, built to withstand waves of change, generation by generation. Its red brick sides rose to four solid stories. The black steel fire escapes snaked up its back like an exposed vertebra. A chain-link fence surrounded its concrete playground. Members of the elite safety patrol, older kids, sixth graders mainly, stood at each of its entrances, wearing their fluorescent white belts that criss-crossed their chests and their metal badges. No one was allowed in the building until the bell rang, not even on rainy or bitter-cold days. Only the safety-patrol stayed warm.

13 My mother stood in front of the main entrance with me and a growing crowd of noisy children. She looked like one of us, being no taller than the sixth-grade girls. She held my hand so tightly that my fingers cramped. When the bell rang, she walked me into the building and kissed my cheek. Apparently my father had done all the paperwork for my enrollment, because the next thing I remember was being led to my third-grade classroom by a black girl who had emerged from the principal's office.

14 Though I had learned some English at home during my first years in Paterson, I had let it recede deep into my memory while learning Spanish in Puerto Rico. Once again I was the child in the cloud of silence, the one who had to be spoken to in sign language as if she were a deaf-mute. Some of the children even raised their voices when they spoke to me, as if I had trouble hearing. Since it was a large troublesome class composed mainly of black and Puerto Rican children, with a few working-class Italian children interspersed, the teacher paid little attention to me. I re-learned the language quickly by the immersion method. I remember one day, soon after I joined the rowdy class when our regular teacher was absent and Mrs. D., the sixth-grade teacher from across the hall, attempted to monitor both

classes. She scribbled something on the chalkboard and went to her own room. I felt a pressing need to use the bathroom and asked Julio, the Puerto Rican boy who sat behind me, what I had to do to be excused. He said that Mrs. D. had written on the board that we could be excused by simply writing our names under the sign. I got up from my desk and started for the front of the room when I was struck on the head hard with a book. Startled and hurt, I turned around expecting to find one of the bad boys in my class, but it was Mrs. D. I faced. I remember her angry face, her fingers on my arms pulling me back to my desk, and her voice saying incomprehensible things to me in a hissing tone. Someone finally explained to her that I was new, that I did not speak English. I also remember how suddenly her face changed from anger to anxiety. But I did not forgive her for hitting me with that hard-cover spelling book. Yes, I would recognize that book even now. It was not until years later that I stopped hating that teacher for not understanding that I had been betrayed by a classmate, and by my inability to read her warning on the board. I *instinctively understood then that language is the only weapon a child has against the absolute power of adults*.

15 I quickly built up my arsenal of words by becoming an insatiable reader of books.

Inquiring into the Essay

Explore, explain, evaluate, and reflect on Cofer's "One More Lesson."

1. In the 1950s and 1960s, many saw America as a "melting pot." The idea then was that although we may have many different immigrant backgrounds, we should strive toward some common "Americanism." For some, this is still a powerful idea, but for others the melting pot is a metaphor for cultural hegemony or even racial prejudice, a demand that differences be ignored and erased rather than celebrated. In your journal, write about your own feelings on this controversy. Tell the story of a friend, a relative, a neighbor who was an outsider. Tell about your own experience. What did it mean to assimilate, and at what cost?
2. Personal essays, like short fiction, rely heavily on narrative. But unlike fiction, essays both *show* and *tell;* that is, they use story to reveal meaning (*show*) and they also explain that meaning to the reader (*tell*). Identify several places in the essay where Cofer "tells." What do you notice about the placement of these moments of reflection?
3. Does this essay make an evaluation, and if so, what is it asserting about cultural assimilation in America during the 1950s and 1960s? Is Cofer's evaluation still relevant?
4. One of the most common reasons students cite for liking a story is that "they could relate to it." Does that criterion apply here? Reflect on whether it's a standard you often use as a reader to judge the value of something. What exactly does it mean to "relate to" a text?

SEEING THE FORM

SELF-PORTRAIT BY FRANCES BENJAMIN JOHNSTON

In the striking self-portrait that follows, American photographer Frances Benjamin Johnston represents herself in ways in which most nineteenth-century women wouldn't dare. Her skirts are hiked up to her knees, she holds a burning cigarette between her fingers, and she clutches a beer mug on her lap. Johnston carefully composed the picture to offer a very particular version of herself. Photographic self-portraits like this one are similar to personal essays in a number of respects. They often tell a story, and the photographer, like the essayist, is a subject of the work, sometimes *the* subject. We also consider a photograph to be "authentic." We assume, for instance, that this is the real Frances Benjamin Johnston, not someone else's impression or interpretation of her. When we read a personal essay, a work of nonfiction, we also assume that the *I* of the essay is the author of the piece, not some character or other invention.

Frances Benjamin Johnston, *Self-Portrait*, 1896.

As writers of personal essays, don't we attempt to represent ourselves as authentically and honestly as we can? Aren't we basically trying to present verbal pictures of ourselves and our experiences? But how accurate are these self-representations? And if the comparison between a self-portrait such as Johnston's picture and the personal essay is an accurate one, what does it imply about how we might write our own essays, but also how we might read the personal essays of other people?

Inquiring into the Details

THE LITERACY NARRATIVE

Some of the great personal essays of the last 500 years were what we now call "literacy narratives," stories about how the author came to understand him or herself as a writer, reader, or speaker. Montaigne, Virginia Woolf, Fredrick Douglas, Malcom X, and others have published moving essays about how they each came to understand their relationships to language. This is an enormously useful project for you, too, because it will help you understand what might be at the root of your current beliefs about yourself as a maker and consumer of language.

Literacy narratives vary but like any other personal essay they often include stories or anecdotes that richly describe moments, scenes, or people, but these are chosen to reveal something about what has influenced how you feel about reading and writing. I wrote, for example, in "The Importance of Writing Badly" (p. 43) about Mrs. O'Neil, my seventh and eighth grade English teacher who had a fondness for the red pen and the SRA. I could have just as easily written about moments in the Highland Park Public Library, the sound of my father's typewriter in the next room, or using my first PC to compose an essay.

Literacy narratives also share with other personal essays the need to move from showing—narrating what happened—to telling—commenting on its significance, or answering the "so what?" question. It's particularly important to use this story-telling as an opportunity to reflect on how your experiences shape you *now* as a reader or writer. Specifically, how have these particular events or people in your past influenced how you think about your own relationship to language—are you a lover of words, resistant to English, a hoarder of books, a self-critical writer? How do your experiences contribute to these kinds of beliefs about yourself?

■ THE WRITING PROCESS ■

INQUIRY PROJECT: Writing a Personal Essay

Write a 1,000-word personal essay that explores some aspect of your experience. Your instructor may provide additional details. Choose your topic carefully. Because of the essay's exploratory methods, the best topics are those that you want to write about *not* because you know what you think, but because you want to *discover* what you think. The essay should have the following qualities:

- It must do more than tell a story; there must be a *purpose* behind telling the story that speaks in some way to someone else.
- It should, ultimately, answer the *So what?* question.
- Your essay should include some reflection to explain or speculate about what you understand *now* about something that you didn't understand *then*.
- It should be richly detailed. Seize opportunities to *show* what you mean, rather than simply explain it.

Thinking About Subjects

When you are assigned a personal essay, it's essential to embrace uncertainty and be willing to suspend judgment. This form of inquiry, more than any other, seems most useful when the writer has chosen a subject *because* he doesn't know what he wants to say about it. This is risky. Obviously, one of the risks when you start out with uncertainty is that you also might end up that way; your draft may just seem to go nowhere. This *is* a problem, but it often can be addressed in revision. The key to writing strong personal essays is accepting that first drafts might be real stinkers. But there's a payoff to this risk—the personal essay frequently yields surprise and discovery. You may well find out what you didn't know you knew, and that is among the greatest pleasures of a writer.

As you play with the prompts that follow, then, be particularly vigilant about pursuing subject matter that is confusing to you, that raises the hair on the back of your neck, or just makes you say to yourself, "I'm not sure what I think or feel about that."

Generating Ideas

Begin exploring possible subjects by generating material in your notebook. This should be an open-ended process, a chance to use your creative side, not worrying too much about making sense or trying to prejudge the value of the writing or the subjects you generate. In a sense, this is an invitation to play around.

One Student's Response

MARGARET'S JOURNAL: LISTING QUESTIONS

Is my cat extremely unusual or can any cat be taught to walk and be as needy and attached as her?

Does testosterone really make one more confident? Is there a correlation between high T and aggressiveness?

How did I once find Dr. Laura so compelling?

Why are women seldom loyal to each other? How are female friendships different from male ones? Can women and men be friends without an underlying sexual tension?

Listing Prompts. Lists can be rich sources of triggering topics. Let them grow freely, and when you're ready, use an item as the focus of another list or an episode of fastwriting. The following prompts should get you started.

1. Make a fast list of experiences you've had that you can't forget. Reach into all parts and times of your life.
2. Make a list of questions that have always nagged you about some of the following: school, men or women, fast food, hair, television, public restrooms, shoes, and sports.

Fastwriting Prompts. In the early stages of generating possible topics for an essay, fastwriting can be invaluable, *if* you allow yourself to write "badly." Initially, don't worry about staying focused; sometimes you find the best triggering topics by ranging freely. Once you've tentatively settled on something, use a more focused fastwrite, trying to generate information and ideas within the loose boundaries of your chosen topic. Here are some fastwriting prompts that might yield useful discoveries for a personal essay:

1. Choose an item from any one of the preceding lists as a prompt. Just start fastwriting about the item; perhaps start with a story, a scene, a situation, a description. Just follow the writing to see where it leads.

2. Most of us quietly harbor dreams—we hope to be a professional dancer, a good father, an activist, an Olympic luger, or a novelist. Begin a fastwrite in which you explore your dreams. When the writing stalls, ask yourself questions: *Where did this dream come from? Do I still believe in it? In what moments did it seem within reach? In what moments did it fade?* Plunge into those moments.

3. What was the most confusing time in your life? Choose a moment or scene that stands out in your memory from that time, and, writing in the present

tense, describe what you see, hear, and do. After five minutes, skip a line and choose another moment. Then another. Make a collage.

4. What do you consider "turning points" in your life, times when you could see the end of one thing and the beginning of something else? Fastwrite about one of these for seven minutes.

Visual Prompts. Sometimes the best way to generate material is to see what we think in something other than sentences. Boxes, lines, arrows, charts, and even sketches can help us see more of the landscape of a subject, especially connections between fragments of information that aren't as obvious in prose. The clustering or mapping method is useful to many writers early in the writing process as they try to discover a topic. (See the "Inquiring into the Details" box that follows for more details on how to create a cluster.) Figure 4.1 shows my cluster from the first prompt listed here.

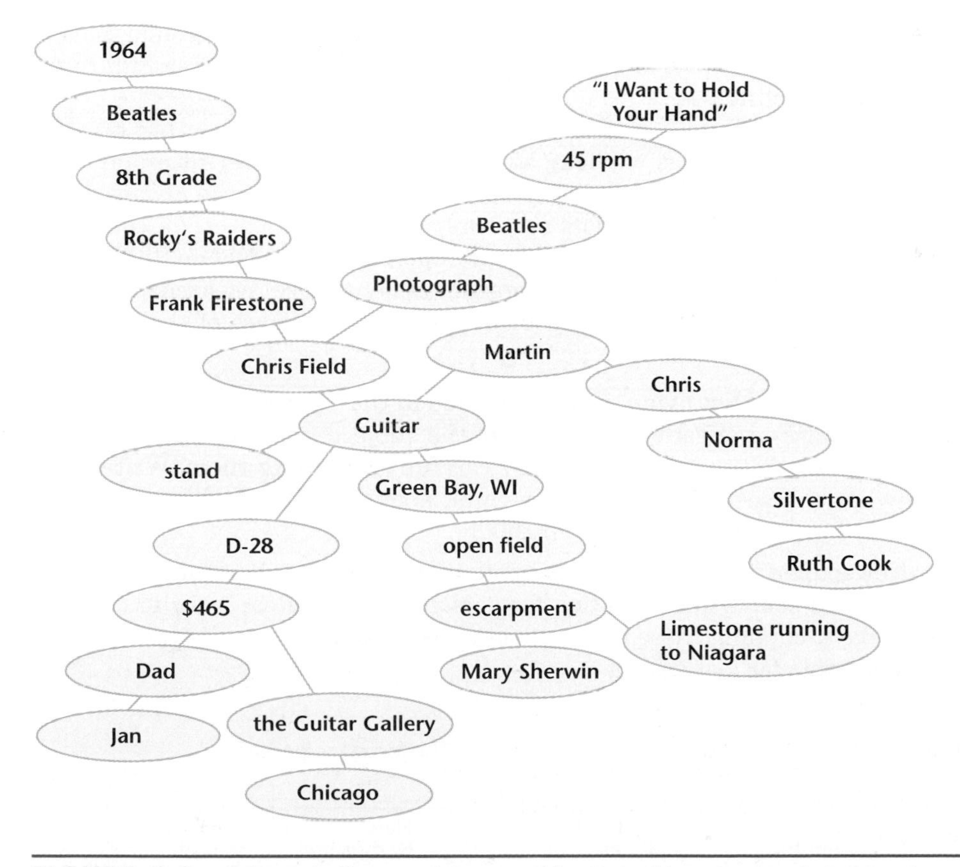

FIGURE 4.1 A cluster built around the one object I would most regret losing in a house fire: my Martin guitar.

1. What objects would you most regret losing in a house fire? The answer would likely reveal something about your passions, your longings, even your regrets. Choose a most-treasured object as the core for a cluster. Build a web of associations from it, returning to the detail in the core whenever a strand dies out. One of the wonderful complexities of being human is that we are sometimes deeply conflicted (I'm not suggesting this is always fun). Pair two opposed feelings that you consider typical of yourself. For example, *ambivalence/commitment, fear/risk taking, lonely/sociable, beautiful/ugly, composed/flaky,* and so on. Use these paired words as a core for a cluster.

2. Draw a long line on a piece of paper in your journal. This is your life. Divide the line into segments that seem to describe what feels like distinct times in your life. These may not necessarily correspond to familiar age categories like adolescence or childhood. More likely, the periods in your life will be associated with a place, a relationship, a dilemma, a job, a personal challenge, and so on, but because this is a timeline, these periods will be chronological. Examine your timeline and, as a fastwrite prompt, put two of these periods in your life together. Explore what they had in common, particularly how the earlier period might have shaped the later one. See Figure 4.2 for a sample timeline.

Research Prompts. Things we hear, see, or read can be powerful prompts for personal essays. It's tempting to believe that personal essays are always about the past, but just as often essayists are firmly rooted in the present, commenting and pondering on the confusions of contemporary life, as Naomi Shihab Nye did in "Long Overdue." In that sense, personal essayists are researchers, always on the lookout for material. Train your eye with one or more of the following prompts.

1. Return to the list of questions you made in the "Listing Prompts" section. Choose one nagging question about any of the subjects you were asked to consider and set aside time to explore it by carefully *observing* them. Write down exactly what you see . . . and what you think about it. (The double-entry notebook method is particularly useful for this.)

2. Newspaper "filler"—short stories often about odd or unusual things—can be a wonderful source of inspiration for personal essays. Read your local paper for a few days, clipping these brief articles. Paste them in your journal and use them as prompts for fastwriting.

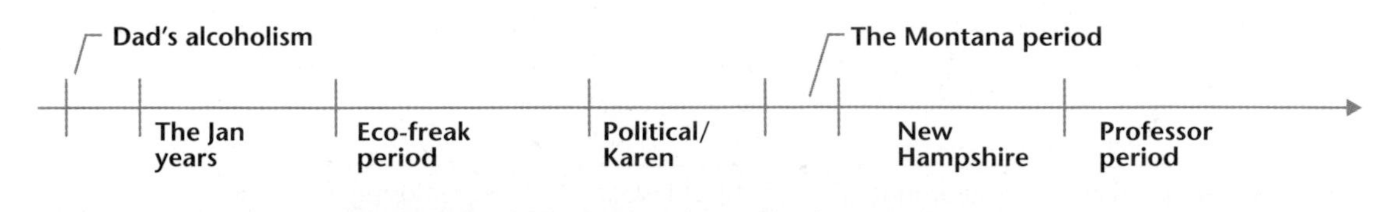

FIGURE 4.2 A sample timeline from my own life.

Inquiring into the Details

CLUSTERING OR MAPPING

One of the virtues of clustering as a method of generating information is that it defies the more linear nature of writing, putting one sentence after another in a chain of thought. When you make a cluster, there are multiple chains, each growing from a core word, phrase, or idea. In Figure 4.1, I clustered the word *guitar*. I'm not just thinking of any guitar, of course, but my 1969 Martin D-28 with Brazilian rosewood and the ding on the front. This is the one object I'd rescue from a fire.

Clusters are in code; each item in the web says more than it says, at least to me, because I'm familiar with its meaning. You don't have that kind of knowledge, obviously, so my cluster wouldn't say much to you. Each strand suggests a story, an idea, or a feeling that I might explore.

Typically, clustering is most useful at the beginning of the writing process as you test a possible subject and want to see its landscape of possibilities. I can see, for example, possible essays about not only the significance of this guitar, but essays on the eighth grade, my old friend Chris Field, and the natural history of limestone. The best clusters are richly suggestive that way, but they're only starting places for more writing. How do you cluster?

1. Begin with a blank page in your journal. Choose a core word, phrase, name, idea, detail, or question; write it in the middle of the page and circle it.
2. Relax and focus on the core word or phrase, and when you feel moved to do so, build a strand of associations from the core, circling and connecting each item. Write other details, names, dates, place names, phrases, and so on—whatever comes to mind.
3. When a strand dies out, return to the core and begin another. Keep clustering until the page looks like a web of associations. Doodle, darkening lines and circles, if that helps you relax and focus.
4. When you feel the urge to write, stop clustering and use one of the strands as a prompt for journal work.

3. Although the Internet offers infinite opportunities for procrastination, with some focus it can also be a great source for jump-starting ideas. What happened to your best friend from kindergarten? Type her name into the Google search engine and find out. (Be sure to put quotation marks around the person's name for a more targeted search.) Think about your favorite vacation—a search for "Grand Canyon" might help jog your memory. Or perhaps checking out "News of the Weird" on Yahoo! might remind you of your own childhood antics.

Judging What You Have

Generating may produce messy, incoherent writing that would earn you bad grades in most classes. Its virtue, however, should be obvious by now: "bad" writing gives a writer material to work with, and it's always better to work from abundance than scarcity. But if this material is going to go anywhere, it must be judged, shaped, and evaluated; the writer must emerge from particulars of his/her experience and find a vantage point to see what, if anything, those particulars add up to.

The initial challenge in producing a first draft is clarifying your topic: What are you really writing about? Later, you'll confront the *So what?* question: What are you trying to *say* about that topic? Don't reject material too soon. Suspend judgment for a bit and work through the following questions as you scrutinize the material you've collected so far in your journal.

What's Promising Material and What Isn't? A good topic for a personal essay need not be dramatic or profound; in fact, some of the most compelling essays are about quite ordinary things. But as you examine your journal writing so far, consider the following:

- **Abundance.** What subject generated the most writing? Do you sense that there is much more to write about?
- **Surprise.** What material did you find most confusing in interesting ways? *Was there something that surprised you*—perhaps a feeling you didn't expect to feel, or a memory that seems charged, or an observation that challenged your preconceptions?
- **Confusion.** What subject raises questions you're not sure you can answer easily? The personal essay is a mode of inquiry that permits uncertainty, and even some inconclusiveness, so it lends itself to material that makes you wonder.
- **Honesty.** What subjects are you willing to write honestly about? The personal nature of the personal essay often leads us to material that may be uncomfortable or even private. However, you should not write essays that make you feel overly vulnerable or unsafe; that stuff should probably stay in your journal. Pursue subjects that you're willing to share.

Questions About Purpose and Audience. Writing should be seen in a particular situation, addressing certain subjects, and serving certain purposes for certain audiences. Knowledge about this rhetorical situation is really the only way a writer can determine what makes a piece good. With open-ended forms like the essay, however, worrying too much about purpose and audience too soon in the writing process can intrude on the development of promising subjects. The personal essay, unlike other genres, directly challenges the writer to work out his or her relationship with a subject, a process that takes place in the open, with the reader as witness. At times, it's a little like dancing nearly naked on a table in a crowded restaurant. *But initially, the essayist is the essay's most*

The personal essay, unlike other genres, directly challenges the writer to work out his or her relationship with the subject, a process that takes place in the open, with the reader as witness.

important audience. The writer's motive is straightforward: *What do I want to understand about this that I don't fully understand now?*

This personal motive will guide you in choosing a topic for your draft, but before long, the rhetorical questions become more urgent. As you evaluate your journal writing and begin to draft your essay, consider these additional questions:

- Did your instructor provide guidelines for the personal essay assignment that might influence your treatment of the material? For example, did he or she specify a certain audience for this draft or a certain structure or approach for the essay? If so, will the material fit those guidelines?
- Who is your audience? If your draft will be peer reviewed, how can this subject be compelling to others in the class? Is it something they would find interesting or relevant?
- Is there a particular question that drives your exploration of this subject? Can you make the question explicit as a way of focusing your draft? For example, *Why was I relieved when my father died?* Or *Why is it true that men never ask directions, consult maps, or read instruction manuals?*

Questions for Reflection. After you've generated enough material on your topic, seize opportunities to reflect. You may do this as you're writing in your journal, thinking about your topic in the shower, or talking about it with friends. Remember that this move to reflect is an essential part of the dialectical thinking that helps writers make sense of things, going back and forth between *what happened* and *what happens,* between *showing* and *telling,* and *observations of* and *ideas about.* In the personal essay, this movement does not occur only in a writer's journal but often appears in the finished essay; in some cases, a reader can clearly see in an essay this movement between showing and telling. If you need help finding reflective distance, questions are the best way to do it. Use one or more of the following questions as prompts for thinking or writing in your journal.

- What do you understand now about this topic that you didn't fully understand when you began writing about it?
- What has surprised you most? Why?
- What seems to be the most important thing you're trying to say so far?
- Focus on how your thinking has changed about your topic. Finish this seed sentence as many times as you can in your notebook: *Once I thought ____________, and now I think ____________.*
- Quickly write a narrative of thought about your topic: *When I began writing about my father's alcoholism, I thought I felt relieved when he died. Then I decided that when he died some part of me died with him, and then I realized that the real truth is . . .*
- Finish this sentence in your journal: *As I look back on this, I realize that . . .* Follow that sentence with another, and another until you feel there's nothing more to say.

Writing the Sketch

It's hard to say when it's time to begin composing the draft, particularly with open-ended forms such as the personal essay. Because the essay invites writers to tackle itchy, confusing subjects, and its mode of inquiry is largely exploratory, it may seem as if you could stay in the shelter of your journal for a long time. On the other hand, you might be uncomfortable with all the time you're spending with "bad" writing and rush to the draft too soon, before you have enough material. Working from abundance is particularly important when you're using writing to discover, the essayist's main motive.

Before you write a full draft, you'll compose a *sketch* or two of what seems to be the most promising material. A sketch is a brief treatment—probably no more than 300 words—that is composed with a sense of audience but not necessarily a clear sense of a thesis, theme, or controlling idea. One of the ways you want to use the sketch is to try out a topic, attempting to clarify your purpose in writing about it. Later, you'll revise a sketch into a draft personal essay.

Your instructor may ask you to write several sketches using the most promising material you've developed from the prompts. *The following guidelines apply to all sketches.*

- *The sketch should have a tentative title*. This is crucial because a title can hint at a possible focus for the revision.
- *The sketch should be approximately 300 to 500 words*. The sketch is a brief look at a topic that may later be developed into a longer essay.
- *The sketch should be a relatively fast draft.* Avoid the temptation to spend a lot of time crafting your sketch. Fast drafts are easier to revise.
- *The sketch may not have a clear purpose or theme.* That's what you hope to discover by writing the sketch.
- *The sketch should have a sense of audience.* You're writing your sketch to be read by someone other than you. That means you need to explain what

WRITING WITH COMPUTERS

CUTTING VERSUS DELETING

Because revision is much more than tinkering with text, it often becomes necessary to remove large portions of text from drafts while revising. A good habit in these situations is to cut passages out of the draft and paste them at the end of the document or into a second document. If you decide to revisit these passages or include portions of them elsewhere in the draft, they are then easy to restore. If you delete these passages completely, they are gone forever (or will have to be retyped from hard copy or memory). Looking at passages you've removed also serves as a record of where you have gone with your thoughts, and sometimes these passages can prompt you into new and more effective directions in your main writing project.

may not be apparent to someone who doesn't know you or hasn't had your experiences.

- *The sketch should be richly detailed.* Personal essays, especially, rely on detail to help the writer, and later, the reader, see the possible meanings of events or observations. Essayists are inductive, working from particulars to ideas. In early drafts especially, it's important to get down the details by drawing on all your senses: what exactly was the color of the wallpaper, how exactly did the beach smell at low tide, how exactly did the old man's hand feel in yours, what exactly did the immigration officer say?

STUDENT SKETCH

A hundred years ago, death was relatively common in most American communities. The infant mortality rate was high, and people—especially men—typically did not live into their seventies. In fact, the mortality rate declined an incredible 83 percent from 1920 to 1973 for those twenty-five or younger in America. Some call ours a death-free society because we are so insulated from its realities. Someone else cares for the bodies prior to cremation and burial, and when we do see the dead, they are made to look as if they are alive.

All of this may help explain why we struggle so when death visits us, as it inevitably will. The difficulty of sorting through our feelings about the loss of a family member or a friend makes it an excellent topic for a personal essay. The form encourages writers to explore ambiguities and attempt to work out mysteries. In the student sketch that follows, Lana Kuchta does just that, trying to think through the wisdom of the advice many of us have received when faced with dying relatives: to remember them as they were, avoid seeing them as they are. Like most sketches, this one doesn't arrive at an answer to the writer's questions. There is no theme or thesis yet. But it does tease out a great deal of specific information that Lana can work with later.

THE WAY I REMEMBER

Lana Kuchta

In the past months three people I knew fairly well have died. All of these deaths were expected to some degree because the people had terminal illnesses. This whole thing is really hard for me to grasp right now—the sheer volume of death surrounding me confuses me about how I feel about death and these friends and how I should remember 1 them. Invariably when we talk about someone who is terminally ill, we say that we hope the person goes quickly for their sake as well as the sake of their family. After all, no one wants to have memories of a prolonged death. We want to remember the person as they were before they got sick.

2 I haven't always felt this way. For a long time after my grandpa died, I was angry that my family wouldn't let me see him in the days before his death. They had good reason for not wanting me to venture into that hospital room where death hung like pea-soup fog over his bed. I was eight months pregnant with my second son, Elliot. I was already dilated to 3.5 cm and Nora, the midwife, wanted me to wait a little longer before I had him. She felt that the stress of my grandpa's condition would send me into full-blown labor.

3 I saw my Grandpa for the last time on a Monday. He was in a lot of pain, but the doctors hadn't increased the pain medication yet. He was still himself that day. We talked briefly about my job and the baby and Austin, my other son who wasn't quite a year old yet. It was hard for me to see him this way and as we sat silently searching for things to say I counted contractions. I know he is going to die soon; I can feel it, I hope that he will live long enough to meet the baby I am carrying. He was tired and when a nurse came to do something, I left and said I would see him in a couple of days. I didn't mean to lie about this; I really did expect that I would see him again. His condition worsened and no one would let me into his room. They told me it was better for me to remember him the way he was.

4 And they were right, but even if they weren't I don't think the images that would come to mind when I thought of my grandpa would be the last image I have of him in the hospital. The last image of him I like to remember is just a month or so before he went into the hospital. I am at his house for a visit. It is July in Redding, California and every day that month was over 110 degrees. My grandpa and grandma have air conditioning and it is just what my bloated pregnant body needed. We sat in their living room with the big picture window that overlooked the Sacramento River. My grandpa plays with Austin on the floor. Austin is crawling around, exploring, and pulling himself up on the furniture. Grandpa tickles him and they both laugh. Watching them play on the floor is nice, but I know that grandpa is sick again. The cancer is back and I know it even though none of us know this yet. But I am happy to be sitting in the air-conditioned house, watching grandpa play with my son.

5 I need to believe that it was better that I didn't get to see him one last time because it is all I have to hold onto now. Anything else is obviously too painful, and I realize this as I write through blurry tears that threaten to roll down my face and smear the inside of my glasses. I know my grandpa would hate this public display of emotion. He was a no bullshit kind of guy and had a very low tolerance for crying. I try to think about other things like the way he was always moving. His hands were always jingling the change in his pocket or he was drumming his fingers on some piece of furniture. He was loud and opinionated, but it was a good thing.

6 He showed that he had a passion for life and he wasn't afraid to speak up for what he believed in.

He was generous, but he expected you to work hard for what you had. He wouldn't just hand money over to you, but he would give you a low interest loan with easy payback terms. 7

Just as I am now glad that I didn't see him just before he died. There are things about my life since he died that I'm glad he didn't have to see. I'm glad he didn't know that my first marriage ended in a messy divorce. 8

It has been fourteen years since he died and four since my grandma died. My uncle now lives in their house on the Sacramento River. I went back to that house this summer for the first time since my grandma died. I was nervous about this. I didn't know what to expect, what I would feel, what I would say. The house was different, yet the same in so many ways. When the kids and I got into the car, Austin said that it was weird being there because the house still smells the same after four years. 9

In the end though I am glad to have the memories of change rattling in a pocket, dirty jokes, Neapolitan ice cream, the river, the smell of cut lumber, and all the other things that remind me of him. 10

Moving from Sketch to Draft

A sketch is often sketchy. It's generally underdeveloped, sometimes giving the writer just the barest outline of his or her subject. But as an early draft, a sketch can be invaluable. It might hint at what the real subject is, or what questions seem to be behind your inquiry into the subject. A sketch might suggest a focus for the next draft, or simply a better lead. Learning to read your sketches for such clues takes practice.

Evaluating Your Own Sketch. Initially, you're the most important reader of your own sketches. It's likely that you're in the best position to sense the material's promise because you understand the context from which it sprang better than any reader can. What are the clues you should look for in a sketch?

1. What surprised you? Might this discovery be the focus of the draft? Chances are, if it surprised you, it will surprise your readers.
2. What is the most important line in the sketch? What makes it important? Might this line be a beginning for more fastwriting? Might it be the theme or controlling idea of the draft?
3. What scene, moment, or situation is key to the story you're telling? Could this be the lead in the draft?
4. What's your favorite part of the sketch? What would happen if you cut it?

Questions for Peer Review. If you'll be sharing your sketch with one or more of your classmates, you'll likely need the most help with clarifying your purpose and focus for a draft. It's less helpful in these early stages to receive editorial comments about sentences, especially questions about grammar and mechanics.

Here are some useful questions that might guide peer responses to your personal essay sketches.

- What does the writer seem to want to say but doesn't quite say in the sketch?
- What line appears most important to the meaning of the sketch, as you understand it?
- What was most surprising about what the writer said or showed?
- What part of the story seems most important? What part might need to be told and isn't?

Methods for Peer Review of Sketches

1. Choose a partner, exchange sketches, read, and comment both in writing and through conversation.
2. Create a pile of sketches in the middle of the classroom. Everyone takes one (not his or her own, obviously), provides written comments, returns it to the pile, and takes another. Repeat this until everyone has read and commented on at least four sketches.
3. Share sketches online on the class Web site.

Reflecting on What You've Learned. Before you begin working on the draft of your personal essay, take a few minutes in your journal to think about your thinking. Finish the following sentence, and follow it in a fastwrite for at least five minutes. *The thing that struck me most about writing and sharing my sketch on ____________ was. . . .* When you finish, quickly complete the following sentences:

1. The *real* story I seem to be trying to tell is ________________.
2. So what? I'd answer that question by saying ________________.
3. The main thing I'm planning to do in the draft is ________________.

Research and Other Strategies: Gathering More Information

You may be itching to move on with the draft. That's understandable. If everything has gone well so far, then your sketch has already given you a sense of direction and some ideas about how to develop your topic. But remember the importance of that dialectical movement between sea and mountain, or collecting and composing. Now that you have a topic and a tentative sense of purpose for your personal essay, journal work can be even more valuable because it can be *more focused.* Before you begin composing the draft—or during that process—consider using the following prompts to generate more information in your notebook:

- *Explode a moment.* Choose a scene or moment in the story or stories you're telling that seems particularly important to the meaning of the essay. Re-enter that moment and fastwrite for a full seven minutes, using all your senses and as much detail as you can muster.
- *Make lists.* Brainstorm a list of details, facts, or specifics about a moment, scene, or observation. List other experiences that seem connected to this one (see the "*Cluster*" point that follows).
- *Research.* Do some quick-and-dirty research that might bring in other voices or more information that will deepen your consideration of the topic. For example, find out exactly how long that solar eclipse was back in 1983, and whether it was in July as you seem to remember. Interview a local expert on your topic. (For more information on where to look for information, see Chapter 9, "Research Techniques.") Do some background reading.
- *Cluster.* In your journal, try to move beyond narrating a single experience and discover other experiences, moments, or scenes that might help you see important patterns. Use the preceding list of related experiences or observations and fastwrite about those, or develop a cluster that uses a key word, phrase, or theme as its core, and build a web of associations. For example, let's say your sketch is about your experience working with the poor in Chile. Have you had other encounters with extreme wealth or extreme poverty? Can you describe them? What do they reveal about your feelings or attitudes about poverty or your reactions to what happened in Chile? See Figure 4.3.

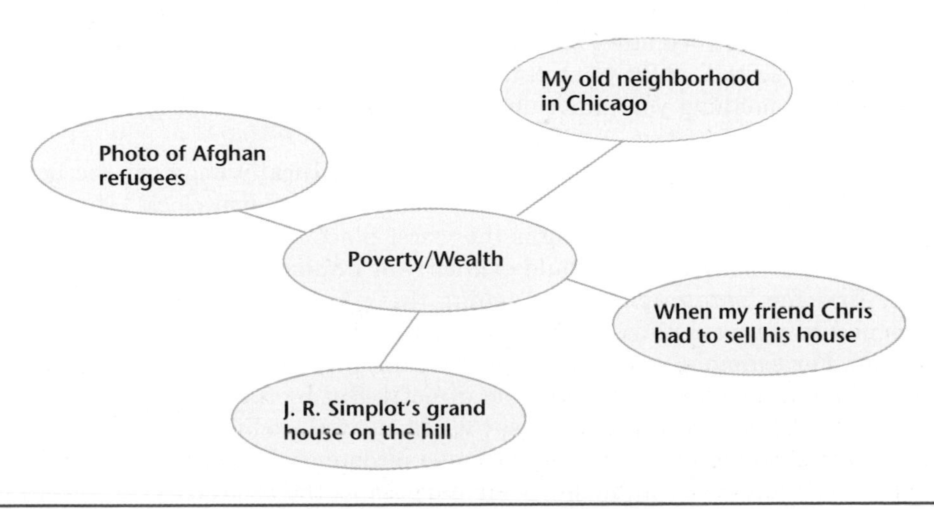

FIGURE 4.3 The start of a cluster built around Poverty/Wealth.

Composing the Draft

Some of my students get annoyed at all the "stuff" I encourage them to do before they begin a first draft of a personal essay. In some cases, all the journal work isn't necessary; the writer very quickly gets a strong sense of direction and feels ready to begin composing. But from the beginning I've encouraged you to gravitate toward topics that you find confusing, and with that kind of material exploratory writing is time well spent. Remember, too, that journal writing counts as writing. It not only offers the pleasures of surprise, but it can ultimately make the drafting process more efficient by generating material that you won't have to conjure up during those long, painful periods of staring at the computer screen wondering what to say next. This front-end work may also help abbreviate the end of the writing process—essentially, all this work in your journal and sketches is revision (see Chapter 11 for more on prewriting as a method of revision).

As you begin drafting, keep in mind what you've learned from your writing so far. For example:

- What is the question(s) behind your exploration of this topic?
- What do you understand now that you didn't understand fully when you started writing about it?
- How can you show *and* explain how you came to this understanding?
- Have you already written a strong first line for the draft? Can you find it somewhere in all your journal writing?

Methods of Development. How might you use some of the typical forms of development to develop your subject?

Narrative. The backbone of the personal essay is often, but not always, narrative. Remember, however, that narrative can work in an essay in at least three ways: (1) you tell an extended story of what happened, (2) you tell one or more anecdotes or brief stories, or (3) you tell the story of your thinking as you've come to understand something you didn't understand before. Often a single essay uses all three types of narrative.

When we tell a story of what happened, we naturally begin at the beginning: "I awoke startled by the unearthly buzz of the alarm clock." But sometimes beginning at the beginning is the worst place to begin. (See Chapter 11 for more about "leads.") You should explicitly or implicitly establish your focus in the first few paragraphs, and opening the essay with the first thing that happened may reveal nothing about your purpose. It just establishes that you woke up. For example, some essays, like Naomi Shihab Nye's "Long Overdue," do not state their purpose quickly and directly. But by the end of the first two sections, we know that this is an essay about the failure of language.

Consider beginning your draft with an anecdote or the part of the story you want to tell that best establishes your purpose in the essay. If you're writing about the needless destruction of a childhood haunt by developers, then consider opening with the way the place looked *after* the bulldozers were done with it.

Naomi Shihab Nye's essay illustrates how a personal essay can stitch together not just one narrative but several stories, all of which are connected by the essay's theme or question. Notice as well how the stories defy chronology. Time in writing is nothing like real time. You can write pages about something that happened in seven minutes or cover twenty years in a paragraph. You can ignore chronology, if it serves your purpose, too. The key is to tell your story or stories in ways that emphasize what's important. Ask yourself, *What does the reader most need to know to understand my thinking and feelings about this topic? What should I show about what happened that gives a reader a clear sense of what* happens?

Using Evidence. How do you make your essay convincing, and even moving to an audience? It's in the details. This form thrives, like most literary genres, on particularity: what exactly did it look like, what exactly did she say, what exactly did it sound and smell like at that moment? Evidence that gives a personal essay authority are details that make a reader believe the writer can be trusted to observe keenly and to remember accurately. All of the professional essays in this chapter are rich in detail—there is the curt monologue of the elderly theatergoer in Nye's "Long, Long Overdue," and the wilting banana leaves that curl around the coconut candy in Cofer's "One More Lesson." This focus on the particular—what it *exactly* looked like, smelled like, felt like, sounded like—makes an essay come alive for both writer and reader.

As you draft your essay, remember the subtle power of details. Tell, but always show, too.

Workshopping the Draft

If your draft is subject to peer review, think carefully about the kind of responses you need from readers at this point in the process. In general, you should encourage comments that make you want to write again.

Reflecting on the Draft. To prepare for workshop, make an entry in your journal that explores your feelings about the draft:

- What do you think worked?
- What do you think needs work?

Following the workshop session, do a follow-up entry in your notebook that summarizes what you heard, what made sense and what didn't, and how you plan to approach the next draft. Your instructor may ask you to share this information in a cover letter submitted with the revision.

Questions for Readers. A writer can structure responses to a draft in many ways. The key is to find a way to get what you need *at this stage in the writing process* that will be most helpful as you revise.

There are a few questions, however, that you might pose to your group that are particularly relevant to the personal essay:

1. Is there a story I'm telling that I need to develop more? Is there a story I'm not telling that I should?
2. What do you think is the *real* story? In other words, what idea or theme lurks beneath the accounts of my experiences and observations?
3. What seems the most important detail, the one that seems to say more than it says, that *reveals* some important feeling, attitude, or idea? What detail seems less important, less revealing?
4. Do my reflective observations seem obvious or overly abstract and general? If so, what questions do you have about what I say that might direct back into the essay's details, where I'm more likely to have better insights?
5. Do I explain things that are unnecessary to explain, that are better told through *showing* rather than *telling?*

Revising the Draft

As I discussed earlier in the book, one of the most misunderstood aspects of revision is that you only do it at the end of the writing process. In fact, up to this point, you should have been revising your work all along, from the first few journal exercises when you chose a topic and played with possible angles on it, to the journal work you might have done to prepare to write the sketch, and then again with your efforts to turn your sketch into a more developed draft. Revision is literally "re-seeing," and every time you create the conditions that allow you to discover something new about how you see or what you think about your subject, you are, in fact, engaged in the act of revision. In a sense, then, each writing assignment you undertake is one long act of revision, from start to finish.

But once you've completed a draft, the revision process becomes more focused. You are mostly working with material that should be somewhat settled, with purposes that might be clearer, and ideas that may have more shape. At this point, the biggest temptation is to tell yourself you are largely done and what revision remains is merely a matter of "fixing things"—tinkering with sentences, correcting typos, and running a spell-checker. In the survey from Chapter 1 (see page 18), 70 percent of students admitted as much. "I usually just tidy things up" was ranked first or second by students who were asked what they do most often when they revise an academic paper.

These activities are certainly an element of revision—and an important one—but as the word revision implies, it's important to "re-see" both what you are trying to say as well as how you try to say it, even at this stage in the process. Chapter 11, "Revision Strategies," is a useful introduction to the revision process for any essay, including the personal essay. It emphasizes ways writers can break the bonds that limit their ability to find new ways of seeing the draft.

GUIDE TO REVISION STRATEGIES		
Problems in the Draft (Chapter 11)	**Part**	**Page Number**
Unclear purpose ■ Not sure what the essay is about? Fails to answer the *So what?* question?	1	420
Unclear thesis, theme, or main idea ■ Not sure what you're trying to say?	2	425
Lack of information or development ■ Needs more details; more showing and less telling?	3	432
Disorganized ■ Doesn't move logically or smoothly from paragraph to paragraph?	4	436
Unclear or awkward at the level of sentences and paragraphs ■ Seems choppy or hard to follow at the level of sentences or paragraphs?	5	442

Personal essay drafts typically have some of the following problems:

- They don't answer the *So what?* question. Are you telling a story but don't help your readers understand *why* you're telling it?
- There is too much showing and not enough telling. In other words, do you *reflect* sufficiently in the draft, contributing your new understandings of what happened?
- There isn't enough detail. Because personal essays often rely heavily on narrative, they should show as well as tell. That is, help readers not only understand the significance of your experiences but in some small way experience those significant moments themselves.

Refer to Chapter 11, "Revision Strategies," for ideas addressing the problems outlined in the accompanying table and how to revise your draft following your workshop. Remember that a draft may present problems in more than one category.

Polishing the Draft

After you've dealt with the big issues in your draft—is it sufficiently focused, does it answer the *So what?* question, is it organized, and so on—you must deal with the smaller problems. You've carved the stone into an appealing figure but now you need to polish it. Are your paragraphs coherent? How do you manage transitions? Are your sentences fluent and concise? Are there any errors in spelling or syntax? Section 5 of Chapter 11 can help you focus on these issues.

Before you finish your draft, work through the following checklist:

- Every paragraph is about one thing.
- The transitions between paragraphs aren't abrupt.
- The length of sentences varies in each paragraph.
- Each sentence is concise. There are no unnecessary words or phrases.
- You've checked grammar, particularly for verb agreement, run-on sentences, unclear pronouns, and misused words (*there/their, where/were,* and so on).
- You've run your spell-checker and proofed your paper for misspelled words.

STUDENT ESSAY

In my part of the country, the seasonal migration of field workers occurs quietly; most of us rarely notice the cars parked on the country roads and the children sitting in the shade waiting near them. We don't notice the bent backs in the fields, moving methodically from row to row. We are dimly aware, of course, that seasonal workers are key to the beet and potato harvests, but these men and women are largely invisible to us.

Julia Arredondo's essay, "Beet Field Dreams," provides a glimpse of this life. She migrated from Texas to Idaho with her family for nearly fourteen years, where they worked the fields from May to October. For many years, when assigned the ubiquitous topic "What I Did on My Summer Vacation" in school, Julia made up stories about another Julia, one with a "normal" life of picnics, barbecues, and days spent at amusement parks. In this personal essay, the Julia who migrated "like a goose" comes to terms with the truth of those summers, and what they have come to mean.

BEET FIELD DREAMS

Julia C. Arredondo

1 I was born in Welsaco, Texas and for my entire childhood I considered myself Tejana—a Texan. It was true that I didn't live my entire life—or even my childhood—in the Rio Grande Valley of Southern Texas, but El Valle was my home, where my family and I lived on our own, where I went to school, where we celebrated the major holidays—Thanksgiving, Christmas, New Year's, and everyone's birthdays. Yet the Mini-Cassia, Magic Valley, area of Southern Idaho was also my home—and in a

way, not my home—as a child. My father's parents—and their parents before them—were all migrant, seasonal farm workers. This was more than a kind of tradition; it was a way of life, a way of survival, and after a time, it began to feel that it was what my family was meant to do in this world.

2 Every year from late May to August my parents worked alongside my extended family hoeing sugar beets in the fields of Burley, Rupert, Heyburn, Paul, Oakley, and Twin Falls, Idaho. It was either thinning and chopping down beets to make room for more or searching for weeds to eliminate and protect the beets. From September to late October they worked in the spud harvest. Twelve to fourteen hour days picking clots out of the clusters of potatoes that flashed before their eyes, and they worked on combines, as if that's what God had put them here to do. And so we migrated. And migrated. And migrated.

* * *

3 School usually started in early September, but by the time we returned to Texas, Alamo public schools had been running for at least a couple of months. I hated being the new kid in school every year and I especially hated it when people started asking where I'd been, why I was coming into the semester late.

4 It was the infamous "How I spent my summer vacation" essay assignment that would always make me lie like Pinocchio. When the essay topic was assigned, I would panic and begin to feel my heart beat faster. I couldn't tell them what I had really being doing all five months of summer. I could not help it; I'd write about a stranger's summer: picnics, vacations, amusement parks, barbecues. A family trip to Fiesta Texas was the biggest, fictional vacation my elementary mind could conjure up and I think I believed the trip myself. I raved in my essay about how we'd spent an entire week in the San Antonio amusement park, how the rides were awesome and how much fun I had had—all the while hoping, praying that no one would uncover the lies, and wishing that the teacher would never really read it. After all, they were only dreams that would never come true. I never told about the car. About the fields. Instead, I continued with the grand fabrications.

* * *

5 We slept in the car, of course. No hotels. Abandoned parking lots. Grocery store parking lots. My Dad liked to park the car somewhere where there was always a lot of light shining. One year in Moab, Utah we had a really hard time finding a resting spot. First we stopped at a store on the main road that ran through the small town; but then a police officer came around and asked us to keep on moving. He said it was illegal for people driving through to just park anywhere to sleep and pointed us toward a rest area just on the edge of Moab. We went there. Dad parked the car under the only light post in the middle of the dirt parking lot. Then, he got off the car and walked to the pay phone just out of reach of the glowing light. Only a few minutes later, a large truck roared into the empty parking lot. Men's voices shouted and hollered from within as they circled our car, picking up speed, raising up dust clouds, tying a knot in

my throat. And then just like that, they were gone. My dad came back to the car, got in, and we drove off.

6 After that, we mostly slept in truck stops. They were always lit, always alive. They were twenty-four-hour oases for travelers on the go. We had bathrooms available—no matter what time my bladder decided I needed to pee. We had hot food within reach. Hot coffee. So whenever Pa wanted to wake up and drive his family on, he could have a cup. It was almost as convenient as a hotel except that we slept amongst the trucks, their thunderous vibrations never really let me sleep. We'd put towels up as curtains, to block out some of the light—noise. But sometimes when I woke up in the middle of the night, and everyone in the car was asleep, I would look out and wonder where these monsters were going and whether they were as driven as we were to move.

* * *

7 As a kid I'd wake up on most summer mornings to the sound of doors slamming shut and cool breezes of fresh morning wind sweeping into the car, making me shiver. I could feel the weight of the car shift as the grown-ups pulled their hoes from the trunk. Their voices lingered outside the vehicle for minutes as they prepared for the day's work, waiting for the first light of day to guide their strokes. I'd lay still and listen as their voices became distant, then I would slowly drift back to my dreams.

8 Some mornings, when the sun wasn't quite strong enough to warm us up, my sister Debra and I would stay inside the car. I'd lounge around in the front seat—a place I hardly ever got to ride in—and impatiently wait for the adults to return to the *caheceras*. From the car they looked miniature as they moved at a hurried pace along the mile long rows. Debra and I would guess which one was Ma and which one was Pa. Sometimes we were right. Sometimes I'd drift back to sleep and miss them reaching our end of the field. I'd awake to find they were already halfway back across the field and feel my heart weigh down.

9 I was always looking for a reason to join them in their hard labor; years later when I would have to really start working I knew exactly how hard it was. Still, I'd mention to my parents how I could work too, how we'd make more money that way. I'd ask them to break a hoe in half and let me have it. They only laughed and said when the time came for me to work I wasn't going to want to, so for me to just enjoy this time.

10 Sometimes near the field there would be a farmhouse from which laughter floated down towards us. Sometimes we could spot kids that looked our age jumping on their trampoline, swimming in their pool and I'd find myself longing to be them. Normal. Playing on a lawn, instead of a field. Waking in a bed, instead of a car's backseat. Eating lunch at a table, instead of from tin foil while I sat in the dirt on the shady side of the car to avoid the hot sun.

* * *

11 When I was fourteen we finally stopped moving. Field work continued being our main source of income, but we made Idaho our permanent home. And as the years passed, returning to Texas became preposterous; we were always too afraid to fall back

into the old migrating lifestyle. Yet, even today I am migrant. And it's not merely the fact that I've spent more than half my life migrating—like a goose—according to the seasons, but because it was a lifestyle that penetrates and becomes part of who I am for the rest of my life. As I grew older, I began to slowly acknowledge to others the kind of lifestyle my family lived during my childhood. Though no longer on the move, I will always be a migrant and sugar beet dreams will always haunt my sleep.

Evaluating the Essay

Discuss or write about your response to Julia Arredondo's essay using some or all of the following questions.

1. What is the essay's greatest strength? Is this something you've noticed in your own work, or the drafts of classmates?
2. Is the balance between exposition and narration, showing and telling, handled well in "Beet Field Dreams?" Does it read fairly quickly or does it drag at points?
3. The essay uses line breaks between sections. What do you think of this technique? What are its advantages and disadvantages?
4. What would you recommend to Arredondo if she were to revise "Beet Field Dreams"?

Using What You Have Learned

My students often love writing personal essays. At its best, the genre is a rare opportunity to reexamine our lives and better understand our experiences. The insights we earn are often reward enough, but what have you learned in this assignment that you might apply in other writing situations?

1. The personal essay you wrote relies heavily on narrative and personal experience. How might an ability to tell a good story, using your experiences or the experiences of others, be a useful academic skill? How might you use it to write a paper for another class?
2. The personal essay is a deeply subjective form, which would seem to put it at odds with formal academic writing, which seems to strive for "objectivity." Are they at odds?
3. Based on your experience writing a personal essay, what do you think are its most important qualities? If you were to write more personal essays, what would you strive to do next time?

French movie poster for *Amelie.*

5

Writing a Review

WRITING THAT EVALUATES

What You'll Learn in This Chapter

- The role of evaluation in a review.
- How feelings and reason can form the basis of evaluation.
- How to develop criteria for making judgments.
- Questions that will help you revise a review.

One of the occasions when I feel fairly stupid is after watching a movie with my wife, Karen. She always wants to know what I think. I don't have much of a problem arriving at a gut reaction—I loved the movie *Amelie,* for example, but I have a hard time saying why. Beyond statements such as, "It was pretty good," or "It was pure Hollywood," a comment I mean to be critical, the conversation scares me a little because Karen is wonderfully analytical and articulate when describing her feelings about a film. In comparison, I stutter and stammer and do my best to go beyond a simple judgment.

Essentially, Karen is asking me to evaluate a film, to make a judgment about its quality. This is something we do all the time. Buying a pair of jeans involves evaluating the reputation of the manufacturer, the quality of the denim and its particular design, and especially aesthetic judgments about how the jeans look on us when we wear them. I think most of us like to think these decisions are quite rational. On the contrary, many of our evaluations are more emotional than logical. We *really do* buy that pair of jeans because an ad suggests that we'll look sexy or attractive in them. Or consider this: How would you evaluate the quality of your mother or father's parenting? Will this be a rational judgment? It's unlikely. Even though we're qualified to make such a judgment—after all, who is a better authority on the parenting skills of parents than their children—often our views toward our parents are always awash in feelings.

You remember evaluation as one of the four ways of inquiring, and you've already practiced it in Chapter 3 and responses to the readings in other chapters. You know, then, that part of the challenge of evaluating something is keeping an open mind, sometimes *despite* our initial feelings about it. Because all evaluation stems from what are essentially subjective value judgments, a tension always exists between our *desire* to prove our point and our *need or willingness* to learn more about the subject.

That emotion figures into our judgments of things isn't a bad thing. It's a human thing. But one of the reasons it's useful to consciously consider *how* we make such judgments is that we're more likely to introduce logical considerations in mostly emotional evaluations, or emotional considerations in mostly logical ones. This awareness also helps us suspend judgment long enough to get a more balanced look at something.

Evaluation involves three things:

1. *Judgment.* Something is good or bad, useful or not useful, relevant or not relevant, convincing or not convincing, worth doing or not worth doing, or perhaps shades in between.

2. *Criteria.* These form the basis by which we judge whether something is good or bad, useful or not useful, and so on. If we evaluate a car, for example, our criteria might be performance or appearance or cost or any combination of the three. Often our criteria are implicit; that is, we aren't even consciously aware of the criteria that inform judgments. The more familiar we are with the thing—say, cars, movies, or mystery novels—the more elaborate and sophisticated the criteria become.

3. *Evidence.* Criteria provide the principles for making a judgment, but evidence—specific details, observations, or facts about the thing itself—is what makes an evaluation persuasive. That's why simply saying, "This assigned reading is boring," produces blank stares from your instructor. What exactly makes it dull? Is the language of the article filled with jargon, and which passage exactly illustrates this well?

If this sounds a lot like making an argument, you're right, because evaluation is the basis of argument. But I suspect that emotion, at least initially, figures more in our judgments of things than our reasoned arguments about them. In fact, evaluation can be a way of seeding the field of argument because it helps you identify the things about which you have strong opinions.

MOTIVES FOR WRITING A REVIEW

I rarely write reviews. But evaluative writing is one of the most common kinds of writing I do, from commenting on student papers, to writing reference letters for former students, to writing a memo to my colleagues about a proposed departmental policy. Evaluative writing is an enormously practical form, relevant in all sorts of situations in and out of school. Quite simply, we turn to it when we are asked to make a judgment of value, and then develop that judgment into something that goes beyond a gut reaction and unstated assumptions.

Beginning in Chapter 3, you were introduced to some of the opening questions that might guide your thinking and seeing: *What's my judgment of this?*

What are my reasons? All things considered, what's most convincing here? What's least convincing? What do I see that supports what I believe? What do I see that complicates or contradicts what I believe?

All of these questions imply that evaluation is a pretty logical process, but more often it begins with a feeling—which, again, is not a bad thing—and evaluative writing helps you work from that feeling outward into reason, which will make your judgment persuasive to others *and* help shape your future judgments about other, similar things. That's why my conversations with Karen about movies, once I stop feeling stupid, can be so helpful because she challenges me to find reasons for what I feel, reasons that I am slowly learning to apply to my judgments of other films.

If you feel strongly about something, turn to evaluative writing and thinking as a way to help yourself and others understand why.

If you feel strongly about something, turn to evaluative writing and thinking as a way to help yourself and others understand why.

THE REVIEW AND ACADEMIC WRITING

We don't usually think of the review as an academic form, although you may be asked to review a film you're shown in an English class or perhaps a performance in a theater class. But evaluative writing, a process you'll practice when writing a review, is among the most common types of writing in all kinds of college classrooms. Here are just a few examples:

- In a literature class, you may be asked to evaluate the effectiveness of a story or a character.
- In a theater class, you may write a review of a dramatic performance.
- In a science class, you may need to evaluate the methodology of an experiment.
- In a composition class, you're often asked to evaluate the writing of peers.
- Philosophy frequently involves the evaluation of arguments.
- Business writing may require evaluation of a marketing strategy, a product, or a business plan.

Once you start thinking about evaluative writing, you'll find it everywhere—the book reviews in the Sunday *Times,* the music reviews in *Spin,* the analysis of Web sites on WebSitesThatSuck.com. It's probably the most common form of workplace writing, too, from assessing the performance of an employee to evaluating a plan to preserve historic buildings.

FEATURES OF THE FORM

Like all forms of writing, evaluation genres vary widely. Perhaps the least likely form is one in which the writer formally announces a judgment, lists criteria, and then offers evidence using the criteria. That is, at least, an approach that you'll have a hard time finding outside school. Much evaluative writing is more subtle than that—and much more interesting—because the writer blends judgments, criteria, and evidence seamlessly throughout. If you've ever read a review of a band, a computer, or a book, you probably never noticed its structure because if the review is well written the structure isn't noticeable. But most reviews share some features, and many of them are a part of all kinds of evaluative writing.

- *A review is usually clear about categories.* Of course, the effectiveness of all writing depends on responding to a certain situation, but evaluative writing is particularly sensitive to the *category* of thing you're writing about. For example, the inverted pyramid in Figure 5.1 shows the narrowing of categories of film, working toward a more limited category—say, feature films about space travel. It's easier to come up with convincing criteria to judge a narrower category than a broad, general one. Reviewers are often very careful to state clearly the kind of thing they're reviewing.
- *Reviews usually describe the thing they evaluate.* How much you describe depends on your readers' knowledge of what you're evaluating. If they haven't seen the performance, don't know the actor, haven't read the book,

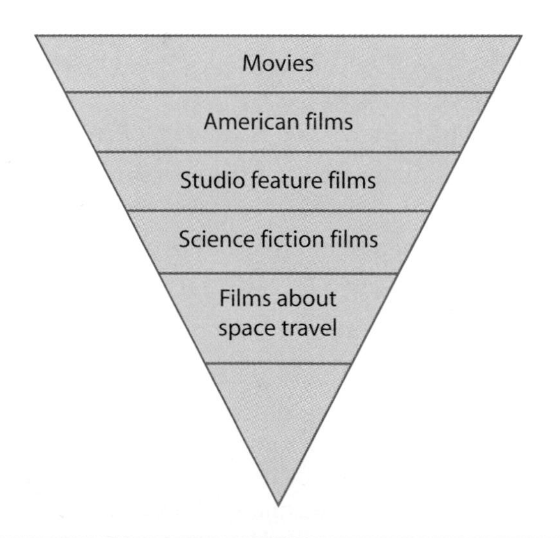

FIGURE 5.1 Narrowing the category of evaluation. One of the keys for developing useful and relevant criteria for judging something is making sure that you're focusing on the neighborhood, not the globe. In this example, it's much more helpful to talk about what makes a good Hollywood science fiction film about space travel than attempt to describe the qualities of the much broader category, all movies. After all, what makes a foreign art film effective is probably different from what makes a romantic comedy effective.

or don't know the type of product you're reviewing, then readers need the necessary background to understand what exactly you're talking about. Summaries can be vital. For example, a review of Ani DiFranco's latest CD might explain that her music seems to straddle folk and rock, and that she's known for her intricate lyrics and political convictions. Some of this description may also be part of the evidence you offer.

- *Evaluation criteria are matched to purpose, category, and audience.* Obviously, a writer has reasons for making a judgment about something. Always in the back of the writer's mind is the purpose of the evaluation: what exactly he or she is writing about (and *not* writing about). If your aim is to help businesses understand which Web sites are likely to sell the most T-shirts, your criteria will be different from those used to evaluate the Web sites nonprofit groups might use to educate people about world hunger. Like all persuasive writing, the review is shaped by its audience. This can affect your approach in several ways. If you're writing a review for an audience that hasn't read Elise Blackwell's novel *Hunger,* you'll need to spend more time providing background on the book than you would if you were writing for an audience—perhaps your instructor—who is familiar with it. In addition, always analyze whether your readers might already have opinions—positive or negative—toward the thing you're reviewing. If you're praising the virtues of Microsoft's new operating system to an audience of Mac users, your pitch—the amount and quality of evidence you offer, and so on—needs to be much stronger than if you are writing for Windows lovers.

Like all persuasive writing, the review is shaped by its audience.

- *In reviews, feelings often lead judgment but they are never enough.* Although evaluation is a form of argument, reason doesn't always lead judgment. Frequently, we first *feel* something—the Web site turns us off, or the new music video is captivating, or the reading assignment puts us to sleep. These feelings often lead us to an initial judgment—something we might acknowledge to readers—but they are never enough. The challenge of persuasive evaluation is to introduce reason into the process.
- *Judgments range from an overall assessment (it was good or bad, helpful or useless, and so on) to more specific commentary on particular evidence or aspects of the thing.* These judgments don't reside in one place in some kind of grand thesis, but are scattered throughout a review essay, working toward a more complicated assessment of the movie, book, or performance you're evaluating. For example, Lester Bangs's review of the book *Lost Highway: Journeys and Arrivals of American Musicians* (see page 129) begins immediately with a judgment—the book inspires "awe" and a "(non-jingoistic) patriotism." But that merely is the launching place for Bangs's evaluation, including his argument that this is "a book about defeat . . . [that is] so beautiful."

- *Reviews frequently attempt to offer a balanced assessment.* Hey, it can't be *all* bad. (Okay, sometimes it is.) The most persuasive negative evaluations tend to include some positive judgments, and positive evaluations frequently make some concessions about a thing's flaws. This isn't just a rhetorical ploy, but recognition that things are never that simple.
- *Criteria may be stated or unstated.* You'll rarely find a piece of evaluative writing that neatly lists all the criteria used to judge the thing; in fact, some criteria may be implicit. Why? A common reason is that the writer and audience *share* certain assumptions about how to judge the value of a thing. It goes without saying, for example, that a writer for the conservative magazine *National Review* would be critical of a proposal for national health care that advocates a new federal government program. Generally speaking, conservatives oppose the growth of federal government, so why state it as a criterion for rejecting the proposal?
- *Relevant comparisons may form the backbone of a review.* Our fascination with winners and losers is reflected in one of the most ubiquitous evaluations in American culture: rankings. We rank cars, movies, music videos, celebrities' tastes in fashion, colleges, cameras, diets, and Web sites. All of these kinds of evaluations fundamentally depend on identifying a certain class of things—a particular car type or a kind of music—and comparing things that belong to that class. The key, of course, is making sure that the things you're comparing do indeed belong in the same class, that you're comparing apples to apples and not apples to oranges.

REVIEW

Lester Bangs is called by some the "founding voice of rock criticism." Sadly, he died in 1982 at age forty-four of an accidental drug interaction while treating himself for a cold, but in his brief career Bangs wrote for many of the most important venues for rock critics: *Rolling Stone*, *The Village Voice*, and the Detroit-based rock magazine *Creem*, which stopped publishing in the late eighties. He is credited with coining the term *punk.*

Bangs's work was celebrated not only for its breezy, breathless, and blunt style, but for his extensive knowledge of rock genres. He was a scholar of rock music who could write about it like an ordinary fan. In the review that follows, Bangs writes about *Lost Highway: Journeys and Arrivals of American Musicians*. While the book was published twenty-five years ago, Bangs's review is a timeless example of both his style of criticism and the reach of his understanding of American popular music. While the essay focuses on *Lost Highway*, Bangs finds ways to make this a meditation on the difficulty of being a commercial artist in the United States, challenges that remain today.

Review of Peter Guralnick's *Lost Highway: Journeys and Arrivals of American Musicians*

Lester Bangs

It's not often these days that anything makes you feel genuine awe, much less (non-jingoistic) patriotism. But those are two of the most pertinent words which come to mind when I think of Peter Guralnick's new book *Lost Highway*. As in his previous *Feel Like Going Home*, his subject is the fathers of American music—here, twenty-one seminal figures in the by now all but lost arts of blues, rhythm 'n' blues, country and western, and the original rock 'n' roll. 1

You put the book down feeling that its sweep is vast, that you have read of giants who walked among us, inspired by the truly mighty dreams and possibilities of the kind of place where any kid could grow up to become Elvis Presley. Hence the patriotism. Which feels even stranger to say than it would anyway, because this book's main theme is how these men were buried by those very dreams, Elvis being only the most obvious case in point. Ernest Tubb, Hank Snow, Bobby Bland, Waylon Jennings, Hank Williams, Jr., Howlin' Wolf, Merle Haggard, Charlie Rich and the others less famous written of here have all probably lost something of themselves in the bone-wearying life of musicians on the road—possibly best summed up by a friend of Ernest Tubb who says, "I think Ernest will die right in the back of that damn bus." 2

In a very real sense this is a book about a bunch of defeated men, commercial success or failure seeming to make very little difference. Like Guralnick, the reader is struck by the way in which the pursuit of success seriously, inevitably distorted the very core of their being, as well as the music itself. To paraphrase Little Richard, they all got (or didn't get) what they wanted but almost invariably lost what they had. 3

The amazing thing is that a book about defeat could be so beautiful. In part this is because Guralnick understands so well and expresses so eloquently the forces that grind many of America's greatest artists to dust. But it's also because he never loses sight of the dream that set them all on that highway in the first place. Thus we see Ernest Tubb, for instance, go from first hearing the Call—"The thought of being a professional musician never entered his mind," writes Guralnick, ". . . until he heard Jimmie Rodgers' first Blue Yodel, which came out on the Victor Label in 1927 when he was thirteen. From that day on he knew exactly what he wanted to be"—to being a victim of Nashville's recent "cultural schizophrenia" in which the present can no longer come to terms with a past it has always at least nominally venerated. 4

"Cultural schizophrenia," in fact, is a major recurrent theme of the book: urban and rural, black and white, the realities of the road vs. songs celebrating home and family life. "All of 'em were totally nuts," says an admiring insider of 5

Elvis, Jerry Lee Lewis and the rest of the progenitors of rockabilly on Sam Phillips's Sun Records. "I think every one of them must have come in on the midnight train from nowhere. I mean, it was like they came from outer space." Years later, Johnny Cash will sing "I Wish I Was Crazy Again" with Waylon Jennings, and Jerry Lee will have a hit called "Middle Age Crazy." What getting "crazy," "real gone," being a "bopcat" was all about, though, was a historically inevitable racial confluence: "I recall one jockey telling me that Elvis Presley was so country he shouldn't be played after five A.M.," said Sam Phillips. "And others said he was too black for them." There are scenes of white and black dancers on opposite sides of cordoned-off rooms in southern jukejoints, literally dancing the barriers down; perhaps the most extreme example of American music as racial melting pot is Stoney Edwards, number-two-ranked "black" country and western singer behind Charley Pride, who say, "I grew up not knowing what I was, Negro, Indian, or white. . . . I can't see anything in my future to equal the pain I been through. . . . I was never really accepted by anyone until I started singing country music." More lucky (or willful) was Big Joe Turner, who turned down a job singing with Count Basie because he would have had to stop shouting the blues during the brass parts, and of whom Guralnick writes: "He remained a free man. When boogie woogie fell into decline, Big Joe Turner became known as a blues shouter. When rock 'n' roll came into vogue, he was a rock 'n' roller. He did it, as he explains, without ever changing his style."

6 And in fact the figures in the book who come off best (meaning happiest) are those with sheer indomitable will like Turner, or Howlin' Wolf who got up from a car accident which sent him flying through a windshield at the age of sixty-three, went right back on the road and toured for the rest of his life with severe kidney damage, stopping off at a hospital in every city he played for dialysis treatment. Others developed a strategy that kept 'em guessing, like Merle Haggard, of whom Guralnick writes: "His whole career, in fact, can be looked upon as a series of deliberate avoidances [walking out on "The Ed Sullivan Show," quitting a network production of *Oklahoma!*], instinctive retreats from the obvious, and restatements of his central role as an outsider. . . . Perhaps this is what has enabled him to create the astonishing body of work that represents the 'career' of Merle Haggard." For country boys who went looking for an elusive but palpable American dream and inevitably if unintentionally cut themselves off from their roots in the process, accommodation simply does not work.

7 Perhaps the saddest example of this in the book is Charlie Rich, who started off as one of the original Sun Records bopcats with "Lonely Weekends" in the fifties, went through years of alcoholism and obscurity, hit again in the mid-sixties with the almost-novelty "Mohair Sam," followed it up with a song he truly cared about which flopped, and has been a deeply cautious and troubled man ever since, even though he climbed out of obscurity once again in the mid-seventies with "Behind Closed Doors." Today he is, seemingly against all odds, enshrined as the Silver Fox, a veritable country music institution, with a seldom broken string of hit singles and albums.

8 Yet we realize his sadness (and Guralnick pulls off the nigh-impossible, making us feel for the problems of somebody richer and more "successful" than we are)

when we see him going to the Village Vanguard in New York City and encountering racial hostility and a fusion-jazz group that has nothing to do with jazz as he has known and played it ("I just wanted to show you, it's not . . . the way it was," he says), and later when his wife, who has kept him together through decades of failures and successes, says,

> "I think it's almost a tragedy when you lose your enthusiasm for something that suited you. . . . It turns into a business, and it just about destroys your creativity. . . . Sometimes I wish he was just playing somewhere for free, playing piano alone or with a small group, just so he could enjoy the music."
>
> "I did that for about twenty years," Charlie protests softly. His broad, melancholy face always has a slightly hurt look about it. It is at once more mobile and more handsome in its private grief than in the countless grins and strained grimaces he has learned to adopt for TV appearances and ads. "When I first started working those little clubs in Memphis, I could play anything I wanted to for ten or fifteen dollars a night. Then when I went to Sun Records I went with the idea that I would do just about anything, as long as I could keep close to the music. I thought I could work the studio gig, make a little bit, and play my jazz at home. . . . You know, when you have a wife and a family, you have to sacrifice a little bit. . . . But there comes a time when you've been working at something so long, trying so long and so hard, that you reach a point where you get scared. And you start thinking to yourself, what am I going to be doing when I'm sixty-five? I don't want to be playing the Nightlighter Club when I'm sixty-five years old. Which could very easily have been the end result. And still could be."

Lost Highway is a book of lives, real lives in America, that are at once larger-than-life and human and humble. Maybe you will come away saying, as Guralnick does in his introduction, "I love the music as much as I ever did, but I have a public confession to make: I don't want to be a rock 'n' roll star any more." Yet he consistently gives us scenes along the road that are so strange and haunting (Hank Williams, Jr., as a teenager, driving around in the very same car his daddy died in, after having it customized and souped-up), or touching (Stoney Edwards confessing, "I ain't never found anything that was more exciting than making corn whiskey"), that they make the whole trip worthwhile. And when it's done, you may find yourself feeling, as Elvis's producer Felton Jarvis said upon learning of Presley's death, "It's like someone just came up and told me there aren't going to be any more cheeseburgers in the world." Or you may conclude, about all these people, America, and even yourself, what Guralnick concludes of Nashville legend/madman/producer Cowboy Jack Clement: "Maybe it's the journey, not the arrival, that matters." 9

Inquiring into the Essay

Use the four ways of inquiring—exploring, explaining, evaluating, and reflecting—to consider your response to Bangs's review.

1. Brainstorm a short list of music or musicians that influenced your life in some way. Choose one work or musician or band and fastwrite in your

journal about that time in your life, and how the music or musician influenced you. At some point, explore how you feel about that work or musician today. What would be your judgment of its quality?

2. Like the original readers of this piece, you likely haven't read the book reviewed here. Explain how Bangs addresses that problem in his review.
3. Bangs liked *Lost Highway,* and he takes time to explain why. But behind these reasons are assumptions or criteria about what, in Bangs's view, are the qualities of a good book about music. What are these assumptions or criteria? Do you agree with them?
4. Bangs seems to be a guy who has no problem arriving at and expressing an opinion. What about you? Do you have a difficult time judging things—from movies to people—or are you pretty opinionated? Reflect on your personal experiences with making judgments. Were you encouraged to express your opinion at home or at school? When have your judgments gotten you into trouble, and can you imagine ways you could have avoided it? What bothers you about others who are judgmental? Whose judgments do you respect? Why? Fastwrite about these questions in your journal.

REVIEW

Dog food companies sell dog food to people, not to dogs, and so it isn't too surprising that one company might boast that its dog food is a "Premium Oven Baked Lamb Recipe," or that another will tantalize dogs with "rich, beefy gravy." Pet food is an $11 billion dollar industry in the United States, and apparently the competitive edge goes to companies that can convince pet owners that Buster or Tabitha will dine at least as well as the rest of the family.

The fine print, of course, tells a different story. Most dog foods have "by-products," or all the remains of chickens and/or cows that aren't thought fit for human consumption—intestines, gizzards, bones, lungs, and ligaments. Rendered restaurant grease gives some dog foods that delightful scent.

Ann Hodgman decided she would take the advertising claims of several pet food companies at face value. If Gravy Train dog food creates a really "rich, beefy gravy," then shouldn't it taste good to the pet owner as well as the pet? In the essay that follows, "No Wonder They Call Me a Bitch," Hodgman reports on her experiences taste-testing some of the more popular brands. Her review of her experience eating some of the major brands makes us all regret ever sampling that dog bone from the bag when we were too young to know better.

Before you start reading the essay, consider following the procedure described in the first question in "Inquiring into the Essay" at the end of the piece.

No Wonder They Call Me a Bitch

Ann Hodgman

I've always wondered about dog food. Is a Gaines-burger really like a hamburger? Can you fry it? Does dog food "cheese" taste like real cheese? Does Gravy Train actually make gravy in the dog's bowl, or is that brown liquid just dissolved crumbs? And exactly what *are* by-products? 1

Having spent the better part of a week eating dog food, I'm sorry to say that I now know the answers to these questions. While my dachshund, Shortie, watched in agonies of yearning, I gagged my way through can after can of stinky, white-flecked mush and bag after bag of stinky, fat-drenched nuggets. And now I understand exactly why Shortie's breath is so bad. 2

Of course, Gaines-burgers are neither mush nor nuggets. They are, rather, a miracle of beauty and packaging—or at least that's what I thought when I was little. I used to beg my mother to get them for our dogs, but she always said they were too expensive. When I finally bought a box of cheese-flavored Gaines-burgers—after 20 years of longing—I felt deliciously wicked. 3

"Dogs love real beef," the back of the box proclaimed proudly. "That's why Gaines-burgers is the only beef burger for dogs with real beef and no meat by-products!" The copy was accurate: meat by-products did not appear in the list of ingredients. Poultry by-products did, though—right there next to preserved animal fat. 4

One Purina spokesman told me that poultry by-products consist of necks, intestines, undeveloped eggs and other "carcass remnants," but not feathers, heads or feet. When I told him I'd been eating dog food, he said, "Oh, you're kidding! Oh no!" (I came to share his alarm when, weeks later, a second Purina spokesman said that Gaines-burgers *do* contain poultry heads and feet—but *not* undeveloped eggs.) 5

Up close my Gaines-burger didn't much resemble chopped beef. Rather, it looked—and felt—like a single long, extruded piece of redness that had been chopped into segments and formed into a patty. You could make one at home if you had a Play-Doh Fun Factory. 6

I turned on the skillet. While I waited for it to heat up I pulled out a shred of cheese-colored material and palpated it. Again, like Play-Doh, it was quite malleable. I made a little cheese bird out of it; then I counted to three and ate the bird. 7

There was a horrifying rush of cheddar taste, followed immediately by the dull tang of soybean flour—the main ingredient in Gaines-burgers. Next I tried a piece of red extrusion. The main difference between the meat-flavored and cheese-flavored extrusions is one of texture. The "cheese" chews like fresh Play-Doh, whereas the "meat" chews like Play-Doh that's been sitting out on a rug for a couple of hours. 8

Frying only turned the Gaines-burger black. There was no melting, no sizzling, no warm meat smells. A cherished childhood illusion was gone. I flipped the patty into the sink, where it immediately began leaking rivulets of red dye. 9

As alarming as the Gaines-burgers were, their soy meal began to seem like an old friend when the time came to try some *canned* dog foods. I decided to try the Cycle 10 foods first. When I opened them, I thought about how rarely I use can openers these days, and I was suddenly visited by a long-forgotten sensation of can-opener distaste. *This* is the kind of unsavory place can openers spend their time when you're not watching! Every time you open a can of, say, Italian plum tomatoes, you infect them with invisible particles of by-product.

11 I had been expecting to see the usual homogeneous scrapple inside, but each can of Cycle was packed with smooth, round, oily nuggets. As if someone at Gaines had been tipped off that a human would be tasting the stuff, the four Cycles really were different from one another. Cycle-1, for puppies, is wet and soyish. Cycle-2, for adults, glistens nastily with fat, but it's passably edible—a lot like some canned Swedish meatballs I once got in a care package at college. Cycle-3, the "lite" one, for fatties, had no specific flavor; it just tasted like dog food. But at least it didn't make me fat.

12 Cycle-4, for senior dogs, had the smallest nuggets. Maybe old dogs can't open their mouths as wide. This kind was far sweeter than the other three Cycles—almost like baked beans. It was also the only one to contain "dried beef digest," a mysterious substance that the Purina spokesman defined as "enzymes" and my dictionary defined as "the products of digestion."

13 Next on the menu was a can of Kal-Kan Pedigree with Chunky Chicken. Chunky chicken? There were chunks in the can, certainly—big, purplish-brown chunks. I forked one chunk out (by now I was becoming more callous) and found that while it had no discernible chicken flavor, it wasn't bad except for its texture—like meat loaf with ground-up chicken bones.

14 In the world of canned dog food, a smooth consistency is a sign of low quality—lots of cereal. A lumpy, frightening, bloody, stringy horror is a sign of high quality—lots of meat. Nowhere in the world of wet dog foods was this demonstrated better than in the fanciest I tried—Kal Kan's Pedigree Select Dinners. These came not in a can but in a tiny foil packet with a picture of an imperious Yorkie. When I pulled open the container, juice spurted all over my hand, and the first chunk I speared was trailing a long gray vein. I shrieked and went instead for a plain chunk, which I was able to swallow only after taking a break to read some suddenly fascinating office equipment catalogs. Once again, though, it tasted no more alarming than, say, canned hash.

15 Still, how pleasant it was to turn to *dry* dog food! Gravy Train was the first I tried, and I'm happy to report that it really does make a "thick, rich, real beef gravy" when you mix it with water. Thick and rich, anyway. Except for a lingering rancid-fat flavor, the gravy wasn't beefy, but since it tasted primarily like tap water, it wasn't nauseating either.

16 My poor dachshund just gets plain old Purina Dog Chow, but Purina also makes a dry food called Butcher's Blend that comes in Beef, Bacon, and Chicken flavor. Here we see dog food's arcane semiotics at its best: a red triangle with a *T* stamped into it is supposed to suggest beef; a tan curl, chicken; and a brown *S*, a piece of bacon. Only dogs understand these messages. But Butcher's Blend does have an endearing slogan: "Great Meaty Tastes—without bothering the Butcher!" *You know, I wanted to buy some meat, but I just couldn't bring myself to bother the butcher. . . .*

17 Purina O.N.E. ("Optimum Nutritional Effectiveness") is targeted at people who are unlikely ever to worry about bothering a tradesperson. "We chose chicken as a primary

ingredient in Purina O.N.E. for several reasonings," the long, long essay on the back of the bag announces. Chief among these reasonings, I'd guess, is the fact that chicken appeals to people who are—you know—*like us*. Although our dogs do nothing but spend 18-hour days alone in the apartment, we still want them to be *premium* dogs. We want them to cut down on red meat, too. We also want dog food that comes in a bag with an attractive design, a subtle typeface and no kitschy pictures of slobbering golden retrievers.

Besides that, we want a list of the Nutritional Benefits of our dog food—and we get it on O.N.E. One thing I especially like about this list is its constant references to a dog's "hair coat," as in "Beef tallow is good for the dog's skin and hair coat." (On the other hand, beef tallow merely provides palatability, while the dried beef digest in Cycle provides palatability *enhancement*.) 18

I hate to say it, but O.N.E. was pretty palatable. Maybe that's because it has about 100 percent more fat than, say, Butcher's Blend. Or maybe I'd been duped by the packaging; that's been known to happen before. 19

As with people food, dog snacks taste much better than dog meals. They're better-looking too. Take Milk-Bone Flavor Snacks. The loving-hands-at-home prose describing each flavor is colorful; the writers practically choke on their own exuberance. Of bacon they say, "It's so good, your dog will think it's hot off the frying pan." Of liver: "The only taste your dog wants more than liver—is even more liver!" Of poultry: "All those farm fresh flavors deliciously mixed in one biscuit. Your dog will bark with delight!" And of vegetable: "Gardens of taste! Specially blended to give your dog that vegetable flavor he wants—but can rarely get!" 20

Well, I may be a sucker, but advertising *this* emphatic just doesn't convince me. I lined up all seven flavors of Milk-Bone Flavor Snacks on the floor. Unless my dog's palate is a lot more sensitive than mine—and considering that she steals dirty diapers out of the trash and eats them, I'm loath to think it is—she doesn't detect any more difference in the seven flavors than I did when I tried them. 21

I much preferred Bonz, the hard-baked, bone-shaped snack stuffed with simulated marrow. I liked the bone part, that is; it tasted almost exactly like the cornmeal it was made of. The mock-marrow inside was a bit more problematic: in addition to looking like the sludge that collects in the treads of my running shoes, it was bursting with tiny hairs. 22

I'm sure you have a few dog food questions of your own. To save us time, I've answered them in advance. 23

Q. *Are those little cans of Mighty Dog actually branded with the sizzling word* BEEF, *the way they show in the commercials?* 24

A. You should know by now that that kind of thing never happens.

Q. *Does chicken-flavored dog food taste like chicken-flavored cat food?*

A. To my surprise, chicken cat food was actually a little better—more chickeny. It tasted like inferior canned pâté.

Q. *Was there any dog food that you just couldn't bring yourself to try?*

A. Alas, it was a can of Mighty Dog called Prime Entree with Bone Marrow. The meat was dark, dark brown, and it was surrounded by gelatin that was almost black. I knew I would die if I tasted it, so I put it outside for the raccoons.

Inquiring into the Essay

Use the four ways of inquiring to develop your responses to "No Wonder They Call Me a Bitch."

1. Explore your reaction to Hodgman's essay by reading and responding to it in three separate fastwrites.
   a. First, read the first or lead paragraph and then go to your notebook and spend three minutes exploring your first thoughts: How does the author come across? What do you expect will come next? What questions does the beginning raise?
   b. Stop halfway through the article, after you finish the paragraph that begins, "In the world of canned dog food . . ." Fastwrite for another three minutes, telling the story of your thinking about the piece up to this point: How has your thinking changed since the beginning? Do you have a clearer sense of what the writer is trying to say? Where do you expect the essay will go from here?
   c. Finally, fastwrite for another three to five minutes after you finish the essay. Now what do you think? What seems to be Hodgman's point? Were your expectations met and your questions answered?
2. How effective is the ending of Hodgman's essay? Why might she choose such an unconventional ending?
3. This is an interesting review because Hodgman uses the pet food companies' own advertising claims as criteria for judging their products. Do you think her approach is balanced and fair? Is it persuasive?
4. It's nearly impossible to resist the pun that the title, "No Wonder They Call Me a Bitch" is in bad taste. All right, it is impossible. Does Hodgman overdo it? Under what circumstances can description of disgusting things be effective in writing, and under what circumstances does it become ineffective?
5. If you responded episodically to the essay, following the directions in Question 1, what did you notice about how your expectations shaped your response to Hodgman's essay? Is the writer entirely responsible for shaping your expectations as a reader? What do you contribute?

Seeing the Form

Choosing the Best Picture

When documentary photographer Dorothea Lange encountered Florence Thompson and her family camped by a frozen pea field, she came away with one of the most indelible images of the Depression, a picture that was later titled *Migrant Mother.* It is the photograph at the beginning of Chapter 3. But Lange

Six photographs Dorothea Lange took of Florence Thompson.

took multiple pictures that day, and only one of them became famous. Why? If you were charged with evaluating all six shots that Lange took of Thompson and her family that you see here, on what basis would you choose the best shot? What criteria would you use for making such a judgment?

▪ THE WRITING PROCESS ▪

INQUIRY PROJECT: Writing a Review

Write a 1,000- to 1,200-word review. You choose the subject—a performance, a book, a Web site, a consumer product, a film, whatever. Just make sure your review has the following qualities:

- You're able to put your subject in a manageable category for more useful comparisons; for example, rather than evaluating a Web site against all others, you're going to focus on Web sites for classroom use.
- The essay has all three elements of evaluation: judgment, criteria, and evidence.
- The criteria are reasonable and appropriate for what you're evaluating; they aren't overly idealistic or general.
- The evaluation seems balanced and fair.

Thinking About Subjects

Possible subjects for a review abound. What will you choose? Perhaps you're a sports fan who regularly seeks information on the Web. Which sites strike you as the most informative? Which would you recommend? Or maybe you are interested in photography, but really don't have any idea how to evaluate the landscape shots you took during a recent trip to Maine. Are they any good? The best inquiry projects begin with a question, not an answer, so try to choose a topic because you want to discover what you think instead of one about which you already have a strong opinion. You'll learn more and probably write a stronger, more balanced, more interesting essay.

Evaluation can be a way of seeding the field of argument because it helps you identify the things about which you have strong opinions.

Generating Ideas

Begin exploring possible subjects for a review by generating material in your notebook. This should be an open-ended process, a chance to use your creative side without worrying too much about making sense or trying to prejudge the value of the writing or the subjects you generate. In a sense, this is an invitation to play around.

Listing Prompts. Lists can be rich sources of triggering topics. Let them grow freely, and when you're ready, use an item as the focus of another list or an episode of fastwriting. The following prompts should get you started.

1. Fold a piece a paper into four equal columns. You'll be making four different brainstormed lists. In the first column, write "Things I Want." Spend two minutes making a quick list of everything you wish you had but don't—a new computer, a classical guitar, a decent boyfriend, and so on. In the next

column, write "The Jury is Still Out." In this column, make a fast list of things in your life that so far are hard to judge—the quality of the school you attend, this textbook, your opinion about the films you saw last month, how well Susie cuts your hair, and so on. In the third column, write "My Media." Devote a fast list to particular films, TV shows, books, Web sites, or musicians you like or dislike—jot down whatever you watch, listen to, or read regularly. Finally, make a list of "Things of Questionable Quality." Try to be specific. Don't worry if any of these lists contain some of the same items; there are plenty of overlaps between them.

Fastwriting Prompts. Remember, fastwriting is a great way to stimulate creative thinking. Turn off your critical side and let yourself write "badly."

1. Choose an item from any of the four preceding lists as a prompt for a seven-minute fastwrite. Explore your experience with the subject, or how your opinions about it have evolved.

2. Begin with the following prompt, and follow it for five minutes in a fastwrite: *Among the things I have a hard time judging is* _____ . . . If the writing stalls, shift subjects by writing, *And another thing I can't judge is* _____ . . .

Visual Prompts. Sometimes the best way to generate material is to see what we think represented in something other than sentences. Boxes, lines, webs, clusters, arrows, charts, and even sketches can help us see more of the landscape of a subject, especially connections between fragments of information that aren't as obvious in prose.

1. On a blank page in your journal, cluster the name of an artist, musician, film, book, author, performance, band, building, academic course or major, restaurant, university bookstore, PDA, computer, food store, or pizza joint. Cluster the name of anything about which you have some sort of feeling, positive or negative. Build a web of associations: feelings, details, observations, names, moments, facts, opinions, and so on. Look for a single strand in your essay that might be the beginning of a review.

2. Draw a sketch of what you think is an *ideal version* of something you need or use often: a computer, a classroom, a telephone, a wallet or handbag, and so on. If you could design such a thing, what would it look like? Use this as a way of evaluating what is currently available and how it might be improved.

Research Prompts. The depth of a review depends on the writer's knowledge of the criteria and evidence through which she judges her subject. Unless she is already an expert on her subject, then, research of some form will be a necessity. At this stage in the writing process, a little advance research can help you find a subject.

1. Do an Internet or library search for reviews on one of your favorite films, books, sports teams, artists, and so on. Do you agree with the evaluations? If not, consider writing a review of your own that challenges the critics.

2. Take a walk. Look for things to evaluate that you see as you wander on and off campus—downtown architecture, the quality of local parks, paintings in the art museum, neighborhoods, coffee shops. You'll be amazed at how much is begging for a thoughtful judgment.

3. Here's an entertaining generating activity: Plan a weekend of movie watching with a few friends. Ask each of them to contribute two or three titles of their favorite films, then rent a slew of them, and when you're thoroughly spent watching movies, discuss which might be most interesting to review.

WRITING WITH COMPUTERS

SPELLING, GRAMMAR, AND STYLE CHECKERS

The spell-checker on word-processing and related software can be a useful tool during the polishing process, but it's important to recognize the weaknesses of such programs and never become too dependent on them. Spell-checkers are limited by their inability to examine language as humans do. They cannot identify misuses of homonyms (words that sound alike, such as *bore* and *boar*) or typos that result in the creation of unintended words (for example, the accidental typing of "top" instead of "too"). Spell-checkers are also restricted to the words in their dictionaries, which are usually limited. The writing in many academic disciplines tends to employ advanced vocabulary and jargon that is not part of the standard dictionary of a spell-checker, so it is important to ensure that you have spelled such terms correctly before adding them to your spell-checker's dictionary. Many spell-checkers immediately underline misspelled words as you type so that it's not necessary to initiate a spell-check review. If you are a writer who becomes preoccupied with copyediting while you are first composing your thoughts, you might consider turning off this feature of your spell-checker so that you are not distracted from writing.

Grammar and style checkers are even more problematic than spell-checkers. Grammar checkers attempt to fit sentences into prescribed patterns of language (much like diagramming sentences in school). If the checker can't "diagram" a sentence, it usually flags it as incorrect. Grammar and style checkers are decent at pointing out structural problems, but often their suggested solution is just as incorrect. Long and complex sentences are difficult for the grammar and style checker to fit into set patterns, so they may be flagged as erroneous when they are not.

Most grammar and style checkers have settings that allow you to explicitly state which conventions of style and grammar your paper requires. For instance, is passive voice prohibited or encouraged (as in the case of some scientific writing)? Is the first person ("I" and "we") to be avoided? When do you spell out numbers or use numerals? Is it acceptable to split infinitives? Do you wish to use the Oxford comma at the end of a list, or leave it off as many journalists do? The style checker options allow you to check boxes for all the possible "rules" that you wish to follow. The settings for the style checker are often buried in the interface of most word processors, so the easiest way to find them is to use the help feature on your word processor. The style checker is fairly effective at helping authors conform to these types of style rules.

Judging What You Have

Generating may produce the messy, incoherent writing that would earn you bad grades in most classes. Its virtue, however, should be obvious by now: "bad" writing gives a writer material to work with. Remember that it's always better to work from abundance than scarcity. But if this material is going to go anywhere, it must be judged, shaped, and evaluated.

What's Promising Material and What Isn't? My favorite coffee shop in my hometown of Boise, Idaho, is a place called the Flying M. It's a funky place with an odd assortment of furniture, overstuffed couches, worn armchairs, and wobbly tables. On the walls, there's work from local artists, mostly unknowns with talent and unusual taste. There are other coffee places in town, including the ubiquitous Starbucks, and another more local chain called Moxie Java. I don't find much difference in the coffee at any of these places, and they're all rather pleasant. What makes me prefer the Flying M?

I've never really thought about it. That's one of the reasons I liked the idea of reviewing my favorite local coffeehouse when the Flying M appeared on one of my lists. The best inquiry-based projects begin when you're not quite sure what you think and want to explore a topic to find out.

- *Is there anything in your lists and fastwrites that you might have an initial judgment about but really haven't considered fully?* For example, you really dislike the sixties architecture that dominates your campus but you're not quite sure what it is about it that leaves you cold.
- *As you consider possible subjects for your review, do some clearly offer the possibility of comparison with other, similar things in that category?* Often judgment is based on such comparisons (remember Ann Hodgman's "No Wonder They Call Me a Bitch"?), although we may not really think about it much. Comparison isn't always essential, however, but it can be helpful. For instance, while I can't really distinguish the coffee served at Starbucks, Moxie Java, or the Flying M—it's all good—I'm pretty sure that my preferences have more to do with the atmosphere. If there were only one place to get a latte in town then this wouldn't be an issue, but because there are many, I have the luxury of comparison. The pleasant but orderly and efficient atmosphere of Starbucks is strikingly different from the mildly chaotic, nearly Bohemian feel of the Flying M, and it's through the contrast that I'm aware of my preferences.
- *Do any of your possible subjects offer the possibility of primary research, or research that might involve direct observation?* Can you listen to the music, attend the performance, read the novel, examine the building, visit the Web site, look at the painting? If I were doing this assignment, I'd choose a review of local cafés over other possible topics because it would give me an excuse to drink coffee and hang out in some of my favorite haunts. This is called research. Seriously.

Questions About Audience and Purpose. If I write a review of Boise's coffeehouse scene, I can immediately think of where I could publish it. *The Boise Weekly* is a local alternative magazine that frequently features food reviews and has an audience that certainly includes a high percentage of gourmet coffee drinkers. Many readers of the *Weekly* have direct experience with the coffeehouses I'd review and may even have judgments of their own about which are best. I'm reasonably confident that they might care about what I have to say on the topic.

Although you likely won't publish your review, consider which topics might be relevant to your intended audience, which in this case might be others in your composition class. Might they already have some kind of *stake* in considering your judgments about it? Because gourmet coffee drinkers abound these days, my topic seems to meet this criterion. But don't necessarily reject a topic because your readers aren't already interested in it. In some cases, your review can persuade readers that they *do* have a stake in the thing you're evaluating, though they may not know it. For example, your review of a local garage band may argue, among other things, that their music is potentially influential far beyond their limited local fans, and all lovers of rock should take note. However, certain more arcane topics, such as your judgment about the best motherboard for a gaming computer, may have a very limited audience, no matter what you say.

EXERCISE 5.1

From Jury to Judgment

Writing an evaluation of a thing requires that you become something of an expert about it. As you complete the following steps of the exercise, you'll generate material to work with that will make writing the draft much easier.

STEP ONE: Begin with a focused fastwrite that explores your initial feelings and experiences, if any, about your subject. In your notebook, use one of the following prompts to launch an exploration of your personal experiences with your topic. If the writing stalls, try another prompt to keep you going for five to seven minutes.

- *Write about your first experience with your subject.* This might be, for example, the first time you remember visiting the restaurant, or hearing the performer, or seeing the photographs. Focus on scenes, moments, situations, and people (see "One Student's Response: Christy's Journal: From Jury to Judgment").
- *Write about what you think might be important qualities of your subject.* Ideally, this would be what the thing should be able to do well or what effects it should have on people who use it or see it. Say you're evaluating laptop computers for college students—under which conditions would a laptop be most useful? What have you noticed about the way you use one? In which common situations do student laptops prove vulnerable to

damage? What have you heard other people say they like or dislike about their machines?

- *Write about how the thing makes you feel.* So much of our evaluation of a thing begins with our emotional responses to it. You love the photography of Edward Weston, or the music of Ani DiFranco, or you really dislike Hitchcock movies. Explore not just your initial good, bad, or mixed feelings about your subject but from where those feelings arise. For instance, when you listen to DiFranco's lyrics, do they move you in some way, are they emotionally suggestive, do they trigger certain feelings and memories and associations?
- *Compare the thing you're evaluating with something else that's similar.* I appreciate the Flying M café largely because it's so different from Starbucks. Focus your fastwrite on a relevant comparison, teasing out the differences and similarities and thinking about how you feel about them.

STEP TWO: Research your subject on the Web, gathering as much relevant background information as you can.

- *Search for information on product Web sites or Web pages devoted specifically to your subject.* If your review is on Ford's new electric car, visit the company's Web site to find out what you can about the vehicle. Find Green Day's home page or fan site for your review of the band's new CD.
- *Search for existing reviews or other evaluations on your subject.* One way to do this is to use a search engine such as Google, using the keyword "review or reviews" (or "how to evaluate") along with your subject. For example, "laptop reviews" will produce dozens of sites that rank and evaluate the machines. Similarly, there are countless reviews on the Web of specific performers, performances, CDs, consumer products, and so on.

STEP THREE: If possible, interview people about what they think. You may do this formally, by developing a survey, or informally by simply asking people what they like or dislike about the thing you're evaluating. Also consider whether you might interview someone who's an expert on your subject. For example, if you're evaluating a Web site, ask people in the technical communications program what they think about it, or what criteria they might use if they were reviewing something similar.

STEP FOUR: This may be the most important step of all: *Experience* your subject. Visit the coffeehouses, examine the Web site, listen to the music, attend the performance, read the book, view the painting, visit the building, look at the architecture, watch the movie. As you do this, gather your impressions and collect information. The best way to do this methodically is to collect field notes, and the double-entry journal is a good note-taking system for this purpose. Put your observations on the left page and explore your impressions and ideas on the opposing right page of your notebook.

One Student's Response

CHRISTY'S JOURNAL

EXERCISE 5.1

STEP ONE: FROM JURY TO JUDGMENT

Ah, *Casablanca,* the word itself rolls off the tongue like a poem. It's a film I've known of for years now. Years. And it has endured as a widely loved favorite for years and years. Only a little over a month ago, it was a film I had never seen. It used to be a film I didn't especially want to see. I don't think. I never made any effort to take it in. "Here's looking at you, kid." A line I think everyone in America must know. I knew it, and I knew where it came from. From the nonchalant voice of Humphrey Bogart. But besides that line and an utterance about "of all the gin joints in all the world . . ."—something to that effect (a line I actually did find particularly fascinating), I knew nothing of the film's contents. It's an old movie, I thought. A mushy classic. Potentially interesting, but nothing I'm in a hurry to see. But then a friend recommended it to me. One of his favorites, he said. This surprised me, and from this particular source's recommendation, I knew that this wasn't just some trying-to-make-you-wanna-cry flick in black-and-white. So I watched. And I liked it. Why?

The characters were complex—thus realistic. The plot was pretty complex—thus realistic. And thus, it seems that my criteria for a good movie includes the element of realism.

STEP FOUR: DOUBLE-ENTRY NOTES ON *CASABLANCA*

She walks in—catches Sam's gaze.	Both seem surprised.
She is with Laszlo. They are approached almost immediately by a freedom fighter.	Ilsa is dealing with much—seeking safety for her husband, and walks into a place where she may be confronted with someone of the past . . .
Renault approaches them—Ilsa asks about Sam, and about the owner of the café.	
Confronted by Nazis . . .	
Ilsa's concern for Laszlo is quite apparent—	Note juxtaposition of concern—a switch
When Laszlo leaves the table she searches, with her eyes, the room.	
Eventually talks with Sam. Asks about Rick. "Leave him alone—you're bad luck to him.	Sam conveys Rick's hurt without making it explicit.
"Play it, Sam. Play 'As Time Goes By.'"	Soft shot of her—apparently reminiscing.

Rick storms in. Demands that song stops.	Interesting how profoundly music affects people.
The reunion, of sorts.	
Rick sits with Laszlo and Ilsa.	That Rick drinks with them and buys their drinks indicates a shift in heart . . .
Rick and Ilsa subtly revisit the last time they saw each other.	Intensity—and he remembers everything. Not so detached now.
After café closes—Rick drinks alone. Waiting for her. Sam tries to convince him to leave the café	

By now, you have some background information on your subject and have gathered observations and impressions that should shape your judgment about it. Maybe you've decided the film is a stinker, the CD is the best one you've heard, or the student union isn't meeting students' needs. After comparing Starbucks and the Flying M—and visiting both places—I'm even more convinced about which one I prefer. But why? This is a key stage in process of evaluation—on what basis do you make the judgment? In other words, what *criteria* are you using? (see "One Student's Response: Christy's Journal: Double-Entry Notes on *Casablanca*").

Thinking About Criteria

Professional reviewers—say, consultants who evaluate marketing plans or people who write film reviews—may not sit down and make a list of their criteria. They're so familiar with their subjects that they've often internalized the criteria they're using, and their clients and readers may not insist on knowing on what they base their judgments. But it can be enormously helpful at this stage in the process to try to articulate your criteria, at least as a way of thinking more thoroughly about your subject. Okay, so you think your university's student union fails to meet students' needs, but why? One way to think about criteria is to try to establish the qualities of something *good* in the category you're reviewing. For example, what does a good university student union—in other words, one that does meet students' needs—look like? What are some of its features?

Criteria might be quite personal. There are certain things that *you* think are important about a coffeehouse, student union, modern dance performance, fusion jazz CD, and so on. These opinions are what make the review yours, and not somebody else's. But they should be reasonable to others. Your criteria for judgment shouldn't set an unrealistic standard or seem nitpicky or irrelevant.

I asked my daughter Rebecca, a dancer, what criteria she would use to judge a modern performance (see the accompanying box). I don't completely understand all of the criteria she listed because I know little about dance, but her list seems sensible and I can imagine how it might guide her in evaluating the next performance of the Balance Dance Company. What I don't understand, she can explain to me.

As you write your sketch, keep your criteria in mind. You may not mention all of them, or even any of them in your draft, but they'll help direct you to the evidence you need to make your judgment seem persuasive to others.

Becca's Criteria

A good modern dance performance has . . .

1. Interesting features—props, comedy or music?
2. Something improvised
3. Visible expressions of the dancers' enjoyment
4. Interesting variation
5. Good balance in choreography between repetition and randomness
6. Beginning, middle, and end, seamlessly joined

Writing the Sketch

As with the other inquiry projects, begin with a sketch of your review. This should be about 500 to 600 words (two to three double-spaced pages) and include the following:

- A tentative title
- An effort to help readers understand why they might have a stake in the thing you're evaluating. What's significant about this particular CD, book, performance, place, or product?
- Specific evidence from the thing itself to help explain and support your judgment of it.

STUDENT SKETCH

My daughter Julia announced the other day that she hates black-and-white films. Becca, her older sister, then forced her to watch her favorite Bette Davis movie, *All About Eve.* We all wrapped ourselves around pillows and spent the next ninety minutes reveling in legendary lines—"You better fasten your seatbelts, it's going to be a bumpy night"—and legendary actors—Marilyn Monroe makes her first major screen appearance in the film.

In the sketch that follows, Christy Claymore has a similar experience, and in her sketch she explores what might be the timeless appeal of one of the best films Hollywood ever made, *Casablanca.* She uses the sketch to surface some of her preconceptions about old films, and then discovers how many of these are challenged by the film she chose to review. In particular, Christy focuses on the complexity of the characterization in *Casablanca*, something she didn't expect in a film from this era. Notice how some of these themes are later developed in her essay on page 155.

CASABLANCA ENDURES: EVEN AS TIME GOES BY

Christy Claymore

1 "Of all the gin joints in all the towns in all the world, she walks in to mine," is a phrase that many people in varying ways and forms can relate to. It's a line I placed in an essay of mine that spoke of "chance" meetings—the miracle it is that such a big world can be made so small when we stumble onto certain paths, or into particular establishments, running into specific persons. Though I could relate to this line, and though I knew the line came from *Casablanca*, I never felt compelled to see this movie. But when I finally gave it a chance, I realized why it was a classic, and not just some dusty old feel-good flick. It has depth and complexity that reaches into the fabric of humanity, and transcends the decades that rest between the time it was made and our present era.

2 I never thought myself a youth who felt the past irrelevant, but I think that is what has kept me from viewing various old films. I can't explain why—I've really had no solid basis for feeling this way. Just impressions I garnered in passing, I guess. The weak heroine fainting at her macho hero's feet. Good guys always defeating the villains. Outrageous lines bursting forth from the actors followed by tears or kisses. I've seen these things in film documentaries, mostly. The documentaries fascinated me more than the films because they gave me the "real" scoop. The off-camera spats, the real character and chemistry of the actors. I guess I hunger for the real. Or, at least, the realistic. Something that conveys actions and emotions I can believe; actions and emotions that prompt a response of sincerity that I can feel for myself. I guess that's my primary criteria for judging whether a film is "good" or not. And from what I saw, mostly from mere clips, old movies did not seem realistic. And so, I think, such an impression is what delayed my viewing of classics like *Casablanca*.

3 And then a friend got me to watch it. And I was shocked by the complexity of the characters, and of the overall plot. It had a good ending—not necessarily a "happy" one. The lovers do not head off into the sunset together. They do not even get a goodbye kiss in the final moments that they have in each other's presence. But deep down inside they know it is all for the best. And the audience knows it, too. And as it is with life, a situation that turns out for the best is not one that always leaves one feeling warm.

4 What ended with a complex intermingling of emotion began and developed with a series of complex characters. Captain Renault (Claude Rains) was one of the first main characters to enter the story. He was not the hero of the story—but his part was key as his interaction with the characters brought out not only his fickle personality, but also highlighted the nuances of others' characters. His personality was mixed with shadiness,

as well as insight. He was a crooked cop, but one who could see the true heart of a person. "I suspect that under that cynical shell, you are, at heart, a sentimentalist," he conveys to Rick (Humphrey Bogart). At this point in the movie, it's hard to see that about Rick, but as soon as the comment is made, I am somehow inclined to believe Renault, despite his already apparent shiftiness, because he says it with a sort of sincerity. Besides Rick, he is the quintessential human throughout the movie—for he displays with great dexterity and degree the paradoxal moods we all, even if only slightly, pass through from time to time.

5 There is, in fact, no ideal "hero" in this movie. Rick ultimately makes the morally admirable decision that punctuates the climax of the film, but his life, one can tell, has not been characterized by acts of virtue. However, though many of Hollywood's leading men seem to enjoy their womanizing and their booze, and other exhibitions of debauchery—such exploits are not glamorized in this movie as they are in others. Rick is never seen enjoying these things. He escorts one of his protesting, broken-hearted beauties out of his bar with what appears to be some somberness, and he sits alone, hunched over his drinks, never taking them with well-meaning customers. And then she walks in—Ilsa—the former flame, the one woman who seems to have gained his sincere affections. And it is at this point, when the audience sees Rick start to grapple with pain and with hope, that Renault's early suspicion is proven accurate. The tough guy is a sentimentalist—or at least possesses a heart of flesh rather than of stone.

6 Renault and Rick, along with the other characters, were remarkably developed, and this development added not only depth, but also realism, to the plot. There was something in each of the characters that an audience member could relate to because the people on the screen seem to us people we can know, because the people on the screen display so vividly the motions of humanity, and thus, at least abstractly, we view some truths about ourselves.

Moving from Sketch to Draft

A sketch usually gives the writer just the barest outline of his or her subject. But as an early draft, a sketch can be invaluable. It might hint at what the real subject is, or what questions seem to be behind your inquiry into the subject. A sketch might suggest a focus for the next draft, or simply a better lead. Learning to read your sketches for such clues takes practice. The following suggestions should help.

Evaluating Your Own Sketch. A sketch is an early draft; it should help expose gaps that you can fill in revision. Begin evaluating your sketch by looking for the following possible omissions:

1. Do you provide enough background about what you're reviewing so that readers unfamiliar with the subject know enough to believe and understand your claims?
2. Did you feel that your treatment of the topic was balanced? For example, did you include perspectives that differ from yours?
3. Do you use any helpful comparisons?

4. Are your judgments supported by specific evidence? Is there enough of it?
5. Having written the sketch, has your judgment changed at all? Should you strengthen, qualify, or elaborate on it? Do you feel as if it would be more honest to change it altogether?

Questions for Peer Review. Because a review is a form of persuasive writing, comments from other readers are crucial. In your workshop session, get your peers to comment on how persuasive they find your sketch by asking some of the following questions:

- After reading the sketch, what one thing do you remember most?
- Do you agree with my review of______ ? If so, what did you find *least* convincing? If you disagreed, what did you find *most* convincing?
- What criterion seemed key to my judgment? Are there others that you thought I might mention but didn't?
- How do I come across in the sketch? Do I seem to know what I'm talking about? Or does it seem like a rant?

Reflecting on What You've Learned. Following your workshop session, write for five to seven minutes in your journal, beginning with a fastwrite in which you try to remember everything that you heard. Do this double-entry style, on the left page of your notebook. It will help you remember if you tell the story of your workshop session: *The workshop began when . . . And then, . . . And then, ...* When you're done trying to recall everything you can about what group members said to you, shift to the opposing right page and fastwrite about your reactions to what they said. What made sense? What didn't? How might you try one or more of the suggestions you like in the next draft?

Research and Other Strategies: Gathering More Information

If your workshop went well, you might feel ready to start the next draft. But remember this: it is always best to work from an abundance of information. It almost always pays off to resist the temptation to rush the draft and spend a little more time collecting information that will help you write it. Consider the following:

Re-Experience. Probably the single most useful thing you can do to prepare for the next draft is to collect more observations of your subject. That might be impossible if you're reviewing a onetime event like a concert. But if you can collect more information at the coffeehouse, or find more Web sites to compare, or watch the video of the film again, you're likely to learn a lot that will help you write the draft. Why? You're much more focused now on what you think, what criteria most influence that judgment, and what particular evidence you were lacking in the sketch that will make your review more convincing.

Interview. If you opted not to spend much time talking to people, you should strongly consider collecting the comments, opinions, and observations of others about the subject of your review. If you reviewed a concert or other event, find others who attended to interview. If you reviewed a film, get a small group of friends to watch the movie with you and jot down their reactions afterward. If it would be helpful to collect data on how people feel, consider designing a brief survey.

Also consider interviewing someone who is an expert on the thing you're reviewing. Talk to the architect who designed the student union building you find so student unfriendly. Interview Web designers about the do's and don'ts of informational Web sites; ask them what they think of the sports site you admire so much. Talk to a professional musician or salesperson who loves the acoustic guitar you reviewed.

Read. Go to the library and search for information about your subject. That will make you more of an expert. Look for books and articles in the following categories:

- *Information about how it's made or designed.* You love Martin's newest classical guitar but you really don't know much about the rosewood used in it. Search for books and articles on the qualities of wood that guitar makers value most.
- *Other reviews.* Search the Web and the library for other reviews of your subject. If you're reviewing a consumer product or some aspect of popular culture, check a database of general-interest periodicals such as *The General Reference Center* or *Reader's Guide Abstracts.* Also check newspaper databases. Has anyone else written about your topic?
- *Background information on relevant people, companies, traditions, local developments, and so on.* For example, if you're reviewing Bob Dylan's new CD, it would be helpful to know more about the evolution of his music. Check the electronic book index for a Dylan biography. Reviewing a modern dance performance? Find out more about the American tradition in the genre by checking the *Encyclopedia of Dance and Ballet* in the library's reference room.

Composing the Draft

One of my favorite writers is essayist E. B. White, author of the familiar children's books *Stuart Little* and *Charlotte's Web.* In a less famous work, an essay that reviewed the work of Don Marquis, White focuses on a book of poetry written by a cockroach, *archy and mehitabel.* This cockroach (Marquis's creation, of course) spent the nighttime hours banging on the keys of a typewriter composing poems and conversing with a cat who was Cleopatra in another life. Because he couldn't reach the shift key, the cockroach wrote everything in lowercase. You probably don't know this book or this author, but after reading this lead don't you want to know more about both?

> Among books of humor by American authors, there are only a handful that rest solidly on the bookshelf. This book about Archy and Mehitabel, hammered out at such awful cost by the bug hurling himself at the keys, is one of those books. It is funny, it is wise; it goes right on selling, year after year. The sales do not astound me; only the author astounds me, for I know (or think I do) at what cost Don Marquis produced these gaudy and irreverent tales.

Like all good leads, White's begins by raising questions. A book produced at "awful cost" about *a bug* "hurling himself at the keys"? Certainly we can see how this is costly labor for the insect, but why for its human author? In just a few sentences, White has given us a reason to want to know more about a book we've probably never heard of. One of the challenges of writing a good review is exactly this one: How can you quickly establish two things—that the thing you're evaluating is a significant subject, and that you can be trusted to review it thoughtfully and fairly?

White does this by raising interesting questions and by implying that he has inside knowledge about his subject, Don Marquis, that he promises to share. There are many ways to begin an essay that create reader interest in your subject and establish your credibility as an evaluator.

Here are some other approaches to a strong lead for a review:

- Begin with a common misconception about your subject and promise to challenge it.
- Begin with an anecdote that reveals what you like or dislike.
- Help readers realize the relevance of your subject by showing how it's used, what it says, or why it's needed in a familiar situation.
- Provide interesting background that you readers may not know.

Methods of Development. What are some ways to organize your review?

Narrative. You only have to remember Ann Hodgman's earlier review of dog food to see how you might use narrative in a review. If you're reviewing a performance or any other kind of experience that has a discrete beginning and end, then telling a story about what you saw, felt, and thought is a natural move. Another way to use narrative is to tell the story of your thinking about your subject, an approach that lends itself to a delayed thesis essay where your judgment of final claim comes late rather than early. For example, you began the book admiring Stephen King's storytelling skill but that admiration shifted as you read it. Your review, then, essentially becomes the story of that change in perspective and what exactly influenced it.

Comparison/Contrast. You already know that comparison of other items in the same category you're evaluating—say, other science fiction films, or other electric cars, or laptops—can be a useful approach to writing an evaluation. If comparison is an important element, you might structure your essay around it, looking first at a comparable item and then contrasting it with another. For example, one way to write my review of Boise coffeehouses is to compare Starbucks and the Flying M. Because Starbucks is the corporate version of the American coffee franchise, I could begin my essay by establishing Starbucks as the standard against which I evaluate my locally owned coffee place. If it is useful, I could keep drawing on that contrast throughout the essay, or establish it just at the beginning, focusing more on the Flying M's qualities.

Question to Answer. One of the most straightforward methods of structuring a review is to simply begin by raising the question we explored earlier: *What makes _____ good?* This way, you make your criteria for evaluation explicit. From there, the next move is obvious—how well does the thing you're evaluating measure up? If the question is what makes a modern dance performance memorable, the answer for Rebecca is the five or six things she listed—spontaneity, variation, interesting scene or costume changes, seamless shifts between the beginning, middle, and end. Now she can apply these criteria to what she saw at the Balance Dance Company's performance last night.

Using Evidence. The most important evidence in an evaluation is your observations of the thing itself. These should be specific. Who was the best performer, or who was the worst? When did that become obvious during the show? What did he or she say or do? What exactly do I mean by the "nearly Bohemian" atmosphere of the Flying M? What does "nearly Bohemian" look like? Which lyrics suggest that Britney Spears is a poor writer? You will most likely obtain this evidence through *primary research.* You'll attend the concert, listen to the CD, or visit the coffeehouse. You may also use evidence from secondary sources; for example, what did another critic say or observe? But in general, the most authoritative evidence in an evaluation comes from direct observation.

Workshopping the Draft

The following journal activities and questions should help you make the most of your opportunity to get peer feedback on your work in progress.

Reflecting on the Draft. Prepare for peer review of your draft by spending three minutes fastwriting in your journal from the following prompt: *The thing that I liked most about this draft was . . .* Now fastwrite for three more minutes beginning with the following prompt: *The thing that bothered me most about this draft was . . .*

Finally, choose one part of your draft that you are *least* sure of; perhaps you think it's unconvincing or cheesy or unclear. Present this passage to your workshop group and ask what they think without initially voicing your concerns about it.

ONE STUDENT'S RESPONSE

CHRISTY'S JOURNAL

REFLECTING ON THE DRAFT

The thing I liked most about this draft is the introduction. However, it does need some work structurally. But I feel I came in strong. The next paragraph gives the reader some clue as to what my criteria are, which gives me a foundation and a slant for the rest of the paper.

The thing I liked least about the paper is the ending. The conclusion needs to be bulked up a bit, and I think I need to say a little more about Ilsa's character. I need to look at thoughts that might be a little too condensed, and try to elaborate on them.

Questions for Readers. Because evaluative writing is meant to be persuasive, pose some questions for your workshop group that help you gauge how convincing your draft is.

1. At what point in the draft did you think my argument was most effective?
2. When was it least effective?
3. Did you care about what I was evaluating? If not, how might I make you care more?
4. How do I come across as a speaker in this essay? What descriptive words would you use to describe me (*fair, critical, serious, nitpicky,* and so on)?
5. Is there a relevant comparison I might have made here but didn't?

Option for Review Essay Workshop

1. Divide each workshop group into two teams—believers and doubters.
2. Believers are responsible for presenting to doubters why the writer's review is convincing and fair.
3. Doubters challenge the writer's judgments and respond to the believer's claims.
4. The writer observes this conversation without participating.
5. After five minutes, believers and doubters drop their roles and discuss with the writer suggestions for revision.

Revising the Draft

As I discussed earlier in the book, one of the most common misconceptions about revision is that you do it only at the end of the writing process. In fact, up to this point, you should have been revising your work all along, from the first few journal exercises when you chose a topic and played with possible angles on it, to the journal work you might have done to prepare to write the sketch, and then again with your efforts to turn your sketch into a more developed draft. Revision is literally "re-seeing," and every time you create the conditions that allow you to discover something new about how you see or what you think about your subject, you are, in fact, engaged in the act of revision. In a sense, then, each writing assignment you undertake is one long act of revision, from start to finish.

But once you've completed a draft, the revision process becomes more focused. You are mostly working with material that should be somewhat settled, with purposes that might be clearer, and ideas that may have more shape. At this point, the biggest temptation is to tell yourself you are largely done and what revision remains is merely a matter of "fixing things"—tinkering with sentences, correcting typos, and running a spell-checker. In the survey from Chapter 1 (see page 18), 70 percent of students admitted as much. "I usually just tidy things up" was ranked first or second by students who were asked what they do most often when they revise an academic paper.

These activities are certainly an element of revision—and important ones—but as the word *revision* implies, it's important to "re-see" both what you are trying to say and how you try to say it, even at this stage in the process. Chapter 11, "Revision Strategies," is a useful introduction to the revision process for any essay, including the review. It emphasizes ways writers can break the bonds that limit their ability to find new ways of seeing the draft.

Review drafts also have some fairly typical problems, most of which can be addressed by repeating some of the steps in this chapter or selecting appropriate revision strategies in Chapter 11.

- Do you provide enough background on your subject for readers who aren't as familiar with it as you?
- Is the draft's *ethos* effective? In other words, does the writer come across as judgmental yet fair, authoritative yet cautious? Is the tone or voice of the draft persuasive to its audience?
- Is there enough evidence? Does the draft offer enough specific information about its subject so that the reader can understand exactly why the writer makes a particular judgment about it?
- Does the writer go beyond a simple assessment of the subject—"it was good or bad because . . ." and offer a range of commentary on the subject's strengths and weaknesses?

Use the accompanying table as a guide to the appropriate revision strategies. Remember that a draft may present problems in more than one category.

Polishing the Draft

After you've dealt with the big issues in your draft—is it sufficiently focused, does it answer the *So what?* question, is it well organized, and so on—you must deal with the smaller problems. You've carved the stone into an appealing figure but now you need to polish it. Are your paragraphs coherent? How do you manage transitions? Are your sentences fluent and concise? Are there any errors in spelling or syntax? Section 5 of Chapter 11 can help you focus on these issues.

Before you finish your draft, work through the following checklist:

- Every paragraph is about one thing.
- The transitions between paragraphs aren't abrupt.
- The length of sentences varies in each paragraph.
- Each sentence is concise. There are no unnecessary words or phrases.
- You've checked grammar, particularly verb agreement, run-on sentences, unclear pronouns, and misused words (*there/their, where/were,* and so on). (See the handbook at the end of the book for help with these grammar issues.)
- You've run your spell-checker and proofed your paper for misspelled words.

GUIDE TO REVISION STRATEGIES		
PROBLEMS IN THE DRAFT (CHAPTER 11)	**PART**	**PAGE NUMBER**
Unclear purpose ■ Not sure what the essay is about? Fails to answer the *So what?* question?	1	420
Unclear thesis, theme, or main idea ■ Not sure what you're trying to say? Judgment isn't clear?	2	425
Lack of information or development ■ Needs more details; more evidence from the review subject? ■ Criteria need work?	3	432
Disorganized ■ Doesn't move logically or smoothly from paragraph to paragraph?	4	436
Unclear or awkward at the level of sentences and paragraphs ■ Seems choppy or hard to follow at the level of sentences or paragraphs?	5	442

STUDENT ESSAY

Christy's sketch on *Casablanca* (page 147) proves fertile ground for the draft that follows. Notice how she uses her initial resistance to old films like this one—something that she writes about in her sketch—as the foundation for her essay. Her review essentially argues that *Casablanca*, at least, brings that prejudice "to its knees." Notice also the care Christy takes to clearly explain the plot, correctly assuming that her readers may not have seen the movie or may not remember it. However, the most important moments in any review are when the writer steps forward and says what she thinks.

Casablanca Endures, Even as Time Goes By

Christy Claymore

1 The specifics of situations vary from person to person, and yet human experience is universal and so is woven with threads that are, in essence, quite similar despite the differences of place and time. We all feel hope as well as disappointment. We all experience clarity and confusion, courage and fear, love and heartbreak. The film *Casablanca* (1942), although taking place in both an era and a place that are great distances from where we are now, encapsulates life traits that are quite real to many—even in our own present time and place.

2 I never thought myself a person who felt the past irrelevant, but I think some sentiment like this must have kept me from viewing old films. In the documentaries I watched, typically these films seemed to portray weak heroines fainting at their macho hero's feet, or good guys always defeating the villains, or outrageous lines accompanying actors' melodramatic tears or overindulgent kisses. I guess I hunger for the real, or at least the realistic. My fulfillment lies in something that conveys actions and emotions I can believe; actions and emotions that prompt a response of sincerity that I can feel for myself. And from what I saw from these clips, old movies did not seem to capture this necessary, personal realism. Such an impression is what delayed my viewing of classics like *Casablanca.*

3 Just under a month ago, through the recommendation of a friend, I watched the film. By the middle of this first viewing, my stereotype of older films had fallen to its knees. There is some of the old-time melodrama, language, and sentimentality in the film, but the complexity of plot and character development in *Casablanca* outshines everything that I might ordinarily find silly.

4 The story is set in the Moroccan city of Casablanca during the early years of the Second World War. Casablanca at this time was administered by the French Vichy government, which itself was subject to the oversight of Nazi Germany. The city was a place where refugees from the war in Europe fled with the hope of escaping still further off, many to the United States. The obstacle the film presents these would-be escapees (though it was supposedly fabricated to generate more dramatic tension) was that they needed to obtain special visas in order to leave Casablanca, visas that were very difficult and expensive to acquire. In the midst of this tense atmosphere is the character of Rick Blaine (Humphrey Bogart), an expatriate American owner of a swank and swinging saloon. Rick lets himself seem quite untouched by the motion around him. He initially keeps to himself, refusing even to share a drink with his well-meaning customers. However, as the shady Captain Renault (Claude Rains) observes of his friend in the first fourth of the movie, under his "cynical shell" Rick, "at heart, is, a sentimentalist."

5 This becomes apparent when Ilsa Lund (Ingrid Bergman) enters the picture, or in the case of her relationship with Rick, re-enters the picture. Ilsa walks into Rick's café along with Victor Laszlo (Paul Henreid), a renowned freedom fighter who is under the scrutiny of the Nazis, who are as much a despicable part of Casablanca as its oppressive heat and suffocating amorality. Moments after stepping into the unfamiliar café, Ilsa notices Sam, the piano player. Their mutual glance is one of surprise, and as soon as the glance is exchanged, it is apparent that there is a history between the characters. After some tense conversations with Captain Renault and some Nazi officers, Ilsa is given an opportunity to chat with the piano player. She asks about Rick.

6 "Leave him alone," pleads Sam. "You're bad luck to him."

7 After she has persuaded Sam to play "As Time Goes By," Rick bursts into the room to tell Sam to quit playing the song. His anger is immediately subdued when he sees Ilsa, and we as an audience find—in the midst of wartime drama and tense politics—that the heart of Casablanca begins to beat with this reunion. It is here that the complexity of plot and character begin to grow as the audience discovers

Renault's observation was in fact correct: Rick, the hard and unscrupulous American tough guy, has a softer heart than he chooses to reveal.

8 After a series of meetings and misunderstandings, Ilsa, who is, it turns out, the wife of Victor Laszlo, confronts Rick, demanding that he give them the visas that were put in his possession earlier in the movie. However, this particular confrontation turns from fury to passion, as she confesses her enduring love for Rick. Ilsa does care for her husband, Laszlo—she respects him, but it is quite apparent that her heart is not for him. Not once in the entire framework of the film does she ever reciprocate or offer freely an "I love you" regarding her husband, choosing instead to disclose such feelings exclusively to Rick.

9 This is Rick's chance to take back what was lost to him years ago at the train station in Paris, where Ilsa stood him up. However, it is not an opportunity Rick chooses to indulge. He proclaimed early on in the movie that he "sticks his neck out for nobody." But this hard-nosed, hard-drinking character transforms as the movie progresses. Rick is not a clear-cut good guy (his vices are revealed prior to Ilsa's arrival) but as an age-old truism states, "love does not seek its own," and the man who once wouldn't "stick his neck out for nobody" sacrifices his chance to regain Ilsa in order to spare her husband, their marriage, promote Laszlo's cause, and prevent any future regrets that might surface if he had chosen otherwise.

10 So Ilsa and Rick part ways, perhaps for the last time. Ilsa leaves Casablanca with her husband, ultimately, and without argument, standing by her commitment to him, and to the cause that drives him. Meanwhile, Rick finishes business with Major Strasser (Conrad Veidt), the Nazi who was pursuing Laszlo. Rick's sacrifice would seem to leave him facing dire consequences as Ilsa and her husband escape Casablanca, but Renault, rising above his customary self-interest, intervenes to spare Rick and as the movie closes the two become good friends.

Rick says his famous good-bye to Ilsa in *Casablanca.*

11 The ending is the best part of the film. Not that I was eager for the film to end, but that is when the complexity of the characters is most dramatically and successfully portrayed. The ending is good, although not necessarily "happy." The lovers do not head off into the sunset together. They do not even get a goodbye kiss in their final, heartbreaking moments, but they do recognize their decision is for the best. And the audience knows it, too. And as it is with life, a situation that turns out for the best is not one that always leaves one feeling warm.

12 What ended with an ingenious intermingling of emotion began with a series of complex characters and, as I've already described, an extraordinary plot. The people of Casablanca seem like people we might know ourselves, people who struggle to live with their choices. Sentiment might easily overrun such a theme, particularly in a movie made in this era. But Casablanca never succumbs to this, in part because it strikes a magic balance between seriousness and wit. This is perhaps best exemplified in the following exchange between Rick and Renault, as Rick explains why he ended up in Casablanca.

13 "It was for my health. I came to Casablanca for the waters."

14 "What waters? We're in the desert."

15 "I was misinformed."

16 The complex and metamorphosing characters along with the brilliant, multifaceted plot cause the long-ago and far-away to impress profoundly upon the present day. Consequently, the relevance of this "old" film is something that must be acknowledged, regardless of the time of its creation. Casablanca has a depth that reaches into the fabric of humanity, transcending the decades between the day it first emerged on the big screen and our own era. In the eyes of many, myself now included, the film is timeless.

Evaluating the Essay

1. Christy argues that the "complexity of plot and character development" in *Casablanca* defied her low expectations of "old-time melodrama." Does the draft deliver on the implied promise to show this complexity to the reader?
2. Photocopy two pages of Christy's essay, and then use a colored highlighter to mark lines and passages in which she actively interprets, comments, evaluates, asserts, or argues. Unmarked passages will be material in which Christy is less active, reporting background information, explaining the plot, summarizing others' views, and so on. What do you notice about the pattern of highlighted and unmarked material? What about the balance between the two? Do this with your own draft.
3. If an evaluation of something depends on criteria for judgment, what are the criteria behind this review of *Casablanca*?
4. If you were going to suggest that Christy incorporate research into the next draft, what would you suggest?

Using What You Have Learned

1. A review is a form of argument. Spend 60 seconds making a focused list of everything you learned about how to write persuasively from this assignment.
2. Judgments aren't always rational; in fact, we often have gut reactions that guide our evaluations of people and things. What have you learned in this chapter about how you might approach judgments in ways that combine both feelings and reason?
3. Suppose you had to evaluate the methodology of a biology experiment, or the effectiveness of a business plan. What are the first three things you would do?

The United States is the second-largest producer of cotton but the shirt on your back was probably made somewhere in Southeast Asia and may have poisoned children in Iran. While a good proposal challenges you to see a problem where you didn't see one before, it also leads you to realistic solutions.

Writing a Proposal

WRITING ABOUT PROBLEMS AND SOLUTIONS

A small group of students sits around the round table in my office. Two are college sophomores, one is a junior, and the other is about to graduate. We're talking about problems each of us would love to solve. "I've got a short story due at three this afternoon and I've only written three pages," says Lana. Everyone nods sympathetically. "I'd really like to feel better about work," confides Amy, who works as a chef at a local restaurant. "Most days I just don't want to go." Margaret, who sits across the table from me, is a history major, familiar with the making and unmaking of nations and other grand narratives of colonialism, war, and social change. Her problem, however, is a bit more local. "I can't get my boyfriend to clean up the apartment," she says.

What about you, they ask me?

"The problem I most want to solve today is how to avoid getting scalded in the shower when someone in my house flushes the toilet," I say, getting into the spirit of things.

This conversation had not gone quite the way I expected. I know these students are socially engaged, politically aware, and academically gifted people. When I asked about problems that need solutions I expected that they might mention local issues such as housing developments that threaten the local foothills, or perhaps the difficulty of non-traditional students adjusting to the university, or possibly budget cuts that threaten the availability of courses next semester. If they had been thinking on a larger scale, say nationally or even internationally, perhaps the conversation would have turned to the spiraling federal deficit, the conflict in Darfur, or perhaps even some of the little-known problems associated with the use of cotton in the garment industry. Of course, I hadn't asked them to suggest social or economic problems. I had simply asked them what problems most vexed them at the moment.

What You'll Learn in This Chapter

- How to define a problem so that your readers have a stake in the solution.
- How to write a research proposal.
- What makes a proposal persuasive.
- Questions that will help you revise a proposal.

I should not have been surprised that these would be boredom with work, too little time, and a messy boyfriend. These problems are quite real, and they demand attention, now. One was easy to solve. Lana would carve out extra time in the afternoon to finish her story—"I already know what I need to do," she says. But the other two problems—disenchantment with work and a boyfriend who's a slob—well, both Amy and Margaret saw these not so much as problems but realities they had to live with. In fact, all the students admitted that they rarely look at the world from the perspective of problem solving.

"What if you did?" I ask.

"Then I guess I'd ask myself if there was an opportunity to learn something," says Amy.

Problems of Consequence

While not all problems are equally solvable, the process of seeking and proposing solutions can be rewarding if you see, as Amy did, the opportunity to learn. There's another motivation, too: if the problem is shared by others, whatever you discover may interest them. Part of the challenge is recognizing problems *of consequence.* What makes a problem consequential?

1. It potentially affects a number of people.
2. The solution may not be simple.
3. There may be multiple solutions and people disagree about which is best.

My problem with getting scalded in the shower if somebody flushes a toilet is certainly a problem of consequence for me. It's painful. And I know that more than a few people have this problem. But the solution isn't complicated; all I need to do is go to Ace Hardware and buy a device for the shower head that senses dramatic temperature change. Problem solved. But what about Margaret's problem with her boyfriend? Is that a problem of consequence? Undoubtedly there are lots of people with messy mates, the solution is not at all obvious (just ask Margaret), and there are likely multiple ways of dealing with the problem. But has anyone else said anything about the topic? Like many other forms of inquiry, problem solving usually requires some research. After all, if we already knew the solution we wouldn't have the problem. A final consideration, then, is whether anyone else has said something about the problem that might help you think about the best ways to solve it.

Like many other forms of inquiry, problem solving usually requires some research.

A quick search of the Web and several of the university library's databases of articles produced an article on the psychological need of some women for tidiness, a Web page with advice on "Living with a Messy Man," and several scholarly articles on orderliness in the workplace and perceptions of messiness. That's not a bad beginning for background on an essay that looks at the problem and proposes some possible solutions. While Margaret may not succeed in her effort to get her boyfriend to pick up his socks, she will probably learn a few things about how to deal with the problem.

Problems of Scale

While our personal problems are very real, and they can be problems of consequence, the challenges of world hunger, war, environmental destruction, economic development, and human rights matter to far more people on the planet. These are also among the most complex problems to solve. I'm always delighted when writers in my classes are passionate about these issues, and they certainly can be great topics for writing. But as always, narrowing the topic to something manageable—with a limited focus that allows you to decide what *not* to consider—is a crucial first step. Obviously, you're not going to have anything meaningful to say about solving the world's hunger problems in a five-page essay (see Figure 6.1). But it might be possible to write a focused essay about the troubles over food production in Zimbabwe, once one of Africa's most productive agricultural nations. Even better, narrow the topic further and investigate the particular U.S. aid policies that are failing to help feed hungry Zimbabwe children. Your interest in hunger can also easily lead to topics with a local angle—say, the reluctance of some hungry families in your community to use food stamps because of a local supermarket's policies. By focusing on the narrower problem you can often reveal aspects of the larger problem much more powerfully.

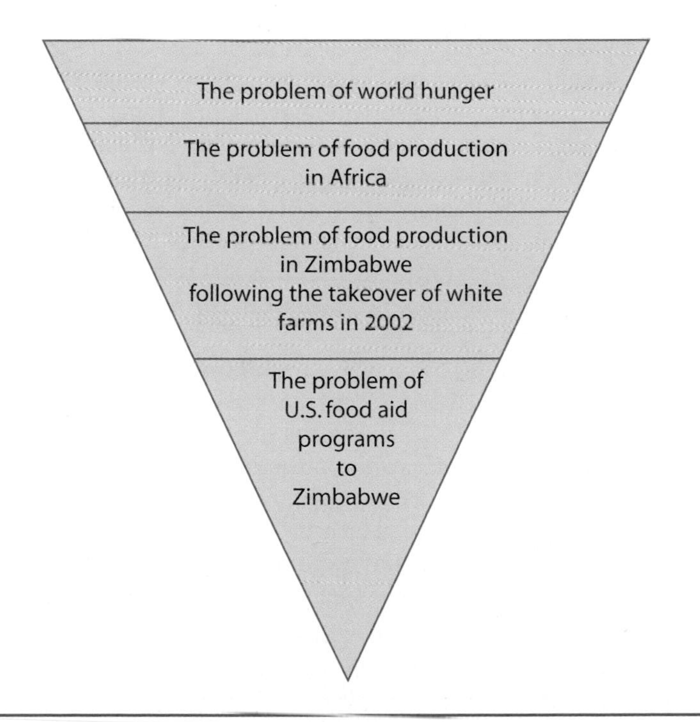

FIGURE 6.1 **Narrowing the focus of the problem.** Most of us want to find solutions to the big problems of the world, but big problems such as world hunger are complicated and do not readily yield to simple solutions. Unless you are writing a book-length proposal, it is better to narrow the focus of the problem to which you will propose solutions.

The *scale* of the problems that you choose to explore, and their potential consequence, are two initial considerations when writing to solve problems. But why would you want to write about a problem in the first place?

MOTIVES FOR WRITING A PROPOSAL

The most obvious motive for using this form of inquiry is because *you care about something*—perhaps avoiding procrastination, having a more obedient dog, reducing air pollution in the valley, helping non-native speakers transition more successfully to the university, or investigating hunger in southern Africa. There might be something in your personal life, your community, or the world that you'd like to change. One of the great things about seeing through the framework of problem solving is that it can transform what once seemed like an intractable, frustrating difficulty into something that you can fix, resolve, or change for the better. It's a way of finding hope, as well as an opportunity for learning.

Because presenting a problem and offering solutions is another form of persuasion—after all, you may want to convince others that your solutions are reasonable and effective—another motive for using problem/solution forms is to change people's behavior and attitudes. In most cases, you're writing about a topic because it's a real problem, and if so, then there's usually an audience for the solution. In that sense, writing that solves problems is a very practical form of inquiry, as well as fairly common one. The explosion of "how to" and "self-help" books and articles is evidence of the popularity of writing that attempts to solve problems. People often write proposals, another form of writing that solves problems, to companies, to foundations, or to governments. The writer's motives in these and similar works are often to persuade readers to do something differently, to encourage particular consumer, political, or social behaviors.

A final motive for choosing to focus on problems and solutions is to explore. Perhaps you're concerned with the retention rate of fellow Latino students at your university following their freshman year. You're aware that the dropout rate is high. You also know that the solutions to this problem are complicated, and at this stage of learning about the problem you're most interested in discovering what other universities have done. In some cases, you might be as interested in the problem as you are in its solutions, particularly if it's a problem you don't fully understand or weren't even aware of.

One of the great things about seeing through the framework of problem solving is that it can transform what once seemed like an intractable, frustrating difficulty into something that you can fix, resolve, or change for the better.

Whatever your motive—to explore, persuade, or learn—writing about problems and solutions is a way of making a difference in things as personal as procrastination or as worldly as African famine. It can be a way to take control over problems that seemed distant or intractable or simply inevitable, and hope is always a good thing.

THE PROPOSAL AND ACADEMIC WRITING

Numerous academic situations involve writing to solve problems. The case study approach, popular in business, medicine, and some social sciences, is essentially the presentation of a real-world problem for you to solve. Related to this is the growing popularity of problem-based learning, particularly in the sciences. Problem-based learning is an approach to inquiry that begins with a messy problem, rather than a question, and involves learners in coming up with tentative solutions. In these cases, writers' intentions may be less to persuade readers that certain solutions are best than to suggest a range of possibilities to consider.

In some classes, you'll be asked to write proposals. For example, political science courses may include an assignment to write a policy proposal, or an essay that looks at a specific public policy problem—say, the organization of the city government, or the state's role in wolf management (a big issue here in Idaho)—and suggest some possible solutions. In a marketing class, you might be asked to draft a proposal for dealing with a particular management problem. How do you motivate workers in a period when wages and benefits are flat? Research proposals are very common in the natural and physical sciences. These identify a particular problem—air pollution inversions in the valley, energy inefficiencies in buildings, declining populations of bull trout—and then propose a certain research program to study it. All of these forms of the proposal differ in the details but share many features and certainly an overall purpose: to get people to do something differently.

FEATURES OF THE FORM

The proposal is an academic form but it's even more common in everyday settings and situations. You can find writing that solves problems in the brochure at your doctor's office that suggests ways to deal with depression; you'll find it in your local newspaper in editorials that back a tax to create more parks; you'll find it in the case studies on marketing a new toy in your business textbook; you'll find it in the countless magazine articles and books that focus on "how to" and "self-help," on topics from anorexia to removing water marks on antique furniture.

The proposal is one of the most common forms of writing about problems and solutions. Here are some of its features:

- *Proposals usually deal with* both *problems and solutions.* What's interesting is seeing how the emphasis on each varies (see the next two points).

- *Proposals that emphasize solutions usually work from the premise that there is agreement on the problem.* That brochure in the doctor's office on depression may devote a single panel to describing the various ways the illness presents itself, and the rest of the brochure to what those who suffer from depression can do about it. Everybody agrees that depression is a problem, so it isn't necessary to persuade readers of the fact; therefore the emphasis is on solutions.

- *Proposals that emphasize the problem usually work from the premise that the problem isn't well known or well understood.* I recently read an article in *The New York Times* that described, at length, the problem that teen stars like Britney Spears have in holding their audience as they get older. Apparently, it's a problem shared by virtually all people who become celebrities as children, and "the majority don't get to the next level." Much of the article explored the nature of this problem because it isn't widely understood. The discussion of solutions was relatively brief, and of course featured an analysis of Madonna's many successful transformations.

- *The writer usually includes outside perspectives on the problem or its solutions.* If you're writing about a problem of consequence, then other people have said something about it or will have something to say if you ask them. Occasionally, the writer might be an expert on the topic and won't think it's necessary to do much research. But more often, we learn about the problem as we seek to solve it and actively seek outside perspectives and ideas.

- *Proposals that advocate certain solutions often use visual rhetoric.* If a main motive is to persuade people to buy something, support something, fund something, vote for something, or otherwise change their behavior, then writers may focus on the many visual ways they might get their point across. Some proposals use graphic devices such as bulleted lists or boldfaced headlines and other techniques for emphasis, drawing readers' attention to elements of the proposal that make it easier to read or more convincing, or give the impression that the writer is professional.

- *Proposals justify their solutions.* You know, of course, that any claim is more convincing with supporting evidence, and solutions are a kind of argumentative claim. Typically proposals that offer certain solutions over others offer evidence—or justifications—for why. A proposal that calls for a memorial statue that pays tribute to Vietnam veterans rather than creating a rose garden in their name might feature evidence from interviews with local vets or information about the success of similar monuments in other communities. Successful grant proposals depend on a convincing justification that would persuade a foundation or agency to fund one solution over competing ones.

PROPOSAL

Binge drinking on college campuses is epidemic. That's not news. But what should we do about the problem? In the essay that follows, Barrett Seaman, a former editor at *Time* and author of *Binge: What Your College Students Won't Tell You,* offers a counterintuitive proposal: lower the drinking age to make alcohol use a less covert activity. Is that a reasonable solution? See what you think.

How Bingeing Became the New College Sport

Barrett Seaman

In the coming weeks, millions of students will begin their fall semester of college, with all the attendant rituals of campus life: freshman orientation, registering for classes, rushing by fraternities and sororities and, in a more recent nocturnal college tradition, "pregaming" in their rooms. 1

Pregaming is probably unfamiliar to people who went to college before the 1990s. But it is now a common practice among 18-, 19- and 20-year-old students who cannot legally buy or consume alcohol. It usually involves sitting in a dorm room or an off-campus apartment and drinking as much hard liquor as possible before heading out for the evening's parties. While reporting for my book *Binge*, I witnessed the hospitalization of several students for acute alcohol poisoning. Among them was a Hamilton College freshman who had consumed 22 shots of vodka while sitting in a dorm room with her friends. Such hospitalizations are routine on campuses across the nation. By the Thanksgiving break of the year I visited Harvard, the university's health center had admitted nearly 70 students for alcohol poisoning. 2

When students are hospitalized—or worse yet, die from alcohol poisoning, which happens about 300 times each year—college presidents tend to react by declaring their campuses dry or shutting down fraternity houses. But tighter enforcement of the minimum drinking age of 21 is not the solution. It's part of the problem. 3

Over the past 40 years, the U.S. has taken a confusing approach to the age-appropriateness of various rights, privileges and behaviors. It used to be that 21 was the age that legally defined adulthood. On the heels of the student revolution of the late '60s, however, came sweeping changes: the voting age was reduced to 18; privacy laws were enacted that protected college students' academic, health and disciplinary records from outsiders, including parents; and the drinking age, which had varied from state to state, was lowered to 18. 4

Then, thanks in large measure to intense lobbying by Mothers Against Drunk Driving, Congress in 1984 effectively blackmailed states into hiking the minimum drinking age to 21 by passing a law that tied compliance to the distribution of federal-aid highway funds—an amount that will average $690 million per state this year. 5

There is no doubt that the law, which achieved full 50-state compliance in 1988, saved lives, but it had the unintended consequence of creating a covert culture around alcohol as the young adult's forbidden fruit.

6 Drinking has been an aspect of college life since the first Western universities in the 14th century. My friends and I drank in college in the 1960s—sometimes a lot but not so much that we had to be hospitalized. Veteran college administrators cite a sea change in campus culture that began, not without coincidence, in the 1990s. It was marked by a shift from beer to hard liquor, consumed not in large social settings, since that is now illegal, but furtively and dangerously in students' residences.

7 In my reporting at colleges around the country, I did not meet any presidents or deans who felt that the 21-year age minimum helps their efforts to curb the abuse of alcohol on their campuses. Quite the opposite. They thought the law impeded their efforts since it takes away the ability to monitor and supervise drinking activity.

8 What would happen if the drinking age was rolled back to 18 or 19? Initially, there would be a surge in binge drinking as young adults savored their newfound freedom. But over time, I predict, U.S. college students would settle into the saner approach to alcohol I saw on the one campus I visited where the legal drinking age is 18: Montreal's McGill University, which enrolls about 2,000 American undergraduates a year. Many, when they first arrive, go overboard, exploiting their ability to drink legally. But by midterms, when McGill's demanding academic standards must be met, the vast majority have put drinking into its practical place among their priorities.

9 A culture like that is achievable at U.S. colleges if Congress can muster the fortitude to reverse a bad policy. If lawmakers want to reduce drunk driving, they should do what the Norwegians do: throw the book at offenders no matter what their age. Meanwhile, we should let the pregamers come out of their dorm rooms so that they can learn to handle alcohol like the adults we hope and expect them to be.

Inquiring into the Essay

Explore, explain, evaluate, and reflect on "How Bingeing Became the New College Sport" in your notebook or in class discussion using some of the following questions.

1. Fastwrite for seven minutes in your notebook about your own experience with drinking on campus, as either a participant or an observer. Begin with a story. Can you remember the moment when you were first introduced to the drinking culture on this campus? Describe it as if you were there.
2. How does this essay employ the "Features of the Form" described earlier in the chapter (see page 165)?
3. Seaman's thesis is simple: the best way to address the problem of alcohol abuse on college campuses is to lower the drinking age. Do you agree with this thesis? How convincing is Seaman's evidence to support it?

4. As readers, we pick up cues in a piece of writing that tell us we're reading an argument of some sort. Consider for a moment reading a personal essay like those in Chapter 4 or a work of short fiction. These aren't forms we usually consider persuasive. What cues do you pick up on in an essay such as "How Bingeing Became the New College Sport" that suggest you're reading an argument that you don't notice in those other forms? Reflect on how you therefore read them differently. What makes you feel comfortable or receptive to an argument? Is that different from what makes you believe a personal essay or short story?

PROPOSAL

The competition for a memorial to New York's 9/11 victims attracted more than 5,000 proposals from around the world. The winning selection by a New York City Housing Authority architect and a landscape architect from California is titled "Reflecting Absence." The memorial is slated to be finished in 2009. The winning proposal is described in the following selection.

Imagine the rhetorical challenge the competition presented to those who submitted designs. Not only were they competing against thousands of the world's best architects, but competitors had to propose a design that would somehow address the intense emotion of those directly affected by the tragedy, and the millions more who see the 9/11 attacks as the defining public event of their lives.

Reflecting Absence

Michael Arad and Peter Walker

1 This memorial proposes a space that resonates with the feelings of loss and absence that were generated by the destruction of the World Trade Center and the taking of thousands of lives on September 11, 2001 and February 26, 1993. It is located in a field of trees that is interrupted by two large voids containing recessed pools. The pools and the ramps that surround them encompass the footprints of the twin towers. A cascade of water that describes the perimeter of each square feeds the pools with a continuous stream. They are large voids, open and visible reminders of the absence.

2 The surface of the memorial plaza is punctuated by the linear rhythms of rows of deciduous trees, forming informal clusters, clearings and groves. This surface consists of a composition of stone pavers, plantings and low ground cover. Through its annual cycle of rebirth, the living park extends and deepens the experience of the memorial.

3 Bordering each pool is a pair of ramps that lead down to the memorial spaces. Descending into the memorial, visitors are removed from the sights and sounds of the

city and immersed in a cool darkness. As they proceed, the sound of water falling grows louder, and more daylight filters in from below. At the bottom of their descent, they find themselves behind a thin curtain of water, staring out at an enormous pool. Surrounding this pool is a continuous ribbon of names. The enormity of this space and the multitude of names that form this endless ribbon underscore the vast scope of the destruction. Standing there at the water's edge, looking at a pool of water that is flowing away into an abyss, a visitor to the site can sense that what is beyond this curtain of water and ribbon of names is inaccessible.

4 The names of the deceased will be arranged in no particular order around the pools. After carefully considering different arrangements, I have found that any

An artist's rendering of the completed memorial and surrounding structures.

arrangement that tries to impose meaning through physical adjacency will cause grief and anguish to people who might be excluded from that process, furthering the sense of loss that they are already suffering.

5 The haphazard brutality of the attacks is reflected in the arrangement of names, and no attempt is made to impose order upon this suffering. The selfless sacrifices of rescue workers could be acknowledged with their agency's insignia next to their names. Visitors to the site, including family members and friends of the deceased, would be guided by on-site staff or a printed directory to the specific location of each name. For those whose deceased were never physically identified, the location of the name marks a spot that is their own.

6 In between the two pools is a short passageway that links them at this lower level. A single alcove is located along this passageway, containing a small dais where visitors can light a candle or leave an artifact in memory of loved ones. Across from it, in a small chamber, visitors might pause and contemplate. This space provides for gatherings, quiet reflection, and memorial services.

7 Along the western edge of the site, a deep fissure exposes the slurry wall from plaza level to bedrock and provides access via a stairway. Descending alongside its battered surfaces, visitors will witness the massive expanse of the original foundations. The entrance to the underground interpretive center is located at bedrock. Here visitors could view many preserved artifacts from the twin towers: twisted steel beams, a crushed fire truck, and personal effects. The underground interpretive center would contain exhibition areas as well as lecture halls and a research library.

8 In contrast with the public mandate of the underground interpretive center is the very private nature of the room for unidentified remains. It is situated at bedrock at the north tower footprint. Here a large stone vessel forms a centerpiece for the unidentified remains. A large opening in the ceiling connects this space to the sky above, and the sound of water shelters the space from the city. Family members can gather here for moments of private contemplation. It is a personal space for remembrance.

9 The memorial plaza is designed to be a mediating space; it belongs both to the city and to the memorial. Located at street level to allow for its integration into the fabric of the city, the plaza encourages the use of this space by New Yorkers on a daily basis. The memorial grounds will not be isolated from the rest of the city; they will be a living part of it.

Inquiring into the Essay

Use the four ways of inquiring to think through your response to Arad and Walker's proposal, "Reflecting Absence."

1. We don't often think of how we are affected by the spaces we occupy. It takes an architect to remind us. Explore the room you're in at this very

moment. Look around, and in your journal write about how the room makes you feel and speculate about what makes it feel that way. Imagine through writing your ideal space for writing, studying, or thinking. What would it look like?

2. Explain what you believe is the strongest justification provided by the architects for this particular design.

3. Visit the Web site for the memorial competition, which was sponsored by the Lower Manhattan Development Corporation, or search the Web for other 9/11 memorial proposals. In comparison with other proposals, how would you evaluate the choice of "Reflecting Absence" as the winner?

4. Imagine that you were going to submit a design to this competition. Reflect on the various audiences you would need to satisfy. What dilemmas would this create for you in the design of your proposal?

PROPOSAL

One of the most common academic proposals is a research proposal. A range of academic disciplines and programs ask that before their students launch a research project—a study or paper—they must first describe what they plan to do. Aside from the obvious benefits to the writer—you can think through your purposes and review what you've already learned about your topic—a research proposal is also a persuasive document. You have to convince others that your project is worthwhile and practical.

While the elements of a research proposal differ somewhat between disciplines, the research proposal that follows, "Effect of Infant's Perceived Gender on Adolescents' Ratings of the Infant," has some features that are typical: a clear statement of purpose, a review of the literature, a hypothesis, and a description of methodology (see "Inquiring into the Details: Writing a Research Proposal" on page 184). This isn't necessarily entertaining reading; it isn't meant to be. But the proposed project—to study how teens respond to cues about a baby's gender—is really interesting, and the approach the writer describes here is a study most of us could do, even without advanced degrees in psychology. This proposal follows APA citation guidelines.

A Research Proposal: Effect of Infant's Perceived Gender on Adolescents' Ratings of the Infants

Julie Ann Homutoff

Abstract

To explore the role of the perceived gender of an infant and the gender of adolescents on ratings of the infant, 36 junior high students (18 boys and 18 girls) will view a photograph of a 3-month-old infant. Written instructions accompanying the photograph will identify the infant as "Laurie," "Larry," or "this infant." Each student will rate the infant on six bipolar adjective scales (firm/soft, big/little, strong/weak, hardy/delicate, well coordinated/awkward, and beautiful/plain). The hypotheses are that both the name assigned to the infant and the students' gender will affect ratings. The predicted results have implications both for parenting and for future research. 1

Background

Many researchers agree that gender role socialization begins at the time of an infant's birth (Haugh, Hoffman, & Cowan, 1980; Honig, 1983). Most parents are extremely interested in learning whether their newborn infant is a boy or a girl, and intentionally or not, this knowledge elicits in them a set of expectations about sex role appropriate traits (Rubin, Provenzano, & Luria, 1974). Empirical research suggests that these initial expectations, which form the basis of gender schemas (Leone & Robertson, 1989), can have a powerful impact on parents' perceptions of and behavior toward infants (Fagot, 1978; Lewis, 1972). Gender contributes to the initial context within which adults respond to an infant and may become an influential agent in the socializing process and the development of the child's sense of self (Berndt & Heller, 1986). 2

Stereotyped expectations may influence gender role socialization and the acquisition of sex-typed behavior through a self-fulfilling prophecy process (Darley & Fazio, 1980). Preconceived gender-based expectations may cause the parent to elicit expected behavior from the infant and to reinforce expected behavior when it occurs, thus confirming the parents' initial expectations. 3

Several studies (Condry & Condry, 1976; Culp, Cook, & Housley, 1983; Delk, Madden, Livingston, & Ryan, 1986; Rubin et al., 1974) have explored the effects of infant gender on adult assignment of sex-typed labels and have demonstrated that adults sex-type infants. These studies have examined a variety of subject populations and included infants of varying ages. Parents in one study, for example, rated and described their newborns shortly after birth, when the primary source of information 4 about the baby was his or her gender (Rubin et al., 1974). Although the infants did not differ on any objective measures, parents rated girls as smaller, softer, more fine-featured, and more attentive than boys. Other studies have revealed that parents treat male and female infants differently. Culp et al. (1983) found that both male and female parents behave differently toward unfamiliar infants on the basis of perceived sex. This study suggests that adults are inclined to perceive traits in an infant that are consistent with an infants' gender label. Also, Fagot (1978) observed that parents of toddlers reacted differently to boys' and girls' behavior. Parents responded more positively to girls than boys when the toddlers played with dolls, and more critically to girls than boys when the toddlers engaged in large motor activity.

5 As a group, these studies suggest that adult responses coincide with culturally specified sex stereotypes associated with the gender label assigned to an infant and independent of actual infant gender differences. These studies have addressed how expectations associated with the gender label assigned to the infant might affect both perceptions and behaviors.

6 Although many studies have examined sex stereotyping of infants by adults, particularly parents, very few studies have examined children's or adolescents' sex-typing of infants (Haugh et al., 1980; Vogel, Lake, Evans, & Karraker, 1991). Stern and Karraker (1989) reviewed available studies of sex-biased perceptions of infants who were labeled either male or female, and concluded that knowledge of an infant's sex often did not influence adults' perceptions; however, young children were found to rate infants in a sex-stereotyped fashion much more frequently than were adults. None of the studies included in the review examined sex stereotyping of infants by older children and adolescents. One question motivating this study, therefore, was how sex-stereotyped perceptions of infants change during the early adolescent period, particularly junior high (middle school) age.

7 The purpose of this present study is to systematically examine the effects of gender of adolescents and infants' perceived gender on adolescents' ratings of the infant. Several studies suggest that differences in the ratings of a perceived male or perceived female infant are a function of the gender of the observer (Condry & Condry, 1976; Vogel et al., 1991). For example, when there is a choice between the adjectives *plain* and *beautiful*, girls tend to rate infants as more beautiful than boys do. Bell and Carver (1980) found that older women, particularly mothers, tend to give more positive ratings than others.

Hypothesis

8 I will select participants for the present study to represent the adolescent age period (12- to 14-year-olds). Consistent with the findings of Haugh et al. (1980) and the studies reviewed here, I expect that the act of labeling infants with gender-typed first names will elicit responses of learned attributes associated with the infant gender labels. First, I predict that if adolescents receive minimal information about an infant, they will use gender cues (i.e., name of infant) to make evaluations

about the infant. Second, I predict that males and females will rate the infant differently regardless of the name assigned to the infant. Third, I predict that the effect of the infant name label will depend on the adolescents' gender (an interaction effect).

Method

Participants. Participants will include 36 junior high students (12- to 14-year-olds) attending a public school in West Covina, California. The school is located in a predominantly middle-lower-class neighborhood. I will obtain informed consent from parents or legal guardians, and I will use an incentive to motivate students to get the informed consent papers signed. 9

Design. This study is a 2 (gender of the adolescent) × 3 (infant name condition) between-subjects factorial design. The gender of the adolescents has two levels (male or female), and the infant name condition has three levels ("Laurie," "Larry," and "this infant"). The dependent measures are the adolescents' ratings of the infant on each of six bipolar adjectives. 10

Materials. I will use a color image of a 3-month-old infant for all the conditions. I will photocopy the infant's image on 8.5 × 11 in. (21.6 × 27.9 cm) paper. Below the photo, there will be several bipolar adjective pairs. I chose the six bipolar adjective pairs (firm/soft, big/little, strong/weak, hardy/delicate, well coordinated/awkward, and beautiful/plain) for this study based on previous studies that used similar adjectives (Haugh et al., 1980; Rubin et al., 1974; Stern & Karraker, 1989; Vogel et al., 1991). Except for the infant name, all materials are exactly the same across conditions. I will assign the infant a gender-typed first name of "Laurie" in one condition, a gender-typed first name of "Larry" in another condition, and refer to the infant as "this infant" in the control condition. 11

Procedure. I will randomly assign 12 adolescents to each of the three infant gender-typed name conditions. I will balance the gender of the students across the conditions and test students in groups on three consecutive days. I will tell students and parents that the study's purpose is to see how an infant's traits can be detected from its physical appearance. 12

I will test each group on a separate day. On that day, I will tell students of the importance of not telling other potential participants about the details of the study. I will also tell them that they will receive additional information when the study is completed. 13

I will test all students in the same classroom, using study carrels. I will ask the students to be quiet and to not distract other students. I will distribute the materials and will read the directions to the students. I will emphasize that there are no right or wrong answers and that answers should be based on their opinions. I will answer any questions before the students begin rating the materials. After each student is finished and the testing materials are collected, I will thank the student for participating in the research. 14

Results

15 The adolescents will rate the six pairs of bipolar adjectives in each condition of the independent variable. Students will rate the infant on each bipolar adjective pair with a number ranging from 1 to 5. For example, on the firm/soft adjective pair, students will rate the infant from 1 (firm) to 5 (soft). I will analyze scores on each of the bipolar adjectives and obtain the mean and standard deviation of the ratings for each bipolar adjective pair for each condition of the independent variable. I will analyze ratings on each bipolar adjective pair using a 2 (gender of the adolescent) × 3 (infant name condition) between-subjects factorial ANOVA.

Discussion

16 I will restate the results of this study and evaluate them in light of the initial hypotheses. If the results are as predicted, researchers can extend the generality of sex-stereotyped perceptions of infants to the population of adolescents. I will also discuss how the results relate to previous research and to the theoretical issues discussed in the introduction. I will also consider practical implications of the results for parenting.

17 I will identify limitations of the current research, along with suggestions for how future research can build upon the findings of the current study. One limitation to the generalizability of the findings is the use of only one photograph of one infant of a particular age. Future research could utilize photographs of infants of a variety of ages to establish the robustness of the results of the present study.

References

Bell, N. J., & Carver, W. (1980). A reevaluation of gender label effects: Expectant mothers' responses to infants. *Child Development*, 51, 925–927.

Berndt, T. J., & Heller, K. A. (1986). Gender stereotypes and social inferences: A developmental study. *Journal of Personality and Social Psychology*, 50, 889–898.

Condry, J., & Condry, S. (1976). Sex differences: A study of the eye of the beholder. *Child Development*, 47, 812–819.

Culp, R. E., Cook, A. S., & Housley, P. C. (1983). A comparison of observed and reported adult-infant interactions: Effects of perceived sex. *Sex Roles*,9, 475–479.

Darley, J. M., & Fazio, R. H. (1980). Expectancy confirmation processes arising in the social interaction sequence. *American Psychologist*, 35, 867–881.

Delk, J. L., Madden, R. B., Livingston, M., & Ryan, T. T. (1986). Adult perceptions of the infant as a function of gender labeling and observer gender. *Sex Roles*, 15, 527–534.

Fagot, B. I. (1978). The influences of sex of child on parental reactions to toddler children. *Child Development*, 49, 459–465.

Haugh, S. S., Hoffman, C. D., & Cowan, G. (1980). The eye of the very young beholder: Sex typing of infants by young children. *Child Development*, 51, 598–600.

Honig, A. S. (1983). Sex role socialization in early childhood. *Young Children*, 38, 57–70.

Leone, C., & Robertson, K. (1989). Effects of sex-linked clothing and gender schema on stereotyping of infants. *Journal of Social Psychology*, 129, 609–619.

Lewis, M. (1972). An analysis of mother-infant interaction as a function of sex. *Merrill-Palmer Quarterly*, 18, 95–121.

Martin, C. L. (1987). A ratio measure of sex stereotyping. *Journal of Personality and Social Psychology*, 52, 489–499.

Rubin, J. Z., Provenzano, F. J., & Luria, Z. (1974). The eye of the beholder: Parents' views on sex of newborns. *American Journal of Orthopsychiatry*, 44, 512–519.

Scanzoni, J., & Fox, G. L. (1980). Sex roles, family and society: The seventies and beyond. *Journal of Marriage and the Family*, 42, 743–756.

Skrypnek, B. J., & Snyder, M. (1982). On the self perpetuating nature of stereotypes about women and men. *Journal of Experimental Social Psychology*, 18, 277–291.

Stern, M., & Karraker, K. H. (1989). Sex stereotyping of infants: A review of gender labeling studies. *Sex Roles*, 20, 501–522.

Vogel, D. A., Lake, M. A., Evans, S., & Karraker, K. H. (1991). Children's and adults' sex-stereotyped perception of infants. *Sex Roles*, 24, 605–616.

Inquiring into the Essay

Explore, explain, evaluate, and reflect on the research proposal "Effect of Infant's Perceived Gender on Adolescents' Ratings of the Infant."

1. The subject of Homutoff's project is pretty interesting—how do we consciously or unconsciously respond to knowledge of gender among infants? In your journal explore your own experience with this. If you have children, can you remember times when you actively tried to avoid certain kinds of gendered responses to your kids? How did your parents treat you in that respect when you were young? Fastwrite about this for five minutes, and then be prepared to answer this question: *Do you think what Homutoff finds out from this study makes any difference?*
2. Explain exactly where in the proposal Homutoff establishes how her research will fill a gap in the current understandings of gender and socialization. Is there logic to that placement?
3. Evaluate the effectiveness of the argument in the proposal. In particular, how would you assess how well the writer establishes her authority in the proposal? How does the writer come across to you a reader, and how does that affect your sense of whether she'll pull off her project?
4. This research proposal, like others in its genre, is written in academic prose. What was your experience reading it? Was that experience typical of how you feel when you read difficult texts?

SEEING THE FORM

THE FACES OF METH USE

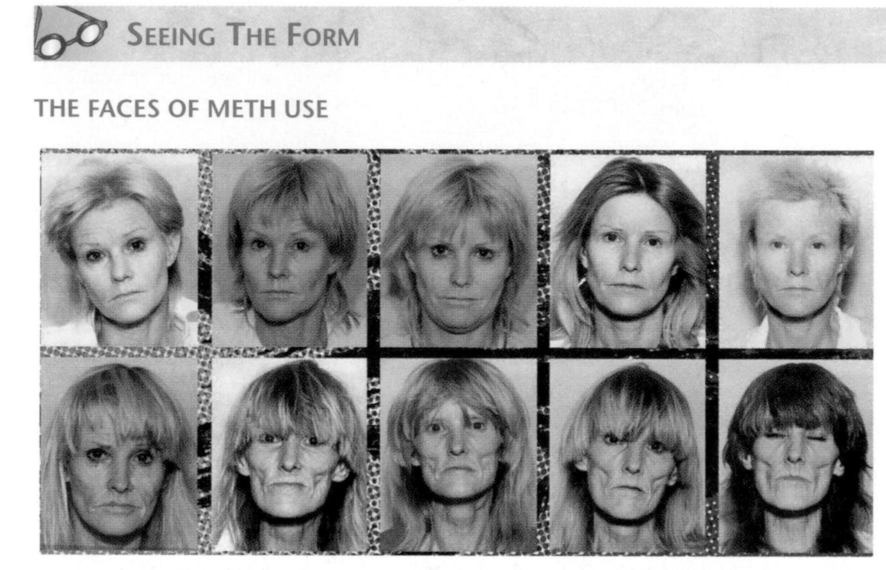

A sequence of photographs showing the transformation of a meth addict over the course of ten years.

Perhaps one of the most effective sites on the Web devoted to ending the abuse of methamphetamines is sponsored by Oregon's Multnomah County Sheriff's Office. The "Faces of Meth" features a gallery of before and after pictures of confirmed meth users who have been repeatedly arrested. The ten photos included here show one woman's decade-long disintegration while addicted to meth. Proposals frequently use visuals to dramatize the problem or highlight a solution. It's hard to imagine a more effective means of dramatizing the health impacts of the drug. But are fear appeals like this one effective?

■ THE WRITING PROCESS ■

INQUIRY PROJECT: Writing a Proposal

A problem needs to be solved and you have an idea how to do it. That's the general purpose of this assignment. Ultimately, you'll write a 1,000- to 1,500-word draft that has the following features:

- It addresses a problem of consequence, and is written to an audience that might be interested in solutions.
- It is a problem of local concern. In other words, the scale of the problem is limited to those that in some way affect your community.
- You justify the solutions you propose.
- The form of your proposal is linked to your purpose and audience.

Thinking About Subjects

Amy, Lana, and Margaret, the three students with whom I talked about problems at the start of this chapter, didn't have much trouble coming up with them: Amy hates her work, Lana procrastinates, and Margaret has a messy boyfriend. Initially, each problem seemed a relatively private matter, hardly a suitable topic for a proposal. But it became apparent later that at least one of them—Margaret's problem with her boyfriend—was actually something that was both shared by other women and a topic about which something had been said.

The explosion of "how to" and "self help" books and articles is evidence of the popularity of writing that attempts to solve problems.

Perhaps you already have a topic in mind for your proposal. But if you don't, or you want to explore some other possibilities, begin by generating a list of problems you'd like to solve without worrying about whether they're problems of consequence. Also don't worry too much yet about whether you have solutions to the problems you're generating. You can come up with those later. Try some of the generating exercises that follow.

Generating Ideas

Play with some ideas about subjects for the proposal assignment. Remember not to judge the material at this stage.

Listing Prompts. Lists can be rich sources of triggering topics. Let them grow freely, and when you're ready, use an item as the focus of another list or an episode of fastwriting. The following prompts should get you started.

1. In your journal, spend three minutes brainstorming a list of problems in your personal life that you'd like to solve. Let the ideas come in waves.

2. Spend three minutes brainstorming a list of problems *on your campus, at your workplace,* or *in the local community* that affect you in some way, or that you feel something about. Don't worry about repeating items from the list you made in Listing Prompt 1.

3. Explore some possible causes of the problem by finishing the following sentence as many times as you can: *This is a problem because* ______________.

One Student's Response

CAESAR'S JOURNAL

LISTING PROMPTS

Problems in my life

Procrastination
Can't stick to a budget
Credit card debt
Hate the winter
Failing calculus
Girlfriend prefers Hector

Balancing studying and social life
Can't afford to travel
Work too much

Problems on campus
No sense of community
Drying up of work-study funds
Not enough diversity
Lines at the registrar
Recent tuition hike
Legislature underfunds higher education
Lousy food at the SUB

Textbooks are too expensive
Waiting list for child-care center

Problems in community
Overdevelopment of foothills
Litter and degradation of Boise River
Too few child-care options
Hate crimes
Concert venues inadequate
Traffic
Air pollution in Valley
Smell from sugar beet factory
Range fires

Fastwriting Prompts. In the early stages of generating possible topics for an essay, fastwriting can be invaluable, *if* you allow yourself to write badly. Initially, don't worry about staying focused; sometimes you find the best triggering topics by ranging freely. Once you've tentatively settled on something, use a more focused fastwrite to try to generate information and ideas within the loose boundaries of your chosen topic.

1. Pick any of the items from the preceding lists as a launching place for a five-minute fastwrite. Explore some of the following questions:
   - When did I first notice this was a problem?
   - What's the worst part about it?
   - What might be some of its causes?
   - What moment, situation, or scene is most typical of this problem? Describe it as if you're experiencing it by writing in the present tense.
   - How does this problem make me feel?
   - What people do I associate with it?

2. Depending on how familiar you are with a problem that interests you, do a five-minute focused fastwrite that explores solutions, beginning with the sentence *I think one of the ways to deal with* ______________ *is* ______________. Follow that sentence as long as you can. When the writing stalls, use the following prompt: *Another possible solution to the problem of* ______________ *might be* ______________. Repeat these prompts as often as you can for ten minutes.

ONE STUDENT'S RESPONSE

GINA'S JOURNAL: FASTWRITE

I first became aware of how wasteful the modern lifestyle is about three years ago, when I first started dating Vinnie. What's bad is that most people aren't aware of the destruction they cause the environment, believe there is no other way, or are too lazy to think progressively. It's unfortunate when people choose to follow old habits instead of making daily active choices. This problem makes me feel dread, helplessness, and anger. I feel angry because I know that people can make a difference; I believe change is possible in the smallest and easiest of actions. I think the cause of this problem is the example the government leads, some of the media, and the influence parents have on their children. One specific example of this problem and how one small decision could greatly impact the Earth is with the restaurant chain, Subway. Right now, Subway wraps every sandwich it makes for customers in paper and then places it in a plastic bag. The plastic bags create an enormous amount of waste. If Subway merely made the decision to ask people if they wanted a bag, then less plastic would pollute the Earth. I believe many people wouldn't want a bag because they are immediately going to eat their sandwich and throw the bag away anyway.

One solution to this problem is being open to change and new modes of thinking. People would need to question everything and think through the logistics completely. Some people may not know how to start, in which case I recommend reading literature and magazines that propose solutions such as *Ode*, *Back Home*, and *Mother Jones*. They could also attend renewable energy festivals and take workshops if they want to increase their awareness even further. I think one of the ways to deal with modern thinking and living styles is providing a good example for others. Make your choices wisely and don't give in to the "easy" decision.

Visual Prompts. Cluster a problem that concerns you. Build associations that help you think about people you associate with the problem, situations when it's most obvious, how it makes you feel, things that might cause the problem, and even possible solutions.

Research Prompts. Research—reading, observing, and talking to people—can be enormously generative at any stage in the inquiry process, including the beginning. It's one of the best ways to discover a topic, and almost always generates information you can use later in your essay once you've chosen a topic. Try some of the following research prompts to help you along.

1. Interview your classmates about what they think are the biggest problems facing them as students. Interview student or faculty leaders or administrators about what they think are the biggest problems facing the university community. Do the same with community leaders.

2. Design an informal survey targeted to a particular group that you're interested in—students, student-athletes, local businesspeople, sports fans, migrant workers, and so on. This group may or may not be one to which you belong. Discover what they believe are the most serious problems they face.

3. Become a student of a local newspaper. In particular, pay attention to the letters to the editor and the local community pages. What seems to be a recurrent problem that gets people's attention? Clip articles, letters, or editorials that address the problem.

Judging What You Have

Feeling a little overwhelmed? See problems everywhere? It can be wearing to focus on what's wrong with your life, your university, and your community. But remember that your ultimate goal is to write a proposal that suggests ways these problems might be resolved. You may have already explored some of these solutions, but if you haven't, don't worry; you'll get the chance later. Begin by scrutinizing the material you generated for possible topics.

What's Promising Material and What Isn't? We've talked about some initial judgments you can make. Now look at the material you generated in the fastwrites, lists, research, or clusters and ask yourself which of the problems listed *do you care about the most,* or which *are you most interested in?* Once you've selected some tentative topics for your proposal, narrow them down using the following questions:

- *Is it a problem of consequence?* Remember that you want to develop a proposal that addresses a problem that isn't merely a private matter but one that others care about, too. To be sure, private problems can be problems of consequence; for example, more than a few women have boyfriends who are slobs, if the number of pages on the Web that address the problem is any indication. But campus and community problems are much more likely to be problems of consequence. How do you know whether your topic qualifies? Ask yourself this question: Do more than a few people recognize the problem and take it seriously?
- *Is there an identifiable audience for proposals about how to solve the problem?* A key part of the assignment is writing your proposal with a particular audience in mind. Can you readily identify who that audience might be? An audience for a proposal about addressing tuition hikes might be the administration of your school, or even the president of the university. You might also write to fellow students, or more narrowly, the student governing body.
- *If you're not already an expert on the problem, or have few ideas about solutions, have others said something on the subject?* One reason to choose a particular problem is that you're an expert on it. Say you know a lot about the problems of being a nontraditional student on your campus because

you just happen to be one. You may also have ideas about how to address the problems you care about. But sometimes, even if you know a lot about the problem, you may be pretty clueless about solutions. That's when research comes in. Quickly search the Web and relevant library databases to see if others have written about the problem, directly or indirectly. Also consider whether there might be experts to interview about the problem and its solutions.

- *Which subject offers you the most opportunity for learning?* Amy saw problem solving as an opportunity to learn. This is most likely to occur if you choose to write about something that you may not fully understand. These are almost always the best topics for an inquiry-based project.

Questions About Audience and Purpose. This assignment asks you to identify an audience for your proposal. When you do, consider what exactly might be your purpose with respect to that audience. Do you want to:

- *Inform* them about the problem and explore possible solutions?
- *Advocate* certain solutions as the best ways to solve the problem?
- *Inform and advocate,* dramatizing the problem because your audience may not fully appreciate and understand it, and then persuade them to support the solutions you favor?

Depending on which of the preceding purposes describe your intentions, your approach to writing the proposal may differ. For instance, if your purpose is to advocate certain solutions, then you may assume that your readers are already familiar with the problem. The emphasis of your draft, therefore, will be to provide clear explanations and justifications for the solutions you propose. You might also exploit visual rhetoric—photographs of the problem—to better make your points. In an advocacy proposal, the key question to ask first is, *Who has the power to implement the solutions I advocate?* That's the audience you want to address.

On other hand, your audience may simply need to better understand the true nature of the problem you're writing about. You'll likely still address the audience in a position to do something about the problem, but you might lavish more attention on informing them about the problem before you propose solutions. The essay on bingeing you read earlier is a good example of a proposal like this. While we all might assume that we understand the problem of bingeing, the writer's research revealed some new aspects of the problem, including an activity called "pregaming."

If your purpose is to inform readers about the problem and explore possible solutions, then your treatment of the topic may vary. Not only might you spend time helping readers appreciate the problem, your proposal might also emphasize a whole range of possible solutions. The tone of the piece might also be more tentative.

Questions of Form. Although it might be premature to decide *the form* your proposal will take, sometimes an awareness of purpose and audience will suggest an approach. For example, if Cheryl's purpose is to advocate for a new nontraditional student center on campus, and her audience is school administrators, then she'll need to consider how best to get her message across. She might, for example, write her proposal in the form of a letter to the university's president. Gerald's proposal on how to deal with Internet plagiarism on campus might be written as a Web page that could be used as a link on the writing program or writing center's site.

INQUIRING INTO THE DETAILS

WRITING A RESEARCH PROPOSAL

A research proposal is a kind of action plan that explains your research question, what you expect might be the answer, how your investigation contributes to what has already been said on the topic, and how you will proceed.

While the format varies, most research proposals aim to persuade readers that (1) the project is reasonable given the investigator's time and resources, (2) the research question or problem is significant, and (3) the researcher has a good plan for getting the job done.

The following elements are typically included in a research proposal:

- *Title.* Short and descriptive.
- *Abstract.* A brief statement of what you intend to do, including your research question and hypothesis, if you've got one.
- *Background or context.* Why is the project worth doing? What problem does it solve, or how does it advance our understanding of the subject? This key section establishes where your question fits into the ongoing conversation about your topic, in your class, in the academic literature, or both. You also want to demonstrate that you've done your homework—you've got a handle on the relevant literature on your topic and understand how you might build on it.
- *Methodology or research design.* How will you try to answer your research question? How will you limit your focus? What information will you need to gather, and how will you do it?
- *Results.* This isn't a common section for proposals in the humanities, but it certainly is in the sciences. How will you analyze the data you collect?
- *References or works cited.* Almost all research proposals, because they review relevant literature, include a bibliography. Sometimes you may be asked to annotate it.

Because the research proposal is a persuasive document, craft it to keep your reader engaged; find a good balance between generalities and detail, avoid jargon, and demonstrate your curiosity and eagerness to pursue your question.

Research Considerations. Research provides crucial support for most proposals and it is not too soon to do a little even at this early stage in the process. For example, say your topic is diversity on your campus. What have other universities done to create a curriculum that is "friendly" to minorities? What kinds of course offerings do successfully diverse campuses feature? A quick search on Google produced a whole range of relevant documents, including a description of a new degree program that emphasizes diversity, a profile of about fifty colleges and their efforts to promote it, and useful definitions of diversity and multiculturalism, including how these might be stated as goals of a college curriculum.

While it's useful to do some quick and dirty research on your topic (for which the Web is ideal), avoid the temptation to while away the hours doing it. Collect just enough information to get you thinking and to give you relevant material you might incorporate in the sketch.

Writing the Sketch

Begin by drafting a sketch of your proposal. It should:

- be at least 500 to 600 words
- have a tentative title
- be written with the appropriate audience in mind
- not only dramatize the problem, but advocate or explore solution(s)

You might also develop this sketch in a form that you think might be particularly effective given your purpose and audience. Perhaps your sketch will be a letter, for example, or the text of a brochure, or an ad, or an essay.

STUDENT SKETCH

Gina's journal work kept pointing her to a potential problem—the wastefulness of American consumerism. Initially, we often circle subjects like birds lifted high on thermals, seeing an entire landscape below us. This is especially true when we focus on problems we think need to be solved. Gina had the good sense to know that consumerism was too large to work with, so she descended quickly and in her sketch landed on something far more focused: clothing. Later, in her draft, notice how she narrows this topic even further.

Clothing Optional

Gina Sinisi

1 Should you wear your green T-shirt and corduroys today or your leather jacket and combat pants? Perhaps you feel like wearing your good old trustworthy blue jeans instead. No matter what you choose, you must choose something because in American society getting dressed is not an option. While you are not allowed to roam freely in your birthday suit, whatever suit you do wear is your decision, as is where you get your clothes and what they are made of. It's easy to drive to the mall and consume to your heart's desire, but what about these traditional American clothing stores? Are they the best shopping option? What if I told you your blue jeans are deadly? Literally. Are they worth the life of another person? Would you trade them for your mom? It's important to know what you're wearing, who made it, and where it came from. It's also important to know you have choices.

2 Blue jeans are the favorite pants of Americans, but because of the toxic dyeing processes used to make them and the unfortunate chemical-laden cotton growing practices, they put their creators in dangerous situations. I believe in the good old "Do unto others as you would have done to yourself" mantra, and like I mentioned earlier, would you trade your mom for your jeans? No? Then why ask someone else to do the same?

3 If you are attached to wearing jeans, and your old ones are too worn out for your liking, then it is still possible to find some new ones. One great alternative to buying new clothes is buying secondhand, used, or vintage clothing. This option is the most environmentally friendly one because it's reusing what already exists and doesn't add to material waste. Secondhand shopping is also a great bargain and usually incredibly cheap. Garage sales are a great means for selling or buying new clothes and it's usually possible to bargain over the price. If you really get excited about clothes and know people who have enviable wardrobes, organizing a clothing swap is another option. This way, you can always borrow something back if you miss it too much, and you also know your clothes can be found on friendly bodies.

4 If you have a fair budget and you feel that secondhand shopping doesn't always suit your needs, then buying clothing made out of organic cotton or hemp is another agriculturally responsible decision. Typical cotton production is toxic and dangerous. "Because the cotton plant is susceptible to disease and pests, it's usually doused with a potent mix of agricultural chemicals. Some of these poisons are carcinogenic; others have been linked to headaches, dizziness, lung infections, asthma, depression and birth defects" (Visscher 22). While hemp is a much more sustainable plant than cotton and grows easily almost anywhere, the government unfortunately doesn't allow farmers to grow it in the States, so if you buy a product made of hemp, understand that you are not buying locally or nationally, but instead supporting a different country and contributing to major transportation costs.

5 While searching through the racks at secondhand stores and reading labels takes more time than bouncing from store to store at the mall, it is kind of like a treasure hunt and the harder you work at searching for the treasure the better

the treasure is. You have to get dressed. You don't have an option. You do, however, have the option of deciding what to wear and what role you want to play in the American clothing industry.

Works Cited

Visscher, Marco. "Imps & Elfs: Fashion Sense." *Ode* April 2006: 22–24.

Moving from Sketch to Draft

Prepare to revise your sketch by assessing it yourself and inviting comments from peers in workshop.

Evaluating Your Own Sketch. Before your proposal is subject to peer review, answer the following questions. Your instructor may ask you to hand in your responses with your sketch or simply make an entry in your notebook.

1. Assume that you're a reader who might be critical of your proposals. What do you say in the sketch that such a reader might disagree with? What might those objections be? Have you adequately responded to them or addressed them in the sketch?
2. Are there parts of the problem you're addressing here that you don't understand yet? Are there things about the solutions you propose that you need to know more about? What are they?
3. Have you changed your mind about anything on this topic after writing the sketch? If so, what?

One Student's Response

GINA'S JOURNAL

1. A reader might disagree with my idea that the current American clothing industry is harmful to the environment and human health. I did not support my claims with enough factual evidence to be believable and get the reader's attention. It seems that I devoted more time to proposing solutions than exploring the problem.
2. There is one part of the problem that I don't quite understand which is the dyeing process of blue jeans. I'm not sure where current factories are located and what methods they use. I have only heard negative rumors regarding current practices. I have also heard opposing information regarding synthetic dyes versus natural indigo. I'm not sure which is worse or better. I would also like to know more about hemp, which is one of the solutions I propose.
3. I have slightly changed my mind regarding this topic and that is because I'm not sure about natural and synthetic dyes. I used to think synthetic ones were more harmful, but now I'm not sure.

Questions for Peer Review. Because the assignment asks you to draft your proposal with a particular audience in mind, your workshop discussions may require a bit more imagination than usual. As when you evaluated your own sketch, you may have to ask your peer reviewers to imagine themselves as the readers you want them to be. For example, suppose your proposal addresses the need for more student housing on and around campus. Who has the power to implement this solution—an off-campus housing complex—that you propose? Probably not fellow students. Your proposal might be a letter to administrators at the school or perhaps the president of the university or the dean of student services. In that case, the students in your peer group should know that they need to transform their identities to fully appreciate what you're trying to say. They have to imagine themselves a dean or president. How might such a person respond to your proposal?

Begin your peer review session by clarifying your audience. Then the group might discuss the following questions about your sketch.

- After reading the sketch, can you say back the problem you believe that the sketch is addressing and why this solution(s) is the best one?
- Is the solution(s) offered sufficiently justified?
- Can you imagine other solutions the writer might consider?
- What part of the proposal did you find most interesting?
- Given the purpose and audience of the proposal, is there another form it might take?

Reflecting on What You Learned. While your proposal sketch is being peer reviewed, record the comments. Draw a line down the middle of a journal page, and on the left side jot down every suggestion or comment about the sketch that you hear—everything, even if you don't agree with it. Following the workshop, fastwrite on the right side about the suggestions that make the most sense to you. Explore how you might follow those suggestions and how they might change your approach to the next draft.

Research and Other Strategies: Gathering More Information

Unless you're an expert on the problem you're writing about, you're going to need to do more research. While the quick and dirty research you did earlier might have given you enough information to draft the sketch, at the very least you'll likely need to fill gaps in your explanation of the problem or more fully justify or explore alternatives to the solutions you propose. Where should you look?

- *Exploit local publications.* Because the assignment asks you to choose a topic of local interest, then sources such as the local daily newspaper, government reports, and university policies may be important sources for your proposal. Some of these, such as local newspapers and government documents, may be available in your campus library. For example, my school has microfilm copies of the Boise paper, the *Idaho Statesman,* indexed on electronic database. Many school policies and reports are also offered on university Web pages.

Writing with Computers

TRACKING CHANGES TO A DRAFT

Most word processors have a function to track changes made to a draft. This function is usually found on the tools menu, but many word processors have dedicated toolbars of buttons for tracking changes too. After enabling the track changes option, you can edit a draft as usual. The computer will keep track of all your changes. Typically, the computer underlines added text and strikes out deletions (or places them in marginal balloons). Most also score the left margin of lines that have changes made to them. However, you don't have to keep these editorial marks visible. In fact, they can sometimes become distracting.

Most word processors allow you to change the viewing mode while tracking changes. You can change the view to show the draft with no tracking marks visible, which would make editing seem no different than usual. At any time you can switch your view to reveal the changes you have made. When you print your draft you can choose to show the annotated changes or hide them to print a presentable draft without removing the tracked changes. When printing, go to File, then Print, and near the bottom of the print dialog box there is usually a "Print what:" option. You can click the dropdown arrow to choose to print the document with or without the markups.

There are a few advantages to using tracked changes. First, if you are writing collaboratively, the track changes feature can help authors see what their partner(s) have changed in a manuscript. Many word processors even show different authors' changes in different colors as a manuscript moves from computer to computer. Second, you can accept or reject individual changes. When writing collaboratively, this means you can undo changes from partners while leaving others intact.

An additional feature of tracking changes is the ability to compare and merge different drafts. If you have multiple drafts of a manuscript and have lost track of the changes in them, you can open one copy and then use the compare and merge option (usually on the tools menu) to open the second copy. When both copies are open, the computer uses the same track changes markups to show changes made between the two drafts.

- *Interview experts.* One of the most efficient ways to collect information for your revision is to talk to people who have knowledge about the problem. These may be experts who have researched the problem or people affected by it. A proposal on dealing with binge drinking on campus, for example, would benefit enormously from information gleaned from an interview with a professor who studies student behavior or someone at the local hospital who has dealt with alcohol poisoning. Interviews with students who indulge in binge drinking might also be useful. What do they think of the solutions you propose?
- *Search for experience with similar solutions elsewhere.* If your proposal calls for an education program on binge drinking, what other universities might

have tried it? What was their experience? Some of this information is on the Web. Search for information using keywords that describe the problem you're writing about ("binge drinking"), and try adding a phrase that describes the solution ("binge drinking education programs"). Also check library databases that might lead you to articles in newspapers, magazines, and journals on the problem and its solutions. A quick search on one database at my own library, InfoTrack, produced 154 documents on binge drinking on campus.

Composing the Draft

Several of the proposals you read earlier in the chapter begin by dramatizing or explaining a problem. For example, Barrett Seaman's essay, "How Bingeing Became the New College Sport," opens with a look at "pregaming," a new ritual among underage college students that involves bingeing in their rooms before going out to party. One Hamilton College student apparently suffered alcohol poisoning from drinking twenty-two shots of vodka in her dorm room.

Establishing the problem your proposal addresses and possibly even dramatizing the problem is a very common way to begin the form. As you begin your draft, consider how much you need to say in the beginning about the problem. If your readers aren't aware of the problem, should you dramatize it in some way, perhaps telling a story of someone who is a victim of the problem, or forcefully describing its effects?

Alternatively, you might want to begin the next draft by establishing your solution, a particularly strong beginning if your motive is advocacy and your audience already recognizes the problem. For example, everyone agrees that 9/11 is a national tragedy. There's no need to make that argument in a proposal for a memorial, so the architects proposing "Reflecting Absence" begin simply:

> *This memorial proposes a space that resonates with the feelings of loss and absence that were generated by the destruction of the World Trade Center and the taking of thousands of lives on September 11, 2001 and February 26, 1993.*

Here are some possible approaches to beginning the next draft:

1. Consider opening with an anecdote, image, description, or profile that dramatizes the problem you're writing about.

2. Lead with an explicit explanation of your proposal, simply stating the problem and advocating your solution.

3. Sometimes the form will influence your method of beginning. For example, if you're writing a brochure, the front panel—the first part readers will see—might include very little text and perhaps a graphic. A Web page might have similar constraints. A grant proposal might begin with an abstract. Choose a beginning that is appropriate to the form or genre of your proposal.

4. Frame the question or pose the problem. What is the question that you're trying to answer, or what part of the problem most needs a solution?

Methods of Development. What are some ways you might organize your proposal?

Problem to Solution. This is the most straightforward way to structure the draft, one that you'll commonly find in proposals of all kinds. In its simplest form, a proposal that works from problem to solution will devote varying emphasis to each, depending on how aware the intended audience is of the problem the proposal addresses. Obviously, more emphasis will be placed on establishing the problem or helping readers understand it if they lack awareness. In fact, some proposals, particularly those that are intended to be more exploratory than persuasive, might place considerable emphasis on problem posing. Other topics, such as binge drinking among college students or messy boyfriends, are well known. What the audience most wants to know is, *What are we going to do about it?* In those cases, the proposal might spend very little time discussing the problem and a great deal offering solutions.

The problem–solution structure need not be a simple two-step performance—first problem, then solution—but rather a two-part harmony in which the writer moves back and forth between discussion of an aspect of the problem and a solution that addresses it. For example, Barrett Seaman spends the first few paragraphs of his essay on college bingeing dramatizing one symptom of the problem—"pregaming"—then shifts to the history of dealing with college drinking in the last forty years, including a previous solution he believes didn't work: raising the drinking age. In his final paragraphs, Seaman finally arrives at the solution he believes *will* work—a return to a 1960s solution that was undone by 1980s reformers, lowering the drinking age. This structure is particularly well suited to a problem that has a number of dimensions and multiple solutions.

Cause and Effect. It's only natural when presented with a problem to ask, *What causes it?* This can be an essential part of explaining the problem, and also a way to introduce solutions; after all, most proposals address in some way the causes of the problem. If one of the causes of procrastination is perfectionism, then a solution will be to have more realistic expectations, perhaps by lowering your standards.

Conventions of the Form. Because this assignment encourages you to consider writing a proposal that might depart from the usual essay form, the method of development might be determined, in part, by the conventions that govern that genre. For example, a proposal for a new course, say, on Chicano literature, written for the English department's curriculum committee, might have to follow a certain format, beginning with the course description followed by a justification. Sometimes these conventions might be more subtle or flexible. Web pages have no strict format, but Web designers do work from some general principles that you'd do well to learn before you design one. This can be one aspect of your research for this assignment. Sometimes merely looking closely at examples of a genre helps you infer some of the basic techniques of writing in that form.

Combining Approaches. As always, the methods of development often involve combining these and other approaches to structuring your draft. The sample proposals in this chapter are a mix of problem to solution, cause and effect, and genre-specific ways of organizing the material.

Using Evidence. What kind of evidence and how much of it you provide to justify the solutions you propose depends, as it often does, on your audience. *How much* evidence you need to provide depends on whether your intended audience is likely to be predisposed to agree or disagree with the solutions you propose. Obviously, if readers need convincing, you need to offer more justification. The "Inquiring into Details: Evidence—A Case Study" box illustrates how the *type* of evidence you provide is a function of audience, too. As you compose your draft, consider who your readers will be and the kinds of evidence they will find most persuasive.

INQUIRING INTO THE DETAILS

EVIDENCE—A CASE STUDY

Suppose a proposal argues that the university needs an alternative or independent film series. The proposal, in the form of a memo, is written to the Student Activities Board, a group of students who decide how to spend student fee money collected at registration. Which of the following types of evidence used to justify such a film series would be *most* persuasive to that audience?

1. The writer's personal enjoyment of foreign films.
2. A petition signed by 100 people that supports the idea.
3. A quotation from Woody Allen about the educational and cultural virtues of independent films.
4. Information about the success of the independent film theater in town.
5. A quote from an English professor supporting the idea.
6. Estimate that shows that the cost of renting five independent films is half the cost of renting the same number of Hollywood films.
7. A survey of 200 students that indicates that 60 percent support the idea.
8. Data on good attendance at a similar series at another, larger university.

Choosing the strongest evidence in a proposal is an exercise in audience analysis. Is your audience likely to favor your idea, oppose it, or have no opinion? If they're neutral or opposed then you better be sure you not only have *appropriate* evidence but a lot of it. What makes evidence appropriate for a particular audience? *It is evidence they are most likely to believe.*

Workshopping the Draft

The following journal activities and questions should help you make the most of your opportunity to get peer feedback on your work in progress.

Reflecting on the Draft. After you've finished the draft, make an entry in your journal that follows these prompts:

- *If I were going to write this over again, the one thing I think I'd do would be . . .*
- *The most important thing I learned about writing a proposal so far is . . .*
- *The most difficult part of the process for me was . . .*
- *The biggest question I have about the draft is . . .*

Your instructor may ask you to hand in your responses to these prompts with your draft.

Following the workshop session, repeat the method of reflection you used following peer review of your sketch, drawing a line down the middle of a notebook page and recording your group's comments and suggestions on the left side and later, your reactions on the right.

Questions for Readers. Again remind your workshop group about the particular audience you had in mind for your proposal. The group might then consider the following questions as they discuss the draft.

1. On a scale from 1 to 5, with 5 being "extremely serious" and 1 being "not serious at all," how would you describe your feelings about the severity of the problem addressed in this draft? Discuss the reasons for your ranking. Remember to imagine that you're the audience for whom the proposal was intended.

2. On the same scale, rank how convinced you were that the solutions proposed in the draft were the best ones. A 5 would indicate that you were totally convinced and a 1 would indicate that you weren't convinced at all. Discuss what was convincing and/or how the solutions offered could be more convincing. Be specific.

3. What questions did you have that weren't adequately answered in the draft?

Revising the Draft

As I discussed earlier in the book, one of the most common misconceptions about revision is that you do it only at the end of the writing process. In fact, up to this point, you should have been revising your work all along, from the first few journal exercises when you chose a topic and played with possible angles on it, to the journal work you might have done to prepare to write the sketch, and then again with your efforts to turn your sketch into a more developed draft. Revision is literally "re-seeing," and every time you create the conditions that allow you to discover something new about how you see or what you think about your subject, you are, in fact, engaged in the act of revision. In a sense, then, each writing assignment you undertake is one long act of revision, from start to finish.

But once you've completed a draft, the revision process becomes more focused. You are mostly working with material that should be somewhat settled, with purposes that might be clearer, and ideas that may have more shape. At this point, the biggest temptation is to tell yourself you are largely done and what revision remains is merely a matter of "fixing things"—tinkering with sentences, correcting typos, and running a spell-checker. In the survey from Chapter 1 (see page 18), 70 percent of students admitted as much. "I usually just tidy things up" was ranked first or second by students who were asked what they do most often when they revise an academic paper.

These activities are certainly an element of revision—and important ones—but as the word *revision* implies, it's important to "re-see" both what you are trying to say and how you try to say it, even at this stage in the process. Chapter 11, "Revision Strategies," is a useful introduction to the revision process for any essay, including the proposal. It emphasizes ways writers can break the bonds that limit their ability to find new ways of seeing the draft.

Proposals also have some fairly typical problems at this stage in the process, most of which can be addressed by repeating some of the steps in this chapter or selecting appropriate revision strategies in Chapter 11. Here are some questions to consider as you decide which of these strategies might be most helpful.

- Have you done enough to dramatize the problem if you're writing for an audience that may not recognize the problem? Should you do more to establish how your readers have a stake in solving the problem?
- How well have you justified your solution? Is there enough evidence? Is it appropriate evidence for your audience?
- Have you overemphasized one solution at the expense of others? Would your proposal be more balanced and persuasive if you considered alternatives, even if you ultimately reject them?

When you refer to Chapter 11, "Revision Strategies," for ideas on how to revise your draft following your workshop, use the following table as a guide. Remember that a draft may present problems in more than one category.

GUIDE TO REVISION STRATEGIES

Problems in the Draft (Chapter 11)	Part	Page Number
Unclear purpose ▪ Not sure what the essay is about? Fails to answer the *So what?* question?	1	420
Unclear thesis, theme, or main idea ▪ Not sure what you're trying to say? Proposal isn't clear?	2	425
Lack of information or development ▪ Needs more information to justify proposed solution? ▪ Evidence offered isn't persuasive enough?	3	432
Disorganized ▪ Doesn't move logically or smoothly from paragraph to paragraph?	4	436
Unclear or awkward at the level of sentences and paragraphs ▪ Seems choppy or hard to follow at the level of sentences or paragraphs?	5	442

Polishing the Draft

After you've dealt with the big issues in your draft—is it sufficiently focused, does it answer the *So what?* question, is it well organized, and so on—you must deal with the smaller problems. You've carved the stone into an appealing figure but now you need to polish it. Are your paragraphs coherent? How do you manage transitions? Are your sentences fluent and concise? Are there any errors in spelling or syntax? Section 5 of Chapter 11 can help you focus on these issues.

Before you finish your draft, work through the following checklist:

- Every paragraph is about one thing.
- The transitions between paragraphs aren't abrupt.
- The length of sentences varies in each paragraph.
- Each sentence is concise. There are no unnecessary words or phrases.
- You've checked grammar, particularly verb agreement, run-on sentences, unclear pronouns, and misused words (*there/their, where/were,* and so on). (See the handbook at the end of the book for help with these grammar issues.)
- You've run your spell-checker and proofed your paper for misspelled words.

STUDENT ESSAY

It's August in Boise and cotton is king. I'm sitting here clothed from head to toe in 100 percent cotton, but until I read Gina Sinisi's essay on the problems of cotton production I never imagined that these shorts, manufactured in Sri Lanka, might have contributed to obscenely low wages in foreign manufacturing plants and health problems among American workers who harvest the crop. But Gina's essay, like all good proposals, doesn't leave it at that. There are things we can do, beginning with being aware that our consumer choices echo into other people's lives, some of whom live on the other side of the world.

Clothing Optional

Gina Sinisi

1 Should you wear your green T-shirt and corduroys today or your leather jacket and combat pants? Perhaps you feel the urge to strut in your trustworthy blue jeans instead. While you are not allowed to roam freely in your birthday suit, whatever suit you do choose is up to you, along with where you get it and what it is made of. It is easy to drive to the mall and consume to your wardrobe's content, but what about these traditional North American clothing stores? Are they the best shopping option? What if I told you your blue jeans are deadly? Literally. Are they worth the life of another person? Would you trade them for your mom? Your dad? It's important to know what you're wearing, who made it, and where it came from. It's also imperative to know you have choices. The impact of your political and social ideals on the clothing industry begins with your underwear.

2 The United States yields to the high demand of cotton by closely following China as the number two producer of cotton in the world, growing enough to manufacture about 9 billion t-shirts ("Clothes for a Change"). The good news is that North Americans can support local farmers by purchasing cotton grown in the United States; the downside is that North American citizens are also the ones directly affected by the chemicals sprayed on the cotton. According to the World Health Organization, pesticide poisoning annually afflicts three million people, killing between 20,000 and 40,000 of them ("Clothes for a Change"). While this statistic doesn't single out cotton as a cause of human health problems, the crop does require unusually high applications of pesticides. While as an agricultural product, cotton only takes up 3% of the world's farmland, it demands a quarter of the globe's pesticides and fertilizers ("Cotton and the Environment"). According to Visscher, "Because the cotton plant is susceptible to disease and pests, it's usually doused with a potent mix of agricultural chemicals. Some of

these poisons are carcinogenic; others have been linked to headaches, dizziness, lung infections, asthma, depression and birth defects" (22).

3 I believe in the familiar credo, "Do unto others as you would have done to yourself," and to repeat my earlier question, would you trade your mom for your jeans? No? Then why ask someone else to do the same?

4 Not only does cotton contribute to poor environmental and health standards, but also poor working conditions. Because the majority of consumers are not willing to pay higher prices for well-made clothing, and instead prefer cheap clothing that changes with the seasons, most manufacturers have "outsourced" their production to countries like Viet Nam and China, where workers are paid extremely low wages,"as low as 13 cents an hour" ("Clothes for a Change"). If you buy these products you are condoning unacceptable work ethics. You can choose otherwise.

5 If you feel that common cotton growing and production practices are unnecessary and hazardous but can't detach yourself from cotton clothing and blue jeans, there is an agriculturally responsible decision you can make. Organic cotton is being grown in more than 18 countries worldwide, including the United States ("Clothes for a Change"), and worldwide sales are increasing by about 25% annually (Eshelby). If you can't find clothing made from organic cotton in your city, there are hundreds of clothing stores available online that support humane and environmentally conscious clothing practices.

6 A second alternative to traditional cotton clothing is buying hemp clothing products. Before the industrial revolution, hemp was a popular fiber in the United States because it is strong and grows quickly and easily in a variety of soil types. The first paper was made from hemp, and, ironically, some say the Declaration of Independence was written on hemp paper.

7 Growing hemp in the United States is currently illegal because it is frequently confused with marijuana. While pot and hemp are the same plant species, hemp contains "virtually no" THC, the ingredient in marijuana that makes users "high." Most likely, hemp is illegal because it would dramatically drown the cotton industry and because of the ignorance that surrounds its false connection with marijuana.

8 While it is currently illegal to grow hemp in the United States, it is legal to sell hemp clothing products. A few clothing stores do exist throughout the country, but once again, it is always possible to easily find these products online. Unlike some rumors that declare hemp is itchy and rough on your skin, it is actually softer, more absorbent, extremely breathable and significantly longer lasting than clothing made from cotton.

9 One dilemma you must face when deciding to buy hemp products is whether or not you want to support a nonlocal product and all of the energy it takes to get the product from its point of origination to your body. Hemp has a high rate of "embodied energy," which is a term used to define all of the energy a product uses to be created and then transported to its final destination.

10 If you have a hard time choosing between the damage caused by cotton practices, the embodied energy included in hemp, and the petroleum base in many synthetic

fabrics, and don't like ordering organic cotton clothing online without being able to try it on first, there is one final solution: A great alternative to buying new clothes is buying secondhand or vintage clothing. This option is the most environmentally friendly one because it's reusing what already exists and doesn't add to material waste. Secondhand shopping is usually incredibly cheap and a great means for selling or buying new clothes. It's usually possible to haggle for a lower price, too.

11 Vintage clothing is often more sturdy and durable than recently produced clothing; you also don't need to worry about anyone else showing up to a party wearing the same outfit as you. If you are a fashion fox and know people who have enviable wardrobes, organizing a clothing swap is another option. This way, you can always borrow something back if you miss it too much, and you also know your clothes can be found on friendly bodies. A final reason why it is better to buy used clothing is because old clothes no longer off-gas their chemicals into your skin and the air you breathe. They are safer, cheaper, and readily available.

12 While searching through the racks at secondhand stores and reading labels takes more time than bouncing from store to store at the mall, it is time well spent. When you know your clothes come from a righteous source, you can flaunt them with pride and revel in your own good health. You have to get dressed. You don't have an option. You do, however, have the option of deciding what to wear and what role you want to play in the clothing industry. Does the day call for an organic cotton T-shirt with hemp shorts, or a vintage tunic with Salvation Army jeans? You decide.

Works Cited

Eshelby, Kate. "Organic Cotton." *Ecologist* 36.1 (2006): 34–39. Academic Search Premier. Ebsco Research Databases. Albertson's Lib. 7 Aug. 2006 <http://www.ebscohost.com>.

"Clothes for a Change." *Organic Consumers Association*. 1 Aug. 2006 <http://www.organicconsumers.org/clothes/background.cfm>.

"Cotton and the Environment." *Organic Trade Association*. 1 Aug. 2006 <http://www.ota.com/organic/environment/cotton_environment.html>.

Visscher, Marco. "Imps & Elfs: Fashion Sense." *Ode* April 2006: 22–24.

Evaluating the Essay

1. The authority of a proposal depends on the evidence. Assess the evidence Gina provides to make her case that non-organic cotton production is a serious problem. Do you find it convincing?
2. Is the solution she offers—use of organic cottons, hemp, or "vintage" clothing—a viable one? How could she strengthen the case for her proposal?
3. Can you imagine how this essay might have incorporated visuals—pictures, graphs, tables, and so on—that would have enhanced the argument?

Using What You Have Learned

1. Think about the proposal draft you've written, and all those that you've read, both in this chapter and in your workshop group. Spend one minute answering, in writing, the following question: *What do you need to know to write an effective proposal?*
2. Draw a line down the middle of the page of your journal. Compare the proposal with another genre of writing you've tried in this book, looking specifically at the following:
   - degree of difficulty (which was harder, and why?)
   - audience awareness (when and how much did you consider who you were writing for?)
   - level of discovery (how much did you learn about your subject, or about yourself?)
   - application to other situations (how much and what might you use from this form of writing and apply in other writing situations?)
3. What approaches or ideas will you borrow from proposal writing that you can apply to other forms of writing and other writing situations? Can you imagine revising an essay you've already written in another genre using what you've learned here?

Tammany, a political machine that dominated New York City politics for nearly a hundred years, is lampooned here in an 1871 cartoon by Thomas Nast. The head of Tammany at the time was the corrupt William "Boss" Tweed. Testifying to the power of visual argument exemplified by Nash's cartoon, Tweed reportedly said "I don't care what the newspapers publish about me—most of my constituents can't read anyway. But them dam' pictures!—everybody can read them."

7

Writing an Argument

What You'll Learn in This Chapter

- New ways to understand the purpose of argument.
- Some differences between formal and informal arguments.
- The basic argument strategies most writers use.
- How to map an argument.
- How to avoid common logical fallacies.
- Revision strategies to fine-tune your argument.

WRITING TO PERSUADE PEOPLE

Where I live, public arguments about wolf reintroduction, saving salmon, growing property taxes, and the need for a local community college are waged on the editorial pages of the local newspaper, *The Idaho Statesman.* The paper's editorials and so-called op-ed articles (short persuasive essays that are literally on the opposite page from editorials) present usually well-reasoned arguments of 250 to 600 words, but the real slugfest takes place in the letters to the editor. Reading letters to the editor is a form of recreation here. One correspondent complained a few years ago that the song "Rain, Rain, Go Away" was objectionable because it made her children dislike precipitation. Another letter writer, an angry animal rights activist, is a regular who always generates heated rebuttals here in cattle country. Last week, she railed about the evils of "Rocky Mountain oysters" (fried cattle testicles), which were served up at the Eagle Fire Department fund-raiser. I can't wait to see the responses to that one.

Letters to the editor, while an important opinion forum, frequently feature great examples of flawed arguments, including logical fallacies, poor reasoning, and a pitiful lack of audience awareness. In the hands of a good writer, however, a short persuasive essay like the op-ed can move people to think and act. It is a genre that attracts some of the best nonfiction writers in the country—Ellen Goodman, George Will, Bob Greene, Anna Quindlen, and others—but op-ed essays are also written by anyone with an idea about a public problem. Across the United States, newspapers and magazines publish the opinion pieces of ordinary citizens, and these essays are among our liveliest forums for public debate.

While we often think of persuasive writing as stiff and formal, the op-ed essay is usually lively and engaging. Here's a sample of some opening lines from published op-ed pieces:

> Many of the hundreds of thousands of Hispanic demonstrators who poured out into the streets on Monday may not know much English, but they've learned the language of American politics: Flags. Tons of flags. And make them American.
>
> —"Immigrants Must Choose," Charles Krauthammer

> Maybe it was at the moment I found myself on my knees in my bathrobe, carefully prying tiny shards of paper out of the immobilized teeth of the shredder, that it finally hit me: The shredder had a paper jam. I had an info jam.
>
> —"C'mon, America, Fire Up Those Shredders," Lisa Johnston

> On the premise that spring is too beautiful for a depressing topic like Iraq, I thought I'd take up a fun subject—global warming.
>
> —"Global Warming: What Me Worry?" Molly Ivins

Persuasive essays like the op-ed are a great way to participate in public debates that affect your campus and community, and even your nation.

While these essays are often informal, they are still persuasive forms, and as you'll see later, they often employ the same methods of more formal arguments. However, unlike formal arguments—the kind you might write in a logic or philosophy course—persuasive essays of this kind have a much larger audience, and they are a great way to participate in public debates that affect your campus and community, and even your nation. In this chapter, you'll learn how to use some principles of argument to write persuasive essays like the op-ed that will give voice to things you care about, and that will increase the likelihood that voice will be heard.

Getting into Arguments

In 1990, the book *You Just Don't Understand* became a runaway best-seller. Written by Deborah Tannen, a linguistics professor, the book analyzed the range of ways in which men and women struggle to communicate with each other. *You Just Don't Understand* made its author famous, and before long she was on the talk show circuit and the subject of newspaper profiles. Despite the many benefits of this exposure, Tannen became increasingly disturbed by how some of the TV shows were orchestrated. Some producers "insisted on setting up a television show as a fight," pitting Tannen against the host or another guest. Newspaper reporters aggressively pursued Tannen's colleagues trying to get them to criticize the book, and some in her discipline obliged, often misrepresenting her work. This experience inspired her 1997 book, *The Argument Culture,* in which she claims that the pervasive "adversarial spirit" in American culture subverts cooperation and community, and reduces complex issues to opposing sides. "Approaching situations like warriors in battle," Tannen writes, "leads to the assumption that intellectual inquiry, too, is a game of attack, counterattack, and self-defense."

Tannen doesn't believe that arguments are things to be avoided, but maintains that there are other ways of approaching subjects that deserve more attention. While this seems like a reasonable position, it's hard to avoid the feeling that being a good debater is what counts most in academia. Yet is argument really "war"?

It sometimes seems that way. It certainly *felt* that way to me at the dinner table those many years ago when I'd walk away from an argument with my dad and feel angry and defeated. Yet my mom's side of the family is Italian American, and my best friends growing up came from predominantly Jewish households. In many of my relatives' and friends' homes, arguments were commonplace, raised voices the norm. At times I would find this upsetting, and wonder, "Why can't these people just get along?" But they often *were* getting along because argument and conflict in some cultures is an expression of commitment and caring. For example, Deborah Tannen notes that in many western European countries "agreement is deemed boring." I've often admired, for example, the French and Italian passion for national politics and their eagerness to share political views with each other, particularly disagreements. On the other hand, what Tannen calls "cultures of harmony," such as those of Japan and China, view open conflict and disagreement as a threat to the group. That does not mean that people always agree, but arguing is indirect, and sometimes undetectable to Western ears.

Obviously, culture influences our response to argument. In the United States, by and large, we argue a lot and in the open. We are a litigious society, and even children in the schoolyard threaten to "sue" each other. Combat metaphors are among the most common ways of talking about conflict—we attempt to "win" an argument, "find more ammunition" to support our position, "leap into the fray," or "attack" our opponent's position. It's hard for the gun-shy among us to feel comfortable participating in such verbal combat, one reason why some of my students retreat into silence when class discussion becomes the least bit combative.

For many of us, then, argument in civic and private discourse is bound by our *feelings* about argument—how comfortable we are with conflict, how confident we are in our ability to say what we think, and how strongly we feel about our opinions. These feelings are complicated by our beliefs about the purpose of argument. Sorting through these beliefs can help us discover new, perhaps more productive ways of approaching argument. Does argument make you uncomfortable? What do you consider a "good" argument? What is a "bad" argument?

Argument and Inquiry

There's often a tension between argument and inquiry. Most people see argument as a closed process—you already have strong opinions about something and therefore the task is to find support for existing beliefs (see Figure 7.1). In contrast, inquiry is an open-ended process. Your motive is not necessarily to simply reinforce existing opinions but to test your ideas against evidence or discover new ways of thinking about a topic.

Yet argument is an essential part of inquiry. When scientists seek to understand something about the way the world works, they often begin with a hypothesis—for

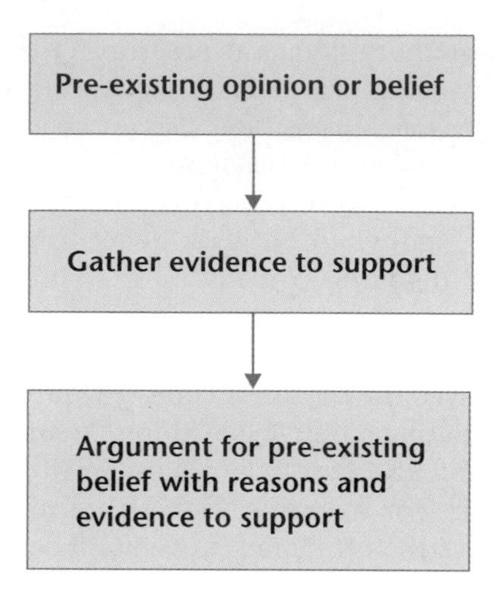

FIGURE 7.1 Many people consider argument to be a closed process like this model.

example, *the rate at which glaciers are melting in the Chilean Andes cannot be explained by natural cycles of atmospheric warming and cooling.* They then design an experiment to collect data that is meant to determine the truth of the hypothesis. That evidence may lead them in several directions: to believe the original hypothesis is true or false, or to consider yet another hypothesis that better explains the results (see Figure 7.2).

Argument can be a similar process of discovery—only instead of proposing hypotheses, you're making claims, testing their truth against what you learn from your research, observations, interviews, and experience.

Argument is also useful when you move from the initial open-ended investigation of your subject, discover what you think about it, and then want to convince others that your ideas are valid.

In the first case, you begin with a belief (hypothesis) and use the process of argument to reinforce the belief, revise it, or abandon it altogether. In the second case, you begin the process with no opinion about your subject, explore the issue to discover what you believe, and then build a case for it.

Making Claims

Arguments make claims, or assertions about which reasonable people might disagree. Argument expert Richard Fulkerson suggests that a claim (or *proposition,* to use his term) is a statement in which the response "I disagree" or "I agree" is a sensible reply. For example, "I have a headache" is a statement but not a claim because it would be goofy to agree or disagree with it.

Obviously, we make claims all the time: "Robert is a narcissist." "That textbook is boring." "Osama bin Laden misread the Qur'an." It is human nature to make

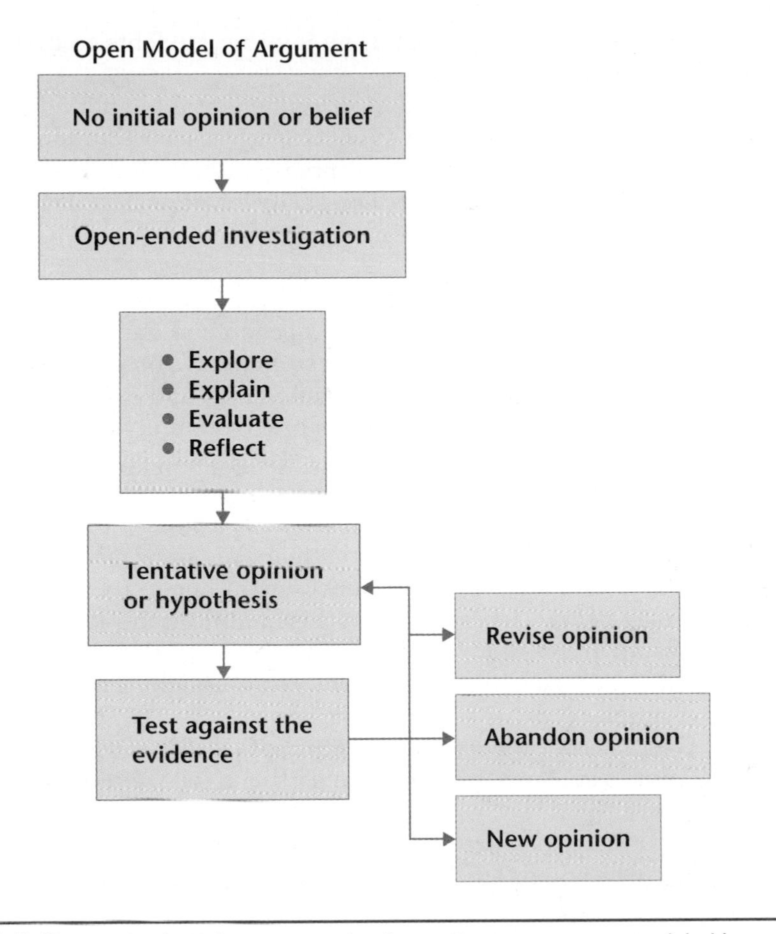

FIGURE 7.2 Inquiry-based argumentation favors the open process modeled here.

judgments, interpretations, and assertions about the people, things, and events that swirl around us. Since the beginning of this book, you have been encouraged to use evaluation as a way of inquiring as you responded to readings, images, your own work, and the work of others, asking questions such as, *What's my take on this? What do I find convincing? Do I see things any differently?* We usually describe this as the process of forming opinions.

But we rarely examine the *assumptions* or *reasons* that lurk behind these opinions or claims, those often shadowy ideas that provide the platform from which we make our assertions about the way things are. For example, if Robert is a narcissist, what does the speaker assume are the behaviors that qualify for such a label? In other words, what *definition* of narcissism seems to provide the basis for the claim about poor Robert? If bin Laden "misreads" the Qur'an, what does that assume about the "proper" reading of that holy text?

One way to discover these assumptions is to use the word *because* before or after the claim. For example, "That textbook is boring *because* it spends too much time explaining things and not enough time inviting students to participate in the learning."

Evaluation is a way of inquiring that is fundamental to all kinds of persuasive writing. In this chapter, however, you'll learn to use evaluation along with other techniques for analyzing how to best present what you think. You'll learn to *build* an argument. And that doesn't necessarily mean picking a side and then developing your case, as you'll discover in the next section.

Two Sides to Every Argument?

TV talk shows stage "discussions" between proponents of diametrically opposed positions. Academic debating teams pit those for and those against. We are nurtured on language like *win* or *lose, right* and *wrong,* and *either/or.* It's tempting to see the world this way, as neatly divided into truth and falsehood, light and dark. Reducing issues to two sides simplifies the choices. But one of the things that literature—and all art—teaches us is the delightful and nagging complexity of things. By inclination and upbringing, Huck Finn is a racist, and there's plenty of evidence in *Huckleberry Finn* that his treatment of Jim confirms it. Yet there are moments in the novel when we see a transcendent humanity in Huck, and we can see that he may be a racist, *but* . . . It is this qualification—this modest word *but*—that trips us up in the steady march toward certainty. Rather than *either/or,* can it be *both/and*? Instead of two sides to every issue, might there be thirteen?

Here's an example:

One side: General education requirements are a waste of time because they are often irrelevant to students' major goal in getting a college education—getting a good job.

The other side: General education requirements are invaluable because they prepare students to be enlightened citizens, more fully prepared to participate in democratic culture.

It's easy to imagine a debate between people who hold these positions, and it wouldn't be uninteresting. But it *would* be misleading to think that these are the only two possible positions on general education requirements in American universities. One of the reasons why people are drawn to arguing is that it can be a method of discovery, and one of the most useful discoveries is some side to the story that doesn't fall neatly into the usual opposed positions. The route to these discoveries is twofold: *initially withholding judgment* and *asking questions.*

For instance, what might be goals of a university education other than helping students get a good job and making them enlightened citizens? Is it possible that a university can do both? Are general education courses the only route to enlightenment? Are there certain situations in which the vocational motives of students are inappropriate? Are there certain contexts—say, certain students at particular schools at a particular point in their education—when general education requirements might be waived or modified?

All of these questions, and more, tend to unravel the two sides of the argument and expose them for what they often are: *starting points* for an inquiry into the question, *What good are general education requirements?*

To argue well is an act of imagination, not a picking of sides.

In presenting their arguments, then, the best argument essays make a clear claim, but they do it by bowing respectfully to the complexity of the subject, examining it from a variety of perspectives, not just two opposing poles. And you will come to appreciate that wonderful complexity by keeping an open mind.

MOTIVES FOR WRITING AN ARGUMENT

Classical rhetoricians like Plato, Aristotle, and Cicero had a great deal to say about how to argue well, and while their focus was largely on public speaking, their ideas are foundational for a modern understanding of argument. For Aristotle, there were three arenas for persuasion—before the courts, before legislators and others who make public policy, and at social occasions. The purpose of each varied. For example, court arguments involved defending or accusing someone, or arguing about past events; the purpose of legislative persuasion was to exhort or dissuade about a future action; and persuasion at social occasions focused on praise or blame, or arguments about the present.

Of course, there are plenty of other reasons to argue. In academic writing, the purpose of argument is usually to establish the truth of something. Modern advertising, the most common medium of modern persuasion, attempts to influence people's behaviors. Generally speaking, you can distinguish between these two purposes—to establish the validity of a certain way of seeing things and the desire to move people to action—but because the persuasive essay you will be writing in this chapter can do both, we won't make much of the distinction between these two purposes here.

Whatever its purpose, people often have quite strong feelings about arguing. Some of these feelings may originate, like mine, in negative experiences with a parent or other adult who seemed condescending when we expressed naive or poorly developed opinions. Some scholars maintain that *agonistic* forms of argument, or those that seem to emphasize the contest between ideas and those who hold them, are particularly masculine approaches because they focus on power rather than cooperation, and proclaiming rather than listening. Yet some people have always loved arguing. My father did, and not just because he was confident in the game; my father genuinely enjoyed matching wits and logic, looking for faulty reasoning or indefensible claims.

Arguing is a civic duty. In fact, it is an essential activity in any democratic culture, and it's certainly a major element of academic discourse; academic argument is one of the key means of making new knowledge. Argument is also commonplace in relationships. Who hasn't argued with a spouse, a partner, a friend? In fact, one Web site on the Internet sponsored by the magazine *Psychology Today,* http://psychologytoday.psychtests.com/tests/arguing_style r_access.html, offers an arguing style test that analyzes how constructive you are in dealing with relationship conflicts. Therapists and counselors share the conviction that arguing is a natural part of intimate relationships and that much more harm can come from *avoiding* conflict rather than facing it. It's all in *how* you do it, they say.

Knowing how to argue well has practical value, even if you don't become a lawyer. It might help you make the best case to a local legislator to support the bill providing tuition relief to students, or even bargaining with the used-car dealer for a better price on that black convertible Mazda Miata. Understanding argument helps you find the flaws in *other people's* arguments as well. Knowing how to analyze an argument gives me a language to talk about the flawed arguments in the letters to the editor in *The Idaho Statesman,* and it also helps me thoughtfully and critically read articles and essays that make claims.

Finally, the most important motive behind writing and studying argument is that you care about something. Throughout this book, I've argued that the personal motive for writing is the most powerful one of all; in this case, you're passionate about a question or an issue, and building a written argument channels that passion into prose that can make a difference.

THE ARGUMENT AND ACADEMIC WRITING

Argumentative writing is one of the most common of all academic forms. One reason for this is that the ability to argue well requires some command of subject matter. But there is another motive for mastering argument in academic settings, however, and it has less to do with proving that you know your stuff. Argument is really about trying to get at the truth.

This is an open-ended as well as a closed process; it involves suspending judgment *and* coming to conclusions, hearing what has already been said *and* discovering what you think. Dialectical thinking—a process you've applied to all kinds of writing in *The Curious Writer,* from the personal essay to the proposal—is just as useful in crafting an argument. It will help you discover what you think, consider other points of view, and shape your work so it's convincing to others. The dialectical process, along with those habits of mind central to academic inquiry—particularly suspending judgment and tolerating ambiguity—will help you as a writer get to the truth of things as you see it.

Argument is an essential activity in any democratic culture, and it's certainly a major element of academic discourse; academic argument is one of the key means of making new knowledge.

In college, the audiences for your arguments are often your instructors. As experts in a particular discipline, professors argue all the time. They're not simply trying to be contrary but trying to get at the truth. Arguing is the main way that the academic community makes knowledge.

Notice I used the word *make.* While it often seems that the facts we take for granted are immutable truths—as enduring as the granite peaks I can see through my office window—things aren't often that way at all. Our knowledge of things—how the planet was formed, the best ways to save endangered species, the meaning of a classic novel, how to avoid athletic injuries—are all ideas that are *contested.* They are less mountains than the glaciers that carved them, and in some cases the sudden earthquakes that bring them down. The primary tool for shaping and even changing what we know is argument.

Richard Fulkerson writes that he "wants students to see argument in a larger, less militant, and more comprehensive context—one in which the goal is not victory, but a good decision, one in which all arguers are at risk of needing to alter their views, one in which a participant takes seriously and fairly the views different from his or her own." This is how I'd like you to approach argument within the persuasive essay. This form will challenge you to make arguments that might be convincing to a range of readers, including those who might not agree with your claims. The argument essay is also an invitation to consider how you feel about local issues and controversies as well as national or even international debates that might have some effect on how you live.

FEATURES OF THE FORM

Generally speaking, persuasive writing can take many forms. Indeed, reviews and proposals, two essays addressed earlier in this book, both represent different types of persuasive writing. The argument essay we are covering in this chapter, however, more obviously embodies persuasive writing than either of these two other forms. This essay typically makes explicit claims and backs them up with hard evidence. It also employs the well-established rhetorical devices and the reasoning of formal argumentation in the effort to sway readers to its point of view. However, unlike more formal academic papers, the argument you'll be writing in this chapter is intended for a more general audience. It's the kind of piece you might see in your local newspaper, or in a magazine. *Newsweek*'s "My Turn" column is an excellent example. (See Figure 7.3 for a comparison of argument essays.)

Rhetorical Context	Academic Argument Essay	Informal Argument Essay
Audience	Academic discourse community	Publication's readers
Speaker	You as a member of above	You as an authority on subject
Purpose	To demonstrate your authority	To make something happen
Subject	Of academic interest	Of community interest
Voice	Conventional, academic	Personal, informed
Research	Always	Usually
Citations	Yes	No
Length	Varies, usually 8–25 pages	Varies, usually 500–1,000 words
How to read	Slowly, thoughtfully	Rapidly, mining for meaning

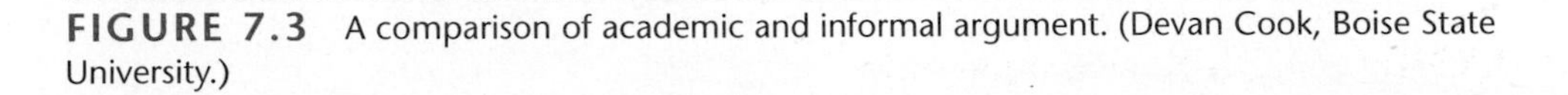

FIGURE 7.3 A comparison of academic and informal argument. (Devan Cook, Boise State University.)

Here are some the features of the informal argument essay:

- *Op-ed essays are often relatively brief treatments of a topic.* Readers of newspapers and many magazines read fast. They want to quickly get the gist of an essay or article and move on to the next story. In addition, space is often limited, particularly in newspapers. As a result, the op-ed or opinion piece rarely exceeds 1,000 words, or about four double-spaced manuscript pages. Longer arguments may be harder to write because you have to provide deeper analysis of your key claims and more evidence, but don't underestimate the difficulty of writing persuasive essays like the op-ed. They must be concise, direct, and well-crafted.
- *Subject matter often focuses on issues of public concern.* The magazines and newspapers that publish argument essays typically report on news, events, or issues that might affect a lot of people. Not surprisingly, then, writers of these essays are keen observers of public debates and controversies. While a nationally syndicated essayist such as George Will may write about the federal budget deficit or the need for more troops in Iraq, a locally grounded writer may focus on an issue affecting a university campus, city hall, or state government, although sometimes writers find a local angle on a national controversy.
- *An op-ed piece has a central claim or proposition.* Sometimes we also call this a *thesis,* a term that's a holdover from the scientific terminology that dominated American scholarship from the end of the nineteenth century. Classical arguments, the kind many of us wrote in high school, usually state this central claim or thesis in the introduction. But many arguments, particularly op-ed essays that rely on narrative structure or explore the answer to a question or problem, may feature the thesis in the middle or at the end of the essay.
- *The central claim is based on one or more premises or assumptions.* You already know something about this from the discussion earlier in the chapter. Basically, a premise suggests that something is true *because* of something else; it expresses the relationship between *what* you claim and *why* you believe that claim to be true. This is discussed at greater length later in the chapter.
- *The op-ed essay relies on evidence that a general audience will believe.* All arguments should use evidence appropriate for a particular audience. Academic writers in marine biology, for example, rely on data collected in the field and analyzed statistically because this kind of evidence is most persuasive to other marine biologists. Anecdotes or personal observation alone simply won't cut it in the *Journal of Marine Biology.* But the persuasive essay's more general audience finds a greater range of evidence convincing, including personal experience and observation. Writers of persuasive essays are likely to do the kind of research you

use to write research papers—digging up statistics, facts, and quotations on a topic.

- *Op-ed essays sometimes invite or encourage a response.* Earlier I noted a broad distinction between the purposes of argument: (1) to establish the validity of a writer's way of seeing what's true and (2) to move or persuade an audience to act a certain way. The second purpose is most obvious in the advertisement, which is a visual argument that asks viewers to *do* something—buy a Jeep or change toilet bowl cleaners. But op-ed essays sometimes ask for or imply a course of action readers should take. An op-ed piece might attempt to change the views and behaviors of political leaders, or influence how people vote for them. It might urge support for a school bond issue, or encourage fellow students to protest against the elimination of an academic program. But even academic articles invite reader response in several ways: they encourage other scholars to examine some part of the question that wasn't addressed by the present research, or they offer claims that can be contested in other articles. Put simply, most argumentative forms are out to change people's behavior and attitudes.
- *Readers won't respond unless they know what's at stake.* An essential element of argument is establishing why a certain action, policy, or idea *matters.* How will opposition to the administration's strip-mining policies in West Virginia and Kentucky make a difference in the quality of life in those states, but even more important, why should someone in Boise, Idaho, care? The best arguments are built to carefully establish, sometimes in quite practical terms, how a certain action, belief, or idea might make a difference in the lives of those who are the argument's audience.

ARGUMENT

Ellen Goodman, whose op-ed essays appear in more than 375 newspapers nationwide, often writes about the intersection between public events and her personal life, and the following essay, "Getting Real in the Classroom," is no exception. While her essay, like many, is sparked by the release of a new public report—in this case on the challenges boys face in the classroom—she finally bends her discussion towards her own grandchildren. What Goodman concludes from watching her granddaughter, 4, and grandson, 3, is that "differences among boys and among girls are greater than the differences between boys and girls." A sharply honed line like that is typical of Goodman's writing. But so is the clarity of her reasoning. In the essay that follows, notice how much time she takes to come to conclusions about the issue. Along the way, she assembles evidence that unravels the argument that there is a "boy crisis" in schools, preparing us for her argument that the underperformance of boys is not really the problem.

Getting Real in the Classroom

Ellen Goodman

1 Too bad the study came out during summer vacation. We tend to forget whatever we learned by the time school rolls around again. But there's something worth retaining over the long, lazy days: The "boy crisis" in education is not what it was cranked up to be.

2 Let's go to the videotape. The first salvo in the battle of the classroom sexes probably came six years ago with the publication of "The War Against Boys." Christina Hoff Sommers's screen opened with the dire warning: "It's a bad time to be a boy in America."

3 Since then, things have gone from "bad" to worse. We've had documentaries and cover stories, psychologists and sociologists, scholars and ideologues offering a horror story of boys in academic free-fall.

4 On the seesaw of this school playground, the message is that as girls went up, boys went down. The social changes that were good for the goose were bad for the gander. The common wisdom is that boys have fallen behind. Behind girls.

5 The causes and cures for the boy crisis are all over the map. The problem is either feminism that demonizes boyishness, or sexism that boxes boys in. It's either nature that hard-wires the boy brain to learn differently, or nurture that creates what has been called a "biologically disrespectful model of education." It's that boys need more discipline, or less.

6 Last December, Doug Anglin, a senior from Milton High School in Massachusetts, filed a lawsuit claiming sex discrimination in the whole system. "If you sit down, follow orders and listen to what they say, you'll do well and get good grades," he complained. "Men naturally rebel against this." (Where? In the Army?)

7 Now a Washington think tank, the Education Sector, has performed a crisis intervention. "The real story," it reports, "is not bad news about boys doing worse; it's good news about girls doing better." Using data from the National Assessment of Educational Progress—a.k.a. "the nation's report card"—the report found that girls score higher in reading and writing and boys score higher in math and science. But girls are closing the math gap faster than boys are closing the writing gap. It turns out that boys aren't doing worse in school. They are doing better than ever. But girls—with apologies to the grammar police—are doing more better.

8 In college, too, more men than ever are enrolling, but at a slower pace than women. Women do get 57 percent of the bachelor's degrees—including a large number of older women returning to school—but the gap at traditional four-year colleges is much less and, let us remember, boys are still a majority in the Ivy League.

9 The "boy crisis" isn't exactly a myth, says Sara Mead, author of the report. It's a "some boys crisis." Race and class are the real issues. In Boston, for example, 100 white males graduate for every 104 white females. But 100 black males graduate for 139 black females. "It's sexier to think about gender," says Mead. "It's something people like debating." Americans, she fears, "have gotten used to thinking poor and minority students do poorly in school. Whereas if you hear that boys are doing worse, it's startling." Especially to the middle-class object of this anxiety attack.

As the besotted grandmother of a 4-year-old girl and a 3-year-old boy, I'm not about to deny gender differences. Moreover, I'm uneasy about the massive drugging of little boys for whatever is labeled attention deficit disorder. And we know too little about the different pace of development or the meaning of new brain research. I also worry that something in the culture is teaching poor Hispanic and African-American boys that being smart isn't masculine. Remember when being smart wasn't feminine? Is that message percolating up through the boy culture? 10

But in the same grandmother role, I see that differences among boys and among girls are greater than differences between boys and girls. And I don't think the "boy crisis" should let us stop worrying about why girls lose their interest in math or why women with those bachelor's degrees still earn less than their male counterparts. 11

Last week, there was some good news from New York, a city with a high school graduation rate of only 58 percent. The 15 small schools started in the city in an experiment posted a graduation rate of 73 percent. Could size and personal attention matter more than gender? 12

The battle of the sexy ideas is a distraction from the struggle for the minds of the younger generation. We need to worry more about children one by one. And less about whether boys are losing their place at the head of the class. 13

Inquiring into the Essay

Explore, explain, evaluate, and reflect about "Getting Real in the Classroom."

1. The performance of boys versus girls in school is a topic you already know something about, though you probably haven't thought about it much. After all, you're either a boy or girl and you've spent years in school. In your journal, explore your own experience of the ways you've noticed gender matters in school. As a boy, or as a girl, were you discouraged from doing or achieving something academically? Were there ever moments that you felt being one sex or the other gave you certain advantages or disadvantages? Fastwrite about this. If you can, begin with a story. At the end of five to seven minutes, skip a line, and compose an answer to this question: *Based on your experience in school, how would you respond to the claim that boys in school are falling behind partly because girls are advancing?*
2. Analyze Goodman's argument and explain two things: her main claim(s) and the premises or assumptions behind it (them). To refresh your memory about these terms and what they mean, consult "Features of the Form" earlier in the chapter. What basic argument strategies does Goodman seem to use? (See the "Inquiring into the Details: Some Basic Argument Strategies" box.)
3. A critic of Goodman's argument here might claim that she's being hypocritical. When girls were academically behind, the women's movement made much about how gender was a factor in their performance. Teachers, for example, were said to discourage girls from pursuing science

while encouraging boys. Now Goodman is too quick to dismiss arguments that gender is a factor in boys' scholastic performance, and that seems unfair. How would you evaluate this claim?

4. Do at least one more full reading of the essay, from beginning to end. While you do, pay attention to what you notice in the essay while rereading it that you didn't really notice in earlier readings. How does your own opinion about an author's argument influence the way you reread it? Do you read more selectively? Does the rereading reinforce what you already think or challenge it in some way?

INQUIRING INTO THE DETAILS

SOME BASIC ARGUMENT STRATEGIES

- **Argument from Generalization:** What I've seen or observed of a particular group is true of the group as a whole. *Risk: Are you sure that what you've observed is typical of the larger population?*
- **Argument from Analogy:** If it is true in one situation it's likely true in another similar situation. *Risk: Are the situations* really *similar?*
- **Argument from Cause:** If one thing always seems present with something else, then one probably causes the other. *Risk: Is cause and effect* really *the relationship between the two things?*
- **Argument from Authority:** If an expert said it, it's true. *Risk: Is the expertise of the authority* really *relevant to the question at issue?*
- **Argument from Principle:** This general principle (which most of us agree with) applies in this case. *Risk: Is there* really *agreement on the rightness of the principle, and does it actually apply in this specific context?*

Adapted from Richard Fulkerson, *Teaching the Argument in Writing*. Urbana, IL: National Council of Teachers of English, 1996.

ARGUMENT

With grace and intelligence, conservative columnist George F. Will writes about a range of topics from the federal budget to baseball. In this essay, Will strikes close to home for me—and possibly for you, too—when he sharply criticizes writing instruction in the United States, an approach he calls the "growth model," one that Will argues offers no "defensible standards" for good writing and emphasizes the "undirected flowering of the student's personality." He bemoans the absence of instruction in grammar and style.

You are the students Will is talking about in this op-ed essay. Does he accurately describe your experience in this and other writing classes? For example, do you also sense that process matters more than content in composition? Do you agree with Will's basic premise that students graduating from high school are "functionally illiterate"?

The "Growth Model" and the Growth of Illiteracy

George F. Will

Summertime, and the living is easy. Schools are empty, so the damage has stopped. During this seasonal respite from the education system's subtraction from national literacy, consider why America may be graduating from its high schools its first generation worse educated than the generation that came before. Particularly, why is it common for high school graduates to be functionally illiterate, uncertain when reading, and incapable of writing even a moderately complicated paragraph? 1

Heather Mac Donald knows one reason: More and more schools refuse, on the basis of various political and ethical and intellectual theories, to teach writing. Her essay, "Why Johnny Can't Write," in the summer 1995 issue of *The Public Interest* quarterly, is a hair-raising peek into what she calls "one overlooked corner of the academic madhouse." 2

Mac Donald, a contributing editor of the Manhattan Institute's *City Journal*, explains how the teaching of writing has been shaped by "an indigestible stew of 1960s liberationist zeal, 1970s deconstructionist nihilism, and 1980s multicultural proselytizing." Indeed many teachers now consider the traditional idea of teaching to be intellectually suspect and morally offensive because it is tainted by the authoritarian idea that there are defensible standards and by the inegalitarian idea that some people do things better than others. 3

At a 1966 conference organized by the Modern Language Association and the National Conference of Teachers of English, the "transmission model" of teaching composition was rejected in favor of the "growth model." The idea of transmitting skills and standards was inherently threatening to the values of that decade—spontaneity, authenticity, sincerity, equality, and self-esteem. Education in the new era of enlightenment was to be not a matter of putting things into students—least of all putting in anything that suggested a hierarchy of achievement—but of letting things out. Nothing must interfere with the natural, undirected flowering of the student's personality. One interference would be a teacher cast as an authority figure rather than in the role of supportive, nurturing friend. 4

The "growth model" was, Mac Donald notes, impeccably liberationist: Who was to judge anyone else's "growth"? And that model "celebrated inarticulateness and error as proof of authenticity." This was convenient for evolving racial policies. In 1966 the City University of New York began the first academic affirmative action program. Open admissions would soon follow, as would the idea that it is cultural imperialism to deny full legitimacy to anything called "Black English." Simultaneously came the idea that demands for literacy oppress the masses and condition them to accept the coercion of capitalism. 5

"Process" became more important than content in composition. Students would "build community" as they taught each other. A reactionary emphasis on the individual was replaced by a progressive emphasis on the collectivity. But, says Mac Donald, 6 there have been difficulties: "Students who have been told in their writing class to let their deepest selves loose on the page and not worry about syntax, logic, or form have trouble adjusting to other classes." Thus a student at St. Anselm's College complains that in her humanities class, "I have to remember a certain format and I have to back up every general statement with specific examples."

7 Academic fads have followed hard upon one another, all supplying reasons why it is unnecessary—no, antisocial—to teach grammar and style. The deconstructionists preached that language is of incurably indeterminate meaning. The multiculturalists, who preach the centrality of identity politics in every endeavor, argue that the rules of language are permeated by the values of the dominant class that makes society's rules and also makes victims. Mac Donald says, "The multicultural writing classroom is a workshop on racial and sexual oppression. Rather than studying possessive pronouns, students are learning how language silences women and blacks."

8 As student writing grows worse, Mac Donald notes, the academic jargon used to rationalize the decline grows more pompous. For example, a professor explains that "postprocess, postcognitive theory . . . represents literacy as an ideological arena and composing as a cultural activity by which writers position and reposition themselves in relation to their own and others' subjectivities, discourses, practices, and institutions."

9 Nowadays the mere mention of "remedial" courses is coming to be considered insensitive about "diversity," and especially insulting and unfair to students from American "cultures" where "orality" is dominant. So at some colleges remedial courses are now called ESD courses—English as a Second Dialect.

10 The smugly self-absorbed professoriate that perpetrates all this academic malpractice is often tenured and always comfortable. The students on the receiving end are always cheated and often unemployable. It is summertime, and the nation is rightly uneasy about autumn.

Inquiring into the Essay

Use the four methods of inquiry to think about Will's essay.

1. For five minutes, fastwrite about your own experience with writing instruction by telling the story of the teacher or teachers that had the most impact on how you think about yourself as a writer and reader.
2. Describe the argument that Will makes in this essay. Begin with a summary of one of his basic claims, then a reason behind the claim, and then list the evidence he offers to support them both. Compare these with other students in the class and analyze the effectiveness of Will's argument. What are the strongest elements of his argument? The weakest?
3. Compose a 250-word letter to the editor that responds in some way to Will's article.

4. Reflect on your own experiences in this composition course. Would Will be scornful of this course—and perhaps this text—and its approach to teaching writing? What have been the most and least effective approaches to teaching reading and writing that you've experienced in high school, or perhaps even in this class?

ARGUMENT

When Erin Aubry Kaplan was hired by *The Los Angeles Times* to be one of their regular columnists, it was a historic move; unlike most other major metropolitan newspapers, the *Times* had never employed an African American op-ed writer. While her work often focuses on issues of race, a relevant topic in such a diverse city as Los Angeles, Kaplan has also written on the arts, parenting, and other topics. Her early personal essay, "Blue Like Me," on race and depression, won Kaplan an award for literary journalism, and she was runner-up recently for Los Angeles Columnist of the Year.

In the essay that follows, Kaplan writes about the "politics of hair." She condemns the move by some corporations and even black colleges to enforce bans on certain kinds of hairstyles, especially those like dreadlocks and braids, that these institutions see as "threatening." The essay is built on a number of assumptions, one of which is that there is, in fact, a "politics of hair," particularly for African Americans, and that this is closely tied to feelings about racial identity. Do you share this assumption?

Still Trying to Kick the Kink

Erin Aubry Kaplan

1 When I was young, one of the first things I learned about myself was that I had "good" hair. It was curly and close enough to the texture of a white person's hair to not need pressing, hot-combing, greasing or some other method of straightening that extremely curly black hair—also known as kinky or "bad" hair—needed before it could venture out in public. Yet even my hair was not quite good enough.

2 Every Sunday my mother washed it, set it on rollers the size of frozen orange-juice cans and put me under a hairdryer for a couple of hours. When it was over, I had the ultimate "do"—smooth and swingy, with none of the wayward curl or frizz that would have confirmed my blackness as much as the Marlo Thomas look cleverly denied it.

3 I eventually learned early that this "denial" look was the ideal for black girls and women, and though I had to do less denying than most, I was not exempt. I also learned that good hair on black people was considered good for reasons much deeper than convenience—it connoted assimilation, sophistication, intelligence, refinement, success. Even when I jettisoned the whole hair ritual and got a short, punky cut, I did it more to reject the limitations of an old paradigm than to celebrate a new one.

4 I might have saved my protest. Denial is still at the core of black hair fashion, which in turn is at the still-unstable core of black identity and acceptability in the United States

in 2006. Although braids, dreadlocks and other natural black hairstyles have become more visible, perms, weaves and extensions for black women have become ubiquitous.

5 In short, the debate about the best choices for "black hair," always charged, is flaring up again. A Louisiana sheriff said last week that anyone on the streets in dreadlocks "can expect to be getting a visit from a sheriff's deputy" because a murder suspect answering that description remained at large. In April, Susan L. Taylor, the iconic editorial director of *Essence* magazine, canceled a campus speech when she discovered the college forbids its students to wear "unusual" hairstyles—including braids, which are Taylor's signature look. This was noteworthy because the college was Hampton University, one of the nation's oldest historically black campuses. Then it was discovered that *Black Enterprise* magazine had a similar ban for student interns.

6 The message is clear. If blacks want to have a chance in the increasingly unforgiving corporate world, they will have to shave off their edges—starting with their hair. To Taylor and to many others, including me, such a message implies a false choice between assimilation and self-affirmation. What looks like practicality is, in fact, more denial.

7 What's troubling is that, by being forced to change their hair, black people once again are being forced to shoulder the burden of proof: We're not as fearsome as we look. It's up to us to mitigate our dark skin and ethnic features by framing them with hair that's as neat and unethnic as possible.

8 That the requirement comes from black institutions only makes it more disturbing. Yes, they are inherently conservative institutions, but they understand the political significance of hair. They should know that this is not the same as a dress code that calls for a suit and tie (understandable), or a Cosby-like antipathy toward trendy, sloppy, vaguely criminal black fashion such as baggy pants or expensive sneakers (understandable, but misplaced).

9 Unlike any of those looks, braids and other natural styles have long been associated with socially conscious and self-confident black people, the kind who would fit nicely in corporate settings that like to say diversity is a priority. But companies tend not to hire them, and black people with those hairstyles tend to gravitate toward work that's necessarily non-corporate. Yet surely we have all earned the right to wear our hair as we please. The freedom we're still working toward is supposed to be aesthetic as well as economic.

10 Mablean Ephriam, the black TV judge from Fox's popular "Divorce Court"—who says she lost her contract this year partly because of irreconcilable hair differences with the company—perhaps said it best in a contentious parting statement that concluded with a quote from Maya Angelou: "And still I rise." I trust she meant her hair.

Inquiring into the Essay

Explore, explain, evaluate, and reflect on Kaplan's essay.

1. You don't have to be an African American to feel that there are social meanings to certain hairstyles. Explore your own experience with this. Tell yourself a story about a time in your life when you were most interested in what your hair said about you, or when you witnessed the effects of the "politics of hair." Fastwrite for five minutes in your notebook, and

then skip a line, and compose an answer to the following question: *Based on your experience, would you agree with the assumption that there is a "politics of hair," and that this is something worth being concerned about?*

2. In the beginning of the essay, Kaplan concedes that there was a time when she engaged in the "denial look," or styling her hair to present a muted racial identity. How does this concession affect the persuasiveness of her essay? Explain what impact a writer's concession that she might be a part of the problem she's discussing has on the strength of her argument. When might such concessions be unnecessary?
3. I mentioned earlier that one assumption behind this essay is that hairstyles do have political and social meanings. Evaluate Kaplan's argument by identifying other assumptions on which her essay rests. Are there any of these that most readers might not necessarily agree with? Should these, if any, have been explicitly discussed to make her argument more persuasive?
4. If you're not African American or a minority of any kind, reading an essay like this one can be challenging because it might feel presumptuous to believe that you truly understand the Other's experience. Did you feel this way reading Kaplan's essay? How does one bridge this gap when encountering readings from writers of other races or other cultures?

Seeing the Form

THE "IMAGETEXT" AS ARGUMENT

While model Kate Moss is likely disturbed by the appropriation of her image by advocates in the pro-anorexia ("pro-ana") movement, Moss's picture along with those of other celebrities such as Calista Flockhart, Mary-Kate Olsen, and Keira Knightley appear as "thinspiration" on Web sites that argue that eating disorders are a "lifestyle choice," not a disease. Some of these images (though not this one) are digitally altered to make the models seem even thinner than they really are. In a recent article on the "imagetexts" used by these controversial Web sites, Robin Jensen observes that images rarely argue in isolation, a phenomenon that is particularly relevant to the Web, which often combines pictures and verbal texts. Jensen notes that when pictures like this one of Kate Moss are given a new "visual frame," quite different from the one originally intended, the meaning of the picture can be manipulated. Imagine, for instance, that the Kate Moss photograph appeared in a "thinspiration" gallery of celebrity photographs on a "pro-ana" Web site, and included the following caption: "Maintaining a weight that is 15 percent below your expected body weight fits the criteria for anorexia, so most models, according to medical standards, fit into the categeory of being anorexic." Analyze this "imagetext" rhetorically. How does this picture of Moss combined with the caption serve the purpose of the "pro-ana" movement? What message is it meant to convey and is it persuasive to its intended audience?

Kate Moss in ultra-thin pose.

THE WRITING PROCESS

INQUIRY PROJECT: Writing an Argument

Now that you've explored various approaches to persuasion and argument, try your hand at writing an argument essay. Remember that these are brief (700- to 1,000-word) essays meant for a general audience. Imagine, for example, that you're writing an op-ed piece for the campus newspaper, the local daily, or *The New York Times.* Your essay should be lively and logical, with a strong personal voice, and also have the following features:

- It focuses implicitly or explicitly on a question. This is always the starting point for inquiry in any genre. In an argumentative essay, you are providing evidence to support a particular answer to this question.
- The essay makes clear premises and claims, including one central claim around which the draft is organized. In other words, *the essay should be clear about what it is asking its readers to do or to believe.*
- It provides specific and appropriate evidence in support of the claims, including research when relevant.
- The essay should address one or more of the counterarguments offered by those who take a different position from yours.

Thinking About Subjects

If you haven't yet figured out a way to make your composition instructor's eyes roll, announce that you want to write an argument essay on gun control. Gun control, abortion rights, and other hot-button public controversies often make the list of banned topics for student essays. This is not because they aren't important public debates. Instead, the problem is much more that the writer has likely already made up his mind and sees the chance to ascend a soapbox. In addition, polarized debates produce such a mass of information that it's difficult for a writer to locate some territory in the topic that isn't already filled with voices repeating the same things to each other. There is so much background noise that it's almost impossible to hear yourself think.

Now, I have my own favorite soapboxes; people with strong convictions do. But as you think about subjects for your essay, consider that the soapbox may not be the best vantage point for practicing dialectical thinking. If you've already made up your mind, will you be open to discovery? If you just want to line up ducks—assembling evidence to support an unwavering belief—will you be encouraged to think deeply or differently? Will you be inclined to filter the voices you hear rather than consider a range of points of view?

The best persuasive essays often emerge from the kind of open-ended inquiry that you might have used writing the personal essay. What do you want to understand better? What issue or question makes you wonder? What controversies are you and your friends talking about? Be alert to possible subjects that you might write about *not* because you already know what you think, but because you want to find out. Or consider a subject that you might have feelings about but feel uninformed, lacking the knowledge to know exactly what you think.

The best argument essays make a clear claim, but they do it by bowing respectfully to the complexity of the subject, examining it from a variety of perspectives, not just two opposing poles.

Generating Ideas

Begin exploring possible subjects for an argument essay by generating material in your notebook. This should be an open-ended process, a chance to use your creative side without worrying too much about making sense or trying to prejudge the value of the writing or the subjects you generate. In a sense, this is an invitation to play around. Later, you can judge the material you've generated and choose a topic that interests you.

Listing Prompts. Lists can be rich sources of triggering topics. Let them grow freely, and when you're ready, use an item as the focus of another list or an episode of fastwriting. The following prompts should get you started.

1. In your journal, make a quick list of issues that have provoked disagreements between groups of people in your hometown or local community.

2. Make a quick list of issues that have provoked disagreements on your college's campus.

3. Make another list of issues that have created controversy between groups of people in your state.

4. Think about issues—local, statewide, regional, national, or even international—that have touched your life, or could affect you in some way in the following areas: environmental, health care, civil rights, business, education, crime, or sports. Make a quick list of questions within these areas you wonder about. For example, *Will there be enough drinking water in my well if the valley continues to develop at this rate?* Or *Will I be able to afford to send my children to the state college in twelve years?* Or *Do new domestic antiterrorism rules threaten my privacy when I'm online?* Or *Will I benefit from affirmative action laws when I apply to law school?*

5. Jot down a list of the classes you're taking this semester. Then make a quick list of topics that prompt disagreements among people in the field that you're studying. For example, in your political science class, did you learn that there are debates about the usefulness of the electoral college? In your biology class, have you discussed global warming? In your women's studies class, did you read about Title 9 and how it affects female athletes?

Fastwriting Prompts. Remember, fastwriting is a great way to stimulate creative thinking. Turn off your critical side and let yourself write "badly." Don't worry too much about what you're going to say before you say it. Write fast, letting language lead for a change.

1. Write for five minutes beginning with one of the questions you raised in Question 4 in the "Listing Prompts" section. Think through writing about when you first began to be concerned about the question, how you think it might affect you, and what you currently understand are the key questions this issue raises. Do you have tentative feelings or beliefs about it?

2. In a seven-minute fastwrite, explore the differences between your beliefs and the beliefs of your parents. Tell yourself the story of how your own beliefs about some question evolved, perhaps moving away from your parents' position. Can you imagine the argument you might make to help them understand your point of view?

3. Choose an item from any of the lists you generated in the "Listing Prompts" section as a starting place for a fastwrite. Explore what you understand about the issue, what are the key questions, and how you feel about it at the moment.

One Student's Response

BEN'S JOURNAL

FASTWRITE

WHY DO STUDENTS SEEM SO APATHETIC ABOUT POLITICS?

We're in the midst of presidential elections and I can't seem to get anyone interested in talking about it. I wonder why that is? Are college students more cynical about politics and politicians than other groups? It seems like it to me. I can think of a few reasons right off the bat. First, college students are mostly young (though certainly not all at this school) so they don't have the habit of going to the polls. Whenever a generation loses the habit of voting, I'll bet the next generation is even more likely to be apathetic. I also think my generation has seen so few effective politicians. My dad talks about being inspired by the likes of JFK but I can't think of too many national politicians that have inspired me as much as JFK inspired him. I also wonder if there is that basic sense of powerlessness. We just don't feel like much of anything makes a difference. I wonder if that is also reflected in volunteerism. Do students volunteer less than they used to? Have to check on that. I guess I just find politics kind of interesting. I wonder why? Hmmm . . . I think it had something to do with my Dad. But I guess I also have this basic belief in voting as an important part of being a citizen. Seems like one of the best ways to be patriotic . . .

Visual Prompts. Sometimes the best way to generate material is to see what we think represented in something other than sentences. Boxes, lines, webs, clusters, arrows, charts, and even pictures and sketches can help us see more of the landscape of a subject, especially connections between fragments of information that aren't as obvious in prose.

Find an advertisement, poster, or other image with a persuasive purpose and create an argument map (see Figure 7.4, which maps the Guess.com ad on page 234). Choose an image that bothers you for some reason. By visually graphing its implicit argument, you might discover ways to offer a critique or a counterargument in your own essay. Use the first box of the argument map to summarize the main claim of the image you've selected. In the next box, list the (often implicit) reasons or premises behind the claim. Use the word *because* to tease this out. In the next box put the two together, creating a premise and a claim, and then follow this up by listing the evidence the image provides to support the premises and claim. Now use your map to generate a list of quick responses to some of the following questions: *Do you agree with the claim? Do you agree with the premises? Which seems most suspect? Why? What might be a more truthful claim? What might be more accurate premises? Is this an argument you've seen elsewhere? Do the claims and premises represent a way of seeing the world typical of a particular social group? How would you redesign the ad to make it more truthful? What is your argument against this argument?* Use the lists and fastwrites generated from analyzing your argument map to develop an argument of your own.

Research Prompts. By definition, argument essays deal with subjects in which people beyond the writer have a stake. And one of the best ways to collect ideas about such issues is to do a little quick and dirty research. Try some of the following research prompts:

1. Spend a few days reading the letters to the editor in your local paper. What issue has people riled up locally? Is there one that you find particularly interesting?

2. Do a Web search to find op-ed essays written by one or more of the following national columnists: Ellen Goodman, Cal Thomas, George Will, David Broder,

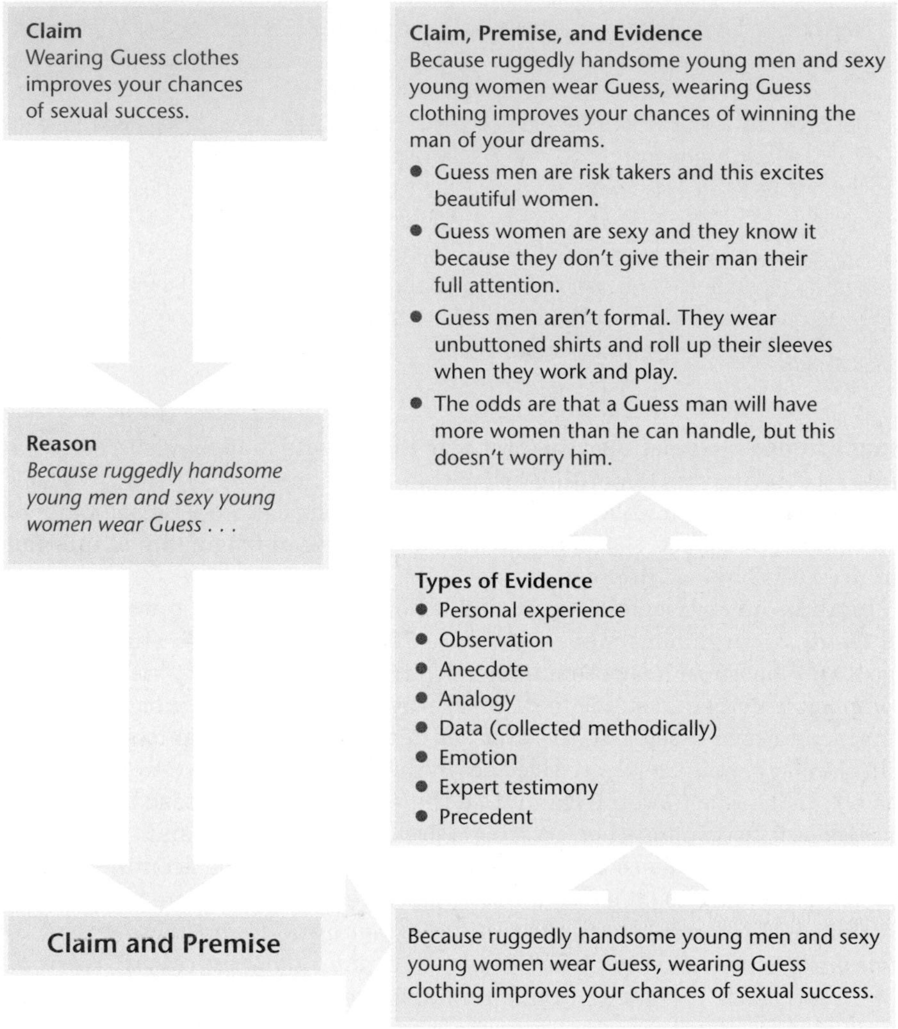

Claim
Wearing Guess clothes improves your chances of sexual success.

Reason
Because ruggedly handsome young men and sexy young women wear Guess . . .

Claim and Premise

Because ruggedly handsome young men and sexy young women wear Guess, wearing Guess clothing improves your chances of sexual success.

Types of Evidence
- Personal experience
- Observation
- Anecdote
- Analogy
- Data (collected methodically)
- Emotion
- Expert testimony
- Precedent

Claim, Premise, and Evidence
Because ruggedly handsome young men and sexy young women wear Guess, wearing Guess clothing improves your chances of winning the man of your dreams.
- Guess men are risk takers and this excites beautiful women.
- Guess women are sexy and they know it because they don't give their man their full attention.
- Guess men aren't formal. They wear unbuttoned shirts and roll up their sleeves when they work and play.
- The odds are that a Guess man will have more women than he can handle, but this doesn't worry him.

FIGURE 7.4 An argument map (see page 234 for Guess.com ad).

Nat Hentoff, Mary McGrory, Molly Ivins, Bob Herbert, or Clarence Page. Read their work with an eye toward topics that interest you.

3. Do a Google search on terms or phrases on an issue that interests you, such as "global warming Greenland glaciers" or "pro-anorexia Web sites." Did you produce any results that make you curious, or make you feel something about the issue, one way or another?

4. Interview people you know—on campus or off—about the public issues that they care most about.

WRITING WITH COMPUTERS

ARGUMENTS ON THE INTERNET

The Internet is a repository of ideas. It is almost always useful to make the Internet a first stop when starting a new writing project in order to determine what others think or believe about a topic. Web sites of organizations reveal how organized cooperative groups treat an issue, Web pages or Web logs (blogs) show the thoughts of individuals, and discussion boards and comments to blog postings can show how multiple people negotiate and debate a topic. Unlike traditional publications, such as books and journals, many of the arguments found on the Internet have not been evaluated or screened by editors. Remember, anyone with a computer and Internet connection can publish ideas and arguments on the Internet. This dynamic gives almost everyone equal access to share beliefs and arguments. This means that new and innovative ideas are often found alongside shallow and unsupported arguments. Always evaluate arguments found on the Internet with a critical viewpoint. If possible, try to validate them with traditional sources.

Judging What You Have

Shift back to your more critical mind and sift through the material you generated. Did you discover a topic that might be interesting for your argument essay? Did you stumble over some interesting questions you'd like to explore further? Did anything you wrote or read make you *feel* something? Evaluate the raw material in your journal and keep the following things in mind as you zero in on a topic for your argument essay.

What's Promising Material and What Isn't? Let's take a critical look at the subjects you've generated so far; what promising topics might be lurking there for an argumentative essay? Consider some of the following as you make your choice.

- *Interest.* This almost goes without saying. But you were warned earlier about seizing on a topic if you already have strong convictions about it. Do you already know what you think? If so, why not choose a topic that initially invites more open-ended inquiry? On the other hand, it matters a lot whether you *care.* What topic might touch your life in some way? Do you have some kind of stake in how the questions are answered?
- *Brevity.* One of the most common flaws of student drafts in all genres is that they attempt to cover too much territory. A more *limited* look at a larger landscape is always best. Because these argument essays are brief, consider topics that you can do justice to in less than a thousand words. As you review potential topics for your essay, can you see how some aspect of a larger question can be addressed by asking a smaller question? For example, the topic of spending on athletic programs at American universities relative to spending

on academic programs raises this obvious question: *Is too much spent on sports?* It's not very difficult to see how this large question can be focused for an effective argument. For example, *Does Boise State University spend too much on its athletic programs and too little on its academic ones?* You can't write a short piece about the negative impact of affirmative action policies on the nation's colleges and universities, but you can write a brief op-ed about the specific impacts on your school.

- *Disagreement.* A topic lends itself to argumentative writing if it leads to disagreement among reasonable people. *Is smoking bad for your health?* was once a question that was debatable, but now pretty much everyone concedes that this question has been answered. *Did the Holocaust really happen?* is a question that only blockheads debate. But the question, *What are the motives of people who deny the Holocaust?* is a question that would generate a range of views.
- *Information.* Is sufficient information available on the topic for you to make a reasonable judgment about what is true? Is it accessible? One great advantage of choosing a local question as the focus for an argumentative essay is that often the people are close by and the relevant information can easily be had. It's also essential that you can obtain information from more than just a single viewpoint on the question.
- *Question.* What makes a topic arguable is that it raises questions to which there are multiple answers. Which of them makes the most sense is at issue. But some questions are merely informational. For example, *How do greenhouse gases contribute to global warming?* is a question that will likely lead to explanations rather than argument. On the other hand, *Is the U.S. rejection of the Kyoto accords on global warming a responsible policy?* is an arguable, rather than informational, question.

Questions About Audience and Purpose. Persuasive writing is a very audience-oriented form. *To whom* you make your case in an argument matters a lot in *how* you make it, but audience also matters in *whether* one topic is a better choice for an essay than another topic. The op-ed essay is written for a more general audience. Your readers are unlikely to be experts on your topic, and they are likely to read your essay quickly rather than slowly and thoughtfully. What does this imply about the best subjects?

- *Do your readers have a stake in the question you're answering?* The word *stake* can be broadly considered. For example, a topic may directly affect the readers of your essay; say you're writing for fellow college students on your campus, all of whom pay tuition, and your topic addresses whether a 12 percent hike in fees is justified. Sometimes, however, you choose a topic because readers need to know that they *do* have a stake in how a question is answered. For instance, the argument that new antiterrorist rules threaten online privacy is something you believe your readers, most of whom surf the Web, should consider.

- *Can you identify what your readers might already believe?* One of the key strategies of persuasion is to find ways to link the values and attitudes of your audience with the position you're encouraging them to believe. Does your potential topic lend itself to this kind of analysis?
- *Is your purpose not only to inform readers but also to encourage them to believe or do something?* As you know by now, one of the things that distinguishes argument essays such as the op-ed piece from other forms of writing is the writer's intention to change his or her audience. Frequently this purpose is quite explicit and even behavioral: vote a certain way, support a certain policy, or *don't* do something like buy a gas-guzzling SUV. Other times, persuasive writing attempts to persuade readers to believe something that may lead to some kind of behavior.

Research Considerations. So you want to look into the controversy over oil drilling in the Arctic National Wildlife Refuge? Your gut reaction is against proposals that would allow oil companies to drill test wells. It seems to be a real can of worms—if you allow testing and then there's momentum for full-scale development, you wonder if the environmental risks will be worth the gain in oil. But you really don't know very much. What are the risks? Is there a significant promise of oil production? How might it affect your region, your state, or the prices at your local Chevron? This is a big subject, of course, and there is lots of information out there. Where do you begin?

Maybe you believe you already know a lot about your topic—you've had enough experience and observations, or perhaps read enough to feel pretty well informed. But if you took my advice to choose a topic about which you might *feel* something but not really know what you *think,* then once you have selected your topic your next step in the process is to collect information.

While writing this argument essay does involve some research, it isn't exactly a research paper. A research paper is a much more extended treatment of a topic that relies on more detailed and scholarly information than is usually needed for an argument essay. In Chapter 9, you'll find information on research strategies that will help you with this project, especially how to conduct effective Internet searches and how to evaluate the sources you find. The section on library research, particularly key references, may also be valuable.

But for the purpose of this essay, you can have a more modest research agenda, and that's when the Web can be especially useful. Because many of the topics ripe for a good argument essay are current, a major source of information will be publications such as newspapers and magazines. As more of these print sources have gone online, the Web has become a central source for topical information. It's a great place to start learning about your topic, but there are hazards. First, the Web can be a trap. Searching and surfing can suck up an enormous amount of time; it can easily become obsessive—"I need just a few more sources and then I'll quit"—or even worse, digressive—"Gee, I just stumbled on a game site . . . it's got Super Mahjongg!" Either of these can become an excuse not to write. The other hazard is the reliability of information on the Web, which is uneven (see "Evaluating Web Sources" in Chapter 9).

Address these pitfalls by making your Web research efficient. Magazines and newspapers are key sources for op-ed essays, and they're likely the best place to begin looking for background information. National issues such as oil drilling in the Arctic National Wildlife Refuge are addressed by national newspapers, which are usually reliable sources of information. Search sites such as *The New York Times* or *The Washington Post* for information on your topic if you think that it might have garnered national attention. In addition, the useful site at http://www.refdesk.com/paper.html lists links for newspapers by state and around the world.

Magazines online are good sources as well, but access to their archives may be limited to subscribers. The university library is useful because it not only subscribes to many magazines but allows you to search them; you may be able retrieve full articles electronically or read them on microfilm. Access to your college's database of magazines is likely online, too, so check the library Web site for more information.

A general search engine such as http://www.google.com will help you find newspapers, magazines, Web sites, and other online publications for background on your topic. Be ready for an avalanche, however. For example, a Google search on the Arctic National Wildlife Refuge turned up nearly 3,000 links.

If you're writing about a campus or community issue, the Web can still be useful, particularly if your campus or local newspapers have sites. State and local governments also post information on the Web (for information on sites, visit State and Local Governments on the Net at http://www.statelocalgov.net/index.cfm). But campus and local issues often call for a different kind of research: basic footwork. The best way to become knowledgeable is to talk to people who are affected by the topic, perhaps people you've identified with particular points of view about it or even other students in your class who may have some knowledge. The local public library, as well as the campus library, can be a valuable source of information on local issues as well.

Narrowing the Question. I've been vaguely aware of the crisis in Medicaid funding—federal health care support for the poor—but the issue really came home when officials told Dorothy Misner, a ninety-two-year-old woman in nearby Nampa, that she would have to gum her food because the state refused to pay for dentures. Probably the best way to make a larger controversy a manageable writing topic is to find a local angle. In this case, for example, the larger question—*Should the national Medicaid program do more to support the poor without health insurance?*—becomes a much narrower question: *Is the state's Medicaid program failing people like Dorothy Misner?* Whenever possible, make big issues smaller by finding some connection to the local.

That isn't always possible, however. Unless you live in Alaska, for instance, the debate over development of the Arctic National Wildlife Refuge is hard to cut as a local issue. Then it becomes important to find a narrower question, something that may not be possible until after you've done a little research. For example, the question, *Should the Arctic National Wildlife Refuge be open to oil development?* could be narrowed by asking, *Are oil company claims about the potential of recoverable oil in the refuge reasonable?*

Another way to narrow the focus of an argument is to find a useful case study, anecdote, or example that somehow typifies some aspect of the issue you want to examine. Suppose you want to write about the impact of oil development on native subsistence hunting in the wildlife refuge. The story of one family, or one local native community's reliance on the nearby caribou population, can anchor an extended discussion of the risks oil development poses to people like them.

Finally, do what journalists do: peg your essay to a recent event related to the issue you're writing about. George Will's approach to many of his op-ed essays is to use a newly released study, report, academic article, or interview with an expert as the anchor for his piece. He then takes off on his own from there. Other events might include a relevant hearing, a protest, a court decision, a crime, an accident, and so on.

Writing the Sketch

Now draft a sketch of roughly 500 to 600 words with the following elements:

- It has a tentative title.
- It makes at least one claim and offers several reasons that support the claim.
- It presents and analyzes at least one contrasting point of view.
- The sketch includes specific evidence to support (or possibly complicate) the reasons offered in support of the claim, including *at least* several of the following: an anecdote or story, a personal observation, data, an analogy, a case study, expert testimony, other relevant quotations from people involved, or a precedent.

STUDENT SKETCH

Inspiring young voters isn't easy. In my own classes, I almost never hear younger students talk casually about elections. On the rare occasions that I actually see a button on a backpack for one candidate or another, I'm always a little surprised. Are young voters apathetic? And if they are, what should be done about it? Those were Ben Bloom's questions, both of which arose from a fastwrite. Here is his sketch on the topic. Where should he go from here? What should he research before the next draft? What should he consider that he doesn't consider here?

How to Really Rock the Vote

Ben Bloom

1 MTV sponsors "Rock the Vote." Presidential candidates swing through college campuses wearing blue jeans and going tieless. There's even an organization called "Kid's Vote" that tries to get high school students involved in the political process. It's pretty clear that student vote matters but are these efforts paying off?

2 It doesn't seem so. On my own campus, fewer than a few hundred students vote in the annual elections for the Student Senate. I can't even get my roommate to talk about the Presidential election, much less who's running for student body president.

3 What seems typical is the following comment from a college-age columnist: "On the issue of voter apathy, I look at myself first. I'm not even registered to vote, which is as apathetic as it gets. I do, however, educate myself about presidential candidates and their proposed policies—I just never have thought my one, lonesome vote could matter. I've neglected registering because it has never seemed logical to inconvenience myself, through the registration process, only to give another drop of water to an ocean (to add one vote to millions)."

4 "Never seemed logical to inconvenience" yourself to participate in the most basic part of the democratic process? Has it gotten this bad?

5 The student journalist above was responding to a survey that came out two years ago from a group called Project Vote Smart. It found what I suspected from my own experiences: young voters are staying away from the polls.

6 According to the study, there has been a decline in the numbers of 18- to 25-year-olds voting by 13% over the last twenty-five years. Actually, I think the situation is worse than that. The main reason they cite is that young people don't think their votes make a difference.

7 What should be done about this? How can we convince young voters to believe in the power of their vote? Are organizations like "Rock the Vote" or "Project Vote Smart" going to convince students like the guy who finds voting "inconvenient" that it's worth the effort?

8 In my opinion, celebrities and rock stars won't make a difference. The key is for political candidates to find a way to talk about issues so that young voters overcome their apathy and actually *feel* something. In the sixties, it was the draft. I'm not sure what the issues with emotional impact are these days. But the people who want students to vote have got to find them.

Moving from Sketch to Draft

A sketch is often sketchy. It's generally underdeveloped, sometimes giving the writer just the barest outline of his subject. But as an early draft, a sketch can be invaluable. It might hint at what the real subject is, or what questions seem to be behind your inquiry into the subject. A sketch might suggest a focus for the next draft, or simply a better lead. Here are some tips for finding clues in your sketch about directions you might go in the next draft.

Evaluating Your Own Sketch. You've read and written about an issue you care about. Now for the really hard part: getting out of your own head and into the heads of your potential readers, who may not care as much as you do. At least not yet. Successful persuasion fundamentally depends on giving an audience the right reasons to agree with you, and these are likely both logical and emotional, involving both *logos* and *pathos* (see the "Inquiring into the Details: *Ethos, Pathos,* and *Logos* and the Rhetorical Situation" box).

Another element of argument is the way the writer comes across to readers—his or her *ethos.* What's the ethos of your sketch? How might you be perceived by a stranger reading the sketch? Is your tone appealing, or might it be slightly off-putting? Do you successfully establish your authority to speak on this issue, or do you sense that the persona you project in the sketch is unconvincing, perhaps too emotional or not appearing fair?

Inquiring into the Details

ETHOS, PATHOS, AND *LOGOS* AND THE RHETORICAL SITUATION

Persuasion theory may have begun with Aristotle's *Rhetoric,* but modern communication researchers have made it a science. Still, Aristotle and other classical rhetors laid the foundation for the study of persuasion. One of Aristotle's most important contributions to our understanding of argument is shown in Figure 7.5, a variation of the rhetorical triangle you learned about in the beginning of the book.

Each of these terms—*ethos, logos,* and *pathos*—represents different kinds of persuasive appeals. *Ethos* refers to the character of the speaker (or writer), and how he or she comes across to the audience. *Logos* is the logic and methods of reason used to make an argument. *Pathos* is an appeal to the audience's (or reader's) emotion.

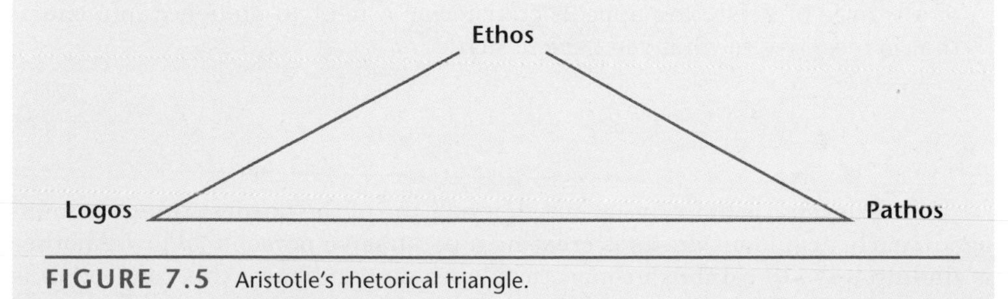

FIGURE 7.5 Aristotle's rhetorical triangle.

Disposition of Audience	*Ethos*	*Pathos*	*Logos*
Resistant	Most important	Least important	Most important
Neutral	Important	Important	Important
Receptive	Least important	Most important	Least important

FIGURE 7.6 Audience and the balance of ethos, logos, and pathos.

All arguments are an artful combination of *ethos, logos,* and *pathos*. As always, what is the most effective combination depends on the rhetorical situation. One way of analyzing a situation is to consider the initial disposition of the audience. Figure 7.6 broadly describes the balance between Aristotle's three categories of appeals in the three most common rhetorical situations: when an audience is resistant to what you're trying to say, neutral about it, or receptive. For instance, direct-mail marketers, particularly those trying to raise money for nonprofit groups and political causes, make a living buying and cultivating lists of people who might be receptive to their messages. Direct-mail letters, therefore, are strong on emotional appeals (*pathos*): The humane society will include photographs of a sad-looking abandoned puppy, a conservative political action group will raise fears about threats to "family values," and so on. There's no need to spend a great deal reasoning (*logos*) with an audience that already agrees with your message. Move them with emotion!

In contrast, resistant audiences immediately suspect the credibility of speakers or writers (*ethos*), and so their challenge is to establish some common ground with their audiences. Emotional appeals will be unlikely to move this audience, at least initially.

Neutral audiences may be difficult to gauge. Sometimes an emotional appeal will spark their interest. Sometimes a well-reasoned argument (*logos*) will move them, and sometimes a neutral audience will be persuaded by the credibility of the speaker. Frequently, a careful combination of all three of Aristotle's appeals transforms a neutral audience into one that is receptive to what you have to say.

As we develop convictions about an issue, one of the hardest things to manage in early argument drafts is creating a persuasive persona *(ethos)*. Another is finding ways to establish connections with our audience; this connection is not just between writers and readers but creating some common ground between readers and *the topic.* There are many ways to do this, including the following:

1. Connecting your readers' prior beliefs or values with your position on the topic.
2. Establishing that readers have a *stake,* perhaps even a personal one, in how the question you've raised is answered; this may be self-interest, but it may also be emotional (remember the advertiser's strategy).
3. Highlighting the common experiences readers may have had with the topic and offering your claim as a useful way of understanding that experience.

As you look over your sketch, evaluate how well you create this common ground between your topic and your intended audience. Might you revise it by exploiting one or more of the strategies listed here?

Finally, is there enough evidence to support the reasons you've provided to support your claims? Initial drafts commonly lack enough specifics. Do you see places in the sketch that could be developed with specific information in the next draft?

Questions for Peer Review. Because the argument essay is such an audience-oriented form, these initial peer reviews of your sketch are invaluable in helping you get your bearings. Much of what you might have felt about how you managed the ethos and connections with readers can be confirmed or challenged by this first public reading. Ask your workshop group some of the following questions:

- How is the *ethos* of the sketch? Do I come across in the sketch as an advocate for my position? For example, am I *passionate, preachy, reasonable, one-sided, sympathetic, overbearing, intimate, detached, objective, subjective, uncaring, empathetic, humorous, serious, angry, mellow, contemptuous, approachable, patronizing, respectful, thoughtful, presumptuous, fair,* or *judgmental?*
- In your own words, what do you think was my central claim?
- Which reasons did you find most convincing? Which were least convincing?
- What do you think was the best evidence I offered in support of my reasons? Where exactly did you feel that you needed more evidence?
- What were the stated or unstated "warrants" behind the claims? What do you need to assume is true to believe in their validity (see "Inquiring into the Details: Using Toulmin to Analyze Arguments")?

Reflecting on What You've Learned. Spend a few minutes following your peer review workshop to generate a list of everything you heard, and then begin a five-minute fastwrite that explores your reaction to these suggestions and your tentative plan for revision. In particular, what will you change? What will you add, and what will you cut in the next draft? What problems were raised that

Guess.com advertisement—a not too subtle yet insidiously persuasive form of visual argument.

you don't yet know how to solve? What problems *weren't* raised that you expected might be? Do you still need to worry about them? End your fastwrite by writing about what you understand now about your topic, and your initial beliefs about it, that you didn't fully understand when you began writing about it.

Research and Other Strategies: Gathering More Information

Here's a mortifying thought: You've completely changed your mind about what you think about your topic and what you want to say in your argument. That's unsettling, but it's also a sign that you're willing to allow things to get a bit messy before they get sorted out. This is good because it's much more likely to result in an essay that gets at the truth of what you feel than if you doggedly stick to a particular point of view, come what may. If you *have* changed your mind, you have a lot of collecting to do. Return to the Web sites of current publications and search for information that might be relevant to your emerging idea.

Another research strategy can be helpful whether you change your mind or not: the interview. People who are somehow involved in your topic are among the best sources of new information and lively material. An interview can provide ideas about what else you should read or who else you might talk to, and it can be a source of quotations, anecdotes, and even case studies that will make the next draft of your argument essay much more interesting. After all, what makes an issue matter is how it affects people. Have you sufficiently dramatized those effects?

Inquiring into the Details

USING TOULMIN TO ANALYZE ARGUMENTS

Stephen Toulmin, an English philosopher, has had an enormous influence on how argument is analyzed and taught. He proposes that most arguments, no matter what the subject or discipline, include *claims, evidence, warrants,* and *backing.* You're likely familiar with at least two of these terms: claims and evidence.

But the most penetrating aspect of Toulmin's approach is the idea that *warrants*—assumptions about the way things are—are key to the logical relationship between evidence and claims. For example, my friend and colleague, Dr. Michelle Payne, asks students to make claims about what type of person she is based on the contents of her handbag. What does the fact that she has three credit cards say about her? Some students say she probably has a lot of money, while others suggest the opposite—that she must carry a lot of debt. Michelle prompts students to state the warrants by asking, *What do you need to believe is true if your claims from the evidence are valid? Backing* is evidence that supports a warrant. For those who claim that the number of Michelle's credit cards is evidence that she might struggle with debt, the warrant is clear: One has to believe that there is a relationship between the numbers of credit cards and debt—the more you have, the more you spend beyond your means. A quick search on the Web uncovered backing for such a warrant. Apparently consumer debt and numbers of cards *are* related, making the original claim more convincing.

Warrants are either stated or unstated. Typically, writers or speakers who believe that their audience shares the assumptions behind their warrants don't explicitly discuss them. Advertisers are expert at this. While it seems logically silly to accept the warrant in a Guess ad that wearing their jeans will help guarantee sexual and social success, we tend not to question the assumption. If we did, we might demand backing: do habitual Guess jeans wearers who are single spend fewer Saturday nights at home alone than those of us who wear Levis?

Can you see how this method allows you to analyze the effectiveness of all kinds of arguments—including visual arguments—particularly by trying to tease out the warrants behind the claims? Toulmin can also help you generate information that will help you write an argument more effectively by challenging you to state your warrants and provide backing when necessary.

Suppose you read a recent poll that considerably more people today believe in the possibility that someone can start poor and get rich in America than they did in 1983. Of the many possible claims that might arise from this evidence, Figure 7.7 presents two: more people believe that the U.S. is the land of opportunity, or Americans apparently choose to ignore the widening gap between rich and poor in this country. In other words, we are either inspired optimists or complete dupes. If you ask yourself what you have to assume is true for each claim to be valid you'll surface some warrants that might be worth questioning. I've listed one warrant for each claim in Figure 7.7.

The effectiveness of arguments rise and fall with the persuasiveness of their warrants. If you think the warrants behind your claim might not reflect assumptions that readers share, then finding backing for your warrants is an important research strategy. Do you think warrant #2 below needs backing?

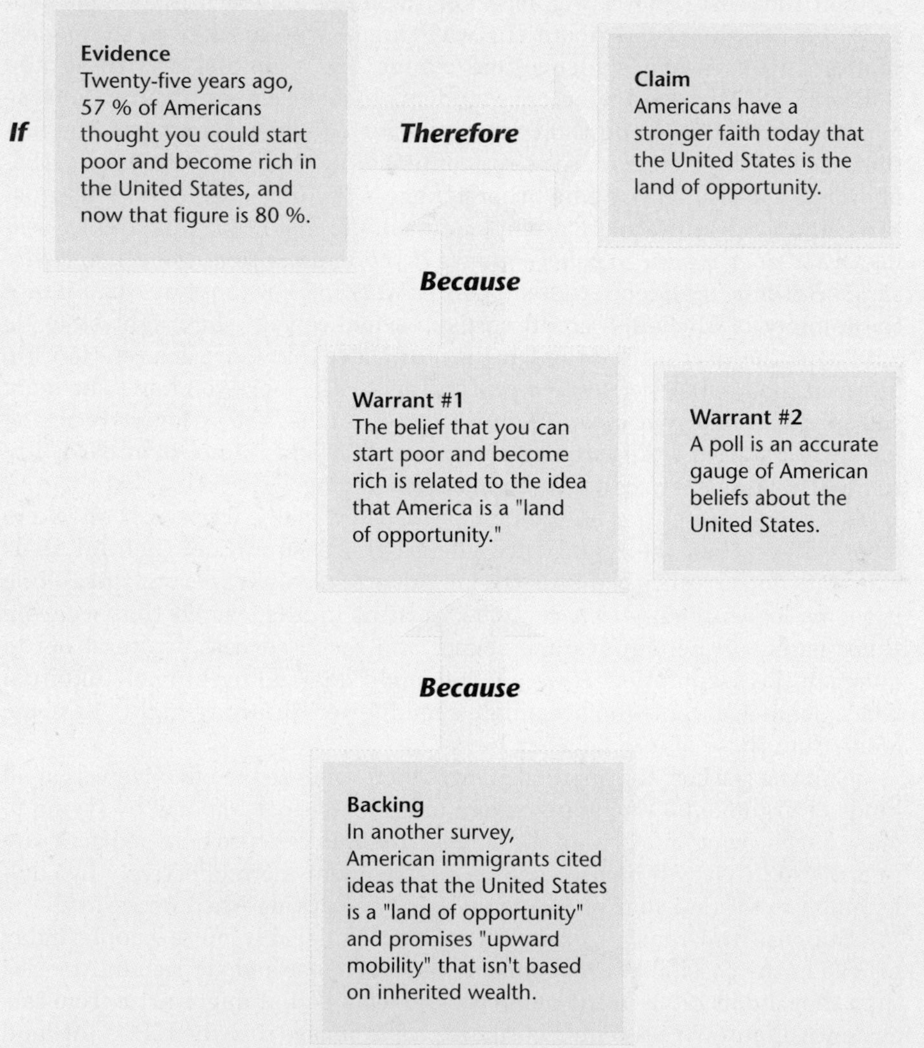

If

Evidence
Twenty-five years ago, 57 % of Americans thought you could start poor and become rich in the United States, and now that figure is 80 %.

Therefore

Claim
Americans have a stronger faith today that the United States is the land of opportunity.

Because

Warrant #1
The belief that you can start poor and become rich is related to the idea that America is a "land of opportunity."

Warrant #2
A poll is an accurate gauge of American beliefs about the United States.

Because

Backing
In another survey, American immigrants cited ideas that the United States is a "land of opportunity" and promises "upward mobility" that isn't based on inherited wealth.

FIGURE 7.7 You can use the Toulmin model to guide your research efforts when you revise.

For more information on face-to-face interviewing, see Chapter 9, "Research Techniques." The Internet can also be a source for interview material. Look for e-mail links to the authors of useful documents you found on the Web and write them with a few questions. Interest groups, newsgroups, or electronic mailing lists on the Web can also provide the voices and perspectives of people with something to say on your topic. Remember to ask permission to quote them if you decide to use something in your draft. For leads on finding Web discussion groups on your topic, visit the following sites:

- **Google Groups,** http://groups.google.com, allows you to search for online discussion groups on virtually any topic.
- **Yahoo Groups** offers a similar service, allowing you to search for groups by keyword. Find it at http://groups.yahoo.com.
- **Catalist,** the official catalog of electronic mailing lists, http://www.lsoft.com/lists/listref.html, has a database of about 15,000 discussion groups.

One of the most useful things you can do to prepare for the draft is to spend forty-five minutes at the campus library searching for new information on your topic. Consider expanding your search from current newspapers and periodicals to books or government publications (see Chapter 9 for more information about searching for government documents). In addition you can refer to almanacs such as *Infoplease* (http://www.infoplease.com) and the *CIA World Factbook* (http://www.odci.gov/cia/publications/factbook/) and statistical information available from sources such as the U.S. Census Bureau's *American Fact Finder* (http://factfinder.census.gov/home/saff/main.html?_lang = en), which is a wonderful resource that draws on the agency's massive database of information on U.S. trends.

Composing the Draft

As always, it's best to work from abundance rather than scarcity. If you don't have enough evidence to support your argument, find more. But if you're feeling reasonably well prepared to develop your argument essay from a sketch (or proposal) to a longer draft, then begin by crafting a strong lead. There are so many ways to begin an essay like this one; which is best? As always, think of a beginning that not only might interest your readers in your topic but hints at or states your purpose in writing about it. Through tone, your beginning also establishes your relationship with your readers. Here's instructor Andrew Merton's lead in "The Guys Are Dumbing Down," a piece that argues that students' baseball caps in class indicate something other than studiousness.

> Here is the big social note from the campus of the University of New Hampshire, where I teach: Dumbing down is in. For guys.

Merton's tone is a strong element of this lead. He begins casually—"Here is the big social note . . ."—suggesting some friendly, almost chatty relationship with his readers. This lead also does what many argument essay beginnings do: it states the writer's main claim. You may assume it is always required to state your thesis in your introduction, but this isn't true at all. Some argument essays, especially op-ed pieces, have a delayed thesis, in which the writer works methodically toward his or her point. Which approach should you use in your draft? In part, that depends on your method of development.

Methods of Development. What are some of the ways you might organize the next draft?

Narrative. Telling a story is an underrated way of developing an argument. One of my favorite persuasive essays is George Orwell's "A Hanging," a piece most don't consider a persuasive essay at all. Orwell's essay is his eyewitness account of a man who is hanged at a squalid prison in colonial Burma. "A Hanging" argues against capital punishment by focusing on about eight minutes of the event—the most dramatic eight minutes obviously—and only in the middle does Orwell break with his story to state his position on the issue. The story is so compelling it's hard to even notice that Orwell is trying to persuade the reader to believe something. Can you imagine a way to turn your topic into an extended story, perhaps by focusing on the experience of a particular person or group of people, in a particular place, at a particular time? Somehow the story must, like Orwell's, be logically linked to your claim; obviously, just any old story won't do.

There are other ways to use narrative, too. Anecdotes, or brief stories used to illustrate an idea or a problem, are frequently used in argument essays. One effective way to begin your essay might be to tell a story that highlights the problem you're writing about or the question you're posing.

Question to Answer. Almost all writing is an attempt to answer a question. In the personal essay and other open forms of inquiry, the writer may never arrive at a definite answer, but an argument essay usually offers an answer. An obvious method of development, therefore, is to begin your essay by raising the question and end it by offering your answer. This can work in a number of ways. For example, an Ellen Goodman essay on recent proposals to bring back publicly funded single-sex schools is organized around what she thinks are some of the key questions this raises. She asks those questions throughout her essay, and answers each before moving on to the next. Following a beginning that provides some background on the proposal, Goodman asks, *How did we get here?* She then explains the "odd coalition" that supports the proposal, describes their arguments and methodically rebuts them. By the middle of her essay, Goodman asks a second question, *Can you have separate but equal schools?* The remainder of her piece examines the answer to this question, and by the end she arrives at her main claim: The solution to poor schools is not an end to coeducation but innovation in teaching.

Are there several key questions around which you might organize your draft, leading, as Goodman does, to your central claim at the end?

Problem to Solution. This is a variation on the question-to-answer structure. But it might be a particularly useful organization strategy if you're writing about a topic readers may know very little about. In that case, you might need to spend as much time establishing what exactly the problem is—explaining what makes it a problem and why the reader should care about it—as you do offering your particular solution. That's what George Will did earlier in the chapter in his argument on the failure of writing instruction. He spent a fair amount of time explaining what he believed were the indefensible current theories of teaching students to write, ideas most of his readers would know little about.

Effect to Cause or Cause to Effect. At the heart of some arguments is the *relationship* between two things, and often what is at issue is pinpointing the real causes for certain undesirable effects. Once these causes are identified, then the best solutions can be offered. Sadly, we know the effects of terrorism, but what are its causes? If you argue, as some do, that Islamic radicalism arose in response to U.S. policies toward Israel and the Palestinians, then the solution offered might be a shift in foreign policy. The international debate over global warming, for some participants, is really an argument about causes and effects. If you don't believe, for example, that U.S. contributions to atmospheric carbon dioxide in the next ten years will match contributions from the developing world, then the U.S. refusal to sign the Kyoto treaty—one proposed solution—may not matter that much. Some arguments like these can be organized simply around an examination of causes and effects.

Combining Approaches. As you think about how you might organize your first draft, you don't necessarily have to choose between narrative, problem-to-solution, or cause-to-effect structures. In fact, most often they are used together. We can easily see that in Erin Aubry Kaplan's essay earlier in the chapter on the politics of hair. The piece begins with a narrative account of her hair straightening efforts as a child, and then shifts to an exploration how recent events highlight a return to the "denial" look in African American hairstyle.

Using Evidence. All writing relies on evidence, usually some specific information in relationships with general ideas (see the "Inquiring into the Details: What Evidence Can Do" box.) Evidence in an argumentative essay often has a *particular* relationship to ideas; most often it is offered to support ideas the writer wants the reader to believe. What *kind* of evidence to include is a rhetorical question. To whom are you writing, and what kind of evidence will they be more likely to believe? Generally speaking, the narrower and more specialized the audience, the more particular they will be about the types of evidence they'll find convincing.

For example, as you write more academic papers in your chosen major, the types of evidence that will help you make a persuasive argument will be more and more prescribed by the field. In the natural sciences, the results of quantitative studies count more than case studies; in the humanities, primary texts count more than secondary ones. The important thing for this argument essay, which you're writing for a more general audience, is that you attempt to *vary* your evidence. Rather than relying exclusively on anecdotes, include some quotes from an expert as well.

Inquiring into the Details

WHAT EVIDENCE CAN DO

Usually we think of using evidence only to support an idea or claim we're making. But evidence can be used in other ways, too. For example, it can do the following:

- *support* an idea, observation, or assertion
- *refute* or challenge a claim with which you disagree
- *show* that a seemingly simple assertion, problem, or idea is really more complex
- *complicate* or even contradict an earlier point you've made
- *contrast* two or more ways of seeing the same thing
- *test* an idea, hypothesis, or theory

Workshopping the Draft

The following journal activities and questions should help you make the most of your opportunity to get peer feedback on your work in progress.

Reflecting on the Draft. After you've finished the draft, prepare for peer review by making a journal entry that explores your experience writing the essay.

- What proved hardest?
- What most surprised you about the process?
- What did you find particularly gratifying? What was especially frustrating?
- How did your process for writing this type of essay differ from writing the personal essay or some other form?
- If you were going to start all over again, what would you do differently?

Discuss the insights that might have emerged from this open-ended writing in class or in your workshop group. After your draft has been discussed, make some notes in your journal in response to the following questions:

- What most surprised you about your group's response to your essay?
- What did you hear that most made you want to write again?
- What specifically do you think you need to do in the next draft?

Questions for Readers. Here are some questions that might prompt members of your workshop group to offer helpful advice on your argument draft.

1. What was the most interesting part of the draft? What was the least interesting?

2. What did you believe about my topic before you read the draft? What did you believe after you read it?
3. What reason most strongly supported my main point? What reason seemed the weakest?
4. What was the most convincing evidence I offered? What was the least convincing?

Inquiring into the Details

COMMON LOGICAL FALLACIES

An important way to evaluate the soundness of an argument is to examine its logic and, in particular, look for so-called logical fallacies that may lead writers' reasoning astray. Aristotle was one of the first to point out many of these, and a quick search on the Web using the term "logical fallacies" will reveal dozens and dozens of them that plague public argument. Many of them have indecipherable Latin names, testifying to their ancient origins.

Here are ten of the most common logical fallacies. I think they cover about 90 percent of the ways in which writers stumble when making an argument.

1. **Hasty generalization:** We're naturally judgmental creatures. For example, we frequently make a judgment about someone after just meeting them. Or we conclude that a class is useless after attending a single session. All of these are generalizations based on insufficient evidence. Hasty generalizations *might* be true—the class might turn out to be useless—but you should always be wary of them.

2. **Ad hominem:** When arguments turn into shouting matches, they almost inevitably get personal. Shifting away from the substance of an argument to attack the person making it, either subtly or explicitly, is another common logical fallacy. It's also, at times, hard to resist.

3. **Appeal to authority:** We all know that finding support for a claim from an expert is a smart move in many arguments. But sometimes it's a faulty move because the authority we cite isn't really an expert on the subject. A more common fallacy, however, is when we cite an expert to support a claim without acknowledging that many experts disagree on the point.

4. **Straw man:** One of the sneakiest ways to sidetrack reason in an argument is to misrepresent or ignore the actual position of an opponent. For example, one way I might criticize George Will's earlier essay on writing instruction is to point out that he conveniently misrepresents the actual goals and practices of what he calls the "growth model" of teaching writing. Therefore he creates a "straw man" that is easy to knock down. When writing critically about the ideas of another, we must always be careful to represent those ideas as accurately as we can.

5. **False analogy:** Analogies can be powerful comparisons in argument. But they can also lead us astray when the analogy simply doesn't hold. Are A and B *really* similar situations? For example, when a critic of higher education argues that a public university is like a business and should be run like one, are the two really analogous? Fundamentally, one is nonprofit and the other is designed to make money. Is this a really useful comparison?

6. **Post hoc or false cause:** Just because one thing follows another doesn't necessarily mean one *causes* the other. It might be coincidence, or the cause might be something else entirely. For example, if you're really keen on arguing that losing the football coach was the cause of the team's losing record, you might link the two. And it's possible that you're right, but it's also just as possible that the injury to the quarterback was one of the real reasons.

7. **Appeal to popularity:** In a country obsessed by polls and rankings, it's not hard to understand the appeal of reasoning that argues that because it's popular it must be good or true. Advertisers are particularly fond of this fallacy, arguing that because their brand is most popular it must be best. In fact, this might not be the case at all. The majority can be wrong.

8. **Slippery slope:** I love the name of this one because it so aptly describes what can happen when reasoning loses its footing. You might start out reasonably enough, arguing, for example, that a gun control law restricts the rights of some citizens to have access to certain weapons, but pretty soon you start sliding toward conclusions that simply don't follow, such as that a gun control law is the beginning of the end of gun ownership in the country. Now you might really believe this, but logic isn't the route to get there.

9. **Either/or fallacy:** In a black-and-white world, something is right or wrong, true or false, good or bad. But ours is a colorful world with many shades. For instance, while it might be emotionally satisfying to say that opponents of the war in Iraq must not support the troops there, it is also possible that the war's opponents are against the war *because* they're concerned about the lives of American service people. Rather than *either/or* it might be *both/and.* We see this fallacy often in arguments that suggest that there are only two choices and each are opposites.

10. **Begging the question:** This one is also called *circular reasoning* because it assumes the truth of the arguer's conclusion without bothering to prove it. An obvious example of this would be to say that a law protecting people from Internet spam is good because it's a law, and laws should be obeyed. But *why* is it a good law?

Revising the Draft

As I discussed earlier in the book, one of the most common misconceptions about revision is that you do it only at the end of the writing process. In fact, up to this point, you should have been revising your work all along, from the first few journal exercises when you chose a topic and played with possible angles on it, to the journal work you might have done to prepare to write the sketch, and then again with your efforts to turn your sketch into a more developed draft. Revision is literally "re-seeing," and every time you create the conditions that allow you to discover something new about how you see or what you think about your subject, you are, in fact, engaged in the act of revision. In a sense, then, each writing assignment you undertake is one long act of revision, from start to finish.

But once you've completed a draft, the revision process becomes more focused. You are mostly working with material that should be somewhat settled, with purposes that might be clearer, and ideas that may have more shape. At this point, the biggest temptation is to tell yourself you are largely done and what revision remains is merely a matter of "fixing things"—tinkering with sentences, correcting typos, and running a spell-checker. In the survey from Chapter 1 (see page 18), 70 percent of students admitted as much. "I usually just tidy things up" was ranked first or second by students who were asked what they do most often when they revise an academic paper.

These activities are certainly an element of revision—and important ones—but as the word *revision* implies, it's important to "re-see" both what you are trying to say and how you try to say it, even at this stage in the process. Chapter 11, "Revision Strategies," is a useful introduction to the revision process for any essay, including the argument essay. It emphasizes ways writers can break the bonds that limit their ability to find new ways of seeing the draft.

Draft argument essays have some typical problems at this stage in the process. Do any of these apply to yours?

- Is your central claim or thesis stated clearly?
- Do you employ any logical fallacies? See "Inquiring into the Details: Common Logical Fallacies."
- Do you have sufficient evidence or information to make your assertions convincing? Do you need to gather more facts?
- Have you considered any counterarguments in your essay? This is especially important if you think the audience for your essay might not be inclined to initially agree with your position.
- Have you clearly established what stake your readers have in the issue you're writing about?
- Does the draft use *pathos, logos,* and *ethos* effectively? (See Figure 7.6.)

Chapter 11, "Revision Strategies," can help you address most of these problems. Refer to the following table to find specific strategies for ideas on how to revise your draft following your workshop. Remember that a draft may present problems in more than one category.

GUIDE TO REVISION STRATEGIES		
Problems in the Draft (Chapter 11)	**Part**	**Page Number**
Unclear purpose ▪ Not sure what the paper is about?	1	420
Unclear thesis, theme, or main idea ▪ Not sure what you're trying to say?	2	425
Lack of information or development ▪ Need more convincing evidence? Need to check for logical fallacies?	3	432
Disorganized ▪ Doesn't move logically or smoothly from paragraph to paragraph?	4	436
Unclear or awkward at the level of sentences and paragraphs ▪ Seems choppy or hard to follow at the level of sentences or paragraphs?	5	442

Polishing the Draft

After you've dealt with the big issues in your draft—is it sufficiently focused, does it answer the *So what?* question, is it well organized, and so on—you must deal with the smaller problems. You've carved the stone into an appealing figure but now you need to polish it. Are your paragraphs coherent? How do you manage transitions? Are your sentences fluent and concise? Are there any errors in spelling or syntax? Section 5 of Chapter 11 can help you focus on these issues.

Before you finish your draft, work through the following checklist:

- Every paragraph is about one thing.
- The transitions between paragraphs aren't abrupt.
- The length of sentences varies in each paragraph.
- Each sentence is concise. There are no unnecessary words or phrases.
- You've checked grammar, particularly verb agreement, run-on sentences, unclear pronouns, and misused words (*there/their, where/were,* and so on). (See of the handbook at the back of the book for help with these grammar issues.)
- You've run your spell-checker and proofed your paper for misspelled words.

STUDENT ESSAY

Many Americans are fond of talking about our country's native people in the past tense. We admire the tribal cultures as they existed a century or two ago, and borrow freely from them, engaging in "vision quests" and drumming circles. We feel the tug of nostalgia for these lost tribes, and yes, guilt for the sad history of relations between the mostly white immigrants who dispossessed the tribes and the Indian people who were confined to reservations. It's convenient to assume that the problems were in the past because contemporary Native Americans are largely invisible to us—except if you happen to drive through a reservation as Kelly Sundberg would on her way to visit friends at a nearby university.

Confronting Native Americans in the present tense forced Kelly to examine her own prejudices, and in the essay that follows she argues that the route to understanding begins at school.

I Am Not a Savage

Kelly Sundberg

Salmon, Idaho, is named after the river that runs through it, a river that is filled with turbulent whitewater punctuated by deep and calm pools and shallow riffles. In the spring, I have looked into these riffles and seen waves of silver and red moving gently just underneath the surface of the water. 1

We call them "reds"—spawning salmon. Nowadays, they are diminished in numbers, but at one time the river was full of them, and full of abundance as well for the Lemhi Indians who once lived on the banks. For the Lemhi, the salmon was not solely for sustenance, but also an integral part of their culture and spirituality. 2

Today there are few "reds" and almost no Lemhi left in the valley. 3

The initial influx of Mormon settlers followed by migrations of Californians and Midwesterners forced Native Americans out of the valley. Still, upon entering the Salmon city limits from Highway 28, a large sign proclaims, "Welcome to Salmon, Idaho. Birthplace of Sacagawea!" In a time when anything related to Lewis and Clark means profit, the city of Salmon, my hometown, has now chosen to capitalize on this marketable heritage, even though they once ignored it or treated it derisively. 4

My high school mascot is the "Salmon Savage." The marquee in front of the school has a picture with an Indian warrior on it, and when the football team scores a touchdown a white girl wearing war paint and a "made in China" headdress will ride a horse around the track in celebration. 5

I never questioned the integrity or intent of these symbols until I was a sophomore at the school. For Civil Rights Day, the school invited Rosa Abrahamson, a Lemhi Indian, to speak to the students. She cried as she spoke about the injustice of the name "savage." "My people are not savages," she said. "We are peaceful and do 6 not take pride in that name." When she finished speaking the applause was polite but subdued.

7 The next speaker was a rancher named Bud, who lit into a tirade about the government subsidizing "lazy Indians." As he finished with fists raised into the air, he was greeted by a standing ovation. For the first time in my life, I felt ashamed to be a part of the community.

8 It wasn't that those of us in the gym had consciously made the decision to be racist. It was simply ignorance. Despite the history of the Lemhi in the valley, our ideas of their culture are shaped from drives through the reservation on the way to campus visits at the University of Idaho. Our perceptions were safely gleaned from inside of an automobile and never involved real interaction with Native Americans.

9 Once, when asked to write our opinions about reservations in a U.S. government class, I wrote that I thought the government was making it "too easy on the Native Americans and they had become apathetic and unmotivated because of subsidies."

10 I got a better glimpse at my Lemhi neighbors recently reading Sherman Alexie's novel The Lone Ranger and Tonto Fistfight in Heaven. Alexie, a member of the Spokane/Coeur d'Alene tribes, conveys the opposition between contemporary and traditional Native American culture. His characters are torn and struggle to reconcile the two: "At the halfway point of any drunken night, there is a moment when an Indian realizes he cannot turn back toward tradition and that he has no map to guide him toward the future."

11 My own community struggles to reconcile two conflicting ideas as well—we embrace the symbols of savagery to inspire the football team, yet in order to make a profit we proudly claim Sacagawea as one of our own. Still, when the Lemhi wanted to build a school near Sacagawea's birthplace, the county refused to sell them the land, claiming it would become a "mini-reservation."

12 Ironically, Salmon shares more than it cares to admit with its neighbors on the reservation. Poverty, alcoholism, and depression are a way of life for many Salmon residents. Yet the perception in the community is that an alcoholic white man is somehow superior to a "drunk Indian."

13 In Salmon, all students are required to take an Idaho history class, yet this class makes almost no mention of Native American history in the valley. None of the readings in Advanced Placement English classes are by Native American authors, and government classes don't address Native American issues at all.

14 Is it any wonder that racism persists?

15 The local school system needs to lead. English teachers should require readings by authors like Alexie, they should provide field trips to local and national archeological sites, and they should bring in Native American interpreters to speak about local history. By letting go of negative and outdated ideas, the city of Salmon and the Lemhi can take the first step toward healing.

Evaluating the Essay

Discuss or write about your responses to Kelly Sundberg's essay using some or all of the following questions:

1. What is the thesis of the essay? Where in the piece is it most clearly stated?
2. Refer to the box that lists ten common logical fallacies and reread Sundberg's essay. Do you suspect there are any logical fallacies in "I Am Not a Savage"?
3. Consider the *ethos* of this essay. How does the writer come across? Is her persona effective?
4. What do you think is the most effective paragraph in the essay? Why? What is the least effective?

Using What You Have Learned

You've read published op-ed essays and a student draft. You've also worked on your own argument essay, a genre that may be new to you. Take a moment to consider how you might use what you've learned.

1. Reflect on how your thinking about argument and argumentative writing may have changed because of the reading and writing in this chapter by finishing the following sentence in your journal at least four times: *Before I began this chapter I thought ________, but now I think ________.*
2. The personal essay (discussed in Chapter 4) and the argument essay might seem at first to be fundamentally different kinds of writing. Do you see any connections between the two genres now?
3. Examine the letters to the editor or the editorial in your local newspaper. How do you read these pages differently after studying and writing an argument? Clip a letter or editorial that might best demonstrate what you've learned.

The poet Grace Butcher, pictured here at a reading in Ohio, sometimes writes about crows, which are quite ordinary birds, unless they fly through the imagination of a writer like Butcher. The best literature often finds the extraordinary significance in familiar things.

8

Writing a Critical Essay

WRITING ABOUT LITERATURE

A voice mail message on my machine from Katie, who works in the English department office, said that she had received a message meant for me. "Stay on and you can listen to it," she said. "Hello," said a stranger's voice. "This is Grace Butcher. And I'm looking for the Bruce Ballenger or Michelle Payne who edited a collection called *The Curious Reader*. There's an essay about me in it."

My heart sank. Oh God, I thought, maybe we made some mistake and she's angry. But I didn't sense that from the sound of her voice; it sounded velvety, warm. "I'm calling because I wanted to tell the student who wrote the essay how delighted and moved I was by her piece. I'd like to know how to get in touch with the student, Peggy Jordan."

I suddenly remembered. Peggy Jordan, a former student of my colleague Michelle, had written an autobiographical/critical essay about the poet Grace Butcher in *The Curious Reader*, a book I co-authored with Michelle. Jordan wrote about attending a reading by Butcher when she was sixteen, and now, twenty-eight years later, finds herself returning to those poems as she struggles with middle age. It's a brutally honest essay—Jordan says there's little to like about growing older, that even if you have a good attitude about it, the body is a nagging reminder of new limitations. But Butcher's poetry, particularly one poem, "What the Crow Does Is Not Singing," helped Peggy Jordan find a new voice, and new wings, which will carry her more gracefully into old age.

I reread the Jordan essay and thought—this is what literature can do. Reading essays, stories, and poems can help us slowly unroll the tightly bound threads of feeling—our fears, joys, desires, or sorrows—and help us follow them back to the heart and out into the world. Literature helps us understand ourselves, and in attending to the

What You'll Learn in This Chapter

- How literary texts differ from other kinds of writing.
- Methods for finding the questions that drive a critical essay.
- Common literary devices.
- Useful sources for writing about literature.

experiences of others as they are represented in strings of words, we can see how we're delicately tethered to others. Peggy Jordan can see in Butcher's poems that there is a way to grow older that she hadn't yet imagined. But would she have seen this as clearly if she hadn't written about it? I don't think so.

MOTIVES FOR WRITING A CRITICAL ESSAY

By now you understand that writing is a means of thinking and learning, so when your writing comes in contact with the writing of others, the conversation illuminates them both. Sometimes, this dialogue has very personal dimensions. It did for Peggy Jordan because she reread Grace Butcher's poem with an open heart and mind, and because Jordan chose a form of the critical essay—autobiographical criticism—that actively encourages such personal connections. But even more formal critical essays, those that don't involve self-disclosure or first-person writing, can offer personal revelation. After all, what draws you to a certain author, essay, story, or poem is often a feeling, a response that is initially closer to the heart than the head. From there you sustain an intimate encounter with the material, reading closely and reflecting on what it might mean.

It isn't necessary that the story you're writing about be an experience you can relate to, or even about a person anything like you. Reading about different lives, strangely, can help us understand ourselves in unexpected ways. Like a carnival mirror, stories, essays, and poems about others can cause us to reflect on ourselves in ways that make us seem strange, sometimes almost unrecognizable, to ourselves. We see ourselves as others see us. We might read James Baldwin's "Notes of a Native Son" and understand how an African American might have felt in the 1950s or 1960s when seeing an approaching white face; a sense, Baldwin writes, that "one was never looked at but was simply at the mercy of the reflexes the color of one's skin caused in other people." Of course, if we're white we learn a little something about being black in America, but we also learn something about how our own faces might appear to someone who is black. Suddenly, the familiar seems strange.

These are personal reasons for writing about literature, but there are other motives as well. One is that the writing can, simply, help us *understand* what we read, and appreciate it much more. You've already practiced methods such as the double-entry journal, in which you create conversations with all kinds of texts—essays, excerpts, and even photographs. When it works, this process helps you figure out what you think and what you might want to say about the thing you're looking at. This is also true when that thing is a literary text, and it becomes even more important to structure these written conversations because what makes texts literary is their complexity.

Most of us are pretty literal, which is why one response to reading, say, a short story is to simply declare, "It's *just a story!* Why do we have to squeeze some deep meaning out of it?" It's a pretty common view that English teachers have created an industry out of squeezing water from stones, of demanding that readers look more deeply at the things they read and consider what might be implied rather than what is explicit. This can be annoying at times, but the intentions are good. To fully appreciate what authors are saying or what effects they're trying to create in an essay, poem, or story, you often need to look closely, and in doing so, you see beyond the obvious. When you make this reading an act of imagination you consider possible meanings that weren't necessarily immediately apparent. In the conversation between what a text says and what it *might* be saying, you discover fresh understandings of what you read. You share these discoveries by writing about them.

To fully appreciate what authors are saying or what effects they're trying to create in an essay, poem, or story, you often need to look closely, and in doing so, you see beyond the obvious.

This is not really impersonal, even if you never mention yourself in your essay, because to do this well you need to bring yourself to the encounter. Whatever interpretations or ideas you discover about a poem, story, or essay are shaped by who you are—the personal experiences, the feelings, the dreams, and the ideas—that lead you to notice some things but not others in a text. You imagine in your own particular ways. How productive this is, however, depends on *how* you read and how you use writing to help you understand and interpret texts. The *process* of reading and writing about literary texts, the subject of this chapter, involves a range of choices, something that you can individualize, too.

THE CRITICAL ESSAY AND ACADEMIC WRITING

Summarizing a work, something that made *CliffsNotes* an industry, is a useful activity, and often is a step in the process, but rarely is it the purpose of a critical essay. Most forms of critical essays are organized around *the writer's ideas* about a text.

In that sense, a critical essay is like most of the other inquiry projects we've discussed so far, with one important difference: the main source of information for the writing is a text, usually a work of literature. Yet the process of thinking and writing is much the same with critical essays as it is in a personal essay, an argument, and a review: You begin with questions, explore possible answers, make judgments and interpretations, and offer evidence that supports, qualifies, or complicates your judgments. You apply all the habits of mind we've discussed throughout the book: dialectical thinking, suspending judgment, and so on. In that sense, writing critical essays prepares you for many other kinds of academic writing, especially if it involves working with published texts.

You will encounter various forms of the critical essay mostly in English classes. They might include the following:

- *Short response papers.* As an initial response to reading, you may be asked to write fairly brief analytical, exploratory, or personal responses. These, by our definition, are essentially sketches that may or may not lead to longer essays. Sometimes a response paper focuses on explication of a certain aspect of the essay, poem, or story, like explaining or analyzing use of metaphor or character.

- *Autobiographical criticism.* Personal and sometimes fairly open-ended responses to literary works, such as Peggy Jordan's essay mentioned at the beginning of the chapter, are sometimes encouraged by English instructors. This type of personal criticism makes the critic's emotional relationship to texts explicit, but seeks to illuminate both the writer and the text.
- *Formal critical analysis.* Among the most common forms is the critical essay that makes an argument about the text. Like all other forms, these essays begin with questions: Does Ken Kesey's *One Flew over the Cuckoo's Nest* use Big Nurse as a misogynistic symbol? Does E. B. White's essay "Once More to the Lake" comment on mortality and identity? These critical essays generally offer a central claim or thesis, and then, using the literary text as evidence, try to make that claim or thesis convincing. Alice Hall Petry's critical essay "Who is Ellie? Oates' 'Where Are You Going, Where Have You Been?,' " which follows later in the chapter, is a good example of this.

FEATURES OF THE FORM

Although the critical essay can exhibit considerable variation, certain conventions hold true for the form. These include the following:

- *The text is the most important source of information.* In a personal response, you might write about how a particular experience helps you understand some aspect of an essay, story, or poem, but even then, everything must be anchored firmly to the text you're writing about or things (letters, interviews, and so on) the writer has said about it. While so-called secondary sources—books or articles written by other critics—may be useful in supporting your interpretation, the best evidence in a critical essay is nearly always material (quotes of passages, summaries, and so on) drawn directly from the text or author you're writing about.
- *Most critical essays make an argument.* Critical essays are built around a main idea, claim, or interpretation you are making about a text. It's like interpreting a painting; however, instead of looking at things such as line, hierarchy, and color, you'll be using literary devices such as theme, character, symbol, scene, and other literary concepts to support and develop your ideas. The arguments you make frequently focus on a problem or pattern in the work. What doesn't quite fit or is puzzling? What elements are repeated? Response essays may be more exploratory and open ended rather than argumentative.

Critical essays are built around a main idea, claim, or interpretation you are making about a text.

- *What has already been said often forms the context for the writer's question.* Typically a critical essay initially establishes what other critics have claimed about the aspect of the essay, poem, or story on which the writer is focusing. How, for example, have other critics interpreted the haunting song that ends "Lullaby," Leslie Silko's short story? These other sources provide the context for putting forward your own take on the question, and establish the ongoing conversation (if any) about the writer or the work.

- *Most critical essays assume readers* are not *familiar with the text.* Unless the literary work is extremely well known, critics generally assume that an audience needs to have its memory refreshed. That means that there may be some background information on the essay, story, or poem, and possibly on the author and his or her other similar works. Frequently this means adding a summary of the story or background on the poem or novel. However, in certain circumstances, such as those involving response essays about a text your entire class has read, this assumption about audience will not apply.

SHORT STORY

Leslie Marmon Silko was raised on the Laguna Pueblo reservation in New Mexico, a place she came to know through stories that were told to her by her father, her aunt, and her grandmother. The storytelling tradition, much of it oral rather than written, is often a powerful element in Native American tribes, preserving certain ways of knowing and helping members recognize their connection to the tribe. But these stories are often living things, adapting and changing to reflect tribal members' struggles to adapt to an often hostile world. They can even be a source of healing, as in the short story "Lullaby" you're about to read here.

Silko is widely recognized as one of the finest living Native American writers, and her novel *Ceremony,* published in 1977, received critical acclaim. She's also a talented poet and essayist. Above all, Leslie Marmon Silko is a storyteller in the Laguna tradition, using a kind of narrative that in many ways will be familiar to non-native readers. There are characters and scenes and a significant event, but also notice how landscape figures into the telling of this story, and in particular what the narrator's relationship is with the natural world. One of the motives for telling a story like this is to deal with loss by seeking recovery through balance or harmony. This may not be at all obvious when you read this story, which on the surface is an unrelentingly sad tale. Do you see redemption or perhaps resistance here?

Lullaby

Leslie Marmon Silko

The sun had gone down but the snow in the wind gave off its own light. It came in thick tufts like new wool—washed before the weaver spins it. Ayah reached out for it like her own babies had, and she smiled when she remembered how she had laughed at them. She was an old woman now, and her life had become memories. She sat 1 down with her back against the wide cottonwood tree, feeling the rough bark on her back bones; she faced east and listened to the wind and snow sing a high-pitched Yeibechei song. Out of the wind she felt warmer, and she could watch the wide fluffy snow fill in her tracks, steadily, until the direction she had come from was gone. By the light of the snow she could see the dark outline of the big arroyo a few feet away. She was sitting on the edge of Cebolleta Creek, where in the springtime the thin cows would graze on a grass already chewed flat to the ground. In the wide deep creek bed where only a trickle of water flowed in the summer, the skinny cows would wander, looking for new grass along winding paths splashed with manure.

2 Ayah pulled the old Army blanket over her head like a shawl. Jimmie's blanket—the one he had sent to her. That was a long time ago and the green wool was faded, and it was unraveling on the edges. She did not want to think about Jimmie. So she thought about the weaving and the way her mother had done it. On the tall wooden loom set into the sand under a tamarack tree for shade. She could see it clearly. She had been only a little girl when her grandma gave her the wooden combs to pull the twigs and burrs from the raw, freshly washed wool. And while she combed the wool, her grandma sat beside her, spinning a silvery strand of yarn around the smooth cedar spindle. Her mother worked at the loom with yarns dyed bright yellow and red and gold. She watched them dye the yarn in boiling black pots full of beeweed petals, juniper berries, and sage. The blankets her mother made were soft and woven so tight that rain rolled off them like birds' feathers. Ayah remembered sleeping warm on cold windy nights, wrapped in her mother's blankets on the hogan's sandy floor.

3 The snow drifted now, with the northwest wind hurling it in gusts. It drifted up around her black overshoes—old ones with little metal buckles. She smiled at the snow which was trying to cover her little by little. She could remember when they had no black rubber overshoes; only the high buckskin leggings that they wrapped over their elkhide moccasins. If the snow was dry or frozen, a person could walk all day and not get wet; and in the evenings the beams of the ceiling would hang with lengths of pale buckskin leggings, drying out slowly.

4 She felt peaceful remembering. She didn't feel cold any more. Jimmie's blanket seemed warmer than it had ever been. And she could remember the morning he was born. She could remember whispering to her mother, who was sleeping on the other side of the hogan, to tell her it was time now. She did not want to wake the others. The second time she called to her, her mother stood up and pulled on her shoes; she knew. They walked to the old stone hogan together, Ayah walking a step behind her mother. She waited alone, learning the rhythms of the pains while her mother went to call the old woman to help them. The morning was already warm even before dawn and Ayah smelled the bee flowers blooming and the young willow growing at the springs. She could remember that so clearly, but his birth merged into the births of the other children and to her it became all the same birth. They named him for the summer morning and in English they called him Jimmie.

It wasn't like Jimmie died. He just never came back, and one day a dark blue sedan with white writing on its doors pulled up in front of the boxcar shack where the rancher let the Indians live. A man in a khaki uniform trimmed in gold gave them a yellow piece of paper and told them that Jimmie was dead. He said the Army would try to get the body back and then it would be shipped to them; but it wasn't likely because the helicopter had burned after it crashed. All of this was told to Chato because he could understand English. She stood inside the doorway holding the baby while Chato listened. Chato spoke English like a white man and he spoke Spanish too. He was taller than the white man and he stood straighter too. Chato didn't explain why; he just told the military man they could keep the body if they found it. The white man looked bewildered; he nodded his head and he left. Then Chato looked at her and shook his head, and then he told her, "Jimmie isn't coming home anymore," and when he spoke, he used the words to speak of the dead. She didn't cry then, but she hurt inside with anger. And she mourned him as the years passed, when a horse fell with Chato and broke his leg, and the white rancher told them he wouldn't pay Chato until he could work again. She mourned Jimmie because he would have worked for his father then; he would have saddled the big bay horse and ridden the fence lines each day, with wire cutters and heavy gloves, fixing the breaks in the barbed wire and putting the stray cattle back inside again. 5

She mourned him after the white doctors came to take Danny and Ella away. She was at the shack alone that day they came. It was back in the days before they hired Navajo women to go with them as interpreters. She recognized one of the doctors. She had seen him at the children's clinic at Cañoncito about a month ago. They were wearing khaki uniforms and they waved papers at her and a black ball-point pen, trying to make her understand their English words. She was frightened by the way they looked at the children, like the lizard watches the fly. Danny was swinging on the tire swing on the elm tree behind the rancher's house, and Ella was toddling around the front door, dragging the broomstick horse Chato made for her. Ayah could see they wanted her to sign the papers, and Chato had taught her to sign her name. It was something she was proud of. She only wanted them to go, and to take their eyes away from her children. 6

She took the pen from the man without looking at his face and she signed the papers in three different places he pointed to. She stared at the ground by their feet and waited for them to leave. But they stood there and began to point and gesture at the children. Danny stopped swinging. Ayah could see his fear. She moved suddenly and grabbed Ella into her arms; the child squirmed, trying to get back to her toys. Ayah ran with the baby toward Danny; she screamed for him to run and then she grabbed him around his chest and carried him too. She ran south into the foothills of juniper trees and black lava rock. Behind her she heard the doctors running, but they had been taken by surprise, and as the hills became stepper and the cholla cactus were thicker, they stopped. When she reached the top of the hill, she stopped to listen in case they were circling around her. But in a few minutes she heard a car engine start and they drove away. The children had been too surprised to cry while she ran with them. Danny was shaking and Ella's little fingers were gripping Ayah's blouse. 7

8 She stayed up in the hills for the rest of the day, sitting on a black lava boulder in the sunshine where she could see for miles all around her. The sky was light blue and cloudless, and it was warm for late April. The sun warmth relaxed her and took the fear and anger away. She lay back on the rock and watched the sky. It seemed to her that she could walk into the sky, stepping through clouds endlessly. Danny played with little pebbles and stones, pretending they were birds eggs and then little rabbits. Ella sat at her feet and dropped fistfuls of dirt into the breeze, watching the dust and particles of sand intently. Ayah watched a hawk soar high above them, dark wings gliding; hunting or only watching, she did not know. The hawk was patient and he circled all afternoon before he disappeared around the high volcanic peak the Mexicans called Guadalupe.

9 Late in the afternoon, Ayah looked down at the gray boxcar shack with the paint all peeled from the wood; the stove pipe on the roof was rusted and crooked. The fire she had built that morning in the oil drum stove had burned out. Ella was asleep in her lap now and Danny sat close to her, complaining that he was hungry; he asked when they would go to the house. "We will stay up here until your father comes," she told him, "because those white men were chasing us." The boy remembered then and he nodded at her silently.

10 If Jimmie had been there he could have read those papers and explained to her what they said. Ayah would have known then, never to sign them. The doctors came back the next day and they brought a BIA policeman with them. They told Chato they had her signature and that was all they needed. Except for the kids. She listened to Chato sullenly; she hated him when he told her it was the old woman who died in the winter, spitting blood; it was her old grandma who had given the children this disease. "They don't spit blood," she said coldly. "The whites lie." She held Ella and Danny close to her, ready to run to the hills again. "I want a medicine man first," she said to Chato, not looking at him. He shook his head. "It's too late now. The policeman is with them. You signed the paper." His voice was gentle.

11 It was worse than if they had died: to lose the children and to know that somewhere, in a place called Colorado, in a place full of sick and dying strangers, her children were without her. There had been babies that died soon after they were born, and one that died before he could walk. She had carried them herself, up to the boulders and great pieces of the cliff that long ago crashed down from Long Mesa; she laid them in the crevices of sandstone and buried them in fine brown sand with round quartz pebbles that washed down the hills in the rain. She had endured it because they had been with her. But she could not bear this pain. She did not sleep for a long time after they took her children. She stayed on the hill where they had fled the first time, and she slept rolled up in the blanket Jimmie had sent her. She carried the pain in her belly and it was fed by everything she saw: the blue sky of their last day together and the dust and pebbles they played with; the swing in the elm tree and broom stick horse choked life from her. The pain filled her stomach and there was no room for food or for her lungs to fill with air. The air and the food would have been theirs.

She hated Chato, not because he let the policeman and doctors put the screaming children in the government car, but because he had taught her to sign her name. Because it was like the old ones always told her about learning their language or any of their ways: it endangered you. She slept alone on the hill until the middle of November when the first snows came. Then she made a bed for herself where the children had slept. She did not lie down beside Chato again until many years later, when he was sick and shivering and only her body could keep him warm. The illness came after the white rancher told Chato he was too old to work for him anymore, and Chato and his old woman should be out of the shack by the next afternoon because the rancher had hired new people to work there. That had satisfied her. To see how the white man repaid Chato's years of loyalty and work. All of Chato's fine-sounding English talk didn't change things. 12

It snowed steadily and the luminous light from the snow gradually diminished into the darkness. Somewhere in Cebolleta a dog barked and other village dogs joined with it. Ayah looked in the direction she had come, from the bar where Chato was buying the wine. Sometimes he told her to go on ahead and wait; and then he never came. And when she finally went back looking for him, she would find him passed out at the bottom of the wooden steps at Azzie's Bar. All the wine would be gone and most of the money too, from the pale blue check that came to them once a month in a government envelope. It was then that she would look at his face and his hands, scarred by ropes and the barbed wire of all those years, and she would think, this man is a stranger; for forty years she had smiled at him and cooked his food, but he remained a stranger. She stood up again, with the snow almost to her knees, and she walked back to find Chato. 13

It was hard to walk in the deep snow and she felt the air burn in her lungs. She stopped a short distance from the bar to rest and readjust the blanket. But this time he wasn't waiting for her on the bottom step with his old Stetson hat pulled down and his shoulders hunched up in his long wool overcoat. 14

She was careful not to slip on the wooden steps. When she pushed the door open, warm air and cigarette smoke hit her face. She looked around slowly and deliberately, in every corner, in every dark place that the old man might find to sleep. The bar owner didn't like Indians in there, especially Navajos, but he let Chato come in because he could talk Spanish like he was one of them. The men at the bar stared at her, and the bartender saw that she left the door open wide. Snowflakes were flying inside like moths and melting into a puddle on the oiled wood floor. He motioned to her to close the door, but she did not see him. She held herself straight and walked across the room slowly, searching the room with every step. The snow in her hair melted and she could feel it on her forehead. At the far corner of the room, she saw red flames at the mica window of the old stove door; she looked behind the stove just to make sure. The bar got quiet except for the Spanish polka music playing on the jukebox. She stood by the stove and shook the snow from her blanket and held it near the stove to dry. The wet wool smell reminded her of new-born goats in early March, brought inside to warm near the fire. She felt calm. 15

16 In past years they would have told her to get out. But her hair was white now and her face was wrinkled. They looked at her like she was a spider crawling slowly across the room. They were afraid; she could feel the fear. She looked at their faces steadily. They reminded her of the first time the white people brought her children back to her that winter. Danny had been shy and hid behind the thin white woman who brought them. And the baby had not known her until Ayah took her into her arms, and then Ella had nuzzled close to her as she had when she was nursing. The blonde woman was nervous and kept looking at a dainty gold watch on her wrist. She sat on the bench near the small window and watched the dark snow clouds gather around the mountains; she was worrying about the unpaved road. She was frightened by what she saw inside too: the strips of venison drying on a rope across the ceiling and the children jabbering excitedly in a language she did not know. So they stayed for only a few hours. Ayah watched the government car disappear down the road and she knew they were already being weaned from these lava hills and from this sky. The last time they came was in early June, and Ella stared at her the way the men in the bar were now staring. Ayah did not try to pick her up; she smiled at her instead and spoke cheerfully to Danny. When he tried to answer her, he could not seem to remember and he spoke English words with the Navajo. But he gave her a scrap of paper that he had found somewhere and carried in his pocket; it was folded in half, and he shyly looked up at her and said it was a bird. She asked Chato if they were home for good this time. He spoke to the white woman and she shook her head. "How much longer?" he asked, and she said she didn't know; but Chato saw how she stared at the boxcar shack. Ayah turned away then. She did not say good-bye.

17 She felt satisfied that the men in the bar feared her. Maybe it was her face and the way she held her mouth with teeth clenched tight, like there was nothing anyone could do to her now. She walked north down the road, searching for the old man. She did this because she had the blanket, and there would be no place for him except with her and the blanket in the old abode barn near the arroyo. They always slept there when they came to Cebolleta. If the money and the wine were gone, she would be relieved because then they could go home again; back to the old hogan with a dirt roof and rock walls where she herself had been born. And the next day the old man could go back to the few sheep they still had, to follow along behind them, guiding them, into dry sandy arroyos where sparse grass grew. She knew he did not like walking behind old ewes when for so many years he rode big quarter horses and worked with cattle. But she wasn't sorry for him; he should have known all along what would happen.

18 There had not been enough rain for their garden in five years; and that was when Chato finally hitched a ride into the town and brought back brown boxes of rice and sugar and big tin cans of welfare peaches. After that, at the first of the month they went to Cebolleta to ask the postmaster for the check; and then Chato would go to the bar and cash it. They did this as they planted the garden every May, not because anything would survive the summer dust, but because it was time to do this. The journey passed the days that smelled silent and dry like the caves above the canyon with yellow painted buffaloes on their walls.

He was walking along the pavement when she found him. He did not stop or turn around when he heard her behind him. She walked beside him and she noticed how slowly he moved now. He smelled strong of woodsmoke and urine. Lately he had been forgetting. Sometimes he called her by his sister's name and she had been gone for a long time. Once she had found him wandering on the road to the white man's ranch, and she asked him why he was going that way; he laughed at her and said, "You know they can't run that ranch without me," and he walked on determined, limping on the leg that had been crushed many years before. Now he looked at her curiously, as if for the first time, but he kept shuffling along, moving slowly along the side of the highway. His gray hair had grown long and spread out on the shoulders of the long overcoat. He wore the old felt hat pulled down over his ears. His boots were worn out at the toes and he had stuffed pieces of an old red shirt in the holes. The rags made his feet look like little animals up to their ears in snow. She laughed at his feet; the snow muffled the sound of her laugh. He stopped and looked at her again. The wind had quit blowing and the snow was falling straight down; the southeast sky was beginning to clear and Ayah could see a star. 19

"Let's rest awhile," she said to him. They walked away from the road and up the slope to the giant boulders that had tumbled down from the red sand-rock mesa throughout the centuries of rainstorms and earth tremors. In a place where the boulders shut out the wind, they sat down with their backs against the rock. She offered half of the blanket to him and they sat wrapped together. 20

The storm passed swiftly. The clouds moved east. They were massive and full, crowding together across the sky. She watched them with the feeling of horses—steely blue-gray horses startled across the sky. The powerful haunches pushed into the distances and the tail hairs streamed white mist behind them. The sky cleared. Ayah saw that there was nothing between her and the stars. The light was crystalline. There was no shimmer, no distortion through earth haze. She breathed the clarity of the night sky; she smelled the purity of the half moon and the stars. He was lying on his side with his knees pulled up near his belly for warmth. His eyes were closed now, and in the light from the stars and the moon, he looked young again. 21

She could see it descend out of the night sky: an icy stillness from the edge of the thin moon. She recognized the freezing. It came gradually, sinking snowflake by snowflake until the crust was heavy and deep. It had the strength of the stars in Orion, and its journey was endless. Ayah knew that with the wine he would sleep. He would not feel it. She tucked the blanket around him, remembering how it was when Ella had been with her; and she felt the rush so big inside her heart for the babies. And she sang the only song she knew to sing for babies. She could not remember if she had ever sung it to her children, but she knew that her grandmother had sung it and her mother had sung it: 22

The earth is your mother,
  she holds you.
The sky is your father,
  he protects you.

Sleep,
sleep.
Rainbow is your sister,
  she loves you.
The winds are your brothers,
  they sing to you.
Sleep,
sleep.
We are together always
We are together always
There never was a time
when this
was not so.

Inquiring into the Story

Use the methods of inquiry—exploring, explaining, evaluating, and reflecting—to discover what you think about Silko's short story, and move toward your own interpretations. The following questions might serve as journal prompts and triggers for class discussion.

1. On the left page of your notebook, jot down at least five lines or passages that you believe were key to your understanding of the story. These may include details that seem important, moments that signify turning points, or feelings or ideas suggested by the narrator or another character. On the opposing right page, openly fastwrite about the passages you collected. What do they seem to suggest about possible themes for the story? What do you notice about Ayah, the main character and narrator? What do you consider the significant events that affect all the characters and how do they change them?
2. Explain the significance of the poem that ends "Lullaby."
3. A recurring detail in the story is the blanket that Ayah received from her son, Jimmie. Trace every mention of the blanket in the story. What accumulated meaning does this detail acquire in the story?
4. Some critics have argued that "Lullaby" is a story of healing and recovery. Do you agree or disagree? What evidence in the story would you point to that either supports or contradicts that contention?
5. One of the most common responses we have to stories we enjoy is to say that we "could relate to it." Did you feel that way about "Lullaby" even though you might not be Native American? Certainly the story helps those

of us who are not Native American understand an aspect of the Indian experience in America, but does it also help us understand ourselves?

ONE STUDENT'S RESPONSE

NOEL'S JOURNAL

DOUBLE-ENTRY JOURNAL RESPONSE TO "LULLABY"

"It was worse than if they had died: to lose the children and to know that somewhere, in a place called Colorado, in a place full of sick and dying strangers, her children were without her."	I think this sets the tone of the whole story. She loses one son to the war and the other two were taken from her. Knowing that one son had died and wouldn't ever come home again. The other two were alive and well but they would not grow up with their mother and were kept from their own culture by the government.
"She stayed on the hill where they had fled the first time, and she slept rolled up in the blanket Jimmie had sent her."	After she lost all her children she finds comfort in the blanket her older son had sent her. She sleeps in the place where she spent the last moments with her other two children. She carries the blanket with her wherever she goes. This is how she spent her time mourning her loss and memories . . .

SHORT STORY

Joyce Carol Oates is among our most prolific writers and gifted literary masters. She has published more than thirty-seven novels or novellas, twenty-three collections of short stories, and many essays. Her success began early. As a nineteen-year-old at Syracuse University, Oates won a national short story contest sponsored by *Mademoiselle* magazine. Since then, she has repeatedly been a finalist for the Pulitzer and National Book awards. Oates currently teaches in the creative writing program at Princeton.

"Where Are You Going, Where Have You Been?" published in 1970, is one of Joyce Carol Oates's most anthologized works of short fiction. The story is set in a time of cultural change and turmoil in the United States, but there are only hints of this in the story. In some ways, the tensions here are timeless—a young girl in an uneasy relationship with her mother, the seductive power of music, and the dark power of a stranger who changes everything. Some critics have called the story "allegorical," a narrative with symbolic undertones, which is one reason, of course, that it is ripe for analysis.

WHERE ARE YOU GOING, WHERE HAVE YOU BEEN?

Joyce Carol Oates

for Bob Dylan

1 Her name was Connie. She was fifteen and she had a quick, nervous giggling habit of craning her neck to glance into mirrors or checking other people's faces to make sure her own was all right. Her mother, who noticed everything and knew everything and who hadn't much reason any longer to look at her own face, always scolded Connie about it. "Stop gawking at yourself. Who are you? You think you're so pretty?" she would say. Connie would raise her eyebrows at these familiar old complaints and look right through her mother, into a shadowy vision of herself as she was right at that moment: she knew she was pretty and that was everything. Her mother had been pretty once too, if you could believe those old snapshots in the album, but now her looks were gone and that was why she was always after Connie.

2 "Why don't you keep your room clean like your sister? How've you got your hair fixed—what the hell stinks? Hair spray? You don't see your sister using that junk."

3 Her sister June was twenty-four and still lived at home. She was a secretary in the high school Connie attended, and if that wasn't bad enough—with her in the same building—she was so plain and chunky and steady that Connie had to hear her praised all the time by her mother and her mother's sisters. June did this, June did that, she saved money and helped clean the house and cooked and Connie couldn't do a thing, her mind was all filled with trashy daydreams. Their father was away at work most of the time and when he came home he wanted supper and he read the newspaper at supper and after supper he went to bed. He didn't bother talking much to them, but around his bent head Connie's mother kept picking at her until Connie wished her mother was dead and she herself was dead and it was all over. "She makes me want to throw up sometimes," she complained to her friends. She had a high, breathless, amused voice that made everything she said sound a little forced, whether it was sincere or not.

4 There was one good thing: June went places with girl friends of hers, girls who were just as plain and steady as she, and so when Connie wanted to do that her mother had no objections. The father of Connie's best girl friend drove the girls the three miles to town and left them at a shopping plaza so they could walk through the stores or go to a movie, and when he came to pick them up again at eleven he never bothered to ask what they had done.

5 They must have been familiar sights, walking around the shopping plaza in their shorts and flat ballerina slippers that always scuffed the sidewalk, with charm bracelets jingling on their thin wrists; they would lean together to whisper and laugh secretly if someone passed who amused or interested them. Connie had long dark blond hair that drew anyone's eye to it, and she wore part of it pulled up on her head

and puffed out and the rest of it she let fall down her back. She wore a pull-over jersey blouse that looked one way when she was at home and another way when she was away from home. Everything about her had two sides to it, one for home and one for anywhere that was not home: her walk, which could be childlike and bobbing, or languid enough to make anyone think she was hearing music in her head; her mouth, which was pale and smirking most of the time, but bright and pink on these evenings out; her laugh, which was cynical and drawling at home—"Ha, ha, very funny,"—but highpitched and nervous anywhere else, like the jingling of the charms on her bracelet.

6 Sometimes they did go shopping or to a movie, but sometimes they went across the highway, ducking fast across the busy road, to a drive-in restaurant where older kids hung out. The restaurant was shaped like a big bottle, though squatter than a real bottle, and on its cap was a revolving figure of a grinning boy holding a hamburger aloft. One night in midsummer they ran across, breathless with daring, and right away someone leaned out a car window and invited them over, but it was just a boy from high school they didn't like. It made them feel good to be able to ignore him. They went up through the maze of parked and cruising cars to the bright-lit, fly-infested restaurant, their faces pleased and expectant as if they were entering a sacred building that loomed up out of the night to give them what haven and blessing they yearned for. They sat at the counter and crossed their legs at the ankles, their thin shoulders rigid with excitement, and listened to the music that made everything so good: the music was always in the background, like music at a church service; it was something to depend upon.

7 A boy named Eddie came in to talk with them. He sat backwards on his stool, turning himself jerkily around in semicircles and then stopping and turning back again, and after a while he asked Connie if she would like something to eat. She said she would and so she tapped her friend's arm on her way out—her friend pulled her face up into a brave, droll look—and Connie said she would meet her at eleven, across the way. "I just hate to leave her like that," Connie said earnestly, but the boy said that she wouldn't be alone for long. So they went out to his car, and on the way Connie couldn't help but let her eyes wander over the windshields and faces all around her, her face gleaming with a joy that had nothing to do with Eddie or even this place; it might have been the music. She drew her shoulders up and sucked in her breath with the pure pleasure of being alive, and just at that moment she happened to glance at a face just a few feet from hers. It was a boy with shaggy black hair, in a convertible jalopy painted gold. He stared at her and then his lips widened into a grin. Connie slit her eyes at him and turned away, but she couldn't help glancing back and there he was, still watching her. He wagged a finger and laughed and said, "Gonna get you, baby," and Connie turned away again without Eddie noticing anything.

8 She spent three hours with him, at the restaurant where they ate hamburgers and drank Cokes in wax cups that were always sweating, and then down an alley a mile or so away, and when he left her off at five to eleven only the movie house was still open at the plaza. Her girl friend was there, talking with a boy. When Connie came up, the

two girls smiled at each other and Connie said, "How was the movie?" and the girl said, "You should know." They rode off with the girl's father, sleepy and pleased, and Connie couldn't help but look back at the darkened shopping plaza with its big empty parking lot and its signs that were faded and ghostly now, and over at the drive-in restaurant where cars were still circling tirelessly. She couldn't hear the music at this distance.

9 Next morning June asked her how the movie was and Connie said, "So-so."

10 She and that girl and occasionally another girl went out several times a week, and the rest of the time Connie spent around the house—it was summer vacation—getting in her mother's way and thinking, dreaming about the boys she met. But all the boys fell back and dissolved into a single face that was not even a face but an idea, a feeling, mixed up with the urgent insistent pounding of the music and the humid night air of July. Connie's mother kept dragging her back to the daylight by finding things for her to do or saying suddenly, "What's this about the Pettinger girl?"

11 And Connie would say nervously, "Oh, her. That dope." She always drew thick clear lines between herself and such girls, and her mother was simple and kind enough to believe it. Her mother was so simple, Connie thought, that it was maybe cruel to fool her so much. Her mother went scuffling around the house in old bedroom slippers and complained over the telephone to one sister about the other, then the other called up and the two of them complained about the third one. If June's name was mentioned her mother's tone was approving, and if Connie's name was mentioned it was disapproving. This did not really mean she disliked Connie, and actually Connie thought that her mother preferred her to June just because she was prettier, but the two of them kept up a pretense of exasperation, a sense that they were tugging and struggling over something of little value to either of them. Sometimes, over coffee, they were almost friends, but something would come up—some vexation that was like a fly buzzing suddenly around their heads—and their faces went hard with contempt.

12 One Sunday Connie got up at eleven—none of them bothered with church—and washed her hair so that it could dry all day long in the sun. Her parents and sister were going to a barbecue at an aunt's house and Connie said no, she wasn't interested, rolling her eyes to let her mother know just what she thought of it. "Stay home alone then," her mother said sharply. Connie sat out back in a lawn chair and watched them drive away, her father quiet and bald, hunched around so that he could back the car out, her mother with a look that was still angry and not at all softened through the windshield, and in the back seat poor old June, all dressed up as if she didn't know what a barbecue was, with all the running yelling kids and the flies. Connie sat with her eyes closed in the sun, dreaming and dazed with the warmth about her as if this were a kind of love, the caresses of love, and her mind slipped over onto thoughts of the boy she had been with the night before and how nice he had been, how sweet it always was, not the way someone like June would suppose but sweet, gentle, the way it was in movies and promised in songs; and when she opened her eyes she hardly knew where she was, the back yard ran off into weeds and a fence-like line of trees and behind it the sky was perfectly blue and still. The asbestos ranch house that was now three years old startled her—it looked small. She shook her head as if to get awake.

It was too hot. She went inside the house and turned on the radio to drown out the quiet. She sat on the edge of her bed, barefoot, and listened for an hour and a half to a program called XYZ Sunday Jamboree, record after record of hard, fast, shrieking songs she sang along with, interspersed by exclamations from "Bobby King": "An' look here, you girls at Napoleon's—Son and Charley want you to pay real close attention to this song coming up!" 13

And Connie paid close attention herself, bathed in a glow of slow-pulsed joy that seemed to rise mysteriously out of the music itself and lay languidly about the airless little room, breathed in and breathed out with each gentle rise and fall of her chest. 14

After a while she heard a car coming up the drive. She sat up at once, startled, because it couldn't be her father so soon. The gravel kept crunching all the way in from the road—the driveway was long—and Connie ran to the window. It was a car she didn't know. It was an open jalopy, painted a bright gold that caught the sunlight opaquely. Her heart began to pound and her fingers snatched at her hair, checking it, and she whispered, "Christ. Christ," wondering how bad she looked. The car came to a stop at the side door and the horn sounded four short taps, as if this were a signal Connie knew. 15

She went into the kitchen and approached the door slowly, then hung out the screen door, her bare toes curling down off the step. There were two boys in the car and now she recognized the driver: he had shaggy, shabby black hair that looked crazy as a wig and he was grinning at her. 16

"I ain't late, am I?" he said. 17

"Who the hell do you think you are?" Connie said. 18

"Toldja I'd be out, didn't I?" 19

"I don't even know who you are." 20

She spoke sullenly, careful to show no interest or pleasure, and he spoke in a fast, bright monotone. Connie looked past him to the other boy, taking her time. He had fair brown hair, with a lock that fell onto his forehead. His sideburns gave him a fierce, embarrassed look, but so far he hadn't even bothered to glance at her. Both boys wore sunglasses. The driver's glasses were metallic and mirrored everything in miniature. 21

"You wanta come for a ride?" he said. 22

Connie smirked and let her hair fall loose over one shoulder. 23

"Don'tcha like my car? New paint job," he said. "Hey." 24

"What?" 25

"You're cute." 26

She pretended to fidget, chasing flies away from the door. 27

"Don'tcha believe me, or what?" he said. 28

"Look, I don't even know who you are," Connie said in disgust. 29

"Hey, Ellie's got a radio, see. Mine broke down." He lifted his friend's arm and showed her the little transistor radio the boy was holding, and now Connie began to hear the music. It was the same program that was playing inside the house. 30

"Bobby King?" she said. 31

"I listen to him all the time. I think he's great." 32

33 "He's kind of great," Connie said reluctantly.

34 "Listen, that guy's *great*. He knows where the action is."

35 Connie blushed a little, because the glasses made it impossible for her to see just what this boy was looking at. She couldn't decide if she liked him or if he was just a jerk, and so she dawdled in the doorway and wouldn't come down or go back inside. She said, "What's all that stuff painted on your car?"

36 "Can'tcha read it?" He opened the door very carefully, as if he were afraid it might fall off. He slid out just as carefully, planting his feet firmly on the ground, the tiny metallic world in his glasses slowing down like gelatine hardening, and in the midst of it Connie's bright green blouse. "This here is my name, to begin with, he said. ARNOLD FRIEND was written in tarlike black letters on the side, with a drawing of a round, grinning face that reminded Connie of a pumpkin, except it wore sunglasses. "I wanta introduce myself, I'm Arnold Friend and that's my real name and I'm gonna be your friend, honey, and inside the car's Ellie Oscar, he's kinda shy." Ellie brought his transistor radio up to his shoulder and balanced it there. "Now, these numbers are a secret code, honey," Arnold Friend explained. He read off the numbers 33, 19, 17 and raised his eyebrows at her to see what she thought of that, but she didn't think much of it. The left rear fender had been smashed and around it was written, on the gleaming gold background: DONE BY CRAZY WOMAN DRIVER. Connie had to laugh at that. Arnold Friend was pleased at her laughter and looked up at her. "Around the other side's a lot more —you wanta come and see them?"

37 "No."

38 "Why not?"

39 "Why should I?"

40 "Don'tcha wanta see what's on the car? Don'tcha wanta go for a ride?"

41 "I don't know."

42 "Why not?"

43 "I got things to do."

44 "Like what?"

45 "Things."

46 He laughed as if she had said something funny. He slapped his thighs. He was standing in a strange way, leaning back against the car as if he were balancing himself. He wasn't tall, only an inch or so taller than she would be if she came down to him. Connie liked the way he was dressed, which was the way all of them dressed: tight faded jeans stuffed into black, scuffed boots, a belt that pulled his waist in and showed how lean he was, and a white pull-over shirt that was a little soiled and showed the hard small muscles of his arms and shoulders. He looked as if he probably did hard work, lifting and carrying things. Even his neck looked muscular. And his face was a familiar face, somehow: the jaw and chin and cheeks slightly darkened because he hadn't shaved for a day or two, and the nose long and hawklike, sniffing as if she were a treat he was going to gobble up and it was all a joke.

47 "Connie, you ain't telling the truth. This is your day set aside for a ride with me and you know it," he said, still laughing. The way he straightened and recovered from his fit of laughing showed that it had been all fake.

48 “How do you know what my name is?” she said suspiciously.

49 “It’s Connie.”

50 “Maybe and maybe not.”

51 “I know my Connie,” he said, wagging his finger. Now she remembered him even better, back at the restaurant, and her cheeks warmed at the thought of how she had sucked in her breath just at the moment she passed him how she must have looked to him. And he had remembered her. “Ellie and I come out here especially for you,” he said. “Ellie can sit in back. How about it?”

52 “Where?”

53 “Where what?”

54 “Where’re we going?”

55 He looked at her. He took off the sunglasses and she saw how pale the skin around his eyes was, like holes that were not in shadow but instead in light. His eyes were like chips of broken glass that catch the light in an amiable way. He smiled. It was as if the idea of going for a ride somewhere, to someplace, was a new idea to him.

56 “Just for a ride, Connie sweetheart.”

57 “I never said my name was Connie,” she said.

58 “But I know what it is. I know your name and all about you, lots of things,” Arnold Friend said. He had not moved yet but stood still leaning back against the side of his jalopy. “I took a special interest in you, such a pretty girl, and found out all about you—like I know your parents and sister are gone somewheres and I know where and how long they’re going to be gone, and I know who you were with last night, and your best girl friend’s name is Betty. Right?”

59 He spoke in a simple lilting voice, exactly as if he were reciting the words to a song. His smile assured her that everything was fine. In the car Ellie turned up the volume on his radio and did not bother to look around at them.

60 “Ellie can sit in the back seat,” Arnold Friend said. He indicated his friend with a casual jerk of his chin, as if Ellie did not count and she should not bother with him.

61 “How’d you find out all that stuff?” Connie said.

62 “Listen: Betty Schultz and Tony Fitch and Jimmy Pettinger and Nancy Pettinger,” he said in a chant. “Raymond Stanley and Bob Hutter—”

63 “Do you know all those kids?”

64 “I know everybody.”

65 “Look, you’re kidding. You’re not from around here.”

66 “Sure.”

67 “But—how come we never saw you before?”

68 “Sure you saw me before,” he said. He looked down at his boots, as if he were a little offended. “You just don’t remember.”

69 “I guess I’d remember you,” Connie said.

70 “Yeah?” He looked up at this, beaming. He was pleased. He began to mark time with the music from Ellie’s radio, tapping his fists lightly together. Connie looked away from his smile to the car, which was painted so bright it almost hurt her eyes to look at it. She looked at that name, ARNOLD FRIEND. And up at the front fender was an expression that was familiar—MAN THE FLYING SAUCERS. It was an

expression kids had used the year before but didn't use this year. She looked at it for a while as if the words meant something to her that she did not yet know.

71 "What're you thinking about? Huh?" Arnold Friend demanded. "Not worried about your hair blowing around in the car, are you?"

72 "No."

73 "Think I maybe can't drive good?"

74 "How do I know?"

75 "You're a hard girl to handle. How come?" he said. "Don't you know I'm your friend? Didn't you see me put my sign in the air when you walked by?"

"What sign?"

76 "My sign." And he drew an X in the air, leaning out toward her. They were maybe ten feet apart. After his hand fell back to his side the X was still in the air, almost visible. Connie let the screen door close and stood perfectly still inside it, listening to the music from her radio and the boy's blend together. She stared at Arnold Friend. He stood there so stiffly relaxed, pretending to be relaxed, with one hand idly on the door handle as if he were keeping himself up that way and had no intention of ever moving again. She recognized most things about him, the tight jeans that showed his thighs and buttocks and the greasy leather boots and the tight shirt, and even that slippery friendly smile of his, that sleepy dreamy smile that all the boys used to get across ideas they didn't want to put into words. She recognized all this and also the singsong way he talked, slightly mocking, kidding, but serious and a little melancholy, and she recognized the way he tapped one fist against the other in homage to the perpetual music behind him. But all these things did not come together.

77 She said suddenly, "Hey, how old are you?"

78 His smile faded. She could see then that he wasn't a kid, he was much older—thirty, maybe more. At this knowledge her heart began to pound faster.

79 "That's a crazy thing to ask. Can'tcha see I'm your own age?"

80 "Like hell you are."

81 "Or maybe a couple years older. I'm eighteen."

82 "Eighteen?" she said doubtfully.

83 He grinned to reassure her and lines appeared at the corners of his mouth. His teeth were big and white. He grinned so broadly his eyes became slits and she saw how thick the lashes were, thick and black as if painted with a black tarlike material. Then, abruptly, he seemed to become embarrassed and looked over his shoulder at Ellie. "*Him*, he's crazy," he said. "Ain't he a riot? He's a nut, a real character." Ellie was still listening to the music. His sunglasses told nothing about what he was thinking. He wore a bright orange shirt unbuttoned halfway to show his chest, which was a pale, bluish chest and not muscular like Arnold Friend's. His shirt collar was turned up all around and the very tips of the collar pointed out past his chin as if they were protecting him. He was pressing the transistor radio up against his ear and sat there in a kind of daze, right in the sun.

84 "He's kinda strange," Connie said.

85 "Hey, she says you're kinda strange! Kinda strange!" Arnold Friend cried. He pounded on the car to get Ellie's attention. Ellie turned for the first time and Connie

saw with shock that he wasn't a kid either—he had a fair, hairless face, cheeks reddened slightly as if the veins grew too close to the surface of his skin, the face of a forty-year-old baby. Connie felt a wave of dizziness rise in her at this sight and she stared at him as if waiting for something to change the shock of the moment, make it all right again. Ellie's lips kept shaping words, mumbling along with the words blasting in his ear.

"Maybe you two better go away," Connie said faintly. 86

"What? How come?" Arnold Friend cried. "We come out here to take you for a ride. It's Sunday." He had the voice of the man on the radio now. It was the same voice, Connie thought. "Don'tcha know it's Sunday all day? And honey, no matter who you were with last night, today you're with Arnold Friend and don't you forget it! Maybe you better step out here," he said, and this last was in a different voice. It was a little flatter, as if the heat was finally getting to him. 87

"No. I got things to do." 88

"Hey." 89

You two better leave." 90

"We ain't leaving until you come with us." 91

"Like hell I am—" 92

"Connie, don't fool around with me. I mean—I mean, don't fool *around*," he said, shaking his head. He laughed incredulously. He placed his sunglasses on top of his head, carefully, as if he were indeed wearing a wig, and brought the stems down behind his ears. Connie stared at him, another wave of dizziness and fear rising in her so that for a moment he wasn't even in focus but was just a blur standing there against his gold car, and she had the idea that he had driven up the driveway all right but had come from nowhere before that and belonged nowhere and that everything about him and even about the music that was so familiar to her was only half real. 93

"If my father comes and sees you—" 94

"He ain't coming. He's at a barbecue." 95

"How do you know that?" 96

"Aunt Tillie's. Right now they're uh—they're drinking. Sitting around," he said vaguely, squinting as if he were staring all the way to town and over to Aunt Tillie's back yard. Then the vision seemed to get clear and he nodded energetically. "Yeah. Sitting around. There's your sister in a blue dress, huh? And high heels, the poor sad bitch—nothing like you, sweetheart! And your mother's helping some fat woman with the corn, they're cleaning the corn—husking the corn—" 97

"What fat woman?" Connie cried. 98

"How do I know what fat woman, I don't know every goddamn fat woman in the world!" Arnold Friend laughed. 99

"Oh, that's Mrs. Hornsby. . . . Who invited her?" Connie said. She felt a little lightheaded. Her breath was coming quickly. 100

"She's too fat. I don't like them fat. I like them the way you are, honey," he said, smiling sleepily at her. They stared at each other for a while through the screen door. He said softly, "Now, what you're going to do is this: you're going to come out that door. You re going to sit up front with me and Ellie's going to sit in the back, the hell with Ellie, right? This isn't Ellie's date. You're my date. I'm your lover, honey." 101

102 "What? You're crazy—"

103 "Yes, I'm your lover. You don't know what that is but you will," he said. "I know that too. I know all about you. But look: it's real nice and you couldn't ask for nobody better than me, or more polite. I always keep my word. I'll tell you how it is, I'm always nice at first, the first time. I'll hold you so tight you won't think you have to try to get away or pretend anything because you'll know you can't. And I'll come inside you where it's all secret and you'll give in to me and you'll love me."

104 "Shut up! You're crazy!" Connie said. She backed away from the door. She put her hands up against her ears as if she'd heard something terrible, something not meant for her. "People don't talk like that, you're crazy," she muttered. Her heart was almost too big now for her chest and its pumping made sweat break out all over her. She looked out to see Arnold Friend pause and then take a step toward the porch, lurching. He almost fell. But, like a clever drunken man, he managed to catch his balance. He wobbled in his high boots and grabbed hold of one of the porch posts.

105 "Honey?" he said. "You still listening?"

106 "Get the hell out of here!"

107 "Be nice, honey. Listen."

108 "I'm going to call the police—"

109 He wobbled again and out of the side of his mouth came a fast spat curse, an aside not meant for her to hear. But even this "Christ!" sounded forced. Then he began to smile again. She watched this smile come, awkward as if he were smiling from inside a mask. His whole face was a mask, she thought wildly, tanned down to his throat but then running out as if he had plastered make-up on his face but had forgotten about his throat.

110 "Honey—? Listen, here's how it is. I always tell the truth and I promise you this: I ain't coming in that house after you."

111 "You better not! I'm going to call the police if you—if you don't—"

112 "Honey," he said, talking right through her voice, "honey, I'm not coming in there but you are coming out here. You know why?"

113 She was panting. The kitchen looked like a place she had never seen before, some room she had run inside but that wasn't good enough, wasn't going to help her. The kitchen window had never had a curtain, after three years, and there were dishes in the sink for her to do—probably—and if you ran your hand across the table you'd probably feel something sticky there.

114 "You listening, honey? Hey?" "—going to call the police—"

115 "Soon as you touch the phone I don't need to keep my promise and can come inside. You won't want that."

116 She rushed forward and tried to lock the door. Her fingers were shaking. "But why lock it," Arnold Friend said gently, talking right into her face. "It's just a screen door. It's just nothing." One of his boots was at a strange angle, as if his foot wasn't in it. It pointed out to the left, bent at the ankle. "I mean, anybody can break through a screen door and glass and wood and iron or anything else if he needs to, anybody at all, and specially Arnold Friend. If the place got lit up with a fire, honey, you'd come runnin' out into my arms, right into my arms an' safe at home—like you knew I was

your lover and'd stopped fooling around. I don't mind a nice shy girl but I don't like no fooling around." Part of those words were spoken with a slight rhythmic lilt, and Connie somehow recognized them—the echo of a song from last year, about a girl rushing into her boy friend's arms and coming home again—

Connie stood barefoot on the linoleum floor, staring at him. "What do you want?" she whispered. 117

"I want you," he said. 118

"What?" 119

"Seen you that night and thought, that's the one, yes sir. I never needed to look anymore." 120

"But my father's coming back. He's coming to get me. I had to wash my hair first—" She spoke in a dry, rapid voice, hardly raising it for him to hear. 121

"No, your daddy is not coming and yes, you had to wash your hair and you washed it for me. It's nice and shining and all for me. I thank you sweetheart," he said with a mock bow, but again he almost lost his balance. He had to bend and adjust his boots. Evidently his feet did not go all the way down; the boots must have been stuffed with something so that he would seem taller. Connie stared out at him and behind him at Ellie in the car, who seemed to be looking off toward Connie's right, into nothing. This Ellie said, pulling the words out of the air one after another as if he were just discovering them, "You want me to pull out the phone?" 122

"Shut your mouth and keep it shut," Arnold Friend said, his face red from bending over or maybe from embarrassment because Connie had seen his boots. "This ain't none of your business." 123

"What—what are you doing? What do you want?" Connie said. "If I call the police they'll get you, they'll arrest you—"

"Promise was not to come in unless you touch that phone, and I'll keep that promise," he said. He resumed his erect position and tried to force his shoulders back. He sounded like a hero in a movie, declaring something important. But he spoke too loudly and it was as if he were speaking to someone behind Connie. "I ain't made plans for coming in that house where I don't belong but just for you to come out to me, the way you should. Don't you know who I am?" 124

"You're crazy," she whispered. She backed away from the door but did not want to go into another part of the house, as if this would give him permission to come through the door. "What do you . . . you're crazy, you. . . ." 125

"Huh? What're you saying, honey?" 126

Her eyes darted everywhere in the kitchen. She could not remember what it was, this room. 127

"This is how it is, honey: you come out and we'll drive away, have a nice ride. But if you don't come out we're gonna wait till your people come home and then they're all going to get it." 128

"You want that telephone pulled out?" Ellie said. He held the radio away from his ear and grimaced, as if without the radio the air was too much for him. 129

"I toldja shut up, Ellie," Arnold Friend said, "you're deaf, get a hearing aid, right? Fix yourself up. This little girl's no trouble and's gonna be nice to me, so Ellie keep to 130 yourself, this ain't your date right? Don't hem in on me, don't hog, don't crush, don't bird dog, don't trail me," he said in a rapid, meaningless voice, as if he were running through all the expressions he'd learned but was no longer sure which of them was in style, then rushing on to new ones, making them up with his eyes closed. "Don't crawl under my fence, don't squeeze in my chipmonk hole, don't sniff my glue, suck my popsicle, keep your own greasy fingers on yourself!" He shaded his eyes and peered in at Connie, who was backed against the kitchen table. "Don't mind him, honey, he's just a creep. He's a dope. Right? I'm the boy for you, and like I said, you come out here nice like a lady and give me your hand, and nobody else gets hurt, I mean, your nice old bald-headed daddy and your mummy and your sister in her high heels. Because listen: why bring them in this?"

131 "Leave me alone," Connie whispered.

132 "Hey, you know that old woman down the road, the one with the chickens and stuff—you know her?"

133 "She's dead!"

134 "Dead? What? You know her?" Arnold Friend said.

135 "She's dead—"

136 "Don't you like her?"

137 "She's dead—she's—she isn't here any more—"

138 "But don't you like her, I mean, you got something against her? Some grudge or something?" Then his voice dipped as if he were conscious of a rudeness. He touched the sunglasses perched up on top of his head as if to make sure they were still there. "Now, you be a good girl."

139 "What are you going to do?"

140 "Just two things, or maybe three," Arnold Friend said. "But I promise it won't last long and you'll like me the way you get to like people you're close to. You will. It's all over for you here, so come on out. You don't want your people in any trouble, do you?"

141 She turned and bumped against a chair or something, hurting her leg, but she ran into the back room and picked up the telephone. Something roared in her ear, a tiny roaring, and she was so sick with fear that she could do nothing but listen to it—the telephone was clammy and very heavy and her fingers groped down to the dial but were too weak to touch it. She began to scream into the phone, into the roaring. She cried out, she cried for her mother, she felt her breath start jerking back and forth in her lungs as if it were something Arnold Friend was stabbing her with again and again with no tenderness. A noisy sorrowful wailing rose all about her and she was locked inside it the way she was locked inside this house.

142 After a while she could hear again. She was sitting on the floor with her wet back against the wall.

143 Arnold Friend was saying from the door, "That's a good girl. Put the phone back."

144 She kicked the phone away from her.

145 "No, honey. Pick it up. Put it back right."

146 She picked it up and put it back. The dial tone stopped.

147 "That's a good girl. Now, you come outside."

She was hollow with what had been fear but what was now just an emptiness. All that screaming had blasted it out of her. She sat, one leg cramped under her, and deep inside her brain was something like a pinpoint of light that kept going and would not let her relax. She thought, I'm not going to see my mother again. She thought, I'm not going to sleep in my bed again. Her bright green blouse was all wet. 148

Arnold Friend said, in a gentle-loud voice that was like a stage voice, "The place where you came from ain't there any more, and where you had in mind to go is cancelled out. This place you are now—inside your daddy's house—is nothing but a cardboard box I can knock down any time. You know that and always did know it. You hear me?" 149

She thought, I have got to think. I have got to know what to do. 150

"We'll go out to a nice field, out in the country here where it smells so nice and it's sunny," Arnold Friend said. "I'll have my arms tight around you so you won't need to try to get away and I'll show you what love is like, what it does. The hell with this house! It looks solid all right," he said. He ran a fingernail down the screen and the noise did not make Connie shiver, as it would have the day before. "Now, put your hand on your heart, honey. Feel that? That feels solid too but we know better. Be nice to me, be sweet like you can because what else is there for a girl like you but to be sweet and pretty and give in?—and get away before her people come back?" 151

She felt her pounding heart. Her hand seemed to enclose it. She thought for the first time in her life that it was nothing that was hers, that belonged to her, but just a pounding, living thing inside this body that wasn't really hers either. 152

"You don't want them to get hurt," Arnold Friend went on. "Now, get up, honey. Get up all by yourself." 153

She stood.

"Now, turn this way. That's right. Come over here to me.— Ellie, put that away, didn't I tell you? You dope. You miserable creepy dope," Arnold Friend said. His words were not angry but only part of an incantation. The incantation was kindly. "Now come out through the kitchen to me, honey, and let's see a smile, try it, you're a brave, sweet little girl and now they're eating corn and hot dogs cooked to bursting over an outdoor fire, and they don't know one thing about you and never did and honey, you're better than them because not a one of them would have done this for you." 154

Connie felt the linoleum under her feet; it was cool. She brushed her hair back out of her eyes. Arnold Friend let go of the post tentatively and opened his arms for her, his elbows pointing in toward each other and his wrists limp, to show that this was an embarrassed embrace and a little mocking, he didn't want to make her self-conscious. 155

She put out her hand against the screen. She watched herself push the door slowly open as if she were back safe somewhere in the other doorway, watching this body and this head of long hair moving out into the sunlight where Arnold Friend waited. 156

"My sweet little blue-eyed girl," he said in a half-sung sigh that had nothing to do with her brown eyes but was taken up just the same by the vast sunlit reaches of the land behind him and on all sides of him—so much land that Connie had never seen before and did not recognize except to know that she was going to it. 157

Inquiring into the Story

Explore, explain, evaluate, and reflect on Oates's story "Where Are You Going, Where Have You Been?"

1. Choose one passage from "Where Are You Going, Where Have You Been?" that you think is central to what you believe the story is really about. Write that on the left page of your notebook. On the right page, fastwrite for five minutes about why you chose that particular passage. How does it seem to point to larger themes or ideas?
2. Oates makes no direct references to time or place in this story. We can infer when it happened from references to a transistor radios and a convertible jalopy, but there are few hints about where the story is set. Why would Oates decide to omit such information?

   Some have argued that Oates's story was "dedicated" to Bob Dylan, and in particular his song, "It's All Over Now, Baby Blue." The song's lyrics, which you can easily find online, hauntingly relate the experience of being forced to leave the familiar world for an unknown, but seemingly more perilous, future. What might you say about the juxtaposition of the following passages from the story and the lyrics of the Dylan song. Do they speak to each other in any revealing ways?

   - *Connie felt a wave of dizziness rise in her at this site and she stared at him as if waiting for something to change the shock of the moment, make it all right again.*
   - *"My sweet little blue-eyed girl," he said in a half-sung sigh that had nothing to do with her brown eyes but was taken up just the same by the vast sunlit reaches of the land behind him and on all side of him—so much land that Connie had never seen before and did not recognize except to know that she was going to it.*

3. Want to know a secret? You can easily buy a critical paper on this short story on the Web. That's plagiarism, of course, and unethical, and you wouldn't do it. Reflect on why some people would.

CRITICAL ESSAY

Writing about literature is like rock climbing—you're always looking for a handhold or the right place to sink your piton. Fortunately, good stories offer writers plenty of places to grasp. You can focus on a particular character, the significance of a scene, a particular motif, or the overall themes of the story. The only essential is that your critical essay be firmly anchored to the story itself—what characters say or do, specific details, particular scenes or passages.

In the essay that follows, Alice Hall Petry focuses on a character who rarely gets much attention in criticism on Joyce Carol Oates' story—Arnold Friend's sidekick, Ellie Oscar. Her essay on Ellie is pretty narrowly focused but it works well because Petry finds plenty of evidence in the story to support her thesis that Ellie is an Elvis prototype. This critical essay, which appeared in the journal *Studies in Short Fiction,* nicely illustrates some the qualities of good critical writing: a narrow focus, a clear argument, and extensive use of the text as evidence.

Who is Ellie? Oates' "Where Are You Going, Where Have You Been?"

Alice Hall Petry

1 Understandably enough, most of the attention generated by Joyce Carol Oates' "Where Are You Going, Where Have You Been?" (*Epoch*, Fall, 1966; collected, *The Wheel of Love*, 1970) has focused on the characters of 15-year-old Connie and her seducer/killer, Arnold Friend. Friend in particular has inspired a series of essays which delineate his resemblance to the Devil,[1] and, curiously enough, Tom Quirk's study of Friend's real-life prototype, Charles Howard Schmid of Tucson, has enhanced rather than qualified the earlier discussions of Friend's allegorical ramifications.[2] Virtually no attention, however, has been paid to Friend's laconic accomplice, Ellie Oscar, a character whose appearance, personality, and behavior suggest he is the incarnation of the darker side of the admitted idol of Friend's prototype: Elvis Presley.

2 Consider Ellie's appearance. The first things Connie notices about him are the lock of hair "that fell onto his forehead" and his "sideburns", [3] both of which call to mind Presley, whose trademark appearance was much imitated by his "cool" male admirers in the late 1950s and early 1960s. Equally significant is Ellie's attire: "His shirt collar was turned up all around and the very tips of the collar pointed out past his chin"; further, his shirt was "unbuttoned halfway to show his chest"—elements which even years after Presley's death in 1977 are still immediately associated with "the King." Other elements are also reminiscent of Presley. Ellie's omnipresent radio—without which he "grimaced, as if . . . the air was too much for him"—reminds us that the phenomena of Presley and the transistor radio were not only simultaneous but also symbiotic: each owed its popularity to the other, and both helped to usher in the hollow, illusory netherworld of adolescence so brilliantly limned in "Where Are You Going?" Likewise, the equally omnipresent sunglasses, that "told nothing about what [Ellie] was thinking", suggest not only Elvis's cool persona, but also the increasingly secretive, mysterious life he was leading at Graceland, his Memphis mansion, by the mid-1960s.

3 Presley was no killer, but certain aspects of his personality are clearly evident in the murderous Ellie. Chief among them is an apparent ambivalence in sexual identity and motivation. The points of Ellie's shirt look "as if they were protecting him";

that unbuttoned shirt reveals not intimidating pectorals, but a "pale, bluish chest"; and those sideburns give Ellie "a fierce, embarrassed look". The ambivalence evident in Ellie—vulnerable and aggressive, "fierce" and "embarrassed"—was in many ways the key to Presley's own immense attraction. As *Newsweek* columnist Jack Kroll noted at the time of Presley's death, a close observer could perceive "an almost androgynous softness and passivity in his punk-hood persona. Elvis and his revolution were vulnerability disguised as bravado."[4] The man who sang saccharine teen love songs such as "Teddy Bear" (1957) and "Good Luck Charm" (1961) also sang the hard-driving "[You're the] Devil in Disguise" (1963) and "Hard-Headed Woman" (1958); in his personal life, Presley collected Teddy bears—and guns. This bizarre combination of a child-like, almost effeminate innocence, plus an insistently adult, male aggressiveness, is quite evident in Ellie, whose very name (clearly a sweet-sounding, juvenile, feminine diminutive of "Elvis") neatly disguises—at least for the nonce—his role as an accomplice in rape and murder. It is not for nothing that the demonic Arnold—posing as Connie's "Friend"—would have as his accomplice a man with the chillingly ambivalent "face of a forty-year-old baby". Ellie *seems* passive: he never gets out of the golden car, and he says very little; but that seeming passivity is undermined by the facts that there is no real need for him to help Arnold (the control over Connie is absolute) and that his only words are an ominous suggestion presented as a helpful offer: " 'You want that telephone pulled out?' ". As with Elvis, Ellie projects an ambivalent sexual/motivational message which leaves his intended victim—a sexually mature but inexperienced adolescent girl—unsure of whether to perceive him as innocuous or sinister, and that unsureness renders her far more vulnerable than if he seemed only threatening.

4 And that is Oates' point. As Marie Mitchell Olesen Urbanski suggests, "the recurring music . . ., while ostensibly innocuous realistic detail, is [,] in fact, the vehicle of Connie's seduction [;] and because of its intangibility, not immediately recognizable as such."[5] More to the point, Tom Quirk argues that the dedication of "Where Are You Going?" to Bob Dylan

> is honorific because the history and effect of Bob Dylan's music had been to draw youth away from the romantic promises and frantic strains of a brand of music sung by Buddy Holly, Chuck Berry, Elvis Presley and others. It was Bob Dylan, after all, who told us that the "times they are a changin'," and one of Oates's aims in her short story is to show that they have already changed. It is the gyrating, hip-grinding music of people like Elvis Presley, whom Schmid identified as his "idol," which emanates from Ellie's transistor radio, the "hard, fast, shrieking" songs played by the disc jockey "Bobby King" rather than the cryptic, atonal folk music of Bob Dylan.[6]

5 And what more forceful way to suggest the dangerous illusions and vacuousness generated by "the romantic promises and frantic strains of a brand of music sung by . . . Elvis Presley" than to have an Elvis-figure participate in the rape and murder of an innocent 15-year-old girl?

1. Joyce M. Wegs, "Don't You Know Who I Am?: The Grotesque in Oates's 'Where Are You Going, Where Have You Been?,'" *Journal of Narrative Technique*, 5 (January 1975), 66–72;

Marie Mitchell Olesen Urbanski, "Existential Allegory: Joyce Carol Oates's 'Where Are You Going, Where Have You Been?,'" *Studies in Short Fiction*, 15 (Spring 1978), 200–03; Joan D. Winslow, "The Stranger Within: Two Stories by Oates and Hawthorne," *Studies in Short Fiction*, 17 (Summer 1980), 263–68.

2. Tom Quirk, "A Source for 'Where Are You Going, Where Have You Been?,'" *Studies in Short Fiction*, 18 (Fall 1981), 413–19.

3. "Where Are You Going, Where Have You Been?" in *The Wheel of Love and Other Stories* (New York: The Vanguard Press, 1970). All page references are to this edition.

4. Jack Kroll, "The Heartbreak Kid," *Newsweek*, August 29, 1977, p. 49.

5. Urbanski, 201.

6. Quirk, 417–18. The same blend of vulnerability and aggressiveness which is evident in Ellie and Elvis may be seen in the disc jockey, "Bobby King," whom both Connie and Arnold admire, and whose voice Arnold acquires. The name "Bobby" suggests a non-threatening, little-boy persona, while "King" (perhaps another veiled reference to Presley) suggests the enormous power wielded by males associated with rock music.

Inquiring into the Essay

Use the four ways of inquiring—exploring, explaining, evaluating, and reflecting—to think about your response to Petry's essay.

1. Explore your own sense of Ellie Oscar. To refresh your memory, consider rereading the story or the passages in which Ellie is featured, then set the story aside and fastwrite for five or six minutes about the character. What strikes you about him? How does Ellie's presence change the story? What would happen if he wasn't in it? Do you find Petry's argument plausible?
2. Using the list in the "Features of the Form" section, explain how this essay exemplifies some of the features.
3. Reread Petry's essay, and for a few minutes play the "doubting game." Where might you find fault in her reasoning? What doesn't she consider about Ellie? What might be some alternative explanations for his apparent resemblance to Elvis?
4. My students often complain that English teachers dig deeply for meaning in stories when it isn't really there. What do you think of this? Do you agree? Would Petry's essay be an example of this?

Seeing the Form

Christina's World by Andrew Wyeth

If a photograph can be thought of as a form of nonfiction, then a painting compares well with fiction or poetry. The painting certainly has a strong relationship to the real; after all, the painter sees the world we all live in and expresses that

Andrew Wyeth, *Christina's World,* 1948. Tempera on gessoed panel, $32^1/_4$″ × $47^3/_4$″. The Museum of Modern Art, New York. Purchase. (16.1949), © Andrew Wyeth.

vision in the work. That expression may be realistic, impressionistic, or abstract, but it is firmly rooted in things that can be seen, smelled, heard, and touched. Yet unlike photographers who work with the visual materials presented to them through the viewfinder, the painter can transform these materials through invention. If it works better that the woman's dress is pink rather than blue, then pink it shall be. Similarly, fiction writers' primary obligation is to the story, not reality, and they invent characters and make them do things that contribute tension and meaning to the narrative.

Interpreting a painting, then, like Andrew Wyeth's famous work *Christina's World,* is much like interpreting fiction. The painting acts as a text that, like a short story, is a complete invention and whose meaning is implicit rather than explicit. Therefore "reading" Wyeth's painting should involve the kind of interpretive moves you might employ in reading any literature.

In analyzing *Christina's World* and other paintings, it can be helpful to consider the following basic terms and concepts:

- *Line.* In artistic composition, the line is the direction the viewer's gaze travels when looking at the painting, something that is managed by the placement of forms and their relative size. In a good painting, the viewer's eye is directed to the main focal point of the picture, and away from unimportant elements. Some questions to ask about line include whether the painting succeeds in encouraging your gaze to move smoothly to the main objects of interest, or whether the line is confusing, making you feel as if you're not quite sure where to look. Do things flow visually?

- *Hierarchy.* Do you sense that some visual elements are more important than others? In a well-composed painting, you should. Artists can manage this in a number of ways, including the size and location of various objects in the painting, and in doing so they are communicating something important about the overall theme of the work. What, for example, might the emphasis on certain objects in the painting imply about its meaning? What is the relationship among these things, and what does that imply?
- *Color.* The arrangement of color in a painting influences its mood. Certain colors are cool—blues, greens, purples, and their many combinations—and these tend to recede in a painting. Other colors—yellows, oranges, and reds—are warm and can be perceived as coming forward. Color is obviously enormously expressive when handled well. How do the colors the artist chose affect the mood of the work? How might that mood contribute to its overall theme or idea?
- *Value.* To create the sense of dimension, artists use light and dark tones. In a black-and-white drawing, these tones are white to black and all the shades of gray in between. In a color painting, value is often managed by using various shades of a color. Without value, a painting looks flat, one-dimensional. With it, the subjects look more realistic. How much emphasis is there on value in the painting? How realistic is the image?
- *Composition.* All of these qualities—line, color, value, hierarchy—and more contribute to a painting's composition. One of the key qualities of composition is balance, and this can be achieved in a number of ways, including arranging visual elements symmetrically, asymmetrically, or using something called the

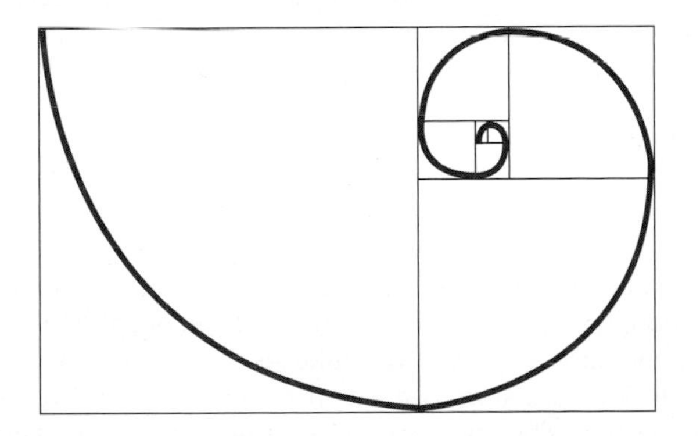

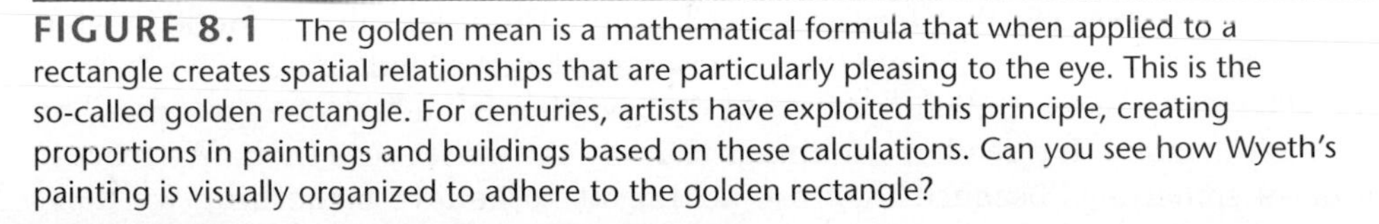

FIGURE 8.1 The golden mean is a mathematical formula that when applied to a rectangle creates spatial relationships that are particularly pleasing to the eye. This is the so-called golden rectangle. For centuries, artists have exploited this principle, creating proportions in paintings and buildings based on these calculations. Can you see how Wyeth's painting is visually organized to adhere to the golden rectangle?

"golden mean," an ancient mathematical concept that has historically influenced art and architecture, and which represents proportions often seen in nature, including the spiral of a sea shell, and the proportions of the human body (see Figure 8.1 on page 279). What do you notice about the composition of the painting? How is it arranged to influence your feelings, and how does it seem to contribute to the overall theme or idea?

THE WRITING PROCESS

INQUIRY PROJECT: Writing a Critical Essay

Look at a story, essay, or poem, possibly one of the works in this chapter. Interpret it as you did Wyeth's painting, looking closely at what the literary work says and how it says it, and, using some of the elements of literary analysis, offer readers a way of understanding the work that they would find convincing. The full draft should be about 1,000 to 1,500 words. You should do the following:

- Organize the essay around a question you're trying to answer about the text and its possible meanings. (For example: *Is Silko's "Lullaby" a story that highlights the power of women in Navajo culture?*)
- Use your question as a guide for reading the story selectively.
- As you shape your answer to the question, rely mostly on passages and other information from the primary work—the story or essay—as a source of evidence.
- If possible, use research with secondary sources (articles about the author, published criticism about the work, and so on) to help you revise your paper.

Thinking About Subjects

It's likely that your instructor will ask you to write a critical essay on one or more of the readings in this chapter, or perhaps an assigned reading from another book. If you can choose among the three readings here, consider which work you found most moving. Although analysis often demands a level of detachment and cool logic, literary works are usually intended to make us *feel.* This is a wonderful starting place for a closer look at the story because it's sensible to wonder what it was that made you feel something. The answer will be found in the text, of course, by looking at how the author tells the story and what he says. But it will also be found in what you bring to the text—your own experiences, associations, and values.

The writer Joan Didion once wrote that writing is an "act of aggression," an implicit demand that readers see things the way the writer sees them. We react to stories sometimes because they are asking us to believe something we don't believe, or don't want to believe, or they are imagining us as readers we don't want to be. A good starting point, then, for choosing to write about a work is to choose it because you find yourself resisting it in some way, rather than "relating to it."

On the other hand, it is also true that we are drawn to stories that seem to confirm our sense of how the world works. Choosing a literary text because you can relate to it is fine. But the challenge is to do more than simply express agreement. Write about such a story because you want to more fully understand what you're agreeing to.

In the conversation between what a text says and what it might be saying, you discover fresh understandings of what you read.

Generating Ideas

Spend some time in your notebook generating material for possible essays. The following prompts will invite you to first play around, and even write "badly." Approach this material initially in an open-ended way. When you can, let the writing lead thought. The following prompts will be general enough to apply to any text, even if it isn't one of the three in this chapter.

Listing Prompts. Lists can be rich sources of triggering topics. Let them grow freely, and when you're ready, use an item as the focus of another list or an episode of fastwriting. The following prompts should get you started.

1. Brainstorm a list of questions about the work that you find puzzling.

2. List the names of every important character or person in the story or essay. Choose one or two that seem most important. Under each name, make two new headings: Dreams and Problems. Under Dreams, list the things that character seems to desire most, even if he or she isn't fully aware of it. Under Problems, list everything that seems to be an obstacle to that character's achieving those desires.

3. List details or particulars from the story that seem to say more than they say. In other words, do any details recur? Do any objects have particular significance to one or more characters? Do any descriptions suggest the feelings, dispositions, or values of a particular character?

Fastwriting Prompts. Remember, fastwriting is a great way to stimulate creative thinking. Turn off your critical side and let yourself write "badly."

1. Write a narrative of thought. Begin with *When I first read this story or essay I thought . . . And then I thought . . . And then . . . And then . . .*

2. Choose three lines or passages that are key to your current understanding of the themes or ideas behind the story or essay. Write these down on the left page of your notebook. On the opposing right page, fastwrite about each, beginning with *The first thing I notice about this passage is . . . And then . . . And then . . . And then . . .* When the writing stalls, write about the next line or passage until you've written about all three.

Visual Prompts. Sometimes the best way to generate material is to see what we think represented in something other than sentences. Boxes, lines, webs, clusters, arrows, charts, and even sketches can help us see more of the landscape of a subject, especially connections between fragments of information that aren't as obvious in prose.

1. Create a cluster using the name of the main character as the core word. Reread the story and then build as many associations as you can from that character. Think about feelings and ideas you associate with that person as well as any particulars you remember from the story.

2. Make a visual map of the story. Begin by placing a brief description of what you believe is the most significant moment in the story at the center of a blank page. This might be a turning point, or the point of highest tension, or perhaps the moment when the main character achieves his or her desires and dreams. Consider that moment the destination of the story. Now map out events or details in the narrative that threaten to lead the protagonist away from that destination, and those that appear to lead the protagonist toward it.

Research Prompts. When writing a critical essay, the most important research you do is carefully reading and rereading the primary text, or the poem, story, or essay you're writing about. But secondary sources can be a great help, too. A background article on the writer might help you understand his or her motives in writing the piece. A little historical research can give you a deeper understanding of the setting.

1. Put the story or essay in a biographical context. First, search the Web for anything you can find about the author. Begin by searching on the term "authors" in Google. You'll find a listing of a range of Web pages with biographical information about authors; one or more might feature yours. Several library databases are also useful, including The Literary Index.

2. Put the story or essay in a historical context. Search the Web for background information about the period, place, or events relevant to the story. For example, if you were writing about "Lullaby," search for information about life among the Navajo in the late 1940s.

INQUIRING INTO THE DETAILS

COMMON LITERARY DEVICES

Many key concepts provide useful frameworks for analyzing literature. The key is to see the following ideas as an angle for seeing an essay, story, or poem, much as you might move around a subject with a camera. Each provides a different way of seeing the same thing. In addition, each becomes a platform from which to pose a question about a text.

- **Plot and significant event.** This is what happens in a story that moves it forward. One way of thinking about plot is to consider this: What are the key moments that propel the story forward? Why do you consider them key? How do they add tension to the story? In an essay, these moments often give rise to the question the writer is exploring. In short stories, there is often a significant event that may happen in or outside of the story, but the entire narrative and its characters act or think in response to that event. This significant event may be dramatic (a baby has died, perhaps) or not seem so at all (a surprise birthday cake is brought to a quiet couple's table in a crowded restaurant). Naming that significant event becomes a way of seeing how everything in the story revolves around it, exposing the logic (and sometimes lack of logic) in why characters behave the way they do.
- **Characters.** Imagine a still pond upon which small paper boats float. Someone throws a rock in the pond—big or small—and the ripples extend outward, moving the boats this way and that. Depending on the size of the ripples, some of the boats may list or capsize, sinking slowly. Characters in a short story are like those boats, responding in some way to something that happened, some significant event that is revealed or implied. They move almost imperceptibly, or quite noticeably, or even violently. Is there logic to their response? How exactly are they changed? How do they relate to each other? In essays, characters live both inside and outside the text. In nonfiction, they are (or were) real people, which imposes an additional burden on them: Are nonfiction characters believable? Are they accurate?
- **Setting.** Where a story takes place can matter a lot or a little, but it always matters. Why? Because where a story takes place signals things about characters and who they are. A story set in rural Wyoming suggests a certain austere, ranching culture in which the characters operate. Even if they're not ranchers, they must somehow deal with that culture. Similarly, a story set in Chicago's predominantly black south side introduces another set of constraints within which characters must operate. In some cases, setting even might become a kind of character.
- **Point of view.** In nonfiction essays, point of view is usually straightforward—we assume the narrator is the author. But in fiction, it's much more complicated; in fact, *how* a story is told—from what perspective—is a crucial aesthetic decision. For instance, stories told from the first-person point of view in the present tense give the story a sense of immediacy—this feels like it's happening *now*—but at the same time limit our understanding of other characters because we can't get into their heads. We can only know what the first person narrator knows.

  So-called omniscient narrators can introduce a feeling of distance from the action, but they are also gratifyingly godlike because they can see everything, hovering above all the action and even entering characters' minds at will. Omniscient narrators can also choose to limit their access to characters and events as well. Why might an author have chosen a particular point of view? Is the narrator trustworthy? What might be his or her biases and how might they affect the telling?

- **Theme.** One way to understand a story or essay is to consider that everything—character, point of view, and setting—all contribute to a central meaning. In a good story, everything is there for a purpose—to say something to the reader about what it means to be human. In essays, this theme may be explicit because essays both show *and* tell. Short stories and especially poems are often short on explanation of theme, operating with more ambiguity. The writer hopes the reader can *infer* certain ideas or feelings by paying close attention to what he *shows* the reader. To get at the theme, begin with the simple question: *So what?* Why is the author telling this story or sharing this experience? What significance are we supposed to attach to it?
- **Image.** Stories and poems ask us to see. When I read them, I imagine that writers take my face in their hands and gently—or sometimes brutally—direct my gaze. What are they insisting that I look at and how do they want me to see it? Images that recur may also be significant. For example, in the short story, "Where Are You Going, Where Have You Been?" Joyce Carol Oates takes great care to describe Arnold Friend's jalopy. Why might she lavish such attention on it if the car wasn't a revealing element of the story?

Judging What You Have

Now it's time to look more critically at what you've generated. Do you see some possible directions you could follow in a sketch? Are there tentative ideas and interpretations you might develop? Are there potential beginnings you could follow? The following suggestions use material generated by the prompts in the preceding section.

What's Promising Material and What Isn't? If your assignment is to write about one of the stories in this chapter, by now you should have a sense of which one interests you most. That initial sense usually starts with a gut reaction—the story makes you *feel* something. That's a good starting point, but the generating prompts should give you a fuller sense of *why* you feel something. As you examine the material you generated, consider the following:

- *What's your question?* Remember that your aim in the assignment is to build your essay around a question you want to answer about the story or essay. You may have found one already. A good opening question is specific enough to guide your rereading of the work, encouraging you to look at certain parts rather than the whole thing.

- *What surprised you?* In your fastwrites, do you find that the writing led you from an initial impression or interpretation of the story but then took you toward ideas you didn't expect? Did you find a lot to say about the significance of certain passages?
- *Does a character in the story seem to emerge as a focus?* A helpful way to write about a story is to focus on the actions and motivations of a particular character. This might have become obvious when you generated lists or clusters about characters, and especially when you generated ideas about a character's dreams and problems. *How* the character attempts to overcome obstacles in the way of his desires can say a lot about the meaning of the story.
- *Is there a recognizable significant event in the story and how do the important characters respond to it?* When you mapped out the story, did you find a scene or moment that seemed to alter the course of the narrative or its characters? How did this change the characters and how did it change their relationships with others in the story? What does this say about what the author seems to be saying about the human condition?
- *Does the story's context help explain the author's purpose?* Literature isn't created in a vacuum. Like all art, it is often a response to things that are going on with and around the artist. It makes an enormous difference that Leslie Marmon Silko is a member of the Laguna Pueblo and has a keen interest in tribal culture and survival. It also helps to know what concerns her and any related historical events to which the writer may be responding. Do these contexts help you to read the story differently? What questions do they raise about its meanings?
- *Do you feel ready to answer the* So what? *question?* Stories aren't merely entertainment. Authors always have certain purposes—ideas they're exploring, comments they want to make, or questions they're trying to answer. In fiction and poems, these intentions are often implicit; that is, stories and poems are often ambiguous and leave us wondering what they're really about. Essays are often much more explicit because authors frequently say what they mean. Answering the *So what?* question—speculating on what authors seem to be saying or implying about being human—is a key move in interpretation. After generating material, you may be ready to finish this sentence, *What I think this story or essay is* really *saying is . . .* If you like what you come up with, turn it into a question that will help organize your rereading of the story.

Questions about Audience and Purpose. Why analyze a work of literature? For the same reason that some of us want to talk about anything complicated, whether it's a relationship gone south or a wrenching movie about war: we simply want to understand. It's fundamentally human to try to make sense of things, and reassuring when we can. Of course, we are drawn to some literature for sheer enjoyment and pleasure, and there's nothing wrong with that, but the best literary works offer readers so much more than that if they're willing to look closely. The best stories offer a glimpse at the human spirit—at what makes people tick, at their longings and fears and possibilities. Ultimately, we learn about ourselves and our own humanity.

Critical analysis of literature is simply a method of discovering these things. In the same way you used some tools of art criticism to interpret Wyeth's painting *Christina's World,* using literary elements of stories such as character, significant event, setting, and especially theme help you think about what a story is trying to do. You can use these tools for several purposes. The most basic is to simply write a summary of what happens to whom in a story. Often called a plot summary, this is useful as a way of initially understanding the work, but it isn't often a college assignment. In general, however, critical essays offer some *interpretation* of what the story or essay seems to be saying, a move that often begins with a question.

In the broadest sense the opening question is simple: *What might this story mean?* But to be really useful, the question needs to be more specific. For example, a slightly more specific question might be, *What are the racial themes in Silko's story "Lullaby"?* Will such a question allow you to read Silko's story selectively? Probably not. What about this: *What is the significance of the recurring image of the blanket in "Lullaby"?* Is this too specific? Possibly. But it's not a bad starting point for your inquiry into the story because the question gives you direction about where to look to find the answers.

Critical essays don't simply ask questions; they attempt to answer them. There are a range of methods for doing that, including the following:

1. You can focus on a particular element such as character, setting, or plot development, analyzing how it contributes to one or more of the story's themes.

2. You can put the story in relevant contexts—perhaps the biography of the author, background about the story's time and place, or certain kinds of theories or ideas about literature—and exploit these as a way of unraveling the story's themes and ambiguities.

3. You can argue for an interpretation of a story's meaning, and use *both* particular elements such as character and setting and relevant contexts to help you make your interpretation convincing to others.

Each approach implies a different emphasis on certain kinds of information in the essay. *But no matter what angle you use, the text of the story—the words, phrases, passages, and ideas that make up the story—will always be the most important source of evidence.* I want to emphasize this because one of the most common weaknesses of writing about a reading is that it fails to mine material from the text itself.

The audience for a critical essay, as for any form of writing, will make a big difference in what you say and how you say it. Scholarly criticism, which is not what you're attempting here, is written for an audience of fellow critics, most of whom are familiar with the work as well as some of its contexts. For the assignment that follows, assume you're writing for an audience of peers. Ask your instructor whether you should assume that your audience is familiar with the work you're writing about (which might be the case if you're all writing about the same story or essay), or assume that your readers are unfamiliar with the work. If the latter is the case, then you'll obviously have to do some summarizing about the plot and characters that wouldn't be necessary if your readers knew your story or essay.

Writing the Sketch

We'll begin again with an early draft, a sketch that represents an initial attempt to discover what you want to focus on and what you might have to say about the literary work you've chosen.

Develop your sketch with the following things in mind:

- It should have a tentative title. This time, the title should be the question about the work you're trying to answer. (For example, *What is the significance of Ayah's relationship to nature in Silko's "Lullaby"?*)
- It should be at least 500 to 600 words.
- Write it with the appropriate audience in mind. Are you writing for readers who are familiar with the text?
- Explore your question by paying close attention to what the story you're writing about says.

STUDENT SKETCH

When Julie Bird read Leslie Marmon Silko's short story "Lullaby" for the first time, she found it deeply moving. "It almost made me cry," she said. In class, we talked a little about some of the traditions in Native American literature, and you can see in her sketch how she tries out several of the ideas we talked about: the importance of the storytelling tradition, the ways in which identity is tied to going home, and the healing power of the natural world. There are all kinds of literary traditions that are lenses through which you can read a story. Some, like this one, have to do with the race, ethnicity, or culture of the writer. Others have more to do with larger literary movements tied to historical events and histories of thought—for example, realism, modernism, or postmodernism.

But the most important thing is to pay close attention to the text itself. What *exactly* does the story say, and what might it mean? Julie Bird doesn't incorporate many passages from "Lullaby" in her sketch; she's thinking through some ideas about key themes in the story. She underlines several ideas that emerged in this first look. Now she has to return to the story and test the ideas against what the text actually says.

What Is the Role of Nature in 'Lullaby'?

Julie Bird

1 "Lullaby," written by Leslie Marmon Silko, is an intriguing story about the life of a Navajo woman by the name of Ayah and her life. Ayah bared her soul to tell this story, an act of special meaning in a culture that passes on history by oral means. The Navajos often connect their identity to family, home, and nature. When the white man came to take away her children, Ayah, not fully understanding why, grabbed them and ran up the long slope of the mesa, to wait for her husband to come home. While she was waiting, she allowed the sun to relax her and felt as if "she could walk into the sky, stepping through clouds endlessly." The connection of peace to the natural world is key to the essay's theme.

2 Ayah, using the wool blanket as an instrument, created strong parallels between her mother (the past) and her son Jimmie (her present). This generational timeline establishes her identity by correlating the comfort of the past with the warmth of the present. The wool blanket is the object of that unbroken line. At the end of the story, Ayah is searching for her husband and she is thinking, "She did this because she had the blanket, and there would be no place for him except with her and the blanket in the old abode barn near the arroyo." The blanket is significant to the characters in revealing the importance of family ties to the Navajos.

3 The overall theme of the essay relates to the sorrow and loss Ayah feels at the hands of the white man, and her inability to do anything about it. First, a government man comes to tell her that her son Jimmie was killed at war. Next, more government officials dupe her into signing her name in order to take away her children. To this she states, "Because it was like the old ones always told her about learning their language or any of their ways: it endangered you." When Chato was too old to work the rancher made them move out of their home, and they had to go to the barn.

4 Through all of the sorrow put upon her, Ayah was able to turn to her identity and connection with her heritage, nature, and roots to find peace and strength to continue on.

Moving from Sketch to Draft

Prepare to revise your sketch by first evaluating it yourself and then sharing it in a small group workshop.

Evaluating Your Own Sketch. Among the key concerns in evaluating this early draft of your critical essay is whether you've discovered a workable focus and whether you're beginning to get some clear idea of what you're trying to say. In your journal or on a separate sheet you can provide to your instructor when you hand in the sketch, try to answer the following questions:

1. Did the question you were asking about the text help you focus on certain parts of the story? What were they? Was the question too broad or too specific? What might be a more refined question as a focus for the next draft, or are you happy with the original question you posed?

2. Can you summarize in a sentence or two how you might now answer the question you pose in your sketch? Can you summarize an answer to another question that emerged that interests you more?

3. Based on what you tentatively seem to be saying in the sketch about the text you're writing about, what do you think you might do in the rewrite?

Questions for Peer Review. Workshop groups that are discussing the sketches should consider the following questions:

- If you're unfamiliar with the text the writer is analyzing, do you have enough information about the story or essay to understand what the writer is saying about it? What else would you like to know?
- Does the sketch seem to answer the question it's asking? In your own words, what do you think the writer seems to be saying?
- Where is the sketch most convincing? Where is it least convincing?
- Are there any questions or approaches that seem like good alternatives to the one the writer chose?

Reflecting on What You've Learned. To make the best use of the workshop, try to listen without commenting to the discussion of your sketch. Use the double-entry journal approach of taking notes during the discussion. On the left page of your notebook, record all the comments and suggestions you hear, whether you agree with them or not. Later, on the right page, fastwrite your reactions and thoughts about the comments you recorded on the opposing page.

Research and Other Strategies: Gathering More Information

Before you wrote your sketch, you did some initial research that may have helped provide a *context* for the work you're writing about. You may have learned a little biographical information about the author, or perhaps some things about the period, time, or place he or she was writing about. Now it's time to dig a little deeper. How deep you dig depends on the scope of your project and the details of the assignment.

This time, your campus library, rather than the Web, will be the focus of your investigations, although many of the following sources and databases are probably accessible through your library's Web pages.

- *Researching the author.* Check the online book index to find biographies of your author. You can also gather biographical information on the author you're writing about by consulting the following references at your university library:

- *Author's Biographies Index.* A key source to 300,000 writers of every period.
- *Biography Index: A Cumulative Index to Biographical Material in Books and Magazines.* Remarkably extensive coverage, which includes biographies, as well as autobiographies, articles, letters, and obituaries.
- *Contemporary Authors.* Up-to-date information on authors from around the world.

• *Researching the critics.* What do other people say about your author or the work you're writing about? Check these references or databases:

- *MLA International Bibliography.* The most important database in which to find articles by others on the work or author you're writing about.
- *Literary Index.* A database of author biographies.
- *Contemporary Literary Criticism.* Excerpts of criticism and reviews published in the last twenty-five years.
- *Magill's Bibliography of Literary Criticism.* Citations, not excerpts, of criticism on more than 2,500 works.
- *Book Review Index.* Citations for tens of thousands of book reviews on even fairly obscure works.

• *Researching the genre or tradition.* The type of writing—short story, novel, personal essay—that you're analyzing is another useful context for thinking about the work. For example, Leslie Marmon Silko is among the most famous of contemporary Native American writers. Native American writing is an identifiable "tradition" of literary works, and much has been written about certain patterns in these stories and certain ways of understanding them. Several reference resources in your library will help you research these traditions. For example, *American Indian: Language and Literature* lists books and articles on the topic. Similarly, *Afro-American Literature* explores the place of black writers and works in American literature. These references can be enormously helpful. Ask your reference librarian about useful books or electronic databases on the tradition you're writing about.

Composing the Draft

Before you begin writing the draft, make sure that you have a workable focusing question that will drive the draft. A workable question needs to be specific enough to allow you to reread the story or essay you're writing about selectively, focusing on certain parts rather than the whole thing. But it also needs to be general enough to allow you to develop the answer in 1,000 to 1,500 words. For example, here's a question that is too general: *What are the main themes in Silko's "Lullaby"?* You can certainly answer that question in four or five pages, but the essay will be so general, leaping from one part of the story to the next, that it will be vague and uninteresting. Consider this question: *What is the significance of Arnold Friend's name in "Where Are You Going, Where Have You Been?"*

This type of question—one that focuses on a particular detail or aspect of plot development—can work extremely well as a focus for a short critical essay. But unless that detail or development seems attached to other details, developments, and themes in the story, it probably won't do.

Here's a good focusing question for a literary analysis, one that strikes a nice balance between specificity and generality: *Why does Silko end with the poem at the end of "Lullaby," and how does it figure in Ayah's efforts to confront her losses?* It seems as if there might be a lot to say about this without resorting to generalities. The question focuses on a particular part of the Silko story, yet also expands outward into other aspects of the work, particularly those relevant to the theme of recovery.

Methods of Development. What are some of the ways you might organize your critical essay?

Narrative. An entirely different approach is to use your question as the starting point for a story you tell about how you arrived at an answer. This approach is more essayistic in the sense that it provides the story of *how* you came to know rather than reporting *what* you think. A narrative essay might also involve relevant autobiographical details that influenced your reading of the literary work, explaining your interest in certain aspects of the story or the question you're asking about it. As always, however, it's critical to read the work closely and discuss your evolving understandings of certain details, passages, or ideas from it.

Question to Answer. Because the assignment is designed around a question you're trying to answer about a literary work, the question-to-answer design is an obvious choice. Consider spending the first part of your essay highlighting the question you're interested in. You can do this in several ways. You can put it in context by demonstrating how your question is relevant to the ongoing conversation that other critics have posed about the story, author, or tradition you're writing about. You can also put it in the context of the research you've done about that tradition, or perhaps what you know about the life and interests of the author. Alternatively, establish the importance of the question by highlighting your understanding of the story's meaning or the author's intentions, or perhaps even how the question arises out of your own personal experiences with the events or subjects in the work. The key is to convince readers that yours is a question worth asking, and that the answer might be interesting to discover.

Compare and Contrast. Critical essays often benefit from this method of development. The approach might be to compare and contrast certain elements within the story or essay—perhaps several characters, symbols or metaphors, plot developments, and so on—or you might compare the work to others by the same or even different authors. For example, it might be interesting to explore the significance of the nature imagery in Leslie Marmon Silko's "Lullaby" by examining other essays by the author. Do similar references appear in some of her other stories? These comparisons have to be relevant to the question you're asking.

Combining Approaches. Frequently a critical essay uses several or even all of the methods of development mentioned here—question to answer, comparison and contrast, and narrative. Consider how you might put them all to work, especially in certain sections of your draft.

Using Evidence. You need to consider two main kinds of evidence in a critical essay: evidence that comes from so-called *primary* sources, especially the work itself, but also letters or memoirs by the author; and evidence that comes from *secondary* sources, or books, articles, and essays by critics who are also writing about the work or author. Primary sources are generally most important. In more personal literary responses, however, your personal associations, anecdotes, stories, or feelings may be used as evidence, if they're relevant to the question you're posing.

Workshopping the Draft

When you finish revising your sketch you should have a more developed draft with a clearer purpose and focus. After all this work, you may feel pretty good about it. But don't worry if you're not satisfied yet; you still have the opportunity to make further changes to your draft. Before you submit your draft for further peer review, explore your own feelings and tentative ideas about what you need to do in the next, and probably final revision.

Reflecting on the Draft. Take a look at the draft before you and circle the passage you think is the best in the essay so far. Now circle the passage that you think is weakest.

In your notebook, fastwrite for five minutes about both passages. What seems to be working in the better passage? What problems to do you notice about the weaker one? Does either one address the question you're writing about? If so, how? If not, how might it? When you compare the two passages, what do you notice about the differences? How might you make the weaker passage more like the stronger one? How might you make the rest of the essay stronger?

Questions for Readers. Share your essay in small groups before you begin the final revision. Group members might consider the following questions about each draft they discuss:

1. If you're unfamiliar with the story or essay the writer is writing about, do you have enough background information about it to understand the draft?

2. Does the draft stay focused, from beginning to end, on the focusing question? If not, where exactly does it seem to stray?
3. Do you find the interpretation of the literary work convincing? Where is the draft most convincing? Where is it least convincing?
4. Where exactly could the writer use more evidence?
5. What part of the draft was most interesting? What part was least interesting?

Revising the Draft

As I discussed earlier in the book, one of the most common misconceptions about revision is that you do it only at the end of the writing process. In fact, up to this point, you should have been revising your work all along, from the first few journal exercises when you chose a topic and played with possible angles on it, to the journal work you might have done to prepare to write the sketch, and then again with your efforts to turn your sketch into a more developed draft. Revision is literally "re-seeing," and every time you create the conditions that allow you to discover something new about how you see or what you think about your subject, you are, in fact, engaged in the act of revision. In a sense, then, each writing assignment you undertake is one long act of revision, from start to finish.

But once you've completed a draft, the revision process becomes more focused. You are mostly working with material that should be somewhat settled, with purposes that might be clearer, and ideas that may have more shape. At this point, the biggest temptation is tell yourself you are largely done and what revision remains is merely a matter of "fixing things"—tinkering with sentences, correcting typos, and running a spell-checker. In the survey from Chapter 1 (see page 18), 70 percent of students admitted as much. "I usually just tidy things up" was ranked first or second by students who were asked what they do most often when they revise an academic paper.

These activities are certainly an element of revision—and important ones—but as the word *revision* implies, it's important to "re-see" both what you are trying to say and how you try to say it, even at this stage in the process. Chapter 11, "Revision Strategies," is a useful introduction to the revision process for any essay, including the critical essay. It emphasizes ways writers can break the bonds that limit their ability to find new ways of seeing the draft.

Critical essays typically have some of the following problems to solve. Do any of these apply to your draft?

- When you make an assertion about the significance or importance of something in the work, is it supported by specific evidence from the work itself?
- Are you clear about your audience? Do you assume that readers are familiar or unfamiliar with the story, and have you written the draft with that assumption in mind?

- When you quote a passage from the work, do you analyze it with your own commentary? In particular, are you clear about the relevance of the passage to the argument you're making about the work?
- Is your thesis clear? By the end of your essay, could a reader state without much confusion the main thing you're trying to say about the poem, story, or essay?

For help addressing some of these questions and others refer to Chapter 11, "Revision Strategies." Use the following table as a guide to the appropriate revision strategies. Remember that a draft may present problems in more than one category.

GUIDE TO REVISION STRATEGIES

Problems in the Draft (Chapter 11)	Part	Page Number
Unclear purpose ■ Not sure what the paper is about? ■ Not focused enough?	1	420
Unclear thesis, theme, or main idea ■ Not sure what you're trying to say?	2	425
Lack of information or development ■ Need more convincing evidence?	3	432
Disorganized ■ Doesn't move logically or smoothly from paragraph to paragraph?	4	436
Unclear or awkward at the level of sentences and paragraphs ■ Seems choppy or hard to follow at the level of sentences or paragraphs?	5	442

Polishing the Draft

After you've dealt with the big issues in your draft—is it sufficiently focused, does it answer the *So what?* question, is it well organized, and so on—you must deal with the smaller problems. You've carved the stone into an appealing figure, but now you need to polish it. Are your paragraphs coherent? How do you manage transitions? Are your sentences fluent and concise? Are there any errors in spelling or syntax? Section 5 in Chapter 11 can help you focus on these issues.

Before you finish your draft, work through the following checklist:

- Every paragraph is about one thing.
- The transitions between paragraphs aren't abrupt.
- The length of sentences varies in each paragraph.
- Each sentence is concise. There are no unnecessary words or phrases.
- You've checked grammar, particularly verb agreement, run-on sentences, unclear pronouns, and misused words (*there/their, where/were,* and so on). (See the handbook at the back of this book for help with these grammar issues.)
- You've run your spell-checker and proofed your paper for misspelled words.

STUDENT ESSAY

Julie Bird's sketch earlier in this chapter about Leslie Marmon Silko's short story "Lullaby" showed traces of the ideas behind this draft. Bird touches on the question behind her inquiry into the story—how does the character Ayah recover from her many losses?—and finds a tentative answer: Ayah finds peace in nature. Sketches are just that—roughly drawn glimpses into our own thinking about something. When they're most helpful, this "bad" writing can help us discover what we want to say, as it did here for Bird.

But notice how Julie takes the idea that nature is a powerful force in the story and extends and deepens it in the draft. The result is that her thesis is richer and more interesting. How did she do this? By returning to the dialectical process—that motion between creative thinking and critical thinking—and immersing herself in the story itself. Bird also did some research on Silko and Native American literature, testing her assertions. She found not only evidence to support them, but new ways of thinking about what she wants to say.

Nature as Being: Landscape in Silko's "Lullaby"

Julie Bird

1 Leslie Marmon Silko, the author of "Lullaby," is a Native American writer from the Laguna Pueblo culture in New Mexico. Silko's story is about a Navajo woman, Ayah, and how she copes with the loss of her children—one dies in war, several others die in infancy, and two more are taken by the "white doctors" who suspect the children may have been exposed to tuberculosis. How is Ayah, condemned to poverty and surrounded by white indifference or hatred, able to recover from these losses?

2 Reflecting the "interrelatedness of man and nature that permeates Native American literature" (Schweninger 49), it is in the landscape that Ayah finds peace in old age. Arizona's natural environment, such as snow and the slope of the mesa, is an integral character in "Lullaby" that shows the intricate relationship between humans and the natural world.

3 Even the structure of the story echoes these themes. Silko writes her story from the end, to the beginning, to the end in the same cyclical fashion as life in the natural world and on the reservation. The writer portrays this cyclical structure of storytelling beautifully when describing Ayah as an old woman, as she reflects on the birth of her children through to the death of her husband.

4 Trying to find peace in the harmony of the natural world, Ayah turned herself to the memories of a happier past, and the rituals and rhythms of the earth's cycle. When saddened by thoughts of her dead son Jimmie, lost in some faraway war, Ayah wraps herself in a wool blanket that he had sent to her. This unconscious gesture invariably brings the memory of sitting with her grandma and mother and combing twigs from the freshly washed wool while they weaved it into blankets. Ayah fondly remembers that "the blankets . . . were soft and woven so tight that rain rolled off them like birds' feathers" (Silko 44). Through Ayah's reference to the feathers, Silko is making the connection to her own beliefs in the natural world. In a sense, Ayah becomes a bird.

5 When Ayah runs into the foothills of the "juniper trees and black lava" (45) in order to get her children away from the white doctors, she is seeking the place of refuge that is a constant source of comfort. It is her ritual to return to this spot. Ayah comes to the mesa when her son Jimmie dies, when she buries her children who died too soon, when the doctors take her children; in other words, when she is looking for balance. To Ayah, "the sun's warmth relaxed her and took the fear and anger away. . . . It seemed to her that she could walk into the sky, stepping through clouds endlessly" (46).

6 This harmony that Ayah shares with the natural world is what makes her who she is; it is her identity as a Navajo woman. This is especially obvious at the end of the story when she is sitting with her dying husband, a man crushed by hopelessness and alcoholism. Silko writes that "The light was crystalline. . . . She breathed the clarity of the night sky; she smelled the purity of the half moon and the stars" (51). Silko was making a point that upon the death of her husband, Ayah at last felt a clear ("crystalline") understanding. With the passing of the storm, "steely blue-gray horses startled across the sky" (51), and with the passing away of the last of her family, Ayah was finally free to find her own peace. In old age, Ayah finally achieved her balance with the harmony of nature and was ready for it.

7 Just hearing the word snow evokes images of "freezing" and "icy," but Silko uses snow to project Ayah's feelings of warmth and comfort. Music, like nature, is a very integral part of some Native American cultures, and Silko expresses the correlation between music and the natural world throughout the story. For example, when Ayah is waiting for her husband to return home from a bar, she "sat down with her back

against the wide cottonwood tree . . . and listened to the wind and snow sing a high-pitched Yeibechei song" (43).

8 We learn from Silko that the Yeibechei song is the Navajo Night Chant and is a ceremony of healing. The fact that the snow sings such a song further reinforces the idea that nature is a healing force in the story. When Ayah is watching as the "snow drifted . . . with the northwest wind hurling it in gusts," and "she smiled at the snow which was trying to cover her little by little" (44), Silko suggests that the snow, like the blanket, is a source of comfort to Ayah. And when Ayah is sitting next to her dying husband, the snow storm clears up and the night is still and clear. This is significant in that it parallels the clearing of Ayah's troubles, the passing of the figurative storm within herself.

9 At the end, Ayah sings her lullaby: "The earth is your mother, . . . the sky is your father, . . . rainbow is your sister, . . . the winds are your brothers" (51). It is hard to miss the balance of nature with humanity that is a part of the Navajo heritage. But Ayah's lullaby also points to Silko's particular vision of the role of nature. Landscapes aren't something to be looked at as separate from people. As the critic Karen E. Waldron notes, "Silko's poems, essays, and novels manifest the relationship between the human being and his or her surroundings as one of *being* rather than viewing" (179) [emphasis added].

10 The most interesting, but subtle way in which the story is written deals with Silko's use of color, scent, and smell to make the story come alive and to further reinforce the images of nature as a benign and loving force. When describing the birth of one of Ayah's children, Silko writes, "The morning was already warm even before dawn and Ayah smelled the bee flowers blooming and the young willow growing at the springs" (44). This passage correlates birth with the smell of spring flowers, very much in tradition of human harmony with the natural world.

11 Silko, in trying to show Ayah's relationship to the natural world, uses every sense at her disposal to paint a vivid picture to the reader. When reading "Lullaby" you can feel the snow landing gently about you, hear the screech of the hawk as it patiently circles above, and smell the pungent odor of the juniper trees. Silko is also able to make the reader feel the intense pain of loneliness associated with the loss of Ayah's family and culture at the hands of the white man. In the story, Silko weaves the natural world into every nook and cranny of the narrative so the reader is unaware of its existence but can feel its essence as its own entity; in this case it's an entity that is not separate from Ayah but merges with her. Both are "beings"; both share consciousness. And in the end, she finds comfort in that.

Works Cited

Silko, Leslie Marmon. "Lullaby." Storyteller. New York: Arcade, 1981. 43–51.

Schweninger, Lee. "Writing Nature: Silko and Native Americans as Nature Writers." Mellis 18 (1993): 47–60.

Waldron, Karen E. "The Land as Consciousness." Such News of the Land: U.S. Women Nature Writers. Ed. Thomas S. Edwards and Elizabeth A. De Wolfe. Hanover, NH: UP of New England, 2001. 179–190.

Evaluating the Essay

1. Compare Bird's earlier sketch and her draft. What do you notice about her revisions? In particular, do you think the draft is more insightful than the sketch? Why?
2. One of the temptations in writing about Native American literature (or any literature by someone from another or unfamiliar culture) is to make assumptions about what "they" believe or how "they" think. Many of these are based on certain cultural commonplaces that we pick up without thinking much about them. One of these is that Indians have strong ties to nature. Does Bird find support for her assumptions about that? How do you avoid simply accepting such assumptions?
3. When you write about literature, the most important source of information is the text you're writing about—the story, poem, essay, or novel. How well does Bird use evidence from "Lullaby" to convince you that what she says about the story is a reasonable interpretation?

Using What You Have Learned

Although literary texts are quite different from the kinds of texts you usually read in school for other classes, practice with writing the critical essay can be useful even if you're not an English major. But how?

1. Think about your experience with this assignment. Can you point to something about *the process* that you could apply to another writing situation? What did you do here that you've done for other assignments in *The Curious Writer?*
2. Compare one of the short stories in this chapter with the research essay in Chapter 10. What are the differences between these two kinds of texts—literary fiction and expository writing, a short story and a research essay? What are the similarities? Do you read them differently? Do you read them in similar ways?
3. In sixty seconds, generate a focused list that describes the most important things you've learned about writing a critical essay. How many of these things apply to writing other kinds of papers?

The cavernous stacks in the library at Trinity College, Dublin. This may seem a daunting place to find a book, but in a library human knowledge is organized, evaluated, and cataloged. In contrast, the Internet is a great sea of information that can be a navigator's nightmare.

Research Techniques

What You'll Learn in This Chapter

- How librarians organize knowledge.
- How to use library and Internet sources to develop a working knowledge of your topic.
- How to craft the best search terms for the library and the Internet.
- How to use more advanced research strategies to build on your working knowledge and develop a deep knowledge of your topic.
- How to evaluate sources and decide what you should use in your writing and what you should ignore.
- Methods of note taking that promote a conversation with sources.
- Techniques for developing surveys and conducting interviews.

METHODS OF COLLECTING

One sure sign that research is an integral part of our everyday lives is the fact that Google, the name of an Internet search engine, is now a verb. Someone can say, "I Googled it" or "I Googled that" and there's a good chance someone else will respond, "Oh really? What did you find?" The Internet makes research easy. It's even fun sometimes. This is a far cry from the experience many of us have had doing academic research at the library, wandering through the stacks trying to find a book that's supposed to be but isn't there, or impatiently waiting in line to commandeer the one photocopy machine on the fifth floor, wondering whether that pocketful of change will be enough to copy Chapter 10 of *The Dreaming Brain.*

But I can also remember moments as a college student—well before the Web—when I hunkered down until midnight in a study carrel in the campus library, reading my way through articles and books that opened doors on the subject I was researching. On rare occasions, I was even blinded by the light that suddenly poured in. Research is a process that, like writing, can be filled with discovery. And it should be, particularly if you've found questions that really interest you about your subject and you don't have to spend too much time learning the technicalities of how to find what you need.

This chapter should help you know everything you need to know about finding what you need in the university library and on the Web. It is particularly useful for collecting information for research essays, but research is a source of information that can make *any* essay stronger. Every assignment in *The Curious Writer,* therefore, includes suggestions for research as you're searching for a topic and writing your draft. Research also can be an especially useful revision strategy for any essay.

Use this chapter much as you would a toolbox—a handy collection of tips and research tools that you can use for any assignment. Refer to it whenever you discover a topic that raises questions that research can help answer, or whenever it would be helpful to hear what other people say about the things you're thinking about.

RESEARCH IN THE ELECTRONIC AGE

The problem used to be not finding enough information on a research topic. Now, according to some librarians, students are so swamped with information that they pretty much print out the first few things they find and rush off to write their papers. "Google has won," lament some librarians. Like any other technological advance, the wide availability of electronic databases is a mixed blessing. On the one hand, these databases are really wonderful. They are searchable not only from the library reference room but also from the comfort of students' own computers in their dorms or apartments. They allow researchers to search twenty years or more of journals and magazines in seconds, something that took hours and hours in the old days when bound indexes were all that was available.

The downside of the Internet and electronic databases is that student researchers can quickly produce such long lists of possible sources that they simply skim off the top, going for the first few that offer full-text versions and ignoring the rest, many of which might be better. The companies that create and sell databases to your university library are aware of this fondness for full-text articles, so they keep adding more and more. This isn't a bad thing, necessarily, except that there is little thought about which sources would be most valuable to academic researchers. In fact, the more useful sources, often articles from the most important journals in a discipline, are still least likely to be served up as full-text articles. The buffet of electronic information is heavy on high-calorie, low-protein offerings, stuff that satisfies your immediate cravings but leaves you hungry later.

This is especially true of the Web. About 80 percent of the Web is dominated by commercial sites. These are great if you're trying to get the best price on an answering machine, but commercial sites usually don't have much value for academic research. Even if you do weed through the dot-com offerings after a Google search, you shouldn't feel at all confident that your search has been comprehensive. Although Google and Yahoo! are remarkable search engines, they don't actually search the entire World Wide Web. What they search is their *own* databases of Web pages, and while these can be quite substantial, they're only a very small fraction of what's out there. In fact, some experts believe that most of the Internet is invisible to conventional search engines. That doesn't mean that this information, much of which is quite useful for academic research, is completely inaccessible; you just have to know how to find it.

Research is easier, faster, and, at times, more pleasant in the electronic age. But it demands new electronic literacies.

Research is easier, faster, and, at times, more pleasant in the electronic age. But it demands new *electronic literacies* that include knowledge about how to exploit the technology to find relevant information and new ways of thinking about how to evaluate and analyze what you find.

Magic Words That Open Doors

One of the key electronic literacies is something that seems so simple you might wonder why I bring it up first: *the words you choose to search for information.* Consider that in 1850 the Harvard library, the first academic library in the nation, had only 84,200 volumes, and many of those were kept behind locked cabinets. To search these stacks, a student would plead with a librarian for a look. Today, my own university's library has more than a half million books and access to millions more through interlibrary loan. In addition, it has tens of thousands of periodicals on microfilm, and access to millions more through electronic databases. Then there's the World Wide Web; it's impossible to know its actual size, but the number of pages is certainly in the billions. All this information can make a researcher giddy, except for this: How do you find your needle in that gargantuan haystack?

In 1850, the Harvard librarian was familiar with the books in the stacks and could lead you to what you wanted. Today, librarians must trust in the language systems and codes they've created to organize knowledge; to find anything, you have to know those language systems. And while information on the Web isn't nearly as organized as it is in the library—for one thing, there isn't any librarian in charge, although there are some Internet directories that librarians maintain—the software that searches the Web also uses a language logic. Using it well means the difference between getting 1 million "hits" on a topic search, which you will never be able to read through, or getting 300 hits, many of which will be relevant to your topic.

How Librarians Organize Books

The Dewey decimal system and the Library of Congress system are the two systems for classifying books. Dewey decimal is what your hometown library uses; Library of Congress is the approach used in the university library. How much do you need to know about a system for shelving books? Not a whole lot, except that you should be familiar with its logic because it will save you time. The key thing to understand is that the letters on the spines of books actually mean something about the structure of knowledge. In the accompanying Library of Congress system table, you'll note that each letter suggests a division of human knowledge; you'll never memorize this, but it does help you to know, for instance, that when you're browsing books in the B's you're in the world of psychological knowledge.

LIBRARY OF CONGRESS SYSTEM	
ORGANIZATION OF BOOKS BY LETTER	
A General Works	**L** Education
B Philosophy, Psychology, Religion	**M** Music
C Auxiliary Sciences of History	**N** Fine Arts
D History: General and Europe	**P** Language and Literature
E History: America	**Q** Science
F History: America	**R** Medicine
G Geography, Anthropology, Recreation	**S** Agriculture
	T Technology
H Social Sciences	**U** Military Science
J Political Sciences	**Y** Naval Science
K Law	**Z** Library Science and Reference

These letters, used in combination with other letters and numbers, make up the call numbers that will help you locate a book in the library. For instance, suppose you're looking for a book about study habits, and your library's book search tool lists a book called *What You Need to Know about Developing Study Skills, Taking Notes and Tests, Using Dictionaries and Libraries* (see Figure 9.1). The call number is LB2395.C65 1991. What may seem like just a bunch of letters and numbers actually gives a lot of information about the book, including the body of knowledge from which it came, when it was published, and the first letter of the author's last name.

But you want to find it. Your library will place books on specific floors or areas of your library according to the first one or two call letters. There should be an index of these locations on the wall. Once you've generally located the book using the letters on the first line (e.g., LB), the second line (e.g., 2395) tells you where it is in relation to the books next to it (see Figure 9.2 and Figure 9.3).

Library of Congress Subject Headings

The *Library of Congress Subject Headings* (*LCSH*) conveniently lists the words that librarians use to index information. This underappreciated and much ignored multivolume book is the key to efficiently finding what you're looking for when using electronic indexes. It holds the magic words to successful searches. For example, if you are writing about the history of arm wrestling you could simply type in *arm wrestling, history* as a subject search in your library's online search form. You might come up with something, but if you turned up nothing, might you give up on the topic? The *LCSH* can help out because it suggests a broader term (BT) for *arm wrestling, history* that might produce some results: *sports records.* Would that have occurred to you on your own? Here's another example: My student Gracie's topic is bipolar disorder. Without checking the

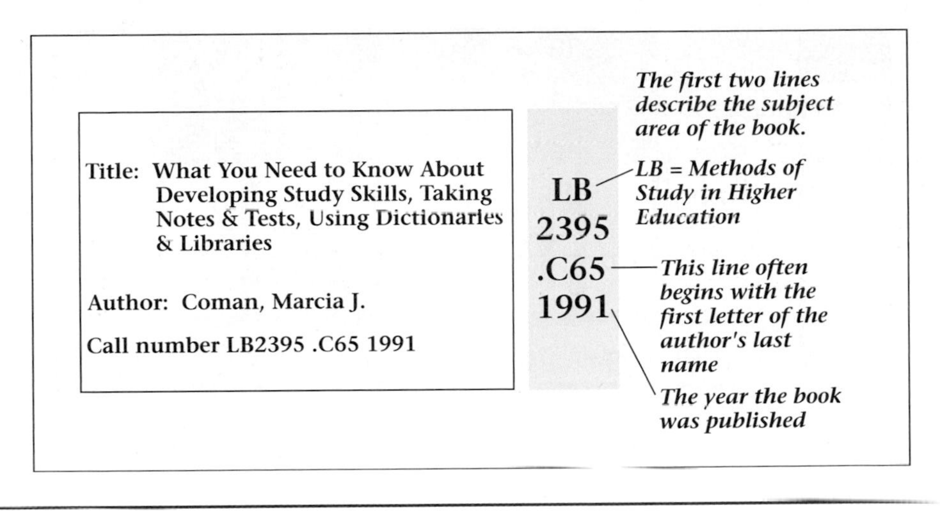

FIGURE 9.1 The library call card.

LCHS, she would quite naturally use *bipolar disorder* to search for books and articles on the subject, and no doubt she'd find some material. But if she checked the *LCSH* under *bipolar disorder,* Gracie would discover that the term preferred by librarians is *manic-depressive illness.* Searching with that term will open up many more doors for her.

The *LCHS* will not only help you find books. Many of the companies that develop databases of articles use Library of Congress terms, too. Equally important, however, for searching these periodical databases is Boolean operators.

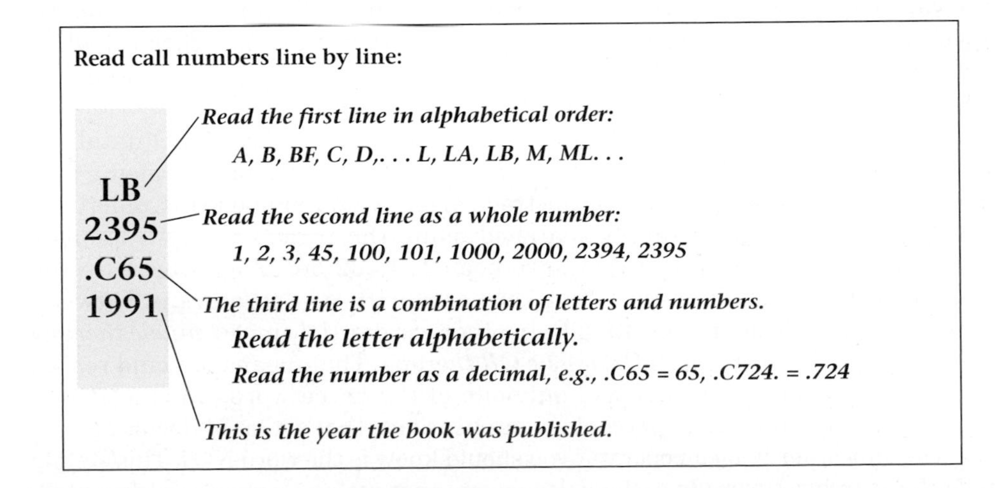

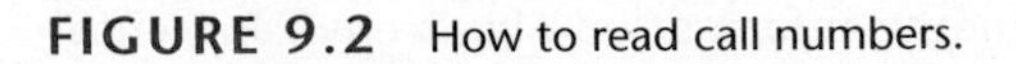
FIGURE 9.2 How to read call numbers.

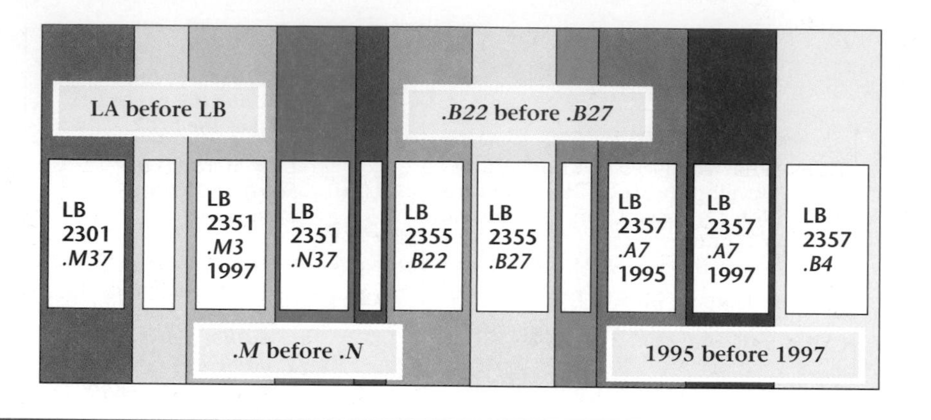

FIGURE 9.3 How books are arranged on the library shelf.

Google Your Boole

George Boole is the eighteenth-century mathematician who came up with the system for using the words AND, OR, and NOT to help researchers design logical queries. Boole's professional legacy is something every modern college researcher should know. Consider Paul's situation. His grandmother has Alzheimer's disease, and his initial research question was, *What are the best therapies for treating Alzheimer's?* When Paul consulted PsycINFO, a popular database of citations from journals relating to psychology, his instinct was simply to enter the word *Alzheimer's* in the online search form. The result was 13,392 citations, and only a portion of these were relevant. But when Paul put the word AND between two key terms from his research question—*Alzheimer's AND therapy*—he managed to reduce his results to 1,955 more relevant citations. As he was looking over his results, Paul became interested specifically in music therapies. His next search was even more focused when he typed in the words *Alzheimer's AND therapy AND music.* That produced 74 citations, and nearly all of these seemed promising.

The Boolean operator AND helped Paul search the PsycINFO database much more efficiently because it asked the computer to look for documents that had all three words in the title or abstract. What would happen if Paul left the AND operators out and simply searched using the three terms *Alzheimer's music therapy?* The result would have been 184,532 documents because the search software would assume that keywords with no operators in between them imply the Boolean operator OR. In other words, *Alzheimer's music therapy* is interpreted as *Alzheimer's OR music OR therapy*. That means it would return citations for documents that had only one of the three words in the title or abstract. For a database of psychology publications, that's a lot of documents.

The only other Boolean operator you should know is the word NOT. This simply tells the search software to exclude documents that include a particular keyword. For example, if you were interested in finding information about environmental organizations in Washington State rather than Washington, D.C., you might construct a query like this: *environmental AND organizations AND Washington NOT D.C.*

The real art of designing queries using the Boolean system is combining the operators to refine your search. For example, let's take the last search on environmental groups in Washington State. Suppose the previous query didn't produce enough results. Let's broaden it a bit: *(environmental OR conservation) AND organizations AND Washington NOT D.C.* This search would find documents that use either *environmental* or *conservation* in the title or abstract, probably returning a longer list. The parentheses simply group the keywords *environmental OR conservation* together as an expression that the search software evaluates first. You can use multiple parentheses in a query to control the order in which expressions are evaluated, beginning with the innermost parenthetical expressions. Librarians call the use of parenthesis to group keywords in this manner *nesting.*

Increasingly, search pages for databases make it easy to exploit Boolean language in a search. For example, in the accompanying photo you can see how the advanced search page for Academic Search Premier, an EBSCOhost database, allows you to enter search terms, and then use drop-down menus to add the Boolean connectors AND, OR, or NOT. The search page adds even more refinement by allowing you to relate a particular term to a type or source or search. For example, you might want to search for Alzheimer's articles by a particular author whose work is relevant to your project. Using the advanced search page, you could simultaneously use *Alzheimer's* as a subject search, with *Smith* as an author search.

Knowing your Boolean operators will help you search library databases because most of the search software relies on the system. Some Web search

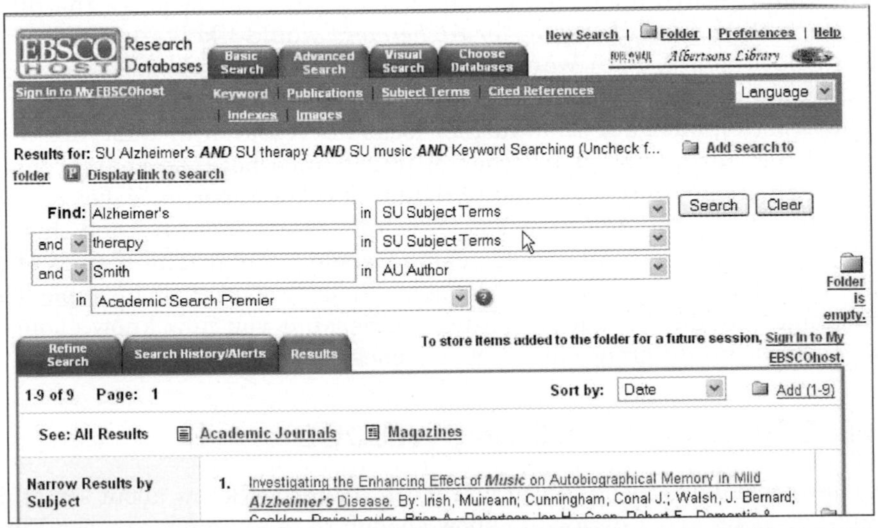

Advanced search pages such as the EBSCOhost database allow you to exploit Boolean terms using drop-down menus. Further refinements allow the researcher to link terms to different kinds of searches or sources.

SEARCH TERMS: BOOLEAN AND THEIR EQUIVALENTS IN GOOGLE			
Boolean	**Example**	**Google**	**Example**
OR	*Romeo OR Juliet*	Add connector between keywords	*Hansel OR Gretel*
AND	*Romeo AND Juliet*	Plus sign in front of keyword, or omit connector	*Hansel + Gretel; Hansel Gretel*
NOT	*Romeo NOT Juliet*	Minus sign in front of keyword	*Hansel – Gretel*
( )	*(Romeo and Juliet)*	No equivalent	
No equivalent		Quotation marks around exact phrase	*"Hansel and Gretel"*

engines do, too. But more often, search engines such as Google use a somewhat different language that accomplishes the same thing. The accompanying table shows both Boolean and typical Web search engine search terms.

Today, search engines such as Google have an advanced search option that allows you to simply fill in a form if you want to search for certain keywords or phrases. I've found that, by far, the most useful syntax to use when searching the Web is quotation marks—an exact phrase search—and carefully ordered keywords, if possible more than three. For example, let's return to Paul's topic of Alzheimer's therapy. If he searched the Web using Google and the keywords *Alzheimer's therapy,* a syntax that implies an AND between the two words, Google would return about 9.9 million documents. But because the phrase *Alzheimer's therapy* or *therapies for Alzheimers* would likely appear in many relevant documents, Paul would be better off to try a phrase search. The result? Searching for *Alzheimer's therapy* produced 10,000 sites.

That's better, but Paul could further focus his research by querying Google with multiple terms, listed in order of importance because search engines usually evaluate keywords from left to right in level of importance. For example, Paul could try this: *+ Alzheimer's + research "music therapy,"* and this time focus the search on journal articles using Google Scholar. The results of this search were about 900 sites and a rich list of scholarly sources on his topic. There is much more to know about composing queries, but you now know enough to make a significant difference in the effectiveness of your searches.

DEVELOPING WORKING KNOWLEDGE

Every day we make decisions about how much we need to know about something. Twenty-five years ago, I decided to know enough to tune up my own car. Fifteen years ago I decided I was't interested in keeping up with the changes in electronic ignitions and fuel injection, so now I leave car repair to Davey at State Street Auto. A scholar is someone who, like Davey, has committed their professional

Writing with Computers

RESEARCHING ONLINE

Today's researchers can conduct scholarly research over the Internet, but their strategy must be more sophisticated than just using Internet search engines. Internet search engines search only items in public places on the Internet. Most college and research libraries have sophisticated Web sites with large subscription-based databases. Internet search engines can't access this information. Generally, you can search the library's holdings in a catalog database. In addition, many libraries subscribe to third-party article indexes. These indexes catalog articles published in magazines, journals, and other periodicals. They can help scholars identify individual articles. The researcher can then use the library's catalog to find the physical location of the journal that contains the article. Large strides in the digitizing of journals over the last few years have made it possible for researchers to find full-text and electronic versions of many articles directly in the indexes or through the library's full text databases. Just ten years ago a college student would have to spend hours in the library pulling hardbound journals or spooling microfilm to access such information. Today's college student can eliminate most of this tedious labor by becoming familiar with his or her library's database services. Currently the digitizing of journals is not universal, so students must still use traditional library bindings and microfilm, but in the near future students may be able to complete all of their research without leaving their computers.

Beyond the databases and indexes of libraries, some scholarly projects place their research on the Internet. These projects use the Internet as a means of immediately displaying their ongoing discoveries and results. One example of such a project is Making of America (http://www.hti.umich.edu/m/moagrp/), which contains scanned images from books, journals, and newspapers from the nineteenth century. This database allows researchers to see the actual pages of rare publications with historical significance. Often search engines aren't able to return results from within these projects or place them in the context of individual search queries. A good researcher should attempt to discover such projects and conduct research directly on these Web sites. If you're unaware of specific online projects in a particular academic field, ask your professor for suggestions.

lives to keeping up with the knowledge in his or her field. College professors possess *expert knowledge* of their discipline (see Figure 9.4). Five hundred years ago, the French writer Montaigne was a "scholar of the self," proposing that self-knowledge was the important kind of knowing of all. If you wrote a personal essay in Chapter 4, you also tapped expert knowledge.

How much we need to know about a subject is, in part, a personal choice, but a college education does at least two things: Challenge you to develop new knowledge about things that will make you a better citizen and more productive professional, and teach you *how* to better acquire the new knowledge that you might seek by choice. A research project like this is driven by both goals—you'll be challenged to go beyond superficial knowledge about a meaningful topic, and you'll learn some of the methods for doing that.

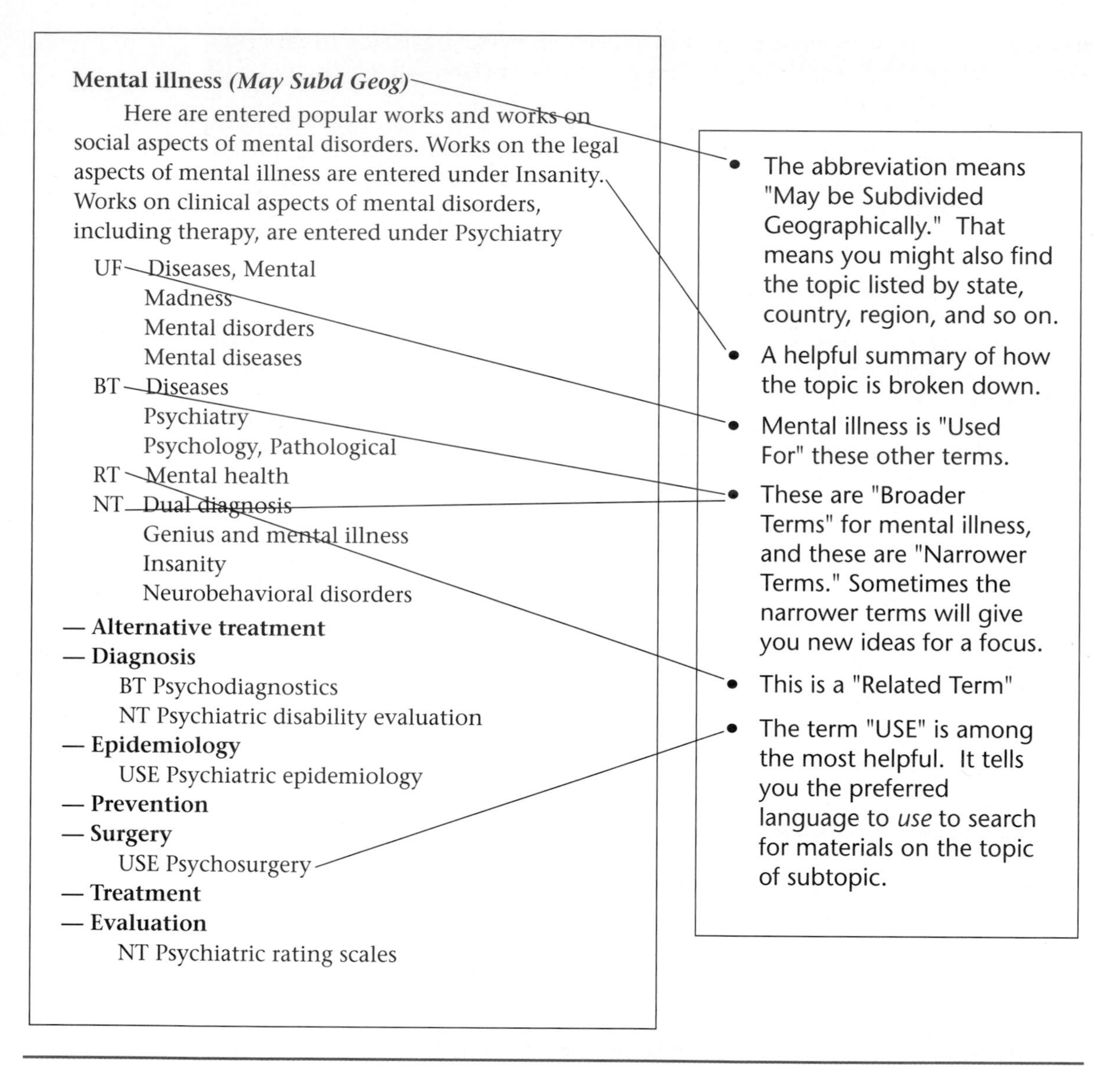

FIGURE 9.4 How to read a Library of Congress Subject Headings entry. At first glance, the *Library of Congress Subject Headings* (*LCSH*) looks like a secret code, one reason that such a valuable research tool initially puts off some student researchers. But using the terms suggested by the *LCSH* can make your research more efficient, particularly when looking for library books or searching databases. Look at the example here. If you are looking for information on bipolar disorder, you might first look in the *LCHS* under *mental disorders*, but because the preferred term is *mental illness*, the book refers you to this page. What does it tell you? A lot.

You will not end up a scholar on anorexia, college dating, the medical effects of music, or whatever topic you're researching. But you will go way beyond superficial knowledge of your subject, and when you do, it will be like opening a door and entering a crowded room of intelligent strangers, all deep in conversation about your topic. At first you simply listen in before you speak, and that begins with a *working knowledge*.

Before you actually start researching a topic, it's unlikely that you could talk about it for one minute without stopping or repeating yourself. But when you can, according to librarian William Badke, you have a "working knowledge" of your topic. Depending on the nature of your project, a working knowledge may be quite enough. For example, suppose you're writing a personal essay about being the target of relational aggression, or to put it less technically, being victimized by a group of girls who express their aggression in often subtle ways. Because of the genre (the personal essay) and your purpose in writing about the topic—say, to come to a clearer understanding why a best friend turned against you—you probably don't need to know a great deal about research done in this field. It would probably be enough to understand the basic theory of relational aggression, a few people who have interesting things to say about it, and perhaps something about how other victims handled their feelings.

You might go beyond a working knowledge of your topic and develop "focused knowledge," the kind often required if you're writing a research essay (focused knowledge is discussed later in this chapter). But if you don't know much about your topic you will always develop a working knowledge first. It's the foundation for further research.

The material that follows will help you develop a working knowledge of a topic using the university library and the Internet. In addition to helping you know enough to talk for a minute without repeating yourself, a working knowledge of a topic helps you understand the following:

1. How your topic fits into the *context* of other subjects. Where does it fall relative to larger and smaller categories of relevant knowledge? This is helpful to know because it can help you narrow your topic.
2. Some of the areas of controversy, debate, questions, or unresolved problems that ripple through the ongoing published conversations about your topic. What, generally, are the people who know something about your topic talking about?

Steps for Developing Working Knowledge

1. Frame a research question or identify your topic as narrowly as you can.
2. Find appropriate search terms in the *Library of Congress Subject Headings*.
3. Check general and specialized encyclopedias.
4. Consult the *Guide to Reference Books* for other references.
5. Do a subject search and a keyword search on the World Wide Web.

Searching Key Library References

Your first inclination when starting research is probably to boot up your computer and do a Web search on your topic. You should resist this temptation, however; laying some groundwork in the library at the start of your research will save you time later. Begin in the reference room of your university library. As a first step, before you begin researching your topic, describe it briefly in a phrase or a sentence, or write out your tentative research question in your journal. It helps enormously to know from the start, if possible, that your topic covers a smaller part of the entire landscape. There's a big difference between wanting to know about *college athletics* versus *college football recruiting practices*.

A good next step is to consult the *Library of Congress Subject Headings.* These several fat volumes are often set out on a table or shelved near the reference desk. Ask a librarian where they are. Because you're probably not familiar with the *LCSH*, you may have to skim the introduction in the front. But basically, try to look up your topic in the book's alphabetically arranged index. Each heading often has lists of subheadings. These may suggest broader terms (BT) or narrower terms (NT) (see Figure 9.4 for an example). You might also notice the abbreviations UF and USE. UF means "used for," or less suitable terms for the topic; USE indicates the standard Library of Congress wording and the one you should use in your library searches. Write down any headings that the *LCSH* suggests for your topic. There may be more than one.

Laying some groundwork in the library at the start of your research will save you time later.

We all grew up with encyclopedias, and while they are pretty useful for that eighth-grade paper on China, general encyclopedias such as *Encyclopaedia Britannica* are less useful as major sources for a college paper. Yet encyclopedias are a good thing to check when developing a working knowledge of your topic. There are, of course, computer-based encyclopedias such as *Encarta,* but these don't hold a candle to the venerable bound version of *Encyclopaedia Britannica*, also in your reference room.

Begin by looking for your topic in a Britannica's *Macropaedia,* a kind of index and abstract of subjects that may point you to longer treatments in the *Micropaedia*. Sometimes you will also find information about your topic *within* articles about other subjects.

Alternatively, see if you can find a specialized encyclopedia in your topic's subject area. These are more focused, obviously, and often have a wealth of information on a topic that's lacking in the more general encyclopedia. Ask the reference librarian whether your library has a specialized encyclopedia in your subject area. A list of some of the more common of these can be found in the accompanying table.

SOME COMMON SPECIALIZED ENCYCLOPEDIAS

Humanities
Encyclopedia of World Art
Encyclopedia of Religions
Encyclopedia of Philosophy
Encyclopedia of African-American Culture and History
Encyclopedia of Social History

Social Sciences
Encyclopedia of Marriage and Family
Encyclopedia of Psychology
The Blackwell Encyclopedia of Social Psychology
Encyclopedia of Educational Research
Encyclopedia of Sociology
Encyclopedia of Social Work
Encyclopedia of World Cultures
Encyclopedia of Democracy
Guide to American Law: Everyone's Legal Encyclopedia
Worldmark Encyclopedia of the Nations

Science
Encyclopedia of the Environment
Concise Encyclopedia of Biology
Encyclopedia of Bioethics
Encyclopedia of Science and Technology
Macmillan Encyclopedias of Chemistry and Physics
Food and Nutrition Encyclopedia

Sports
The Baseball Encyclopedia
Encyclopedia of Women and Sports
Encyclopedia of World Sport
Encyclopedia of Sports Medicine and Science

When you find interesting or relevant information in an encyclopedia, jot down the encyclopedia where you found it and record the information by summarizing it, paraphrasing it, or quoting it directly (see the "Inquiring into the Details: Methods of Recording Information" box). You may find using the double-entry journal method here particularly useful for coming up with ideas and questions you will want to explore in your essay. Summarize, paraphrase, and quote information on the left page of your journal and then fastwrite some of your thoughts in response to that information on the right page. Use questions to direct your fastwriting: *What strikes you most about this information? What do you find interesting? How does the information challenge your initial assumptions about your topic?*

As a final step in the library, consult the *Guide to Reference Books.* This is another one of those incredibly useful and woefully underused reference books that can lead you to a mother lode of sources. The *Guide* includes more than 16,000 indexes, bibliographies, special encyclopedias, almanacs, and other references in several thousand general topic areas. It's organized by field of study (Humanities, Social and Behavioral Sciences, History, Science and Technology, and so forth), but probably the best place to begin is with the index at the back. Try to locate your topic directly, or find some larger subject category that seems relevant. The General Works section in each subject category is a great place to begin if the index at the back fails you.

Inquiring into the Details

METHODS OF RECORDING INFORMATION

The default mode for many student researchers is to simply quote information from a book, article, or Web page, writing down excerpts word for word. Jotting down quotations is fine. But it's often far more useful to summarize and paraphrase a source in your own words. Here's a brief description of each method.

1. **Summary.** One of the more useful ways of taking notes because it challenges you to condense, in your own words, a longer text, capturing key concepts or claims.
2. **Paraphrase.** This also tests your understanding of what you read, prompting you to translate a passage from a source into your own words; your paraphrase will be roughly the same length as the original.
3. **Quotation.** A perennial favorite approach to note taking because it's mere transcription, ranging from a few key words to several paragraphs. Remember to always transcribe the words of the original source exactly.
4. **"Paraquote."** One of the most useful methods of note taking is to cast part of an original passage in your own words, and then integrate a key term or phrase in quotations. For example: *Ballenger claims that the "paraquote," a combination of paraphrase and quotation in a single sentence, is "one of the most useful methods of note taking."*

Write down the name and publication information about any reference source listed in the *Guide* that seem promising on your topic; find out if your library has it, and if it's an encyclopedia, almanac, or some other general reference source, do some reading on your topic. Again, consider using the double-entry journal method to get the most out of the information.

Conducting Subject Surveys on the Web

One of the useful qualities of the World Wide Web is how much it offers researchers who want to quickly develop a working knowledge of their topics. The Web is probably where you wanted to start your research rather than in your library's reference room, but if the campus library reflects reference librarians' passion for order and logic in a chaotic universe, the Web is more like the mind of my nine-year-old daughter Julia. She has lots of passions, but one look at her bedroom and it's clear that order isn't one of them. She does try from time to time, as the bins in her closet show: the contents of each bin roughly corresponds to an area of interest, but the stuff is often mixed up and I'm not surprised when she can't find what she's looking for.

Librarians and scholars have tried to bring some order to the similar chaos of the Internet, perhaps with more success. They've introduced plastic bins, too, and these are subject directories such as the Virtual Library, or the Internet Public Library. Unfortunately, these sites are often ignored by student researchers who opt instead to begin with a Google search, an effort that will produce some useable results that will be scattered among much less reliable documents. Consulting the subject directories may not generate as much information, but what you find will be better quality for academic research.

A good way to start your research on the Web is to visit one or more of the following subject directories:

- Academic Info (http://www.academicinfo.net)
- Infomine (http://infomine.ucr.edu)
- The Librarians Index to the Internet (http://lii.org)
- Best Information on the Net (http://library.sau.edu/bestinfo/Default.htm)
- The Internet Public Library (http://www.ipl.org)
- Virtual Library (http://vlib.org)
- The Google Directory (http://directory.google.com)
- Yahoo! Directory (http://dir.yahoo.com)

The way to use the directories is to work from the general to the specific, beginning with broad subject categories relevant to your topic and then mouse-clicking your way down to narrower categories until you find a good match with your topic. If one directory yields little, try another.

Print out copies of any useful documents you find, and consider composing one- or two-paragraph summaries, or *annotations,* for each of the sources you find. *What are the key ideas? What seems most important and relevant to your project?* If your instructor requires you to develop a working bibliography or annotated bibliography on your topic, this might be the beginning of it (see the "Inquiring into the Details: The Working Bibliography" box).

Finish your Web research by using so-called metasearch engines. This software deploys multiple search engines in the service of a single search. For example, when you type your keywords into Dogpile it simultaneously searches using Google, Yahoo!, LookSmart, Ask.com, MSN Search, and others. If this

INQUIRING INTO THE DETAILS

THE WORKING BIBLIOGRAPHY

A working bibliography lists sources you've collected that you think will be helpful when you draft your essay. These may include annotations, or brief summaries of what the source says that you find relevant to your research question. Consider the following examples:

Topic: Relational Aggression

Print Sources

Simmons, Rachel. *Odd Girl Out: The Hidden Culture of Aggression in Girls.* New York: Harcourt, 2002.

Simmons argues that the "secret world of girls' aggression"—the backstabbing, the silent treatment, the bartering of friendship for compliance to a group's "rules"—can be just as bad as the less subtle aggression of boys. Her basic thesis is that girls in American culture are supposed to be "nice," and therefore have no outlet for their anger except for exploiting the one thing they do covet: relationships. Because my essay focuses on the popularity phenomenon in high school—How does it affect girls when they are adults?—Simmons's chapter on parents of these girls seems particularly useful because it shows how the parents' responses are often shaped by their own experiences in school.

Web Sources

"What Is Relational Aggression?" *The Ophelia Project.* 22 Sept. 2003 <http://www.opheliaproject.org/issues/issues_RA.shtml>.

The page defines relational aggression by contrasting it with physical aggression. It argues that most research, naturally, has focused on the latter because of need to limit physical injury between children. But girls tend to avoid physical aggression and instead indulge in actions that harm others by disrupting their social relationships, like giving someone the silent treatment. The Ophelia Project is a nonprofit group created in 1997 by parents who wanted to address the problem.

sounds too good to be true, it is; metasearch engines tend to skim off the top of the results for each individual search engine, so you often get a breadth of results but not depth. Still, metasearches are worth doing because they help extend your coverage of the Web.

Use one or more of the following metasearch engines to search on your topic:

- Metacrawler (http://www.metacrawler.com)
- Dogpile (http://www.dogpile.com)
- Mamma (http://www.mamma.com)
- Search.com (http://www.search.com)

Remember to play around with the number and order of keywords to get the best results. Several of these sites also provide subject searches. You might try one of those as well.

Add promising sites or documents to your working bibliography, writing summaries or annotations for each individual source. Be sure to list the bibliographic information on each source following the appropriate documentation style (see Chapter 10 for MLA and APA guidelines).

A working knowledge may be all you need, depending on your project. With a working knowledge, you know enough to search with more efficiency and read with more understanding if you want or need to learn more. If you are writing a research paper, you will need to develop focused knowledge about your topic, discussed later in the chapter. But first, consider this: How do you determine which sources you can trust, and which will be most persuasive for your readers? The next sections should help you decide.

EVALUATING LIBRARY SOURCES

One of the huge advantages of finding what you need at the campus library is that nearly everything there was chosen by librarians whose job it is to make good information available to academic researchers. Now that many of the university library's databases are available online, including full-text articles, there really is no excuse for deciding to exclusively use Web pages you downloaded from the Internet for your essays. But even in the campus library, some sources are more authoritative than others. The "Pyramid of Library Sources" (see Figure 9.5) gives you a general idea of the hierarchy of authority for most library sources.

In general, the more specialized the audience for a publication, the more authoritatively scholars view the publication's content. Academic journals are at the bottom of this inverted pyramid because they represent the latest thinking and knowledge in a discipline, and most of the articles are reviewed by specialists in the field before they are published. At the top of the inverted pyramid are general encyclopedias and general-interest magazines such as *Newsweek* and *Time.* These have broader audiences and feature articles that are written

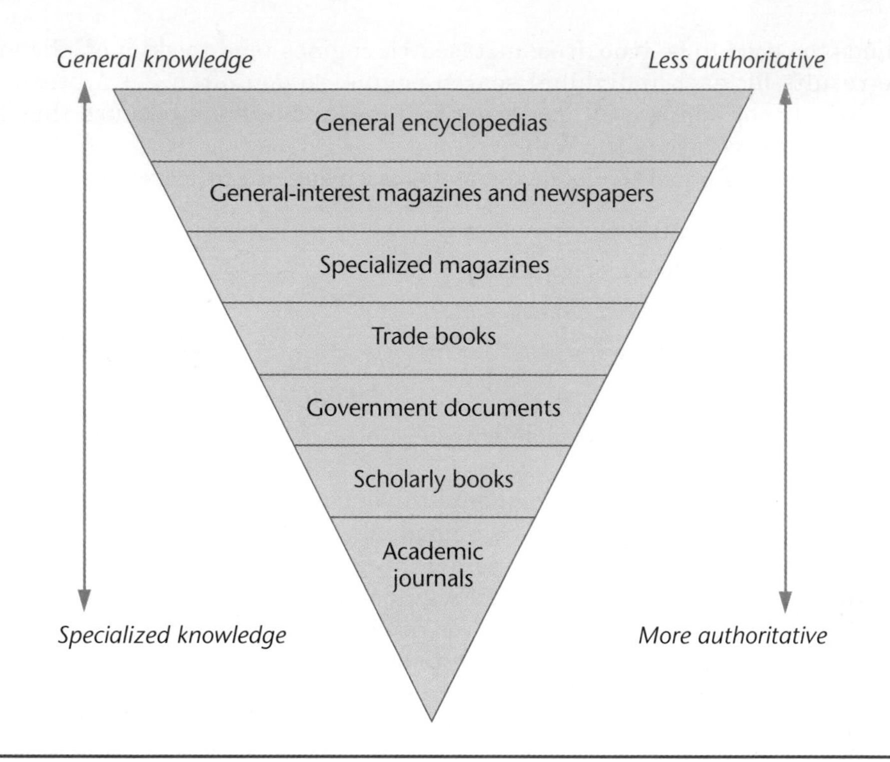

FIGURE 9.5 A hierarchy of sources places the most credible at the bottom of an inverted pyramid. For academic research, these are usually articles and books that are reviewed by other experts before they're published.

by nonspecialists. They are rarely peer reviewed. As a rule, then, the lower you draw from this inverted pyramid, the more authoritative the sources from an academic point of view. Here are some other guidelines to consider:

- *Choose more recent sources over older ones.* This is particularly good advice, obviously, if your subject is topical; the social and natural sciences also put much more emphasis on the currency of sources than humanities disciplines.
- *Look for often-cited authors.* Once you've developed a working knowledge of your topic, you'll start noticing that certain authors seem to be mentioned or cited fairly frequently. These are likely to be the most listened-to authors, and may be considered the most authoritative on your topic.
- *If possible, use primary sources over secondary sources.* In literary research, primary sources are the original words of writers—their speeches, stories, novels, poems, memoirs, letters, interviews, and eyewitness accounts. Secondary sources would be articles that discuss those works. Primary sources in other fields might be original studies or experiments, firsthand newspaper accounts, marketing information, and so on.

EVALUATING WEB SOURCES

One of the more amusing sites on the Web is titled "Feline Reactions to Bearded Men." At first glance, the site appears to be a serious academic study of the physiological responses of cats—heartbeat, respiration, and pupil dilation—to a series of photographs of men with beards. The researchers are listed with their affiliations with respected universities. The article includes an abstract, methodology, and results section, as well as a lengthy list of works cited.

The conclusions seem genuine and include the following:

1. Cats do not like men with long beards, especially long dark beards.
2. Cats are indifferent to men with shorter beards.
3. Cats are confused and/or disturbed by men with beards that are incomplete and to a lesser degree by men whose beards have missing parts.

The study is a hoax, a fact that is pretty obvious to anyone who critically examines it. For one thing, it was "published" in the *Annals of Improbable Research*, but I can usually fool about a third of my class with the site for five to ten minutes as I discuss the conventions of academic research, some of which are accurately reproduced in the "study."

A cat reacts to a picture of a bearded man from the study "Feline Reactions to Bearded Men."

Everyone knows to be skeptical of what's on the Web. But this is even more crucial when using Web sources for college writing. Because it's dominated by commercial sites, much of the World Wide Web has limited usefulness to the academic researcher, and although very few online authors are out to fool researchers with fake scholarship, many have a persuasive purpose. Despite its "educational" mission, for example, the purpose of the Web site ConsumerFreedom.com is to promote industry views on laws relating to food and beverages. That doesn't make the information it offers useless, but a careful researcher would be wary of the site's claims and critical of its studies. At the very least, the information on ConsumerFreedom.com should be attributed as a pro-industry view.

Imagine as you're researching on the Web that you've been dropped off at night in an unfamiliar neighborhood. You're alert. You're vigilant. And you're careful about whom you ask for directions. You can also be systematic about how you approach evaluating online sources. In general, follow these principles:

- *Favor governmental and educational sources over commercial ones.* These sites are more likely to have unbiased information. How can you tell which are institutional sites when it's not obvious? Sometimes the domain name—the abbreviation *edu*, *org*, or *gov* at the end of an Internet address—provides a strong clue, as does the absence of ads on the site.
- *Favor authored documents over those without authors.* There's a simple reason for this: You can check the credentials of authors if you know who they are. Sometimes sites provide e-mail links so you can write to authors, or you can do a search on the Internet or in the library for other materials they've published.
- *Favor documents that are also available in print over those available only online.* Material that is published in both forms generally undergoes more scrutiny. An obvious example would be newspaper articles, but also some articles from journals and magazines are available electronically and in print.
- *Favor Web sources that document their claims over those that don't.* This familiar academic convention is strong evidence that the claims an online author is making are supported and verifiable.
- *Favor Web pages that were recently updated over those that haven't changed in a year or more.* Frequently at the bottom of a Web page there is a line indicating when the information was posted to the Internet and/or when it was last updated. Look for it.

For a more systematic approach to evaluating Web sources, follow the steps in Figure 9.6. This method begins by dividing Web documents into two broad categories: those with authors and those without authors. Web sites that list authors for documents are generally more trustworthy because you can evaluate who the authors are and whether they have appropriate expertise or a particular bias. But many Web documents have no stated authors, forcing you to resort to other ways of evaluating them.

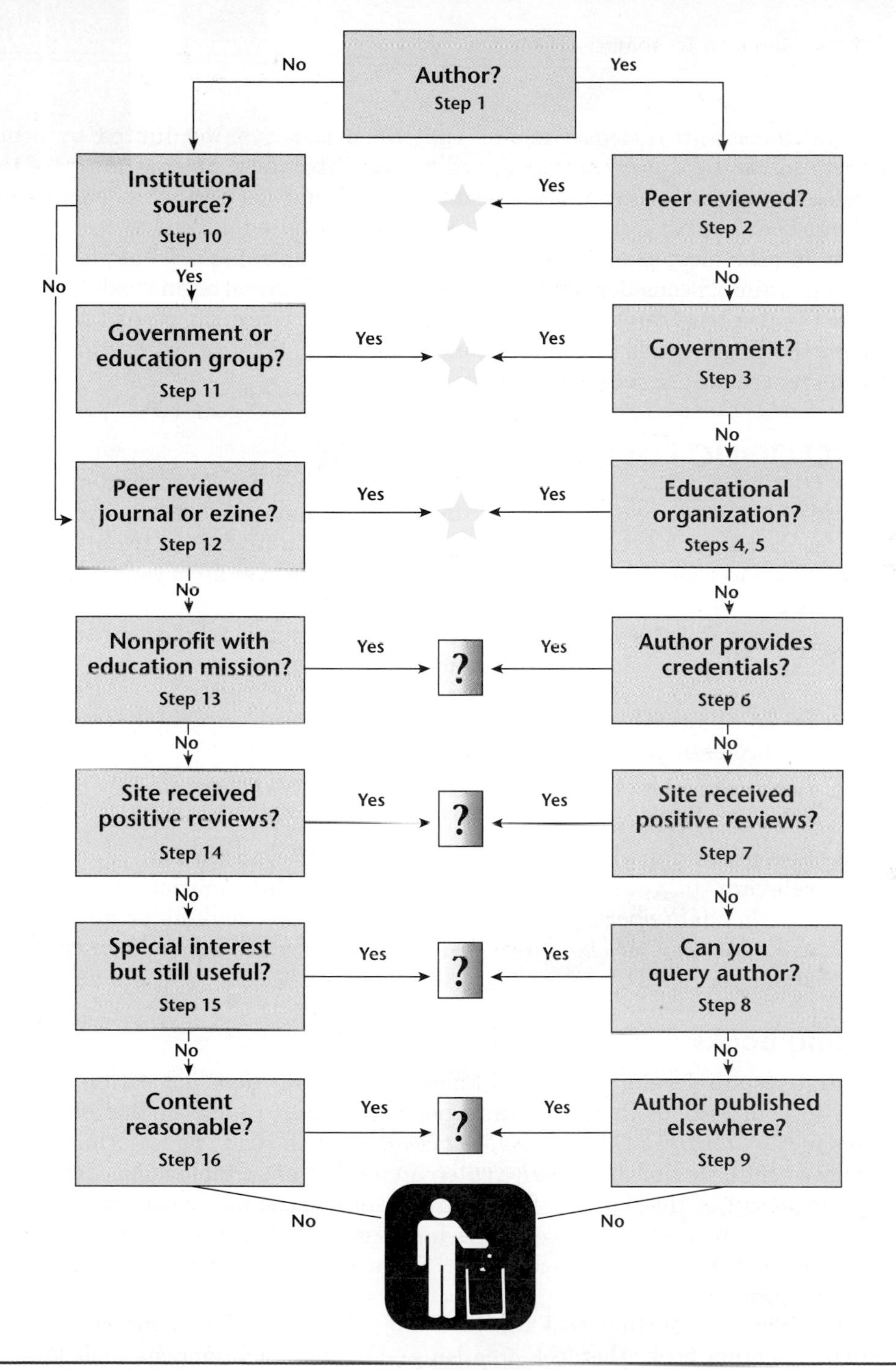

FIGURE 9.6 Steps for evaluating Web sources. Begin by trying to find an author of a Web document, and then follow one of the two columns. If subsequent answers to the questions that follow lead you to a star, then you've probably found a credible source. A question mark suggests one that may be useful, depending. If you end up at the trash can at the bottom, well, the implication is clear.

The term *peer reviewed* means that an article was evaluated by other experts in the field and was published because it passed muster. Many of the articles in academic journals are peer reviewed, but very few Web documents undergo that kind of scrutiny; if they were, they usually tell you so.

By far, the most common method of analyzing the value of what you find on the Web is simply considering the source: Is it a commercial or an academic institution? Is it a lone ranger with no affiliations or government group? Are there ads on the page (which suggests a commercial site) or none (which suggests a noncommercial organization)?

DEVELOPING FOCUSED KNOWLEDGE

If working knowledge equips you to sustain a one-minute monologue on your topic, then focused knowledge is enough for you to make a fifteen- to twenty-minute presentation to your class. You'll probably be able to answer all of your classmates' questions, too.

On acquiring focused knowledge on your topic, you won't become an expert but you should know enough to do the following:

1. Be familiar with some of the *key people* who have participated actively in the professional conversation about your topic.
2. Put your research question in the context of *what has already been said* about your topic.
3. Recognize quickly whether any information you find on your topic is relevant to your project. If it is relevant information, you'll know whether it *supports or develops* a claim you are making or an idea you are exploring, or *challenges or complicates* what you've been thinking about your topic.

Finding Books

The first step in developing focused knowledge in your topic is locating relevant books in your campus library. Here's where your effort to find productive search terms in the *Library of Congress Subject Headings* will really pay off. During your earlier consultation of the *LCSH,* you created a list of suitable subject headings on your topic. Use that list now to search the online book index in your university library. You can probably access this index on any Internet-enabled campus computer or from your home computer. Try several subject headings until you generate promising results.

Next, find two or three books on your subject in your school's library—making note of any other books that look promising—and jot down complete bibliographic information, a summary of the book's basic argument or approach, and why it seems relevant to your research question (see the "Inquiring into the Details: How to Annotate a Book" box). Use this information to start a working bibliography on your topic if you haven't done so already. If you managed to find a particularly good book on your topic, don't forget to check the book's bibliography, if it has one, for more relevant books and articles.

Finding Periodicals

Your campus library contains at least three kinds of periodicals: general-interest magazines such as *Time, Harper's,* and *People;* special-interest magazines such as *PC World, Outside*, and *Sports Illustrated*; and scholarly journals such as *Journal of Mass Communication* and *American Sociologist.* Depending on your topic, you may end up using all three types of periodicals; remember, though, that the scholarly ones are considered more authoritative for college research.

Steps for Developing Focused Knowledge

1. Find relevant books on your topic.
2. Find relevant articles in periodicals on your topic.
3. Find relevant newspaper articles on your topic.
4. Find relevant sources on the Web.
5. Synthesize source information and your own ideas using techniques such as the double-entry journal and research log.

Inquiring into the Details

HOW TO ANNOTATE A BOOK

The brevity of articles and most Web pages makes them much easier to annotate than a book. You can usually summarize the argument or relevant ideas of such sources fairly easily. But how do you do that with a book that may have hundreds of pages of information and an extended argument? Read strategically.

1. To summarize a book's approach or basic argument, skim the preface and introduction. Sometimes there's a concluding chapter that neatly summarizes things, too. Even the back cover or jacket flap can be helpful for this overview.
2. To explain the relevance of the book to your research question or topic, you may focus on a particular chapter or chapters. Again, at this point you can probably skim the text quickly to discover its relevance. Later, you may do a more careful reading.
3. Evaluate *part* of the author's treatment of your topic rather than the whole book. Search the table of contents for what you suspect are the most relevant chapters, and focus your reading on those.

These days, searching for periodicals is easier than ever. Your university library likely has a Web page that includes a long list of databases that index periodicals by discipline (for example, PsycINFO) or that cover periodicals in a range of subjects (for example, Reader's Guide Abstracts or Academic Search Premier).

Find your library's Web site that lists databases for periodicals and choose a subject-specific database relevant to your topic or a general subject database. In fact, consider checking both. Again, your knowledge of Boolean logic and your familiarity with search terms suggested by the *Library of Congress Subject Headings* will give you a head start when using the search forms for each database.

As you did before with the books you found, add promising articles to your working bibliography, jotting down the bibliographic information on each article (see Chapter 10 for MLA and APA guidelines) and annotating each entry with a brief paragraph describing the article.

Finding Newspapers

Newspaper databases are also available online at your university library. The most common of these include the National Newspaper Index, Newspaper Source, and Proquest National Newspapers. Most such databases index major newspapers such as The *New York Times*, The *Wall Street Journal*, and The *Washington Post*, but you might find a database for the local or state paper as well.

Search for newspaper articles on your topic. This will be a particularly important search if you're interested in a current topic, something that has drawn the attention of daily news reporters or columnists. Some of the databases will provide you with full-text articles online, but more often you'll need to find the article on microfilm in the reference room of your university library. As before, add noteworthy newspaper articles to your working bibliography, citing bibliographic information and annotating each article.

Finding Sources on the Web

Build on the working knowledge of your topic that you developed during your preliminary search on the Web. You can maximize your coverage of the Web using various individual search engines. But why bother when a single popular search engine such as Google has such an enormous database? The extra effort is worthwhile because the overlap between individual search engines actually is quite small, particularly if your topic is uncommon.

Search the Web using at least two or three of the following popular search engines:

- Google (http://www.google.com)
- MSN Search (http://search.msn.com)
- AltaVista (http://www.altavista.com)
- Yahoo! (http://www.yahoo.com)
- Hotbot (http://www.hotbot.com)
- Search.com (http://www.search.com)

- AllTheWeb.com (http://www.alltheweb.com)
- Ask.com (http://www.ask.com)

Remember that whenever possible, you should use three or more words in a keyword search, listing the most important term first. Phrases, usually enclosed in quotation marks, can be especially helpful in generating useful results.

Writing in the Middle: Synthesizing Source Information and Your Own Ideas

It's not news that there is an epidemic of plagiarism and it's not just a problem on the college campus. Recently, several well-known historians admitted to being a bit sloppy about giving their sources proper credit. Naturally, a lot of people assume that the problem of plagiarism has to do with ethics. Students cheat. They confuse means and ends. And so on. There's some truth to this, but I contend that the real cause of the problem comes not from what students do, but what they don't do—they don't "write in the middle."

The plagiarism problem usually surfaces when writers are rushed, madly composing drafts at the last minute, and they simply haven't made the time to make the information they've collected their own. As a result, they're controlled *by* the information rather than controlling it for their own purposes. "How can I improve on what this guy says?" The thinking goes, "I guess I should just get it down in my paper." The result is sometimes unintentional plagiarism—some quotation marks were omitted or the paraphrase was too close to the original—but more often the paper suffers from another problem: the absence of an author. The writer doesn't seem to be in charge of where the essay goes and what it says.

There's a solution to this that is really quite simple. Write about what you're reading *as you collect it.*

Note cards aren't what I have in mind unless you use them to do more than simply jot down what a source says. Instead, I strongly recommend that you keep a double-entry journal or a research log that will serve two purposes: collecting information and exploring your reactions to what you've found. This is merely an extension of what I've been suggesting from the beginning of *The Curious Writer*—that you can move dialectically from creative thinking to critical thinking and back again—but this time you'll be creatively exploring information and then reflecting on how it addresses your research question.

The suggestion that you take time to write about the information you have collected in the middle of the process may come across as needing a pretty tough sell. *Save the writing for the draft,* you're thinking. But you are essentially *beginning* your draft with thoughtful note taking, which will save you time later.

Double-Entry Journal. You already are familiar with the double-entry journal. This approach uses opposing pages of your notebook to encourage dialectical thinking. On the left page take notes—paraphrases, summaries, and quotations—as you might usually do with conventional note taking, and on the opposing right

Writing with Computers

PLAGIARISM AND THE INTERNET

Plagiarism is theft of intellectual property without acknowledging the source. Most students think of plagiarism as copying words, but plagiarism includes unacknowledged acquisition of another's words, ideas, information, or even structural presentation. Plagiarism is an academic crime with serious consequences, including expulsion. In academic circles, plagiarism can have a destructive effect on careers.

Unfortunately, the Internet makes plagiarism easier than ever before. It also increases the potential for accidental plagiarism because the efficiency of quickly finding large quantities of information causes many students to overlook proper management of their source material. The convenience of copying and pasting also causes some students to fail to distinguish outside sources from their own work. Accidental plagiarism can be avoided through diligent research practices.

The Internet also facilitates intentional plagiarism. Many Web sites collect and distribute essays. Some Web sites charge for essays while others operate under a reciprocity agreement by which a student can copy an essay from the database after uploading one of his or her own. Some services even offer to write original papers for a fee.

While the Internet might seem like a plagiarist's dream, it also makes detecting plagiarism easy. Internet services allow teachers to upload manuscripts and search for similar copies online. Most of these databases are sophisticated enough to search past minor textual changes that a coy plagiarist might make to avoid detection. These services then send a highlighted report showing where suspected similarities occur and direct the teacher to the source Web sites. Keep in mind too, that because the Internet is not regulated like traditional publications, plagiarism is rampant within Internet publications, so an essay or source material may be found on multiple Web sites, increasing the chance that a plagiarist might be caught.

If you publish on the Internet, you can reasonably assume that others may plagiarize your work. While you cannot completely protect your own intellectual property, the low cost and convenience of Internet publication appeals to many writers. A service called Copyscape.com helps writers control their work. A free version of the service allows writers to search for Web sites that have duplicated their work. A subscription version continuously monitors the Internet for duplications and notifies authors if duplicates are found on other Web sites. For those who enjoy self-publishing on the Internet, the fee of such a service might be well worth it.

page *explore* your responses, reactions, and questions about the information you've collected on the left page (for a full description of the double-entry notebook method, see "Using the Double-Entry Journal" in Chapter 2).

Research Log. Another method of note taking that also exploits dialectical thinking is the research log. Rather than using opposing pages, you'll layer your notes and responses, one after another. This is a particularly useful method for those who would prefer to work with a keyboard rather than a pencil. Here's how it works:

1. Begin by taking down the full bibliographic information on the source, something you may already have in your working bibliography.

2. Read the article, book chapter, or Web page, marking up your personal copy as you typically do, perhaps underlining key facts or ideas or information relevant to your research question.

3. Your first entry in your notebook or on the computer will be a fastwrite, an open-ended response to the reading under the heading What Strikes Me Most. As the title implies, you're dealing with first thoughts here. Consider some of the following approaches to this initial response to the source:

- First play the believing game, exploring how the author's ideas, arguments, or findings seem sensible to you. Then shift to the doubting game, a more critical stance in which you look for gaps, raise questions, or express doubts about what the source says.
- What strikes you as the most important thing the author was trying to say?
- What do you remember best? What surprised you most after reading the source?
- What seemed most convincing? Least convincing?
- How does the source change your thinking on the topic? What do you understand better now than you did before you read the piece?
- How does it compare to other things you've read?
- What seems most relevant to your research question?
- What other research possibilities does it suggest?

4. Next, take notes on the source, jotting down summaries, paraphrases, quotations, and key facts you glean from it. Title this section Source Notes.

5. Finally, follow up with another episode of fastwriting. Title this The Source Reconsidered. This is a *more focused* look at the source; fastwrite about what stands out in the notes you took. Which facts, findings, claims, or arguments shape your thinking now? If the writing stalls, skip a line, take another look at your source notes, and seize on something else to write about.

One Student's Response

CLAUDE'S RESEARCH LOG

SOURCE

Source Letawsky, Nicole R., et al. "Factors Influencing the College Selection Process of Student Athletes." *College Student Journal* 37.4 (2003): 604–11. *Academic Search Premier.* EBSCOhost Databases. Albertson's Lib. 5 Apr. 2004.

WHAT STRIKES ME MOST

Really interesting article that studied about 130 student athletes at a large 1-A university. Noted that there have been a lot of research studies on why students choose a particular school but not so much on why student-athletes choose a school. Everyone assumes, of course, that student-athletes go somewhere because they're wined and dined and promised national TV exposure. In other words, it all has to do with the glamour of playing 1-A, particularly the so-called revenue sports like basketball and football. But this study had some surprising findings. They found that the number one reason that student-athletes chose a school was the degree options it offers. In other words, the reasons student-athletes choose a school aren't that much different that the reason regular students choose one. The study also found that the glamour stuff—getting awards, getting on TV, and future professional possibilities—mattered the least to the student-athletes. This study challenges some of the myths about student recruiting, and should be read by recruiters especially. If you want to get a blue-ribbon player at your school, tell them about the academic opportunities there.

SOURCE NOTES (CUT-AND-PASTE FROM ELECTRONIC VERSION)

"This study found that the most important factor for student-athletes was the degree program options offered by the University. Other important factors were the head coach, academic support services, type of community in which the campus is located, and the school's sports traditions. Two of the top three factors were specifically related to the academic rather than athletic environment. This is a key finding and should be understood as recruiting efforts should be broad based, balancing academics and athletics if they are to be effective."

"A somewhat surprising result of the study concerned relatively low ratings associated with factors considered essential to 'Big-Time College Sports.' Television exposure, perceived opportunity to play immediately, and perceived future professional sporting opportunities were among the lowest-ranked factors. Furthermore, the participants rated athletic rewards (a 5-item survey scale containing these and other reward items) consistently lower than both the campus and athletic environment. These results may be due to the fact that respondents were from each of the sports offered by the University. Many of the sports (e.g., swimming, track), although funded and supported similar to the other sports, do not receive the national attention, large crowds, and television exposure."

SOURCE RECONSIDERED

This article did more than anything I've read so far to make me question my thesis that big-time college sports recruiting is way out of control. It's pretty convincing on the point that athletes care about the academic programs when they're choosing a school. But then the second quotation has an interesting part that I just noticed. This study surveyed athletes in all sports, not just the big-time sports like football and basketball at the university where the study was conducted. It seems to me that that would really skew the findings because someone participating in a sport like tennis that doesn't get a lot of attention and doesn't necessarily lead to professional opportunities after school *would* be more interested in academics. They're not dreaming of making a name for themselves, but getting a scholarship to pay for school. Seems like a better study would focus on the big-time sports . . .

Whichever note-taking method you choose—the double-entry journal or the research log—what you are doing is taking possession of the information and making it yours by evaluating it for your own purposes. One of the hardest parts of writing with outside sources is doing exactly that—using someone else's ideas or information in the service of your own questions. And that's why taking the time to write in the middle is so important: you're doing the most important intellectual work *as* you encounter the perspectives of others. This will make writing the draft much easier, and will also, I believe, lower the risk of unintentional plagiarism, a mistake that often occurs in the mad rush to begin writing the draft the night before it's due.

INTERVIEWS

Tethered as we are these days to the electronic world of the Web and the increasingly digital university library, it's easy to forget an old-fashioned source for research: a living, breathing human being. People are often the best sources of information because you can have a real conversation rather than the imagined one simulated by the double-entry notebook. Some kinds of writing, such as the profile, fundamentally depend on interviews; with other genres, such as the personal essay or the research paper, interviews are one of several sources of information. But they can be central to bringing writing to life because when we put people on the page, abstract ideas or arguments suddenly have a face and a voice. People on the page make ideas matter.

The principal advantage of doing interviews is that you ask the questions that you are most interested in learning the answers to.

Arranging Interviews

Whom do you interview? Basically, there are two kinds of interviews: (1) the interviewee is the main subject of your piece, as in a profile, and (2) the interviewee is *a source of information* about another subject.

The interviewee as a source of information is the far more common type of interview, and it usually involves finding people who either are experts on the topic you're writing about or have been touched or influenced in some way by it. For example, Tina was writing a research essay on the day care crisis in her community. Among those affected by this issue are the parents of small children, their day care teachers, and even the kids themselves; all were good candidates for interviews about the problem. Experts were a little more difficult to think of immediately. The day care teachers might qualify—after all, they're professionals in the area—but Tina also discovered a faculty member in the College of Health and Social Sciences who specialized in policies related to child care. Interviewing both types of people—experts and those influenced by the issue—gave Tina a much richer perspective on the problem.

How do you find experts in your topic? Here are a few strategies for locating potential interviewees:

- *Check the faculty directory on your campus.* Many universities publish an annual directory of faculty and their research interests, which may be online. In addition, your university's public information office might have a similar list of faculty and areas of expertise.
- *Ask friends and your instructors.* They might know faculty who have a research interest in your topic, or might know someone in the community who is an expert on it.
- *Check the phone book.* The familiar Yellow Pages can be a gold mine. Want to find a biologist who might have something to say about the effort to bring back migrating salmon? Find the number of the regional office of U.S. Fish and Wildlife Service in the phone book and ask for the public information officer. He or she may help you find the right expert.
- *Check your sources.* As you begin to collect books, articles, and Internet documents, note their authors and affiliations. I get calls or e-mails from time to time from writers who came across my book on lobsters, posing questions I love to try to answer because no one in Idaho gives a hoot about lobsters. Google searches of authors who are mentioned in your sources may produce e-mail addresses or Web sites with e-mail links that you might query.
- *Check the* Encyclopedia of Associations. This is another underused book and database in your university's reference room that lists organizations in the United States with interests as varied as promoting tofu and saving salmon.

Conducting the Interview

The kinds of questions you ask fundamentally depend on what type of interview you're conducting. In a profile, your questions will focus on the interview subject. To some extent, this is also true when you interview nonexperts who are *affected* by the topic you're writing about. For example, Tina is certainly interested in what the parents of preschoolers *know* about the day care crisis in her town, but she's also interested in the feelings and *experiences* of these people. Gathering this kind of information leads to some of the questions you may have used in a profile, but with more focus on the subject's experience with your topic:

- What was your first experience with ____________? What has most surprised you about it?
- How does ____________ make you feel?
- Tell me about a moment that you consider most typical of your experience with ____________.

More often, however, your motive in an interview will be to gather information. Obviously, this will prompt you to ask specific questions about your topic as you try to fill in gaps in your knowledge. But some more general, open-ended questions may be useful to ask. For example:

- What is the most difficult aspect of your work?
- What do you think is the most significant popular misconception about ____________?
- What are the significant current trends in ____________?
- If you had to summarize the most important thing you've learned about ____________, what would that be?
- What is the most important thing other people should know or understand?
- What do you consider the biggest problem?
- Who has the power to do something about it?
- What is your prediction about the future? Ten years from now, what will this problem look like?

Once you have a list of questions in mind, be prepared to ignore them. Good interviews often take turns that you can't predict, and these journeys may lead you to information and understandings you didn't expect. After all, a good interview is like a good conversation; it may meander, speed up or slow down, and reveal things about your topic and your interview subject that you don't expect. But good interviewers also attempt to control an interview when the turns it's taking aren't useful. You do this through questions, of course, but also more subtle tactics. For example, if you stop taking notes most interview subjects notice, and the astute ones quickly understand that what they're saying has less interest to you. A quick glance at your watch can have the same effect.

E-mail interviews produce a ready-made text with both your questions and the subject's answers. This is pretty wonderful. Live interviews, on the other hand, require more skill. It's usually a good idea to use a tape recorder (with your subject's permission), but never rely exclusively on it especially since machines can fail and batteries can expire unexpectedly. *Always take notes.* Your notes, if nothing else, will help you know where on the tape you should concentrate later, transcribing direct quotations or gathering information. Note taking during interviews is an acquired skill; the more you do it, the better you get, inventing all sorts of shorthand for commonly occurring words. Practice taking notes while watching the evening news.

Most of all, try to enjoy your interview. After all, you and your interview subject have something important in common—you have an interest in your topic—and this usually produces an immediate bond that transforms an interview into an enjoyable conversation.

Using the Interview in Your Writing

Putting people on the page is one of the best ways to bring writing to life. This is exactly what information from interviews can do—give otherwise abstract questions or problems a voice and a face. One of the most common ways to use interview material is to integrate it into the lead or first paragraph of your essay. By focusing on someone involved in the research question or problem you're exploring, you immediately capture reader interest. For example, here's the beginning of a *Chronicle of Higher Education* essay, "What Makes Teachers Great?"[1] Quite naturally, the writer chose to begin by profiling someone who happened to be a great teacher, using evidence from the interviews he conducted.

> When Ralph Lynn retired as a professor of history at Baylor University in 1974, dozens of his former students paid him tribute. One student, Ann Richards, who became the governor of Texas in 1991, wrote that Lynn's classes were like "magical tours into the great minds and movements of history." Another student, Hal Wingo, the editor of *People* magazine, concluded that Lynn offered the best argument he knew for human cloning. "Nothing would give me more hope for the future," the editor explained, "than to think that Ralph Lynn, in all his wisdom and wit, will be around educating new generations from here to eternity."

This is a strong way to begin an essay because the larger idea—the qualities that make a great teacher—is grounded in a name and a face. But information from interviews can be used anywhere in an essay—not just at the beginning—to make an idea come to life.

Information from interviews can also provide strong evidence for a point you're trying to make, especially if your interview subject has expertise on the topic. But interviews can also be a *source* of ideas about what you might want to say in an essay. The essay on great teaching, for instance, offers seven qualities that great teachers embrace in their classrooms, things such as "create a natural critical learning environment" and "help students learn outside of class." All of these claims grew from interviews with sixty professors in a range of disciplines.

The principal advantage of doing interviews is that *you* ask the questions that you're most interested in learning the answers to. Rather than sifting through other sources that may address your research questions briefly or indirectly, interviews generate information that is often relevant and focused on the information needs of your essay. In other words, interviews are a source of data that can also be a *source* of theories or ideas on your topic. And this is often the best way to use interview material in your essay.

SURVEYS

The survey is a fixture in American life. We love surveys. What's the best economical laptop? Should the president be reelected? Who is the sexiest man alive? What movie should win Best Picture? Some of these are scientific surveys with carefully crafted questions, statistically significant sample sizes, and carefully chosen target audiences. In your writing class, you likely won't be

1. Ken Bain, "What Makes Teachers Great?" *Chronicle of Higher Education* (April 9, 2004): B7–B9.

conducting such formal research. More likely it will be like Mike's—fairly simple, and although not necessarily statistically reliable, your informal survey will likely be more convincing than anecdotal evidence or your personal observation, particularly if it's thoughtfully developed.

Defining a Survey's Goals and Audience

A survey is a useful source of information when you're making some kind of claim regarding "what people think" about something. Mike observed that his friends all seem to hate pennies, and he wanted to generalize from this anecdotal evidence to suggest that most people probably share that view. But do they? And which people are we really talking about? As we discussed this in his writing group, Mike pointed out that his grandfather grew up during the Great Depression, and that he has a very different perspective on money than Mike. "So your grandfather would probably pick up a penny in the parking lot, right?" I asked. Probably, Mike said.

Quickly, Mike not only had a survey question but began to think about qualifying his claim. Maybe younger adults—Mike's generation—in particular share this attitude about the lowly penny. To confirm this, Mike's survey had both a purpose (to collect information about how people view pennies) and an audience (students on his campus). If he had the time or inclination, Mike could conduct a broader survey of older Americans, but for his purposes the quad survey would be enough.

Types of Survey Questions

You can typically ask two types of questions on a survey: *open-ended questions* and *direct questions*. Open-ended questions often produce unexpected information, while direct questions are easier to analyze. Open-ended questions are like those on the narrative evaluations students might fill out at the end of the semester, such as, "What did you learn in this course?" and "What were the instructor's strengths and weaknesses?" Direct questions are the kind used on quizzes and tests, the kind that have a limited number of answers. The simplest, of course, would be a question or statement that people might agree or disagree with: "Would you pick up a penny if you saw it lying on the street?" Yes? No? You don't know?

How do you decide which types of questions to ask? Here are some things to consider:

- *How much time do you have to analyze the results?* Open-ended questions obviously take more time, while direct questions often involve mere tabulation of responses. The size of your sample is a big factor in this.
- *How good are you at crafting questions?* Direct questions need to be more carefully crafted than open-ended ones because you're offering limited

responses. Are the responses appropriate to the question? Have you considered all the alternative ways of responding?

- *Do you want statistical or qualitative information?* Qualitative information—anecdotes, stories, opinions, case studies, observations, individual perspectives—are the stuff of open-ended questions. This can be wonderful information because it is often surprising, and it offers an individual's voice rather than the voiceless results of statistical data. On the other hand, statistical information—percentages, averages, and the like—is easily understood and can be dramatic.

Crafting Survey Questions

To begin, you want to ask questions that your target audience can answer. Don't ask a question about a campus alcohol policy that most students in your survey have never heard of. Second, keep the questions simple and easy to understand. This is crucial because most respondents resist overly long survey questions and won't answer confusing ones. Third, make sure the questions will produce the information you want. This is a particular hazard of open-ended questions. For example, a broad open-ended question such as, "What do you think of the use of animals in the testing of cosmetics?" will probably produce a verbal shrug or an answer of "I don't know." A better question is more focused: "What do you think about the U.S. Food and Drug Administration's claim that animal testing by cosmetic companies is 'often necessary to provide product safety'?"

Such a question could be an open-ended or direct question, depending on the kind of responses you're seeking. Focusing the question also makes it more likely to generate information that will help you compose your essay on the adequacy of current regulations governing animal testing. Also note that the question doesn't necessarily betray the writer's position on the issue, which is

INQUIRING INTO THE DETAILS

TYPES OF SURVEY QUESTIONS

These are a few of your options when deciding what type of questions to ask in a survey.

1. Limited choice

Do you believe student fees should be used to support campus religious organizations?

☐ Yes

☐ No

☐ I'm not sure

At what point in the writing process do you usually get stuck?

- ☐ Getting started
- ☐ In the middle
- ☐ Finishing
- ☐ I never get stuck
- ☐ Other________________________.

2. Scaled response

The Student Film Board should show more foreign films.

- ☐ Strongly agree
- ☐ Agree
- ☐ Neither agree or disagree
- ☐ Disagree
- ☐ Strongly disagree

3. Ranking

Which of the following do you consider important in designing a classroom to be conducive to learning? Rank them from 1 to 5, with the most important a "1" and the least important a "5."

Comfortable seating	
Natural light from windows	
Carpeting	
Effective soundproofing	
Dimmable lighting	

4. Open-ended

Describe three things you learned in this course.

What steps do you think the university should take to increase attendance at women's soccer games?

essential—a good survey question isn't biased or "loaded." Imagine how a less neutral question might skew the results: "What do you think of the federal bureaucrats' position that animal testing for cosmetics is 'often necessary to provide product safety'?" An even more subtle bias might be introduced by inserting the term *federal government* rather than *Food and Drug Administration* in the original question. In my part of the world, the Rocky Mountain West, the federal government is generally not viewed favorably, no matter what the issue.

Keep your survey questions to a minimum. It shouldn't take long—no more than a few minutes at most—to complete your survey, unless you're lucky enough to have a captive audience such as a class.

Finally, consider beginning your survey with background questions that establish the identity of each respondent. Typical information you might collect includes the gender and age, or, with student-oriented surveys, the class ranking of the respondent. Depending on your topic, you might be interested in particular demographic facts, such as whether someone has children or comes from a particular part of the state. All of these questions can help you sort and analyze your results.

Conducting a Survey

People who design surveys for a living always test them first. Invariably this turns up problems: a survey is too long, a question is poorly worded, the response rate to a particular question is low, and so on. You won't be able to test your draft survey nearly as thoroughly as the experts do, but before you put your faith in an untested survey, ask as many people as you can to try it out and describe their experience answering your questions. Was there any confusion? How long did it take? Is the survey generating relevant information?

Once you're confident in the design of your survey, plan how you'll distribute it. How do you reach the audience you've selected for your survey? Professional pollsters have all sorts of methods, including computerized dialing in some regions of the country and purchasing mailing lists. Your project is much more low tech. Begin by asking yourself whether your target audience tends to conveniently gather in a particular location. For example, if you're surveying sports fans, then surveying people by the main gate at the football stadium on Saturday might work. If your target audience is first-year college students and your university requires freshman English composition, then surveying one or more of those classes would be a convenient way to reach them.

In some situations, you can leave your survey forms in a location that might produce responses from your target audience. For example, a student at my university wanted to survey people about which foothill's hiking trails they liked best, and she left an envelope with the forms and a pencil at several trailheads.

A new possibility for tech-savvy students is the online survey. Software for designing online surveys is available now, but unless the survey is linked to a Web site that is visited by the target audience whose opinions you seek, the response rates can be low. Telephone surveys are always a possibility, but they are often time consuming and unless you can target your calls to a specific audience—say, people living in the dorms on your campus—it's hard to reach the people you most want to query. Postal mail is usually too slow and expensive, although intercampus mail can be an excellent option for distributing surveys. Response rates, however, may not meet your expectations.

Using Survey Results in Your Writing

The best thing about conducting an informal survey is that you're producing original and interesting information about your topic's local relevance. This can be an impressive element of your essay and will certainly make it more interesting.

Because analysis of open-ended questions can be time consuming and complicated, consider the simplest approach: as you go through the surveys, note which responses are worth quoting in your essay because they seem representative. Perhaps the responses are among the most commonly voiced in the entire sample, or they are expressed in significant numbers by a particular group of respondents. You might also quote a response because it is particularly articulate, surprising, or interesting.

In a more detailed analysis, you might try to nail down more specifically the *patterns* of responses. Begin by creating a simple coding system—perhaps numbers or colors—that represent the broadest categories of response. For example, perhaps you initially can divide the survey results into two categories: people who disagree with the university's general-education requirements and those who agree with it, Group 1 and Group 2. The next step might be to further analyze each of these groups, looking for particular patterns. Maybe you notice that freshmen tend to oppose the requirement in larger numbers than seniors and voice similar criticisms. In particular, pay attention to responses you didn't expect, responses that might enlarge your perspectives about what people think about your topic.

Direct questions that involve choosing limited responses—true/false, yes/no, multiple choice, and so on—often involve tabulation. This is where knowledge of a spreadsheet program such as Microsoft Excel is invaluable.

Your analysis of the responses to direct questions will usually be pretty simple—probably a breakdown of percentages. What percentage of the sample, for example, checked the box that signaled agreement with the statement that their "main goal for a college education was to get a good job"? In a more sophisticated analysis, you might try to break the sample down, if it's large enough, to certain categories of respondents—men and women, class ranking, respondents with high or low test scores, and so on—and then see if any response patterns correlate to these categories. For example, perhaps a much higher percentage of freshmen than seniors sampled agreed that a good job was the most important reason to go to college.

What might this difference mean? Is it important? How does it influence your thinking about your topic or how does it affect your argument? Each of these questions involves interpretation of the results, and sample size is the factor that most influences the credibility of this kind of evidence. If you surveyed only five freshmen and three seniors about their attitudes toward your school's general-education requirements, then the comparisons you make between what they say are barely better than anecdotal. It's hard to say what the appropriate sample size for your informal survey should be—after all, you aren't conducting a scientific survey and even a small sample might produce some interesting results—but, in general, the more responses you can gather the better.

Using What You Have Learned

You will have countless opportunities, in school and out, to apply your research skills. But have you learned enough about *research techniques* to find good information efficiently? Consider the following situations. What would you suggest to the writer as a good research technique?

1. Casey is revising his essay on the effectiveness and accuracy of Internet voting. His workshop group says he needs more information on whether hackers might compromise the accuracy of computers used for voting. Casey says he's relied pretty heavily on Internet sources. Where else would you suggest he search for information? What search terms might he use?
2. Alexandra needs to find some facts on divorce rates in the United States. Where might she find them fairly easily?
3. The university is proposing to build a new parking lot on a natural area near the edge of campus. Sherry wants to investigate the proposal to write a paper on whether the parking lot might be built with minimal environmental damage. What steps might she take to research the topic? Where should she look for information first? And then?

When researching we often wrestle for control. We gather information from experts, yet as writers we're expected to demonstrate some authority on the topic. Which experts make the most sense? What claims do we find persuasive? Most of all, what do *we* think? The impulse to plagiarize is a form of surrender, a willingness to let the other guy push us around.

Using and Citing Sources

CONTROLLING INFORMATION

The first college paper that really meant something to me was an essay on whaling industry practices and their impacts on populations of humpback and sperm whales. The essay opened with a detailed description of the exploding harpoon, a highly effective and dramatic method of subduing the animals, and was written at a time when the International Whaling Commission exerted little control over the whale harvests of the largest whaling nations. I never forgot that paper because it engaged both my heart and my head; I was intensely curious about the issue and felt strongly that this was a problem that needed to be solved.

Writing from the place of itchy curiosity and strong feelings is a wonderful thing. It will motivate you to read and learn about your topic, and when it comes to writing the draft you might find that you have little trouble enlisting the voices of your sources to make your point. More often, however, you've chosen a topic because you don't know what you think or feel about it—the inquiry-based approach—or you've been assigned a general topic that reflects the content of a course you're taking. In these cases, writing with sources is like crashing a party of strangers that has been going on for a long time. You shyly listen in, trying to figure out what everyone is talking about, and look for an opening to enter the conversation. Mostly you just feel intimidated, so you hang back feeling foolish.

This kind of writing situation is really a matter of control. Will you control the outside sources in your research essay, or will they control you? Will you enter the conversation and make a contribution to it, or will you let others do all the talking? The easiest way to lose control is simply to turn long stretches of your paper over to a source, usually with a long quotation. I've seen a quotation from a single source run more

What You'll Learn in This Chapter

- How to control sources so they don't control you.
- How to properly summarize, paraphrase, and quote source material.
- How to avoid plagiarism.
- Methods of citation in the MLA and APA systems.

than a full page in some drafts. Another way to lose control is to do what one of my colleagues calls a "data dump." Fill the truck with a heavy load of information, back it up to the paper, and dump in as much as you can, without analysis, without carefully selecting what is relevant and what isn't, without much thought at all. The writer in this situation sees his or her essay as a hole that must be filled with information.

USING SOURCES

The appropriate use of sources is really a matter of control. Writers who put research information to work for them see outside sources as serving a clear purpose. There are at least five of these purposes:

1. To use information that provides useful background or a context for understanding the research question.
2. To use information that answers a relevant question.
3. To use information as evidence to support a claim or idea, or in some cases, evidence that seems *not to* support an assertion but might if seen a certain way.
4. To use information from a particular author who is influential in the debate about a topic.
5. To use information to *complicate* a writer's thesis, raising interesting questions.

Let's see how this works in an actual passage. In an essay that asks, "Why Did God Create Flies," writer Richard Conniff argues that the answer might be as a punishment for human arrogance. In the middle of the essay, he draws on research to provide some background for this claim by establishing the long and sometimes unhappy relationship between the housefly and human beings.

> The true housefly, *Musca domestica,* does not bite. (You may think this is something to like about it, until you find out what it does instead.) *M. domestica,* a drab fellow of salt-and-pepper complexion, is the world's most widely distributed insect species and probably the most familiar, a status achieved through its pronounced fondness for breeding in pig, horse, and human excrement. In choosing at some point in the immemorial past to concentrate on the wastes around human habitations, *M. domestica* made a major career move. Bernard Greenberg of the University of Illinois at Chicago has traced human representations of the housefly back to a Mesopotamian cylinder seal from 3000 B.C. But houseflies were probably with us even before we had houses, and they spread with human culture.

Here Conniff demonstrates exquisite control over outside sources, marshalling them in the service of his larger point. But he also does this by not simply quoting extensively or going on and on explaining the relevant information, but by *finding his own way of saying things.* Rather than writing that the housefly's fondness for associating with people had significant ecological implications for the insect, Conniff writes that it was "a major career move."

The sections that follow review the techniques of summarizing, paraphrasing, and quoting. You know these as the three horsemen of note taking. But these should never be thoughtless activities; in fact, they're a great opportunity to exert control over your sources by doing two things:

1. *Taking notes with a particular purpose in mind.* How is the information you're writing about relevant to your purpose in your essay?
2. *Finding your own way of saying things.* By putting other people's words into your own voice, you take possession of the information.

Summarizing

"So basically what you're saying is that we can never win the war on terrorism because it isn't really a war in the conventional sense?"

Imagine that you're in the midst of a conversation with someone about the challenge of defeating terrorism. You've just listened for about a minute to a friend explain in some detail that the battle against terrorism isn't really a battle at all, but a series of surprise attacks that then provoke retaliation, with the two opponents blindly striking out at each other. Your friend adds that the terrorists' tactics are aimed at targets with symbolic rather than military value. Victory for terrorists is not measured in damage inflicted on military forces but in the terror provoked in the civilian population. You listen to all of this and summarize your friend's larger point: This isn't really war as we've historically understood it.

Summary is like making moonshine. You collect some ingredients and distill them into a more concise and powerful concoction, one that accurately captures the main idea of a book, an article, an argument, a chapter, or even a passage. The best summaries involve *thinking.* You're not just searching for a topic sentence somewhere in the source to copy down, but taking it all in as you would information and ideas in a conversation and then trying to find your own way of saying what seems to be at the heart of things.

A summary is usually much shorter than the original. For example, consider the following summary of the earlier extract paragraph about the relationship between houseflies and human beings:

> The common housefly is among the "most familiar" insects because it found its long partnership with human beings, one that goes back thousands of years, extremely beneficial.

Can you see how the summary captures the main idea of the longer paragraph? Also note that when the summary refers to identical language in the original—the phrase "most familiar"—the writer is careful to use quotation marks. Finally, the summary uses original language that breaks with the source, describing the relationship between people and flies as a "long partnership."

Reasons you would want to write a summary rather than quote directly or paraphrase a source include the following:

- Your essay needs not a longer explanation of what a source says but a nugget of an idea, one that might have more impact because of its brevity.
- The original source, while useful, doesn't say things in a particularly distinctive way. It isn't quotable, but distilled it does serve a purpose in your essay.
- The source is making an argument, and what matters most is the gist of that argument rather than a discussion of the details.

Tips for Crafting a Summary

1. If your aim is to summarize an entire work, and if the source isn't a book, read it all once through, marking what seem to be key claims or findings. Academic articles in the social sciences often include abstracts, or ready-made summaries of a study. Books frequently explain their purpose in a preface or introduction. Start there. Then check the concluding chapter.
2. If your aim is to summarize a passage of a longer work, remember to look for the author's most important ideas where he or she is most likely to put them: the first and last sentences of paragraphs or a concluding paragraph.
3. Summary has little to do with your opinion. Save that for the right side of your double-entry journal. Try, as best you can, to capture your understanding of the *source's* meaning or argument.
4. Typically, a summary includes the name(s) of the author or the title of the work, usually attached to a verb that characterizes its nature: so-and-so *argues, finds, explains, speculates, questions,* and so on.

Paraphrasing

Paraphrasing doesn't get any respect. It's like a difficult cousin that shows up at the family picnic and insists on enlisting everyone in a deep discussion. It's hard work, thinking that hard, particularly when there's beer and potato salad and Grandma's homemade chicken potpies. Of the three forms of note taking, paraphrasing requires the most attention and the greatest care. Your goal is to craft a restatement, in your own words, of what an original source is saying, in roughly the same length as the original.

Obviously, we don't paraphrase books or even entire articles. Paraphrasing usually involves closer work—examining a paragraph or a passage and then finding a way to accurately capture the original's ideas and information but in a fresh and original way. This demands not only faith in our own way of saying things—that's hard enough—but a pretty thorough understanding of what exactly the source is trying to say. You simply can't paraphrase a source you don't understand.

That's where the brain work comes in, and the payoff is significant. When you successfully paraphrase a source, you've written a part of your own essay. You've already done the work of comprehending what the source says, and found your own way of writing about it. This is the essence of using outside sources in your own work.

Here's a paraphrase of the earlier extract paragraph on houseflies.

> Houseflies, according to Richard Conniff, have had "a long partnership with human beings." They are also among "the world's most widely distributed insect species," two factors that explain our familiarity with *Musca domesticus,* the housefly's Latin name. This partnership may have been cultivated for thousands of years, or certainly as long as humans—and their animal companions—produced sufficient excrement in which the flies can breed. Ironically, those pests have benefited enormously from their "fondness" for human and animal wastes, and unwittingly we have contributed to their success at our own expense.

A key element of the translation in a paraphrase is trying not to imitate the structure of the original passage. By deliberately setting out to reorganize the information, you'll find writing a paraphrase much easier. And you'll also find it much less likely that you unintentionally plagiarize the material. Notice as well that whenever the paraphrase borrows wording from the original, quotation marks are included. The very last line of the paraphrase seems to cross over into interpretation, pointing out an irony that the original passage may have only hinted at. This is fine. In fact, it's something that you should try to develop as a habit—don't just translate and transcribe the information, try to make something of it. This move is particularly important when quoting material.

Tips for Crafting a Paraphrase

1. If a summary is a macroscopic look at a text, a paraphrase is microscopic, usually focusing on a brief passage. Consequently, the plagiarism danger goes from yellow to red (see Avoiding Plagiarism on page 350). Make sure to find your own way of saying things, quoting phrases that you borrow from the source.
2. Try the "look away" strategy. Carefully read the passage several times, then set it aside. Compose your paraphrase without looking at the source, trusting that you'll remember what's important. Then check the result against the passage, changing or quoting any borrowed language and refining your prose.
3. Like summary, introduce paraphrased material in your essay by attributing the author or the work.

Quoting

Jotting down exactly what a source says—word for word—is relatively mindless work. Beyond selecting *what* you'll write down—a choice that does involve some thought—quoting a source merely involves careful transcription. Is that why it's the most popular form of note taking?

That's not to say that you should never quote a source. Not at all. If you jot down a passage from a source in the left page of your double-entry journal, and then use the right page to explore, analyze, question, and interpret what it says, you're doing the kind of work good research writing demands. Well-selected quotes in an essay can also be memorable. But too often writers turn to transcription alone, and this quoted material simply gets dropped into the draft with virtually no analysis or even explanation. Frequently, I notice a quoted sentence appearing in the middle of a paragraph simply because the writer was too lazy to paraphrase. Then there's the long quotation that's thrown in as an obvious ploy to make the paper longer.

When should you turn to quotation in your essay? There are two main situations:

1. When the source says something in a distinctive way that would be lost by putting it in your own words.
2. When you want to analyze or emphasize a particular passage in the source, and the exact words of the author matter.

I like to tell the story of a moment in the thirteen-hour documentary *Shoah,* a film about the Holocaust. In one scene, the filmmakers are riding the train that took hundreds of Jews to their deaths in one of the concentration camps. Amazingly, the engineer who drove that train back then was still on the job, guiding the train on the same tracks past the ruins of the same camps. The filmmakers interviewed this man, and asked him the obvious question: *How does it feel to still be driving the train on which you led so many people to their deaths?* The engineer paused, and said quietly, "If you could lick my heart, it would poison you."

This is the kind of quotation that could never be paraphrased. To do so would be to rob what the man said of all its emotional power and truth. You will rarely find such a memorable quotation in your sources. Much more often, you encounter a voice in your reading that simply sounds interesting and has a nice way of putting things. For instance, the excerpt from "Why Did God Create Flies" is eminently quotable because Richard Conniff, its author, writes with such a lively voice. Consider his sentence:

When you introduce a voice other than your own, make it clear what this new voice adds to the conversation you have going about your topic.

> The true housefly is the world's most widely distributed insect species and probably the most familiar, a status achieved through its pronounced fondness for breeding in pig, horse, and human excrement.

What is it about this that seems quotable? Maybe the way it goes along with fairly straightforward exposition until the second half of the sentence, when suddenly the fly seeks status and feels fondness for you know what.

Academic writing also resorts to quotation when it's worthwhile to look more closely at what an author says. This is common in the critical essay when analyzing literature. But it's also a good move when working with other sources, perhaps excerpts from a transcript or in analyzing an expert's claim or a striking finding. The key is not just using such quotations sparingly—typically a research essay is no more than 20 percent quotation—but *working with them*.

When you bring someone else's voice into your own writing, it's usually a good idea to introduce the source and provide some justification for making such a move. For instance, you might introduce the preceding quote by saying something like this:

> Richard Conniff, whose popular studies of invertebrate animals have made even leeches lovable, observes that the familiarity of the house fly is no accident. He writes . . .

It's even more important in academic writing to follow up quoted text with your own commentary. What would you like the reader to notice about what the quotation says? What seems most relevant to your own research question or point? How does the quotation extend an important idea you've been discussing or raise an important question? What does it imply? What do you agree with? What do you disagree with? In other words, when you introduce a voice other than your own, make it clear what this new voice adds to the conversation you have going about your topic.

Tips for Handling Quotations

Integrate quoted material in your essay in the following ways:

1. **Separate it**. There are two ways to do this. Provide an introductory tag that ends in a comma or a colon. *According to Carl Elliott (82), the new drug pushers "are officially known as 'pharmaceutical sales representatives' but everyone calls them 'sales reps.'"* Or, *Carl Elliott (82) observes that drug salespeople are easy to spot: "Drug reps today are often young, well groomed, and strikingly good looking. Many are women . . ."*
2. **Embed it.** Integrate quoted material in your own sentence something like this: *Carl Elliott calls drug reps "the best dressed people in the hospital."*
3. **Block it.** Extended quotations (more than 40 words in APA style and more than four lines in MLA) should be indented five spaces in APA style and ten spaces in MLA style in a block. Quotation marks, except those used in the source, are omitted. For instance:

   Carl Elliott, in "The Drug Pushers," highlights the perks doctors have historically received:

   > *Gifts from the drug industry are nothing new, of course. William Helfand, who worked in marketing for Merck for thirty-three years, told me that company representatives were giving doctors books and pamphlets as early as the late nineteenth century. "There is nothing new under the sun," Helfand says, "There is just more of it." The question is: Why is there so much more of it just now? And what changes occurred during the past decade to bring about such a dramatic increase in reps bearing gifts? (86)*

CITING SOURCES

Somewhere in the great hall at Mount Olympus, the mist obscuring his or her ankles, must have been an English teacher. Hardly the right hand of Zeus, this was a minor god. But there were important tasks for this god, for the mortals were careless with their language, running on their sentences and mistaking *their* for *there.* But nothing could make the god's anger flash more brilliantly than a missing citation. There was a special place in Hades reserved for the plagiarist, where the condemned spent eternity composing Works Cited pages of endless stacks of books whose title pages were unreadable.

Of all the rules some of my students believe were invented to torture composition students, requirements that they carefully cite their sources in research papers may cause the most anguish. They rarely question these requirements; they seem like divine and universal law. In fact, these aren't rules but conventions, hardly as old as the Greeks, and historically quite new. For many centuries, writers freely borrowed from others, often without attribution, and the appropriation of someone else's words and ideas was considered quite normal. This is still the view in some non-Western cultures; some students, for example, are quite puzzled in their English as a Second Language classes when they have to cite a source in their research essays.

This convention of explicitly acknowledging the source of an idea, quotation, piece of data, or information with a footnote or parenthetical citation and bibliography arose in the past 150 years. It began when mostly German universities began promoting the idea that the purpose of research was not simply to demonstrate an understanding of what already was known but to *make a contribution of new knowledge.* Researchers were to look for gaps in existing scholarship—questions that hadn't yet been asked—or to offer extensions of what had already been posed by someone else. Knowledge making became the business of the research writer, and like gardeners, scholars saw themselves as tending a living thing, a kind of tree that grew larger as new branches were grafted onto existing limbs.

Just as a child clambering up a tree in the park is grateful for the sturdy limbs under his or her feet, research writers acknowledge the limbs they are standing on that have helped them to see a little more of their subjects. That's why they cite their sources. This is an act of gratitude, of course, but it also signals to readers on whose authority the writer's claims, conclusions, or ideas are based. Citation helps readers locate the writer's work on a specific part of the tree of knowledge in a discipline; it gives a useful context of *what has already been said* about a question or a topic.

Citation helps readers locate the writer's work on a specific part of the tree of knowledge in a discipline; it gives a useful context of what has already been said *about a question or a topic.*

Student writers cite for exactly the same reasons. Not because it's required in most college research writing but because it makes their research writing more relevant and more convincing to the people who read it.

There are quite a few conventions for citing, and these conventions often vary by discipline. Humanities disciplines such as English often use the Modern

Language Association (MLA) conventions, while the social sciences use the American Psychological Association (APA) methods. Both of these documentation styles are detailed later in this chapter. Although there are differences between the two styles, the purpose of each is the same: to acknowledge those from whom you have borrowed ideas and information.

Writing with Computers

CITATION FORMATTING SOFTWARE

Compiling a correctly formatted Works Cited or References page is tedious work. Students whose course of study will involve writing multiple research-based essays might consider investing in citation software such as Daedalus or BiblioCite. Enter the author, title, and publication information of sources, and the software composes an MLA Works Cited page or APA References page. Many of these programs allow you to take notes from your sources and then "link" the citation record to those notes so that you don't have to search for documentation information from poorly organized or missing handwritten notes. This can help you avoid accidental plagiarism, particularly for long and complex projects. When using citation software, be sure to keep it up-to-date because documentation guidelines change.

Avoiding Plagiarism

Modern authors get testy when someone uses their work without giving them credit. This is where the concept of intellectual property comes from, an idea that emerged with the invention of the printing press and the distribution of multiple copies of an author's work. In its most basic form, plagiarism is stealing someone else's words, ideas, or information. Academic plagiarism, the kind that gets a lot of ink these days with the rise of the Internet, usually refers to more specific misdeeds. Your university probably has an academic honesty or plagiarism policy posted on the Web or in a student handbook. You need to look at it. But it probably includes most or all of the following forms of plagiarism:

1. Handing in someone else's work—a downloaded paper from the Internet or borrowed from a friend—and claiming that it's your own.
2. Using information or ideas that are not common knowledge from any source and failing to acknowledge that source.
3. Handing in the same paper for two different classes.
4. Using the exact language or expressions of a source and not indicating through quotation marks and citation that the language is borrowed.
5. Rewriting a passage from a source using minor substitutions of different words but retaining the same syntax and structure of the original.

Most plagiarism is unintentional. The writer simply didn't know or pay attention to course or university plagiarism policies. Equally common is simple carelessness. How can you avoid this trap? Check out the "Tips for Avoiding Plagiarism" box.

Intentional plagiarism, of course, is a different matter. Many Web sites offer papers on thousands of topics to anyone willing to pay for them. College instructors, however, have tools for identifying these downloaded papers. The consequences of buying and handing in online papers are often severe, including flunking the course and even expulsion, an academic Hades of sorts. Moreover, even if a person is not caught committing this academic crime, intentional plagiarism stems from an intellectual laziness and dishonesty that are bound to catch up with the person doing it sooner or later. Just don't go there.

Intentional plagiarism stems from an intellectual laziness and dishonesty that are bound to catch up with the person doing it sooner or later.

Tips for Avoiding Plagiarism

- **Don't procrastinate.** Many careless mistakes in citation or proper handling of source material occur in the rush to finish the draft in the wee hours of the morning.
- **Be an active note taker.** Work in the middle of the process to take possession of the material you read, especially exploring your responses to sources *in your own words* and *for your own purposes.*
- **Collect bibliographic information first.** Before you do anything else, take down complete publication information for each source, including the page numbers from which you borrowed material.
- **Mark quoted material clearly.** Whenever you quote a source directly, make sure that's obvious in your notes.
- **Be vigilant whenever you cut and paste.** The great usefulness of cutting and pasting passages in electronic documents is also the downfall of many research writers. Is the copied material directly borrowed, and if so is it properly cited?

EXERCISE 10.1

The Accidental Plagiarist

Most plagiarism problems are accidental. The writer simply isn't aware that he or she has stumbled into the problem. Here's a low-stakes exercise that can test your understanding of how to avoid the simplest—and most common—types of accidental plagiarism. Get this wrong and the grammar police won't accost you in the middle of the night, throw you against the wall and make you spell difficult words. You'll just learn something.

Using the words and ideas of others in your own writing is essential in most research essays and papers. Doing this without plagiarizing isn't exactly like walking through a minefield, but you do have to step carefully. For example, Beth is exploring the question, "What might explain the high rate of divorce in the early years of marriage?" She's interested in divorce because she just went through one. In her research, Beth encounters Diane Ackerman's book, *The Natural History of Love,* and Beth finds the following paragraph:

> "Philandering," we call it, "fooling around," "hanky-panky," "skirt chasing," "man chasing," or something equally picturesque. Monogamy and adultery are both hallmarks of being human. Anthropologist Helen Fisher proposes a chemical basis for adultery, what she calls "The Four-Year Itch." Studying the United Nations survey of marriage and divorce around the world, she noticed that divorce usually occurs early in marriage, during the couple's first reproductive and parenting years. Also, that this peak time for divorce coincides with the period in which infatuation normally ends, and a couple has to decide if they're going to call it quits or stay together as companions. Some couples do stay together and have other children, but even more don't. "The human animal," she concludes, "seems built to court, to fall in love, and to marry one person at a time; then, at the height of our reproductive years, often with a single child, we divorce them; then, a few years after, we remarry once again."

Beth thought this was pretty interesting stuff, and in her draft she summarized the paragraph in the following way:

> According to Diane Ackerman, a hallmark of being human is "monogamy and adultery," and she cites the period right after infatuation subsides—about four years for most couples—as the time when they call it quits.

STEP ONE: In small groups, analyze Beth's summary. Does Beth plagiarize the original passage, and if so, do you have ideas about how she could fix it? Revise the summary on a piece of newsprint and post it on the wall.

STEP TWO: Discuss the proposed revisions. How well do they address any plagiarism problems you see in Beth's summary?

STEP THREE: Now compare the following paraphrases of the same Ackerman passage. Which has plagiarism problems and which seems okay?

Paraphrase 1

Divorce may have a "chemical basis," something that may kick in after four years of marriage and ironically when partners are reaching their highest potential for having children. Researcher Helen Fisher calls it "The Four-Year Itch," the time that often

Paraphrase 2

When infatuation fades and couples are faced with the future of their relationship, biochemistry may help them decide. According to researcher Helen Fisher, "divorce usually occurs early in marriage, during the couple's first reproductive and parenting years" (Ackerman 165).

signals a shift from infatuation into a more sober assessment of the relationship's future: are they going to stay together or "call it quits"? Most end up deciding to end the relationship.

She suggests that this is often about four years into the relationship, and argues that humans may be designed to behave this way because the pattern seems so entrenched (Ackerman 166).

STEP FOUR: In class, discuss which paraphrase seems acceptable and which does not. Remember that the problems are pretty subtle.

STEP FIVE: Now practice your own *summary* of the following passage, applying what you've learned so far in the exercise about ways to avoid plagiarism when using the words and ideas of other people. This passage in Ackerman's book follows the passage you worked with earlier.

> Our chemistry makes it easy to follow that plan, and painful to avoid it. After the seductive fireworks of first attraction, which may last a few weeks or a few years, the body gets bored with easy ecstasy. The nerves no longer quiver with excitement. Nothing new has been happening for ages, why bother to rouse oneself? Love is exhausting. Then the attachment chemicals roll in their thick cozy carpets of marital serenity. Might as well relax and enjoy the calm and security some feel. Separated even for a short while, the partners crave the cradle of the other's embrace. Is it a chemical craving? Possibly so, a hunger for the soothing endomorphins that flow when they're together. It is a deep, sweet river, just right for dangling one's feet in while the world waits.
>
> Other people grow restless and search for novelty.

MLA DOCUMENTATION GUIDELINES

The professional organization in charge of academic writing in literature and languages, the Modern Language Association (MLA), uses one of the two methods of citing sources that you should know. The second, the American Psychological Association system, is described in the next section. Your English class will most likely use the MLA system. When should you cite your sources?

1. Whenever you quote from an original source.
2. Whenever you borrow ideas from an original source, even when you express them in your own words by paraphrasing or summarizing.
3. Whenever you borrow factual information from a source that is not common knowledge (see the "Inquiring into the Details: The Common Knowledge Exception" box).

INQUIRING INTO THE DETAILS

THE COMMON KNOWLEDGE EXCEPTION

The business about *common knowledge* causes much confusion. Just what does this term mean? Basically, *common knowledge* means facts that are widely known and about which there is no controversy.

Sometimes, it's really obvious whether something is common knowledge. The fact that the Super Bowl occurs in late January and pits the winning teams from the American and National Football Conferences is common knowledge. The fact that former president Ronald Reagan was once an actor and starred in a movie with a chimpanzee is common knowledge, too. And the fact that most Americans get most of their news from television is also common knowledge, although this information is getting close to leaving the domain of common knowledge.

But what about a writer's assertion that most dreaming occurs during rapid eye movement (REM) sleep? This is an idea about which all sources seem to agree. Does that make it common knowledge?

It's useful to ask next, *How common to whom? Experts in the topic at hand or the rest of us?* As a rule, consider the knowledge of your readers. What information will not be familiar to most of your readers or may even surprise them? Which ideas might even raise skepticism? In this case, the fact about REM sleep and dreaming goes slightly beyond the knowledge of most readers, so to be safe, it should be cited. Use common sense, but when in doubt, cite.

Citing Sources

The foundation of the MLA method of citing sources *in your paper* is putting the last name of the author and the page number of the source in parentheses as closely as possible to the borrowed material. For example,

```
Researchers believe that there is an "infatuation chemical" that
may account for that almost desperate attraction we feel when
we're near someone special (Ackerman 164).
```

The parenthetical citation tells a reader two things: the source of the information (for example, the author's name), and where in the work to find the borrowed idea or material. A really interested reader—perhaps an infatuated one—who wanted to follow up on this would then refer to the Works Cited at the back of the paper. This would list the work by the author's last name and all the pertinent information about the source:

Ackerman, Diane. A Natural History of Love. New York: Vintage, 1994.

Here's another example of parenthetical author/page citation from another research paper. Note the differences from the previous example:

> "One thing is clear," writes Thomas Mallon, "plagiarism didn't become a truly sore point with writers until they thought of writing as their trade. . . . Suddenly his capital and identity were at stake" (3-4).

The first thing you may have noticed is that the author's last name—Mallon—was omitted from the parenthetical citation. It didn't need to be included, because it had already been mentioned in the text. *If you mention the author's name in the text of your paper, then you only need to parenthetically cite the relevant page number(s).* This citation also tells us that the quoted passage comes from two pages rather than one.

Where to Put Citations. Place the citation as close as you can to the borrowed material, trying to avoid breaking the flow of the sentences, if possible. To avoid confusion about what's borrowed and what's not—particularly in passages longer than a sentence—mention the name of the original author *in your paper.* Note that in the next example the writer simply cites the source at the end of the paragraph, not naming the source in the text. Doing so makes it hard for the reader to figure out whether Blager is the source of the information in the entire paragraph or just part of it:

> Though children who have been sexually abused seem to be disadvantaged in many areas, including the inability to forge lasting relationships, low self-esteem, and crippling shame, they seem advantaged in other areas. Sexually abused children seem to be more socially mature than other children of their same age group. It's a distinctly mixed blessing (Blager 994).

In the following example, notice how the ambiguity about what's borrowed and what's not is resolved by careful placement of the author's name and parenthetical citation in the text:

> Though children who have been sexually abused seem to be disadvantaged in many areas, including the inability to forge lasting relationships, low self-esteem, and crippling shame, they seem advantaged in other areas. According to Blager, sexually abused children seem to be more socially mature than other children of their same age group (994). It's a distinctly mixed blessing.

In this latter version, it's clear that Blager is the source for one sentence in the paragraph, and the writer is responsible for the rest. Generally, use an authority's last name, rather than a formal title or first name, when mentioning him or her in your text. Also note that the citation is placed *inside* the period of the sentence (or last sentence) that it documents. That's almost always the case, except at the end of a blocked quotation, where the parenthetical reference is placed after the period of the last sentence.

Inquiring into the Details

CITATIONS THAT GO WITH THE FLOW

There's no getting around it—parenthetical citations can be like stones on the sidewalk. Readers stride through a sentence in your essay and then have to step around the citation at the end before they resume their walk. Yet citations are important in academic writing because they help readers know who you read or heard that shaped your thinking.

However, you can minimize citations that trip up readers and make your essay more readable by doing the following:

- Avoid lengthy parenthetical citations by mentioning the name of the author in your essay. That way, you usually have to include only a page number in the citation.
- Try to place citations where readers are likely to pause anyway—for example, the end of the sentence, or right before a comma.
- Remember that you *don't* need a citation when you're citing common knowledge, or referring to an entire work by an author.
- If you're borrowing from only one source in a paragraph of your essay, and all of the borrowed material comes from a single page of that source, don't bother repeating the citation over and over again with each new bit of information. Just put the citation at the end of the paragraph.

The citation can also be placed near the author's name, rather than at the end of the sentence, if it doesn't unnecessarily break the flow of the sentence. For example:

```
Blager (994) observes that sexually abused children tend to be more
socially mature than other children of their same age group.
```

When You Mention the Author's Name. It's generally good practice in research writing to identify who said what. The familiar convention of using attribution tags such as "According to Fletcher . . ." or "Fletcher argues that . . ." and so on helps readers attach a name to a voice, or an individual to certain claims or findings.

When you mention the author of a source, you can drop his or her name from the parenthetical citation and just list the page number. For example,

> Robert Harris believes that there is "widespread uncertainty" among students about what constitutes plagiarism (2).

You may also list the page number directly after the author's name.

> Robert Harris (2) believes that there is "widespread uncertainty" among students about what constitutes plagiarism.

When There Is No Author. Occasionally, you may encounter a source in which the author is anonymous—the article doesn't have a byline, or for some reason the author hasn't been identified. This isn't unusual with pamphlets, editorials, government documents, some newspaper articles, online sources, and short filler articles in magazines. If you can't parenthetically name the author, what do you cite?

Most often, cite the title (or an abbreviated version, if the title is long) and the page number. If you choose to abbreviate the title, begin with the word under which it is alphabetized in the Works Cited. For example:

> According to the Undergraduate Catalog, "the athletic program is an integral part of the university and its total educational purpose" (7).

Here is how this publication would be listed at the back of the paper:

Works Cited

Undergraduate Catalog, Boise State University 2004-2005. Boise, ID: BSU, 2004.

For clarity, it's helpful to mention the original source of the borrowed material in the text of your paper. When there is no author's name, refer to the publication (or institution) you're citing or make a more general reference to the source. For example:

> An article in Cuisine magazine argues that the best way to kill a lobster is to plunge a knife between its eyes ("How to Kill" 56).

or

> According to one government report, with the current minimum size limit, most lobsters end up on dinner plates before they've had a chance to reproduce ("Size at Sexual Maturity" 3-4).

Works by the Same Author. Suppose you end up using several books or articles by the same author. Obviously, a parenthetical citation that merely lists the author's name and page number won't do, because it won't be clear *which* of several works the citation refers to. In this case, include the author's name, an abbreviated title (if the original is too long), and the page number. For example:

> One essayist who suffers from multiple sclerosis writes that "there is a subtle taxonomy of crippleness" (Mairs, Carnal Acts 69).

The Works Cited list would show multiple works by one author as follows:

> Works Cited
>
> Mairs, Nancy. Voice Lessons. Boston: Beacon, 1994.
>
> - - - . Carnal Acts. Boston: Beacon, 1996.

It's obvious from the parenthetical citation which of the two Mairs books is the source of the information. Note that in the parenthetical reference, no punctuation separates the title and the page number, but a comma follows the author's name. If Mairs had been mentioned in the text of the paper, her name could have been dropped from the citation.

Also notice that the three hyphens used in the second entry are meant to signal that the author's name in this source is the same as in the preceding entry.

When One Source Quotes Another. Whenever you can, cite the original source for material you use. For example, if an article on television violence quotes the author of a book and you want to use the quote, try to hunt down the book. That way, you'll be certain of the accuracy of the quote and you may find some more usable information.

Sometimes, however, finding the original source is not possible. In those cases, use the term *qtd. in* to signal that you've quoted or paraphrased a quotation from a book or article that initially appeared elsewhere. In the following example, the citation signals that Bacon's quote was culled from an article by Guibroy, not Bacon's original work:

> Francis Bacon also weighed in on the dangers of imitation, observing that "it is hardly possible at once to admire an author and to go beyond him" (qtd. in Guibroy 113).

Personal Interviews. If you mention the name of your interview subject in your text, no parenthetical citation is necessary. On the other hand, if you don't mention the subject's name, cite it in parentheses after the quote:

> Instead, the recognizable environment gave something to kids they could relate to. "And it had a lot more real quality to it than, say, Mister Rogers . . . ," says one educator. "Kids say the reason they don't like Mister Rogers is that it's unbelievable" (Diamonti).

Regardless of whether you mention your subject's name, you should include a reference to the interview in the Works Cited. In this case, the reference would look like this:

Works Cited

Diamonti, Nancy. Personal interview. 5 Nov. 1999.

Several Sources in a Single Citation. Suppose two sources both contributed the same information in a paragraph of your essay. Or perhaps even more common is when you're summarizing the findings of several authors on a certain topic—a fairly common move when you're trying to establish a context for your own research question. You cite multiple authors in a single citation in the usual fashion, using author name and page number, but separating each with a semicolon. For example,

> A whole range of studies have looked closely at the intellectual development of college students, finding that they generally assume "stages" or "perspectives" that differ from subject to subject (Perry 122; Belenky et al. 12).

If you can, however, avoid long citations because they can be cumbersome for readers.

Sample Parenthetical References for Other Sources. MLA format is pretty simple, and we've already covered some of the basic variations. You should also know five additional variations, as follow:

AN ENTIRE WORK

If you mention the author's name in the text, no citation is necessary. The work should, however, be listed in the Works Cited.

> Leon Edel's Henry James is considered by many to be a model biography.

A VOLUME OF A MULTIVOLUME WORK

If you're working with one volume of a multivolume work, it's a good idea to mention which volume in the parenthetical reference. The following citation attributes the passage to volume 2, page 3, of a work by Baym and three or more other authors. The volume number always precedes the colon, which is followed by the page number:

> By the turn of the century, three authors dominated American literature: Mark Twain, Henry James, and William Dean Howells (Baym et al. 2: 3).

SEVERAL SOURCES FOR A SINGLE PASSAGE

Occasionally, a number of sources may contribute to a single passage. List them all in one parenthetical reference, separated by semicolons:

> American soccer may never achieve the popularity it enjoys in the rest of the world, an unfortunate fact that is integrally related to the nature of the game itself (Gardner 12; "Selling Soccer" 30).[1]

A LITERARY WORK

Because so many literary works, particularly classics, have been reprinted in so many editions, it's useful to give readers more information about where a passage can be found in one of these editions. List the page number and then the chapter number (and any other relevant information, such as the section or volume), separated by a semicolon. Use arabic rather than roman numerals, unless your teacher instructs you otherwise:

> Izaak Walton warns that "no direction can be given to make a man of a dull capacity able to make a Flie well" (130; ch. 5).

When citing classic poems or plays, instead of page numbers, cite line numbers and other appropriate divisions (book, section, act, scene, part, etc.). Separate the information with periods. For example, (Othello 2.3.286) indicates act 2, scene 3, line 286 of Shakespeare's work.

AN ONLINE SOURCE

Texts on CD-ROM and online sources frequently don't have page numbers. So how can you cite them parenthetically in your essay? You have several options.

Sometimes, the documents include paragraph numbers. In these cases, use the abbreviation *par.* or *pars.,* followed by the paragraph number or numbers you're borrowing material from. For example:

> In most psychotherapeutic approaches, the personality of the therapist can have a big impact on the outcome of the therapy ("Psychotherapy," par. 1).

Sometimes the material has an internal structure, such as sections, parts, chapters, or volumes. If so, use the abbreviation *sec., pt., ch.,* or *vol.* (respectively), followed by the appropriate number.

In many cases, a parenthetical citation can be avoided entirely by simply naming the source in the text of your essay. A curious reader will then find the full citation to the article on the Works Cited page at the back of your paper. For example:

> According to Charles Petit, the worldwide effort to determine whether frogs are disappearing will take somewhere between three and five years.

1. Jason Pulsifer, University of New Hampshire, 1991. Used with permission.

Finally, if you don't want to mention the source in text, parenthetically cite the author's last name (if any) or article title:

```
The worldwide effort to determine whether frogs are disappearing
will take somewhere between three and five years (Petit).
```

WRITING WITH COMPUTERS

FORMATTING IN THE MLA STYLE

Using your word processor's formatting options can prevent a great deal of frustration. Always use your word processor's formatting options instead of manually moving text around your document by repeatedly pressing the spacebar, enter key, or tab key. Using the formatting settings allows you to revise without the tedious task of manually altering your document's appearance. These options are under the format menu of your word processor.

Paragraph Formatting

Paragraph formatting sets how text in individual paragraphs appears. Some of the most common paragraph formatting options are spacing (single or double), indentation, and alignment (flush right, centered, etc.).

In MLA format, you can take a few steps to ensure that your formatting is correct:

1. Set your paper to double spacing before typing a single word, and never press the enter key twice in a row. This ensures that you always have proper spacing.
2. Set your paragraphs to have a first line indention of a half inch.
3. On your Works Cited page, use the hanging indent paragraph format setting to automatically indent subsequent lines for each entry. Remember, the Works Cited page is also double spaced with no additional spaces between entries. The hanging indent, not extra spacing, creates the distinctions between entries.

Page Formatting

Page formatting refers to how text appears on a page. Common page formatting options are margins, headers and footers, and orientation. Formatting your page for MLA can also be achieved in a few simple steps.

1. To place your name and page number in the top right corner, use your word processor's header settings instead of manually typing it at the top of each new page. This automatically adds correct page numbers as you write and prevents a manually typed header from interrupting your text as your revise.
2. Keep in mind that many word-processing programs have default margins of 1.25 inches, while MLA requires inch-wide margins. You will need to adjust these margins in the page format options area.
3. If you wish to start a section of your document on a new page (for instance, to start your Works Cited on a new page), press Ctrl + Enter to create a *page break*. This ensures that the text you type is always on a brand-new page no matter how much you revise the preceding text.

If you are unsure how to make any of these settings, use your word processor's help feature. These common word processor settings will be heavily documented.

Format

The Layout. A certain fussiness is associated with the look of academic papers. The reason for it is quite simple—academic disciplines generally aim for consistency in format so that readers of scholarship know exactly where to look to find what they want to know. It's a matter of efficiency. How closely you must follow the MLA's requirements for the layout of your essay is up to your instructor, but it's really not that complicated. A lot of what you need to know is featured in Figure 10.1.

Printing. Compose your paper on white, $8\frac{1}{2}$" x 11" printer paper. Make sure the printer has sufficient ink or toner.

Margins and Spacing. The old high school trick is to use big margins. That way, you can meet your page length requirements with less material. Don't try that trick with this paper. Leave half-inch margins at the top and one inch margins at the bottom and sides of your pages. Indent the first line of each paragraph five spaces and blocked quotes ten spaces. Double-space all of the text, including blocked quotes and Works Cited.

Title Page. Your paper doesn't need a separate title page. Begin with the first page of text. One inch below the top of the page, type your name, your instructor's name, the course number, and the date (see the following). Below that, type the title, centered on the page. Begin the text of the paper below the title.

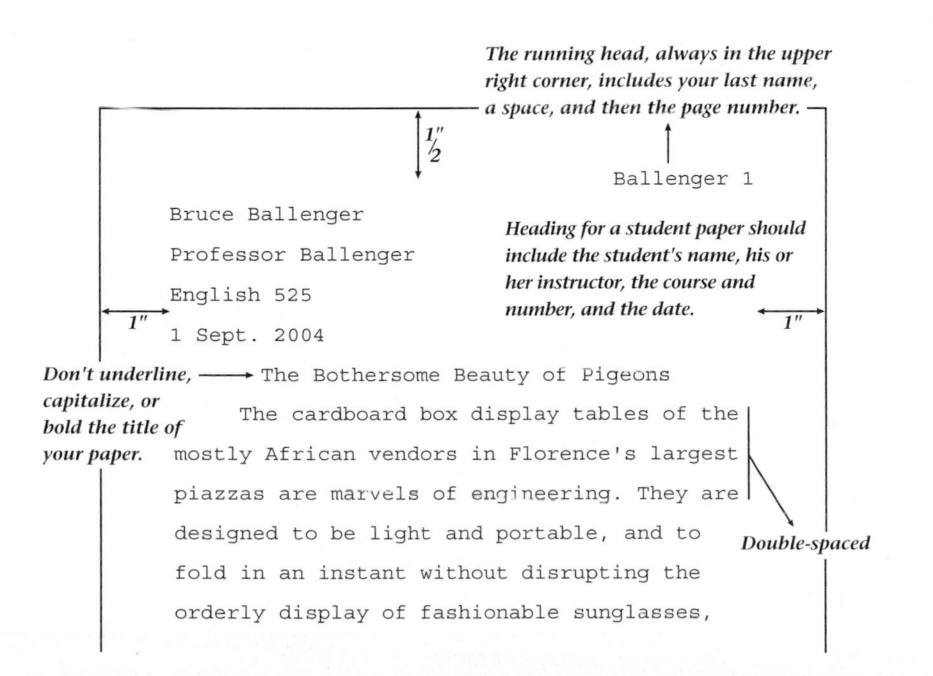

FIGURE 10.1 The basic look of an MLA-style paper.

Julie Bird

Professor Ballenger

English 102

1 June 2004

Nature as Being: Landscape in Silko's 'Lullaby'

Leslie Marmon Silko, the author of "Lullaby," is a Native American writer from the Laguna Pueblo culture . . .

Note that every line is double spaced. The title is not underlined (unless it includes the name of a book or some other work that should be underlined) or boldfaced.

Pagination. Make sure that every page including the first one is numbered. That's especially important with long papers. Type your last name and the page number in the upper right corner, flush with the right margin: Ballenger 3. Don't use the abbreviation *p.* or a hyphen between your name and the number.

Placement of Tables, Charts, and Illustrations. With MLA format, papers do not have appendixes. Tables, charts, and illustrations are placed in the body of the paper, close to the text that refers to them. Number illustrations consecutively (Table 1 or Figure 3), and indicate sources below them (see Figure 10.2). If you use a chart or illustration from another text, give the full citation. Place any table caption above the table, flush left. Captions for illustrations or diagrams are usually placed below them.

Handling Titles. The MLA guidelines about handling titles are, as the most recent *Handbook* observes, "strict." The general rule is that the writer should capitalize the first letters of all principal words in a title, including any that follow hyphens. The exceptions are articles (*a, an,* and *the*), prepositions (*for, of, in, to*), coordinating conjunctions (*and, or, but, for*), and the use of *to* in

TABLE 1

PERCENTAGE OF STUDENTS WHO SELF-REPORT ACTS OF PLAGIARISM

Acts of Plagiarism	Never/ Rarely	Some- times	Often/ Very Freq.
Copy text without citation	71	19	10
Copy paper without citation	91	5	3
Request paper to hand in	90	5	2
Purchase paper to hand in	91	6	3

Source: Scanlon, Patrick M., and David R. Neumann. I nternet Plagiarism among College Students." Journal of College Student Development 43.3 (2002): 379.

FIGURE 10.2 Example of format for a table.

infinitives. These exceptions apply *only if the words appear in the middle of a title;* capitalize them if they appear at the beginning or end.

The rules for underlining a title or putting it in quotation marks are as follows:

1. Underline the Title if it is a book, play, pamphlet, film, magazine, TV program, CD, audiocassette, newspaper, or work of art.
2. "Put the Title in Quotes" if it is an article in a newspaper, magazine, or encyclopedia; a short story; a poem; an episode of a TV program; a song; a lecture; or a chapter or essay in a book.

Here are some examples:

```
The Curious Researcher (Book)

English Online: The Student's Guide to the
     Internet (CD-ROM)

"Once More to the Lake" (Essay)

Historic Boise: An Introduction into the
     Architecture of Boise, Idaho (Book)

"Psychotherapy" (Encyclopedia article)

Idaho Statesman (Newspaper)

"One Percent Initiative Panned" (Newspaper article)
```

Italics and Underlinings. If you are writing your paper on a computer or word processor, you can probably produce italic type, which is slanted to the right, *like this.* Many magazines and books—including this one—use italic type to distinguish certain words and phrases, such as titles of works that otherwise would be underlined. MLA style recommends the use of underlining, not italics. Check with your instructor to see what style he or she prefers.

Language and Style.

Names. Though it may seem as if you're on familiar terms with some of the authors you cite by the end of your research project, it's not a good idea to call them by their first names. Typically, initially give the full names of people you cite, and then only their last names if you mention them again in your essay.

Ellipsis. Those are the three (always three) dots that indicate you've left out a word, phrase, or even whole section of a quoted passage. It's often wise to do this because you want to emphasize only certain parts of a quotation rather than burden your reader with unnecessary information, but be careful to preserve the basic intention and idea of the author's original statement. The ellipsis can come at the beginning of a quotation, in the middle, or at the end, depending where it is you've omitted material. The accepted format for using an ellipsis is to enclose them in brackets. For example,

"After the publication of a controversial picture that shows, for example, either dead or grieving victims [. . .], readers, in telephone calls and in letters to the editor, often attack the photographer for being tasteless [. . .]."

Quotations. Quotations that run more than four lines long should be blocked, or indented ten spaces from the left margin. The quotation should be double- spaced and quotation marks should be omitted. In an exception from the usual convention, the parenthetical citation is placed *outside* the period at the end of the quotation. A colon is a customary way to introduce a blocked quotation. For example,

Chris Sherman and Gary Price, in <u>The Invisible Web</u>, contend that much of the Internet, possibly most, is beyond the reach of researchers who use conventional search engines:

> The problem is that vast expanses of the Web are completely invisible to general-purpose search engines like AltaVista, HotBot, and Google. Even worse, this "Invisible Web" is in all likelihood growing significantly faster than the visible Web that you're familiar with. It's not that search engines and Web directories are "stupid" or even badly engineered. Rather, they simply can't "see" millions of high quality resources that are available exclusively on the Invisible Web. So what is this Invisible Web and why aren't search engines doing anything about it to make it visible? (xxi)

Preparing the Works Cited Page

The Works Cited page ends the paper. Several other lists of sources may also appear at the end of a research paper. An Annotated List of Works Cited not only lists the sources used in the paper but also includes a brief description of each. A Works Consulted list includes sources that may or may not have been cited in the paper but shaped your thinking. A Content Notes page, keyed to superscript numbers in the text of the paper, lists short commentaries or asides that are significant but not central enough to the discussion to be included in the text of the paper.

The Works Cited page is the workhorse of most college papers. The other source lists are used less often. Works Cited is essentially an alphabetical listing of all the sources you quoted, paraphrased, or summarized in your paper. If you have used MLA format for citing sources, your paper has numerous parenthetical references to authors and page numbers. The Works Cited page provides complete information on each source cited in the text for the reader who wants to know. (In APA format, this page is called References and is only slightly different in how items are listed.)

If you've been careful about collecting complete bibliographic information—author, title, editor, edition, volume, place, publisher, date, page numbers—then preparing your Works Cited page will be easy. If you've recorded that information on notecards, all you have to do is put them in alphabetical order and then transcribe them into your paper. If you've been careless about collecting that information, you may need to take a hike back to the library.

Format

Alphabetizing the List. Works Cited follows the text of your paper on a separate page. After you've assembled complete information about each source you've cited, put the sources in alphabetical order by the last name of the author. If the work has multiple authors, use the last name of the first listed. If the source has no author, then alphabetize it by the first key word of the title. If you're citing more than one source by a single author, you don't need to repeat the name for each source; simply place three dashes followed by a period (– – –.) for the author's name in subsequent listings.

Indenting and Spacing. Type the first line of each entry flush left, and indent subsequent lines of that entry (if any) five spaces. Double-space between each line and each entry. For example:

Works Cited

Greeley, Alexandra. "No Tan Is a Safe Tan." Nutrition Health Review: The Consumer's Medical Journal 59 (Summer 1991): 14-15.

Hayes, Jean L. "Are You Assessing for Melanoma?" RN 66.2 (Feb. 2003): 36-40.

Holick, Michael F. "Vitamin D--The Underrated Essential." Life Extension 9.4 (Apr. 2003): 46-48.

Johnson, Rheta Grimsley. "The Rural South These Days Has More Tanning Salons Than John Deeres." Atlanta Journal-Constitution 23 Apr. 2000, home ed.: M1.

"Just the Facts Stats." 36 Expose 17 Sept. 2003 <http://www.stats.org/tanning>.

"The Light Touch." Total Health 14.3 (June 1992): 43.

McLaughlin, Patricia. "Dying for a Tan This Summer?" St. Louis Post-Dispatch 15 June 1995: 02.

Reinhold, Vieth. "Vitamin D Nutrition and Its Potential Health Benefits for Bone, Cancer and Other Conditions." Journal of Nutritional and Environmental Medicine 11 (2001): 275-91.

"Sun Tanning." Cool Nurse 2000-2003 18 June 2003 <http://www.coolnurse.com/tanning.htm>.

Vid, Da. "Sound and Light: Partners in Healing and Transfor mation." Share Guide 5.2 (Winter 1994): 20-21.

Vogel, Phillip J. "A New Light on Vitamin D." Life Extension 9.4 (Apr. 2003): 40-46.

Citing Books. You usually need three pieces of information to cite a book: the name of the author or authors, the title, and the publication information. Occasionally, other information is required. The *MLA Handbook*[2] lists this additional information in the order it would appear in the citation. Remember, any single entry will include a few of these things, not all of them. Use whichever are relevant to the source you're citing.

1. Name of the author
2. Title of the book (or part of it)
3. Number of edition used
4. Number of volume used
5. Name of the series
6. Where published, by whom, and the date
7. Page numbers used
8. Any annotation you'd like to add

Each piece of information in a citation is followed by a period and one space (not two).

Title. As a rule, the titles of books are underlined, with the first letters of all principal words capitalized, including those in any subtitles. Titles that are not underlined are usually those of pieces found within larger works, such as poems and short stories in anthologies. These titles are set off by quotation marks.

2. Joseph Gibaldi, *MLA Handbook for Writers of Research Papers,* 6th ed. (New York: MLA, 2003).

Titles of religious works (the Bible, the Qur'an, etc.) are neither underlined nor enclosed within quotation marks. (See the guidelines in the earlier "Handling Titles" section.)

Edition. If a book doesn't indicate an edition number, then it's probably a first edition, a fact you don't need to cite. Look on the title page. Signal an edition like this: *2nd ed., 3rd ed.,* and so on.

Publication Place, Publisher, and Date. Look on the title page to find out who published the book. Publishers' names are usually shortened in the Works Cited list: for example, *St. Martin's Press Inc.* is shortened to *St. Martin's.*

It's sometimes confusing to know what to cite about the publication place, because several cities are often listed on the title page. Cite the first. For books published outside the United States, add the country name along with the city to avoid confusion.

The date a book is published is usually indicated on the copyright page. If several dates or several printings by the same publisher are listed, cite the original publication date. However, if the book is a revised edition, give the date of that edition. One final variation: If you're citing a book that's a reprint of an original edition, give both dates. For example:

Stegner, Wallace. Recapitulation. 1979. Lincoln: U of Nebraska P, 1986.

This book was first published in 1979 and then republished in 1986 by the University of Nebraska Press.

Page Numbers. You don't usually list page numbers of a book. The parenthetical reference in your paper specifies that. But if you use only part of a book—an introduction or an essay—list the appropriate page numbers following the publication date. Use periods to set off the page numbers. If the author or editor of the entire work is also the author of the introduction or essay you're citing, list her by last name only the second time you cite her. For example:

Lee, L. L., and Merrill Lewis. Preface. Women, Women Writers, and the West. Ed. Lee and Lewis. Troy, MI: Whitston, 1980. v-ix.

Sample Book Citations

A BOOK BY ONE AUTHOR

Keen, Sam. Fire in the Belly. New York: Bantam, 1991.

In-Text Citation: (Keen 101)

A BOOK BY TWO AUTHORS

Ballenger, Bruce, and Barry Lane. Discovering the Writer Within. Cincinnati: Writer's Digest, 1996.

In-Text Citation: (Ballenger and Lane 14)

A BOOK WITH MORE THAN THREE AUTHORS

If a book has more than three authors, list the first and substitute the term *et al.* for the others.

Belenky, Mary Field, et al. Women's Ways of Knowing. New York: Basic Books, 1973.

In-Text Citation: (Belenky et al. 21–30)

SEVERAL BOOKS BY THE SAME AUTHOR

Baldwin, James. Tell Me How Long the Train's Been Gone. New York: Dell-Doubleday, 1968.

– – –. Going to Meet the Man. New York: Dell-Doubleday, 1948.

In-Text Citation: (Baldwin, Going 34)

A COLLECTION OR ANTHOLOGY

Crane, R. S., ed. Critics and Criticism: Ancient and Modern. Chicago: U of Chicago P, 1952.

In-Text Citation: (Crane xx)

A WORK IN A COLLECTION OR ANTHOLOGY

The title of a work that is part of a collection but was originally published as a book should be underlined. Otherwise, the title of a work in a collection should be enclosed in quotation marks.

Bahktin, Mikhail. Marxism and the Philosophy of Language. The Rhetorical Tradition. Ed. Patricia Bizzell and Bruce Herzberg. New York: St. Martin's, 1990. 928–44.

In-Text Citation: (Bahktin 929–31)

Jones, Robert F. "Welcome to Muskie Country." The Ultimate Fishing Book. Ed. Lee Eisenberg and DeCourcy Taylor. Boston: Houghton, 1981. 122–34.

In-Text Citation: (Jones 131)

AN INTRODUCTION, PREFACE, FOREWORD, OR PROLOGUE

Scott, Jerie Cobb. Foreword. Writing Groups:History, Theory, and Implications. By Ann Ruggles Gere. Carbondale: Southern Illinois UP, 1987. ix–xi.

In-Text Citation: (Scott x-xi)

Rich, Adrienne. Introduction. On Lies, Secrets, and Silence. By Rich. New York: Norton, 1979. 9-18.

In-Text Citation: (Rich 12)

A BOOK WITH NO AUTHOR

American Heritage Dictionary. 3rd ed. Boston: Houghton, 1994.

In-Text Citation: (American Heritage Dictionary 444)

AN ENCYCLOPEDIA

"City of Chicago." Encyclopaedia Britannica. 1999 ed.

In-Text Citation: ("City of Chicago" 397)

A BOOK WITH AN INSTITUTIONAL AUTHOR

Hospital Corporation of America. Employee Benefits Handbook. Nashville: HCA, 1990.

In-Text Citation: (Hospital Corporation of America 5-7)

A BOOK WITH MULTIPLE VOLUMES

Include the number of volumes in the work between the title and publication information.

Baym, Nina, et al., eds. The Norton Anthology of American Literature. 5th ed. 2 vols. New York: Norton, 1998.

In-Text Citation: (Baym et al. 2: 3)

If you use one volume of a multivolume work, indicate which one along with the page numbers, followed by the total number of volumes in the work.

Anderson, Sherwood. "Mother." The Norton Anthology of American Literature. Ed. Nina Baym et al. 5th ed. Vol. 2. New York: Norton, 1998. 1115-31. 2 vols.

In-Text Citation: (Anderson 1115)

A BOOK THAT IS NOT A FIRST EDITION

Check the title page to determine whether the book is *not* a first edition (2nd, 3rd, 4th, etc.); if no edition number is mentioned, assume it's the first. Put the edition number right after the title.

Ballenger, Bruce. The Curious Researcher. 5th ed. Boston: Longman, 2007.

In-Text Citation: (Ballenger 194)

Citing the edition is necessary only for books that are *not* first editions. This includes revised editions (*Rev. ed.*) and abridged editions (*Abr. ed.*).

A BOOK PUBLISHED BEFORE 1900

For a book this old, it's usually unnecessary to list the publisher.

`Hitchcock, Edward. Religion of Geology. Glasgow, 1851.`

In-Text Citation: `(Hitchcock 48)`

A TRANSLATION

`Montaigne, Michel de. Essays. Trans. J. M. Cohen. Middlesex, England: Penguin, 1958.`

In-Text Citation: `(Montaigne 638)`

GOVERNMENT DOCUMENTS

Because of the enormous variety of government documents, citing them properly can be a challenge. Because most government documents do not name authors, begin an entry for such a source with the level of government (U.S. Government, State of Illinois, etc., unless it is obvious from the title), followed by the sponsoring agency, the title of the work, and the publication information. Look on the title page to determine the publisher. If it's a federal document, then the *Government Printing Office* (abbreviated *GPO*) is usually the publisher.

`United States. Bureau of the Census. Statistical Abstract of the United States. Washington: GPO, 2005.`

In-Text Citation: `(United States, Bureau of the Census 79–83)`

A BOOK THAT WAS REPUBLISHED

A fairly common occurrence, particularly in literary study, is to find a book that was republished, sometimes many years after the original publication date. In addition, some books first appear in hardcover, and then are republished in paperback. To cite, put the original date of publication immediately after the book's title, and then include the more current publication date, as usual, at the end of the citation. Do it like so:

`Didion, Joan. Slouching toward Bethlehem. 1968. New York: Farrar, 1992.`

In-Text Citation: `(Didion 31)`

AN ONLINE BOOK

Citing a book you found online requires more information than the usual citation for a book you can hold in your hands. As usual, include the author's name (if listed), an underlined title, and publication information. What you include in publication information depends on whether the text was published exclusively online or is also based on a print version. If it is only a digital book, include the date of electronic publication and the group or organization that sponsored it. If the book also appeared on paper, add the usual information (if provided) about the print version (city of publication, publisher, and date). The citation ends, finally, with the date you accessed the book online and the Internet address (URL). For example,

Badke, William. Research Strategies: Finding Your Way through the Information Fog. Lincoln, NE: Writers Club P, 2000. 12 July 2002 <http://www.acts.twu.ca/lbr/textbook.htm>.

In-Text Citation: (Badke)

Citing Periodicals.

Format. Periodicals—magazines, newspapers, journals, and similar publications that appear regularly—are cited similarly to books but sometimes involve different information, such as date, volume, and page numbers. The *MLA Handbook* lists the information to include in a periodical citation in the order in which it should appear:

1. Name of the author
2. Article title
3. Periodical title
4. Series number or name
5. Volume number
6. Date
7. Page numbers

Author's Name. List the author(s) as you would for a book citation.

Article Title. Unlike book titles, article titles are usually enclosed in quotation marks.

Periodical Title. Underline periodical titles, dropping introductory articles (*Aegis,* not *The Aegis*). If you're citing a newspaper your readers may not be familiar with, include in the title—enclosed in brackets but not underlined—the city in which it was published. For example:

Barber, Rocky. "DEQ Responds to Concerns About Weiser Feedlot." Idaho Statesman [Boise] 23 Apr. 2004: B1.

Volume Number. Most academic journals are numbered as volumes (or occasionally feature series numbers); the volume number should be included in the citation. Popular periodicals sometimes have volume numbers, too, but these are not included in the citations. Indicate the volume number immediately after the journal's name. Omit the tag *vol.* before the number.

There is one important variation: Although most journals number their pages continuously, from the first issue every year to the last, a few don't. These journals feature an issue number as well as a volume number. In that case, cite both by listing the volume number, a period, and then the issue number: for example *12.4,* for volume number *12* and issue *4.*

Date. When citing popular periodicals, include the day, month, and year of the issue you're citing—in that order—following the periodical name. Academic journals are a little different. Because the volume number indicates when the journal was published within a given year, just indicate that year. Put it in parentheses following the volume number and before the page numbers (see examples following).

Page Numbers. Include the page numbers of the article at the end of the citation, followed by a period. Just list the pages of the entire article, omitting abbreviations such as *p.* or *pp.* It's common for articles in newspapers and popular magazines *not* to run on consecutive pages. In that case, indicate the page on which the article begins, followed by a " + " (*12+*).

Newspaper pagination can be peculiar. Some papers wed the section (usually a letter) with the page number (*A4*); other papers simply begin numbering anew in each section. Most, however, paginate continuously. See the sample citations for newspapers that follow for how to deal with these peculiarities.

Online sources, which often have no pagination at all, present special problems. For guidance on how to handle them, see the "Citing Online Databases" section.

Sample Periodical Citations

A MAGAZINE ARTICLE

Elliot, Carl. "The New Drug Pushers." <u>Atlantic Monthly</u> Apr. 2006: 82-93.

In-Text Citation: (Elliot 92)

Williams, Patricia J. "Unimagined Communities." <u>Nation</u> 3 May 2004: 14.

In-Text Citation: (Williams 14)

A JOURNAL ARTICLE

For a journal that is paginated continuously, from the first issue every year to the last, cite as follows:

Allen, Rebecca E., and J. M. Oliver. "The Effects of Child Maltreatment on Language Development." <u>Child Abuse and Neglect</u> 6 (1982): 299-305.

In-Text Citation: (Allen and Oliver 299-300)

For an article in a journal that begins pagination with each issue, include the issue number along with the volume number.

Goody, Michelle M., and Andrew S. Levine. "Health-Care Workers and Occupational Exposure to AIDS." <u>Nursing Management</u> 23.1 (1992): 59-60.

In-Text Citation: (Goody and Levine 59)

A NEWSPAPER ARTICLE

Some newspapers have several editions (morning edition, late edition, national edition), and each may feature different articles. If an edition is listed on the masthead, include it in the citation.

Mendels, Pamela. "Internet Access Spreads to More Classrooms." New York Times 1 Dec. 1999, morning ed.: C1+.

In-Text Citation: (Mendels C1)

Some papers begin numbering pages anew in each section. In that case, include the section number if it's not part of pagination.

Brooks, James. "Lobsters on the Brink." Portland Press 29 Nov. 2005, sec. 2: 4.

In-Text Citation: (Brooks 4)

Increasingly, full-text newspaper articles are available online using library databases such as Newspaper Source or through the newspapers themselves. Citing articles from library databases involves adding information about the specific database you use (e.g., Newspaper Source), the provider of that database (e.g., EBSCOhost), where (which library?) and when (date) you accessed the information online, and the Web address of the provider (e.g., http://www.epnet.com). You can find the URLs for most database providers later in this section.

Here's what the citation would look like:

"Lobsterman Hunts for Perfect Bait." AP Online 7 July 2002. Newspaper Source. EBSCOhost. Albertson's Lib., Boise, ID. 13 July 2002 <http://www.epnet.com>.

In-Text Citation: ("Lobsterman Hunts")

Here's an example of a citation for an article I found on the newspaper's own Web site:

Higgins, Michelle. "Forget Legroom. What about More Water?" New York Times on the Web 27 Aug. 2006. 30 Aug. 2006 <http://www.nytimes.com/2006/08/27/travel/27prac.html?_r=1&ref=travel?8dpc&oref=slogin>.

In-Text Citation: (Higgins)

AN ARTICLE WITH NO AUTHOR

"The Understanding." New Yorker 2 Dec. 1991: 34–35.

In-Text Citation: ("Understanding" 35)

AN EDITORIAL

"Downward Mobility." Editorial. New York Times 27 Aug. 2006: 31.

In-Text Citation: ("Downward" 31)

A LETTER TO THE EDITOR

Boulay, Harvey. Letter. Boston Globe 30 Aug. 2006: 14.

In-Text Citation: (Boulay 14)

A REVIEW

Page, Barbara. Rev. of Allegories of Cinema: American Film in the Sixties, by David E. James. College English 54 (1992): 945-54.

In-Text Citation: (Page 945-46)

AN ABSTRACT

It's usually better to have the full text of an article for research purposes, but sometimes all you can come up with is an abstract, or short summary of the article that highlights its findings or summarizes its argument. Online databases frequently offer abstracts when they don't feature full-text versions of an article.

To cite an abstract, begin with information about the full version, and then include the information about the source from which you got the abstract. If the title of the source fails to make it obvious that what you are citing is an abstract (i.e., it's not called something such as "Psychological Abstracts"), include the word *Abstract* after the original publication information, but don't underline it or put it in quotation marks. In this example, the source of the abstract is a periodical database called MasterFILE Premier, provided by the company EBSCOhost. Because I accessed the abstract at my library, I include the library name and its location in the citation. In addition, I include the date of access and the Web address of the database's provider in the citation. (A list of URLs for these providers appears later in this section.)

Edwards, Rob. "Air-Raid Warning." New Scientist 14 Aug. 1999: 48-49. Abstract. MasterFILE Premier. EBSCOhost. Albertson's Lib., Boise, ID. 1 May 2002 <http://www.epnet.com>.

In-Text Citation: (Edwards)

The following citation is from another useful source of abstracts, the *Dissertation Abstracts International.* In this case, the citation is from the print version of the index.

McDonald, James C. "Imitation of Models in the History of Rhetoric: Classical, Belletristic, and Current-Traditional." U of Texas, Austin. DAI 48 (1988): 2613A.

In-Text Citation: (McDonald 2613A)

Citing Nonprint and Other Sources

AN INTERVIEW

If you conducted the interview yourself, list your subject's name first, indicate what kind of interview it was (telephone, e-mail, or personal interview), and provide the date.

`Kelley, Varen. Personal interview. 1 Sept. 2006.`

In-Text Citation: `(Kelley)`

Or avoid parenthetical reference altogether by mentioning the subject's name in the text: `According to Lonny Hall, . . .`

If you're citing an interview done by someone else (perhaps from a book or article) and the title does not indicate that it was an interview, you should, after the subject's name, include *Interview*. Always begin the citation with the subject's name.

Stegner, Wallace. Interview. Conversations with Wallace Stegner. By Richard Eutlain and Wallace Stegner. Salt Lake: U of Utah P, 1990.

In-Text Citation: `(Stegner 22)`

If there are other works by Stegner on the Works Cited page:

(Stegner, Conversations 22)

As radio and TV interview programs are increasingly archived on the Web, these can be a great source of material for a research essay. In the following example, the interview was on a transcript I ordered from the Fresh Air Web site. Note that the national network, National Public Radio, *and* the local affiliate that produced the program, WHYY, are included in the citation along with the air date.

Mairs, Nancy. Interview. Fresh Air. Natl. Public Radio. WHYY, Philadelphia. 7 June 1993.

In-Text Citation: `(Mairs)`

The following citation is for an interview published on the Web. The second date listed is the date of access.

Messner, Tammy Faye Bakker. Interview. The Well Rounded Interview. Well Rounded Entertainment. Aug. 2000. 14 July 2002 <http://www.wellrounded.com/movies/reviews/tammyfaye_intv.html>.

In-Text Citation: `(Messner)`

SURVEYS, QUESTIONNAIRES, AND CASE STUDIES

If you conducted the survey or case study, list it under your name and give it an appropriate title.

Ball, Helen. "Internet Survey." Boise State U, 2006.

In-Text Citation: (Ball)

RECORDINGS

Generally, list a recording by the name of the performer and underline the title. Also include the recording company, catalog number, and year. (If you don't know the year, use the abbreviation *n.d.*)

Orff, Carl. Carmina Burana. Cond. Seiji Ozawa. Boston Symphony. RCA, 6533-2-RG, n.d.

In-Text Citation: (Orff)

TELEVISION AND RADIO PROGRAMS

List the title of the program (underlined), the station, and the broadcast date. If the episode has a title, list that first in quotation marks. You may also want to include the name of the narrator or producer after the title.

All Things Considered. Interview with Andre Dubus. Natl. Public Radio. WBUR, Boston. 12 Dec. 1990.

In-Text Citation: (All Things Considered)

FILMS, VIDEOTAPES, AND DVD

Begin with the title (underlined), followed by the director, the distributor, and the year. You may also include names of writers, performers, or producers. End with the date and any other specifics about the characteristics of the film or videotape that may be relevant (length and size).

Saving Private Ryan. Dir. Steven Spielberg. Perf. Tom Hanks, Tom Sizemore, and Matt Damon. Videocassette. Paramount, 1998.

In-Text Citation: (Saving)

You can also list a video or film by the name of a contributor you'd like to emphasize.

Capra, Frank, dir. It's a Wonderful Life. Perf. Jimmy Stewart and Donna Reed. RKO Pictures, 1946.

In-Text Citation: (Capra)

ARTWORK

List each work by artist. Then cite the title of the work (underlined) and where it's located (institution and city). If you've reproduced the work from a published source, include that information as well.

Homer, Winslow. Casting for a Rise. Hirschl and Adler Galleries, New York. Ultimate Fishing Book. Ed. Lee Eisenberg and DeCourcy Taylor. Boston: Houghton, 1981.

In-Text Citation: (Homer 113)

LECTURES AND SPEECHES

List each by the name of the speaker, followed by the title of the address (if any) in quotation marks, the name of the sponsoring organization, the location, and the date. Only indicate what kind of address it was (*Lecture, Speech,* etc.) when no title is given.

Naynaha, Siskanna. "Emily Dickinson's Last Poems." Sigma Tau Delta, Boise, ID. 15 Nov. 1999.

Avoid the need for parenthetical citation by mentioning the speaker's name in your text.

PAMPHLETS

Cite a pamphlet as you would a book.

New Challenges for Wilderness Conservationists. Washington, DC: Wilderness Society, 2006.

In-Text Citation: (New Challenges)

Citing "Portable" Databases. Nearly every new computer these days is sold with an encyclopedia on CD-ROM. If you're doing research, I don't think they hold a candle to the more extensive bound versions. Still, a CD-ROM encyclopedia is easy to use and, for quickly checking facts, can be quite helpful. While the encyclopedia is the most familiar *portable* database on CD-ROM, there are many others, including full-text versions of literary classics, journal article abstracts, indexes, and periodicals. The number of such portable databases on CD will continue to multiply along with databases on other media, such as diskettes and tapes. Citation of these materials requires much of the usual information and in the usual order. But it will also include these three things: the *publication medium* (for example, *CD-ROM, Diskette,* or *Tape*), the *vendor* or company that distributed it (for example, SilverPlatter or UMI-ProQuest), and the *date of electronic publication* (or the release date of the disk or tape).

There are two categories of portable databases: (1) those that are issued periodically, such as magazines and journals, and (2) those that are not routinely updated, such as books. Citing a source in each category requires some slightly different information.

A NONPERIODICAL DATABASE

This is cited much as a book.

- List the author. If no author is given, list the editor or translator, followed by the appropriate abbreviation (*ed., trans.*)
- Publication title (underlined) or title of the portion of the work you're using (if relevant)
- Name of editor, compiler, or translator (if relevant)
- Publication medium (for example, *CD-ROM, Diskette, Magnetic tape*)
- Edition or release or version

- City of publication
- Publisher and year of publication

For example:

Shakespeare, William. Romeo and Juliet. Diskette. Vers. 1.5. New York: CMI, 1995.

In-Text Citation: (Shakespeare)

"Psychotherapy." Microsoft Encarta. CD-ROM. 2004 ed. Everett, WA: Microsoft, 2003.

In-Text Citation: ("Psychotherapy")

A PERIODICAL DATABASE

Frequently a periodical database is a computer version—or an analogue—of a printed publication. For example, the *New York Times* has a disk version, as does *Dissertation Abstracts.* Both databases refer to articles also published in print; therefore, the citation often includes two dates: the original publication date and the electronic publication date. Note the location of each in the following citations.

Haden, Catherine Ann. "Talking about the Past with Preschool Siblings." DAI 56 (1996). Emory U, 1995. Dissertation Abstracts Ondisc. CD-ROM. UMI-ProQuest. Mar. 1996.

In-Text Citation: (Haden)

Kolata, Gina. "Research Links Writing Style to the Risk of Alzheimer's." New York Times 21 Feb. 1996: 1A. Newspaper Abstracts. CD-ROM. UMI-ProQuest. 1996.

In-Text Citation: (Kolata 1A)

Frequently, a periodically issued electronic source doesn't have a printed analogue. In that case, obviously, you can't include publication information about the printed version.

Citing Online Databases. Citing most online sources is much like citing any other sources, with two crucial exceptions:

1. Electronic source citations usually include at least two dates: the *date of electronic publication* (if available) and the *date of access* (when you visited the site and retrieved the document). There is a good reason for listing both dates: Online documents are changed and updated frequently—so when you retrieve the material matters. If the online document you are using originally appeared in print, it might be necessary to include three dates: the print publication date, the online publication date, and your access date (see the McGrory citation that follows in the "Is It Also in Print?" section).

2. The MLA now requires that you include the Internet address of the document in angle brackets at the end of your citation (for example,

<http: www.cc.emory.edu/citation.formats.html>). The reason is obvious: the Internet address tells your readers where they can find the document.

Other Recent Changes by the MLA. The MLA no longer requires inclusion of a number of items in a citation. For example, it's no longer necessary to include the word *online* in your citations to indicate the publication medium or mention the name of the network or service you used to retrieve the document (for example, *Internet, America Online*). Both are great improvements, I think. Another quirky thing about citing online sources is dealing with page numbers, paragraph numbers, or numbered sections. Many Internet documents simply don't have them. The MLA no longer requires inclusion of the term *n. pag.* when a document lacks pagination.

Is It Also in Print? Databases from computer services or networks feature information available in printed form (such as a newspaper or magazine) and online, or information available exclusively online. This distinction is important. If the online source has a printed version, include information about it in the citation. For example:

McGrory, Brian. "Hillary Clinton's Profile Boosted." Boston Globe 26 June 1996: 1. Boston Globe Online 27 June 1996. 8 July 1998 <http://www.boston.com/80/globe/nat/cgi-bin>.

In-Text Citation: (McGrory 1)

Note that the first date lists when the print version appeared, the second date when the article was published online, and the third when the researcher accessed the document.

Material that only appeared online is somewhat simpler to cite because you'll need to include information only about the electronic version.

Hutchins, Lisa. "The Intelligence of Crows." Pica Productions Mar. 1999. 23 Apr. 2004 <http://www.picaproductions.com/intelligencecrows>.

In-Text Citation: No page or paragraph numbers were used in this document, so simply list the author's last name: (Hutchins). Or avoid parenthetical citation altogether by mentioning the name of the source in your essay (for example: "According to Lisa Hutchins, the crow is . . .").

You may be missing citation information on some Internet material—such as page numbers and publication dates—that are easy to find in printed texts. Use the information that you have. Keep in mind that the relevant information for a citation varies with the type of electronic source (see the citation examples that follow in the "Sample Online Citations" section). To summarize, the basic format for an online citation includes the following information:

1. Author's name (if given). If an editor, translator, or compiler is included, list that name followed by the appropriate abbreviation (*ed., trans., comp.*).

2. Publication information:
   - Title of the document, database, or Web site
   - Title of the larger work, database, or Web site (if any) of which it is a part
   - Name of editor (if any) of the project, database, or Web site (usually different from author)
   - Publication information about print version (if any)
   - Volume, issue, or version number (if any)
   - Date of electronic publication or latest update
   - Page or paragraph numbers (if any)
   - Date of access and electronic address

Address Mistakes Are Fatal. When you include Internet addresses in your citations, you must take great care in accurately recording them. Make sure you get all your slash marks going in the right direction and the right characters in the right places; also pay attention to whether the characters are upper- or lowercase. These addresses are often *case sensitive,* unlike, say, the file names used to retrieve WordPerfect documents. The cut-and-paste function in your word processor is an invaluable tool in accurately transferring Internet addresses into your own documents. One last thing: If an Internet address in your citation must go beyond one line, make sure the break occurs after a slash, not in the middle of a file name, and don't include an end-of-line hyphen to mark the break.

Sample Online Citations

AN ARTICLE

Notice the inclusion of the document length after the publication date in the following example. Sometimes Internet documents number paragraphs instead of pages. Include that information, if available, using the abbreviation *par.* or *pars.* (e.g., "53 pars."). More often, an Internet article has no page or paragraph numbers. Put the title of the article in quotation marks and underline the title of the journal, newsletter, or electronic conference.

Haynes, Cynthia, and Jan R. Holmevik. "Enhancing Pedagogical Reality with MOOs." Kairos: A Journal for Teachers of Writing in a Webbed Environment 1.2 (1996): 1 p. 28 June 1996 <http://english/ttu.edu/kairos/1.2/index.html>.

In-Text Citation: (Haynes and Holmevik 1)

Davis, Robert, and Anthony Barros. "Alcohol and Fire a Deadly Mix." USA Today 30 Aug. 2006. 30 Aug. 2006 <http://www.usatoday.com/news/nation/2006-08-29-campus-fires-cover_x.htm>.

In-Text Citation: (Davis and Barros)

AN ARTICLE OR ABSTRACT IN A LIBRARY DATABASE

One of the great boons to researchers in recent years is the publication of full-text versions of articles as part of the online databases available on your campus library's Web pages. Quite a few databases, such as MasterFILE and Newspaper Source, offer this service, and more are adding it every year. Some that don't offer full-text versions of articles offer abstracts, and even these can be useful. Citing articles or abstracts from library databases requires some information beyond what is usually required for citing other online articles. Specifically, you need

- The name of the database, underlined (e.g., Newspaper Source)
- The name and Web address of the company or organization that provides it to your library (e.g., EBSCOhost)
- The name and location of the library (e.g., Albertson's Library, Boise, ID)
- The date you accessed the database to get the article

All of this information is pretty easy to come up with except information about the company that provides the database. You can usually find that name on the search page of the database. The accompanying table lists the Web addresses of some of the most popular of these providers, along with some of the databases each features. You can use the provider's address in your citation. Note in the following example that information on the print version of the article is provided first, and then information about the database and its provider.

Winbush, Raymond A. "Back to the Future: Campus Racism in the 21st Century." The Black Collegian Oct. 2001: 102-03. Expanded Academic ASAP. Gale Group Databases. U of New Hampshire Lib. 12 Apr. 2002 <http://www.infotrac.galegroup.com>.

In-Text Citation: (Winbush)

URLs OF POPULAR DATABASE PROVIDERS FOR USE IN CITATIONS

The table lists the Web addresses for most of the major companies that provide databases for libraries. This information is vital if you want to cite an article or abstract you found while searching your campus library's databases online. Usually a database has a specific name, such as Expanded Academic ASAP, as shown in the second column, and then a service that provides it, a name that you can usually find somewhere on the search page of the database. For example, Expanded Academic ASAP's provider is called Gale Group Databases, as shown in the first column. You need both pieces of information for a citation, as well as the provider's URL.

(continued)

(continued)

Database Provider	Databases	Web Address
Britannica Online	Encyclopaedia Britannica	http://www.britannica.com
EBSCOhost	Academic Search Elite, Academic Search Premier, Business Source Elite, Computer Source, Health Source, MasterFILE Elite, MasterFILE Premier, Newspaper Source, Nursing and Allied Health Collection	http://www.epnet.com
Gale Group Databases	Book Review Index, Contemporary Authors, Expanded Academic ASAP, General Business File ASAP, General Reference Center, Health Reference Center, InfoTrac, Literary Index	http://www.infotrac.galegroup.com
LexisNexis	Academic, Government Periodicals Universe, History Universe, Statistical	http://www.lexisnexis.com
OCLC First Search	Art Index, Book Review Digest, Contemporary Women's Issues, EconLit, Essay and General Literature Index, Reader's Guide Abstracts, Social Science Index, WorldCat	http://newfirstsearch.oclc.org
ProQuest	ABI/INFORM, Academic Research Library, Newsstand Academic Research Library, Nursing & Allied Health Source, Psychology Journals, Wilson Databases	http://proquest.umi.com/pdgweb
SilverPlatter/Web SPIRS	Agricola, Biological Abstracts, CINHAL, EconLit, Essay and General Literature Index, Philosopher's Index, PsycINFO	http://webspirs.silverplatter.com
Wilson Web	Applied Science and Technology Abstracts, Art Index, Bibliographic Index Plus, Biography Index, Book Review Digest Plus, Education Index, General Science Index, Humanities Index, Reader's Guide, Social Sciences Index, World Authors	http://hwwilsonweb.com

When citing an abstract from a library database, include the word *Abstract* in the citation. For example,

Erskine, Ruth. "Exposing Racism, Exploring Race." Journal of Family Therapy 24 (2002): 282-97. Abstract. EBSCO Online Citations. EBSCOhost. Albertson's Lib., Boise, ID. 3 Dec. 2002.

In-Text Citation: (Erskine)

AN ONLINE BOOK

I can't imagine why anyone would read *The Adventures of Huckleberry Finn* online, but it's available, along with thousands of other books and historical documents in electronic form. If you use an online book, remember to include publication information (if available) about the original printed version in the citation.

Twain, Mark. The Adventures of Huckleberry Finn. New York: Harper, 1912. 22 Aug. 2006 <http://users.telecoma.com/~joseph/finn/finntitl.html>.

In-Text Citation: (Twain)

Or better yet, because there are no page numbers, mention the author in the text rather than citing him parenthetically: In The Adventures of Huckleberry Finn, Twain re-creates southern dialect . . .

When citing part of a larger work, include the title of that smaller part in quotation marks before the title of the work. Also notice that the following cited text is part of an online scholarly project. Include the name of the project, the editor and compiler of the work if listed, and its location.

Service, Robert. "The Mourners." Rhymes of a Red Cross Man. 1916. Project Gutenberg. Ed. A. Light. Aug. 1995. Illinois Benedictine College. 1 July 1998 <ftp://uiarchive.cso.uiuc.edu/pub/text/gutenberg/etext95/redcr10.txt>.

In-Text Citation: (Service)

A PERSONAL OR PROFESSIONAL WEB SITE

Begin with the name of the editor or creator of the site, if listed. Include the title of the site, or, if no title is given, use a descriptor such as the term *Home page*. Also include the sponsoring organization, if any; the date of access; and the electronic address.

Population Ecology. Ed. Alexi Sharev. Virginia Tech U. 30 Aug. 2006 <http://www.ento.vt.edu/~sharov/popechome/welcome.html>.

In-Text Citation: (Population)

Battalio, John. Home page. 26 May 2006 <http://www.boisestate.edu/english/jbattalio/>.

In-Text Citation: (Battalio)

You may cite a document that is part of a Web site. For example:

Cohn, Priscilla. "Wildlife Contraception: An Introduction." Animal Rights Law Center Web Site. 2006. Rutgers U. 27 May 2006 <http://www.animal-law.org/hunting/hunting.htm>.

In-Text Citation: (Cohn)

AN ONLINE POSTING

An online posting can be a contribution to an e-mail discussion group, a posting to a bulletin board or Usenet group, or a WWW forum. The description *Online posting* is included after the title of the message (usually drawn from the subject line). List the date the material was posted, the access date, and the online address as you would for any other online citation.

Alvoeiro, Jorge. "Neurological Effects of Music." Online posting. 20 June 1996. 10 Aug. 2006 <news:sci.psychology.misc>.

In-Text Citation: (Alvoeiro)

The following example is from an e-mail discussion group. The address at the end of the citation is from the group's archives, available on the Web. If you don't have an Internet address for the post you want to cite, include the e-mail address of the group's moderator or supervisor.

Fullwiller, Megan. "Error in Student Writing." Online posting. 29 Aug. 2006. WPA Discussion List. 30 Aug. 2006 <http://lists.asu.edu>.

In-Text Citation: (Fullwiller)

AN E-MAIL MESSAGE

Tobin, Lad. "On Going Home." E-mail to the author. 8 July 2006.

In-Text Citation: (Tobin)

A SOUND CLIP

Greene, Robert. "Checking Up on Federal Promises on Katrina." Natl. Public Radio. 30 Aug. 2006. 30 Aug. 2006 <http://www.npr.org/templates/story/story.php?storyId=5738211>.

In-Text Citation: (Greene)

AN INTERVIEW

Kolbert, Elizabeth. Interview. New Yorker Online. 18 Apr. 2005. 30 Aug. 2006 <http://www.newyorker.com/online/content/articles/050425on_onlineonly01>.

In-Text Citation: (Kolbert)

A Sample Paper in MLA Style

Most of the student essays in *The Curious Writer* use MLA style. For a fully documented research paper in MLA style, see Amy Garrett's essay, "We Need the Sun."

STUDENT ESSAY

Amy Garrett's essay begins with a question that arose from her ordinary life. Should she be obsessive about avoiding the sun? How seriously should she take warnings from the sunscreen industry and others that she should never walk outside without slathering on the sunblock?

Through research, Garrett answers these questions in "We Need the Sun," and in the process she argues that the case for avoiding the sun is overstated. It's a controversial conclusion. Do you think the facts that Garrett gathers effectively support the claim? Does her essay raise other questions about sun tanning that she doesn't address? Finally, how well do you think she weaves in her personal experiences and personal voice along with the factual information? What effect does it have on you as a reader?

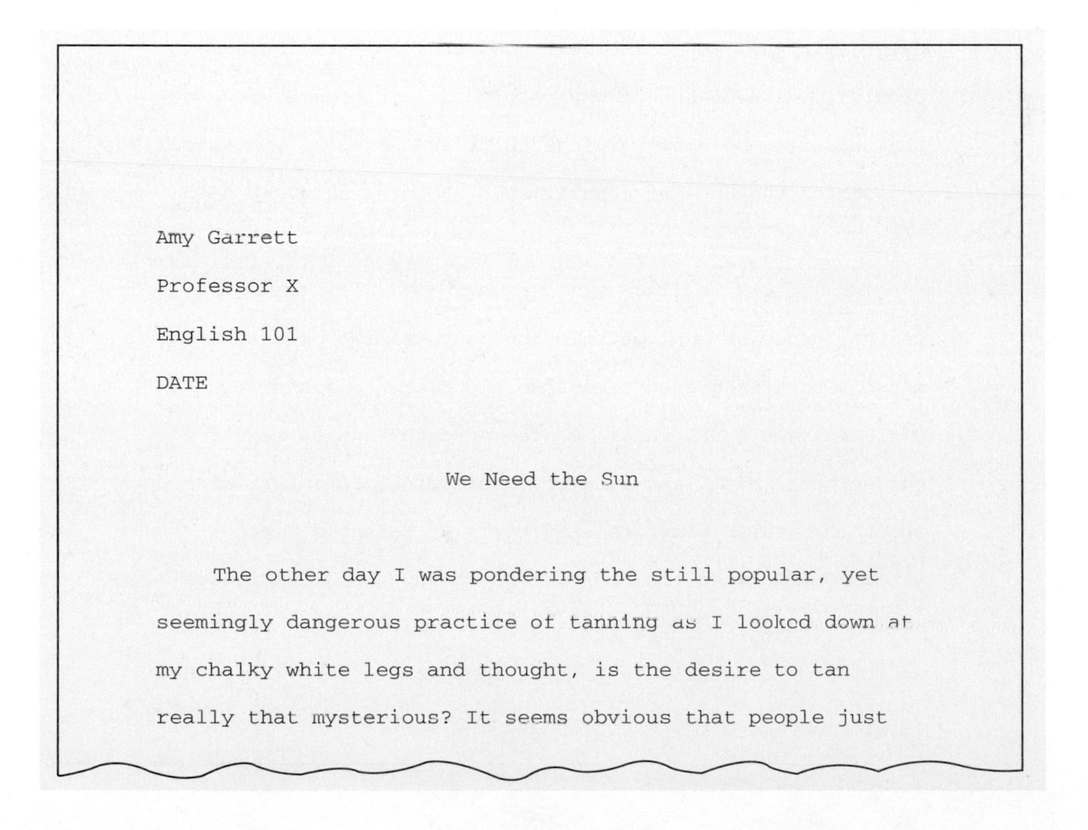

Amy Garrett

Professor X

English 101

DATE

We Need the Sun

The other day I was pondering the still popular, yet seemingly dangerous practice of tanning as I looked down at my chalky white legs and thought, is the desire to tan really that mysterious? It seems obvious that people just like the way it looks to be tan. In fact, one survey of American teenagers revealed that two thirds of them feel "healthier" and "more sophisticated" with a tan (qtd. in "Sun Tanning"). I know I feel better about putting on a bathing suit if I'm not so starkly white that I worry about blinding young children. I also know that it just feels good to be in the sun. The warm rays beating down on my back and shoulders as I work outdoors or go for a hike seem therapeutic and natural. I'll admit I've seen the inside of a tanning booth a few times before I took a spring break trip to California and, yes, that felt good too. As I searched more deeply into the issue of why people tan, it became apparent that despite the dire warnings there is a deeper, biological reason for the undying popularity of bronzed skin. We need the sun.

Actually, the human body is "hard-wired" to need healthy doses of sunlight. Through our skin we process vitamin D, which is gained almost solely from the sun's Ultraviolet B (UVB) rays. We also need the sun to regulate our hormone levels and fend off depression. In an article about the health benefits of vitamin D, Reinhold Vieth explains that when "humans evolved at equatorial latitudes, without modern clothing and shelter, their vitamin D supply would have been equivalent to at least 100/g day" (275). He goes on to explain that today our bodies typically harbor only half that amount of vitamin D at best, but that our current genetic make up was selected at a point in our evolution to demand much higher amounts (275). This is the most important key to understanding our longing for the sun—evolutionarily speaking, we need it.

Almost 100% of our body's necessary vitamin D intake can be gained through sun exposure (Vogel 42). How does this work? When our skin is exposed to the sun's UVB rays, a cholesterol compound in the skin is turned into a catalyst for vitamin D, called vitamin D3. This compound enters circulation and becomes vitamin D. We depend upon vitamin D for absorption of calcium, for bone strength and maintenance and for immunity to many diseases such as cancer, diabetes and multiple sclerosis (Vogel 42).

But, that's not all of the sun's health benefits. According to Vieth, "studies show that higher serum . . . and/or environmental ultraviolet exposure is associated with lower rates of breast, ovarian, prostate and colorectal cancers, [also] lymphoma, and cancer of the bladder, esophagus, kidney, lung, pancreas, rectum, stomach and corpus uteri" (279).

In a study about the relationship between light and sound, Da Vid explains the necessity of the sun's light on the body's maintenance of hormone levels. Through an almost magical process our body literally turns the sun's light into the chemical components that we need to maintain balance. The sun's light enters the body through the optic nerves and then travels through a complex series of reactions, stimulating the pineal gland, which in turn triggers the hypothalamus. These two functions alone are very important. The pineal gland produces neurohormonal agents which are light sensitive. These agents are connected directly to the pineal gland which "mediates from moment to moment all the vital processes of the body" (276). From here the hypothalamus carries the light to the pituitary gland in the form of chromophillic cells. The pituitary gland then turns these cells into hormones which maintain homeostasis (276).

This is one of the major foundations to understanding seasonal depression. We need the sun's light to be happy. Without homeostasis, or balance, we are lost and confused, a mess of delinquent hormones, depressed and unhealthy. No wonder tanning is so popular. Said simply, "Light is a beneficial and vital, biologic resource, affecting everyone medically, psychologically and environmentally" ("Light Touch" 1). Not only is sunlight good for hormone regulation, but it also influences Circadian rhythms and the body's internal clock ("Light Touch" 2).

But, instead of promoting the absorption of healthy levels of vitamin D3 and UVB rays, the health industry frightens us away from the sun. Sales of sun screen, according to Information Resources, topped $416 million in 2002, nearly a 7% increase from the year before ("Just the Facts Stats"); healthy profits apparently means screening consumers from the health benefits of exposure to sunlight. We are taught that the sun is bad, when in fact, a good relationship with the sun is very natural and healthy. We are scared. We hide indoors and watch TV or we are too caught up in the grind, we work too much and never see the light of day. When we do get out, we slather ourselves with sunscreen and block vitamin D production.

Other experts contend that we should simply stay out of the sun altogether. In an article by Alexanra Greely titled, "No Tan is a Safe Tan" she presents her case against spending time in the sun, and especially tanning, with potent statistics and facts. But, I couldn't help wonder if she ever has any fun after reading her closing lines: "In the end, there really is nothing new under the sun, except that perhaps more people are staying out of it, heeding medical warning such as Bergstresser's: 'Less sun is better. No sun is best of all'" (15).

All of this sun bashing *is* based on some well-known dangers. Some of the statistics that Greely used were frightening. She mentioned that in 1990, 600,000 people were diagnosed with basal and squamous cell carcinomas, the leading skin cancers. This was an increase of 200,000 victims in ten years (14). But right after that, she concedes that it can't be blamed directly on the sun. The problem is behavioral. "Those people with the highest light exposure appear to have a lower frequency of melanomas than those who get sunlight more episodically . . . [and] those people who have had severe sunburns at an early age are also at higher risk for melanomas" (14).

These hazards would seem to make the case for slathering on the sunblock at the very least. However, progressive health experts are beginning to question our obsessive use of sunblock (Holick 46). According to several reviews in medical journals wearing sunscreen all of the time is not healthy since our bodies need to produce vitamin D. For example, a study of veiled women in Turkey recently exposed that 82% of women in Turkey aren't exposed enough. Their vitamin D levels were severely depleted and another 8% were moderately deficient. These women all complained of poor muscle strength and weakness and their bones were very fragile at young ages, consistent with other vitamin D deficient subjects (Vogel 43).

This is key: it is healthy and beneficial to enjoy the sun on a regular basis, but getting sunburned, especially at a young age is not. Instead of telling us to be wary of sunburns, the suntan lotion industry and other experts tell us to stay completely out of the sun, which isn't healthy either. The repercussions of vitamin D deficiencies are numerous and very serious.

We must find that middle ground, somewhere between getting cooked or being completely veiled. Granted, with the depletion of the ozone and other studies about the dangers of over-exposure to UVB rays, and the fact that "a single 15- to 30-minute session with artificial tanning equipment exposes the body to the same amount of harmful UV rays as a day at the beach" we should be careful (Hayes 38). We should use good sunscreen and cover up when we are going to be in the sun all day; we all know that by now. But we shouldn't obsess about it either. We need routine unprotected exposure to the sun; in fact, at least 15 minutes a day will provide us with the required amount vitamin D (Holick 47).

So, the most important lesson learned is that we should enjoy the sun regularly, rather than sporadically, which is the only behavior that is proven to lead to skin cancer. We should avoid sunburns and occasional, all-day sun baking and enjoy the sun's rays on a regular basis instead. We should not fear the sun; we should relish every minute of our sweat-drenched, sun-worshipping because, body and soul, we need it.

Garrett 8

Works Cited

Greeley, Alexandra. "No Tan is a Safe Tan." Nutrition Health Review: the Consumer's Medical Journal 59 (Summer 1991): 14-15.

Hayes, Jean L. "Are You Assessing For Melanoma?" RN 66.2 (February 2003): 36-40.

Holick, Michael F. "Vitamin D—The Underrated Essential." Life Extension 9.4 (Apr 2003): 46-48.

Johnson, Rheta Grimsley. "The Rural South These Days Has More Tanning Salons Than John Deeres." The Atlanta Journal-Constitution 23 Apr 2000, home ed.:M1.

"Just the Facts Stats." 36 Expose. 17 September 2003 <http://www.ecrm-online.com/Expose/V6_1/36.pdf>.

McLaughlin, Patricia. "Dying For a Tan This Summer?" St. Louis Post-Dispatch 15 Jun 1995: 02.

"The Light Touch." Total Health 14.3 (June 1992): 43.

Vid, Da. "Sound and Light: Partners in Healing and Transformation." Share Guide 5.2 (Winter 1994): 20-21.

Reinhold, Vieth. "Vitamin D Nutrition and its Potential Health Benefits for Bone, Cancer and Other Conditions." Journal of Nutritional and Environmental Medicine 11 (2001): 275-291.

"Sun Tanning." Cool Nurse 2000-2003. 18 Jun 2003 <http://www.coolnurse.com/tanning.htm.>.

Vogel, Phillip J. "A New Light on Vitamin D." Life Extension 9.4 (Apr 2003): 40-46.

Evaluating the Essay

1. Choose a page of Garrett's research essay, and using a yellow highlighter, mark every line or passage in which she actually *does* something with information rather than simply explain or report what she found. In other words, where does she interpret, argue, analyze, assert, speculate, or evaluate? How much of the page is covered with color?
2. Using Garrett's essay as a model, identify at least one question you have about the proper way to cite sources in a research essay.
3. What is Garrett's thesis and where in the essay does she state it? Did you find it persuasive? Why or why not?

APA Documentation Guidelines

The American Psychological Association's (APA) citation conventions are the other dominant approach to acknowledging sources. If you're headed for courses in the social sciences, then this is the system you'll use. It's no harder than the MLA; in fact, the two systems are quite similar. Both use parenthetical citations. Both organize the bibliography (or References page) in very similar ways. But there are a few significant differences, some of which are summarized in the accompanying table. Detailed descriptions of the APA system then follow.

MLA Versus APA: Some Basic Differences

MLA Approach	APA Approach
(Author page #)—Example:	**(Author, year)—Example:**
`According to Ackerman, there is an infatuation chemical (164).`	`According to Ackerman (1994), there is an infatuation chemical.`
Usually no title page.	Usually title page and abstract. An abstract is a short summary of the paper's content, always less than 120 words in APA style.
Pagination uses writer's last name and page number. For example:	Pagination uses running head and page number. A "running head" is the paper's abbreviated title. For example:
`Smith 5`	`Exporting Jobs 5`
Figures and tables included within the paper.	Figures and tables included in section at the end of the paper.
Bibliography called Works Cited page.	Bibliography called References page.

How the Essay Should Look

Page Format. Papers should be double spaced, with at least one-inch margins on all sides. Number all pages consecutively, beginning with the title page; put the page number in the upper right corner. Above or five spaces to the left of the page number, place an abbreviated title of the paper on every page, in case pages get separated. As a rule, the first line of all paragraphs of text should be indented five to seven spaces.

INQUIRING INTO THE DETAILS

RECENT APA STYLE CHANGES

- Article abstracts should be no longer than 120 words.
- Whenever possible, use italics, rather than underlining.
- When quoting from electronic sources that lack page or paragraph numbers, use chapter or section headings, if available, to pinpoint the location of borrowed material.
- It's okay to use boldface.
- Use the paragraph symbol (¶) or the abbreviation *para.* in the citation to identify the location of borrowed material in an electronic source.
- In the references, list up to six authors. For more than six, list the first six authors then add the abbreviation *et al.*
- Use serif typeface in text, and sans serif in figures, tables, and illustrations.

Source: APA *Publication Manual,* 5th ed.

Title Page. Unlike a paper in MLA style, an APA-style paper has a separate title page, containing the following information: the title of the paper, the author, and the author's affiliation (e.g., what university she is from). Each line of information should be centered and double spaced. See Figure 10.3. At the top of the title page, flush left and in uppercase letters, you may also include a *running head,* or an abbreviation of the title (fifty characters or less, including spaces). A page header, which uses the first two or three words of the title followed by the page number, begins on the title page, too. This is different from the running head, which tends to be longer and appears only on the title page.

Abstract. Although it's not always required, many APA-style papers include a short abstract (no longer than 120 words) following the title page. See Figure 10.4. An abstract is essentially a short summary of the paper's contents. This is a key feature, because it's usually the first thing a reader encounters. The abstract should include statements about what problem or question the paper examines and what approach it follows; the abstract should also cite the thesis and significant findings. Type *Abstract* at the top of the page. Type the abstract text in a single block, without indenting.

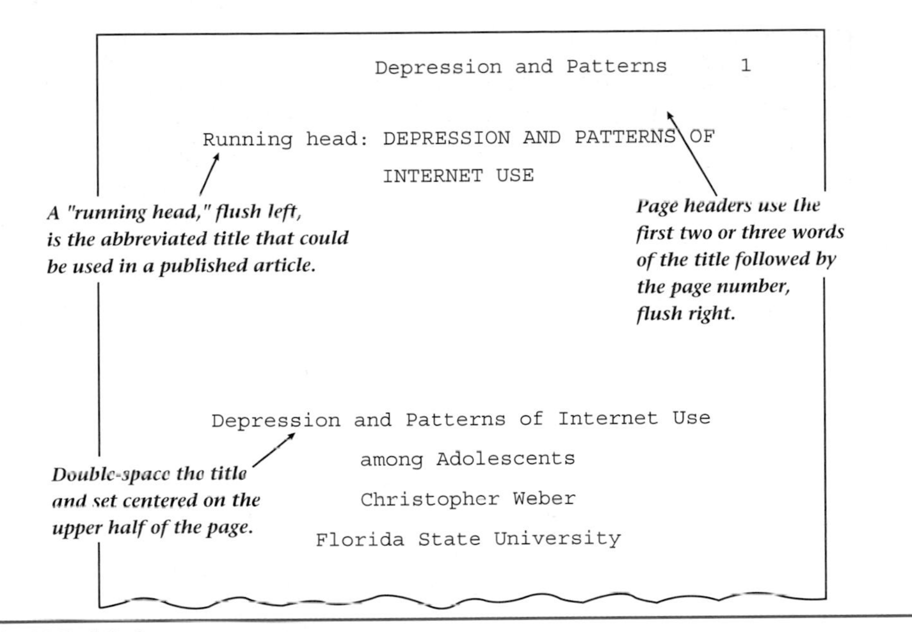

FIGURE 10.3 Title page in APA style.

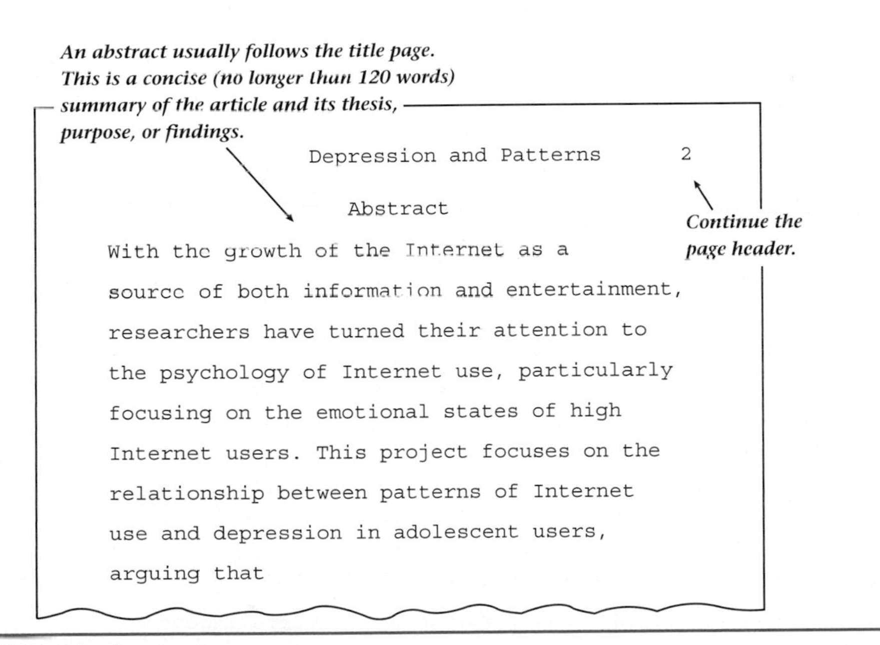

FIGURE 10.4 The abstract page.

Body of the Paper. The body of the paper begins with the centered title, followed by a double space and then the text. A page header (usually an abbreviated title and "3" if the paper has a title page and abstract) should appear in the upper right corner. See Figure 10.5.

Depression and Patterns 3

Depression and Patterns of Internet Use
among Adolescents

Before Johnny Beale's family got a new computer in August 2002, the sixteen-year-old high school student estimated that he spent about twenty minutes a day online, mostly checking his e-mail. Within months, however, Beale's time at the computer tripled, and he admitted that he spent most of his time playing games. At first, his family noticed

Center the title of the paper and double-space to begin the body of the text.

FIGURE 10.5 The body of the paper in APA style.

You may find that you want to use headings within your paper. If your paper is fairly formal, some headings might be prescribed, such as *Introduction, Method, Results,* and *Discussion*. Or create your own heads to clarify the organization of your paper.

If you use headings, the APA recommends a hierarchy like this:

CENTERED UPPERCASE

Centered Upper- and Lowercase

Centered, Italicized, Upper- and Lowercase

Flush Left, Italicized, Upper- and Lowercase

Indented, italicized, initial cap and lowercase; ends with period.

A paper will rarely use all five levels of headings. In fact, for the essays you write in your composition class, you'll likely use no more than two levels, a centered uppercase title, and a centered upper- and lowercase title. For example,

THE INTELLIGENCE OF CROWS

Current Understandings of Crow Intelligence

References Page. All sources cited in the body of the paper are listed alphabetically by author (or title, if anonymous) on the page titled References. See Figure 10.6. This list should begin a new page. Each entry is double spaced; begin each entry flush left, and indent subsequent lines five to seven

Depression and Patterns 10

References

Sanders, C., Tiffany, M., & Diego, M. (2002). The relationship of Internet use to depression and social isolation among adolescents. *Adolescence, 35,* 237-242.

Waestlund, E., Norlander, T., & Archer, T. (2001). Internet blues revisited: Replication and extension of an Internet paradox study. *CyberPsychology & Behavior, 4,* 385-391.

Always start the References on a new page.

Create a five-to seven-space "hanging indent."

FIGURE 10.6 The References page.

spaces. Explanation of how to cite various sources in the references follows in the "Preparing the References List" section.

Appendix. This is a seldom-used feature of an APA-style paper, although you might find it helpful for presenting specific or tangential material that isn't central to the discussion in the body of your paper: a detailed description of a device described in the paper, a copy of a blank survey, or the like. Each item should begin on a separate page and be labeled *Appendix,* followed by *A, B,* and so on, consecutively, if there is more than one item.

Notes. Several kinds of notes might be included in a paper. The most common is *content notes,* or brief commentaries by the writer keyed to superscript numbers in the body of the text. These notes are useful for discussion of key points that are relevant but might be distracting if explored in the text of your paper. Present all notes, numbered consecutively, on a page titled *Footnotes.* Each note should be double spaced. Begin each note with the appropriate superscript number, keyed to the text. Indent each first line five to seven spaces; consecutive lines run the full page measure.

Tables and Figures. The final section of an APA-style paper features tables and figures mentioned in the text. Tables should all be double spaced. Type a table number at the top of the page, flush left. Number tables *Table 1, Table 2,* and so on, corresponding to the order in which they are mentioned in the text. A table may also include a title. Each table should begin on a separate page.

Figures (illustrations, graphs, charts, photographs, drawings) are handled similarly to tables. Each should be titled *Figure* and numbered consecutively.

Captions may be included, but all should be typed on a separate page, clearly labeled *Figure Captions,* and listed in order. For example:

Figure Captions

Figure 1. A photograph taken in the 1930s by Dorothea Lange.

Figure 2. Edward Weston took a series of green pepper photographs like this. This is titled "No. 35."

Language and Style. The APA is comfortable with the italics and bold functions of modern word processors, and underlining is a thing of the past. The guidelines for *italicizing* call for its use when writing the following:

- The title of books, periodicals, and publications that appear on microfilm.
- When using new or specialized terms, but only the first time you use them (e.g., "the authors' *paradox study* of Internet users . . .")
- When citing a phrase, letter, or word as an example (e.g., "the second *a* in *separate* can be remembered by remembering the word *rat*").

The APA calls for quotation marks around the title of an article or book chapter when mentioned in your essay.

Been nagged all your life by the question of whether to spell out numbers or use numerals in APA style? Here, finally, is the answer: numbers less than 10 that aren't precise measurements should be spelled out, and numbers 10 or more should be digits.

Citing Sources in Your Essay

When the Author Is Mentioned in the Text. The author/date system is pretty uncomplicated. If you mention the name of the author in text, simply place the year his work was published in parentheses immediately after his name. For example:

Herrick (1999) argued that college testing was biased against minorities.

When the Author Isn't Mentioned in the Text. If you don't mention the author's name in the text, then include that information parenthetically. For example:

A New Hampshire political scientist (Sundberg, 2004) recently studied the state's presidential primary.

Note that the author's name and the year of her work are separated by a comma.

When to Cite Page Numbers. If the information you're citing came from specific pages, chapters, or sections of a source, that information may also be included in the parenthetical citation. Including page numbers is essential when quoting a source. For example:

> The first stage of language acquisition is called "*caretaker speech*" (Moskowitz, 1985, pp. 50–51), in which children model their parents' language.

The same passage might also be cited this way if the author's name is mentioned in the text:

> Moskowitz (1985) observed that the first stage of language acquisition is called "*caretaker speech*" (pp. 50–51), in which children model their parents' language.

A Single Work by Two or More Authors. When a work has two authors, always mention them both whenever you cite their work in your paper. For example:

> Allen and Oliver (1998) observed many cases of child abuse and concluded that maltreatment inhibited language development.

If a source has more than two authors but less than six, mention them all the first time you refer to their work. However, any subsequent references can include the surname of the first author followed by the abbreviation *et al.* When citing works with six or more authors, *always* use the first author's surname and *et al.*

A Work with No Author. When a work has no author, cite an abbreviated title and the year. Place article or chapter titles in quotation marks, and *italicize* book titles. For example:

> The editorial ("Sinking," 2006) concluded that the EPA was mired in bureaucratic muck.

Two or More Works by the Same Author. Works by the same author are usually distinguished by the date; works are rarely published the same year. But if they are, distinguish among works by adding an *a* or *b* immediately following the year in the parenthetical citation. The reference list will also have these suffixes. For example:

> Douglas's studies (1986a) on the mating habits of lobsters revealed that the females are dominant. He also found that the female lobsters have the uncanny ability to smell a loser (1986b).

This citation alerts readers that the information came from two studies by Douglas, both published in 1986.

An Institutional Author. When citing a corporation or agency as a source, simply list the year of the study in parentheses if you mention the institution in the text:

> The Environmental Protection Agency (2000) issued an alarming report on ozone pollution.

If you don't mention the institutional source in the text, spell it out in its entirety, along with the year. In subsequent parenthetical citations, you can abbreviate the name as long as the abbreviation will be understandable. For example:

```
A study (Environmental Protection Agency [EPA], 2000) predicted dire
consequences from continued ozone depletion.
```

And later:

```
Continued ozone depletion may result in widespread skin cancers (EPA,
2000).
```

Multiple Works in the Same Parentheses. Occasionally, you'll want to cite several works at once that speak to a topic you're writing about in your essay. Probably the most common instance is when you refer to the findings of several relevant studies, something that is a good idea as you try to establish a context for what has already been said about your research topic. For example,

```
A number of researchers have explored the connection between Internet
use and depression (Sanders, Field, & Diego, 2000; Waestlund,
Norlander, & Archer, 2001).
```

When listing multiple authors in the same parenthesis, order them as they appear in the references. Semicolons separate each entry.

Interviews, E-Mail, and Letters. Interviews and other personal communications are not listed in the references at the back of the paper, because they are not *recoverable data,* but they are parenthetically cited in the text. Provide the initials and surname of the subject (if not mentioned in the text), the nature of the communication, and the complete date, if possible.

Nancy Diamonti (personal communication, November 12, 1990) disagrees with the critics of *Sesame Street*.

In a recent e-mail, Michelle Payne (personal communication, January 4, 2000) complained that . . .

New Editions of Old Works. For reprints of older works, include both the year of the original publication and that of the reprint edition (or the translation).

```
Pragmatism as a philosophy sought connection between scientific study
and real people's lives (James, 1906/1978).
```

A Web Site. When referring to an *entire* Web site (see the following example), cite the address parenthetically in your essay. As for e-mail, it isn't necessary to include a citation for an entire Web site in your references list. However, you will cite online documents that contribute information to your paper (see the "Citing Electronic Sources" section).

```
One of the best sites for searching the so-called Invisible Web is the
Librarians Index to the Internet (http://www.lii.org).
```

Preparing the References List

All parenthetical citations in the body of the paper correspond to a complete listing of sources on the References page. The format for this section was described earlier (see the "References Page" section).

Order of Sources. List the references alphabetically by author or by the first key word of the title if there is no author. The only complication may be if you have several articles or books by the same author. If the sources weren't published in the same year, list them in chronological order, the earliest first. If the sources were published in the *same* year, include a lowercase letter to distinguish them. For example:

```
Lane, B. (1991a). Verbal medicine . . .

Lane, B. (1991b). Writing . . .
```

While the alphabetical principle—listing authors according to the alphabetical placement of their last names—works in most cases, there are a few variations you should be aware of.

- If you have several entries by the same author, list them by year of publication, beginning with the earliest.
- Because scholars and writers often collaborate, you may have several references in which an author is listed with several *different* collaborators. List these alphabetically using the second author's last name. For example,

```
Brown, M., & Nelson, A. (2002)
Brown, M., & Payne, M. (1999)
```

Order of Information. A reference to a periodical or book in APA style includes this information, in order: author, date of publication, article title, periodical title, and publication information.

Author. List all authors—last name, comma, and then initials. Invert all authors' names. Use commas to separate authors' names and add an ampersand (&) before the last author's name. When citing an edited book, list the editor(s) in place of the author, and add the abbreviation *Ed.* or *Eds.* in parentheses following the initials. End the list of names with a period.

Date. List the year the work was published, along with the date if it's a magazine or newspaper (see the following "Sample References" section), in parentheses, immediately after the last author's name. Add a period after the closing parenthesis.

Article or Book Title. APA style departs from MLA, at least with respect to periodicals. In APA style, only the first word of the article title is capitalized, and it is not underlined or quoted. Book titles, on the other hand, are italicized; capitalize only the first word of the title and any subtitle. End all titles with periods.

Periodical Title and Publication Information. Italicize the complete periodical title; type it using both uppercase and lowercase letters. Add the volume number (if any), also italicized. Separate the title and volume number with a comma (e.g., *Journal of Mass Communication, 10,* 138–150). If each issue of the periodical starts with page 1, then also include the issue number in parentheses immediately after the volume number (see examples following). End the entry with the page numbers of the article. Use the abbreviation *p.* or *pp.* if you are citing a newspaper. Other APA-style abbreviations include the following:

chap.	p. (pp.)
ed.	Vol.
Rev. ed.	No.
2nd ed.	Pt.
Trans.	Suppl.

For books, list the city and state or country of publication (use postal abbreviations) and the name of the publisher; separate the city and publisher with a colon. End the citation with a period. The following cities do not require state or country abbreviations:

Baltimore	Amsterdam
Boston	Jerusalem
Chicago	London
Los Angeles	Milan
New York	Moscow
Philadelphia	Paris
San Francisco	Rome
	Stockholm
	Tokyo
	Vienna

Remember that the first line of each citation should begin flush left and all subsequent lines should be indented five to seven spaces. Double-space all entries.

Sample References

A JOURNAL ARTICLE

Cite a journal article like this:

Blager, F. B. (1979). The effect of intervention on the speech and language of children. *Child Abuse and Neglect, 5,* 91–96.

In-Text Citations: (Blager, 1979)

If the author is mentioned in the text, just parenthetically cite the year: Blager (1979) stated that . . .

If the author is quoted, include the page number(s):

(Blager, 1979, p. 92)

A JOURNAL ARTICLE NOT PAGINATED CONTINUOUSLY

Most journals begin on page 1 with the first issue of the year and continue paginating consecutively for subsequent issues. A few journals, however, start on page 1 with each issue. For these, include the issue number in parentheses following the volume number:

Williams, J., Post, A. T., & Stunk, F. (1991). The rhetoric of inequality. *Attwanata, 12*(3), 54-67.

First In-Text Citation: (Williams, Post, & Stunk, 1991)

Subsequent citations would use *et al.:* (Williams et al., 1991)

If quoting material, include the page number(s):

(Williams et al., 1991, pp. 55-60)

A MAGAZINE ARTICLE

Maya, P. (1981, December). The civilizing of Genie. *Psychology Today,* 28-34.

In-Text Citations: (Maya, 1981)

Maya (1981) observed that . . .

If quoting, include the page number(s): (Maya, 1981, p. 28)

A NEWSPAPER ARTICLE

Honan, W. (2004, January 24). The war affects Broadway. *New York Times,* pp. C15-16.

In-Text Citations: (Honan, 2004)

Honan (2004) argued that . . .

Honan (2004) said that "Broadway is a battleground" (p. C15).

If there is no author, a common situation with newspaper articles, alphabetize using the first "significant word" in the article title. The parenthetical citation would use an abbreviation of the title in quotation marks, then the year.

A BOOK

Lukas, A. J. (1986). *Common ground: A turbulent decade in the lives of three American families.* New York: Random House.

In-Text Citations: (Lukas, 1986)

According to Lukas (1986), . . .

If quoting, include the page number(s).

A BOOK OR ARTICLE WITH MORE THAN ONE AUTHOR

Rosenbaum, A., & O'Leary, D. (1978). Children: The unintended victims of marital violence. *American Journal of Orthopsychiatry, 4,* 692-699.

In-Text Citations: (Rosenbaum & O'Leary, 1978)

Rosenbaum and O'Leary (1978) believed that . . .

If quoting, include the page number(s).

A BOOK OR ARTICLE WITH AN UNKNOWN AUTHOR

The politics of war. (2004, June 1). *New York Times,* p. 36.

In-Text Citations: ("Politics," 2004)

Or mention the source in the text:

In "The Politics of War" (2004), an editorialist compared Iraq to . . .

If quoting, provide page number(s) as well.

A manual of style (14th ed.). (1993). Chicago: University of Chicago Press.

In-Text Citations: (*Manual of Style,* 1993)

According to the *Manual of Style* (1993), . . .

If quoting, include the page number(s).

A BOOK WITH AN INSTITUTIONAL AUTHOR

American Red Cross. (1999). *Advanced first aid and emergency care.* New York: Doubleday.

In-Text Citations: (*American Red Cross,* 1999)

The book *Advanced First Aid and Emergency Care* (American Red Cross, 1999) stated that . . .

If quoting, include the page number(s).

A BOOK WITH AN EDITOR

Crane, R. S. (Ed.). (1952). *Critics and criticism.* Chicago: University of Chicago Press.

In-Text Citations: (Crane, 1952)

In his preface, Crane (1952) observed that . . .

If quoting, include the page number(s).

A SELECTION IN A BOOK WITH AN EDITOR

McKeon, R. (1952). Rhetoric in the Middle Ages. In R. S. Crane (Ed.), *Critics and criticism* (pp. 260–289). Chicago: University of Chicago Press.

In-Text Citations: (McKeon, 1952)

McKeon (1952) argued that . . .

If quoting, include the page number(s).

A REPUBLISHED WORK

James, W. (1978). *Pragmatism.* Cambridge, MA: Harvard University Press. (Original work published 1907)

In-Text Citations: (James, 1907/1978)

According to William James (1907/1978), . . .

If quoting, include the page number(s).

AN ABSTRACT

The growth of online databases for articles has increased the availability of full-text versions or abstracts of articles. Although the full article is almost always best, sometimes an abstract alone contains some useful information. If the abstract was retrieved from a database or some other secondary source, include information about it. Aside from the name of the source, this information might involve the date, if different from the year of publication of the original article, an abstract number, or a page number. In the following example, the abstract was retrieved from an online database, Biological Abstracts.

Garcia, R. G. (2002). Evolutionary speed of species invasions. *Evolution, 56,* 661–668. Abstract retrieved from Biological Abstracts.

In-Text Citations: (Garcia, 2002), or Garcia (2002) argues that . . .

A SOURCE MENTIONED BY ANOTHER SOURCE

Frequently you'll read an article that mentions another article you haven't read. Whenever possible, track down that original article and read it in its entirety. But when that's not possible, you need to make it clear that you know of the article and its findings or arguments indirectly. The APA convention for this is to use the expression *as cited in* parenthetically, followed by the author and date of the indirect source. For example, suppose you want to use some information from Eric Weiser's piece that you read about in Charlotte Jones's book. In your essay, you would write something like:

Weiser argues (as cited in Jones, 2002) that . . .

It isn't necessary to include information about the Weiser article in your references. Just cite the indirect source; in this case, that would be the Jones book.

A BOOK REVIEW

Dentan, R. K. (1989). A new look at the brain [Review of the book *The dreaming brain*]. *Psychiatric Journal, 13,* 51.

In-Text Citations: (Dentan, 1989)

Dentan (1989) argued that . . .

If quoting, include the page number(s).

A GOVERNMENT DOCUMENT

U.S. Bureau of the Census. (2004). *Statistical abstract of the United States* (126th ed.). Washington, DC: U.S. Government Printing Office.

In-Text Citations: (U.S. Bureau of the Census, 2004)

According to the U.S. Census Bureau (2004), . . .

If quoting, include the page number(s).

A LETTER TO THE EDITOR

Hill, A. C. (2006, February 19). A flawed history of blacks in Boston [Letter to the editor]. *The Boston Globe,* p. 22.

In-Text Citations: (Hill, 2006)

Hill (2006) complained that . . .

If quoting, include page number(s).

A PUBLISHED INTERVIEW

Personal interviews are not cited in the References section of an APA-style paper, unlike published interviews. Here is a citation for a published interview:

Cotton, P. (2004, April). [Interview with Jake Tule, psychic]. *Chronicles Magazine,* 24–28.

In-Text Citations: (Cotton, 2004)

Cotton (2004) noted that . . .

If quoting, include the page number(s).

A FILM OR VIDEOTAPE

Hitchcock, A. (Producer & Director). (1954). *Rear window* [Motion Picture]. Los Angeles: MGM.

In-Text Citations: (Hitchcock, 1954)

In *Rear Window,* Hitchcock (1954) . . .

A TELEVISION PROGRAM

Burns, K. (Executive Producer). (1996). *The west* [Television broadcast]. New York and Washington, DC: Public Broadcasting Service.

In-Text Citations: (Burns, 1996)

In Ken Burns's (1996) film, . . .

For an episode of a television series, use the scriptwriter as the author, and provide the director's name after the scriptwriter. List the producer's name after the episode.

Hopley, J. (Writer/Director), & Shannon, J. (Writer/Director). (2006). Buffalo burrito/Parkerina [Television series episode]. In J. Lenz (Producer), *Mr. Meaty.* New York: Nickelodeon.

In-Text Citations: (Hopley & Shannon, 2006)

Fans were appalled by the second episode, when Hopley and Shannon (2006) . . .

A MUSICAL RECORDING

Wolf, K. (1986). Muddy roads [Recorded by E. Clapton]. On *Gold in California* [CD]. Santa Monica, CA: Rhino Records. (1990)

In-Text Citations: (Wolf, 1986, track 5)

In Wolf's (1986) song, . . .

A COMPUTER PROGRAM

OmniPage Pro 14 (Version 14) [Computer software]. (2003). Peabody, MA: Scansoft.

In-Text Citation: (OmniPage Pro, Version 14, 2003)

Scansoft's new software, OmniPage Pro, (2003) is reputed . . .

Citing Electronic Sources. The ever-changing Internet is forcing continual change on professional organizations such as the APA. The fifth edition of the group's *Publication Manual* significantly expanded instructions on how to cite electronic sources, largely reflecting the growth in the variety of documents on the Web. The APA's Web page, *http://www.apastyle.org,* includes some excerpted information from the *Publication Manual* and is a good source of news for any new changes in documentation methods. But much of what you need to know can be found here. The key in any citation is to help readers find the original sources if they want to, and for Web-based documents, that means the Internet address (the *URL*), has to be accurate. The copy-and-paste function of your word-processing program will be your ally in this.

The essential information when citing an electronic source, in order, includes the following:

- The author(s), if indicated
- The title of the document, Web page, or newsgroup
- A date of publication, update, or retrieval
- The Internet address, or URL

Sample Electronic Sources

AN ELECTRONIC VERSION OF AN ARTICLE ALSO IN PRINT

Because so much scholarly information on the Web is simply an electronic version of an article published in print, some of what you cite will simply list the conventional bibliographic information for any periodical article. But if you viewed only an electronic version, you must indicate that in your citation. For example,

Codrescu, A. (March, 2002). Curious? Untouchable porcelain meets fluttering pigeons [Electronic version]. *Smithsonian, 104.*

In-Text Citation: (Codrescu, 2002), or Codrescu (2002) believes that . . .

If you suspect that the electronic version of an article that appeared in print has been or will be changed in any way, then you should include the date you retrieved the article from the Web and the URL of the document. For example,

Ballenger, B. (1999). Befriending the Internet. *The Curious Researcher,* 59–76. Retrieved July 18, 2002, from http://english.boisestate.edu/bballenger

In-Text Citation: (Ballenger, 1999) *or* Ballenger (1999) features an exercise . . .

AN ARTICLE ONLY ON THE INTERNET

Pearce, F. (2006). Doomsday scenario. *New Scientist.* Retrieved August 30, 2006, from http://www.newscientist.com/channel/earth/climate-change/mg18024225.300

In-Text Citations: (Pearce, 2006)

According to Pearce (2006) . . .

If quoting, include page number(s).

AN ELECTRONIC TEXT

Encyclopedia mythica. (2006). Retrieved December 1, 2006, from http://www.pantheon.org/myth

In-Text Citations: (*Encyclopedia Mythica,* 2006)

The *Encyclopedia Mythica* (2006) presents . . .

If the text is an electronic version of a book published in print earlier, include the original publication date in parentheses following the title: (Original work published 1908).

AN ARTICLE OR ABSTRACT FROM A LIBRARY DATABASE

As mentioned earlier, library databases, often accessed online, increasingly offer not just citations of articles, but full-text versions of abstracts, too. This wonderful service can make a trip to the library superfluous. When citing an article or abstract from a database, simply include the name of the database at the end of the citation followed by a period.

Ullman, S., & Brecklin, L. (2002). Sexual assault history and suicidal behavior in a national sample of women. *Suicide and Life Threatening Behavior, 32,* 117–130. Retrieved October 18, 2002, from Electronic Collections Online database.

In-Text Citations: (Ullman & Brecklin, 2002), or if you like Ullman and Brecklin (2002) argue that . . .

An abstract from an electronic database is cited much the same way except to clarify that the source *is* an abstract. For example,

Warm, A., & Murray, C. (2002). Who helps? Supporting people who self harm. *Journal of Mental Health, 11,* 121–130. Abstract retrieved July 19, 2002, from PsycINFO database.

In-Text Citations: (Warm & Murray, 2002), or According to Warm and Murray (2002) . . .

A PART OF A WORK

Hunter, J. (n.d.). Achilles. In *Encyclopedia mythica.* Retrieved January 4, 2000, from http://www.pantheon.org/myth/achill

In-Text Citations: (Hunter, n.d.)

According to Hunter (no date), Achilles was . . .

If quoting, include the page or paragraph number(s), if any.

AN ONLINE JOURNAL

Schneider, M. (1998). The nowhere man and mother nature's son: Collaboration and resentment in the lyrical ballads of the Beatles. *Anthropoetics, 4*(2), 1-11. Retrieved November 24, 1999, from http://www.humnet.ucla.edu/humnet/anthropoetics/ap0402/utopia.htm

In-Text Citations: (Schneider, 1998)

Schneider (1998) recently observed that . . .

If quoting, include page or paragraph numbers, if any.

A NEWSPAPER ARTICLE

It's not hard anymore to find articles online from all the major American and even international newspapers. As for other nonscholarly periodicals, include more specific information about date of publication in the parentheses following the author's name, and as usual include the date retrieved and the URL.

Broad, J. W. (2002, July 18). Piece by piece a Civil War battleship is pulled from the sea. *New York Times.* Retrieved July 18, 2002, from http://www.nytimes.com

In-Text Citations: (Broad, 2002) or Broad (2002) reports that . . .

A WEB SITE

If you're referring to an entire Web site in the text of your essay, include the address parenthetically. However, there is no need to include it in the reference list. For example:

One of the best sites for searching the so-called Invisible Web is the Librarians Index to the Internet (http://www.lii.org).

DISCUSSION LISTS

Discussion lists abound on the Internet. They range from groups of flirtatious teenagers to those with a serious academic purpose. Although virtually all of these discussion lists are based on e-mail, they do vary a bit. The most useful lists for academic research tend to be e-mail discussion lists. Newsgroups, or Usenet groups, are extremely popular among more general Internet users. Various search engines can help you find these discussion groups on your topic. You can join or monitor the current discussion or, in some cases, search the archives for contributions that interest you. Google is a great search tool for newsgroups and includes an archive for many of them. *If there are no archives, don't include the citation in your references because the information isn't recoverable.* However, you may still cite these in your essay as a personal communication.

The method of citation varies slightly if it's a newsgroup, an online forum, or an electronic mailing list. For example, a newsgroup posting would be cited like this:

Hord, J. (2002, July 11). Why do pigeons lift one wing up in the air? [Msg 5]. Message posted to rec.pets.birds.pigeons

In-Text Citations: (Hord, 2002), or Hord asks (2002) . . .

Note that the citation includes the subject line of the message as the title, and the message number of the "thread" (the particular discussion topic). The prefix for this newsgroup is *rec,* which indicates the list is hobby oriented.

Electronic mailing lists would be cited this way:

Cook, D. (2002, July 19). Grammar and the teaching of writing. Message posted to the CompTalk electronic mailing list, archived at http://listserv.comptalk.boisestate.edu

In-Text Citations: (Cook, 2002), or According to Cook (2002) . . .

E-MAIL

E-mail is not cited in the list of references. But you should cite e-mail in the text of your essay. It should look like this:

In-Text Citations: Michelle Payne (personal communication, January 4, 2000) believes that PDAs are silly . . .

CD-ROM DATABASES AND ENCYCLOPEDIAS

Cite a CD-based database like an online database, including the retrieval date. For example:

Drugs and drug interaction. (1999). *Encyclopaedia Britannica.* Retrieved July 5, 2000, from Encyclopaedia Britannica database.

In-Text Citation: ("Drugs and Drug Interaction," 1999)

Kolata, G. (1996, July 10). Research links writing style to the risk of Alzheimer's. *New York Times.* Retrieved from UMI-ProQuest/Newspaper Abstracts database.

In-Text Citation: (Kolata, 1996)

A Sample Paper in APA Style

For an example of a professional essay formatted using APA style, see "A Research Proposal: Effect of Infant's Perceived Gender" by Julie Ann Hamutoff in Chapter 6.

Using What You Have Learned

The main message you should take from this chapter is that if you don't make the effort to control your sources, your sources will control you, with results ranging from writing that fails to deliver on its promise to accidental plagiarism.

1. List three ways that you can control sources in a research essay so that they don't control you.
2. The concern about plagiarism is growing, and most blame the Internet. Do you agree with both of those premises—that plagiarism is a bigger problem and the Internet is the cause?
3. You won't always be required to cite sources for papers in other classes. In fact, you've probably noticed that some articles in more popular periodicals don't cite information at all, even though the work is clearly a product of research. How do you explain this?

Rewriting necessarily involves some time staring off into space. But the work gets done much more quickly when you're *doing* things—exploring different beginnings, fastwriting in your journal about what seems to be working and what needs work, talking to someone about your topic or ideas, doing fresh research, or pruning sentences to make your writing clear. Revision is work. But it's also an opportunity for surprise. The trick is to see what you have written in ways you haven't seen before.

Revision Strategies

11

What You'll Learn in This Chapter

- How genuine revision involves exactly that: revision, or *re-seeing* your topic.
- Basic revision strategies for "divorcing the draft."
- How to become a reader of your own work.
- The five categories of revision.
- Advanced revision strategies.

RE-SEEING YOUR TOPIC

"I don't really revise," Amy told me the other day. "I'm usually pretty happy with my first draft."

Always? I wondered.

"Well, certainly not always," she said. "But I know I work better under pressure so I usually write my papers right before they're due. There usually isn't much time for revision, even if I wanted to do it, which I don't, really."

Amy is pretty typical. Her first-draft efforts usually aren't too bad, but I often sense tentativeness in her prose, endings that seem much stronger than beginnings, and promises that aren't really kept. Her essay promises to focus on the dangers of genetically engineered foods to teenagers who live on Cheeze-Its and Cheetos, but she never quite gets to saying much about that. The writing is competent—pretty clear and without too many awkward passages—but ultimately it's disappointing to read.

You can guess what I'm getting at here—Amy's work could be much stronger if it were rewritten—but the logic of last-minute writing is pretty powerful: "I really think I need to bump up against a deadline."

The writing process has three phases: prewriting, drafting, and rewriting. Prewriting refers to a range of activities writers might engage in before they attempt to compose a first draft, including fastwriting, listing, clustering, rehearsing lines or passages, preliminary research, conversations, or even the kind of deep thought about a topic that for some of us seems to occur best in the shower. The drafting stage is hardly mysterious. It often involves the much slower, much more focused process of putting words to paper, crafting a draft that presumably grows from some of the prewriting activities. Rewriting is a rethinking of that draft. Although this typically involves tweaking sentences, it's much more than that. Revision, as the name implies, is a *re-seeing* of the paper's topic and the writer's initial approach to it in the draft.

Revision, as the name implies, is a re-seeing *of the paper's topic and the writer's initial approach to it in the draft.*

DIVORCING THE DRAFT

Sometimes I ask my students to generalize about how they approach the writing process for most papers by asking them to divide a continuum into three parts corresponding to how much time, roughly, they devote to prewriting, drafting, and rewriting. Then I play "writing doctor" and diagnose their problems, particularly resistance to revision. Figure 11.1 below depicts a typical example for most of my first-year writing students:

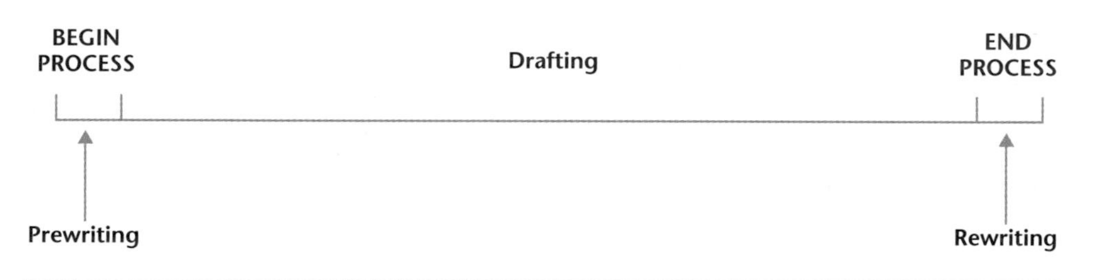

FIGURE 11.1 How some writers who resist revision typically divide their time between the three elements of the writing process: prewriting, drafting, and rewriting. The most time is devoted to writing the first draft, but not much time is given to prewriting and rewriting.

The writing process shown in Figure 11.1 obviously invests lots of time in the drafting stage and very little time in prewriting or rewriting. For most of my students, this means toiling over the first draft, starting and then starting over, carefully hammering every word into place. For students who use this process, strong resistance to revision is a typical symptom. It's easy to imagine why. If you invest all that time in the first draft, trying to make it as good as you can, you'll be either too exhausted to consider a revision, delusional about the paper's quality, or, most likely, so invested in the draft's approach to the topic that revision seems impossible or a waste of time.

There also is another pattern among resistant revisers. Students who tend to spend a relatively long time on the prewriting stage also struggle with revision. My theory is that some of these writers resist revision as a final stage in the process because *they have already practiced some revision at the beginning of the process.* We often talk about revision as occurring only after you've written a draft, which of course is a quite sensible idea. But the process of revision is an effort to *re-see* a subject, to circle it with questions, to view it from fresh angles, and many of the open-ended writing methods we've discussed in *The Curious Writer* certainly involve revision. Fastwriting, clustering, listing, and similar invention techniques all invite the writer to re-see. Armed with these discoveries, some writers may be able to write fairly strong first drafts.

What is essential, however, whether you revise at the beginning of the writing process or, as most writers do, after you craft the draft, is achieving some separation from what you initially thought, what you initially said, and how you said it. To revise well, writers must divorce the draft.

Writing with Computers

WHEN YOUR COMPUTER MAKES IT HARD TO DIVORCE A DRAFT

Divorcing yourself from a draft can be more difficult with a computer. The polished look of text on the screen and in printouts can give you a false sense of completion. After all, the text looks as clean and crisp as a published book or magazine. Because of this polished look, you may limit yourself to editorial changes instead of conducting actual revision. Additionally, because the computer makes it easy to copy, move, delete, insert, and preview multiple arrangements of text, it is easy to think of revision as only a process of rearranging the existing text. Because of this flexibility, writers tend to limit themselves to working only with what is already on the screen. Keep in mind that it may not be possible to repair a passage without writing new material. Being completely divorced from the draft means that you are willing to completely re-envision a sentence, paragraph, or even the whole project and compose completely new material. If a sentence or paragraph doesn't work, open a new document and try a new approach to communicate the same idea. You might be surprised how much more effective starting from scratch can be.

STRATEGIES FOR DIVORCING THE DRAFT

You can do some things to make separation from your work easier, and spending less time on the first draft and more time on the revision process is one of them. But aside from writing fast drafts, what are other strategies for re-seeing a draft that already has a hold on you?

1. **Take some time.** Absolutely the best remedy for revision resistance is setting the draft aside for a week or more. Professional writers, in fact, may set a piece aside for several years and then return to it with a fresh, more critical perspective. Students simply don't have that luxury. But if you can take a week or a month—or even a day—the wait is almost always worth it.

2. **Attack the draft physically.** A cut-and-paste revision that reduces a draft to pieces is often enormously helpful because you're no longer confronted with the familiar full draft, a version that may have cast a spell on you. By dismembering the draft, you can examine the smaller fragments more critically. How does each piece relate the whole? Might there be alternative structures? What about gaps in information? (See Revision Strategy 11.17 later in this chapter for a useful cut-and-paste exercise.)

3. **Put it away.** Years ago I wrote a magazine article about alcoholism. It was about 25 pages long and it wasn't very good. I read and reread that draft, completely

puzzled about how to rewrite it. One morning, I woke up and vowed I would read the draft just once more, then put it away in a drawer and start all over again, trusting that I would remember what was important. The result was much shorter and much better. In fact, I think it's the best essay I've ever written. Getting a troublesome draft out of sight—literally—may be the best way to find new ways to see it.

4. **Ask readers to respond.** Bringing other people's eyes and minds to your work allows you to see your drafts through perspectives other than your own. Other people have a completely different relationship with your writing than you do. They will see what you don't. They easily achieve the critical distance that you are trying to cultivate when you revise.

5. **Write different leads.** The nonfiction writer John McPhee once talked about beginnings as the hardest thing to write. He described a lead as a "flashlight that shines down into the story," illuminating where the draft is headed. Imagine, then, the value of writing a new beginning, or even several alternative beginnings; each may point the next draft in a slightly different direction, perhaps one that you didn't consider in your first draft.

6. **Conduct research.** One of the central themes of *The Curious Writer* is that research isn't a separate activity but a source of information that can enrich almost any kind of writing. Particularly in genres such as the personal essay, in which the writer's voice, perspective, and experience dominate the draft, listening to the voices and knowledge of others about a topic can deepen and shift the writer's thinking and perspectives.

7. **Read aloud.** I often ask students in workshop groups to read their drafts aloud to each other. I do this for several reasons, but the most important is the effect that *hearing* a draft has on a writer's relationship to it. In a sense, we often hear a draft in our heads as we compose it or reread it, but when we read the words aloud the draft comes alive as something separate from the writer. As the writer listens to herself—or listens to someone else read her prose—she may cringe at an awkward sentence, suddenly notice a leap in logic, or recognize the need for an example. Try reading the work aloud to yourself and the same thing may happen.

8. **Write in your journal.** One of the strategies you can use to divorce the draft is to return to your notebook and fastwrite to yourself about what you might do to improve the piece. You can do this by asking yourself questions about the draft and then—through writing—attempt to answer them. The method can help you see a new idea that may become key to the structure of your next draft. Too often we see the journal exclusively as a prewriting tool, but it can be useful throughout the writing process, particularly when you need to think to yourself about ways to solve a problem in revision.

Later in this chapter, we'll build on some of these basic strategies with specific revision methods that may work with particular kinds of writing and with drafts that have particular problems. All of these methods encourage a separation between the writer and his or her draft or rely on that critical distance to be effective.

FIVE CATEGORIES OF REVISION

The following are some characteristics of writers who most need to revise:

1. Writers of fast drafts
2. Writers who compose short drafts
3. Writers who indulge in creative, but not critical, thinking
4. Writers who rarely go past their initial way of seeing things
5. Writers who have a hard time imagining a reader other than themselves
6. Writers who rely on limited sources of information
7. Writers who still aren't sure what they're trying to say
8. Writers who haven't found their own way of saying what they want to say
9. Writers who haven't delivered on their promises
10. Writers who think their draft is "perfect"

These are the usual suspects for revision, but there are many more. In general, if you think there's more to think about, more to learn, more to say, and better ways to say it, then revision is the route to surprise and discovery. Most writers agree that rewriting is a good idea, but where should they start?

Problems in drafts vary enormously. But the diagnosis tends to involve concerns in five general areas: purpose, meaning, information, structure, and clarity and style. Here are some typical reader responses to drafts with each kind of problem:

1. **Problems with Purpose**
   - "I don't know why the writer is writing this paper."
   - "The beginning of the essay seems to be about one thing, and the rest of it is about several others."
   - "I think there are about three different topics in the draft. Which one do you want to write about?"
   - "So what?"
2. **Problems with Meaning**
   - "I can't tell what the writer is trying to say in the draft."
   - "There doesn't seem to be a point behind all of this."
   - "I think there's a main idea, but there isn't much information on it."
   - "I thought the thesis was pretty obvious."
3. **Problems with Information**
   - "Parts of the draft seemed really pretty vague or general."
   - "I couldn't really *see* what you were talking about."
   - "It seemed like you needed some more facts to back up your point."
   - "It needs more detail."

4. **Problems with Structure**
   - "I couldn't quite follow your thinking in the last few pages."
   - "I was confused about when this happened."
   - "I understood your point but I couldn't figure out what this part had to do with it."
   - "The draft doesn't really flow very well."
5. **Problems with Clarity and Style**
   - "This seems a little choppy."
   - "You need to explain this better. I couldn't quite follow what you were saying in this paragraph."
   - "This sentence seems really awkward to me."
   - "This doesn't have a strong voice."

PROBLEMS OF PURPOSE

When you're fulfilling a specific writing assignment for a class—for instance, you are instructed to write on the question, *What were the initial causes of U.S. intervention in Vietnam?*—then you begin, knowing your purpose. Essay exams are a familiar example of this. But more often, even if you've been assigned a topic, one of the early challenges of the writing process is to discover how you're going to answer the *So what?* question. Why exactly are you writing about this? (And you can't answer, "Because I have to.") Quite simply, readers need a reason to read, and if the writer doesn't supply them with one then they'll be understandably frustrated and bored.

It's a little like riding a tandem bike. The writer sits up front and steers while the reader occupies the seat behind, obligated to pedal but with no control over where the bike goes. As soon as the reader senses that the writer isn't steering anywhere in particular, then the reader will get off the bike. Why do all that pedaling if the bike seems to be going nowhere?

Frequently, when you begin writing about something, you don't have any idea where you're headed; that's exactly *why* you're writing about the subject in the first place. When we write such discovery drafts, revision often begins by looking for clues about your purpose. What you learn then becomes a key organizing principle for the next draft, trying to clarify this purpose to your readers. The first question, therefore, is one writers must answer for themselves: "Why am I writing this?" Of course, if it's an assignment it's hard to get past the easy answer—"Because I have to"—but if the work is going to be any good there must be a better answer than that. Whether your topic is open or assigned, you have to find your own reason to write about it, and what you discover becomes an answer to your bike partner's nagging question, yelled into the wind from the seat behind you: "If I'm going to pedal this hard, you better let me know where we're going."

In general, the motives behind writing reflect the four ways of inquiring, but writing can and often does involve more than one of these following four purposes.

1. **To explore.** One way to handle complicated questions is to approach the answers in an open-ended way; the writer writes to discover what he thinks or how he feels and reports to the reader on these discoveries.

2. **To explain.** Much of the writing we encounter in daily life is meant simply to provide us with information: This is how the coffeemaker works or this is the best way to prepare for a trip to New Zealand. Expository writing frequently explains and describes.

3. **To evaluate.** In a sense, all writing is evaluative because it involves making judgments. For instance, when you explain how to plan a New Zealand vacation, you're making judgments about where to go. But when the explicit purpose is to present a judgment about something, the writer encourages readers to see the world the way the writer does. He or she may want the reader to think or behave a certain way: It makes sense to abolish pennies because they're more trouble than they're worth, or you should vote for the bond issue because it's the best way to save the foothills.

4. **To reflect.** Less frequently, we write to stand back from what we're writing about and consider *how* we're thinking about the subject, the methods we're using to write about it, and what we might learn from this writing situation that might apply to others.

Revision Strategy 11.1: What's Your Primary Motive?

It may help to begin revision by attempting to determine your *primary motive* for the next draft. Do you want to explore your topic, explain something to your readers, offer a persuasive judgment, or step back and reflect on what you're saying or how you're saying it? The genre of writing has a great deal to do with this (see the following table). If you're writing a personal essay, your purpose is likely to be exploratory. If you're writing a review, a proposal, a critical essay, or an argument essay, it's likely your primary motives are to evaluate. One way, then, to get some basic guidance for the next draft is to carefully craft the second half of the following sentence: *My primary motive in writing this paper is to explore/evaluate/explain/reflect about ________.*

Genre	Primary Motives
Personal essay	Explore
Profile	Explore or explain
Review	Evaluate
Proposal	Evaluate
Argument	Evaluate
Critical essay	Evaluate
Ethnographic essay	Explore or evaluate
Research essay	Explore or evaluate
Reflective essay	Reflect

Of course, any one essay may involve all four motives, but for the purpose of this exercise, choose your *main* purpose in writing the essay. Composing the second half of the sentence may not be so easy because it challenges you to limit your subject. For instance, the following is far too ambitious for, say, a five-page essay: *My main motive in writing this paper is to evaluate the steps taken to deal with terrorism and judge whether they're adequate.* That's simply too big a subject for a brief persuasive paper. This is more reasonable: *My main motive in writing this paper is to evaluate passenger screening procedures in Europe and decide whether they're better than those in the United States.*

Since largely exploratory pieces often are motivated by questions, a writer of a personal essay might compose the following sentence: *My main motive in writing this essay is to explore why I felt relieved when my father died.*

After you craft your motive sentence, put it on a piece of paper or index card and post it where you can see it as you revise the draft. Periodically ask yourself, *What does this paragraph or this section of the draft have to do with my main motive?* The answer will help you decide what to cut and what needs more development in the next draft. Remember, the essay should be organized around this motive from beginning to end.

Revision Strategy 11.2: What Do You Want to Know About What You Learned?

Because inquiry-based writing is usually driven by questions rather than answers, one way to discover your purpose in a sketch or draft is to generate a list of questions it raises for you. Of course, you hope that one of them might be behind your purpose in the next draft. Try the following steps with a draft that needs a stronger sense of purpose.

1. Choose a draft or sketch you'd like to revise, and reread it.
2. On the back of the manuscript, craft an answer to the following question: *What do I understand about this topic now that I didn't understand before I started writing about it?*
3. Next, if you can, build a list of questions—perhaps new ones—that this topic still raises for you. Make this list as long as you can, and don't censor yourself (see the following "One Student's Response").
4. Choose one or more of the questions as a prompt for a fastwrite. Follow your writing to see where it leads and what it might suggest about new directions for the revision.
5. If you can't think of any questions, or find you didn't learn much from writing about the topic (step 2), you may have several options. One is to abandon the draft altogether. Is it possible that this topic simply doesn't interest you anymore? If abandoning the draft isn't possible, then you need to find a new angle. Try Revision Strategy 11.3.

Revision Strategy 11.3: Finding the Focusing Question

The best topics, and the most difficult to write about, are those that raise questions for you. In a sketch or first draft, you may not know what these questions are. But if your subsequent drafts are going to be purposeful and focused, then discovering the main question behind your essay is essential. This is particularly important in essays that are research based because the drafts are longer and you're often trying to manage a lot of information. This revision strategy works best when it's a class activity.

1. Begin by simply putting your essay topic on the top of a large piece of paper such as newsprint or butcher paper. If yours is a research topic—say, Alzheimer's disease—jot that down. Post your paper on the classroom wall.

2. Spend a few minutes writing a few sentences explaining why you chose to write about this topic in the first place.

3. Make a quick list of everything you *already know* (if anything) about your topic—for instance, surprising facts or statistics, the extent of the problem, important people or institutions involved, key schools of thought, common misconceptions, familiar clichés that apply to the topic, observations you've made, important trends, and typical perspectives. Spend about five minutes on this.

4. Now spend fifteen or twenty minutes brainstorming a list of questions about your topic that you'd love to learn the answers to. Make this list as long as possible.

5. As you look around the room, you'll see a gallery of topics and questions on the walls. You can help each other. Circulate around the room and do two things: add a question that you're interested in about a particular topic, and check the question (yours or someone else's) that seems most interesting.

ONE STUDENT'S RESPONSE

JULIA'S DRAFT

What do I understand about this topic now that I didn't understand before I started writing about it?

After writing this essay, I understand more clearly that there's a relationship between a girl's eating disorders and how her father treats her as a child.

LIST OF QUESTIONS

- Why the father and not the mother?
- What is it about father/daughter relationships that make them so vulnerable to feminine body images?
- Is the father's influence on a girl's body image greater at certain ages or stages in her life?
- How can a father be more informed about his impact on a daughter's body image?

When you return to your newsprint or butcher paper, it should be covered with questions. How will you decide which of them might provide the best focus for the next draft? Consider the following criteria as you try to make this decision:

- **What question do *you* find most intriguing?** After all, it's your essay, and it should be driven by your own interests in the subject.
- **Which question seems most manageable?** This mostly has to do with the level of generality or specificity of the question. You want a focusing question that isn't too general or too specific. For example, a question such as *What causes international terrorism?* is a landscape question—it contains so much possible territory that you'll never get a close look at anything. But a question such as *How effective has the Saudi royal family been in limiting terrorist activities?* is a much more focused, and therefore manageable, question.
- **What question seems most appropriate for the assignment?** For example, if you're assigned a research essay, certain questions are more likely than others to send you to the library. If you're writing a persuasive essay, gravitate toward a question that might point you toward a claim or thesis.
- **What seems most relevant to the information you've already collected?** It would be convenient if information from your research or first draft is relevant to the question that's behind the next draft. While this might make the revision go more quickly, always be open to the possibility that a question that takes you in new directions might simply be more interesting to you.
- **What question is likely to yield answers that interest your readers?** You already have a sense of this from the questions that students in your class added to your newsprint about your topic. The challenge in any piece of writing, of course, is to answer the *So what?* question. Does your focusing question promise to lead you somewhere that readers would care to go?

Revision Strategy 11.4: What's the Relationship?

One of the more common purposes for all kinds of essays is to explore a relationship between two or more things. We see this in research all the time. What's the relationship between AIDS and IV drug use in China? What's the relationship between gender and styles of collaboration in the workplace? What's the social class relationship between Huck and Tom in *The Adventures of Huckleberry Finn?*

One way, then, to clarify your purpose in revision is to try to identity the relationship that may be at the heart of your inquiry. Relationships between things can be described in several different ways.

- **Cause and effect.** What is the relationship between my father's comments about my looks and my eating disorder when I was a teenager? What is the relationship between the second Iraqi war and destabilization in

Saudi Arabia? What is the relationship between the decline of the Brazilian rain forest and the extinction of the native eagles? What is the relationship between my moving to Idaho and the failure of my relationship with Kevin?

- **Compare and contrast.** How is jealousy distinguished from envy? How might writing instruction in high school be distinguished from writing instruction in college? What are the differences and similarities between my experiences at the Rolling Stones concert last month and my experiences at the Stones concert fifteen years ago?

Review your sketch or draft to determine whether what you're really trying to write about is the relationship between two (or more) things. In your journal, try to state this relationship in sentences similar to those listed here. With this knowledge, return to the draft and revise from beginning to end with this purpose in mind. What do you need to add to the next draft to both clarify and develop the relationship you're focusing on? What should you cut that is irrelevant to that focus?

PROBLEMS WITH MEANING

Fundamentally, most of us write something in an attempt to say something to someone else. The note my wife Karen left for me yesterday said it in a sentence: "Bruce—could you pick up some virgin olive oil and a loaf of bread?" I had no trouble deciphering the meaning of this note. But it isn't always that easy. Certain poems, for example, may be incredibly ambiguous texts, and readers may puzzle over them for hours, coming up with a range of plausible interpretations of meaning.

Implicit or Explicit Meaning

Two broad categories of writing are texts that embody *implicit* or *explicit* meaning. Certain literary forms such as poems or short stories are often implicit—writers may not step forward and say what they mean—while much nonfiction prose (although some of it, like the essay, is also literary) may be much more explicit.

College writing is almost always explicit in meaning, and one of the most common complaints I hear about student writing is that it's not explicit enough. Recently, the theater faculty at my university told me that their Theater 101 students have difficulty producing writing that has a clear thesis. "Some of them have never even heard the word," one professor told me. *Thesis,* of course, is only one (scientific) term to describe how meaning can be expressed in a piece of writing. Other terms include *main point, theme, controlling idea,* and *central claim* or *assertion.* I've used some of these words interchangeably in *The Curious Writer* because they basically mean pretty much the same thing: *Most well-written essays have a single dominant meaning that should be clear to the reader.*

In certain genres of academic writing, the thesis is stated very early on in a paper. This was true, for example, of the essays the theater faculty asked students to write in their 101 class. This kind of essay is often called the *thesis/support*

Terms to Describe Dominant Meaning

- Thesis
- Main point
- Theme
- Controlling idea
- Central claim or assertion

paper, and the basic structure is probably familiar to you: Say what you're going to say, say it with supporting evidence, and say it again to conclude.

Other genres, including the personal and even some persuasive essays, may follow a less formal structure, working their way less directly to an important idea or point. Such essays may have a delayed thesis that appears toward the end of the piece. But make no mistake—*all* essays have some kind of controlling idea or question at their hearts. An essay that fails to make that meaning clear will frustrate the reader because the essay will seem pointless.

Looking Beyond the Obvious

Sketches and first drafts often have problems with meaning. Frequently they are written because their authors are trying to discover what they want to say. These discovery drafts then provide guidance about what that meaning might be, and the revision then will be more focused and more explicit about meaning. The challenge, of course, is learning how to read your drafts for clues about your thesis or main idea.

However, sometimes the problem isn't so much that you don't know what you're trying to say as that what you're saying seems obvious. Clichés, conventional wisdoms, or broad generalizations are typical examples of this. You're writing about the performance you saw of Tennessee Williams's *A Streetcar Named Desire* and your draft's thesis is something like, "This was a really sad play." Okay, true . . . but that's pretty obvious. Or perhaps you're writing about losing touch with your childhood buddy, and in the last paragraph of your essay you write, "True friends are hard to find." Well, that sounds familiar. Isn't there more to say that might be a little less obvious?

The revision strategies that follow address each of these problems separately. Featured first are techniques that should help you discover what you're trying to say in a sketch or draft when you're not sure. These are followed by techniques that will help you refine a thesis or theme to make it more insightful (and less obvious) or more accurate and truthful.

Methods for Discovering Your Thesis

Use the following strategies if you're not quite sure whether you know what you're trying to say in a sketch or draft. How can you discover clues about your main point or meaning in what you've already written?

Revision Strategy 11.5: Find the "Instructive Line"

It may seem odd to think of reading your own drafts for clues about what you mean. After all, your writing is a product of your own mind. But often a draft can reveal to us what we didn't know we knew—an idea that surfaces unexpectedly, a question that we keep asking, or a moment in a narrative that seems surprisingly significant. Part of the challenge is to recognize these clues to your own meanings, and understand what they suggest about the revision.

This isn't always easy, which is one reason it's often so helpful to share your writing with other readers; they may see the clues that we miss. However, this revision strategy depends on reading your own drafts more systematically for clues about what your point might be. What do you say in this draft that might suggest what you really want to say in the next one?

1. **Find the "instructive line."** Every draft is made up of many sentences. But which of these is *the most important sentence or passage?* What do I mean by *important?* Which line or passage points to a larger idea, theme, or feeling that seems to rise above much of the draft and illuminates the significance or relevance of many other lines and passages? The writer Donald Murray calls this the "instructive line," the sentence that seems to point upward toward the meaning of what you've set down. Underline the instructive line or passage in your draft. It may be subtle, only hinting at larger ideas or feelings, or quite explicitly stated. In a narrative essay, the instructive line might be a moment of stepping back to reflect—"As I look back on this now, I understand that . . ." In a review or persuasive essay, it might be an assertion of some kind—"American moviegoers are seduced by the 'twist' at the end of a film, and learn to expect it."

2. **Follow the thread of meaning.** If the instructive line is a ball of string, tightly packed with coils of meaning that aren't readily apparent, then to get any guidance for revision you need to try to unravel it. At the top of a journal page, write the line or passage you selected in your draft as most important. Use it as a prompt for five minutes of exploratory writing, perhaps beginning with the following seed sentence: *I think/feel this is true because . . . And also because . . . And also . . . And also . . . .*

3. **Compose a thesis.** Reread your fastwriting in the preceding step and, keeping your original passage in mind, craft a single sentence that best captures the most important idea or feeling you'd like to bring into the next draft. For example, *Because of the expectation, encouraged by Hollywood, that every good movie has a surprise ending, American moviegoers often find even superior foreign films a disappointment.*

4. **Post it.** Put this thesis on the wall above your computer, or use a Post-it note and place the thesis on your computer screen. Revise with the thesis in mind, from beginning to end. Add information that will *illustrate, extend, exemplify, complicate, clarify, support, show, background,* or *prove* the thesis. Cut information from the draft that does none of these things.

Revision Strategy 11.6: Looping Toward a Thesis

I've argued throughout *The Curious Writer* for a dialectical approach to writing, moving back and forth between creative and critical modes of thinking, from your observations of and your ideas about, from generating and judging, from specifics and generalities. This is how writers can make meaning. The approach can also be used as a revision strategy, this time in a technique called *loop writing*. When you loop write you move back and forth dialectically between both modes of thought—opening things up and then trying to pin them down. I imagine that this looks like an hourglass.

1. Reread the draft quickly, and then turn it upside down on your desk. You won't look at it again but trust that you'll remember what's important.

2. Begin a three-minute fastwrite on the draft in which you tell yourself the story of your thinking about the essay. When you first started writing it, what did you think you were writing about, and then what, and then . . . Try to focus on your ideas about what you were trying to say and how it evolved.

3. Sum up what you said in your fastwrite by answering the following question in a sentence: *What seems to be the most important thing I've finally come to understand about my topic?*

4. Begin another three-minute fastwrite. Focus on scenes, situations, case studies, moments, people, conversations, observations, and so on that stand out for you as you think about the draft. Think especially of specifics that come to mind that led to the understanding of your topic that you stated in the preceding step. Some of this information may be in the draft, but some may *not* yet be in the draft.

5. Finish by restating the main point you want to make in the next draft. Begin the revision by thinking about a lead or introduction that dramatizes this point. Consider a suggestive scene, case study, finding, profile, description, comparison, anecdote, conversation, situation, or observation that points the essay toward your main idea (see the "Inquiring into the Details: Types of Leads" box on page 439). For example, if your point is that your university's program to help second-language learners is inadequate, you could begin the next draft by telling the story of Maria, an immigrant from Guatemala who was a victim of poor placement in a composition course that she was virtually guaranteed to fail. Follow this lead into the draft, always keeping your main point or thesis in mind.

Revision Strategy 11.7: Reclaiming Your Topic

When you do a lot of research on your topic you may reach a point when you feel awash in information. It's easy at such moments to feel as if you're losing control of your topic, besieged by the voices of experts, a torrent of statistics and facts, and competing perspectives. Your success in writing the paper depends on making it your own again, gaining control over the information for your own purposes, in the service of your own questions or arguments.

This revision strategy, a variation of Revision Strategy 11.6, should help you gain control of the material you collected for a research-based inquiry project.

1. Spend ten or fifteen minutes reviewing all of the notes you've taken and skimming key articles or passages from books. Glance at your most important sources. If you have a rough draft, reread it. Let your head swim with information.

2. Now clear your desk of everything but your journal. Remove all your notes and materials. If you have a rough draft, put it in the drawer.

3. Now fastwrite about your topic for seven full minutes. Tell the story of how your thinking about the topic has evolved. When you began, what did you think? What were your initial assumptions or preconceptions? Then what happened, and what happened after that? Keep your pen moving.

4. Skip a few lines in your notebook, and write *Moments, Stories, People, and Scenes.* Now fastwrite for another seven minutes, this time focusing more on specific case studies, situations, people, experiences, observations, facts, and so on that stand out in your mind from the research you've done so far, or perhaps from your own experience with the topic.

5. Skip a few more lines. For another seven minutes, write a dialogue between you and someone else about your topic. Choose someone who you think is typical of the audience you're writing for. If it helps, think of someone specific—an instructor, a fellow student, a friend. Don't plan the dialogue. Just begin with the question most commonly asked about your topic, and take the conversation from there, writing both parts of the dialogue.

6. Finally, skip a few more lines and write these two words in your notebook: *So what?* Now spend a few minutes trying to summarize the most important thing you think your readers should understand about your topic, based on what you've learned so far. Distill this into a sentence or two.

As you work your way to the last step, you're reviewing what you've learned about your topic without being tyrannized by the many voices, perspectives, and facts in the research you've collected. The final step, Step 6, leads you toward a thesis statement. In the revision, keep this in mind as you reopen your notes, reread your sources, and check on facts. Remember in the rewrite to put all of this information in the service of this main idea, as examples or illustrations, necessary background, evidence or support, counterexamples, and ways of qualifying or extending your main point.

Revision Strategy 11.8: Believing and Doubting

In persuasive writing such as the argument, review, proposal, or research paper, we often feel that a thesis involves picking sides—"the play was good" or "the play was bad," "the novel was boring" or "the novel was fun to read." Instead of *either/or,* consider *both/and.* This might bring you to a more truthful, more sophisticated understanding of your subject, which rarely is either all bad or all good. One way to do this is to play Peter Elbow's doubting game and believing game.

1. Draw a line down the middle of a page in your notebook. First, on the right side, make a list of the things in response to the following questions:

The Believing Game	**The Doubting Game**
Give the author, performer, text, or performance the benefit of the doubt. Suspend criticism.	Adopt a critical stance. Look for holes, weaknesses, omissions, problems.
1. What seems true or truthful about what is said, shown, or argued?	1. What seems unbelievable or untrue?
2. How does it confirm your own experiences or observations of the same things?	2. What does it fail to consider or consider inadequately?
3. What did you like or agree with?	3. Where is the evidence missing or insufficient, or where do the elements not work together effectively?
4. Where is it strongest, most compelling, most persuasive?	4. How does it fail to meet your criteria for good in this category of thing?
5. How does it satisfy your criteria for being good, useful, convincing, or moving?	5. Where is it the least compelling or persuasive? Why?

2. From this work in your notebook, try to construct a sentence—a thesis—that is more than a simple statement of the worth or worthlessness of the thing you're evaluating, but an expression of *both* its strengths and weaknesses: *Although* _________ *succeeds (or fails) in* _________, *it mostly* _________. For example: *Although reality television presents viewers with an often interesting glimpse into how ordinary people handle their fifteen minutes of celebrity, it mostly exaggerates life by creating drama where there often is none.*

Methods for Refining Your Thesis

You may emerge from writing a draft with a pretty clear sense of what you want to say in the next one. But does this idea seem a little obvious or perhaps too general? Does it fail to adequately express what you really feel and think? Use one or more of the following revision strategies to refine a thesis, theme, or controlling idea.

Revision Strategy 11.9: Questions as Knives

Imagine that your initial feeling, thesis, or main point is like an onion. Ideas, like onions, have layers and to get closer to their hearts you need to cut through the most obvious outer layers to reveal what is less obvious, probably more specific, and almost certainly more interesting. Questions are to ideas as knives are to onions: They help you slice past your initial impressions. The most important question—the sharpest knife in the drawer—is simply *Why? Why* was the Orwell essay interesting? *Why* do you hate foreign films? *Why* should the university do

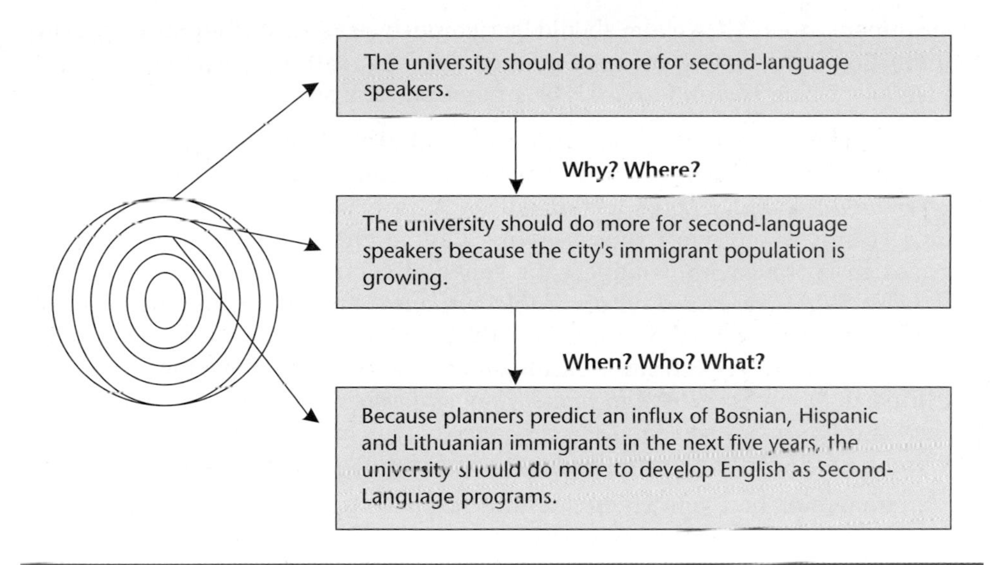

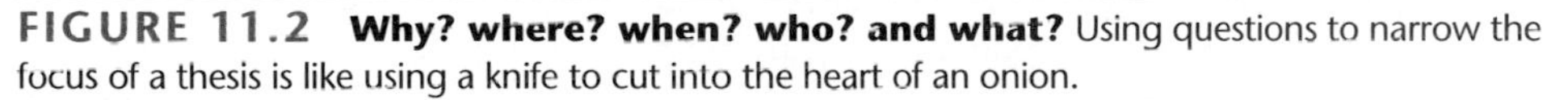

FIGURE 11.2 Why? where? when? who? and what? Using questions to narrow the focus of a thesis is like using a knife to cut into the heart of an onion.

more for second-language speakers? *Why* did you feel a sense of loss when the old cornfield was paved over for the mall?

Why may be the sharpest knife in the drawer, but there are other *W* questions with keen blades, too, including *What, Where, When,* and *Who?* In Figure 11.2 you can see how these questions can cut a broad thesis down to size. The result is a much more specific, more interesting controlling idea for the next draft.

1. Subject your tentative thesis to the same kind of narrowing. Write your theme, thesis, or main point as a single sentence in your notebook.
2. Slice it with questions and restate each time.
3. Continue this until your point is appropriately sliced; that is, when you feel that you've gone beyond the obvious and stated what you think or feel in a more specific and interesting way.

As before, rewrite the next draft with this new thesis in mind, reorganizing the essay around it from beginning to end. Add new information that supports the idea, provides the necessary background, offers opposing views, or extends it. Cut information that no longer seems relevant to the thesis.

Revision Strategy 11.10: Qualifying Your Claim

In your research you discovered that while 90 percent of Americans think that their fellow citizens are too "fat," only 39 percent would describe themselves that way. This evidence leads you to make the following claim: *Although Americans agree that obesity is a national problem, their response is typical: it's somebody else's problem, an attitude that will cripple efforts to promote healthier lifestyles.* This seems like a logical assertion if the evidence is reliable. But if you're going to try to build an argument around it, a claim should be rigorously examined. Toulmin's approach to analyzing arguments provides a method for doing this (see the "Inquiring into the Details: Using Toulmin to Analyze Arguments" box on page 235).

1. Toulmin observes that sometimes a claim should be *qualified* to be more accurate and persuasive. The initial question is simple: *Is what you're asserting always or universally true?* Essentially, you're being challenged to examine your certainty about what you're saying. This might lead you to add words or phrases to it that acknowledge your sense of certainty: *sometimes, always, mostly, in this case, based on available evidence,* and so on. In this case, the claim is already qualified by specifying that it is limited to Americans, but it is also based on evidence from a single source. The claim, therefore, might be qualified to say this: *Although one survey suggests that Americans agree that obesity is a national problem, their response is typical: it's somebody else's problem, an attitude that will cripple efforts to promote healthier lifestyles.*

2. Imagining how your claim might be rebutted is another way to strengthen it. How might someone take issue with your thesis? What might be the exceptions to what you're saying is true? For example, might someone object to the assertion that Americans "typically" respond by putting their heads in the sand when personally confronted with problems? You must decide then whether this clever aside in your claim is something you're prepared to support. If not, cut it.

PROBLEMS WITH INFORMATION

Writers who've spent enough time generating or collecting information about their topics can work from abundance rather than scarcity. This is an enormous advantage because the ability to throw stuff away means you can be selective about what you use, and the result is a more focused draft. But as we revise, our purpose and point might shift, and we may find ourselves in the unhappy position of working from scarcity again. Most of our research, observation, or fastwriting was relevant to the triggering subject in the initial sketch or draft, not to the generated subject we decide is the better direction for the next draft. In some cases, this might require that you research the new topic or return to the generating activities of listing, fastwriting, clustering, and so on that will help provide information for the next draft.

More often, however, writers don't have to begin from scratch in revision. Frequently, a shift in the focus or refining a thesis in a first draft just means emphasizing different information or perhaps filling in gaps in later drafts. The strategies that follow will help you solve this problem.

Revision Strategy 11.11: Explode a Moment

The success of personal essays that rely on narratives frequently depends on how well the writer renders an important scene, situation, moment, or description. When you're telling a story from experience, not all parts of the story are equally important. As always, emphasis in a narrative depends on the writer's purpose in the essay. For example, Matt's essay on the irony of the slow poisoning of Butte, Montana, his hometown, by a copper mine that once gave the city life would emphasize those parts of the story that best highlight that irony. Or a description of the agonizing death of the snow geese that unwittingly landed on the acid pond—their white beauty set against the deadly dark water—might be an important scene in Matt's next draft; it nicely portrays life and death, beauty and ugliness in much the same way the town and the mine might be contrasted. Matt should "explode that moment" because it's an important part of the story he's trying to tell about his Montana home town.

If you're trying to revise a draft that relies on narratives, this revision strategy will help you first identify moments, scenes, or descriptions that might be important in the next draft, and then develop these as more important parts of your story.

1. Choose a draft that involves a story or stories.

2. Make a list in your journal of the moments (for example, scenes, situations, and turning points) that stand out in the narrative.

3. Circle one that you think is most important to your purpose in the essay. It could be the situation that is most telling, a dramatic turning point, the moment of a key discovery that is central to what you're trying to say, or a scene that illustrates the dilemma or raises the question you're exploring in the draft.

4. Name that moment at the top of a blank journal page (for example, *the snow geese on the acid pond*, *when the ice broke*, or *when I saw my grandfather in his coffin*).

5. Now put yourself back into that moment and fastwrite about it for seven full minutes. Make sure that you write with as much detail as possible, *drawing on all your senses.* Write in the present tense if it helps.

6. Use this same method with other moments in the narrative that might deserve more emphasis in the next draft. Remember that real time means little in writing. An experience that took seven seconds can easily take up three pages of writing if it's detailed enough. Rewrite and incorporate the best of the new information in the next draft.

Revision Strategy 11.12: Beyond Examples

When we add information to a draft we normally think of adding examples. If you're writing a research essay on living with a sibling who suffers from Down syndrome, you might mention that your brother typically tries to avoid certain cognitive challenges. Members of your workshop group wonder, "Well, what kind of challenges?" In revision, you add an example or two from your own experience to clarify what you mean. This is, of course, a helpful strategy; examples of what you mean by an assertion are a kind of evidence that helps readers more fully understand your work. But also consider other types of information it might be helpful to add to the next draft. Use the following list to review your draft for additions you might not have thought of for revision.

- **Presenting counterarguments.** Typically, persuasive essays include information that represents an opposing view. Say you're arguing that beyond "avoidance" behaviors, there really aren't personality traits that can be attributed to most people with Down syndrome. You include a summary of a study that says otherwise. Why? Because it provides readers with a better understanding of the debate, and enhances the writer's ethos because you appear fair.

- **Providing background.** When you drop in on a conversation between two friends, you initially may be clueless about the subject. Naturally, you ask questions: "Who are you guys talking about? When did this happen? What did she say?" Answers to these questions provide a context that allows you to understand what is being said and to participate in the conversation. Background information like this is often essential in written communication, too. In a personal essay, readers may want to know when and where the event occurred or the relationship between the narrator and a character. In a critical essay, it might be necessary to provide background on the short story because readers may not have read it. In a research essay, it's often useful to provide background information about what has already been said on the topic and the research question.
- **Establishing significance.** Let's say you're writing about the problem of obesity in America, something that most of us are generally aware of these days. But the significance of the problem really strikes home when you add information from research suggesting that 30 percent of American adults are overweight, up from 23 percent just six years ago. It is even more important to establish the significance of a problem about which there is little awareness or consensus. For example, most people don't know that America's national park system is crumbling and in disrepair. Your essay on the problem needs to provide readers with information that establishes the significance of the problem. In a profile, readers need to have a reason to be interested in someone—perhaps your profile subject represents a particular group of people of interest or concern.
- **Giving it a face.** One of the best ways to make an otherwise abstract issue or problem come to life is to show what it means to an individual person. We can't fully appreciate the social impact of deforestation in Brazil without being introduced to someone such as Chico Mendes, a forest defender who was murdered for his activism. Obesity might be an abstract problem until we meet Carl, a 500-pound 22-year-old who is "suffocating in his own fat." Add case studies, anecdotes, profiles, and descriptions that put people on the page to make your essay more interesting and persuasive.
- **Defining it.** If you're writing about a subject your readers know little about, you'll likely use concepts or terms that readers will want you to define. What exactly do you mean, for example, when you say that the Internet is vulnerable to cyberterror? What exactly is cyberterror anyway? In your personal essay on your troubled relationship with your mother, what do you mean when you call her a narcissist? Frequently your workshop group will alert you to things in the draft that need defining, but also go through your own draft and ask yourself, *Will my readers know what I mean?*

Revision Strategy 11.13: Research

Too often, research is ignored as a revision strategy. We may do research for the first draft of a paper or essay, but never return to the library or search the Web to fill in gaps, answer new questions, or refine the focus of a rewrite. That's crazy, particularly because well-researched information can strengthen a draft of any kind. That has been one of the themes of *The Curious Writer* since the beginning of the book: research is not a separate activity reserved only for the research paper, but a rich source of information for any type of writing. Try some of these strategies:

1. For quick facts, visit http://www.refdesk.com. This enormously useful Web site is the fastest way to find out the exact height of the Great Wall of China or the number of young women suffering from eating disorders in America today.

2. Return to the *Library of Congress Subject Headings*, the reference mentioned in Chapter 9 that will help you pinpoint the language you should use to search library databases on your topic. Particularly if the focus of your next draft is shifting, you'll need some fresh information to fill in the gaps. The *LCSH* will help you find more of it, more quickly.

3. To maximize Web coverage, launch a search on at least three single search engines (for example, Google, MSN Search, and Yahoo!), but this time search using terms or phrases from your draft that will lead you to more specific information that will fill gaps in the draft.

4. Interview someone relevant to your topic. (See Chapter 9.)

5. To ferret out some new sources on your topic, search library databases under author rather than keyword. Focus on authors that you know have something to say on your topic.

6. Return to any of the steps in Chapter 9 that involve developing deep knowledge about your topic.

Revision Strategy 11.14: Backing Up Your Assumptions

Targeted research is particularly important when you're making an argument. In addition to providing evidence that is relevant to your thesis, frequently an argument rests on the assumptions behind that assertion. Stephen Toulmin calls these assumptions *warrants* (see the "Inquiring into the Details: Using Toulmin to Analyze Arguments" box on page 235). For example, suppose your claim is the following: *Although most Americans agree that obesity is a national problem, most don't describe themselves as fat, an attitude that will cripple efforts to promote healthier lifestyles.* Every claim rests on assumptions, or warrants. In other words, what do you have to believe is true to have faith in the accuracy of the claim?

1. Write your claim on the top of a journal page, and then list the assumptions or warrants on which it seems to rest. For example, the claim about obesity includes an assumption that most Americans equate the words *obesity* and *fat.* Also there's an assumption that public attitudes—particularly the view that there is a problem but it isn't my problem—hinder progress on public policy.

2. Which of the warrants behind your claim would be stronger if there were "backing" or evidence to support them? This will give you new direction for research. It might strengthen the argument on the obesity problem, for example, to draw on evidence from the civil rights struggle. Is there any evidence that attitudes toward personal responsibility for racism lagged behind acknowledgment of racial inequality as a national problem? Was progress finally made when this gap narrowed?

PROBLEMS WITH STRUCTURE

When it's working, the structure of a piece of writing is nearly invisible. Readers don't notice how the writer is guiding them from one piece of information to the next. When structure is a problem, the writer asks readers to walk out on a shaky bridge and trust that it will help them get to the other side, but the walkers can think of little else but the shakiness of the bridge. Some professional writers, such as John McPhee, obsess about structure, and for good reason—when you're working with a tremendous amount of information, as McPhee often does in his research-based essays, it helps to have a clear idea about how you'll use it.

Formal Academic Structures

In some academic writing, the structure is prescribed. Scientific papers often have sections—Introduction, Methodology, Results, Discussion—but within those sections writers must organize their material. Certain writing assignments may also require you to organize your information in a certain way. The most common of these is the thesis/support structure. In such essays you typically establish your thesis in the first paragraph, spend the body of the paper assembling evidence that supports the thesis, and conclude the essay with a summary that restates the thesis in light of what's been said.

Thesis/support is a persuasive form, so it lends itself to arguments, critical essays, reviews, proposals, and similar pieces. In fact, you may have already structured your draft using this approach. If so, the following revision strategy may help you tighten and clarify the draft.

Revision Strategy 11.15: Reorganizing Around Thesis and Support

Because the thesis/support structure is fairly common, it's useful to master. Most drafts, even if they weren't initially organized in that form, can be revised into a thesis/support essay. (Personal essays would be an exception.) The order of information in such in an essay generally follows this design:

- **Lead paragraph:** This paragraph introduces the topic and explicitly states the thesis, usually as the last sentence in the paragraph. For example, a thesis/support paper on the deterioration of America's national parks system might begin this way:

    Yellowstone National Park, which shares territory with Idaho, Montana, and Wyoming, is the nation's oldest park, and to some, its most revered. Established on March 1, 1872, the park features the Old Faithful geyser, which spouts reliably every 76 minutes on average. What isn't nearly as reliable these days is whether school groups will get to see it. Last year 60% of them were turned away because the park simply didn't have the staff. This essay will argue that poor funding of our national park system is a disgrace that threatens to undermine the Park Service's mission to preserve the areas "as cumulative expressions of a single national heritage" ("Famous Quotes").

The thesis (underlined) is the final sentence in the paragraph, for emphasis.

- **Body:** Each succeeding paragraph until the final one attempts to prove or develop the thesis. Often each paragraph is devoted to a single *reason* why the thesis is true, frequently stated as the topic sentence of the paragraph. Specific information then explains, clarifies, and supports the reason. For example, here's a typical paragraph from the body of the national parks essay:

One aspect of the important national heritage at risk because of poor funding for national parks is the pride many Americans feel about these national treasures. Newsweek writer Arthur Frommer calls the national park system among the "crowning glories of our democracy." He adds, "Not to have seen them is to have missed something unique and precious in American life" (12). To see the crumbling roads in Glacier National Park, or the incursion of development in Great Smoky Mountains National Park, or the slow strangulation of the Everglades is not just an ecological issue; it's a sorry statement about a democratic nation's commitment to some of the places that define its identity.

The underlined sentence is the topic sentence of the paragraph and is an assertion that supports and develops the thesis in the lead of the essay. The rest of the paragraph offers supporting evidence of the assertion, in this case a quotation from a *Newsweek* writer who recently visited several parks.

- **Concluding paragraph:** This paragraph reminds the reader of the central argument, not simply by restating the original thesis from the first paragraph but by reemphasizing some of the most important points. This may lead to an elaboration or restatement of the thesis. One common technique is to find a way in the end of the essay to return to the beginning. Here's the concluding paragraph from the essay on national park funding:

We would never risk our national heritage by allowing the White House to deteriorate or the Liberty Bell to rust away. As the

> National Park Service's own mission states, the parks are also "expressions" of our "single national heritage," one this paper contends is about not only preserving trees, animals, and habitats, but our national identity. The Old Faithful geyser reminds Americans of their constancy and their enduring spirit. What will it say about us if vandals finally end the regular eruptions of the geyser because Americans didn't support a park ranger to guard it? What will we call Old Faithful then? Old Faithless?

Note that the underlined sentence returns to the original thesis but doesn't simply repeat it word for word. Instead, it amplifies the original thesis, adding a definition of "national heritage" to include national identity. It returns to the opening paragraph by finding a new way to discuss Old Faithful. Revise your draft to conform to this structure, beginning with a strong opening paragraph that explicitly states your thesis and with an ending that somehow returns to the beginning without simply repeating what you've already said.

Revision Strategy 11.16: Multiple Leads

A single element that may affect a draft more than any other is how we begin it. There are many ways into the material, and of course you want to choose a beginning or lead that a reader might find interesting. You also want to choose a beginning that makes some kind of promise, providing readers with a sense of where you intend to take them. But a lead has less obvious effects on both readers and writers. How you begin often establishes the voice of the essay; signals the writer's emotional relationship to the material, the writer's ethos; and might suggest the form the essay will take.

This is, of course, why beginnings are so hard to write. But the critical importance of where and how we begin also suggests that examining alternative leads can give writers more choices and more control over their essays. To borrow John McPhee's metaphor, if a lead is a "flashlight that shines down into the story," then pointing that flashlight in four different directions might reveal four different ways of following the same subject. This can be a powerful revision strategy.

1. Choose a draft that has a weak opening, doesn't have a strong sense of purpose, or needs to be reorganized.

2. Compose four *different* openings to the *same* draft. One way to generate ideas for this is to cluster your topic, and write leads from four different branches. Also consider varying the type of lead you write (see the "Inquiring into the Details: Types of Leads" box).

3. Bring a typed copy of these four leads (or five if you want to include the original lead from the first draft) to class and share them with a small group. First simply ask your classmates to choose the beginning they like best.

4. Choose the lead *you* prefer. It may or may not be the one your classmates chose. Find a partner who was not in your small group and ask him or her the following questions after sharing the lead you chose:

- Based on this lead, what do you predict this paper is about?
- Can you guess the question, problem, or idea I'm writing about in the rest of the essay?
- Do you have a sense of what my thesis might be?
- What is the ethos of this beginning? In other words, how do I come across to you as a narrator or author of the essay?

If the predictions were fairly accurate using the lead you preferred, this might be a good alternative opening to the next draft. Follow it in a fastwrite in your notebook to see where it leads you. Go ahead and use the other leads elsewhere in the revision, if you like.

Inquiring into the Details

TYPES OF LEADS

Writer John McPhee says beginnings—or leads—are "like flashlights that shine down into the story." If you imagine that information about your topic is collected in a darkened room, then where and how you choose to begin an essay will, like a flashlight, illuminate some aspect of that room. Different beginnings point the flashlight in different directions and imply the different directions the essay might develop. Consider a few types of leads:

1. **Announcement.** Typical of a thesis/support essay, among others. Explicitly states the purpose and thesis of the essay.
2. **Anecdote.** A brief story that nicely frames the question, dilemma, problem, or idea behind the essay.
3. **Scene.** Describe a situation, place, or image that highlights the question, problem, or idea behind the essay.
4. **Profile.** Begin with a case study or description of a person who is involved in the question, problem, or idea.
5. **Background.** Provide a context through information that establishes the significance of the question, problem, or idea.
6. **Quotation or Dialogue.** Begin with a voice of someone (or several people) involved or whose words are relevant.
7. **Comparison.** Are there two or more things that, when compared or contrasted, point to the question, problem, or idea?
8. **Question.** Frame the question the essay addresses.

If your reader's predictions were off, the lead may not be the best choice for the revision. However, should you consider this new direction an appealing alternative for the next draft? Or should you choose another lead that better reflects your current intentions rather than strike off in new directions? Either way, follow a new lead to see where it goes.

Revision Strategy 11.17: The Frankenstein Draft

One way to divorce a draft that has you in its clutches is to dismember it; that is, cut it into pieces and play with the parts, looking for new arrangements of information or new gaps to fill. Writing teacher Peter Elbow's cut-and-paste revision can be a useful method, particularly for drafts that don't rely on narrative structures (although sometimes playing with alternatives, particularly if the draft is strictly chronological, can be helpful). Research essays and other pieces that attempt to corral lots of information seem to benefit the most from this strategy.

1. Choose a draft that needs help with organization. Make a one-sided copy.

2. Cut apart the copy, paragraph by paragraph. (You may cut it into smaller pieces later.) Once you have completely disassembled the draft, shuffle the paragraphs to get them wildly out of order so the original draft is just a memory.

3. Now go through the shuffled stack and find the *core paragraph*. This is the paragraph the essay really couldn't do without because it helps answer the *So what?* question. It might be the paragraph that contains your thesis or establishes your focusing question. It should be the paragraph that explains, implicitly or explicitly, what you're trying to say in the draft. Set this aside.

4. With the core paragraph directly in front of you, work your way through the remaining stack of paragraphs and make two new stacks: one of paragraphs that don't seem relevant to your core (such as unnecessary digressions or information) and those that do (they support the main idea, explain or define a key concept, illustrate or exemplify something important, provide necessary background).

5. Put your reject pile aside for the moment. You may decide to salvage some of those paragraphs later. But for now focus on your relevant pile, including the core paragraph. Now play with order. Try new leads, ends, middles. Consider trying some new methods of development as a way to organize your next draft (see the "Methods of Development" box). As you spread the paragraphs out before you and consider new arrangements, don't worry about the lack of transitions; you can add those later. Also look for gaps, places where more information might be needed. Consider some of the information in the reject pile as well. Should you splice in *parts* of paragraphs that you initially discarded?

6. As a structure begins to emerge, begin taping together the fragments of paper. Also splice in scraps in appropriate places that note what you might add in the next draft that is currently missing.

Methods of Development

- Narrative
- Problem to solution
- Cause to effect, or effect to cause
- Question to answer
- Known to unknown, or unknown to known
- Simple to complex
- General to specific, or specific to general
- Comparison and contrast
- Combinations of any of these

Now you've created a Frankenstein draft. But hopefully this ugly mess of paper and tape and scribbled notes holds much more promise than the monster. On the other hand, if you end up with pretty much the original organization, perhaps your first approach wasn't so bad after all. You may at least find places where more information is needed.

Revision Strategy 11.18: Make a PowerPoint Outline

While outlines can be a useful tool for planning a formal essay, they can also help writers revise a draft. One of the best tools for doing this is a program such as PowerPoint that challenges you to develop brief slides in sequence. The ease of moving the slides around, the imperative to be brief and to the point, and the visual display of your logic all combine to make the program an ideal medium for playing with the order of information. This is often helpful even if you don't ever make a presentation.

Your goal in creating a PowerPoint outline isn't to transfer all your text to slides and then move it around, though you could do that if you thought it helpful. Your aim is to exploit the software to help you develop a logical outline. You have several options for doing this. One is to title separate slides using some of the conventional structures of academic essays, and then making bulleted lists of the information you might include in each (see the sample slide). For example, these could be slide titles:

- Abstract, Introduction, Literature Review, Thesis/Purpose, Methods, Results, Discussion, Conclusion
- The Problem/Question, Purpose of the Essay, Claim, Reasons and Evidence (separate slide for each reason), Conclusion
- Introduction, Thesis, Example 1, Example 2, Example 3, etc., Conclusion
- Lead/Introduction, Background, Research Question, Significance of the Problem or Question, Other Voices on the Question, Thesis, Conclusion

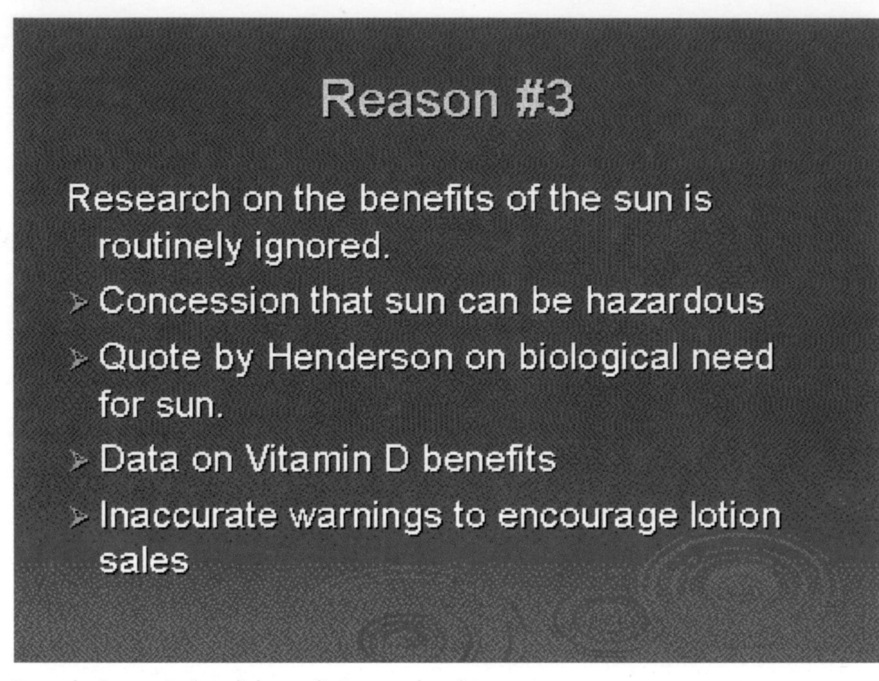

Sample PowerPoint slide outlining a plan for an essay.

Alternatively, you might use less formal methods of parsing the information in the draft onto slides. For example, can you label categories of information? In a narrative essay, it might be a particular scene, description, or reflection. In an argument it might be claims, warrants or assumptions, evidence, and counterarguments. A literary essay might be grouped on slides using key passages, main idea, textual background, information on the author, and so on.

Whichever method you use, once you are able to disassemble your draft onto PowerPoint slides using some logic, don't just play with the order. Consider moving some of the information from slide to slide, too.

PROBLEMS OF CLARITY AND STYLE

One thing should be made clear immediately: problems of clarity and style need not have anything to do with grammatical correctness. You can have a sentence that follows all the rules and still lumbers, sputters, and dies like a Volkswagen bug towing a heavy trailer up a steep hill. Take this sentence, for instance:

> Once upon a point in time, a small person named Little Red Riding Hood initiated plans for the preparation, delivery and transportation of foodstuffs to her grandmother, a senior citizen residing at a place of residence in a wooded area of indeterminate dimension.

This beastly sentence opens Russell Baker's essay "Little Red Riding Hood Revisited," a satire about the gassiness of contemporary writing. It's grammatically correct, of course, but it's also pretentious, unnecessarily wordy, and would be annoying to read if it wasn't pretty amusing. This section of the chapter focuses on revision strategies that improve the clarity of your writing and will help you consider the effects you want to create through word choice and arrangement. Your questions about grammar and mechanics can be answered in the handbook at the back of the book.

Strong writing at the sentence and paragraph levels always begins with clarity.

Maybe because we often think that work with paragraphs, sentences, and words always involve problems of correctness, it may be hard to believe at first that writers can actually manage readers' responses and feelings by using different words or rearranging the parts of a sentence or paragraph. Once you begin to play around with style, however, you will discover that it's much more than cosmetic. In fact, style in writing is a lot like music in movies. Chris Douridas, a Hollywood music supervisor who picked music for *Shrek* and *American Beauty,* said recently that he sees "music as a integral ingredient to the pie. I see it as helping to flavor the pie and not as whip cream on top." Certainly people don't pick a movie for its music, but we know that the music is central to our experience of a film. Similarly, *how* you say it in a piece of writing powerfully shapes the reader's experience of *what* you say.

But style is a secondary concern. Strong writing at the sentence and paragraph levels always begins with clarity. Do you say what you mean as directly and economically as you can? This can be a real problem, particularly with academic writing, in which it's easy to get the impression that a longer word is always better than a shorter word, and the absence of anything interesting to say can be remedied by sounding smart. Nothing could be further from the truth.

Solving Problems of Clarity

Begin by revising your draft with one or more revision strategies that will make your writing more direct and clear.

Revision Strategy 11.19: Untangling Paragraphs

One of the things I admire most in my friends David and Margaret is that they both have individual integrity—a deep understanding of who they are and who they want to be—and yet they remain just as profoundly connected to the people close to them. They manage to exude both individuality and connection. I hope my friends will forgive the comparison, but good paragraphs have the same qualities: alone they have their own identities, yet they are also strongly hitched to the paragraphs that precede and that follow them. This connection happens quite naturally when you're telling a story, but in expository writing the relationship between paragraphs is more related to content than time.

The following passage is the first three paragraphs from Paul de Palma's essay on computers, with the clever title "http://www.when_is_enough_enough?.com." Notice the integrity of each paragraph—each is a kind of mini-essay—as well as the way each one is linked to the paragraph that precedes it.

A paragraph should be unified, focusing on a single topic, idea or thing. It's like a mini-essay in that sense.

In the misty past, before Bill Gates joined the company of the world's richest men, before the mass-marketed personal computer, before the metaphor of an information superhighway had been worn down to a cliché, I heard Roger Schank interviewed on National Public Radio. Then a computer science professor at Yale, Schank was already well known in artificial intelligence circles. Because those circles did not include me, a new programmer at Sperry Univac, I hadn't heard of him. Though I've forgotten details of the conversation, I have never forgotten Schank's insistence that most people do not need to own computers.

Note how the first sentence in the new paragraph links with the last sentence in the preceding one.

That view, of course, has not prevailed. Either we own a personal computer and fret about upgrades, or we are scheming to own one and fret about the technical marvel yet to come that will render our purchase obsolete. Well, there are worse ways to spend money, I suppose. For all I know, even Schank owns a personal computer. They're fiendishly clever machines, after all, and they've helped keep the wolf from my door for a long time.

As before, the first sentence links with the last sentence in the previous paragraph.

It is not the personal computer itself that I object to. What reasonable person would voluntarily go back to a typewriter? The mischief is not in the computer itself, but in the ideology that surrounds it. If we hope to employ computers for tasks more interesting than word processing, we must devote some attention to how they are actually being used, and beyond that, to the remarkable grip that the idol of computing continues to exert.

The final sentence is the most important one in a paragraph. Craft it carefully.

Well-crafted paragraphs like these create a fluent progression, all linked together like train cars; they make readers feel confident that this train is going somewhere. This might be information that clarifies, extends, proves, explains, or even contradicts. Do the paragraphs in your draft work well on their own and together?

1. Check the length of every paragraph in your draft. Are any too long, going on and on for a full page or more? Can you create smaller paragraphs by breaking out separate ideas, topics, discussions, claims?

2. Now examine each paragraph in your draft for integrity. Is it relatively focused and unified? Should it be broken down further into two or more paragraphs because it covers too much territory?

3. In Figure 11.3, note the order of the most important information in a typical paragraph. Is each of your paragraphs arranged with that order in mind? In particular, how strong is the final sentence in each paragraph? Does it prepare readers to move into the next paragraph? In general, each paragraph adds some kind of new information to the old information in the paragraphs preceding it. This new material may clarify, explain, prove, elaborate on, contrast, summarize,

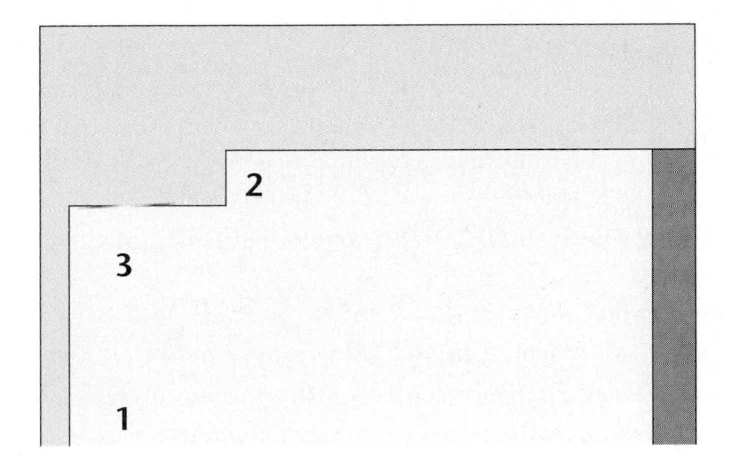

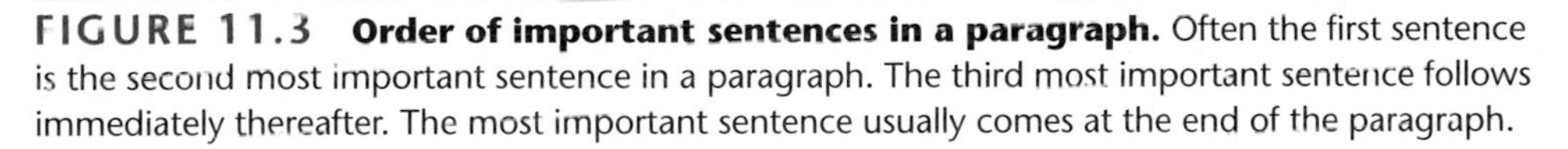

FIGURE 11.3 Order of important sentences in a paragraph. Often the first sentence is the second most important sentence in a paragraph. The third most important sentence follows immediately thereafter. The most important sentence usually comes at the end of the paragraph.

contradict, or alter time. Sometimes you should signal the nature of this addition using transition words and phrases (see the "Inquiring into the Details: Transition Flags" box). Are there any awkward transitions? Should you smooth them using transition flags?

Revision Strategy 11.20: Cutting Clutter

Russell Baker's overinflated version of "Little Red Riding Hood" suffered from what writer and professor William Zinsser called "clutter." This disease afflicts much writing, particularly in academic settings. Clutter, simply put, is saying in three or four words what you might say in two, or choosing a longer word when a shorter one will do just as well. It grows from the assumption that simplicity means simplemindedness. This is misguided. Simplicity is a great virtue in writing. It's respectful of the readers, for one thing, who are mostly interested in understanding what you mean without unnecessary detours or obstacles.

In case Russell Baker's tongue-and-cheek example of cluttered writing isn't convincing because it's an invention, here's a brief passage from a memo I received from a fellow faculty member some years ago. I won't make you endure more than a sentence.

> While those of us in the administration are supporting general excellence and consideration of the long-range future of the University, and while the Faculty Senate and Caucus are dealing with more immediate problems, the Executive Committee feels that an ongoing dialogue concerning the particular concerns of faculty is needed to maintain the quality of personal and educational life necessary for continued educational improvement.

Inquiring into the Details

TRANSITION FLAGS

One way to connect paragraphs is to signal to a reader with words what the relationship is between them.

- **Clarifying:** *For example, furthermore, specifically, also, to illustrate, similarly.*
- **Proving:** *In fact, for example, indeed.*
- **Time:** *First . . . second . . . finally, subsequently, following, now, recently.*
- **Cause or effect:** *Therefore, consequently, so, accordingly.*
- **Contrast or contradiction:** *On the other hand, in contrast, however, on the contrary, despite, in comparison.*
- **Summarizing:** *Finally, in the end, in conclusion, summing up, to conclude.*

That's a 63-word sentence, and while there is nothing inherently wrong with long sentences, I'm pretty sure that at least half of the words are unnecessary. For the fun of it, see if you can cut at least thirty words from the sentence without compromising the writer's intent. Look for ways to say the same things in fewer words, and look for shorter words that might replace longer ones. What kinds of choices did you make to improve the clarity of the sentence?

Now shift your attention to one of your own drafts and see if you can be as ruthless with your own clutter as you were with the memo writer's.

1. One of the most common kinds of clutter is stock phrases, things we mindlessly say because we've simply gotten in the habit of saying them. *Due to the fact that* . . . is the one that drives me most crazy. Why not the simpler word *Because?* The following table lists some of the most common stock phrases used in student writing. Read your draft from beginning to end and when you see one of these, cut it down to size.

Stock Phrase	Simpler Version
Due to the fact that . . .	Because
At the present time . . .	Now
Until such time as . . .	Until
I am of the opinion that . . .	I think
In the event of . . .	When
This is an appropriate occasion to . . .	It's time
Proceed with the implementation of . . .	Begin
Referred to as . . .	Called
Until such time as . . .	Until

Totally lacked the ability to . . .	Couldn't
A number of . . .	Many
In the event of . . .	If
There is a need for . . .	Must

2. Another thing to consider is choosing a shorter, simpler word rather than a longer, more complicated word. For example, why not say *many* rather than *numerous,* or *ease* rather than *facilitate,* or *do* rather than *implement,* or *found* rather than *identified*. Go through your draft and look for opportunities such as these to use simpler, more direct words.

3. In his book *Style: Ten Lessons in Clarity and Grace,* Joseph Williams cleverly calls the habit of using meaningless words "verbal tics." These are words, he writes, that "we use unconsciously as we clear our throats." My favorite verbal tic is the phrase *in fact*, which I park at the front of a sentence when I feel like I'm about to clarify something. Mostly I can do without it. In fact, most of us have verbal tics, and we should learn to recognize them. Williams mentions a few common ones, including *kind of, actually, basically, generally, given, various,* and *certain*—for example, *It's generally assumed that certain students have various reasons for being apolitical these days*. A better version would be, *Students have reasons for being apolitical these days*.

Go through your draft and search for words and phrases that you use out of habit, and cut them if they don't add meaning.

Revision Strategy 11.21: The Actor and the Action Next Door

I live in a relatively urban neighborhood, and so I can hear Kate play her music across the street and Gray powering up his chainsaw to cut wooden pallets next door. I have mixed feelings about this. Kate and I have different taste in music and Gray runs the saw at dusk. But I am never confused about who is doing what. That's less obvious in the following passage:

> A conflict that was greeted at first with much ambivalence by the American public, the war in Iraq, which caused a tentativeness that some experts call the "Vietnam syndrome," sparked protests among Vietnam veterans.

The subject or actor of the sentence (*the war in Iraq*) and the action (*sparked protests*) are separated by a few city blocks. In addition, the subject is buried behind a long introductory clause. As a result, it's a bit hard to remember who is doing what. Putting actor and action next door to each other makes the writing livelier, and bringing the subject up front helps clarify who is doing what.

> The war in Iraq sparked protests among Vietnam veterans even though the conflict was initially greeted with public ambivalence. Some experts call this tentativeness the "Vietnam syndrome."

Review your draft to determine whether the subjects in your sentences are buried or in the same neighborhood as the verbs that modify them. If not, rewrite to bring the actors up front in your sentences and to close the distance between actors and actions.

Improving Style

These revision strategies will improve the style of your writing. In the same way that a John Williams score can make movies such as *Indiana Jones and the Temple of Doom* and *Star Wars* more memorable and moving, style in writing can add to readers' experiences of a text. These are often calculated moves. Writers adopt a style because it serves a purpose, perhaps encouraging a certain feeling that makes a story more powerful, enhancing the writer's ethos to make an essay more convincing, or simply giving certain information particular emphasis. For example, here's the beginning of an article about Douglas Berry, a Marine drill sergeant.

> He is seething, he is rabid, he is wound up tight as a golf ball, with more adrenalin surging through his hypothalamus than a cornered slum rat, he is everything these Marine recruits with their heads shaved to dirty nubs have ever feared or ever hoped a drill sergeant might be.

The style of this opening is calculated to have an obvious effect—the reader is pelted with words, one after another, in a breathless sentence that almost simulates the experience of having Sgt. Douglas Berry in your face. There's no magic to this. It is all about using words that evoke action and feeling, usually verbs or words based on or derived from verbs.

Revision Strategy 11.22: Actors and Actions

My favorite verb yesterday was *shattered.* I often ask my writing students to come to class and share their favorite verb of the day; last spring, my senior seminar consistently selected *graduate* as their favorite.

As you know, verbs make things happen in writing, and how much energy prose possesses depends on verb power. Academic writing sometimes lacks strong verbs, relying instead on old passive standbys such as *the study concluded* or *it is believed.* Not only are the verbs weak, but the actors, the people or things engaged in the action, are often missing completely from the sentence. *Who* or *what* did the study? *Who* believes?

This is called *passive voice,* and while it's not grammatically incorrect, passive voice can suck the air out of a room. While reasons exist for using passive voice (sometimes, for instance, the writer wants the reader to focus on the action, not the actor), you should avoid it in your own writing. One of the easiest ways to locate passive voice in your drafts is to conduct a *to be* search. Most forms of the verb *to be* (see the box on the next page) usually signal passive voice. For example,

> It is well known that medieval eating habits were unsavory by contemporary health standards. Cups were shared, forks were never used, and the same knives used to clean under fingernails or to gut a chicken were used to cut and eat meat.

What is missing, of course, are the actors. To revise into active voice you simply need to add the actors, whenever possible:

> Medieval diners had unsavory eating habits by contemporary health standards. Friends shared cups, never used forks, and they used their knives, the same ones they used to clean under their fingernails or gut a chicken, to cut and eat their meat.

1. Conduct a *to be* search of your own draft. Whenever you find passive construction, try to put the actor into the sentence.

2. Eliminating passive voice is only one strategy for giving your writing more energy. Try to use lively verbs as well. Can you replace weak verbs with stronger ones? How about *discovered* instead of *found,* or *seized* instead of *took, shattered* instead of *broke.* Review every sentence in the draft and when appropriate revise with a stronger verb.

Revision Strategy 11.23: Smoothing the Choppiness

Good writing reads like a Mercedes drives—smoothly, suspended by the rhythms of language. One of the most important factors influencing this rhythm is sentence length, or, more precisely, pauses in the prose that vary as the reader travels from sentence to sentence and paragraph to paragraph. We rarely notice either the cause or the effect, but we certainly notice the bumps and lurches. Consider the following sentences, each labeled with the number of syllables:

> When the sun finally rose the next day I felt young again.(14) It was a strange feeling because I wasn't young anymore.(13) I was fifty years old and felt like it.(10) It was the smell of the lake at dawn that thrust me back into adolescence.(18) I remembered the hiss of the waves.(9) They erased my footprints in the sand.(9)

This really isn't awful; it could pass as a bad Hemingway imitation. But do you notice the monotony of the writing, the steady, almost unvarying beat that threatens to dull your mind if it goes on much longer? The cause of the plodding rhythm is the unvarying length of the pauses. The last two sentences in

---

Forms of *To Be*

- Is
- Are
- Was
- Were
- Has been
- Have been
- Will be

---

the passage each have 9 syllables, and the first two sentences are nearly identical in length as well (14 and 13 syllables, respectively).

Now notice how this choppiness disappears by varying the lengths of the pauses through sentence combining, insertion of other punctuation, and dropping a few unnecessary words.

> When the sun finally rose the next day I felt young again,(14) and it was a strange feeling because I wasn't young.(11) I was fifty years old.(6) It was the smell of the lake at dawn that thrust me back into adolescence and remembering the hiss of the waves as they erased my footprints in the sand.(35)

The revision is much more fluent and the reason is simple: The writer varies the pauses and the number of syllables within each of them—14, 11, 6, 35.

1. Choose a draft of your own that doesn't seem to flow or seems choppy in places.
2. Mark the pauses in the problem areas. Put slash marks next to periods, commas, semicolons, dashes, and so on—any punctuation that prompts a reader to pause briefly.
3. If the pauses seem similar in length, revise to vary them, combining sentences, adding punctuation, dropping unnecessary words, or varying long and short words.

Revision Strategy 11.24: Fresh Ways to Say Things

It goes without saying that a tried-and-true method of getting to the heart of revision problems is to just do or die. Do you know what I mean? Of course you don't, because the opening sentence is laden with clichés and figures of speech that manage to obscure meaning. One of the great challenges of writing well is to find fresh ways to say things rather than relying on hand-me-down phrases that worm their way into our speech and writing. Clichés are familiar examples: *home is where the heart is, hit the nail on the head, the grass is greener,* and all that. But even more common are less figurative expressions: *more than meets the eye, rude awakenings, you only go around once, sigh of relief,* and so on.

Removing clichés and shopworn expressions from your writing will make it sound more as if you are writing from your own voice rather than someone else's. It gives the work a freshness that helps readers believe that you have something interesting to say. In addition, clichés especially tend to close off a writer's thoughts rather than open them to new ideas and different ways of seeing. A cliché often leaves the writer with nothing more to say because someone else has already said it.

1. Reread your draft and circle clichés and hand-me-down expressions. If you're not sure whether a phrase qualifies for either category, share your circled items with a partner and discuss them. Have you heard these things before?

2. Cut clichés and overused expressions and rewrite your sentences, finding your own way to say things. In your own words, what do you really mean by "do or die" or "striking while the iron is hot" or becoming a "true believer"?

Using What You Have Learned

Take a few moments to reflect on what you learned in this chapter and how you can apply it.

1. Which revision strategy has proved most helpful to you so far? Does it address one of your most common problems in your drafts?
2. Here's a common situation: You're assigned a paper for another class and the professor doesn't require you to hand in a draft. She's just interested in your final version. What incentive do you have to work through a draft or two?
3. If revision is rhetorical, then the kinds of revision strategies you need to use depend on the particular situation: to whom you're writing and why, and in what form. The kind of writer you are—and the kinds of problems you have in your drafts—also matters. Consider the following forms: the essay exam, the review, the annotated bibliography, the letter, the formal research paper, and the reading response. Which of the five revision strategies would probably be most important for each form?

CREDITS

Text Credits

Page 77. Frank Bruni. From "It Died For Us" by Frank Bruni from THE NEW YORK TIMES, June 25, 2006. Copyright © 2006 The New York Times Co. Reprinted by permission.

Page 91. "Long Overdue" by Naomi Shihab Nye. Reprinted by permission of the author, Naomi Shihab Nye, 2006.

Page 95. "One More Lesson" is reprinted with permission from the publisher of SILENT DANCING: A PARTIAL REMEMBRANCE OF A PUERTO RICAN CHILDHOOD by Judith Ortiz Cofer (Arte Publico Press—University of Houston, 1990).

Page 127. "Review of Peter Guralnick's 'Lost Highways'" by Lester Bangs from PSYCHOTIC REACTIONS AND CARBURETOR DUNG by Lester Bangs edited by Greil Marcus, Copyright © 1987 by The Estate of Lester Bangs. Used by permission of Alfred A. Knopf, a division of Random House, Inc.

Page 133. Ann Hodgman. "No Wonder They Call Me a Bitch" by Ann Hodgman from SPY MAGAZINE. Copyright © 1989 by Sussex Publishers, Inc. Reprinted by permission of the author.

Page 167. "How Bingeing Became the New College Sport" by Barrett Seaman from Time Magazine, 21 August 2005. Used by permission.

Page 212. Ellen Goodman. "Getting Real in the Classroom" by Ellen Goodman from THE BOSTON GLOBE, July 7, 2006. Copyright © 2006, The Washington Post Writers Group. Reprinted with permission.

Page 215. George Will. "Teach Johnny to Write" by George Will from THE WASHINGTON POST, July 9, 1995. Copyright © 1995, The Washington Post Writers Group. Reprinted with permission.

Page 217. "Still Trying to Kick the Kink" by Erin Aubry Kaplan as appeared in LOS ANGELES TIMES, July 12, 2006. Reprinted by permission of Erin Aubry Kaplan, Op-ed columnist, Los Angeles Times.

Page 253. Leslie Marmon Silko. "Lullaby" from STORYTELLER by Leslie Marmon Silko. Copyright © 1981 by Leslie Marmon Silko reprinted with the permission of The Wylie Agency Inc.

Page 262. Joyce Carol Oates. "Where Are You Going, Where Have You Been?" by Joyce Carol Oates. Copyright © 1970 Ontario Review. Reprinted by permission of John Hawkins & Associates, Inc.

Page 275. "Who Is Ellie? Oates' Where Are You Going, Where Have You Been?" by Alice Hall Petry from STUDIES IN SHORT FICTION 25.2 (Spring 1988): 155–157. Reprinted by permission of the author.

Page 307. © EBSCO Publishing Inc. 2007. All rights reserved.

Photo Credits

Page x. Reg Charity/Corbis

Page 17. AP WideWorld Photos

Page 30. Royalty Free/Corbis

Page 35. Jackson Pollock One (Number 31, 1950) © The Museum of Modern Art/Licensed by SCALA/Art Resource, NY

Page 35. © 2006 The Pollock-Krasner Foundation/Artist Rights Society (ARS), New York

Page 35. Major League Baseball trademarks and copyrights are used with permission of MLB.com. All Rights Reserved.

Page 51. Photofest NYC

Page 53. Kraft Foods

Page 53. The Advertising Archives

Page 55. "All I got was a letter from my girl. He got a tube of non-alcoholic Wildroot Cream Oil!" Item BH0636. Ad*Acess. 1999. Rare book, Manuscript and Special Collections Library, Duke University. http://scriptorium.lib.duke.edu/adaccess

Page 58. Francis G. Mayer/CORBIS

Page 58. Pepper No. 30 Photograph by Edward Weston. Collection Center for Creative Photography. © 1981 Arizona Board of Regents.

Page 58. Swim Ink 2, LLC/CORBIS

Page 59. Swim Ink 2, LLC/CORBIS

Page 59. Photograph by Milton Rogovin, copyright 1952–2002

Page 63. Courtesy of Paramount Pictures

Page 66. Library of Congress Prints and Photographs Division

Page 75. Yann Arthus-Bertrand/CORBIS

Page 78. Ji Lee

Page 99. Getty Images

Page 122. Photos 12.com—Collection Cinema

Page 137. Courtesy of Oakland Museum of California

Page 137. Library of Congress Prints and Photographs Division

Page 137. Library of Congress Prints and Photographs Division

Page 137. Library of Congress Prints and Photographs Division

Page 137. Library of Congress Prints and Photographs Division

Page 137. Library of Congress Prints and Photographs Division

Page 157. Sunset Boulevard/Corbis

Page 160. Joseph Sohm; ChromoSohm Inc./CORBIS

Page 170. Courtesy of the Lower Manhattan Development Corporation

Page 178. Courtesy of Drug Free Arizona, www.drugfreeaz.org

Page 200. Getty Images

Page 220. Photo B.D.V./CORBIS

Page 234. Guess. Advertisement from Guess.com website. Reprinted by permission of GUESS Inc.

Page 278. *Christina's World* 1948 Tempera on Panel © Andrew Wyeth / The Museum of Modern Art / Licensed by SCALA / Art Resource, NY

Page 300. 1996–98 AccuSoft Inc., All Rights/Robert Harding World Imagery/Corbis

Page 307. EBSCO Publishing

Page 319. Robert Bull Design

Page 340. Owen Franken / CORBIS

Page 414. Michael Prince / CORBIS

INDEX

B

C

Q

R

S